THE NEW BLACKWELL COMPANION TO MEDICAL SOCIOLOGY

BLACKWELL COMPANIONS TO SOCIOLOGY

The *Blackwell Companions to Sociology* provide introductions to emerging topics and theoretical orientations in sociology as well as presenting the scope and quality of the discipline as it is currently configured. Essays in the Companions tackle broad themes or central puzzles within the field and are authored by key scholars who have spent considerable time in research and reflection on the questions and controversies that have activated interest in their area. This authoritative series will interest those studying sociology at advanced undergraduate or graduate level as well as scholars in the social sciences and informed readers in applied disciplines.

THE NEW BLACKWELL COMPANION TO

Medical Sociology

EDITED BY
WILLIAM C. COCKERHAM

A John Wiley & Sons, Ltd., Publication

This edition first published 2010
© 2010 Blackwell Publishing Ltd

Blackwell Publishing was acquired by John Wiley & Sons in February 2007. Blackwell's publishing program has been merged with Wiley's global Scientific, Technical, and Medical business to form Wiley-Blackwell.

Registered Office
John Wiley & Sons Ltd, The Atrium, Southern Gate, Chichester, West Sussex, PO19 8SQ, United Kingdom

Editorial Offices
350 Main Street, Malden, MA 02148-5020, USA
9600 Garsington Road, Oxford, OX4 2DQ, UK
The Atrium, Southern Gate, Chichester, West Sussex, P019 8SQ, UK

For details of our global editorial offices, for customer services, and for information about how to apply for permission to reuse the copyright material in this book please see our website at www.wiley.com/wiley-blackwell.

The right of William C. Cockerham to be identified as the author of the editorial material in this work has been asserted in accordance with the Copyright, Designs, and Patents Act 1988.

Library of Congress Cataloging-in-Publication Data

The new Blackwell companion to medical sociology / edited by William C. Cockerham.
    p. cm.
  Includes bibliographical references and index.
  ISBN 978-1-4051-8868-5 (hardcover: alk. paper)
  1. Social medicine.   I. Cockerham, William C.
  RA418.N3885 2010
  362.1'042—dc22

                            2009015234

A catalogue record for this book is available from the British Library.

Set in 10 on 12.5 pt Sabon by SNP Best-set Typesetter Ltd., Hong Kong

Printed in Singapore by Ho Printing Singapore Pte Ltd

1   2010

Contents

Contributors

Ellen Annandale, PhD (Brown University), is Senior Lecturer in the Department of Sociology at the University of Leicester (UK). Her most recent books are *Women's Health and Social Change* (2009) and the *Current Sociology* Monograph, *New Connections: Towards a Gender-Inclusive Approach to Women's and Men's Health* (2009), co-edited with Elianne Riska. She is Vice-President of the Research Committee on Health Sociology of the International Sociological Association and Editor-in-Chief of the journal *Social Science and Medicine*.

George J. Armelagos, PhD (University of Colorado), is Goodrich C. White Professor of Anthropology at Emory University (USA). He is a Wenner-Gren Viking Medalist and the recipient of the Franz Boaz Award from the American Anthropological Association and the Charles Darwin Award from the American Association of Physical Anthropologists.

William R. Avison, PhD (University of Alberta), is Professor of Sociology, Pediatrics, and Epidemiology and Biostatistics at the University of Western Ontario in Canada. He chairs the Child Health and Well-Being Program of the Children's Health Research Institute and is Assistant Director of the Lawson Health Research Institute. He received the James R. Greenley Award for Distinguished Contributions to the Sociology of Mental Health from the Society for the Study of Social Problems and the Leonard I. Pearlin Award for Distinguished Contributions to the Sociological Study of Mental Health from the American Sociological Association. He was Chair of the Section on the Sociology of Mental Health (1998–9) and Chair of the Medical Sociology Section (2009–10) of the American Sociological Association.

Hans A. Baer, PhD (University of Utah), is Senior Lecturer in the School of Philosophy, Anthropology, and Social Inquiry and the Centre for Health and Society at the University of Melbourne in Australia. He has published 14 books and numerous chapters and journal articles on alternative medicine and other topics. His books include *Biomedicine and Alternative Healing Systems in America: Issues of Race,*

Class, Ethnicity, and Gender (2001), *Toward an Integrative Medicine: Merging Alternative Therapies with Biomedicine* (2004), and the co-authored *Global Warming and the Political Ecology of Health: Emerging Crises and Systematic Solutions* (2009).

Carol A. Boyer, PhD (Yale University), is Associate Director of the Institute for Health, Health Care Policy, and Aging Research and a member of the graduate faculty of the Department of Sociology at Rutgers University (USA). Her research focuses on access, utilization, and the content of treatment and services provided to individuals with a diagnosis of schizophrenia and the impact of mental health services on social functioning, symptomatology, and quality of life. Recent publications include a co-authored chapter in *Mental Health, Social Mirror* (2007), and papers in *Psychiatric Services* and the *American Journal of Psychiatry*.

Hannah Bradby, PhD (University of Glasgow), is Co-Director of the Institute of Health and Lecturer in the Department of Sociology and the Medical School at the University of Warwick (UK). She is Editor of the journal *Ethnicity and Health* and her latest book is *Medical Sociology: An Introduction* (2009).

Michael Bury is Emeritus Professor of Sociology at the University of London (UK). He was appointed to a chair in Sociology at the University of London (1991) and served as Head of the Department of Social and Political Science at Royal Holloway (1996–2002). He is a member of the Public Health Interventions Advisory Committee at the National Institute for Health and Clinical Excellence in the UK and completed a four-year term on the Medical Research Council. He was Co-Editor of the journal *Sociology of Health and Illness* (1995–2001) and his most recent book is *Health and Illness* (2005). Professor Bury received an honorary doctorate from the University of Linköping, Sweden, in 2001.

Kathy Charmaz, PhD (University of California, San Francisco), is Professor of Sociology and Coordinator of the Faculty Writing Program at Sonoma State University (USA). She is author of two award-winning books, *Good Days, Bad Days: The Self in Chronic Illness and Time* (1991) and *Constructing Grounded Theory: A Practical Guide Through Qualitative Analysis* (2006). She has recently edited *Health, Illness, and Healing: Society, Social Context and Self* (2007) and co-authored *Developing Grounded Theory: The Second Generation* (2008). Professor Charmaz has served as Chair of the Medical Sociology Section of the American Sociological Association and President of the Pacific Sociological Association. She has received the Feminist Mentors Award and George Herbert Mead Award for lifetime achievement from the Society for the Study of Symbolic Interaction.

William C. Cockerham, PhD (University of California, Berkeley), is Distinguished Professor of Sociology and Co-Director of the Center for Social Medicine at the University of Alabama at Birmingham (USA). He also holds secondary appointments in medicine and public health. Among his recent publications are a co-authored chapter in *Quantifying Theory: Pierre Bourdieu* (2009) and a chapter in *The Sociology of Medical Education* (2009). Recent books include *Social Causes of Health* *and Disease* (2007), *Medical Sociology*, 11th edition (2010), andthe co-authored *Health and Globalization* (2010). He is President of the Research Committee on Health Sociology of the International Sociological Association and a current member of the Editorial Board of the *American Sociological Review*.

Joseph E. Davis, PhD (University of Virginia), is Research Associate Professor of Sociology and Director of Research at the Institute for Advanced Studies in Culture at the University of Virginia (USA). He is editor of *Identity and Social Change* (2000) and author of *Stories of Change: Narratives and Social Movements* (2002) and *Accounts of Innocence: Sexual Abuse, Trauma, and the Self* (2005). He is working on a new book on the self, suffering, and psychopharmacology with a tentative title of *After Psychology: Medication and the Quest for Control of Life*.

Raymond G. DeVries, PhD (University of California, Davis), is Associate Professor in the Bioethics Program, the Department of Obstetrics and Gynecology, and the Department of Medical Education at the University of Michigan Medical School (USA). He is author of *A Pleasing Birth: Midwifery and Maternity Care in the Netherlands* (2005) and Co-Editor of *The View from Here: Bioethics and the Social Sciences* (Blackwell, 2007). He is at work on a critical social history of bioethics and is studying the regulation of science, international research ethics, informed consent and the problem of therapeutic misconception, and the social, ethical, and policy issues associated with non-medically indicated surgical birth.

Robert Dingwall, PhD (University of Aberdeen), is Professor and Director of the Institute for Science and Society at the University of Nottingham (UK). Since 1997, he has directed a graduate and research center for the study of the social, legal, cultural, and ethical implications of science and technology. He has published extensively on issues in medical sociology, the sociology of law, and the sociology of science and technology. Recent work has included projects on the representations of the Human Genome Project, the presentation of evolution in popular TV wildlife programming, public health early warning systems for infectious diseases, and implications of developments in research governance for the social sciences and humanities. Recent publications include *Essays on Professions* (2008) and the edited four-volume work *Qualitative Health Research* (2008). He is Secretary of the Research Committee on Health Sociology of the International Sociological Association.

Kristin N. Harper, PhD (Emory University), is a Robert Wood Johnson Health and Society Scholar at Columbia University (USA). Her current research examines the relationship between nutrition, mutation rates, and disease, with a present focus on the effects of maternal micronutrient deficiencies on offspring risk of developing schizophrenia.

Ellen L. Idler, PhD (Yale University), is Director, Religion and Public Health Collaborative, and Professor of Sociology and Epidemiology, Emory University. She is a Fellow of the Gerontological Society of America. She studies the influence of attitudes, beliefs, and social connections on health and mortality, with numerous publications on the relationship of religious involvement to disability, depression, quality of life, and the timing of death among the elderly. She serves on the Editorial Boards of the *Journal of Gerontology: Social Sciences*, the *Journal of Health and Social Behavior*, the *Journal of Aging and Health*, *Sociological Forum*, the *Slovenian Journal of Aging*, and on the Editorial Committee of Rutgers University Press.

Tania Jenkins is a graduate student in the Department of Sociology at McGill University in Canada as the laureate of a Canadian Graduate Scholarship from the Social Science and Humanities Research Council of Canada (SSHRC). Her research interests include health care systems, with a current focus on access to primary health care in Quebec. Her publications include a paper on the Cuban health care system in *Qualitative Health Research* and a co-authored chapter ("Vieillissement et utilisation des soins: Comment partager les coûts?") in *Le Privé dans lasanté: Les discours et les faits* (2008).

Eero Lahelma, PhD (University of Helsinki), is Professor of Medical Sociology in the Department of Public Health at the University of Helsinki in Finland. He is head of the Helsinki Health Study that compares the health of an occupational cohort in Finland with counterparts in Britain and Japan. He has published extensively on the social determinants of public health, socioeconomic inequalities in health, and international comparisons of inequalities in health.

Nan Lin, PhD (Michigan State University), is the Oscar L. Tang Family Professor of Sociology at Duke University (USA). He has published extensively during a distinguished career and is the author of *Social Capital: A Theory of Social Structure and Action* (2001) and co-editor of *Social Capital: An International Research Program* (2008). His research interests include social networks and social capital, stratification and mobility, stress and coping, and Chinese societies.

Paul A. Martin, DPhil (University of Sussex), is Reader in Science and Technology Studies and Deputy Director of the Institute for Science and Society, University of Nottingham (UK). His research focuses on the ethical, legal, and social issues associated with the emerging genetic technologies, the commercialization of biotechnology, and expectation dynamics in medical innovation. He is on the Editorial Boards of *Sociology of Health and Illness* and *New Genetics and Society*. He has been an advisor on issues surrounding genomics to the European Parliament, the Conseil d'Analyse Economique, the UK Department of Trade and Industry, and the Royal Pharmaceutical Society.

James Y. Nazroo, PhD (University College, London), is Professor of Sociology at the University of Manchester (UK). He has researched ethnic inequalities in health for more than a decade and also studies social and health inequalities in aging populations. His latest book is *Health and Social Research in Multicultural Societies* (2006).

Sarah Nettleton, PhD (University of London), is a Reader in Sociology at the University of York (UK). She is author of *The Sociology of Health and Illness*,

2nd edition (2006). Her current research interests include embodiment, food, illness, and health. She is Senior Editor of *Social Science and Medicine*.

Kristina Orfali, PhD (Ecole des Hautes Etudes en Sciences Sociales), is Associate Clinical Professor of Bioethics in Pediatrics, College of Physicians and Surgeons at Columbia University (USA) and a Faculty Associate at the Center for Bioethics and the Institute for Social and Economic Research and Policy (ISERP). She is a graduate of the Ecole Normale Supérieure in Paris and trained as a sociologist. She has published work on the hospital patient experience and clinician and family decision-making in intensive care units. Her current research is on ethical dilemmas and international variations in medical prognosis in neonatology. She is Co-Editor of *The View from Here: Bioethics and Social Sciences* (Blackwell, 2007).

Bernice A. Pescosolido, PhD (Yale University), is Distinguished Professor of Sociology and Director of the Indiana Consortium for Mental Health Services Research at Indiana University (USA). She is also Co-Director of the Preparing Future Faculty Program and Associate Director of the Mack Center's Institute for the Scholarship of Teaching and Learning. Her research targets social network influences in the health care arena, particularly the ties that serve as important links between communities and treatment systems. She has several major publications and served on the Editorial Boards of leading sociology journals, including the *American Sociological Review* and the *Journal of Health and Social Behavior*. She has been honored with numerous teaching and mentoring awards.

Sharyn J. Potter, PhD (Emory University), MPH, is Associate Professor of Sociology and Co-Director of Prevention Innovations, Research, and Practices for Ending Violence Against Women on Campus at the University of New Hampshire (USA). She has a major role in a large grant award from the Centers for Disease Control and Prevention (CDC) to experimentally evaluate campus violence prevention programs. Her recent publications include co-authored papers in *Violence Against Women*, *Prevention and Intervention in the Community*, *Journal of Applied Gerontology*, and *Social Science and Medicine*.

Stella Quah, PhD (National University of Singapore), is Professor of Sociology at the National University of Singapore. She served as Associate Editor-in-Chief of the six-volume *International Encyclopedia of Public Health* (2008) and is author of *Crisis Preparedness: Asia and the Global Governance of Epidemics* (2007) and *Families in Asia: Home and Kin* (2009). She was Chair of the Research Committee on Health Sociology and Vice-President for Research and Chair of the Research Council of the International Sociological Association. Additionally, she served as Associate Editor of *International Sociology* (1998–2004) and is on the Editorial Boards of several international journals.

Amélie Quesnel-Vallée, PhD (Duke University), is Assistant Professor of Sociology and Epidemiology at McGill University in Canada. She is also Head of the International Research Infrastructure on Social Inequalities in Health (IRIS). In 2005, she received the American Sociological Association Dissertation Award for her

Fulbright-funded doctoral research. She currently studies the impact of public policies on health inequalities. Her recent publications include a co-edited book, *Le Privé dans la santé: Les discours et les faits* (2008) and papers in the *Canadian Medical Association Journal*, the *Journal of Epidemiology and Community Health*, the *American Journal of Epidemiology*, and *Social Science and Medicine*.

Elianne Riska, PhD (State University of New York at Stony Brook), is Professor of Sociology at the University of Helsinki, Finland. Her research focuses on the medical profession and gender and health. Her publications include *Medical Careers and Feminist Agendas: American, Scandinavian, and Russian Women Physicians* (2001) and *Masculinity and Men's Health: Coronary Heart Disease in Medical and Public Discourse* (2004). Most recently, she co-edited a monograph issue on gender and health for *Current Sociology* (2009) with Ellen Annandale and is author of a chapter in *Men's Health: Body, Identity and Social Context* (Wiley-Blackwell, 2009). Professor Riska is Past Chair of the Research Committee on Health Sociology of the International Sociological Association.

Dana Rosenfeld, PhD (University of California, Los Angeles), is Senior Lecturer in the School of Sociology and Criminology at the University of Keele (UK). She is a qualitative sociologist whose research centers on aging and the life course, health, and identity and embodiment. She is author of *The Changing of the Guard: Lesbian and Gay Elders, Identity, and Social Change* (2002) and lead editor of a volume on *Medicalized Masculinities* (2006). Her most recent publications include chapters in *Body/Embodiment: Symbolic Interaction and the Sociology of the Body* (2007) and the *International Handbook of Social Gerontology* (forthcoming). She serves on the Editorial Boards of *Social Theory and Health* and the *Journal of Aging Studies*.

Graham Scambler, PhD (University of London), is Professor of Medical Sociology at University College, London (UK). He has published extensively on social and critical theory, health inequalities, chronic and stigmatizing illness, and the health of sex workers. He is Co-Editor of the international journal *Social Theory and Health* and his recent books include *Health and Social Change: A Critical Theory* (2002), *Sport and Society: History, Power and Culture* (2005), and *Sociology as Applied to Medicine*, 6th edition (2008).

Johannes Siegrist, PhD (University of Freiburg), is Director of the Department of Medical Sociology and Director of the Public Health Program at the University of Düsseldorf in Germany. He has numerous publications. His two main research areas are the adverse health effects of psychosocial stress at work (development of the Effort–Reward–Imbalance model) and the social determinants of health in early old age. Professor Siegrist is Past President of the European Society of Health and Medical Sociology and, among others, Fellow of *Academica Europaea*.

Joonmo Son, PhD (Duke University), is Assistant Professor of Sociology at the National University of Singapore. His areas of research include social capital, social support, and their impact on mental and physical health status. His latest publications (2008) are "Cross-National Comparison of Social Support Structures between Taiwan and the United States" with Nan Lin and Linda K. George in the *Journal of Health and Social Behavior* and "Social Capital and Civic Action: A Network-Based Approach" with Nan Lin in *Social Science Research*.

Lijun Song, PhD (Duke University), is Assistant Professor of Sociology and Assistant Professor of Medicine, Health, and Society at Vanderbilt University. Her research focuses on social networks, social capital, medical sociology, and social stratification. Her paper, "The Cultural Revolution Depressed Educational Homogamy in Urban China," is forthcoming in *Social Forces*.

Fred Stevens, PhD (University of Maastricht), is a sociologist and Associate Professor in the Department of Educational Development and Research, Faculty of Health, Medicine, and Life Sciences (FHML) at the University of Maastricht in the Netherlands. His current teaching and research interests include the comparison of health care systems, medical education and global health, health professions, medical careers, and labor issues. Recent publications include a chapter on European innovations in medical education in the *Sociology of Medical Education* (2009) and papers in the *Sociology of Health and Illness, Medical Education, BMC Health Services Research,* and *Health Policy*.

Stephanie S. Thomas is a graduate student in the Department of Sociology at the University of Western Ontario in Canada. Her research interests are in the sociology of mental health and more particularly in the deinstitutionalization of mental illness, recovery from mental illness, and youth mental illness and suicide.

Jennifer Vanderminden is a graduate student in the Department of Sociology at the University of New Hampshire (USA). She is currently conducting research on the social construction of disability.

Simon J. Williams, PhD (University of London), is a Professor of Sociology in the Department of Sociology, University of Warwick, UK. He has published widely in the fields of medical sociology, sociology of the body, and the sociology of emotion, including a recent co-edited international volume *Pharmaceuticals and Society* (Wiley-Blackwell, 2009) and other forthcoming books on *The Politics of Sleep* and *NeuroFutures in the Making*. His current research is focused on the neurosciences, including on-going work on psychopharmaceuticals for treatment or enhancement, the emergence of neuroculture, and the problems and prospects of integrating neuroscience and social science, with particular reference to emotions/affects. He is also the founder and co-organizer of the new interdisciplinary Neuroscience and Society group at Warwick.

Preface

The New Blackwell Companion to Medical Sociology is the latest book in Black-well's *Companion* series that brings together leading scholars in the various subdis-ciplines of sociology to provide current discussions of the most important issues and research in their respective fields.

This edition continues this process by providing insightful chapters from both established and rising young scholars on health-related topics of central interest in medical or health sociology.

The contributors are from the United States, the United Kingdom, Canada, Australia, France, Germany, Finland, the Netherlands, and Singapore who were carefully selected to write chapters on topics in which they were recognized experts. This edition differs from its predecessor in that all chapters are on substan-tive topics. Country/regional perspectives from around the world are not included since Blackwell's editors felt little significant change in the social organization of health care had occurred in the various countries or regions since the publication of the earlier volume in 2001.

The new chapters not only review relevant empirical research, but are also theo-retically informed. This development is evidence of the fact that medical sociology is increasingly embracing the use of sociological theory in its research agenda on real-world health problems. Some 30 years ago, medical sociology was viewed by some as atheoretical and under the control of the medical profession. If this was once true, it is certainly not the case today, as medical sociology has evolved into a field that is both applied and theoretical, and in control of its own approach to research. This volume begins with an overview of sociological theory in medical sociology by the editor and Graham Scambler (University College, London), Co-Editor of the journal *Social Theory and Health*. Nan Lin (Duke University), a leading theorist on social capital, co-authors a chapter with Lijun Song (Vanderbilt University) and Joonmo Son (National University of Singapore) on social capital and health; Johannes Siegrist (University of Düsseldorf), the proponent of the effort–reward imbalance theory, writes on stress in the workplace; and the editor provides an updated account of his health lifestyle theory. Siegrist is Past President of the European Society of Health and Medical Sociology, while Lin is Past Vice-President of the American Sociological Association. Other chapters in which sociological theory is prominently featured include those by Stella Quah (National University of Singapore), Past Chair of the International Sociological Association Research Council, on health and culture; Sarah Nettleton (York University), a Senior Editor of *Social Science and Medicine*, on the sociology of the body; and Elianne Riska (University of Helsinki), a leading scholar in the field of health occupations and professions.

Four other contributors have also been awarded major prizes and recognition for scholarship. They are George Armelagos (Emory University), Wenner-Gren Viking Medalist and recipient, among others, of the Franz Boaz Award from the American Anthropological Association, who contributes a chapter on infectious diseases in the era of global warming with Robert Wood Johnson Health and Society Scholar Kristin Harper (Columbia University); William Avison (University of Western Ontario), who has received both the James R. Greenley Award from the Society for the Study of Social Problems and the Leonard I. Pearlin Award from the American Sociological Association, joins Stephanie Thomas (University of Western Ontario) to write a chapter on stress; Kathy Charmaz (Sonoma State University), winner of the George H. Mead Award from the Society for the Study of Symbolic Interaction, who writes on chronic illness with Dana Rosenfeld (University of Keele); and Bernice Pescosolido (Indiana University), whose many awards include the Leo G. Reeder Award from the American Sociological Association. Professor Pescosolido and Carol Boyer (Rutgers University) contribute a chapter on the American health care delivery system, including consideration of likely changes by the new Obama administration.

Other contributors are highly recognized scholars in their fields as well. Those selected to address social inequalities in health because of their past work include Ellen Annandale (University of Leicester), the Editor-in-Chief of *Social Science and Medicine*, writing on gender; Eero Lahelma (University of Helsinki), who examines social class; and Hannah Bradby (University of Warwick) and James Nazroo (University of Manchester), analyzing race and ethnicity. These chapters on gender, class, and race provide a European perspective that is usually missing from similar accounts by American medical sociologists. A new scholar is Amélie Quesnel-Vallée (McGill University), who received the American Sociological Association Dissertation Award. She contributes a chapter on social policies and inequality with her co-author Tania Jenkins (McGill University). Another new scholar is Sharyn Potter (University of New Hampshire), who provides us with an update on the changing doctor–patient relationship with her co-author Jennifer Vanderminden (University of New Hampshire).

Additionally, there is an excellent chapter on health and religion by the well-known scholar Ellen Idler (Emory University). There are also interesting chapters on relatively new topics by rising scholars Joseph E. Davis (University of Virginia) on medicalization and Hans Baer (University of Melbourne) on complementary and alternative medicine. Other chapters by leading European medical sociologists include those by Mike Bury (University of London) on the British health care system and Fred Stevens (University of Maastricht) on global health care systems. The concluding section of the volume addresses topics that are increasingly significant in medical sociology, but about which little has yet been published. These chapters by important scholars provide fundamental statements on their subjects. Robert Dingwall (University of Nottingham), former Co-Editor of the journal *Sociology of Health and Illness*, and Paul Martin (University of Nottingham) write on genetics, Kristina Orfali (Columbia University) and Raymond DeVries (University of Michigan) discuss bioethics, and Simon Williams (University of Warwick) introduces the relevance of neuroscience to medical sociologists. Both separately and collectively, these chapters should provide useful information and insight for the current generation of medical sociologists.

Finally, I would like to acknowledge the hard work and very able assistance of Sarah Ballard, Cullen Clark, and Matthew West, doctoral students in medical sociology at the University of Alabama at Birmingham. They were first to edit the manuscripts and were vitally important in making sure the chapters were all of a high quality in the beginning. The academic institutions that employ them in the future will be fortunate. I would also like to thank the efforts of several people at Blackwell in Oxford who had an important role in the development and publication of this book. These include Justin Vaughan, Ben Thatcher, Barbara Duke and Brigitte Lee. This book results from a conversation with Justin in a bar in New York City one pleasant afternoon during the American Sociological Association meeting. Finally, I would like to thank my long- (and still-) suffering wife, Cynthia, who puts up with a lot.

William C. Cockerham
Birmingham, Alabama

Part I

Introduction

1

Medical Sociology and Sociological Theory

William C. Cockerham and Graham Scambler

The link between medical sociology and sociological theory is crucial to the subdiscipline. Theory binds medical sociology to the larger discipline of sociology more extensively than any other aspect of the sociological enterprise. Theory is also what usually distinguishes research in medical sociology from socially oriented studies in allied fields, like public health and health services research. Whereas seminal sociological contributions in quantitative and qualitative data collection and analysis, along with many fundamental concepts of social behavior, have been adopted by multidisciplinary approaches in several fields, sociological theory allows medical sociology to remain unique among the health-related social and behavioral sciences. This could be considered as a somewhat surprising statement because medical sociology has often been described in the past as atheoretical. It is true that much of the work in the field historically has been applied to practical problems rather than theoretical questions. That is, it was intended to help solve a clinical problem or policy issue, rather than develop theory or utilize it as a tool to enhance understanding. Medical sociology was not established until after World War II when the American government provided extensive funding through the National Institutes of Health for joint sociological and medical research projects. The same situation prevailed in Western Europe, where, unlike in the United States, few medical sociologists were affiliated with university sociology faculties and connections to the general discipline of sociology were especially weak (Claus 1982; Cockerham 1983). It was primarily through the stimulus of the availability of government funding that sociologists and health professionals embraced medical sociology as a new subdiscipline. Funding agencies were not interested in theoretical work, but sponsored research that had some practical utility in postwar society as Western governments had come to realize that social factors were important for health.

By the end of the twentieth century, however, this situation had changed significantly. Most research in medical sociology remains oriented toward practical problem solving, but the use of sociological theory in this endeavor is now widespread. There has been a general evolution of work in medical sociology that combines both applied and theoretical perspectives, with the utilization of theory becoming increasingly common as a framework for explaining or predicting health-related social behavior. At the same time, medical sociology moved away from a state of dependence upon medicine for defining and guiding research agendas to a position of relative independence. Although the relationship between medical sociology and medicine has been important, it has not always been harmonious. Medical sociology tended to side with patients and call attention to instances of poor treatment, while some physicians have been contemptuous of medical sociologists in clinical settings. Yet medicine nurtured, funded, and sponsored medical sociology early in its development and continues to do so today. In fact, one could arguably state that medicine has supported medical sociology with funding and job positions to a much greater extent than sociology. It can also be claimed that the increased use of theory in medical sociology represents more of an effort on the part of medical sociologists to establish and reinforce links to the parent discipline than vice versa. In many ways, medicine has been a better ally of medical sociology than sociology.

While medical sociology is moving closer to sociology, it has generally removed itself from a subordinate position to medicine. There are four reasons for this development. First, the shift from acute to chronic diseases as the primary causes of death in contemporary societies has made medical sociology increasingly important to medicine. This is because of the key roles of social behavior and living conditions in the prevention, onset, and course of chronic disorders. Medical sociologists bring more expertise to the analysis of health-related social conditions than physicians, who typically receive little or no training in this area. Second, medical sociology has moved into a greater partnership with medicine as it has matured and fostered a significant body of research literature, much of it relevant to clinical medicine and health policy. Third, success in research has promoted the professional status of medical sociologists, in relation to both medicine and sociology. And fourth, medical sociology has generally set its own research agenda, which includes medical practice and policy as an *object* of study. In the case of malpractice, failure to police incompetent practitioners, limited access to quality care for the poor, and placing professional interest ahead of the public's interest, medical sociologists have been significant critics of medicine. In doing so, they have established themselves as objective professionals.

The movement of medical sociology toward greater connections with general sociology reflects the desire of a mature subdiscipline to expand its analytic capabilities and reinforce its potential. Changing social conditions associated with the transition in society from the postindustrial to the current late modern period requires all of sociology to account for altered circumstances and formulate new concepts. This situation suggests that not only is medical sociology connecting with general sociology, but that sociology is moving toward a closer affiliation with it – given the considerations of health increasingly evident in the everyday social lives of people and medical sociology's capacity for explaining it. Under the current conditions of social change, medical sociologists are making greater use of sociological theory because theory promotes the explanatory power of their empirical findings. This development has led some to suggest that medical sociology may indeed prove to be the "leading edge" in some areas of the development of contemporary theory (Turner 1992). The extent to which this assertion will be fully realized is not yet certain, but it is clear that a considerable amount of theoretical work is taking place in medical sociology (Cockerham 2007a). The remainder of this chapter will provide an overview of the field with respect to theory.

PARSONS, DURKHEIM, AND STRUCTURAL FUNCTIONALISM

From 1946 to 1951, the new field of medical sociology was almost completely an applied area of research. Medical sociologists worked with psychiatrists and other physicians on government-funded projects to largely address medical problems; few were employed in university departments of sociology in the United States and they were generally absent from sociology faculties in Europe and Asia. However, a pivotal event occurred in 1951 that oriented medical sociology toward theoretical concerns and initiated the establishment of its academic credentials. This was the publication of Talcott Parsons' long anticipated book, *The Social System*, which established the author at the time as the dominant figure in American sociology (Ritzer 2008). Anything Parsons published attracted great attention because he was thought to be charting a course for all of sociology. This book, providing a structural-functionalist model of society, contained Parsons' concept of the sick role and was the first time a major sociological theorist included an analysis of the function of medicine in his view of society. Parsons (1951: 428–9) was interested in the differing roles of professionals in capitalist and socialist societies and decided to include physicians and their relationship to their clients in his analysis because this topic was an area of long-standing interest and one in which he felt he had familiarity. Parsons himself had undergone training in psychoanalysis in the 1930s at the Boston Psychoanalytic Institute when he was on the faculty at Harvard University (Smelser 1998).

This experience had grounded him in the theories of Sigmund Freud which became an important influence on his own work, along with the ideas of the classic sociological theorists Emile Durkheim and Max Weber. Parsons had completed his doctoral studies at Heidelberg University in Germany in the mid-1920s where he participated in the "Weber Circle" that continued to meet regularly to discuss sociology after Weber's death at the home of his widow, Marianne Weber. Parsons subsequently translated Weber's book on the *Protestant Ethic and the Spirit of Capitalism* (1958) into English, and reintroduced the work of both Weber and Durkheim to European sociologists after the disruption of their work during World War II. Freud's concepts of transference and counter-transference can be seen in the way Parsons drew analogies between the roles of parent–child and physician–patient important in his notion of the sick role. Freud's structure of the personality and theory of the unconscious are also apparent in his ideas on the motivation of sick persons to either recover or desire the "secondary gain" of privileges and exemption from normal social roles that accompany sick-role legitimation. Parsons likewise incorporates Durkheim's ideas on moral authority and Weber's analysis of religion into his discussion of the normative requirement to visit physicians when sick and the dominant position of the physician in the doctor–patient role relationship.

Parsons' concept of the sick role is a clear and straightforward statement of four basic propositions outlining the normative pattern of physician utilization by the sick and their respective social roles. Parsons not only constructed the first theoretical concept directly applicable to medical sociology, but by utilizing the work of Durkheim and Weber, he did so within the parameters of classical socio-logical theory. His formulation was recognized as "a penetrating and apt analysis of sickness from a distinctly sociological point of view" (Freidson 1970a: 228), which indeed it was. Parsons also influenced the study of professions by using the medical profession as the model for professions based on expertise and a service orientation. Although extensive criticism was to subsequently lessen the acceptance of the Parsonian approach to theory, this outcome does not negate the significant influence Parsons initially had on promoting debate and research in medical sociology. Parsons, more so than any other sociologist of his time, made medical sociology academically respectable by providing it with its inaugu-ral theoretical orientation.

However, structural functionalism, with its emphasis on value consensus, social order, stability, and functional processes at the macro-level of society, had a short-lived period as the leading theoretical paradigm in medical sociology. Robert Merton and his colleagues extended the structural-functionalist mode of analysis to the socialization of medical students in their book *The Student Physician* (1957), but other major works in medical sociology were not forthcoming. Structural function-alism itself was under assault by critics in the 1960s and early 1970s and lost considerable influence.

Durkheim (1950), who was generally responsible for the theory in sociology, emphasized the importance of macro-level social processes, structures, norms, and values external to individuals that integrated them into the larger society and shaped their behavior. People were depicted as constrained in exercising free will by the social order. Durkheim's (1951) only work that had a direct application to medical sociology was his theory of suicide in which the act of taking one's life was deter-mined by the individual's ties to his or her community or society. This is seen in his typology of three major types of suicide: (1) egoistic (social detachment), (2) anomic (state of normlessness), and (3) altruistic (a normative demand for suicide). The merit of his concept is that it shows the capability of the larger society to create stressful situations where people are forced to respond to conditions not of their own choosing. Thus, Durkheim helps us not only to understand the social facets of suicide, but also to recognize that macro-level social events (like economic reces-sions) can affect health in a variety of ways through stress and that the effects of stress can be mitigated through social support (Cockerham 2010). Indirectly, Durkheim (1964) also influenced the study of health professions in noting the transi-tion from mechanical to organic social solidarity, with its emphasis upon specializa-tion, in the modern division of labor.

However, symbolic interactionists objected to the relegation of individuals to relatively passive roles in large social systems, while conflict theorists found struc-tural functionalism inadequate in explaining the process of social change and the social functions of conflict. The theory's emphasis on equilibrium and consensus also seemed to favor maintenance of the status quo and support for dominant elites (Ritzer 2008), at a time (the 1960s) of widespread social protest against authority in the West. Structural functionalism in general and Parsons in particu-lar suffered a serious fall in popularity, although Parsons' work enjoyed a mild resurgence in the 1990s (Callinicos 2007). Parsons' concept of the sick role, however, has remained a central theoretical proposition in medical sociology, despite challenges. It is still utilized as a basic ("ideal-type") explanation for physician–patient encounters in which the model of interaction is primarily that of guidance on the part of the physician and cooperation by the patient in clinics or patient care office settings.

SYMBOLIC INTERACTION

The first major theoretical perspective to challenge Parsons and structural-functionalist theory in medical sociology was symbolic interaction, based largely on the work of George Herbert Mead (1934) and Herbert Blumer (1969). Symbolic interaction maintained that social reality is constructed on a micro-level by individuals interacting with one another on the basis of shared symbolic meanings. Human beings were seen to possess the capacity to think, define situations, and construct their behavior on the basis of their definitions and interpretations. "It is the position of symbolic interaction," states Blumer (1969: 55), "that the social action of the actor is *constructed* by him [or her]; it is not a mere release of activity brought about by the play of initiating factors on his [or her] organization." Social life was therefore produced by interacting agents choosing their own behavior and acting accordingly, not by large-scale social processes and structures channeling behavior down optionless pathways. Symbolic interaction had not only its particular (micro-level) orientation toward theory construction, but also its own qualitative research methodologies of participant observation that focused on small group interaction in natural social settings. A related approach was ethnomethodology, which featured description of taken-for-granted meanings in natural settings, rather than analysis.

The major figures in early medical sociology working in the symbolic interactionist tradition were Anselm Strauss and Erving Goffman. Strauss joined with Howard Becker and others in their now classic study of medical school socialization, *Boys in White* (Becker et al. 1961). Strauss made his own contributions to theory and methods in a number of areas, including seminal work on the social process of death and dying (Glaser and Strauss 1965, 1968); observation of the "negotiated order" of hospital routine featuring a minimum of "hard and fast" regulations and a maximum of "innovation and improvisation" in patient care, especially in emergency treatment (Strauss et al. 1963); and formulation of grounded theory methodology featuring the development of hypotheses from data *after* their collection, rather than before (Glaser and Strauss 1967).

Goffman, who became a major theorist in sociology generally, began his research career in medical sociology by using participant observation to study the life of mental hospital patients. His classic work in this area, *Asylums* (1961), presented the concept of "total institutions" that emerged as an important sociological statement on the social situation of people confined by institutions. His observations also led to the development of his notions of impression management and the dramaturgical perspective in sociology that views "life as a theatre" and "people as actors on a stage," as well as his concept of stigma (Goffman 1959, 1967).

With the introduction of symbolic interactionist research into an area previously dominated by structural functionalism, medical sociology became an arena of debate between two of sociology's major theoretical schools. By the mid-1960s, symbolic interaction came to dominate a significant portion of the literature in the field. One feature of this domination was the numerous studies conducted in reference to labeling theory, a variant of symbolic interaction, and the controversy it provoked. Labeling theory held that deviant behavior is not a quality of the act a person commits but rather is a consequence of the definition applied to that act by others (Becker 1973). That is, whether or not an act is considered deviant depends upon how other people react to it. Although labeling theory pertained to deviance generally, the primary center of argument was focused on the mental patient experience, with Thomas Scheff (1999) the principal proponent of the labeling approach. Labeling theory was also employed in studies of the medical profession as seen in Eliot Freidson's (1970b) alternative concept of the sick role.

By the 1980s, however, symbolic interaction entered a period of decline in medical sociology. Many of its adherents had been "rebels" intentionally subverting the dominant paradigm of structural functionalism and giving voices to women and marginal social groups like mental patients, the physically handicapped, and the aged and their caretakers by entering their social world and observing it. Yet, as Norman Denzin (1991) points out, between 1981 and 1990, the canonical texts in the field had shifted from Mead to Blumer and Blumer himself was under attack on several methodological and substantive issues – but most importantly for not advancing the field to meet his own early criticisms; moreover, practitioners of the perspective were getting older ("the graying of interactionism"), the number of students espousing interactionism was decreasing, and the old enemy (structural functionalism) had been largely vanquished. Elsewhere, in Great Britain, where interactionism had been the dominant theoretical perspective in medical sociology as seen in the majority of published studies (Annandale 1998), a related theoretical perspective – social constructionism – is now the leading theory (Nettleton 2006; Seale 2008).

Unfortunately, symbolic interaction had taken on the image of a "fixed doctrine" and, except for Mead's (1934) concept of the "generalized other," was unable to satisfactorily link small group processes with social phenomena reflecting the behavioral influences of the larger society. It was particularly unable to account for interaction between institutions or societal-level processes that affect each other, not just individuals or groups. In addition, labeling theory, despite its merits in accounting for the powerful behavioral effects of "labels" placed on people, had not been able to explain the causes of deviance (other than the reaction of the social audience), nor whether deviants themselves share common characteristics like poverty, stress, family, or class background.

But it would be a mistake to relegate symbolic interaction to history, as participant observation remains the primary form of qualitative research in medical sociology. Participant observation and ethnomethodology are still the best methods for recording social behavior from the personal standpoint of those being studied and the settings within which they lead their usual lives. Moreover, the observed patterns of behavior and first-person accounts of social situations bring a sense of "real life" to studies that quantitative research is unable to capture. While symbolic interaction theory has not moved far beyond the original concepts of Mead and Blumer, it persists as an important theoretical approach to the study and explanation of social behavior among small groups of people interacting in ways that are relevant for health.

One area of research in medical sociology helping to revive symbolic interaction is the sociology of emotions, a topic neglected in the past. Research in this field seeks to understand the link between social factors and emotions, since emotions are expressed either in response to social relationships or situations or both. Symbolic interactionism fills in the analytic gap between organic or biological approaches to the study of emotions and sociological approaches like social constructionism that ignores biological processes and focuses more or less exclusively on the social and cultural components of emotions (Williams and Bendelow 1996). Interaction between people plays perhaps the major role in the activation and expression of emotions and analyzing interpersonal relations is a strength of symbolic interaction. Emotions, as Simon Williams (1998) points out, are existentially embodied states that also connect "personal troubles" to social structures in ways that affect health and shape patterns of disease. Williams finds, for example, that feelings of stress, helplessness, depression, sense of coherence, insecurity, and lack of control have consistently been shown to be associated with increased levels of mortality and morbidity.

CONFLICT THEORY

Conflict theory, with its roots in the work of Karl Marx and Max Weber, joined symbolic interaction in significantly reducing the influence of structural functionalism, but has yet to establish a major foothold in medical sociology. Conflict theory is based on the assumption that society is composed of various groups struggling for advantage, that inequality is a basic feature of social life, and conflict is the major cause of social change. Marx's perspective in conflict theory is seen in the rejection of the view expressed by structural functionalism that society is held together by shared norms and values. Conflict theory claims that true consensus does not exist; rather, society's norms and values are those of the dominant elite and imposed by them on the less privileged to maintain their advantaged position. Weber adds, however, that social inequality is not based on just money, property, and relationships to the means of production, but also on status and political influence. Since all social systems contain such inequality, conflict inevitably results and conflict, in turn, is responsible for social change.

Whereas the Marxian-oriented features of conflict theory have emphasized class struggle, other theorists have moved toward emphasizing conflicts that occur between interest groups and the unequal distribution of political power (Dahrendorf 1959). According to Turner (1988), modern societies are best understood as having a conflict between the principles of democratic politics (emphasizing equality and universal rights) and the organization of their economic systems (involving the production, exchange, and consumption of goods and services, about which there is considerable inequality). Therefore, while people have political equality, they lack social equality. This unresolved contradiction is relatively permanent and a major source of conflict. Ideologies of fairness are constantly challenged by the realities of inequalities, and they influence governments to try to resolve the situation through politics and welfare benefits.

This situation represents one of conflict theory's most important assets for medical sociology; namely, the capacity to explain the politics associated with health reform. Conflict theory allows us to chart the maneuvers of various entities, like the medical profession, insurance companies, drug companies, the business community, and the public, as they struggle to acquire, protect, or expand their interests against existing government regulations and programs and those under consideration. Other conflict approaches are connected more directly to classical Marxism by relying on class struggle to explain health policy outcomes (Navarro 1994) and the disadvantages of the lower and working classes in capitalist medical systems where the emphasis is on profit (McKinlay 1984; Waitzkin 1983). While a major focus of conflict theory in medical sociology is on the role of competing interests in health care delivery and policy, other interests concern the sources of illness and disability in work environments, working-class health, differences in health lifestyles, and capitalist ideologies in the physician–patient relationship (Blane 1987; McKinlay 1984; Navarro 1986; Waitzkin 1983, 1989, 1991). However, there are inherent limitations in the use of conflict theory in medical sociology. While some health situations are affected by conflict-related conditions, others are not. People may maintain their health or become sick and these outcomes can have little or nothing to do with conflict, politics, interest-group competition, class struggles, and the like. Moreover, Marxism began losing influence from the late 1970s onward. As Alex Callinicos (2007) points out, political events sank Marxist theory in the universities. First, French scholars turned their back on Marxism as a "theory of domination" in response to Soviet labor camps, the Cold War, and the crackdown on Solidarity in Poland in 1981, followed by similar reactions elsewhere in Europe and Latin America. "The process of retreat was slower in the English-speaking world," states Callinicos (2007: 261), "but by the beginning of the 1990s, under the impact of postmodernism and the collapse of 'existing socialism' in Eastern Europe and the Soviet Union, Marx was a dead dog for most intellectuals there as well." As a political doctrine, Marxism–Leninism also failed to construct healthy social conditions and an adequate health care delivery system in the former Soviet Union and the East European socialist countries that experimented with it (Cockerham 1997, 1999, 2000, 2007b). Most of these countries experienced a 30-year decline (1965–95) in male life expectancy and for some – Belarus, Kazakhstan, Russia, and Ukraine – the health crisis is still continuing (Cockerham 2007b; Cockerham et al. 2006a, 2006b). The epicenter of the downturn in life expectancy was in Russia where male longevity fell 5.2 years between 1965 and 2005 and female life expectancy rose only 0.3 years. The theoretical and practical failure of Marxism to produce healthy societies substantially undermines the utility of Marxist-based theories in medical sociology (Cockerham 2007a). The greatest potential of conflict theory for medical sociology thus lies in its non-Marxist aspects, as interest-group competition in welfare states proves more relevant for health concerns than Marxist notions of class struggle.

Max Weber

None of the classical theorists – Comte, Spencer, Simmel, Marx, Durkheim, and Weber – concerned themselves with medical sociology. Weber, however, has had the greatest direct influence on the field. His most important contributions are associated with his concepts of formal rationality and lifestyles. Weber (1978) distinguished between two major types of rationality: formal and substantive. Formal rationality is the purposeful calculation of the most efficient means and procedures to realize goals, while substantive rationality is the realization of values and ideals based on tradition, custom, piety, or personal devotion. Weber described how, in Western society, formal rationality became dominant over its substantive counterpart as people sought to achieve specific ends by employing the most efficient means and, in the process, tended to disregard substantive rationality because it was often cumbersome, time-consuming, inefficient, and stifled progress. This form of rationality led to the rise of the West and the spread of capitalism. It is also linked to the development of scientific medicine and modern social structure through bureaucratic forms of authority and social organization that includes hospitals (Hillier 1987). The rational goal-oriented action that takes place in hospitals tends to be a flexible form of social order based on the requirements of patient care, rather than the rigid organization portrayed in Weber's concept of bureaucracy (Strauss et al. 1963). But his perspective on bureaucracy nevertheless captures the manner in which authority and control are exercised hierarchically and the importance of organizational goals in hospital work (Hillier 1987).

Weber's notion of formal rationality has likewise been applied to the "deprofessionalization" of physicians. Deprofessionalization means a decline in power resulting in a decline in the degree which a profession maintains its professional characteristics. Freidson's (1970a, 1970b) seminal work on the medical profession in the 1970s had captured American medicine's professional dominance in its relations with patients and external organizations. Medicine was *the* model of professionalism, with physicians having absolute authority over their work and ranked at or near the top of society in status. However, Ritzer and Walczak (1988) noted the loss of absolute authority by physicians as their treatment decisions came under increasing scrutiny in the late twentieth century by patients, health care organizations, insurance companies, and government agencies.

Ritzer and Walczak found that government policies emphasizing greater control over health care costs and the rise of the profit motive in medicine identified a trend in medical practice away from substantive rationality (stressing ideals like serving the patient) to formal rationality (stressing rules, regulations, and efficiency). Government and insurance company oversight in reviewing and approving patient care decisions, and the rise of private health care business corporations, decreased the autonomy of medical doctors by hiring them as employees and controlling their work. This, joined with greater consumerism on the part of patients, significantly reduced the professional power and status of physicians. Thus, the "golden age" of medical power and prestige ended, as medicine's efforts to avoid regulation left open an unregulated medical market that invited corporate control and public demands for government control to contain costs. Hafferty and Light (1995: 138) accurately predicted that "the basic overall thrust of professionalism is toward a loss and not a continuation or strengthening of medicine's control over its work."

Weber's work also provides the theoretical background for the study of health lifestyles. Weber (1978) identified life conduct (*Lebensführung*) and life chances (*Lebenschancen*) as the two central components of lifestyles (*Lebensstil*). Life conduct refers to choice or self-direction in behavior. Weber was ambiguous about what he meant by life chances, but Dahrendorf (1979: 73) analyzed Weber's writings and found that the most comprehensive concept of life chances in his terminology is that of "class position" and that he associated the term with a person's probability of finding satisfaction for interests, wants, and needs. He did not consider life chances to be a matter of pure chance; rather, they are the chances that people have in life because of their social situation.

Weber's most important contribution to conceptualizing lifestyles is to identify the dialectical interplay between choices and chances as each works off the other to shape lifestyle outcomes (Abel and Cockerham 1993; Cockerham, Abel, and Lüschen 1993). That is, people choose their lifestyle and the activities that characterize it, but their choices are constrained by their social situation. Through his concept of *Verstehen* or interpretive understanding, Weber seems to favor the role of choice as a proxy for agency over chance as representative of structure in lifestyle selection, although both are important. Weber also made the observation that lifestyles are based not so much on what people produce, but what they consume. By connecting lifestyles to status, Weber suggests that the means of consumption not only *expresses* differences in social and cultural practices between groups, but *establishes* them as social boundaries (Bourdieu 1984).

Health lifestyles are collective patterns of health-related behavior based on choices from options available to people according to their life chances (Cockerham 2005, 2007a; Cockerham, Rütten, and Abel 1997). These life chances include class, age, gender, ethnicity, and other relevant structural variables that shape lifestyle choices. The choices typically involve decisions about smoking, alcohol use, diet, exercise, and the like. The behaviors resulting from the interplay of choices and chances can have either positive or negative consequences for health, but nevertheless form a pattern of health practices that constitute a lifestyle. Although positive health lifestyles are intended to produce good health, the ultimate aim of such lifestyles is to be healthy in order to use (consume) it for something, such as the capability to work, feel and look good, participate in sports and leisure activities, and enjoy life (d'Houtaud and Field 1984). Health lifestyles originated in the upper middle class, yet have the potential to spread across class boundaries in varying degrees of quality (Cockerham, Kunz, and Lüschen 1988). While Weber did not consider the health aspects of lifestyles, his concepts allow us to view them as (1) associated with status groups and principally a collective, rather than individual, phenomenon; (2) patterns of consumption, not production; and (3) formed by the dialectical interplay between choices and chances. His conceptualization of lifestyles provides the foundation for current theorizing on health-related lifestyles (Cockerham 2005, 2007a).

CRITICAL THEORY AND JÜRGEN HABERMAS

The term critical theory has a long history but in sociology has come to be associated with a group of philosophers and social theorists pre-eminent in "culture critique" in Frankfurt in the interwar years and later, with the advent of Nazism, in California. Under the inspiration of Horkheimer and Adorno, and in the 1960s in the USA with Marcuse, the classical contributions of Marx and Weber were reworked and framed in response to fascism, Stalinism, and managerial capitalism (Outhwaite 1996). The name of Adorno, in particular, came to be linked with a profound and remorseless cultural pessimism: the logic of the twentieth century, even of modernity, was seen as one of ineluctable decline. The influential *Dialectic of Enlightenment*, written with Horkheimer during World War II and published in 1947, epitomizes this inexorable sense of decay. One of Adorno's assistants, Jürgen Habermas, did not share the gloom of his mentor and it is his contribution that came to dominate critical theory during the last decades of the twentieth century. Some medical sociologists turned to his work for theoretical inspiration. It was Habermas' concept of rationality that differentiated his theories from those of predecessors like Marx, Weber, Adorno, and Horkheimer. He rejected any suggestion that rationality be subsumed by Weber's *Zweckrationalität*, or instrumental rationality. In other words, rationality is more than that which governs the choice of means to given, usually material, ends. He developed the notion of what he came to call "communicative rationality," which refers to the activity of reflecting on our taken-for-granted assumptions about the world, bringing basic norms to the fore to be interrogated and negotiated. Not only does instrumental rationality bypass these norms, but it is on its own insufficient to capture the nature of either "cultural evolution" or even the economy and state, which are too complex to be seen merely as its product.

Basic to his early work is a distinction between work and interaction. Marx, Weber, and his Frankfurt predecessors had, he felt, fixated on the former and neglected the latter. In the case of Marxian theory, what Habermas understands as the reduction of interaction, or "communicative action," to work, instrumental or "strategic action," dramatically limited its scope both to account for modernity and to ground a project of human emancipation. The two-volume *Theory of Communicative Action*, published in Germany in 1981, took this analysis to a new level of subtlety and comprehensiveness (Habermas 1984, 1987). Locating his theories within the orbit of a "reconstructed" Enlightenment project, Habermas sought to bring together two long-standing, "rival" approaches to social theory. The first analyzes society as a meaningful whole for its participants (*Verstehen* theory); and the second analyzes society as a system that is stabilized behind the backs of the participants (system theory) (Sitton 1996). This goal gave rise to the celebrated distinction between the *lifeworld*, based on social integration, and the *system*, based on system integration.

The lifeworld is characterized by communicative action and has two aspects or sub-systems: the private sphere comprises the rapidly changing unit of the household, while the public sphere represents the domain of popular communication, discussion, and debate. The system operates through strategic action and it too has its sub-systems, the economy and the state. These four sub-systems are interdependent: each is specialized in terms of what it produces but is dependent on the others for what it does not produce. The private sphere of the lifeworld produces "commitment" and the public sphere "influence"; the economy produces "money" and the state "power." These products or "media" are traded between sub-systems. Thus the economy relies on the state to set up appropriate legal institutions such as private property and contract, on the public sphere of the lifeworld to influence consumption patterns, and on the private sphere to provide a committed labor force, and itself sends money into each other sub-system. Habermas argued that in the modern era, system and lifeworld have become "decoupled." Moreover, the system has come increasingly to dominate or "colonize" the lifeworld. Thus decision-making across many areas owes more to money and power than to rational debate and consensus.

This notion of system penetration and colonization of the lifeworld has been taken up in medical sociology (Scambler 2001). It has been suggested that "expert systems" like medicine have become more answerable to system imperatives than to the lifeworlds of patients. Using Mishler's (1984) terms, the "voice of medicine" has grown in authority over the "voice of the lifeworld." Independently of the motivations and aspirations, and sometimes the reflexivity, of individual physicians, they have become less responsive to patient-defined needs, nothwithstanding ubiquitous rhetorics to the contrary. Habermas' framework of system and lifeworld, strategic and communicative action, continues to be used in the twenty-first century to analyze and explain macro-level changes to health care organization and delivery and micro-level changes to physician–patient interaction and communication. Scambler (2002), for example, draws on it to account for (1) Clinton's failure to partially decommodify health care in the US in the early 1990s, and (2) the partial recommodification of the British National Health Service from the 1980s onwards. He deploys it also to address the diminution of patient trust in individual encounters with physicians, a theme of growing importance in health care.

THEORY IN THE TWENTY-FIRST CENTURY

The twentieth century ended with new social realities causing both sociology and medical sociology to adjust and consider new theoretical orientations, as well as adapt older ones to account for the changes. As Pescosolido and Kronenfeld (1995: 9) explain:

> We stand at a transition between social forms. The society that created the opportunity for the rise of a dominant profession of medicine, for a new discipline of sociology, and for a spinoff of the subfield of medical sociology, is undergoing major change. As the larger social system unravels in the face of rapid social change, established problems, solutions, and understandings are challenged because they do not as successfully confront current realities.

With the twenty-first century at hand, we have witnessed the aftermath of the collapse of communism in the former Soviet Union and Eastern Europe, the multi-culturalization of Europe and North America, the rise of cultural and sexual politics, changing patterns of social stratification, the increasing importance of information as an economic commodity, the dominance of the service sector in the global economy, the rise of China as the world's center for manufacturing consumer goods, a global economic recession, and the election of the first black president of the United States. Changing circumstances have resulted in new orientations toward living for many individuals. Crawford (2000), for example, sees a contradiction at the heart of the new "consumer society." He argues that capitalism only functions if people are simultaneously producers and consumers, but that the personalities and ethics of the two are in opposition. To be a producer in the workplace requires self-denial, self-control, rationality, self-discipline, and willpower, while irrational-ity, release, indulgence, and pleasure-seeking characterize consumption. Such "co-presence" is evident in relation to health lifestyle practices like smoking, eating various foods, exercise, drinking alcohol, and so on. These practices have a binary character in that they can be either good or bad, depending on how they affect a person's health. Whereas people may have more or less taken their health for granted in past historical eras, this is no longer the case as health is considered an achievement and everyone is expected to work at being healthy or risk chronic illness and premature death if they do not (Clarke et al. 2003). Changing health-related social conditions signify an adjustment in theoretical approaches for medical sociology or the emergence of new ones so these changes can be taken into account.

Poststructuralism: Michel Foucault

Many current theories are grounded in poststructuralism, which emerged out of a short-lived structuralist perspective popular in France in the 1960s. Structuralism has its roots in linguistics, most notably the semiotic (sign systems) theory of Fer-dinand de Saussure, and is largely based on the work of the anthropologist Claude Lévi-Strauss. Both structuralism and poststructuralism developed theories which analyzed culture in terms of signs, symbolic codes, and language, and took the posi-tion that the individual was not autonomous but constrained by discourse (Best and Kellner 1991). Structuralism depicted social meanings as fixed, not free, and main-tained by traditional and universal structures (deep structures) that formed a stable and self-contained system. Poststructuralists, however, rejected the notion that there were universal rules organizing social phenomena into compact systems, along with structuralism's failure to account for the motivations of users of language and its ahistorical approach to analysis. One major approach to poststructuralism is the work of Jacques Derrida, which helped lay a foundation for the emergence of post-modern theory. Derrida's (1978) analysis (deconstruction) of texts suggested that written language was not socially constraining, nor were its meanings stable and orderly. Depending upon the context in which they were used, meanings could be unstable and disorderly.

The leading representative of poststructuralism is the French theorist Michel Foucault, who focused on the relationship between knowledge and power. Foucault provided social histories of the manner in which knowledge produced expertise that was used by professions and institutions, including medicine, to shape social behavior. Knowledge and power were depicted as being so closely connected that an extension of one meant a simultaneous expansion of the other. In fact, Foucault often used the term "knowledge/power" to express this unity (Turner 1995). The knowledge/power link is not only repressive, but also productive and enabling, as it is a decisive basis upon which people are allocated to positions in society. A major contribution of Foucault to medical sociology is his analysis of the social functions of the medical profession, including the use of medical knowledge as a means of social control and regulation, as he studied madness, clinics, and sexuality. Foucault (1973) found two distinct trends emerging in the history of medical practice: "medicine of the species" (the classification, diagnosis, and treatment of disease) and "medicine of social spaces" (the prevention of disease). The former defined the human body as an object of study subject to medical intervention and control, while the latter made the public's health subject to medical and civil regulation. The surveillance of human sexuality by the state, church, and medicine subjected the most intimate bodily activities to institutional discourse and monitoring. Thus, bodies themselves came under the jurisdiction of experts on behalf of society (Petersen and Bunton 1997; Turner 1992, 1996).

Foucault's approach to the study of the body also influenced the development of a new specialty, the sociology of the body, with Bryan Turner's book *The Body and Society* (1996, originally published in 1984) the seminal work in this area. Theoretical developments concerning the sociological understanding of the control, use, and the phenomenological experience of the body, including emotions, have been most pronounced in Great Britain where this subject has become a major topic in medical sociology. One area of inquiry is the dialectical relationship between the physical body and human subjectivity or the "lived" or phenomenological experience of both having and being in a body. As Lupton (1998: 85) explains: "The body-image shapes the ways in which individuals understand and experience physical sensations and locate themselves in social space, how they conceptualize themselves as separated from other physical phenomena, how they carry themselves, how they distinguish outside from inside and invest themselves as subject or object."

Regardless of its influence on many facets of contemporary theory in medical sociology, poststructuralism and the work of Foucault has its critics. Some suggest that the perspective does not take limits on power into account, nor explain relations between macro-level power structures other than dwell on their mechanisms for reproduction; moreover, there is a disregard of agency in poststructural concepts, especially those of Foucault (Giddens 1987; Münch 1993). Giddens (1987: 98), for example, notes Foucault's history tends to have no active subjects at all and concludes: "It is history with the agency removed." And he (Giddens 1987: 98) goes on to say that the "individuals who appear in Foucault's analyses seem impotent to determine their own destinies." Yet Foucault's knowledge/power equation, applied to social behavior, remains important for a number of topics in medical sociology (Petersen and Bunton 1997). While both structuralism and poststructuralism are now considered dead traditions of social thought, some of the themes associated with them nevertheless remain influential (Giddens 1987) and reappear in social constructionism, feminist theory, especially postmodern theory, and the work of Bourdieu.

Social constructionism

One theoretical area of investigation with links to poststructuralism is social constructionism, which is based on the premise that phenomena are not discovered but socially produced (Turner 2004). That is, things are what they are defined as, even illness. For example, Lorber (1997) and others (Radley 1993) maintain that illness is socially constructed in that the expression of symptoms is shaped by cultural and moral values, experienced through interaction with other people, and influenced by particular beliefs about what constitutes health and illness. The result, claims Lorber, is a transformation of physiological symptoms into a diagnosis which produces socially appropriate illness behavior and a modified social status. When it comes to emotions, social constructionism emphasizes the social, rather than biological, nature of emotional states (James and Gabe 1996). It takes the position that emotions vary cross-culturally and socially in their meaning and expression; consequently, they are first and foremost social and cultural constructions (Williams and Bendelow 1996).

In medical sociology, one branch of the social constructionist approach is closely tied to Foucault and analyzes the body as a product of power and knowledge (Annandale 1998; Bury 1986; Nettleton 2006). It focuses on examining the manner in which people shape, decorate, present, manage, and socially evaluate the body. Shilling (1993), for example, points out that social class has a profound influence on how people develop their bodies and apply symbolic values to particular body forms. Shilling (1993: 140) finds that bodies represent physical capital with their value determined by "the ability of dominant groups to define their bodies and lifestyles as superior, worthy of reward, and as, metaphorically and literally, the embodiment of class." Nettleton (2006) summarizes the Foucauldian wing of social constructionism in medical sociology by emphasizing its three major characteristics. First, it denies the existence of truth and the possibility of arriving at a single valid account of disease and the body. Second, it opposes traditional histories of medicine which suggest steady and continuous progress toward an increasingly valid knowledge of disease. Instead, social constructionism favors a more eclectic approach, focusing on specific and discontinuous arguments. And third, since all types of knowledge, whether based on science or experience, have equal validity, a rethinking of the relationship between medical "experts" and lay persons is required. The notion that all knowledge is socially constructed removes any claim that medical knowledge is always superior to lay knowledge.

The other branch of social constructionism is based on the seminal work of Peter Berger and Thomas Luckmann in their book *The Social Construction of Reality* (1967), which is grounded in symbolic interaction and its emphasis on agency. This approach is also influenced by Eliot Freidson's (1970a, 1970b) analysis of medical professionalization. Freidson examined how the medical profession monopolized power and authority in health matters to advance its own interests. Given the significant differences between Berger and Luckmann in comparison to Foucault, it is obvious that social constructionism lacks a single, unified doctrine. According to Turner (2004: 43), "These different types of constructionism present very different accounts of human agency and thus have different implications for an understanding of the relationship between patients, doctors, and disease entities." The more social constructionist work is influenced by Berger and Luckmann, the more agency ori-ented it is; the closer to Foucault, the less agency has a role.

Feminist theory

Feminist theory in medical sociology also has poststructural roots, especially in regard to social constructionist accounts of the female body and its regulation by a male-dominated society. Social and cultural assumptions are held to influence our perceptions of the body, including the use of the male body as the standard for medical training, the assignment of less socially desirable physical and emotional traits to women, and the ways in which women's illnesses are socially constructed (Annandale and Clark 1996; Clarke and Olesen 1999; Lorber 1997; Lupton 1994). Other feminist theory is grounded in conflict theory or symbolic interaction, and deals with the sexist treatment of women patients by male doctors and the less than equal status of female physicians in professional settings and hierarchies (Fisher 1984; West 1984; Riska and Wegar 1993; Hinze 2004). There is, however, no unified perspective among feminist theorists other than a "woman-centered" perspective that examines the various facets of women's health and seeks an end to sexist orientations in health and illness and society at large (Annandale 1998; Annandale and Clark 1996; Clarke and Olesen 1999; Lengermann and Niebrugge-Brantley 2000; Nettleton 2006).

Postmodern theory

There is considerable disagreement about the nature and definition of postmoder-nity, but a common theme is the breakup of modernity and its postindustrial social system that is bringing new social conditions. Postmodernism was generally ignored by sociologists until the mid-1980s when primarily British social scientists decided it was worthy of serious attention (Bertens 1995). Postmodernism emerged out of poststructuralism as a more inclusive critique of modern sociological theory and grand narratives making sweeping generalizations about society as a whole; it rejected notions of continuity and order and called for new concepts explaining the disruptions of late modern social change (Best and Kellner 1991). Rather, it argued that there was no single coherent rationality and the framework for social life had become fragmented, diversified, and decentralized (Turner 1990). Its sociological relevance rested in its depiction of the destabilization of society and the requirement to adjust theory to new social realities. However, there have been few works to date in medical sociology explicitly adopting postmodern themes. Exceptions include highly abstract and poststructuralist-oriented discourses on health and the definition of the body (Fox 1993), along with works concerning the fragmentation of modern society and medical authority leaving individuals with greater self-control over their bodies (Glassner 1989), increased personal responsibility for their health (Cockerham et al. 1997), and enhanced use of alternative forms of health care (McQuaide 2005). Pescosolido and Rubin (2000) linked postmodern conditions to the deinstitutionalization of the mentally ill in the United States.

The theory reached its highest level of popularity in sociology during the early 1990s and momentarily seemed poised to have an important future in medical sociology. But this did not occur. Use of the theory abruptly declined in the late 1990s and a strong foothold in medical sociology was never achieved (Cockerham 2007c). Why? Postmodern theory turned out to have a number of shortfalls, including its failure to explain social conditions after the rupture with modernity is complete, the lack of an adequate theory of agency, being too abstract and ambiguous, not providing clear conceptualizations, an inability to account for social causation, not having empirical confirmation, and invariably featuring an obtuse jargon that only its dedicated adherents found meaningful and others came to regard as nonsense (Best and Kellner 1991; Cockerham 2007c; Pescosolido and Rubin 2000; Ritzer 2008). While its demise for medical sociology has been announced (Cockerham 2007c; Williams 1999), it is still popular in some circles although its influence has waned considerably in recent years and become less important. The advantage of postmodern theory is that modern society is undergoing a transition, with social conditions different from the recent past (the latter part of the twentieth century), and the perspective provides a theoretical framework, despite its diffuse literature, for examining some of these changes.

Pierre Bourdieu

Once ranked as the leading intellectual in France, Bourdieu (1984) focused on how the routine practices of individuals are influenced by the external structure of their social world and how these practices, in turn, reproduce that structure. Through his key concept of habitus, Bourdieu connects social practices to culture, structure, and power (Swartz 1997). Bourdieu (1990) describes the habitus as a mental scheme or organized framework of perceptions (a structured structure operating as a structuring structure) that predisposes the individual to follow a particular line of behavior as opposed to others that might be chosen. These perceptions are developed, shaped, and maintained in memory and the habitus through socialization, experience, and the reality of class circumstances. While the behavior selected may be contrary to normative expectations and usual ways of acting, behavioral choices are typically compatible with the dispositions and norms of a particular group, class, or the larger society; therefore, people tend to act in predictable and habitual ways even though they have the capability to choose differently. Through selective perception, the habitus adjusts aspirations and expectations to "categories of the probable" that impose boundaries on the potential for action and its likely form.

Of all Bourdieu's works, the one most relevant for medical sociologists remains his book *Distinction* (1984), in which he systematically accounts for the patterns of cultural consumption and competition over definitions of taste of the French social classes. It includes an analysis of food habits and sports that describes how a class-oriented habitus shaped these particular aspects of health lifestyles. Cockerham (1997, 1999, 2000, 2005, 2007b) follows Bourdieu's theoretical framework in his theory of health lifestyles and in identifying negative health lifestyles as the primary social determinant of ongoing downturn in life expectancy in Russia. The group most responsible for reduced longevity are middle-age, working-class males. The living conditions of these men and their relatively low and powerless position in the social structure produced a habitus fostering unhealthy practices (heavy drinking and smoking, disregard for diet, and rejection of exercise) that resulted in a lifestyle promoting heart disease, accidents, and other health problems leading to a shortened life span. These behaviors were norms established through group interaction, shaped by the opportunities available to them, and internalized by the habitus. The structure of everyday life both limited and molded health-related choices to the extent that lifestyles led to premature deaths.

According to Williams (1995), the merit of Bourdieu's analysis for understanding the relationship between class and health lifestyles lies in his depiction of the relative durability of various forms of health-related behavior within particular social classes and the relatively seamless fashion in which he links agency and structure. "In particular," states Williams (1995: 601), "the manner in which his arguments are wedded to an analysis of the inter-relationship between class, capital, taste, and the body in the construction of lifestyles ... is both compelling and convincing." Although Bourdieu has been criticized for overemphasizing structure at the expense of agency and presenting an overly deterministic model of human behavior (Münch 1993), he nevertheless provides a framework for medical sociologists to conceptualize health lifestyles and for sociologists generally to address the agency–structure interface (Cockerham 2005).

Critical realism

Critical realism is a relatively new theoretical perspective that emerged in Great Britain and is based on the work of philosopher Roy Bhaskar (1994, 1998) and sociologist Margaret Archer (1995, 2000, 2003; Archer et al. 1998). Critical realist theory argues that social constructionism does not account for agency and provides an "oversocialized" view of individuals overemphasizing the effects of structure, while other theorists, like Bourdieu and Giddens, opt for a "seamless" approach to agency and structure, but the operations of the two in reality are not synchronized. Consequently, critical realism, in opposition to poststructuralism, treats agency and structure as fundamentally distinct but interdependent dimensions that need to be studied separately in order to understand their respective contributions to social practice. The "analytical decoupling of structure and agency" is necessary, states Williams (1999: 809), "not in order to abandon their articulation, but, on the contrary, so as to examine their *mutual interplay across time*; something which can result both in *stable reproduction* or *change* through the *emergence* of new properties and powers."

Critical realism takes the position that social systems are open to process and change and that people as agents and actors have the critical capacity, reflexivity, and creativity to shape structure, yet, in turn, are shaped by structure. But the key factor for the critical realist is the capacity of the individual to transform structure and produce variable outcomes (Archer 1995). Structure, for its part, is relatively enduring, although it can be modified, and deep structures have generative mechanisms going beyond the observable that influence behavior. A goal of critical realism is to connect agency and structure in a way that the distinctive properties of both can be realistically accounted for without being reduced to a single entity. Among the few studies in medical sociology employing critical realism to date are examinations of the body from the standpoint of chronic illness and disability, which focus on the interrelationship of biological and social factors in shaping outcomes

(Williams 1999), and an attempt to develop a sociology of health inequalities which goes beyond orthodox social epidemiological studies (Scambler 2002).

CONCLUSION

The notion that medical sociology is atheoretical is wrong. This chapter has provided a brief account of the history and variety of viewpoints in sociological theory that have been utilized within the field and provided influential statements on the relationship between society and health. Beginning with Parsons and structural functionalism, medical sociology in reality has a rich theoretical tradition spanning almost 60 years and incorporating the work of both classical and contemporary theorists. Debates in general sociology, such as those involving the opposition of symbolic interactionists and conflict theorists to structural functionalism and the current agency versus structure dispute, became points of theoretical contention in medical sociology as well. During the latter part of the twentieth century, structural theories like structural functionalism were largely abandoned in favor of agency-oriented theories like symbolic interaction, labeling theory, and the agency side of social constructionism. However, improved statistical techniques to measure the effects of structure – such as hierarchical linear modeling – forecast a paradigm shift back to greater considerations of structure and structural approaches to theory (Cockerham 2007a). Although it is too early to determine the ultimate direction of theory in medical sociology this century with exact precision, these improved statistical procedures should provide a more comprehensive approach to research with theory guiding and adjusting to this capability. Already the theoretical basis for work in the field is extensive and its potential explanatory power is likely to increase. Medical sociology has become a theoretical subdiscipline.

References

Abel, Thomas and William C. Cockerham. 1993. "Lifestyle or *Lebensführung*? Critical Remarks on the Mistranslation of Weber's 'Class, Status, Party'." *Sociological Quarterly* 34: 551–6.

Annandale, Ellen. 1998. *The Sociology of Health and Medicine: A Critical Introduction*. Cambridge: Polity Press.

Annandale, Ellen and Judith Clark. 1996. "What is Gender? Feminist Theory and the Sociology of Human Reproduction." *Sociology of Health and Illness* 18: 17–44.

Archer, Margaret S. 1995. *Realist Social Theory: The Morphogenetic Approach*. Cambridge: Cambridge University Press.

Archer, Margaret S. 2000. *Being Human: The Problem of Agency*. Cambridge; Cambridge University Press.

Archer, Margaret S. 2003. *Structure, Agency, and the Internal Conversation*. Cambridge: Cambridge University Press.

Archer, Margaret, Roy Bhaskar, Andrew Collier, Tony Lawson, and Alan Norrie. 1998. *Critical Realism: Essential Readings*. London: Routledge.

Beck, Ulrich. 1992. *Risk Society: Towards a New Modernity*. London: Sage.

Becker, Howard S. 1973. *Outsiders: Studies in the Sociology of Deviance*, 2nd edition. New York: Free Press.

Becker, Howard S., Blanche Greer, Everett Hughes, and Anselm Strauss. 1961. *Boys in White: Student Culture in Medical School.* Chicago: University of Chicago Press.

Berger, Peter L. and Thomas Luckmann. 1967. *The Social Construction of Reality.* New York: Anchor.

Bertens, Hans. 1995. *The Idea of the Postmodern.* London: Routledge.

Best, Steven and Douglas Kellner. 1991. *Postmodern Theory: Critical Interrogations.* New York: Guilford.

Bhaskar, Roy. 1994. *Plato Etc.: The Problems of Philosophy and Their Resolution.* London: Verso.

Bhaskar, Roy. 1998. *The Possibility of Naturalism: A Philosophical Critique of the Contemporary Human Sciences.* London: Routledge.

Blane, David. 1987. "The Value of Labour-Power and Health." Pp. 8–36 in G. Scambler (ed.), *Sociological Theory and Medical Sociology.* London: Tavistock.

Blumer, Herbert. 1969. *Symbolic Interactionism.* Englewood Cliffs, NJ: Prentice-Hall.

Bourdieu, Pierre. 1984. *Distinction: A Social Critique of the Judgement of Taste.* London: Routledge.

Bourdieu, Pierre. 1990. *The Logic of Practice.* Cambridge: Polity Press.

Bury, Michael. 1986. "Social Constructionism and the Development of Medical Sociology." *Sociology of Health and Illness* 8: 137–69.

Callinicos, Alex. 2007. *Social Theory: A Historical Introduction*, 2nd edition. Cambridge: Polity.

Clarke, Adele E. and Virginia L. Olesen (eds.). 1999. *Revisioning Women, Health, and Healing.* London: Routledge.

Clarke, Adele E., Janet K. Shim, Laura Mamo, Jennifer Ruth Fosket, and Jennifer R. Fishman. 2003. "Biomedicalization: Technoscientific Transformations of Health, Illness, and US Biomedicine." *American Sociological Review* 68: 161–94.

Claus, Elizabeth. 1982. *The Growth of a Sociological Discipline: On the Development of Medical Sociology in Europe*, vol. I. Leuven, Belgium: Sociological Research Institute, Katholieke Universiteit Leuven.

Cockerham, William C. 1983. "The State of Medical Sociology in the United States, Great Britain, West Germany, and Austria." *Social Science and Medicine* 17: 1513–27.

Cockerham, William C. 1997. "The Social Determinants of the Decline of Life Expectancy in Russia and Eastern Europe." *Journal of Health and Social Behavior* 38: 117–30.

Cockerham, William C. 1999. *Health and Social Change in Russia and Eastern Europe.* London: Routledge.

Cockerham, William C. 2000. "Health Lifestyles in Russia." *Social Science and Medicine* 51: 1313–24.

Cockerham, William C. 2005. "Health Lifestyle Theory and the Convergence of Agency and Structure." *Journal of Health and Social Behavior* 46: 51–67.

Cockerham, William C. 2007a. *Social Causes of Health and Disease.* Cambridge: Polity Press.

Cockerham, William C. 2007b. "Health Lifestyles and the Absence of the Russian Middle Class." *Sociology of Health and Illness* 29: 457–73.

Cockerham, William C. 2007c. "A Note on the Fate of Postmodern Theory and its Failure to Meet the Basic Requirements for Success in Medical Sociology." *Social Theory and Health* 5: 285–96.

Cockerham, William C. 2010. *Medical Sociology*, 11th edition. Upper Saddle River, NJ: Pearson Prentice-Hall.

Cockerham, William C., Thomas Abel, and Günther Lüschen. 1993. "Max Weber, Formal Rationality, and Health Lifestyles." *Sociological Quarterly* 34: 413–25.

Cockerham, William C., Brian P. Hinote, Geoffrey B. Cockerham, and Pamela Abbott. 2006a. "Health Lifestyles and Political Ideology in Belarus, Russia, and Ukraine." *Social Science and Medicine* 62: 1799–809.

Cockerham, William C., Brian P. Hinote, and Pamela Abbott. 2006b. "Psychological Distress, Gender, and Health Lifestyles in Belarus, Kazakhstan, Russia, and Ukraine." *Social Science and Medicine* 63: 2381–94.

Cockerham, William C., Gerhard Kunz, and Günther Lüschen. 1988. "Social Stratification and Health Lifestyles in Two Systems of Health Care Delivery: A Comparison of the United States and West Germany." *Journal of Health and Social Behavior* 29: 113–26.

Cockerham, William C., Alfred Rütten, and Thomas Abel. 1997. "Conceptualizing Contemporary Health Lifestyles: Moving Beyond Weber." *Sociological Quarterly* 38: 321–42.

Crawford, Robert. 2000. "The Ritual of Health Promotion in the US." Pp. 219–325 in S. Williams, J. Gabe, and M. Calnan (eds.), *Health, Medicine and Society: Key Theories, Future Agendas*. London: Routledge.

Dahrendorf, Ralf. 1959. *Class and Conflict in Industrial Society*. Stanford, CA: Stanford University Press.

Dahrendorf, Ralf. 1979. *Life Chances*. Chicago: University of Chicago Press.

Denzin, Norman K. 1991. *Symbolic Interactionism and Cultural Studies*. Oxford: Blackwell.

Derrida, Jacques. 1978. *Writing and Difference*. Chicago: University of Chicago Press.

d'Houtaud, A. and Mark G. Field. 1984. "The Image of Health: Variations in Perception by Social Class." *Sociology of Health and Illness* 6: 30–59.

Durkheim, Emile. 1950 [1895]. *The Rules of Sociological Method*. New York: Free Press.

Durkheim, Emile. 1951 [1897]. *Suicide: A Study in Sociology*. Glencoe, IL: Free Press.

Durkheim, Emile. 1964 [1893]. *The Division of Labor in Society*. New York: Free Press.

Field, Mark. 1995. "The Health Crisis in the Former Soviet Union: A Report from the 'Post-War' Zone." *Social Science and Medicine* 41: 1469–78.

Fisher, Sue. 1984. "Doctor–Patient Communication: A Social and Micro-Political Performance." *Sociology of Health and Illness* 6: 1–27.

Foucault, Michel. 1973. *The Birth of the Clinic*. London: Tavistock.

Fox, Nicholas J. 1993. *Postmodernism, Sociology and Health*. Buckingham: Open University Press.

Freidson, Eliot. 1970a. *Profession of Medicine: A Study of the Sociology of Applied Knowledge*. New York: Dodd & Mead.

Freidson, Eliot. 1970b. *Professional Dominance*. Chicago: Aldine.

Giddens, Anthony. 1987. *Social Theory and Modern Sociology*. Stanford, CA: Stanford University Press.

Glaser, Barney G. and Anselm M. Strauss. 1965. *Awareness of Dying*. Chicago: Aldine.

Glaser, Barney G. and Anselm M. Strauss. 1967. *The Discovery of Grounded Theory*. Chicago: Aldine.

Glaser, Barney G. and Anselm M. Strauss. 1968. *Time for Dying*. Chicago: Aldine.

Glassner, Barry. 1989. "Fitness and the Postmodern Self." *Journal of Health and Social Behavior* 30: 180–91.

Goffman, Erving. 1959. *The Presentation of Self in Everyday Life*. New York: Anchor.

Goffman, Erving. 1961. *Asylums*. Anchor.

Goffman, Erving. 1967. *Stigma: Notes on the Management of Spoiled Identity*. Engelwood Cliffs, NJ: Prentice-Hall.

Habermas, Jürgen. 1984. *The Theory of Communicative Action. Vol. 1: Reason and the Rationalization of Society*. London: Heinemann.

Habermas, Jürgen. 1987. *The Theory of Communicative Action. Vol. 2: Lifeworld and System: A Critique of Functionalist Reason*. Cambridge: Polity Press.

Hafferty, Frederic W. and Donald W. Light. 1995. "Professional Dynamics and the Changing Nature of Medical Work." *Journal of Health and Social Behavior*, Extra Issue: 132–53.

Hillier, Sheila. 1987. "Rationalism, Bureaucracy, and the Organization of Health Services: Max Weber's Contribution to Understanding Modern Health Care Systems." Pp. 194–220 in G. Scambler (ed.), *Sociological Theory and Medical Sociology*. London: Tavistock.

Hinze, S. 2004. " 'Am I Being Oversensitive?' Women's Experience of Sexual Harassment during Medical Training." *Health* 8: 101–27.

James, Veronica and Jonathan Gabe (eds.). 1996. *Health and the Sociology of Emotions*. Oxford: Blackwell.

Lengermann, Patricia Madoo and Jil Niebrugge-Brantley. 2000. "Contemporary Feminist Theory." Pp. 307–55 in G. Ritzer (ed.), *Modern Sociological Theory*. New York: McGraw-Hill.

Lorber, Judith. 1997. *Gender and the Social Construction of Illness*. London: Sage.

Lupton, Deborah. 1994. *Medicine as Culture: Illness, Disease, and the Body in Western Culture*. London: Sage.

Lupton, Deborah. 1998. "Going with the Flow: Some Central Discourses in Conceptualizing and Articulating the Embodiment of Emotional States." Pp. 82–99 in S. Nettleton and J. Watson (eds.), *The Body in Everyday Life*. London: Routledge.

McKinlay, John (ed.). 1984. *Issues in the Political Economy of Health Care*. London: Tavistock.

McQuaide, M. 2005. "The Rise of Alternative Health Care: A Sociological Account." *Social Theory and Health* 3: 286–301.

Mead, George H. 1934. *Mind, Self, and Society*. Chicago: University of Chicago Press.

Merton, Robert K., George G. Reader, and Patricia Kendall. 1957. *The Student Physician*. Cambridge, MA: Harvard University Press.

Mishler, Elliot. 1984. *The Discourse of Medicine: Dialectics of Medical Interviews*. Norwood, NJ: Ablex.

Münch, Richard. 1993. *Sociological Theory*. Chicago: Nelson-Hall.

Navarro, Vicente. 1986. *Crisis, Health, and Medicine: A Social Critique*. London: Tavistock.

Navarro, Vicente. 1994. *The Politics of Health Policy*. Oxford: Blackwell.

Nettleton, Sarah. 2006. *The Sociology of Health and Illness*, 2nd edition. Cambridge: Polity Press.

Outhwaite, William (ed.). 1996. *The Habermas Reader*. Cambridge: Polity Press.

Parsons, Talcott. 1951. *The Social System*. New York: Free Press.

Pescosolido, Bernice and Jennie J. Kronenfeld. 1995. "Health, Illness, and Healing in an Uncertain Era: Challenges from and for Medical Sociology." *Journal of Health and Social Behavior*, Extra Issue: 5–33.

Pescosolido, Bernice P. and Beth A. Rubin. 2000. "The Web of Group Affiliations Revisited: Social Life, Postmodernism, and Sociology." *American Sociological Review* 65: 52–76.

Petersen, Alan and Robin Bunton (eds.). 1997. *Foucault, Health, and Medicine*. London: Routledge.

Radley, Alan (ed.). 1993. *Worlds of Illness: Biographical and Cultural Perspectives on Health and Disease*. London: Routledge.

Riska, Elianne and Katarina Wegar (eds.). 1993. *Gender, Work, and Medicine*. London: Sage.

Ritzer, George. 2008. *Modern Sociological Theory*, 7th edition. New York: McGraw-Hill.

Ritzer, George and David Walczak. 1988. "Rationalization and the Deprofessionalization of Physicians." *Social Forces* 67: 1–22.

Scambler, Graham (ed.). 2001. *Habermas, Critical Theory and Health*. London: Routledge.

Scambler, Graham. 2002. *Health and Social Change: A Critical Theory*. Buckingham: Open University Press.

Scheff, Thomas J. 1999. *Being Mentally Ill*, 3rd edition. Hawthorne, NY: Aldine de Gruyter.

Seale, Clive. 2008. "Mapping the Field of Medical Sociology: A Comparative Analysis of Journals." *Sociology of Health and Illness* 5: 677–95.

Shilling, Chris. 1993. *The Body and Social Theory*. London: Sage.

Sitton, John. 1996. *Recent Marxian Theory: Class Formation and Social Conflict in Contemporary Capitalism*. New York: State University of New York Press.

Smelser, Neil J. 1998. *The Social Edges of Psychoanalysis*. Berkeley: University of California Press.

Strauss, Anselm, Leonard Schatzman, Danuta Ehrlich, Rue Bucher, and Melvin Sabshin. 1963. "The Hospital and its Negotiated Order." Pp. 147–69 in E. Freidson (ed.), *The Hospital in Modern Society*. New York: Free Press.

Swartz, David. 1997. *Culture and Power: The Sociology of Pierre Bourdieu*. Chicago: University of Chicago Press.

Turner, Bryan S. 1988. *Status*. Milton Keynes: Open University Press.

Turner, Bryan S. 1990. "The Interdisciplinary Curriculum: From Social Medicine to Postmodernism." *Sociology of Health and Illness* 12: 1–23.

Turner, Bryan S. 1992. *Regulating Bodies*. London: Routledge.

Turner, Bryan S. 1995. *Medical Power and Social Knowledge*, 2nd edition. London: Sage.

Turner, Bryan S. 1996. *The Body and Society*, 2nd edition. London: Sage.

Turner, Bryan S. 2004. *The New Medical Sociology: Social Forms of Health and Illness*. London: Norton.

Waitzkin, Howard. 1983. *The Second Sickness: Contradictions of Capitalist Health Care*. New York: Free Press.

Waitzkin, Howard. 1989. "A Critical Theory of Medical Discourse: Ideology, Social Control, and the Processing of Social Context in Medical Encounters." *Journal of Health and Social Behavior* 30: 220–39.

Waitzkin, Howard. 1991. *The Politics of Medical Encounters*. New Haven, CT: Yale University Press.

Weber, Max. 1958 [1904–5]. *The Protestant Ethic and the Spirit of Capitalism*, translated by T. Parsons. New York: Scribner's.

Weber, Max. 1978 [1922]. *Economy and Society*, 2 vols., edited and translated by G. Roth and C. Wittich. Berkeley: University of California Press.

West, Candace. 1984. "When the Doctor is a 'Lady': Power, Status, and Gender in Physician–Patient Encounters." *Symbolic Interaction* 7: 87–106.

Williams, Simon J. 1995. "Theorising Class, Health and Lifestyles: Can Bourdieu Help Us?" *Sociology of Health and Illness* 17: 577–604.

Williams, Simon J. 1998. " 'Capitalising' on Emotions? Rethinking the Inequalities in Health Debate." *Sociology* 32: 121–39.

Williams, Simon J. 1999. "Is Anybody There? Critical Realism, Chronic Illness and the Disability Debate." *Sociology of Health and Illness* 21: 797–819.

Williams, Simon J. and Gillian Bendelow. 1996. "Emotions, Health and Illness: The 'Missing Link' in Medical Sociology." Pp. 25–53 in V. James and J. Gabe (eds.), *Health and the Sociology of Emotions*. Oxford: Blackwell.

2

Health and Culture

STELLA QUAH

Is culture relevant to the study of health and illness? Almost with one voice, sociologists and anthropologists agree that it is. Such a consensus is exceptional in these disciplines, both of which have produced the bulk of systematic research on health-related behavior by applying a wide variety of approaches and conceptual perspectives. Today, we know that culture is not just one of many factors associated with health but rather is the context within which health-related behavior unfolds. This chapter explains why culture is significant in health-related behavior, beginning with an overview of the classic definitions of culture and research trends. Next, we consider the link between culture and health behavior and, finally, focus on the link between culture and healing systems.

THE CLASSICS

The meaning of the term "culture" varies widely across disciplines and conceptual perspectives. To keep within the scope of this volume, the focus is on work in sociology and anthropology. We begin with an historical glance at the efforts made to define and understand "culture." One enduring contribution comes from Emile Durkheim, a pioneer of the discipline of sociology. In his *Rules of Sociological Method*, first published in 1895, Durkheim proposed guidelines for the study of social phenomena as *social facts*. He argued that social facts are "representations" of society in the mind of the individual. They are ways of thinking, feeling, and acting external to the person. Such "facts" include myths, popular legends, religious conceptions, moral beliefs, and social beliefs and practices in general. By treating social values, beliefs, and customs as social facts, Durkheim promoted the systematic study of culture. Durkheim also wrote about the collective social consciousness and social solidarity, both of which encompass culture. He saw social solidarity and, particularly, collective consciousness as reflective of culture and concurrently present within and external to the individual. Taylor and Ashworth (1987: 43) propose that these ideas are applicable to the study of medical sociology phenomena, such as attitudes toward death and the link between "changing forms of social solidarity and changing perceptions of health, disease, and medicine."

Also writing about issues of culture was one of Durkheim's contemporaries, Max Weber. Weber's work during the first two decades of the twentieth century brilliantly marked the initiation of the sociological analysis of culture. Among his voluminous published work, two studies are particularly relevant: *The Protestant Ethic and the Spirit of Capitalism* (1904–5), and *Economy and Society* (first published in English in 1968). Weber highlighted the importance of culture as values and beliefs coexisting and shaping social action within the micro-cosmos of the individual actor as well as at the level of collectivities, institutions, and the larger society. His conceptualizations of *ethnic group* and *traditional action* offer particularly relevant insights into the study of culture. Weber defined *ethnic groups* as human groups characterized by a "subjective belief in their common descent," given their real or perceived similarities in one or more characteristics (physical types or race, customs, language, religion), and in "perceptible differences in the conduct of everyday life" (Weber 1978: 389–90). The impact of these subjectively perceived similarities on social action is heightened by yet another defining feature of ethnicity: "the belief in a specific *honor* of their members, not shared by outsiders, that is, the sense of *ethnic honor*." As Weber (1978: 391) explained:

> palpable differences in dialect and differences of religion in themselves do not exclude sentiments of common ethnicity ... The conviction of the excellence of one's own customs and the inferiority of alien ones, a conviction which sustains the sense of ethnic honor, is actually quite analogous to the sense of honor of distinctive status groups.

Weber's concept of *traditional action* (one of four in his typology of social action) is also relevant to the relationship between culture and health. Weber defines *traditional* action as social action "determined by ingrained habituation." *Traditional* action, he wrote, "is very often a matter of almost automatic reaction to habitual stimuli that guide behavior in a course which has been repeatedly followed. The great bulk of all everyday action to which people have become habitually accustomed approaches this type" (Weber 1978: 4). As will be discussed, the concepts of ethnicity and traditional action, as defined by Weber, elucidate the pervasiveness of customs, beliefs, and practices of different ethnic or cultural communities upon their health-related behavior. Weber's analyses have inspired subsequent research and contributed to the understanding of the pervasiveness of culturally inspired and culturally sustained health practices. Probably because of the profound influence and widespread incorporation of his conceptual insights into the body of general knowledge of sociology, these Weberian contributions are seldom cited directly in current medical sociology research. A notable exception is the analysis of Weber's legacy in medical sociology by Uta Gerhardt (1989) and his concept of lifestyles (Cockerham 2010).

This interest in culture has been passed along to subsequent generations of social scientists. By 1951, Clyde Kluckhohn reported many different definitions of culture and many more have appeared since. Yet, in spite of the plurality of definitions, some common strands that make up the fundamental fabric of this important concept are found in the cumulative work of anthropologists and sociologists. Kluckhohn (1951: 86) defined "culture" in the widest sense as a community's "design for living." He pointed out that despite the wide variety of definitions he and A. L. Kroeber (1952) found, an "approximate consensus" could be developed, in which:

> Culture consists in patterned ways of thinking, feeling, and reacting, acquired and transmitted mainly by symbols, constituting the distinctive achievements of human groups, including their embodiments in artifacts; ... traditional (i.e. historically derived and selected) ideas and especially their attached values. (Kluckhohn 1951: 86)

Kluckhohn proposed that this definition of culture be used as "a map" or "abstract representation" of the distinctive features of a community's way of life. This method is akin to the *ideal type*, the analytical tool introduced by Weber (1946) to identify general characteristics, patterns, and regularities in social behavior.

A direct connection between culture and health was articulated by Bronislaw Malinowski (1944: 37), who considered culture as a functional response to satisfy "the organic and basic needs of man and of the race." He defined culture as "the integral whole" encompassing "human ideas and crafts, beliefs and customs ... A vast apparatus, partly material, partly human and partly spiritual, by which man is able to cope with the concrete, specific problems that face him" (Malinowski 1944: 36). Malinowski saw those problems as human "needs" that prompted "cultural responses." These needs were metabolism, reproduction, bodily comforts, safety, movement, growth, and health. However, in his view, health is implied in all the other six human basic needs, in addition to the explicit need for the "relief or removal of sickness or of other pathological conditions" (1944: 93). The "cultural response" which addresses the problem of health is "hygiene," defined as all "sanitary arrangements" in a community, "native beliefs as to health and magical dangers," "rules about exposure, extreme fatigue, the avoidance of dangers or accidents," and the "never absent range of household remedies" (Malinowski 1944: 91, 108).

Another valuable contribution to the understanding of culture was provided by sociologist Talcott Parsons. Parsons was greatly influenced as a student by Durkheim and Weber. Among his colleagues, he acknowledged the influence of Kluckhohn concerning the problems of culture and its relation to society (Parsons 1970). He conceptualized social action as taking place within a three-dimensional context comprising personality, culture, and the social system. Parsons (1951: 327) defined culture as "ordered systems of symbols" that guide social action and are "internalized components of the personalities of individual actors and institutionalized patterns of social systems." For Parsons (1951: 11), the shared symbolic systems are fundamental for the functioning of the social system and they represent "a *cultural tradition*." Parsons (1951: 326–7) also argued that a cultural tradition has three principal components or systems: value-orientations, beliefs, and expressive symbols.

His preoccupation with a balanced analysis of values and motives that would prevent us from falling into the extremes of "psychological" or "cultural" determinism led him to invest considerable effort into the discussion of culture. Parsons (1951: 15) identified three main features:

First, that culture is *transmitted*, it constitutes a heritage or a social tradition; secondly, that it is *learned*, it is not a manifestation, in particular content, of man's genetic constitution; and third, that it is *shared*. Culture, that is, is on the one hand the product of, on the other hand a determinant of, systems of human interaction.

Parsons' concepts of culture and cultural traditions and his identification of culture as transmitted, learned, and shared, together with the contributions of Durkheim, Weber, Kluckhohn, and Malinowski, form the classical basis for the study of culture. An additional heritage of the study of culture arises out of the cross-fertilization of insights and research between sociology and anthropology. Most current studies on culture and on the link between culture and health have been built on this rich foundation.

By identifying the fundamental components of culture, the collective wisdom inherited from the classics permit us to consider culture and ethnicity as the same phenomenon. Although Margaret Mead (1956) and Benjamin Paul (1963) proposed that cultural differences cut across racial and religious lines, these two factors are very much part of the cultural landscape within which individuals and groups operate. This idea is captured well by Stanley King (1962: 79), who proposed that what constitutes an ethnic group is the combination of "common backgrounds in language, customs, beliefs, habits and traditions, frequently in racial stock or country of origin" and, more importantly, "a consciousness of kind." It is important to keep in mind that, from the perspective of individuals and collectivities, these ethnic similarities may be factual or perceived and may include a formal religion. The sharing of the same geographical settlement is not as important as it was once thought, mainly because large migrations (voluntary or not) of people from different ethnic groups have resulted in the formation of diaspora beyond their ancestral lands and the subsequent increase of multiethnic settlements. The process of assimilation (becoming a member of the host culture) is commonly observed when individuals settle in a new country. Living in close proximity to each other leads individuals from different ethnic groups into another process, *pragmatic acculturation*, that is, the process of culture borrowing motivated by the desire to satisfy specific needs (Quah 1989: 181). Assimilation and *pragmatic acculturation* have been found to influence health behavior significantly. These processes will be discussed in more detail later. But first, let us review some of the contemporary leading ideas on culture and health.

MAIN CONTEMPORARY RESEARCH TRENDS

The contributions of the classics are the foundation of our understanding of culture and of its impact on behavior. As we shall see, studies conducted over the past five decades have supported their interpretation of culture. The corpus of contemporary sociological and anthropological research on culture is expanding rapidly and in different directions. "Neoclassical" approaches emerged from the work of Weber, Durkheim, and Marx but have taken on a life of their own, as seen, for example, in interpretations of religion, studies of social control, and feminist perspectives of the body and gender (Alexander 1990).

Attention to the body as an important subject of social analysis was brought up by Michel Foucault's work on *The Order of Things* (1970), *The Birth of the Clinic* (1973), and *Discipline and Punish* (1977). He eschewed research in favor of formulating assumptions, but his effort at awakening alertness to the symbolic and perceived meaning of the body is, to me, his vital contribution. Research findings over the past two decades show that the symbolic meaning of the body in relation to health and illness, manipulation, completeness and mutilation, varies substantially across cultures. One of the most dramatic illustrations of this finding is the cultural interpretation of female genital cutting (FGC) by Western groups advocating the eradication of FGC as opposed to the symbolic meaning of FGC held by some African communities that are struggling to preserve it (Greer 1999).

On the effort to elucidate how culture affects the individual's behavior, the work of Erving Goffman (1968a, 1968b) using the symbolic-interaction perspective is important. Goffman focuses on the person's subjective definition of the situation and the concept of stigma. He proposes a three stage stigmatization process (1968b): the person's initial or "primary" deviation from a normative framework; the negative societal reaction; and the person's "secondary" reaction or response to the negative reaction that becomes the person's "master-status." It is clear that Goffman's "normative framework" is socially constructed based on the community's predominant culture. Disability and disease, particularly mental illness (1968a), are typically perceived as stigma and trigger the stigmatization process. Unfortunately, Goffman and many of his followers have neglected to apply his conceptual approach fully to their own studies: they overlook cross-cultural comparisons (see, for example, Locker 1983; Scambler 1984; Strauss 1975).

The preceding discussion might lead some readers to believe that there is consensus on what culture is and how to study it. Drawing a sketch of the current situation in cultural studies, Jeffrey Alexander (1990: 25–6) indicates that one point of agreement is "their emphasis on the autonomy of culture from social structure." On the other hand, he finds in the contemporary literature on culture "extraordinary disagreement over what is actually inside the cultural system itself." Is it symbols, or values, or feelings, or metaphysical ideas? He proposes that culture might embrace all these because culture cannot be understood "without reference to subjective meaning" and "without reference to social structural constraints." For the same reason he favors a multidisciplinary approach to the study of culture.

The multidisciplinary approach is indeed one of two main trends in contemporary research on the link between culture and health. Focusing on the understanding of culture and health behavior, the disciplines of sociology and anthropology have produced research findings confirming that culture or ethnicity influence health behavior and attitudes significantly. The body of research advanced over the past five decades is characterized by a second main trend: although several conceptual perspectives on the influence of culture are discussed and explored, no dominant theory has yet emerged to explain that influence systematically and comprehensibly.

Renée Fox (Fox 1976, 1989; Parsons and Fox 1952a, 1952b) has contributed to the search for evidence on the impact of values and beliefs on health behavior at the micro-level through her analysis of individuals and at the macro-level by focusing on institutional aspects of medical care such as the medical school and the hospital. She demonstrated the advantages of close collaboration between sociology and anthropology in the study of health-related behavior, particularly on the aspect of culture. Some of her contributions will be discussed in the subsequent sections.

A final note before moving on to culture and health: The inclusion of ethnicity has become fashionable in medical research in the past three decades but it appears that little is learned from social science research. Reviewing the uses of the ethnicity concept in articles published in the *American Journal of Public Health* from 1980 to 1989, Ahdieh and Hahn (1996: 97–8) found that "there was little consensus in the scientific [biomedical] community regarding the meaning or use of terms such as race, ethnicity or national origin." Efforts have been made to assist health care practitioners to appreciate the complexity of culture (LaVeist 1994; Williams 1994). The social sciences and, in particular, sociology and anthropology remain the disciplines most dedicated to the study of culture or ethnicity per se and of its association with health and illness phenomena.

CULTURE AND HEALTH BEHAVIOR

The conceptual insights of the classic and contemporary sociologists and anthropologists on the significance of culture are confirmed by research on health behavior over the past four decades. A complete review of the vast body of sociological and anthropological literature dealing with the influence of culture upon the individual's health behavior is a formidable task beyond the scope of this chapter. Instead, I will highlight the nuances and significance of cultural variations in health behavior by discussing relevant findings within the framework of three types of health-related behavior, namely, *preventive health behavior, illness behavior, and sick-role behavior*. The former two concepts were proposed by Kasl and Cobb (1966). The concept of *sick-role* behavior was formulated by Talcott Parsons (1951: 436–8).

Preventive health behavior refers to the activity of a person who believes he or she is healthy for the purpose of preventing illness (Kasl and Cobb 1966: 246). Kasl and Cobb labeled this "health behavior" but the term *preventive* differentiates it clearly from the other two types of health-related behavior. Kasl and Cobb (1966: 246) defined *illness behavior* as the activity undertaken by a person who feels ill for the purpose of defining the illness and seeking a solution. In the sense intended for this discussion, *illness behavior* encompasses the time span between a person's first awareness of symptoms and his or her decision to seek expert assistance or "technically competent" help (to borrow Parsons' [1951: 437] term). *Illness behavior*, thus defined, includes activities such as initial self-medication or self-treatment and discussion of the problem with non-expert family members and others within one's primary or informal social network. *Sick-role behavior* is the activity undertaken by a person who considers himself or herself ill for the purpose of getting well (based on Parsons 1951: 436–8). *Sick-role behavior* is typically preceded by *illness behavior* and encompasses the sick person's formal response to symptoms, that is, the seeking of what he or she perceives as "technically competent" help. The sick person may seek technically competent or expert advice from whoever he or she perceives as or believes to be an expert including a traditional healer, modern medical healing practitioners, or a combination of these. *Sick-role behavior* also includes the relation between patient and healer, and the subsequent activity of the person as a patient.

Culture and preventive health behavior

Preventive health behavior refers to the activity of a person who believes he or she is healthy for the purpose of preventing illness (Kasl and Cobb 1966: 246). In addition to the study of healthy individuals, relevant research on preventive health behavior also covers studies on substance addiction or abuse (drugs, alcohol, cigarettes), which seek to understand the path toward addiction and to identify the factors involved. The subjective evaluation of one's own health status may propel or retard preventive action against disease. Many studies on preventive health behavior report data on self-health evaluation but it is not common to report variations in the cultural meaning attached to health status. As health status is, in many respects, a value, cultural variations are commonly found in people's evaluation of their own health status and the way in which they evaluate it.

The study by Lew-Ting, Hurwicz, and Berkanovic (1998) illustrates this phenomenon in the case of the Chinese. The Chinese use the traditional idea of "ti-zhi" or "constitution" to denote "a long-term, pervasive characteristic that is central to their sense of self" and clearly different from the Western concept of health status. The latter is "a more temporal, fluctuating state" that varies with "the experience of illness" (Lew-Ting et al. 1998: 829). This is an illustration of the cultural similarity in the definition of constitution among people of the same ethnic group (Chinese elderly) living in two different parts of the world. In contrast, residing in the same geographical location does not secure a common meaning of health status. For example, significant cultural differences in self-evaluated health status were observed among three cultural groups living in close proximity of each other in south-central Florida (Albrecht, Clarke, and Miller 1998).

Among the latest studies relevant to the prevention of substance abuse, in this example, alcohol, is the work of Gureje, Mavreas, Vazquez-Baquero, and Janca (1997). People in nine cities around the world were interviewed by Gureje and his colleagues on their values and perceptions concerning the meaning of drinking alcohol. The nine cities were Ankara (Turkey), Athens (Greece), Bangalore (India), Flagstaff (Arizona), Ibadan (Nigeria), Jebal (Romania), Mexico City (Mexico), Santander (Spain), and Seoul (South Korea). These authors reported a "remarkable congruence" in the practitioners' criteria to diagnose alcoholism. But they found significant variations among people across the nine cities concerning "drinking norms, especially with regard to *wet* and *dry* cultures" (1997: 209). A *wet* culture, they stated, is one where alcohol drinking is permitted or encouraged by the social significance attached to the act of drinking and to the social context within which drinking takes place. In a *dry* culture, alcohol drinking is discouraged or prohibited altogether. They cited two of the earliest alcohol studies by Bunzel (1940) and Horton (1943), both of which suggested the strong influence of culture on alcohol drinking. Their own study adds to the increasing body of research findings showing that the difficulties encountered in the prevention of alcoholism are greater in some cultures than in others.

The investigation into the relative influence of culture upon alcohol abuse was found by Guttman (1999) to be equivocal in situations where acculturation takes place. Guttman refers to the common definition of acculturation as "the process whereby one culture group adopts the beliefs and practices of another culture group over time" (1999: 175). His study of alcohol drinking among Mexican immigrants in the United States highlighted several problems. He found it difficult to identify clearly the boundaries between cultures sharing the same geographical area. This problem has been overcome in some studies by following the symbolic-interaction postulate of the importance of subjective definition of self and of the situation and correspondingly accepting the subjects' self-identification as members of a given culture (see Quah 1993). Some researchers assume that the length of time spent in the host country leads to acculturation and thus use other indicators, such as the proportion of the immigrant's life spent in the host country (cf. Mandelblatt et al. 1999).

A second and more critical difficulty in the study of preventive and other types of health behavior involving alcoholism and other health disorders among immigrants is their concurrent exposure to multiple cultural influences. In this regard, Guttman's finding in the United States is similar to findings from immigrant studies in other countries. He observed that immigrants "are participants not only in the dissolution of older cultural practices and beliefs but are also constantly engaged in the creation, elaboration, and even intensification of new cultural identities" (Guttman 1999: 175). However, the presence of multiple cultural influences does not necessarily lead to the creation of new identities. Other outcomes are also possible, such as one outcome which I label *pragmatic acculturation*: the borrowing of cultural elements (concepts, ways of doing things, ways of organizing and planning) and adapting them to meet practical needs. Pragmatic acculturation is practiced in the search for ways to prevent illness, or trying different remedies to deal with symptoms (illness behavior), or seeking expert help from healers from other cultures (Quah 1985, 1989, 1993). Individuals "borrow" healing options from cultures other than their own, but they may or may not incorporate those options or additional aspects of the other cultures into their lives permanently. The borrowing and adapting is part of the ongoing process of dealing with health and illness. Solutions from other cultures tend to be adopted, or adapted to one's own culture, if and for as long as they "work" to the satisfaction of the user.

Yet another angle of analysis in the study of culture and health is the identification of cultural differences in health behavior among subgroups of a community or country assumed to be culturally homogeneous. Such is the case with differences commonly found between "rural" and "urban" ways of life and ways of thinking in the same country. One of the numerous illustrations of this phenomenon is the study on preventive health education on AIDS in Thailand by Lyttleton (1993), which documented the urban–rural divide. The message of public preventive information campaigns designed in urban centers was not received as intended in rural villages. The concept of promiscuity that was at the center of the Thai AIDS prevention campaigns was associated by the villagers with the visiting of "commercial sex workers" only and not with the practice of "sleeping with several different village women" (1993: 143). The misperception of preventive public health campaigns occurs between the rural, less educated, and dialect-speaking groups on the one hand, and the urban, educated civil servants and health professionals who design the campaigns, on the other hand. The misperception of the campaign message is not the only problem. An additional serious obstacle to reach the target rural population is the medium used to disseminate preventive health information. The Thai villagers perceived new technology, including television broadcasts from Bangkok, as "belonging to a different world – both physically and socioculturally" and, consequently, "increased exposure to these messages simply reinforces the [villagers'] perception that they are not locally pertinent" (Lyttleton 1993: 144).

Culture and illness behavior

As mentioned earlier, illness behavior refers to the activity undertaken by a person who feels ill for the purpose of defining the illness and seeking a solution (Kasl and Cobb 1966). What people do when they begin to feel unwell, the manner in which people react to symptoms, and the meaning they attach to symptoms have been found to vary across cultures.

Reviewing the work of Edward Suchman (1964, 1965) on illness behavior and ethnicity, Geertsen and his colleagues (1975) concluded that there was indeed an association between the two phenomena. They found that "group closeness and exclusivity increases the likelihood" of a person responding to a health problem "in a way that is consistent with his subcultural background" (1975: 232). Further detailed data on the correlation between ethnicity and illness behavior were reported by, among others, Robertson and Heagarty (1975), Kosa and Zola (1975), and by Sanborn and Katz (1977), who found significant cultural variations in the perception of symptoms. In fact, the relative saturation of the literature regarding the ethnicity–illness behavior link was already manifested in Mechanic's observation in the late 1970s: "Cultures are so recognizably different that variations in illness behavior in different societies hardly need demonstration" (1978: 261).

Nevertheless, the number of studies documenting the association between culture and illness behavior has increased continuously. One of the most common research themes is mental illness, given that mental illness symptoms are primarily manifested through alterations in what is culturally defined as "normal" or "acceptable" social interaction. A prominent contributor to the study of culture and mental illness is Horacio Fabrega (1991, 1993, 1995). Summarizing the crux of current research in sociology and anthropology, Fabrega states that "empirical studies integral to and grounded in sound clinical and epidemiological research methods ... have succeeded in making clear how cultural conventions affect manifestations of disorders, aspects of diagnosis, and responses to treatment" (1995: 380).

The reactions of others, particularly the family and people emotionally close to the symptomatic person, play an important part in determining how the affected person reacts, that is, how he or she defines and handles symptoms. Such reactions vary across cultures. McKelvy, Sang, and Hoang (1997) found that, in contrast to Americans, "the Vietnamese traditional culture has a much narrower definition of mental illness." They are more tolerant of behavioral disturbances triggered by distress. The Vietnamese define someone as mentally ill only if the person is "so disruptive" that he or she "threatens the social order or the safety of others"; even then, the family is the first source of care, which may include "physical restraint."

The person is taken to the hospital only if the family is unable to control him or her (1997: 117).

Research conducted from the perspective of psychiatry tends to put a stronger emphasis on the importance of culture: The cultural definition of symptoms is seen as determining the disease outcome. Hahn and Kleinman (1983) proposed that beliefs in the etiology and prognosis of disease are as important to disease causation as microorganisms or chemical substances. Adler (1994) found this premise evident in the case of the sudden nocturnal death syndrome or SUNDS among the Hmong refugees in the United States. Adler (1994: 26) explains "in the traditional Hmong worldview the functions of the mind and the body are not dichotomized and polarized." Consequently, Adler identified a series of pathological circumstances leading to SUNDS. As refugees, the Hmong lost their traditional social support and were pressed to adapt to a different culture. Adler (1994: 52) found that "severe and ongoing stress related to cultural disruption and national resettlement," as well as "the intense feelings of powerlessness regarding existence in the US," and their "belief system in which evil spirits have the power to kill men who do not fulfill their religious obligations" together led "the solitary Hmong male" to die of SUNDS.

Illness behavior typically involves a "wait-and-see" attitude as the first reaction to symptoms, followed by self-medication; if the problem is judged to have worsened, then the person might be prepared to seek expert advice. In this process, cultural patterns of behavior may be superseded by formal education. In a comparative analysis of Chinese, Malays, and Indians, I found that education explains the practice of self-medication with modern over-the-counter medications better than culture. There was a significant difference among the three groups in the keeping of non-prescription and traditional medications at home. Yet, education served as an "equalizer" for self-medication with modern (i.e., Western) medicines. The more educated a person is, the more inclined he or she would be to practice self-medication with "modern" over-the-counter medicines before (or instead of) seeking expert advice, irrespective of his or her ethnic group (Quah 1985). A similar finding is reported by Miguel and her colleagues (1999) in the treatment of malaria in the Philippines.

Culture and sick-role behavior

To recapitulate what was discussed in the first section, *sick-role behavior* is the activity undertaken by a person who considers himself or herself ill for the purpose of getting well (based on Parsons 1951: 436–8). Sick-role behavior encompasses the sick person's response to symptoms, in particular, the seeking of what he or she perceives as "technically competent" help (to borrow Parsons' term), as well as doctor–patient or healer–patient interaction. Lyle Saunders (1954) was among the first sociologists to observe that cultural differences in medical care manifested in the problems encountered when the physician and the patient were from different ethnic groups.

One of the earliest and most significant investigations on the actual influence of culture on sick-role behavior was Mark Zborowski's (1952, 1969) analysis of cultural differences in responses to pain. Investigating differences among war veterans warded in an American hospital, he observed that the Italian-American and Jewish-American patients differed significantly from the "old American" and Irish-American patients in their expression of pain and description of their symptoms. Zborowski proposed that cultural differences such as socialization, time-orientation, and the array of values outlining what is appropriate behavior in cultural communities explained the differences he observed among the four groups of patients. Along the same line of investigation, Irving Zola (1966) pursued the analysis of how culture shapes the subjective perception of symptoms. His research confirmed the findings reported by Zborowski on the presence of cultural differences in perception of, and reaction to, symptoms and pain. Zola (1973, 1983) continued his probe into the impact of cultural differences on the doctor–patient relationship, the perception of illness, and the importance given to health matters in different cultural communities. Twaddle (1978) conducted an exploratory replication of Zborowski's study, comparing 26 American married males who classified themselves as "Italian Catholics," "Protestants," and "Jewish." Twaddle found that Parsons' configuration of "sick role" varied among these groups. The relevance of cultural differences in responses to pain is well recognized and research on this important dimension continues, as illustrated by the comparative analysis of Black Caribbean and White British cancer patients by Koffman and colleagues (2008).

Later studies continue to confirm the impact of culture on the doctor–patient relation and, correspondingly, on patient outcomes. Nitcher (1994) observed the use of the traditional term "mahina ang baga" (weak lungs) by doctors and lay persons in the Philippines. Nitcher found that doctors use the term when diagnosing tuberculosis in an effort to spare the patient the social stigma of the disease. However, "weak lungs" is a very ambiguous term in everyday discourse; thus, the unintended consequence is a negative patient outcome. Nitcher states "the sensitivity of clinicians to [the] social stigma [of tuberculosis] is laudatory." But he correctly points out that "the use of the term *weak lungs* has [serious] consequences" for public health because the diagnosis "*weak lungs* is not deemed as serious as TB" and thus people, especially the poor, do not comply with the prescribed treatment, which is a "six-month course of medication" (Nitcher 1994: 659).

A major direct implication of the concept of role is the symbolic, perceived, or actual presence of others. Sick-role behavior implies the presence of the healing expert (irrespective of what healing system is at work). A large body of research into the doctor–patient relationship has produced interesting information confirming the relevance of culture. An expected finding is that cultural similarities, such as physical appearance and language, among other characteristics, between doctor (or healer) and patient facilitate the relationship and increase the possibility of positive patient outcomes (Cockerham 2010: 175–205; Kleinman 1980: 203–58). A note of caution, however: Similarities in culture do not secure success in the doctor–patient relationship. Many other aspects come into play, from ecological factors (Catalano 1989) to the differential understanding of metaphors (Glennon 1999). The structural features of the healer–patient relationship, such as how the interaction is conducted and who is involved, also vary across cultures. Haug and her colleagues (1995) found interesting differences in the manner in which the doctor–patient interaction develops in Japan and the United States. Kleinman (1980: 250–310) shows that the relationship is not always a dyad since, in some communities, the patient's family is often directly involved. Furthermore, the quality of the interpersonal relationship built between patient and healer is paramount and may become as significant to the patient as "the technical quality" of the medical care received (Haddad et al. 1998).

Recent publications have addressed the need of physicians and other health care personnel to be informed on the importance of cultural differences that may affect the doctor–patient interaction. Three of the latest works will suffice as illustrations. *The Cultural Context of Health, Illness and Medicine* by Martha O. Loustaunau and Elisa J. Sobo (1997) introduces the role of culture in an easy style devoid of conceptual arguments and thus suitable for health care practitioners who simply wish to improve their interaction with patients. Using a similar approach, the *Handbook of Diversity Issues in Health Psychology* edited by Pamela M. Kato and Traci Mann (1996) offers basic information for practitioners on the impact of ethnicity on health. The third example is Malcolm MacLachlan's (1997) book on *Culture and Health* that covers the analysis of culture in more detail and introduces some conceptual discussion. His book is also addressed to the medical profession but, compared to the other two, MacLachlan's is more suitable for health care practitioners interested in a social science analysis of culture and health. It is relevant to note that MacLachlan is a clinical psychologist but follows (albeit without citations) the sociological and anthropological conceptualization of ethnicity discussed earlier in this chapter: that ethnicity encompasses a way of life and common origin as well as a consciousness of kind.

Following the same premise on the significance of the presence of others, another important aspect of sick-role behavior is the availability of an informal, social support network for the sick individual. The emotional, social, and instrumental support received from one's informal network of family and friends tends to guide the attitudes and actions of the ill person before, during, and after consulting experts. Just as cultural variations are observed among sick people searching for help from healing experts (whether traditional or modern), the seeking of emotional and social support and the presence and quality of informal social support from family and friends also vary across cultures. A recent example of studies supporting these assumptions is the study conducted by Kagawa-Singer, Wellisch, and Durvasula (1997). They compared Asian-American and Anglo-American women's situations after breast cancer diagnosis and found that the subjective meaning of the disease and the presence and use of family as the first source of social support varied between the two groups of patients.

CULTURE AND HEALING SYSTEMS

The options available to people seeking health care vary greatly across countries and cultures. As Cockerham explains (2010: 208), even in a modern, developed country like the United States, people may not look at modern medicine as the only or right option. In the discussion of culture and health, reference must be made to the wide range of healing options found in most societies today. For the sake of clarity and expediency, it is useful to consider all healing options as falling into three general categories: the modern or *Western biomedicine* system; *traditional* medicine systems; and *popular* medicine. A medical system is understood as "a patterned, interrelated body of values and deliberate practices governed by a single paradigm of the meaning, identification, prevention and treatment of ... illness and/ or disease" (Press 1980: 47). Traditional medical systems flourished well before Western biomedicine, and their history goes back more than one millennium. Three ancient healing traditions are considered to be the most important: the Arabic, Hindu, and Chinese healing traditions (Leslie 1976: 15–17). However, there is a revival of interest in cultural traditions today around the two best-known traditional medicine systems: traditional Chinese medicine (Unschuld 1985) and Hindu or Ayurvedic medicine (Basham 1976). Popular medicine refers to "those beliefs and practices which, though compatible with the underlying paradigm of a medical system, are materially or behaviorally divergent from official medical practice" (Press 1980: 48). Popular medicine is also labeled "complementary" and "alternative" medicine or therapies (Quah 2008; Sharma 1990).

In contrast to the modest attention given by researchers to power and dominance in the traditional healing system, the intense concern with the preponderance and power of Western biomedicine is evident in the work of Foucault (1973) and Goffman (1968a, 1968b), and has been documented and analyzed in detail by Freidson (1970), Starr (1982), and Conrad and Schneider (1992) among others. These authors have referred to Western biomedicine as practiced in Western industrialized countries mainly in North America and Western Europe. Interestingly, however, by the end of the twentieth century, the predominance of Western biomedicine is apparent in other countries as well (Quah 1995, 2008).

Healing systems are constantly evolving and two features of their internal dynamics are relevant here: divergence and pragmatic acculturation. Divergence in a healing system is the emergence of subgroups within the system supporting different interpretations of the system's core values. The comparative study of medical schools by Renée Fox (1976) serves as a good illustration of cultural divergence. She investigated the assumed resilience of six value-orientations (in Parsons' sense) at the core of Western biomedicine: rationality, instrumental activism, universalism, individualism, and collectivism, all of which comprise the ethos of science and detached concern, a value she assigned specifically to Western biomedicine practitioners. Fox observed that these values of biomedicine are subject to reinterpretations across cultures. She found "considerable variability in the form and in the degree to which they [the six value-orientations] are institutionalized" (Fox 1976: 104–6) even within the same country, as illustrated by the situation in four major medical schools in Belgium in the 1960s representing basic cultural rifts: "Flemish" versus "French," and "Catholic" versus "Free Thought" perspectives.

A manifestation of pragmatic acculturation in a healing system is the inclination of its practitioners to borrow ideas or procedures from other systems to solve specific problems without necessarily accepting the core values or premises of the system or systems from which they do the borrowing. To illustrate: Some traditional Chinese physicians use the stethoscope to listen to the patient's breathing, or the sphygmomanometer to measure blood pressure, or the autoclave to sterilize acupuncture needles, or a laser instrument instead of needles in acupuncture (see Quah 1989: 122–59; Quah and Li 1989). The study by Norheim and Fonnebo (1998) illustrates the practice of pragmatic acculturation among young Western biomedicine practitioners in Norway who learned and practiced acupuncture. Norheim and Fonnebo (1998: 522) reported that general practitioners were more inclined than specialists to use acupuncture with their patients, and that the majority of all 1,466 practitioners interviewed had "already undergone acupuncture or indicated that they would consider doing so." Pragmatic acculturation has also facilitated the provision of Western biomedical services to peoples from other cultures. Ledesma (1997) and Selzler (1996) studied the health values, health beliefs, and the health needs of Native Americans. These researchers stressed the importance of taking the cultures of Native Americans into consideration for the provision of relevant Western biomedical services to their communities. Adapting the type and mode of delivery of modern health care services to serve the needs of traditional peoples is not a new preoccupation but it is now receiving more serious attention from health care providers. In today's parlance, the process is called making the medical services more "user-friendly." Although pragmatic acculturation requires the Western biomedicine practitioners to change or adapt their usual practices and assumptions, it is deemed worthwhile if it attains the objective of delivering health care to communities in need. An example of research on culture and the accessibility of health services is the study by Harmsen and colleagues (2008) on linguistic and cultural barriers to patients' satisfaction with medical care.

The presence and relative success of groups and institutions (for example, the medical profession, hospitals, and other health care organizations) involved in the provision of health care unfold in the context of culture. Arthur Kleinman (1980) highlights the relevance of the "social space" occupied by health systems. He identified significant differences among ethnic communities and the subsequent impact of cultural perceptions of mental illness upon the structure of mental health services. The influence of culture on the provision of mental health services has been studied widely. In the recent investigation on mental health in Vietnam by McKelvy, Sang, and Hoang (1997: 117), cited earlier, they found that "there is no profession specifically dedicated to hearing the woes of others. Talk therapy is quite alien to the Vietnamese." In addition, the traditional Vietnamese perception of child behavior and their "narrow" definition of mental illness help to explain their skepticism on the need for child psychiatric clinics.

While the long-standing interest of social scientists in the link between culture and health is evident, two comparatively recent developments in the biomedical health system are worth noting. The first development is the systematic discussion of culture within the realm of bioethics, including the nuances of informed consent, and its meaning and interpretation among different ethnic groups (Turner 2005). The second development is that governments and health authorities are recognizing the importance of culture in illness prevention and the provision of health care services. One interesting example is the US Surgeon General's Report on Mental Health (USDHHS 1999) and the supplement report on "Mental Health: Culture, Race and Ethnicity" (USDHHS 2001). The Supplement was intended as a collaborative document with social scientists and it became "a landmark in the dialogue – political and scientific – regarding health disparities in the United States" (Manson 2003: 395); and "more than a government document" as it discusses the significance of ethnicity in the planning and provision of preventive and curative mental health services (Lopez 2003: 420).

The Pervasiveness of Culture

In conclusion, culture has, does, and will continue to influence health-related behavior. There is a wealth of social science and, in particular, medical sociology research demonstrating the pervasiveness of cultural values and norms upon preventive health behavior, illness behavior, and sick-role behavior among individuals and groups as well as at the macro-level of healing systems.

The preceding discussion has highlighted three additional features of the study of culture in health and illness. The first of these features is the remarkable confluence of different and even opposite schools of thought in sociology concerning the need to analyze culture as an independent phenomenon, and the influence of culture upon agency and structure. The affective nature and subjectivity of one's perceived identity as member of an ethnic group and the permeability of cultural boundaries are ideas found implicitly or explicitly in Durkheim, Weber, and Parsons, as well as in Goffman, Foucault, and Habermas, among others. The second feature is the divergence of healing systems. Healing systems are not always internally consistent; different interpretations of the core values or principles of the system may be held by subgroups within the system. The third feature is pragmatic acculturation, that is, the borrowing from other cultures of elements, ways of thinking, and ways of doing things, with the objective of solving specific or practical problems. This borrowing is very prevalent in matters of health and illness and is found in all types of health-related behavior. Finally, a comprehensive review of the relevant literature is not possible in this chapter given the enormous body of medical sociology research on health and culture. Instead, illustrations and the list of references are offered for each main argument in this discussion in the hope that the reader be enticed to pursue his or her own journey into this engaging research topic.

References

Adler, Shelley R. 1994. "Ethnomedical Pathogenesis and Hmong Immigrants' Sudden Nocturnal Deaths." *Culture, Medicine and Psychiatry* 18: 23–59.

Ahdieh, L. and R. A. Hahn. 1996. "Use of Terms 'Race', 'Ethnicity', and 'National Origin': A Review of Articles in the *American Journal of Public Health*, 1980–1989." *Ethnicity and Health* 1: 95–8.

Albrecht, Stan L., Leslie L. Clarke, and Michael K. Miller. 1998. "Community, Family, and the Race/Ethnicity Differences in Health Status in Rural Areas." *Rural Sociology* 63: 235–52.

Alexander, Jeffrey C. 1990. "Analytic Debates: Understanding the Relative Autonomy of Culture." Pp. 1–27 in J. C. Alexander and Steven Seidman (eds.), *Culture and Society: Contemporary Debates*. Cambridge: Cambridge University Press.

Basham, A. L. 1976. "The Practice of Medicine in Ancient and Medieval India." Pp. 18–43 in Charles Leslie (ed.), *Asian Medical Systems: A Comparative Study*. Berkeley: University of California Press.

Bunzel, R. 1940. "The Role of Alcoholism in Two Central American Cultures." *Psychiatry* 3: 361–87.

Catalano, Ralph. 1989. "Ecological Factors in Illness and Disease." Pp. 87–101 in Howard E. Freeman and Sol Levine (eds.), *Handbook of Medical Sociology*, 4th edition. Englewood Cliffs, NJ: Prentice-Hall.

Cockerham, William C. 2010. *Medical Sociology*, 11th edition. Englewoods Cliffs, NJ: Prentice-Hall.

Conrad, Peter and Joseph W. Schneider. 1992. *Deviance and Medicalization: From Badness to Sickness*, expanded edition. Philadelphia: Temple University Press.

Durkheim, Emile. 1938 [1895]. *The Rules of Sociological Method*, 8th edition. New York: Free Press.

Fabrega, Horacio. 1991. "Psychiatric Stigma in Non-Western Societies." *Contemporary Psychiatry* 326: 534–51.

Fabrega, Horacio. 1993. "A Cultural Analysis of Human Behavioral Breakdowns: An Approach to the Ontology and Epistemology of Psychiatric Phenomena." *Culture, Medicine and Psychiatry* 17: 99–132.

Fabrega, Horacio. 1995. "Cultural Challenges to the Psychiatric Enterprise." *Comprehensive Psychiatry* 36: 377–83.

Foucault, Michel. 1970. *The Order of Things: An Archaeology of the Human Sciences*. London: Tavistock.

Foucault, Michel. 1973. *The Birth of the Clinic: An Archeology of Medical Perception*. London: Tavistock.

Foucault, Michel. 1977. *Discipline and Punish: The Birth of the Prison*. London: Allen Lane.

Fox, Renée C. 1976. "The Sociology of Modern Medical Research." Pp. 102–14 in Charles Leslie (ed.), *Asian Medical Systems: A Comparative Study*. Berkeley: University of California Press.

Fox, Renée C. 1989. *Medical Sociology: A Participant Observer's View*. New York: Prentice-Hall.

Freidson, Eliot. 1970. *Profession of Medicine: A Study of the Sociology of Applied Knowledge*. New York: Dodd & Mead.

Geertsen, Reed, Melville R. Klauber, Mark Rindflesh, Robert L. Kane, and Robert Gray. 1975. "A Re-Examination of Suchman's Views on Social Factors in Health Care Utilization." *Journal of Health and Social Behavior* 16: 226–37.

Gerhardt, Uta. 1989. *Ideas about Illness: An Intellectual and Political History of Medical Sociology*. New York: New York University Press.

Glennon, Cheryl D. 1999. "Conceptual Metaphor in the Health Care Culture (Health Communicators)." Unpublished PhD Dissertation. San Diego: University of San Diego.

Goffman, Erving. 1968a. *Asylums: Essays on the Social Situation of Mental Patients and Other Inmates*. Harmondsworth: Penguin.

Goffman, Erving. 1968b. *Stigma: Notes on the Management of Spoilt Identity*. Harmondsworth: Penguin.

Greer, Germaine. 1999. *The Whole Woman*. New York: Knopf.

Gureje, Oye, Venos Mavreas, J. L. Vazquez-Baquero, and Aleksandar Janca. 1997. "Problems Related to Alcohol Use: A Cross-Cultural Perspective." *Culture, Medicine and Psychiatry* 21: 199–211.

Guttman, M. C. 1999. "Ethnicity, Alcohol, and Assimilation." *Social Science and Medicine* 48: 173–84.

Habermas, Jürgen. 1981. *The Theory of Communicative Action. Vol. 1: Reason and the Rationalization of Society*. Cambridge: Polity Press.

Haddad, Slim, Pierre Fournier, Nima Machouf, and Fissinet Yatara. 1998. "What Does Quality Mean to Lay People? Community Perceptions of Primary Health Care Services in Guinea." *Social Science and Medicine* 47: 381–94.

Hahn, Robert A. and Arthur Kleinman. 1983. "Belief as Pathogen, Belief as Medicine: 'Voodoo Death' and the 'Placebo Phenomenon' in Anthropological Perspective." *Medical Anthropology Quarterly* 14: 6–19.

Harmsen, J. A. M., R. M. D. Bernsen, M. A. Bruijnzeels, and L. Meeuwesen. 2008. "Patients' Evaluation of Quality of Care in General Practice: What Are the Cultural and Linguistic Barriers?" *Patient Education and Counseling* 72: 155–62.

Haug, Marie, H. Akiyama, G. Tryban, K. Sonoda, and M. Wykle. 1995. "Self-Care: Japan and the US Compared." Pp. 313–24 in William C. Cockerham (ed.), *The Sociology of Medicine: International Library of Critical Writings in Sociology*. Aldershot: Elgar. Reprinted from *Social Science and Medicine* 33(1991): 1011–22.

Horton, D. J. 1943. "The Functions of Alcohol in Primitive Societies: A Cross-Cultural Study." *Quarterly Studies of Alcohol* 4: 195–320.

Kagawa-Singer, Marjorie, David K. Wellisch, and Ramani Durvasula. 1997. "Impact of Breast Cancer on Asian American and Anglo American Women." *Culture, Medicine and Psychiatry* 21: 449–80.

Kasl, S. V. and S. Cobb. 1966. "Health Behavior, Illness Behavior, and Sick Role Behavior." *Archives of Environmental Health* 12: 246–55.

Kato, Pamela M. and Traci Mann (eds.). 1996. *Handbook of Diversity Issues in Health Psychology*. New York: Plenum Press.

King, Stanley H. 1962. *Perceptions of Illness and Medical Practice*. New York: Russell Sage Foundation.

Kleinman, Arthur. 1980. *Patients and Healers in the Context of Culture*. Berkeley: University of California Press.

Kluckhohn, Clyde. 1951. "The Study of Culture." Pp. 86–101 in Daniel Lerner and Harold D. Lasswell (eds.), *The Policy Sciences: Recent Developments in Scope and Method*. Stanford, CA: Stanford University Press.

Koffman, J., M. Morgan, P. Edmonds, P. Speck, and I. J. Higginson. 2008. "Cultural Meanings of Pain: A Qualitative Study of Black Caribbean and White British Patients with Advanced Cancer." *Palliative Medicine* 22(4): 350–9.

Kosa, J. and I. K. Zola. 1975. *Poverty and Health: A Sociological Analysis*, revised edition. Cambridge, MA: Harvard University Press.

LaVeist, T. 1994. "Beyond Dummy Variable and Sample Selection: What Health Services Researchers Ought to Know about Race as a Variable." *Health Services Research* 29: 1–16.

Ledesma, Rita V. 1997. "Cultural Influences upon Definitions of Health and Health Sustaining Practices for American Indian Children." Unpublished PhD Dissertation. Los Angeles: University of California.

Leslie, Charles (ed.). 1976. *Asian Medical Systems: A Comparative Study*. Berkeley: University of California Press.

Lew-Ting, Chih-Yin, M. L. Hurwicz, and E. Berkanovic. 1998. "Personal Constitution and Health Status among Chinese Elderly in Taipei and Los Angeles." *Social Science and Medicine* 47: 821–30.

Locker, D. 1983. *Disability and Disadvantage: The Consequences of Chronic Illness*. London: Tavistock.

Lopez, Steven R. 2003. "Reflections on the Surgeon General's Report on Mental Health, Culture, Race, and Ethnicity." *Culture, Medicine and Psychiatry* 27: 419–34.

Loustaunau, Martha O. and Elisa J. Sobo. 1997. *The Cultural Context of Health, Illness and Medicine*. Westport, CT: Bergin & Garvey.

Lyttleton, Chris. 1993. "Knowledge and Meaning: The AIDS Education Campaign in Rural Northeast Thailand." *Social Science and Medicine* 38: 135–46.

MacLachlan, Malcolm. 1997. *Culture and Health*. Chichester: Wiley.

Malinowski, Bronislaw. 1944. *A Scientific Theory of Culture and Other Essays*. Chapel Hill: University of North Carolina.

Mandelblatt, Jeanne S., K. Gold, A. S. O'Malley, K. Taylor, K. Cagney, J. S. Hopkins, and J. Kerner. 1999. "Breast and Cervix Cancer Screening Among Multiethnic Women: Role of Age, Health and Source of Care." *Preventive Medicine* 28: 418–25.

Manson, Spero M. 2003. "Extending the Boundaries, Bridging the Gaps: Crafting Mental Health: Culture, Race, and Ethnicity, a Supplement to the Surgeon General's Report on Mental Health." *Culture, Medicine and Psychiatry* 27: 395–408.

McKelvy, Robert S., David L. Sang, and Cam Tu Hoang. 1997. "Is There a Role for Child Psychiatry in Vietnam?" *Australian and New Zealand Journal of Psychiatry* 31: 114–19.

Mead, Margaret. 1956. "Understanding Cultural Patterns." *Nursing Outlook* 4: 260–2.

Mechanic, David. 1978. *Medical Sociology*, 2nd edition. New York: Free Press.

Miguel, Cynthia A., V. L. Tallo, L. Manderson, and M. A. Lansong. 1999. "Local Knowledge and Treatment of Malaria in Agusan del Sur, the Philippines." *Social Science and Medicine* 48: 607–18.

Nitcher, Mark. 1994. "Illness Semantics and International Health: The Weak Lung/TB Complex in the Philippines." *Social Science and Medicine* 38: 649–63.

Norheim, Arne Johan and Vinjar Fonnebo. 1998. "Doctors' Attitudes to Acupuncture: A Norwegian Study." *Social Science and Medicine* 47: 519–23.

Parsons, Talcott. 1951. *The Social System*. London: Routledge & Kegan Paul.

Parsons, Talcott. 1970. *Social Structure and Personality*. New York: Free Press.

Parsons, Talcott and Renée Fox. 1952a. "Introduction." *Journal of Social Issues* 8: 2–3.

Parsons, Talcott and Renée Fox. 1952b. "Illness, Therapy, and the Modern Urban Family." *Journal of Social Issues* 8: 31–44.

Paul, Benjamin. 1963. "Anthropological Perspectives on Medicine and Public Health." *Annals of the American Academy of Political and Social Science* 346: 34–43.

Press, I. 1980. "Problems of Definition and Classification of Medical Systems." *Social Science and Medicine* 14B: 45–57.

Quah, Stella R. 1985. "Self-Medication in Singapore." *Singapore Medical Journal* 26: 123–9.

Quah, Stella R. (ed.). 1989. *The Triumph of Practicality: Tradition and Modernity in Health Care Utilization in Selected Asian Countries*. Singapore: Institute of Southeast Asian Studies.

Quah, Stella R. 1993. "Ethnicity, Health Behavior, and Modernization: The Case of Singapore." Pp. 78–107 in Peter Conrad and Eugene B. Gallagher (eds.), *Health and Health Care in Developing Countries: Sociological Perspectives*. Philadelphia: Temple University Press.

Quah, Stella R. 1995. "The Social Position and Internal Organization of the Medical Profession in the Third World: The Case of Singapore." Pp. 485–501 in William C. Cockerham (ed.), *The Sociology of Medicine: International Library of Critical Writings in Sociology*. Aldershot: Elgar. Reprinted from *Journal of Health and Social Behavior* 30(1989): 450–66.

Quah, Stella R. 2008. "In Pursuit of Health: Pragmatic Acculturation in Everyday Life." *Health Sociology Review* 17: 419–22.

Quah, Stella R. and Jing-Wei Li. 1989. "Marriage of Convenience: Traditional and Modern Medicine in the People's Republic of China." Pp. 19–42 in Stella R. Quah (ed.), *The*

Triumph of Practicality: Tradition and Modernity in Health Care Utilization in Selected Asian Countries. Singapore: Institute of Southeast Asian Studies.

Robertson, Leon and M. Heagarty. 1975. *Medical Sociology: A General Systems Approach*. New York: Nelson Hall.

Sanborn, Kenneth O. and Martin M. Katz. 1977. "Perception of Symptoms Behavior Across Ethnic Groups." Pp. 236–40 in Y. H. Poortinga (ed.), *Basic Problems in Cross-Cultural Psychology*. Amsterdam: International Association for Cross-Cultural Psychology.

Saunders, Lyle. 1954. *Cultural Differences and Medical Care*. New York: Russell Sage Foundation.

Scambler, Graham. 1984. "Perceiving and Coping with Stigmatizing Illness." Pp. 35–43 in Ray Fitzpatrick et al. (eds.), *The Experience of Illness*. London: Tavistock.

Selzler, Bonnie Kay. 1996. "The Health Experiences of Dakota Sioux and Their Perceptions of Culturally Congruent Nursing Care." Unpublished PhD Dissertation. Denver: University of Colorado Health Sciences Center.

Sharma, Ursula M. 1990. "Using Alternative Therapies: Marginal Medicine and Central Concerns." Pp. 127–39 in Pamela Abbot and Geoff Payne (eds.), *New Directions in the Sociology of Health*. London: Falmer Press.

Starr, Paul. 1982. *The Social Transformation of American Medicine*. New York: Basic Books.

Strauss, Anselm L. 1975. *Chronic Illness and the Quality of Life*. St. Louis: Mosby.

Suchman, Edward. 1964. "Socio-Medical Variations Among Ethnic Groups." *American Journal of Sociology* 70: 319–31.

Suchman, Edward. 1965. "Social Patterns of Illness and Medical Care." *Journal of Health and Human Behavior* 6: 2–16.

Taylor, Steve and Clive Ashworth. 1987. "Durkheim and Social Realism: An Approach to Health and Illness." Pp 37–58 in Graham Scambler (ed.), *Sociological Theory and Medical Sociology*. London: Tavistock.

Turner, Leigh. 2005. "From the Local to the Global: Bioethics and the Concept of Culture." *Journal of Medicine and Philosophy* 30: 305–20.

Twaddle, Andrew C. 1978. "Health Decisions and Sick Role Variations: An Exploration." Pp. 5–15 in Howard D. Schwartz and Cary S. Kart (eds.), *Dominant Issues in Medical Sociology*. Reading, MA: Addison-Wesley. Reprinted from *Journal of Health and Social Behavior* 10(June 1969): 105–15.

Unschuld, Paul U. 1985. *Medicine in China: A History of Ideas*. Berkeley: University of California Press.

US Department of Health and Human Services (USDHHS). 1999. *Mental Health: A Report of the Surgeon General*. Rockville, MD: US Department of Health and Human Services, Public Health Service, Office of the Surgeon General.

US Department of Health and Human Services (USDHHS). 2001. *Mental Health: Culture, Race and Ethnicity. A Supplement to Mental Health: A Report of the Surgeon General*. Rockville, MD: US Department of Health and Human Services, Public Health Service, Office of the Surgeon General.

Weber, Max. 1946 [1925]. *From Max Weber: Essays in Sociology*, edited and translated by Hans H. Gerth and C. Wright Mills. New York: Oxford University Press.

Weber, Max. 1958 [1904–5]. *The Protestant Ethic and the Spirit of Capitalism*, translated by Talcott Parsons. New York: Scribner's.

Weber, Max. 1978. *Economy and Society*. Berkeley: University of California Press.

Williams, D. 1994. "The Concept of Race in Health Services Research, 1966–1990." *Health Services Research* 29: 261–74.

Zborowski, Mark. 1952. "Cultural Components in Response to Pain." *Journal of Social Issues* 8: 16–30.

Zborowski, Mark. 1969. *People in Pain*. San Francisco: Jossey-Bass.

Zola, Irving K. 1966. "Culture and Symptoms: An Analysis of Patients' Presentation of Complaints." *American Sociological Review* 31: 615–30.

Zola, Irving K. 1973. "Pathways to the Doctor: From Person to Patient." *Social Science and Medicine* 7: 677–87.

Zola, Irving K. 1983. *Socio-Medical Inquiries: Recollections, Reflections, and Reconsiderations*. Philadelphia: Temple University Press.

3

The Sociology of the Body

SARAH NETTLETON

In Tom Stoppard's (1967) play *Rosencrantz and Guildenstern are Dead*, the two central characters lament the precariousness of their lives. Rosencrantz seeks solace in life's only certainty when he comments that "the only beginning is birth and the only end is death – if we can't count on that what can we count on?" To this he might have added that he could reliably count on the fact that he had a body. The "fact" that we are born, have a body, and then die is of course something that does *seem* to be beyond question. It is something that we can hold on to, as we live in a world that appears to be ever more uncertain and risky (Beck 1992; Giddens 1991). But is this fact so obvious? Ironically, the more sophisticated our medical, technological, and scientific knowledge of bodies becomes, the more uncertain we are as to what the body actually is. For example, technological developments have meant boundaries between the physical (or natural) and social body have become less clear. With the development of assisted conception, when does birth begin? With the development of life-extending technologies, when does the life of a physical body end? With the development of prosthetic technologies, what constitutes a "pure" human? It seems the old certainties around birth, life, bodies, and death are becoming increasingly unstable. It is perhaps not surprising, therefore, that attempts to understand the social and ethical significance of the body have become central to recent sociological debates. Attempts to develop a sociological appreciation of the body have been especially important in the subdiscipline of the sociology of health and illness. The aim of this chapter is to delineate some of the key developments in the sociological theorizing of the body and to assess their sigificance for a number of substantive issues in medical sociology.

To meet this aim, the chapter will first review the main perspectives on the *sociology of the body* and the key social theorists who have informed each of these approaches. Second, the chapter will outline the parameters of the *sociology of embodiment*. Two key concepts which have emerged from these sociologies of the body and embodiment – *body projects* and the *lived body* – will also be discussed. Finally, a number of substantive issues which are central to medical sociology will be discussed with a view to highlighting the value of incorporating the body into the analysis of issues associated with health and illness. These issues are: illness and injury, health care work, medical technology, and health inequalities.

SOCIOLOGICAL PERSPECTIVES ON THE SOCIOLOGY OF THE BODY

There is now a copious literature on the sociology of the body which spans a range of perspectives. There are, however, alternative ways in which the body is understood and analyzed, with the most obvious approaches being rooted within the physical sciences and classified as being part of a naturalistic perspective (Nettleton 2006; Shilling 2003). In this chapter, however, we will focus on three main *sociological* approaches. First, those which draw attention to the *social regulation* of the body, especially the way in which social institutions regulate, control, monitor, and use bodies. Our bodies are, of course, highly politicized. Whilst we might like to think that we own and have control of our own bodies and what we do with them, we do not. This fact has perhaps become most strikingly evident as a result of feminist analyses of the ways in which medicine has controlled the bodies of women (Martin 1989; Oakley 1993; Ussher 2006). It is also evident in contemporary debates on topics such as euthanasia, organ transplantation, and abortion.

A second perspective within the sociology of the body literature focuses on the ontology of the body. A number of theorists have asked the question: What exactly is the body? Their answer is that in late modern societies we seem to have become increasingly *uncertain* as to what the body actually is. For most sociologists the body is to a greater or lesser extent socially constructed. However, there are a number of variants of this view, with some arguing that the body is simply a fabrication – an effect of its discursive context – while others maintain that bodies display certain characteristics (e.g., mannerisms, gait, shape) which are influenced by social and cultural factors.

The third approach pays more attention to the way the body is experienced or lived. Whilst this *phenomenological* approach accepts that the body is to some extent socially fashioned, it argues that an adequate sociology must take account of what the body, or rather embodied actor, actually does. In this sense it is perhaps more accurately described as a *sociology of embodiment* rather than a sociology of the body. This approach to the study of the body has gained much currency in recent years. It has to some extent emerged as a result of critical and creative debates within this field of study which have attempted to counter the dominant structuralist approach that concentrates on the social regulation of bodies (Turner 2008). This research, which has outlined the ways in which bodies are socially regulated and socially constructed, remains crucial for our understanding of the body in society.

Social regulation of bodies

In his book *Regulating Bodies*, Turner (1992) suggests that late modern societies are moving toward what he refers to as a "somatic society"; that is, a social system in which the body constitutes the central field of political and cultural activity. The major concerns of society are becoming less to do with increasing production, as was the case in industrial capitalism, and more to do with the regulation of bodies. Turner (1992: 12–13) writes:

> our major political preoccupations are how to regulate the spaces between bodies, to monitor the interfaces between bodies, societies and cultures ... We want to close up bodies by promoting safe sex, sex education, free condoms and clean needles. We are concerned about whether the human population of the world can survive global pollution. The somatic society is thus crucially, perhaps critically structured around regulating bodies.

The concerns of the somatic society are also evidenced by the way in which contemporary political movements such as feminist groupings, pro- and anti-abortion campaigns, debates about fertility and infertility, disability, and the Green movement coalesce around body matters.

Turner (1992, 2008) examines the ways in which bodies are controlled within society and finds it is the institutions of law, religion, and medicine that are most preoccupied with such regulation. The role of religion, law, and medicine is especially evident at the birth and death of bodies. Whilst the control of bodies by the church has gone into decline, the control of bodies by the medical profession is in the ascendancy. He argues, echoing the earlier writings of Zola (1972) and Conrad and Schneider (1980), that as society has become more secularized it has also become more medicalized, with medicine now serving a moral as well as a clinical function:

> Medical practice in our time clearly does have a moral function, especially in response to AIDS and IVF programmes for unmarried, single women, but these moral functions are typically disguised and they are ultimately legitimized by an appeal to scientific rather than religious authority ... medicine occupies the space left by the erosion of religion. (Turner 1992: 23)

Developing an analytical framework which works at two levels – the bodies of individuals and the bodies of populations – Turner (2008) identifies four basic social tasks which are central to social order. We might refer to these as the four "r"s. First, *reproduction*, which refers to the creation of institutions that govern populations over time to ensure the satisfaction of physical needs, for example the control of sexuality. Second, the need for the *regulation* of bodies, particularly medical surveillance and the control of crime. Third, *restraint*, which refers to the inner self and inducements to control desire and passion in the interests of social organization. Fourth, the *representation* of the body, which refers to its physical presentation on the world's stage.

Turner's conceptualization of these four "r"s owes a great deal to the ideas of Foucault, especially his writings on normalization and surveillance. These draw attention to the ways in which bodies are monitored, assessed, and corrected within modern institutions. A central theme which runs through Foucault's (1976, 1979) work is that the shift from pre-modern to modern forms of society involved the displacement of what he terms *sovereign power*, wherein power resided in the body of the monarch, by *disciplinary power*, wherein power is invested in the bodies of the wider population. Disciplinary power refers to the way in which bodies are regulated, trained, maintained, and understood; it is most evident in social institutions such as schools, prisons, and hospitals. Disciplinary power works at two levels. First, individual bodies are trained and observed. Foucault refers to this as the anatomo-politics of the human body. Second, and concurrently, populations are monitored. He refers to this process as "regulatory controls: a bio-politics of the population" (Foucault 1981: 139). It is these two levels – the individual and the population – which form the basis of Turner's arguments about regulating bodies that we have discussed above. Foucault argues that it is within such institutions that knowledge of bodies is produced. For example, the observation of bodies in prisons yielded a body of knowledge we now know as criminology, and the observation of bodies in hospitals contributed to medical science. In fact, it was the discourse of pathological medicine in the eighteenth century which formed the basis of the bodies in Western society that we have come to be familiar with today. The body, Foucault argued, is a fabrication which is contingent upon its discursive context (see Armstrong 1983).

Through these discussions, we can see that the regulation of bodies is crucial to the maintenance of social order. This observation forms the basis of Mary Douglas's (1966, 1970) work on the representation of the symbolic body. The ideas of Mary Douglas – an anthropologist – have been drawn upon extensively by medical sociologists. She argues that the perception of the physical body is mediated by the social body. The body provides a basis for classification, and in turn the organization of the social system reflects how the body is perceived.

> The social body constrains the way the physical body is perceived. The physical experience of the body, always modified by the social categories through which it is known, sustains a particular view of society. There is a continual exchange of meanings between the two kinds of bodily experience so that each reinforces the categories of the other. As a result of this interaction the body itself is a highly restricted medium of expression. (Douglas 1970: xiii)

Thus, according to Douglas (1966), the body forms a central component of any classificatory system. Working within a Durkheimian tradition she maintains that all societies have elements of both the sacred and the profane, and that demarcation between the two is fundamental to the functioning of social systems. Thus societies respond to disorder by developing classificatory systems which can designate certain phenomena as matter out of place. "Where there is dirt there is system ... This idea of dirt takes us straight into the field of symbolism and promises a link-up with more obviously symbolic systems of purity" (Douglas 1966: 35). Anything which transcends social, or bodily, boundaries will be regarded as pollution. Ideas, therefore, about bodily hygiene tell us as much about our cultural assumptions as they do about the "real" body and our medical knowledge of it. Furthermore, any boundaries that are perceived to be vulnerable or permeable will need to be carefully regulated or monitored to prevent transgressions (Nettleton 1988).

Social changes have bodily correlates in that what bodies are permitted to do, and how people use their bodies, is contingent upon social context. The work of Elias (1978, 1982) demonstrates this on a very grand scale. Elias is concerned with the link between the state and state formations and the behaviors and manners of the individual. He offers a *figurational sociology*; this means that he works at the level of social configurations, rather than societies. In fact, for Elias, societies are the outcome of the interactions of individuals. In his studies of *The Civilizing Process* (first published in 1939 in German), Elias (1978) examines in detail changes in manners, etiquette, codes of conduct, ways of dressing, ways of sleeping, ways of eating, and changing ideas about shame and decency associated with bodies.

According to Elias, the civilizing process began in the Middle Ages within court societies where social mobility became more fluid and people's futures could be determined not only by their birthrights, as had been the case under the feudal system, but also by the extent to which they were in favor with the sovereign or his/her advisors. In short, people were more inclined to be on their best behavior. Medieval personalities were characteristically unpredictable and emotional, they were inclined to be indulgent, and there were virtually no codes surrounding bodily functions. However, within court societies, codes of body management were developed and copious manuals were written on how to and where to sleep and with whom, how to behave at meals, appropriate locations for defecation, and so on. Changes in behavior impacted on social relations and, as social relations transformed, so the compulsions exerted over others became internalized. This process, according to Elias, was accelerated in the sixteenth century. People came to have greater self-control over behaviors associated with the body and a heightened sense of shame and delicacy:

> The individual is compelled to regulate his [*sic*] conduct in an increasingly differentiated, more even and more stable manner.... The more complex and stable control of conduct is increasingly instilled in the individual from his earliest years as an automatism, a self compulsion that he cannot resist. (Elias 1982: 232–3)

This civilizing process involves three key progressive processes (Shilling 2003: 142–6): *socialization, rationalization,* and *individualization. Socialization* refers to the way in which people are encouraged to hide away their natural functions. Thus the body comes to be regarded more in social rather than natural terms. In fact, we find many natural functions offensive or distasteful; for example, if someone sitting next to us on a bus vomits over our clothes or if someone willingly urinates in an "inappropriate" part of our house. *Rationalization* implies that we have become more rational as opposed to emotional and are able to control our feelings. Finally, *individualization* highlights the extent to which we have come to see our bodies as encasing ourselves as separate from others. It is important, therefore, that we maintain a socially acceptable distance between ourselves and others. Furthermore, how we "manage" and "present" our bodies (cf. Goffman 1959) has become especially salient in a late modern context. Some argue that this is because the body has become a prime site for the formation and maintenance of the modern self and identity.

UNCERTAIN BODIES IN LATE MODERN SOCIETIES

Giddens (1991) and a number of other commentators such as Beck (1992) and Douglas (1986) have argued that a key feature of such contemporary societies is risk. Doubt, Giddens argues, is a pervasive feature which permeates into everyday life "and forms a general existential dimension of the contemporary social world." Within our post-traditional societies, our identities and our sense of self are not givens. We can no longer hang on to our "traditional place" in society with respect to our social class, family, gender, locality, and so on. Rather, our self and identity become a "reflexively organised endeavour." Less and less can we rely on continuous biographical narratives. Instead, these tend to be flexible and continually revised (Featherstone and Hepworth 1991). The reflexive self is one that relies on a vast array of advice and information provided by a myriad of sources.

What has all this got to do with the body? Well, a number of theorists have suggested that the body has come to form one of the main sites through which people develop their social identities. Whilst the environment and the social world seem to be "out of control," the body becomes something of an anchor. Giddens points out that the self is embodied and so the regularized control of the body is a fundamental means whereby a biography of self-identity is maintained. Giddens (1991: 218) states:

> The body used to be one aspect of nature, governed in a fundamental way by processes only marginally subject to human intervention. The body was a "given," the often inconvenient and inadequate seat of the self. With the increasing invasion of the body by abstract systems all this becomes altered. The body, like the self, becomes a site of interaction, appropriation and re-appropriation, linking reflexively organised processes and systematically ordered expert knowledge. [...] Once thought to be the locus of the soul ... the body has become fully available to be "worked upon by the influences of high modernity" [...]. In the conceptual space between these, we find more and more guidebooks and practical manuals to do with health, diet, appearance, exercise, lovemaking and many other things.

According to this thesis, therefore, we are more uncertain about our bodies; we perceive them to be more pliable and are actively seeking to alter, improve, and refine them.

The idea that contemporary societies are characterized by change and adaptability has also been articulated by Emily Martin (1994) in her empirical study of contemporary ideas about immunity in North America. By way of data collected via interviews, analyses of documents, participant observation, and informal exchanges, she (Martin 1994: xvii) found that "flexibility is an object of desire for nearly everyone's personality, body and organisation." Flexibility is associated with the notion of the immune system which now underpins our thinking about the body, organizations, machines, politics, and so on. In her interviews with ordinary men and women, the idea of developing a strong immune system appeared to be in common currency. To be effective, that is to protect the body against the threats of disease and illness, the immune system must be able to change and constantly adapt. Martin's study not only provides a valuable analysis of late modernity but also reveals how our accounts and interpretations of our bodies are historically and socially contingent, and that they are not "immune" from broader social transformations (see also the discussion about the work of Elias above). How we experience our bodies is invariably social, and one of the central thrusts of modern times is that we feel compelled to work at creating a *flexible* and therefore adaptable and socially acceptable body.

Shilling (2003) also argues that the body might best be conceptualized as an *unfinished* biological and social phenomenon, which is transformed, within limits, as a result of its participation in society. The body is therefore in a continual state of "unfinishedness"; the body is "seen as an entity which is in the process of becoming; *a project* which should be worked at and accomplished as part of an individual's self-identity" (Shilling 2003: 4). *Body projects* become more sophisticated and more complex in a context where there is both the knowledge and technology to transform them in ways that in the past might have been regarded as the province of fiction. There is now a vast array of medical technologies and procedures to choose from if we want to shape, alter, and recreate our bodies – from various forms of techniques to "assist" conception, to gene therapies, to forms of cosmetic surgery and so on. Shilling points out that there is, of course, an irony here. As we expand our "knowledge" and "expertise," we become more uncertain as to what the body actually is and what its boundaries are. Reviewing the impact of new medical technologies and the body, Williams (1997: 1047) suggests: "From plastic surgery to virtual medicine, our previously held and cherished beliefs about the body and the 'limits' of corporeality are being 'placed in brackets' and the body has thus become 'ever more elusive and problematic'."

Whilst the above discussion has highlighted the body as an unfinished and malleable entity which has become central to the formation of the late modern *reflexive* self, other postmodern analyses have suggested that the body is not so much *uncertain* as *un/hyperreal*. In other words, the body has disappeared – there is no distinction between bodies and the images of bodies. Drawing on the work of Baudrillard, Frank (1992) challenges the conventional idea that the body of the patient forms the basis of medical practice. It is the *image* of the body which now forms the basis of medical care.

> Real diagnostic work takes place away from the patient; bedside is secondary to screen side. For diagnostic and even treatment purposes, the image on the screen becomes the "true" patient, of which the bedridden body is an imperfect replicant, less worthy of attention. In the screens' simulations our initial certainty of the real (the body) becomes lost in hyperreal images that are better than the real body. (Frank 1992: 83)

A high-profile illustration of this is the "Visible Human Project" (VHP), described on the US National Library of Medicine, National Institutes of Health website as:

> the creation of complete, anatomically detailed, three-dimensional representations of the normal male and female human bodies. Acquisition of transverse CT, MR and cryosection images of representative male and female cadavers has been completed. The male was sectioned at one millimeter intervals, the female at one-third of a millimeter intervals. (National Library of Medicine 2008)

Fascinated by this undertaking, Catherine Waldby (2000) subjects the VHP to sociological scrutiny and highlights some intriguing features. Not only do images of the inner reaches of the body become accessible to a wide audience, but also the transformation of bodies into a "digital substance" contributes to the blurring of boundaries between the real and the unreal, the private and the public, and the dead and the living (Waldby 2000: 6). She argues that the whole exercise represents a further extension of Foucault's notion of bio-power. The VHP is at once a means of both examining and experimenting on the body and, therefore, it is also a means by which knowledge of bodies is generated and circulated. In addition, the establishment of knowledge contributes to the production of "surplus value" in that there are significant commercial interests that benefit through the related production of medical technologies, be they equipment, drugs, and so on. This is what Waldby calls "biovalue," which "refers to the yield of vitality produced by the biotechnological reformulation of living processes" (Waldby 2002: 310). Two factors precipitate the generation of biovalue. First, the hope that biotechnologies will result in a better understanding and thereby treatment of disease. Second, the pursuit of exchange value of biomedical commodities – be they patents or pills – that are the yield of the interventions. Indeed, biovalue is "increasingly assimilated into capital value, and configured according to the demands of commercial economies" (Waldby 2000: 34). The counterpart to the VHP, observes Waldby, is the Human Genome Project (HGP) in that both projects are means by which the body comes to form a database, an archive and so a source of bioinformation.

Waldby (2000: 39–40) explains:

> The instrumentation specific to the VHP and the HGP address the body so that it acts as an archive, laying it open as a source of bioinformation. The VHP cuts up the body so that it can act as a visual and morphological archive, while the HGP has a large repertoire of molecular practices (polymerase chain reaction, automated DNA fluorescence sequencing, pulse field gel electophoresis) that make the body's sequences of DNA intelligible and mappable.

There is an ever increasing array of images in the medical clinic – CAT scan images, X-rays, angiograms, magnetic resonance imaging (MRI) videotapes, and so on. The image or the virtual takes precedence over the "real" or at least that which is felt. The image of the body is more legitimate than the body itself. For example, one participant in a study by Rhodes and colleagues who experienced chronic back pain said that the doctors:

> are not listening to what you say … [they] try to tell you backaches are psychosomatic and your back couldn't be hurting, [that] there's nothing, no reason for it to hurt. X-rays don't show anything and you don't really have a backache. Oh yes I do, yes I do … but backaches are hard to see. Unless there's something that's a visible thing, it's kind of your word against who's looking. (Cited in Rhodes et al. 1999: 1191)

Perhaps a more profound impact of the production of images is in relation to pregnancy. Writing in German from a historical perspective, Barbera Duden (1993) argues that the use of technologies which enable the fetus to be visually represented has contributed to the transformation of an unborn fetus into *a life*. The imagining of the unborn has meant that the fetus has become an emblem, a "billboard image," which has come into the limelight. Her study addresses the following puzzle:

How did the female peritoneum acquire transparency? What set of circumstances made the skinning of women acceptable and inspired public concern for what happens in her innards? And finally, the embarrassing question: how was it possible to mobilize so many women as uncomplaining agents of this skinning and as willing? (Duden 1993: 7)

A scanning ultramicroscope produces images which those who are trained appropriately can "read." However, this is something that has to be learned. Duden (1993: 29) describes the experience of a Puerto Rican woman, new to New York, who was asked to look at such images when she visited the antenatal clinic:

The graph that she is asked to look at during her visit to the clinic only serves to mystify her experience. In ways that she cannot fathom, expert professionals claim to know something about her future child, much more, in fact, than she could ever find out by herself.

In an amazingly short space of time, "the scan" became a routine and ubiquitous experience for most pregnant women in many Western societies. In popular discourse, women – and especially men – can be heard to say that "it was only then," when they saw the image of the fetus, that they felt it was "real."

There is a tension here, then, between the way the body is experienced or *lived* and the way the body is observed and described by "medical experts." In those circumstances where the voice of the body is silenced, the person is likely to become alienated from those who aim to "practice" upon his or her body. In some respects this tension captures the difference between a sociology of the body and a sociology of embodiment. This difference is described neatly by Bendelow and Williams (1998: 123), who write:

Whilst the former translates, in corporeal terms, into a treatment of the body as simply one amongst many topics which sociologists can study from "outside" … the latter, in contrast, refuses to slip into this deceptive Cartesian view of the world – one which treats mind and body as distinctly separate entities – taking the embodiment of its practitioners as well as its subjects seriously through a commitment to a lived body and its being in the world.

Sociology of embodiment

A sociology of embodiment has developed out of a critique that the literature on the body has failed to incorporate the voices of bodies as they are experienced or lived (James and Hockey, 2007). Drawing on phenomenological analyses, this approach proposes that much of the existing literature has failed to challenge a whole series of dualisms such as: the split between mind and body; culture and nature; and reason and emotion. Such socially created dualisms are pernicious, not only because they are false, but also because they serve to reinforce ideologies and social hierarchies. "These dualisms," Bendelow and Williams (1998: 1) argue, "have been mapped onto the gendered division of labour in which men, historically, have been allied with the mind, culture and the public realm of production, whilst women have been tied to their bodies, nature, and the private sphere of domestic reproduction." But most important, from a sociological point of view they hinder any effective theorizing which must assume the inextricable interaction and oneness of mind and body. Studies of pain and emotion have, perhaps more than any other, revealed that the body and the mind are not separate entities (Bendelow and Williams 1998; Morris 1991).

Phenomenology: The "lived body"

The phenomenological perspective focuses on the "lived body"; the idea that consciousness is invariably embedded within the body. The human being is an embodied social agent. The work of Merleau-Ponty, in particular his text *The Phenomenology of Perception*, has been revisited, and it is regarded by many as critical to our appreciation of embodiment (Crossley 1995, 2006; Csordas 1994). Essentially, he argued that all human perception is embodied; we cannot perceive anything, and our senses cannot function independently of our bodies. This does not imply that they are somehow glued together, as the Cartesian notion of the body might suggest, but rather there is something of an oscillation between the two. This idea forms the basis of the notion of "embodiment." As Merleau-Ponty (1962) writes:

> Men [*sic*] taken as a concrete being is not a psyche joined to an organism, but movement to and fro of existence which at one time allows itself to take corporeal form and at others moves toward personal acts.... It is never a question of the incomprehensive meeting of two casualties, nor of a collision between the order of causes and that of ends. But by an imperceptible twist an organic process issues into human behaviour, an instinctive act changes direction and becomes a sentiment, or conversely a human act becomes torpid and is continued absent-mindedly in the form of a reflex. (Merleau-Ponty 1962: 88, cited by Turner 1992: 56)

Thus, while the notion that embodied consciousness is central here, it is also highlighted that we are not always conscious or aware of our bodily actions. We do not routinely tell our body to put one leg in front of the other if we want to walk, or to breathe in through our nose if we want to smell a rose. The body in this sense is "taken for granted," or as Leder puts it, the body is "absent."

> Whilst in one sense the body is the most abiding and inescapable presence in our lives, it is also characterised by its absence. That is, one's own body is rarely the thematic object of experience ... the body, as a ground of experience ... tends to recede from direct experience. (Leder 1990: 1)

Within this perspective, the lived body is presumed to both construct and be constructed by, and within, the lifeworld. The lived body is an intentional entity which gives rise to this world. As Leder (1992: 25) writes elsewhere:

> in a significant sense, the lived body helps to constitute this world as experienced. We cannot understand the meaning and form of objects without reference to bodily powers

through which we engage them – our senses, motility, language, desires. The lived body is not just one thing in the world but a way in which the world comes to be.

We can see therefore that it is analytically possible to make a distinction between *having* a body, *doing* a body, and *being* a body. Turner (1992) and others have found the German distinction between *Leib* and *Korper* to be instructive here. The former refers to the experiential, animated, or living body (the body-for-itself), the latter refers to the objective, instrumental, exterior body (the body-in-itself).

This approach highlights that the concept of the "lived body" and the notion of "embodiment" remind us that the self and the body are not separate and that experience is invariably, whether consciously or not, embodied. As Csordas (1994: 10) has argued, the body is the "existential ground of culture and self," and therefore he prefers the notion of "embodiment" to "the body," as the former implies something more than a material entity. It is rather a "methodological field defined by perceptual experience and mode of presence and engagement in the world." This idea that the self is embodied is also taken up by Giddens (1991: 56–7), who also emphasizes the notion of day-to-day *praxis*. The body is not an external entity but is experienced in practical ways when coping with external events and situations. How we handle our bodies in social situations is crucial to our self and identity and has been extensively studied by Goffman, symbolic interactionists, and ethnomethodologists (Heritage 1984). Indeed, the study of the management of bodies in everyday life and how this serves to structure the self and social relations has a long and important history within sociology. It highlights the preciousness of the body as well as the remarkable ability of humans to sustain bodily control through day-to-day situations.

Marrying the work of theorists such as Foucault and Giddens with the insights of the early interactionists, Nick Crossley (2006) has developed the particularly useful concept of "reflexive embodiment." Premised on Cooley's (1902) notion of the "looking glass self" and Mead's (1967) suggestion that we care about, and are influenced by, how we think other people see us, Crossley's thesis is that humans are not merely subjects of regulation but are active agents whose thoughts, actions, and intentions are embedded within social networks. Embodied agents have the capacity to reflect upon themselves and such reflection involves an assessment of what they believe other people (the "generalized other") think of them.

> "Reflexive embodiment" refers to the capacity and tendency to perceive, emote about, reflect and act upon one's own body; to practices of body modification and maintenance; and to "body image." Reflexivity entails that the object and subject of perception, thought, feeling, desire or action are the same. (Crossley 2006: 1)

This notion is central to the experience of health and illness, not least because so many bodily practices and techniques are associated with the maintenance and reproduction of bodies to ensure good health and to manage illness. Many of these themes have been explored by sociologists who have studied how people *experience* illness.

THE SOCIOLOGY OF THE BODY: SOME ILLUSTRATIVE ISSUES

Illness and injury and lived bodies

The literature on the experience of chronic illness and disability drew attention to many of the themes discussed above prior to the more recent emergence of the body and embodiment literature, most particularly the fundamental link between the *self* and the body. A number of researchers (e.g., Charmaz 2000) have documented how this occurs in the case of chronic illness. Here the relationship between the body and self can be seriously disrupted.

Simon Williams (1996) has illustrated this well by drawing on the findings of research into chronic illness. He demonstrates how the experience of chronic illness involves a move from an "initial" state of embodiment (a state in which the body is taken for granted in the course of everyday life) to an oscillation between states of (*dys*)embodiment (embodiment in a dysfunctional state) and "re-embodiment." Attempts to move from a dys-embodied state to a re-embodied state require a considerable amount of biographical work, or what Gareth Williams (1984) terms "narrative reconstruction." This theme is also demonstrated by Seymour (1998) in her empirical study of 24 men and women who experienced profound and permanent body paralysis as a result of spinal injuries. As the title of her book, *Remaking the Body*, suggests, as men and women go about remaking their bodies they "remake their worlds." Through listening to the accounts of these men and women, Seymour argues that she was able to appreciate the crucial role of embodiment in the reconstitution of the self. Whilst the participants she spoke to have had to endure profound bodily changes and difficulties, she maintains that they have retained their "selves." Seymour (1998: 178) states:

> this damage [the spinal injury] has disturbed, but not destroyed, their embodied selves. These people still inhabit and possess their bodies; their bodies are still resources with which they may explore new possibilities and opportunities for re-embodiment.

The problem with the literature on the lived body (from within the sociology of embodiment), and the notion of body projects and the reflexive self (from within the sociology of the body), is that they both assume a competent mind. In a moving paper, David Webb (1998) describes the impact on individuals and their families of traumatic brain injury (TBI), which he describes as a silent epidemic of our modern times. In Britain, 15 people are taken to hospital every hour with a head injury. Most are the result of traffic accidents, and young men are the most common victims. This modern epidemic ironically means that the victims are unable to participate in one of the key aspects of late modernity. As Webb (1998: 545) explains:

> Indeed the case here is that with a physiologically damaged brain comes the likelihood of a fractured mind, and that consequently this will have a bearing on the person's capacity to existentially "live their body" – to reflexively experience it [...] [H]igh modernity revolves around a mentalist discourse in which greater importance is given to the mind than the sociological talk of "body matters" suggests.

Many assumptions are made, therefore, that when we reflect upon the following – how we feel about ourselves, how we view our past, how we assess and plan our futures – we have a socially acceptable, competent mental capacity to do so. Our mental capacity depends upon "normal" functioning of the brain, which in turn may also be contingent upon the acceptable functioning of the rest of our bodies. This issue is explored in the context of hospice care and is discussed in the next section of this chapter.

Health care work

As Twigg (2006) has demonstrated in her elegantly argued book on the body in health and social care, the material body is critical to any adequate analysis of health care in practice. Medicine, health, care, and the body are inextricably interlinked. Analyses of, or policies on, health and social care which overlook the messy realities of the body will invariably be wanting. The rationalistic approach which has tended to dominate policy debates in this area, she concludes, "presents a leached out, abstract, dry account that takes little cognizance of the messy, swampy, emotional world of the body and its feelings" and she suggests that a focus on the body "promises to bring the world of policy into much closer and direct engagement with its central subject" (Twigg 2006: 173). In what ways can theorizations on the body and embodiment help us to make sense of health care in practice? There are some excellent qualitative studies of health care work within formal settings that can help us answer this question. Julia Lawton's (1998) study of care within a hospice is an excellent example. Her ethnographic study sets out to understand why it is that some patients remain within the hospice to die whilst others are more likely to be discharged and sent home to die. To address this health policy puzzle, Lawton argues we need to focus on the *body* of the dying person. She found that those patients cared for within the hospice were those whose bodies became *unbounded*. By this she means that the diseases they were suffering from involved a particular type of bodily deterioration and disintegration requiring very specific forms of symptom control, the most common examples being:

> incontinence of urine and faeces, uncontrolled vomiting (including faecal vomit), fungating tumours (the rotting away of a tumour site on the surface of the skin) and weeping limbs which resulted from the development of gross oedema in the patient's legs or arms. (Lawton 1998: 128)

It is these forms of bodily (dys)functions that people living in Western society cannot tolerate rather than the process of dying itself. Indeed, in those cases where the boundedness of their bodies could be reinstated, patients would be discharged. To address the question of why unbounded bodies are unacceptable in Western society, Lawton draws upon much of the sociological theorizing outlined above – especially the work of Douglas and Elias. The unbounded body is perceived symbolically, according to Douglas, as a source of dirt – it is matter out of place. The increasingly "civilized" body, according to Elias, has become "individualized" and private, and the "natural" functions of the body are removed from public view.

The fact that natural or intimate bodily functions are problematic for health care practitioners has also been explored by Lawler (1991), who again draws upon the ideas developed by Elias and Douglas in her study of nursing care in an Australian hospital. Quintessentially, the work of nurses is about caring for bodies. This becomes a problem when nurses have to attend to those bodily functions (defecating, grooming, etc.) which in a "civilized" society have become taboo. Consequently, nurses have to learn how to negotiate social boundaries and create new contexts so that both the patient and the nurse can avoid feelings of shame and embarrassment.

There is a further fascinating finding highlighted in Lawton's study, and this relates to the link that we have discussed above between the notion of self and physical body. The two are meshed together. We saw in our discussion of Webb's (1998) paper that the functioning reflexive self relied on the competent mind. Lawton's work demonstrates that even where there is a "competent" mind, the lack of bodily controls (see also Featherstone and Hepworth 1991 and Nettleton and Watson 1998: 14–17) affects a person's capacity to continue with their life projects or their reflexive self. In fact, patients who had the least control over their bodily functions exhibited behavior which suggested a total loss of self and social identity once their bodies became severely and irreversibly unbounded. Take Lawton's account of Deborah, for example:

> When Deborah's bodily deterioration escalated, I observed that she had suddenly become a lot more withdrawn. After she had been on the ward for a couple of days she started asking for the curtains to be drawn around her bed to give her more privacy. A day or so later she stopped talking altogether, unless it was really necessary (to ask for a commode, for example), even when her family and other visitors were present. Deborah spent the remaining ten days of her life either sleeping or staring blankly into space. She refused all food and drink.... One of the hospice doctors concluded that "for all intents and purposes she [had] shut herself off in a frustrated and irreversible silence." (Lawton 1998: 129)

Both Webb and Lawton's papers are pertinent to late modern societies, in that the salience of the loss of self is linked to features of contemporary societies. The emphasis was on bodily controls and the boundedness of the body in Lawton's study. In Webb's analysis, by contrast, TBI would clearly alter who a person "is" and his or her capacity to "act" in any context. But its prevalence is related to modern ways of living (fast cars). Webb (1998: 548–50) comments:

> In high modernity the body has a diminishing *productive* significance, and it becomes increasingly a site more of recreational indulgence than labour power as such. In this context, it is catastrophic to be denied the opportunity to participate in the identity constituting reflexivity of late modernity (Giddens 1991). [...] There is, in short, no clarity about the categorisation of those who are head injured. The person becomes "someone else," an everyday recognition that it is the mind (more than the body) which signifies what it is to be a person. If the mind itself is seriously impaired then it is no longer able to mobilise the body to create the *physical capital* which might compensate for the run on *mental capital* occasioned through head injury.

The experience of TBI also brings into sharp relief another feature of late modernity, and that is the fact that (medical) technologies have their limits. As Webb points out, in cases of physical impairment very often technology can offer something – some means by which motor coordination or whatever can be facilitated. This is not so when physical injury impairs the mind; here, technological resolutions to disability are almost invariably impossible (Webb 1998: 547).

Technology and the body

Whilst technological "advances" do have their limits, there is no doubt that they have served to contribute to our reconceptualization of what constitutes the "body" (Shilling 2005). The boundaries between the physical and the social body, between bodies and machines, between human bodies and animal bodies, are being transgressed in novel and innovative ways. These new "hybrid" technologies such as human tissue engineering and xenotransplantation (animal to human transplants) transcend and therefore challenge existing categories and raise political and ethical "problems" which are by no means easy to resolve (Brown et al. 2006). The body becomes fuzzy and messy, and as we have suggested above, we are less certain as to what the body actually is, or has the potential to do. During the last few decades, developments in a number of areas of medical and related technologies have contributed to these uncertainties and even, some would venture, to "reordering life" (Brown and Webster 2004). For example, bodies have bits added to them to enable them to function more effectively. Prosthetics – the use of artificial body parts such as limbs – of course has a long history. But the list of body parts has grown in recent decades to include cardiac pacemakers, valves, ear implants, and even polyurethane hearts. Such developments have become increasingly sophisticated as they have developed in concert with advances in molecular biology. This has led some authors to talk about the emergence of *cyborgs* – the marriage between a human organism and machines (Featherstone and Hepworth 1991) which has been defined thus:

> Cyborgs are hybrid entities that are neither wholly technological nor completely organic, which means that the cyber has the potential to disrupt persistent dualisms that set the natural body in opposition to the technologically recrafted body, but also to refashion our thinking about the theoretical construction of the body as both a material entity and a discursive process. These bodies are multiple constituted parts of cybernetic systems – what we now recognise as social and informational networks. (Balsamo 1996: 11)

Thus the cyborg is neither a "natural body" nor simply a machine.

New reproductive technologies (NRTs) comprise a range of methods to assist conception which have been around for some decades. However, more recent technological developments, in conjunction with the more extended use of technologies such as gamete intrafallopian transfer (GIFT), hormonal treatments, and diagnostic technologies such as pre-implantation genetic diagnosis, have altered the boundaries of what was or was not physically possible for a growing number of women (Edwards et al. 1999; Williams et al. 2008). People are presented with more choices than ever before, people are presented with a wider array of possibilities, and people are also having to learn how to negotiate and deal with new identities. For example, as Edwards et al. (1999: 1) point out:

> To a greater or lesser extent, part of everyone's identity as a person is derived from knowledge about their birth and about how they were brought up [...]. The late twentieth-century development of the means to alter what many would have said were immutable processes of birth has created a new and complex vehicle for conceptualising connections.

The certainties of "birth" as an immutable process are therefore altered. This can make the negotiation of a reflexive identity very complex indeed.

A further "technological" development, affecting our notions of who and what we are, arises from the so-called "new genetics." The Human Genome Project is an international initiative to identify particular genes associated with diseases and, more controversially, behaviors (Conrad and Gabe 1999). This project, completed in 2000, gave rise to a new discourse with which to talk about our selves. It comprises a new twist to the notion that our biology is our destiny. The prospect is that medical science will be able to predict with a significant degree of precision our *predisposition* to a wide range of diseases such as cancers, heart disease, diabetes, and so on.

More knowledge, more information, and yet ever more uncertainty. Although the degree of accuracy, or rather certainty, associated with molecular genetic predictive testing is greater than that of traditional probabilistic clinical genetics, many uncertainties still remain and, in large measure, predictive tests can rarely be completely certain. They also raise a host of social and ethical considerations (see Davison, Macintyre, and Smith 1994 for a thorough exploration of these issues for social researchers). In relation to our discussion here, the main point is that the language of the new genetics has implications for how we think about, talk about, and experience our bodies. When we reflect upon our selves and our identities, we increasingly do so with recourse to our genes. As Spallone (1998) has pointed out, the word "gene" has replaced the looser notions of "the biological" and "hereditary." So rather than say, as we might have done 15 years ago, "it runs in the family," or "it's inherited," we hear ourselves saying, "it must be in their/my genes" (Spallone 1998: 50). Spallone also cites James Watson, the first director of the US Human Genome Initiative, who said: "We used to think our fate was in the stars. Now we know, in large measure, our fate is in our genes."

We noted above how "bits" are added to bodies, but another salient issue is the fact that body organs can be transplanted from one body to another due to advances in *organ donation and transplantation*. In the summer of 1999 in England, a 15-year-old girl who refused consent to a heart transplant had her case overruled by the high court. She was reported to have said: "Death is final – I know I can't change my mind. I do not want to die, but I would rather die than have the transplant and have someone else's heart." Again, as with medical practices associated with the new genetics, this issue raises ethical issues. Who should make decisions about people's bodies – should it be lawyers, medical practitioners, relatives, or the "owner" of the body itself? This issue also highlights the malleability of bodies in the modern age. Is it my body if parts of it belonged to someone else? A study of patients who had undergone organ transplant surgery found these patients felt they needed to work at "restructuring their sense of self' (Sharp 1995). The author reports that there was a tension between the need to both personalize and objectify bodies and organs. Thus, as Williams (1997: 1044) has pointed out, organ transplantation poses many questions about self-identity:

Medical personnel put great stress on objectification; the heart, for example, is "only a pump." Yet recipients experience conflict between this mechanistic/reductionist view of the body and their wider cultural beliefs about the embodied nature of self identity and the "sacred" nature of the heart as the very core of the person.

This albeit brief and partial discussion of medical technological developments and the body serves to highlight a key theme running through this chapter. That is the idea that in late modern contexts, there is a growing array of uncertainties associated with the body. The emergence of sophisticated medical knowledge and practices in fields associated with reproduction, genetics, and immunology has increased the complexities and choices people face when reflecting upon their bodies and their *embodied* identities. But choice is an ideologically powerful term. People make choices but not in circumstances of their own choosing, and the analysis of experiential dimensions of embodiment must always be located within the wider social, political, and economic context. Bodies, body parts, body organs, and body tissue are subject to commercialization, exploitation, and exchange and, as we have seen, yield surplus value (Dickenson 2008). Thus it is perhaps not surprising that sociologists have become increasingly preoccupied with the embodied basis of social action.

There is a further twist to the emerging debates within the sociology of the body and embodied sociology, and this relates to an area of medical sociology which has a much longer history – the study of health inequalities. A vein of research and debate is emerging within this area of study which draws upon the lived body, the physiological basis of the body, and social structure.

Social inequalities and the sociology of embodiment

A basic tenet of medical sociology is that social circumstances – in particular material and social deprivation – become inscribed upon people's bodies. In other words, it is argued that health status is socially determined. The reasons why social circumstances, and more especially social inequalities, impact upon health status have been researched and debated for over a century. Surprisingly, perhaps, the literatures on the sociology of the body and the sociology of embodiment are providing some important clues as to why health is socially patterned in this way. It seems, then, that "unhealthy societies" (Wilkinson 1996), or rather unequal societies, are associated with unhealthy bodies. This is not just a result of *material* deprivation and poverty – the harmful effects of poor housing, poor food, and living conditions per se – though these are undoubtedly important. But what is also important is one's class position. Essentially, those people who are lower down the social hierarchy and who have the least control over their circumstances are more likely to be ill.

The reason for this is that they are more likely to experience prolonged stress and negative emotions, which in turn have physiological consequences. This psychosocial perspective on health inequalities has been summarized by Elstad (1998), who points to a growing body of research that demonstrates how certain aspects of social life, such as a sense of control, perceived social status, strength of affiliations, self-esteem, feelings of ontological insecurity, and so on, lead to variations in health outcomes. This has been most fully explored in relation to male paid employment but also in relation to the housing circumstances of men and women (Nettleton and Burrows 2000).

It seems that how people reflect upon, feel about, and internalize their social position or their social circumstances is critical. Drawing from work in physiological anthropology, in particular studies of non-human primates, researchers have found that primates who were lower down the social hierarchy, and most importantly had least control and power, exhibited more detrimental physiological changes in times of stress. Authors have argued this may help explain the fact that numerous studies have consistently found that people in social environments with limited autonomy and control over their circumstances suffer proportionately poor health. The key issue here is the degree of social cohesion. Greater social cohesion means people are more likely to feel secure and "supported" and are less likely to respond negatively when they have to face difficulties or uncertainties. In turn, it is social inequality that serves to undermine social cohesion and the quality of the social fabric. Freund (1990) has argued that people express "somatically" the conditions of their existence. What he calls "emotional modes of being" are very likely to be linked to one's structural position. He writes:

> Subjectivity, social activity and the social structural contexts interpenetrate. It is this relationship that comes to be physically embodied in many ways. Irregularity of breathing may accompany muscular tension and experiences of ontological insecurity and the anger or fear that is part of this insecurity. (Freund 1990: 461)

Thus, for example, if we are in a social environment which is threatening, we may be "scared stiff." Freund (1990: 471) is able to postulate this theory because he believes that:

> Emotions and the feeling they express are embodied in neurohormonal and other aspects of bodyliness. They form communicative "fields" between the body and between body–mind and social existence.

This link becomes evident when we mesh together the "lived body" and the structural perspectives on the body. How people experience their structural context, the meanings and interpretations they ascribe to it, in turn impacts their physical bodies. This is the new development here. Hitherto, the literature on health inequalities has tended to be limited to the physical body and so works within a Cartesian model which brackets off the mind. Experience and meanings were only elicited to try to understand why people might engage in "unhealthy" activities such as smoking, overeating, and so on (Popay et al. 2003). The lived body approach, which collapses these dualisms, therefore provides us with fresh insights into one of the main concerns for sociologists of health and illness. This said, hitherto the empirical studies have been restricted to class and socioeconomic inequalities rather than others associated with gender and race – where issues of social control and ascribed social status are particularly salient.

CONCLUSION

This chapter has reviewed some of the key theoretical perspectives within the literature on the sociology of the body and the sociology of embodiment. Drawing on these approaches, it has discussed a number of substantive issues which are of interest to those working within medical sociology. Thus, it has attempted to show that a "sociology of the body" and an "embodied sociology" have made an important contribution to matters which have traditionally been of interest to this field of study. A key theme running through this chapter is that the more knowledge and information we have about bodies, the more uncertain we become as to what bodies actually are. Certainties about seemingly immutable processes associated with birth and death, for example, become questioned. Furthermore, how we experience and live our bodies has also become central to how we think about our *selves*. Thus any comprehensive analysis of the experience of health, illness, or health care should take cognizance of the body (whatever that is!) itself.

References

Armstrong, David. 1983. *Political Anatomy of the Body: Medical Knowledge in Britain in the Twentieth Century*. Cambridge: Cambridge University Press.

Balsamo, A. 1996. *Technologies of the Gendered Bodies: Reading Cyborg Women*. London: Duke University Press.

Beck, Ulrich. 1992. *Risk Society: Towards a New Modernity*. London: Sage.

Bendelow, Gill and Simon J. Williams (eds.). 1998. *Emotions in Social Life: Critical Themes and Contemporary Issues*. London: Routledge.

Brown, Nik and Andrew Webster. 2004. *New Medical Technologies and Society: Reordering Life*. Cambridge: Polity Press.

Brown, Nik, Alex Faulkner, Julie Kent, and Mike Michael. 2006. "Regulating Hybridity: Policing Pollution in Tissue Engineering and Transpecies Transplanation." In A. Webster (ed.), *New Technologies in Health Care: Challenge, Change and Innovation*. Basingstoke: Palgrave Macmillan.

Charmaz, Kathy. 2000. "Experiencing Chronic Illness." In G. L. Albrecht, R. Fitzpatrick, and S. Scrimshaw (eds.), *The Handbook of Social Studies in Health and Medicine*. London: Sage.

Conrad, Peter and Jonathon Gabe. 1999. "Introduction: Sociological Perspectives on the New Genetics: An Overview." *Sociology of Health and Illness* 21: 505–16.

Conrad, Peter and J. W. Schneider. 1980. *Deviance and Medicalization: From Badness to Sickness*. St. Louis: Mosby.

Cooley, C. H. 1902. *Human Nature and Social Order*. New York: Charles Scribner & Sons.

Crossley, Nick. 1995. "Merleau-Ponty, the Elusive Body and Carnal Sociology." *Body and Society* 1: 43–64.

Crossley, Nick. 2006. *Reflexive Embodiment in Contemporary Society*. Maidenhead: Open University Press.

Csordas, Thomas J. 1994. *Embodiment and Experience: The Existential Ground of Culture and Self*. Cambridge: Cambridge University Press.

Davison, Charlie, Sally Macintyre, and George Davey Smith. 1994. "The Potential Impact of Predictive Genetic Testing for Susceptibility to Common Chronic Diseases: A Review and a Proposed Research Agenda." *Sociology of Health and Illness* 16: 340–71.

Dickenson, D. 2008. *Body Shopping: The Economy Fuelled by Flesh and Blood*. Oxford: Oneworld Publications.

Douglas, Mary. 1966. *Purity and Danger: An Analysis of the Concepts of Pollution and Taboo*. London: Routledge and Kegan Paul.

Douglas, Mary. 1970. *Natural Symbols: Explorations in Cosmology*. London: Cresset Press.

Douglas, Mary. 1986. *Risk Acceptability According to the Social Sciences*. London: Routledge and Kegan Paul.

Duden, Barbera. 1993. *Disembodying Women: Perspectives on Pregnancy and the Unborn*. London: Harvard University Press.

Edwards, Juliet, Sarah Franklin, E. Hirsch, F. Price, and Marilyn Strathern. 1999. *Technologies of Procreation: Kinship in the Age of Assisted Conception*, 2nd edition. London: Routledge.

Elias, Norbert. 1978. *The Civilizing Process. Vol. 1: The History of Manners*. Oxford: Blackwell.

Elias, Norbert. 1982. *The Civilizing Process. Vol. 2: State Formation and Civilization*. Oxford: Blackwell.

Elstad, Jon I. 1998. "The Psycho-social Perspective on Social Inequalities in Health." *Sociology of Health and Illness* 20: 598–618.

Featherstone, Mike and Mike Hepworth. 1991. "The Mask of Aging and the Postmodern Lifecourse." In M. Featherstone, M. Hepworth, and B. Turner (eds.), *The Body: Social Processes and Cultural Theory*. London: Sage.

Foucault, Michel. 1976. *The Birth of the Clinic: An Archaeology of Medical Perception*. London: Tavistock.

Foucault, Michel. 1979. *Discipline and Punish: The Birth of the Prison*. Harmondsworth: Penguin.

Foucault, Michel. 1981. *The History of Sexuality: An Introduction*. Harmondsworth: Penguin.

Frank, Arthur W. 1992. "Twin Nightmares of the Medical Simulacrum: Jean Baudrillard and David Cronenberg." In W. Stearns and W. Chaloupka (eds.), *Jean Baudrillard: The Disappearance of Art and Politics*. London: Macmillan.

Freund, Pete E. S. 1990. "The Expressive Body: A Common Ground for the Sociology of Emotions and Health and Illness." *Sociology of Health and Illness* 12: 452–77.

Giddens, Anthony. 1991. *Modernity and Self-Identity: Self and Society in the Late Modern Age*. Cambridge: Polity Press.

Goffman, Ervin. 1959. *The Presentation of Self in Everyday Life*. Harmondsworth: Penguin.

Heritage, John. 1984. *Garfinkel and Ethnomethodology*. Cambridge: Polity Press.

James, Alison and Jenny Hockey. 2007. *Embodying Health Identities*. Basingstoke: Palgrave Macmillan.

Lawler, Joclyn. 1991. *Behind the Screens: Nursing Somology and the Problem of the Body*. London: Churchill Livingstone.

Lawton, Julia. 1998. "Contemporary Hospice Care: The Sequestration of the Unbounded Body and 'Dirty Dying'." *Sociology of Health and Illness* 20: 121–43.

Leder, Drew. 1990. *The Absent Body*. Chicago: Chicago University Press.

Leder, Drew. 1992. "Introduction." In D. Leder (ed.), *The Body in Medical Thought and Practice*. London: Kluwer Academic.

Martin, Emily. 1989. *The Woman in the Body: A Cultural Analysis of Reproduction*. Milton Keynes: Open University Press.

Martin, Emily. 1994. *Flexible Bodies: The Role of Immunity in American Culture from the Days of Polio to the Age of AIDS*. Boston: Beacon Press.

Mead, George Herbert. 1967. *Mind, Self and Society*. Chicago: Chicago University Press.

Morris, David. 1991. *The Culture of Pain*. Berkeley: University of California Press.

National Library of Medicine. 2008. "The Visible Human Project." National Library of Medicine, US National Institutes of Health. Retrieved January 13, 2008 (www.nlmnih. gov/research/visible/visible_human.htm).

Nettleton, Sarah. 1988. "Protecting a Vulnerable Margin: Towards an Analysis of How the Mouth Came to be Separated from the Body." *Sociology of Health and Illness* 10: 156–69.

Nettleton, Sarah. 2006. *The Sociology of Health and Illness*, 2nd edition. Cambridge: Polity Press.

Nettleton, Sarah and Roger Burrows. 2000. "When a Capital Investment Becomes an Emotional Loss: The Health Consequences of the Experience of Mortgage Repossession in England." *Housing Studies* 15(3): 463–79.

Nettleton, Sarah and Jonathon Watson (eds.). 1998. *The Body in Everyday Life*. London: Routledge.

Oakley, Ann. 1993. *Essays on Women, Medicine and Health*. Edinburgh: Edinburgh University Press.

Popay, Jenny, S. Bennett, Carol Thomas, and Tony Gatrell. 2003. "Beyond 'Beer, Fags, Eggs and Chips?' Exploring Lay Understanding of Social Inequalities in Health." *Sociology of Health and Illness* 20(5): 619–44.

Rhodes, Lorna A., Carol A. McPhillips-Tangum, Christine Markham, and Rebecca Klenk. 1999. "The Power of the Visible: The Meaning of Diagnostic Tests in Chronic Back Pain." *Social Science and Medicine* 48: 1189–203.

Seymour, Wendy. 1998. *Remaking the Body*. London: Routledge.

Sharp, Lesley A. 1995. "Organ Transplantation as a Transformative Experience: Anthropological Insights into the Restructuring of the Self." *Medical Anthroplogy Quarterly* 93: 357–89.

Shilling, Chris. 2003. *The Body and Social Theory*, 2nd edition. London: Sage.

Shilling, Chris. 2005. *The Body in Culture, Technology and Society*. London: Sage.

Spallone, Pat. 1998. "The New Biology of Violence: New Geneticisms for Old?" *Body and Society* 4: 47–66.

Stoppard, Tom. 1967. *Rosencrantz and Guildenstern are Dead*. London: Faber and Faber.

Toombs, S. K. 1992. "The Body in Multiple Sclerosis: A Patient's Perspective." In D. Leder (ed.), *The Body in Medical Thought and Practice*. London: Kluwer Academic.

Turner, Bryan S. 1984. *The Body and Society*, 1st edition. Oxford: Blackwell.

Turner, Bryan S. 1992. *Regulating Bodies: Essays in Medical Sociology*. London: Routledge.

Turner, Bryan S. 2008. *The Body and Society*, 3rd edition. Oxford: Blackwell.

Twigg, Julia. 2006. *The Body in Health and Social Care*. Basingstoke: Palgrave Macmillan.

Ussher, Jane. 2006. *Managing the Monstrous Feminine: Regulating the Reproductive Body*. London: Routledge.

Waldby, Catherine. 2000. *The Visible Human Project: Informatic Bodies and Post-Human Medicine*. London: Routledge.

Waldby, Catherine. 2002. "Stem Cells, Tissue Cultures and the Production of Biovalue." *Health* 6(3): 305–323.

Webb, David. 1998. "A 'Revenge' on Modern Times: Notes on Traumatic Brain Injury." *Sociology* 32: 541–56.

Wilkinson, Richard. 1996. *Unhealthy Societies: The Afflictions of Inequality*. London: Routledge.

Williams, Clare, Steven Wainwright, Kathy Ehrich, and Mike Michael. 2008. "Human Embryos as Boundary Objects? Some Reflections on the Biomedical Worlds of Embryonic Stem Cells and Pre-Implantation Genetic Diagnosis." *New Genetics and Society* 27: 17–18.

Williams, Gareth. 1984. "The Genesis of Chronic Illness: Narrative Reconstruction." *Sociology of Health and Illness* 6: 175–200.

Williams, Simon. 1996. "The Vicissitudes of Embodiment across the Chronic Illness Trajectory." *Body and Society* 2: 23–47.

Williams, Simon. 1997. "Modern Medicine and the 'Uncertain Body': From Corporeality to Hyperreality?" *Social Science and Medicine* 45: 1041–9.

Williams, Simon and Gill Bendelow. 1998. *The Lived Body: Sociological Themes, Embodied Issues*. London: Routledge.

Zola, Irvine K. 1972. "Medicine as an Institution of Social Control." *Sociological Review* 20: 487–504.

Part II
Health and Social Inequalities

4

Health and Social Stratification

Eero Lahelma

It is an inherent starting point of any medical sociological analysis that health and illness are embedded not only in the biological but equally in the social context. The significance of social and cultural divisions to health-related outcomes was put forward in sociology by Emile Durkheim (1897), who viewed suicide as a "social fact," that is, as dependent on the social and cultural environment and needing sociological explanation within and between countries. Over time, social environmental factors and their divisions have gradually been included in the sociological analysis of health and illness. Currently, the issue of how people's social environments contribute to the onset, course, and consequences of their illness and disease forms a key area of medical sociology (Cockerham 2007; Totman 1979).

Social stratification is a fundamental concept in sociology which directs attention to divisions emerging from people's positioning in the hierarchical social structures of society. Medical sociological analyses on the social production of health, illness, and death are linked to the concepts of social stratification. Traditionally, social class has been the dominant concept within the sociology of stratification. However, in medical sociology and health research at large it has become a convention to call the various domains of social stratification – such as education, occupational social class, and income – socioeconomic position. Divisions of health by social stratification are typically called socioeconomic inequalities in health, or health inequalities for short. In the United States, the term health disparities has also been used to signify health inequalities (Braveman et al. 2005; Galobardes et al. 2006a, 2006b; Townsend and Davidson 1982). Current conventions are followed here: "socioeconomic position" is used to denote positions in social stratification and "health inequalities" to denote disparities in health between socioeconomic positions. Large inequalities in health by socioeconomic position can be regarded as unjust or unfair in particular to the extent that they are avoidable. When health inequalities are viewed from an ethical perspective, the term health (in)equity is also used (Braveman and Gruskin 2003; Whitehead 1992).

Evidence has accumulated confirming that people's positioning across the hierarchical socioeconomic structures of society strongly and persistently determines their health (Bartley 2004; Cockerham 2007; Graham 2007; Townsend and Davidson 1982). A health divide not only exists between poor people and the rest of the population, but also those gradually better positioned in the stratification of society tend to have gradually better health and longer survival. Thus, socioeconomic inequalities in health typically follow a gradient. The main message from this work can be encapsulated in what can be called "the health inequalities invariance": the poorer the socioeconomic position, the poorer the health.

It is the task of this chapter to illuminate how subsequent research has elaborated the nature of this association and suggested reasons for health inequalities. It will do this by drawing on medical sociological analysis of socioeconomic inequalities in health, illness, and death, focusing on the overarching significance of social stratification for health. In addition to presenting the hierarchical socioeconomic inequalities in health, the possible reasons for these inequalities are discussed. Evidence is drawn from Europe and the United States, and reference is also made to international comparative analyses.

THE CHALLENGES

Health inequalities provide a major challenge for medical sociologists and public health actors as well as wider circles of people. While health inequalities are well known to many medical sociologists and other scholars, they are not necessarily as well known among lay people. In some countries, such as Britain, the Netherlands, and Sweden, health inequalities have been much debated in the public and political arenas. This has also led to initiatives to tackle health inequalities in these countries (Mackenbach and Bakker 2002). However, the public debates may not reach lay people very effectively, and the lay and expert construction of ill health as resulting from adverse social conditions is likely to be different. While lay people may be less prone to attribute ill health to adverse social conditions, for most medical sociologists it is a starting point that health, illness, and death are profoundly determined by the unequally stratified conditions in which people live (Blaxter 1997).

Nevertheless, socioeconomic inequalities in health have also been challenged by scholars. For example, the American sociologist Charles Kadushin (1964: 75) predicted over 40 years ago that health inequalities would disappear as "in modern western countries the relationship between social class and the prevalence of illness is certainly decreasing and most probably no longer exists." His conclusion was based on the disappearance of the problem of absolute subsistence, which nevertheless is a limited perspective on the social stratification of living conditions and resources. Subsequent research has not confirmed this predicted egalitarian health development.

A later scholarly challenge comes from the sociological debate on late modernism or postmodernism where arguments were presented for the death of class. That would imply that class inequalities give way to new divisions in society (Lee and Turner 1996; Scambler and Higgs 1999). It makes sense to argue that social structures and stratification are under constant change and this will affect the social determinants of health as well. In addition to social stratification across socioeconomic positions, further divisions related to employment status, consumption patterns, gender, ethnicity, and identity have gained importance. Consequently, medical sociological theories, concepts, and empirical approaches to health and social stratification also need to be constantly rethought (Scambler and Higgs 1999). However, it would be a very profound transformation of industrial and postindustrial societies if universal social stratification and the related stratification of inequalities lost their significance for these novel divisions. In fact, health provides an interesting case study to examine the challenges cast by the persistence of universal socioeconomic inequalities.

THE INTERNATIONAL TRADITION

It has long been known that poor health emerges from poor living conditions. The origins of examining health and social stratification can be traced back to early sociomedical analysis of ill health and mortality. Such analysis later contributed to the emergence of medical sociology as well. This tradition has its deepest roots in Britain, where documenting and monitoring of social divisions in the population's health was initiated by such scholars as John Graunt and William Petty in the seventeenth century. In one of the first studies from 1662, Graunt reported those living in London had a shorter life than those living in the countryside due to poor living conditions such as pollution in the city (Whitehead 1997).

The early nineteenth century saw a breakthrough in British public health policies and documenting health divisions in the population, marked by the publication of the General Report on the Sanitary Conditions of the Labouring Population of Great Britain by Edwin Chadwick in 1842. This report showed stark mortality inequalities in Liverpool, where the average age at death was 35 years for the gentry and professionals, 22 years for tradesmen, and 15 years for laborers, mechanics, and servants. Chadwick's report is a seminal work for all subsequent examination of health and social stratification (Macintyre 1997; Rosen 1993). His analysis emphasized the prevention of infectious diseases by using proximal hygienic measures. Another simultaneous analysis by William Farr, in turn, emphasized more distal social and economic determinants of health (Hamlin 1995). These early analyses strongly influenced the monitoring of health divisions in the population. For example, the British report Decennial Supplement on mortality by social class was inaugurated. The different emphases on determinants of health extend their significance even to current debates. While medical sociology examines a variety of social structural determinants, such as stratification shaping health in the population at large, the dominant (bio)medical model examines specific programs directed toward the treatment of those already at risk or affected by diseases.

British developments were paralleled in the mid-nineteenth-century United States, where much attention was given to health problems in the urban slums expanding due to immigration. Chadwick's influence was clearly seen in a study by John Griscom in New York in 1845 in which he concluded that "there is an immense amount of sickness, physical disability and premature mortality among the poorer classes" (Rosen 1993: 238). The emerging statistical evidence enabled such conclusions and provided important tools for analyzing population health by key social divisions, such as poverty, social class, and ethnicity. These developments were important steps in American public health policies and analysis; their influences extended for several decades ahead.

In Germany, the founder of modern cellular pathology, Rudolf Virchow, writing in the revolutionary months of 1848, drew a connection between a typhoid epidemic and living conditions among the mining population in Upper Silesia. This marked a new relationship between medicine and sociology which Virchow encapsulated by stating that "Medicine is social science and politics nothing but medicine on a grand scale." In other words, its task was to contribute to the health and well-being of the population, not only to the treatment of those already hit by diseases. According to Virchow, health must be a democratic right rather than a privilege of the well-positioned few. Virchow's work has provided far-reaching incentives for the emergence of modern medical sociology and the examination of health and social stratification (Gerhardt 1989).

In the Nordic countries a special feature was the early development of population statistics. The Swedish empire was probably the first country to initiate nationwide population statistics in 1749. These statistics were immediately utilized in research (Lahelma, Karisto, and Rahkonen 1996). For example, Abraham Bäck, Sweden's chief medical officer, reported in 1765 that:

> The poverty-stricken are ravaged by pestilence while few of the wealthier fall ill …
> When I consider the causes behind diseases and excessive mortality among the peasantry, and the worse-off in towns, the first and foremost are poverty, misery, lack of bread, anxiety and despair. (Fritzell and Lundberg 2005: 177)

Thus also in Sweden, health and social stratification was very early identified as a key issue for public health.

Even in mid-nineteenth-century Finland, then under Russian rule, an early wave of sociomedical research emerged. In the early twentieth century, the chief medical officer of Finland, Akseli Koskimies, summarized the research tradition and set a future program for sociomedical research, which "was to examine a person as member of a particular class, economic group; as such a person is susceptible to the health hazards common and characteristic to one's own class" (Lahelma et al. 1996: 90). This exemplifies how the sociomedical tradition gradually evolved into research on health and social stratification, which simultaneously was close to the roots of medical sociology.

However, a socioeconomic research program had to wait for several decades to be seriously pursued. The early twentieth century saw a relative decline of socio-economic research as medicine adopted a new biomedical paradigm and differentiated into narrow subspecialties (Claus 1983; Krieger and Fee 1996; Rosen 1993).

More practical developments in research emerged in the United States, where an important innovation was the population-based survey on health and illness. This method complemented the earlier sources of information on health mostly based on vital statistics, official records, and clinical experience. Such surveys were started by Edgar Sydenstricker in the 1920s, and they provided statistical evidence on US socioeconomic inequalities and ill health (Krieger, Williams, and Moss 1997). Since this beginning, population surveys have gradually became a standard instrument in monitoring health and well-being in the social context.

An equally influential innovation took place in Britain, where the Registrar General, T. H. C. Stevenson, developed an occupational class scheme in the early 1920s to be used in analyses of vital statistics and other studies. The first study to use this classification showed a clear social class gradient in infant mortality. These findings were debated to find out the reasons for such a gradient. Darwin's ideas of natural selection were applied to health and social stratification by hereditarians and eugenicists to reduce social class to genetic endowment, arguing that poor health among the lower classes was due to high proportions of men and women from "tainted stock." Stevenson represented contrasting environmentalist ideas and argued poor health and premature death emerged from poor living conditions that were unequally distributed among people. A further point emphasized in the debate was that unhealthy or feckless behaviors were likely to contribute to poor health. Thus, this debate for the first time articulated three different types of explanations for class inequalities in health, namely, the selectionist-hereditarian, the social environmental, and the behavioral explanation (Macintyre 1997).

The three types prefigured the explanations presented by the British Black Report on Inequalities in Health (Macintyre 1997; Townsend and Davidson 1982), which 60 years after Stevenson's studies "refound" socioeconomic inequalities in health and death and put the issue back on the research agenda. The Black Report marked a strong incentive for research and monitoring all over the developed world (Davey Smith, Bartley, and Blane 1990; Macintyre 1997) and it also influenced international health policies aimed at improving equity in health (WHO 1985). We have thus proceeded in a long tradition analyzing health inequalities over 300 years and ended in a boom of medical sociological research on health inequalities since the late twentieth century. This long tradition has raised several methodological, analytical, and substantial issues to be pursued by contemporary scholars. We are today facing the challenge of inequalities in health between and within countries all over the world (Marmot 2005).

THE GLOBAL CONTEXT

As a background for our main focus on within-country health inequalities, we first examine global health inequalities in terms of the variation of life expectancy between countries at different levels of affluence. The global perspective provides us information on the deepest and most comprehensive health divide. That health measured by life expectancy is unequally divided between the rich and the poor countries is shown in Figure 4.1 by arranging countries along their gross domestic product (GDP) per capita, measuring affluence, and their life expectancy, measuring the average age people are expected to reach in a given population (Deaton 2003). In addition to placing countries along the curve showing the association of affluence and life expectancy, the size of the population of each country is presented by the diameter of the circle.

This global analysis first shows that among the poorest countries the length of life expectancy is closely dependent on the country's affluence as measured by GDP. The poorer the country, the shorter is the average life expectancy. However, there

Life expectancy, 2000

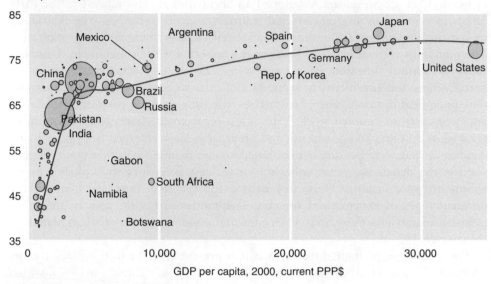

Figure 4.1 The association of wealth and life expectancy.
Source: Deaton 2003.

are outliers and some sub-Saharan countries have very short life expectancy even if they are not among the poorest of the poor countries. Second, among many mid-range countries, even at a relatively low level of affluence, the average life expectancy is fairly long, reaching 65 years or more. But the dependence of life expectancy on affluence is not straightforward, and it is weaker among this intermediate group of countries than among the poorest countries. The mid-range countries include large countries such as China and India, which cover substantial segments of the world's population. Third, among the richest countries the dependence of life expectancy on affluence levels off. Some countries have clearly longer (Argentina, Japan) and some countries shorter (South Korea, United States) average life expectancy than could be expected on the basis of their GDP level.

There are large overall inequalities in life expectancy by affluence among the world's countries. However, this relationship is strongest among the poorest coun-tries and to a lesser extent the mid-range countries. Among the richest countries, factors other than wealth per se contribute to the variation of the average length of life expectancy.

Our global analysis shows that health inequalities in life expectancy are huge between the rich and the poor countries. For example, a girl in Lesotho can expect to live 42 years less than her Japanese counterpart (WHO 2008). Global analyses typically rely on mortality-based measures such as life expectancy. They provide country-level data such as average life expectancy by affluence in Figure 4.1. To better understand the nature and production of inequalities in health, illness and mortality information indicating within-country divisions would also be needed, for example, how various domains of health are distributed across various domains of socioeconomic position. Unfortunately, global information on various domains of health is lacking, and for the time being we have to be satisfied with data sources mostly limited to affluent countries.

THE DOMAINS OF HEALTH

The traditional and current global evidence on health inequalities comes from vital statistics and concerns mortality and causes of death. Even information on gender may be absent or only men are included. Mortality is an indispensable indicator of population health. Of course, mortality-based data do have great advantages, and they are available from practically all countries. Mortality data are more reliable and valid in most countries than any other information on health. Mortality also allows reliable comparisons between countries.

However, mortality data do have limitations. The sources and quality of mortality data vary a lot between countries. In some countries, notably the European Nordic ones, the use of unique personal identification numbers allows accurate analyses of health inequalities as population register data on socioeconomic position can be linked at the individual level to data on causes of death with practically no dropout. A drawback with mortality data is that deaths do not adequately reflect the burden of ill health among currently living people. The causes of death do not necessarily correspond to the illnesses and diseases contemporary people suffer from. There are also health problems that cause a lot of pain and suffering as well as costs for sick leave, treatment, and care, but which may not be fatal. These include, for example, musculoskeletal and common mental disorders, both prevalent in the adult population. To be able to cover people's well-being and functioning, we also need data on the manifold domains of health, illness, sickness, and disease.

Information used in analysis of health inequalities is often derived from population surveys using interviews or mail questionnaires. Surveys have great advantages as a broad variety of determinants can be asked. However, survey measures of health are by their very nature self-reported and subjective, instead of being medically confirmed conditions. Self-reports are subject to possible reporting bias, but working directly with people's own reports is an inherent characteristic of many medical sociological studies, which do not aim at treatment but rather at people's own accounts of their well-being and ability to fully participate in everyday life.

In addition to mortality, three other key domains of health – the subjective, functional, and medical – can be distinguished (Blaxter 1989). Together these domains of health open a comprehensive view for the examination of health inequalities, complementing that for mortality (Graham 2007).

First, the subjective domain reflects an illness concept of health, and it is subjective since data on health are based purely on people's own assessments of their health. Measures of self-rated health or any long-standing health problems are typically subjective and generic health measures indicating health irrespective of the context or nature of the health problem. Self-rated health mostly indicates physical ill health (Manderbacka 1998) and does have predictive validity as it is strongly associated with subsequent mortality (Heistaro et al. 2001). Further subjective measures include, for example, pain, aches, and mental symptoms. Subjective measures of illness are frequently used in medical sociological studies on health inequalities.

Second, the functional domain of health reflects the sickness concept. It is functional since the focus is on abilities and inabilities to perform daily tasks with regard to health status and environment (Bowling 1991, 1995). Limiting long-standing health problems, ability to work as well as physical and mental functioning are typical measures of the functional domain of health. The functional domain is sociologically important since attention is devoted not only to the health status of a person, but also to the social and physical environments and consequences of ill health. Functional measures of health are also common in medical sociological analyses of health inequalities (Blaxter 1989).

Third, the medical domain of health reflects the disease concept based on the (bio)medical model of health. Medically confirmed diseases or diagnoses, often classified along the International Statistical Classification of Diseases and Related Health Problems (ICD-10) by the World Health Organization (WHO), are typical measures for the medical domain. Causes of death are equally based on the ICD classification. Measures based on diagnoses or causes of death are much used in health care and provide important data for research purposes as well. Self-reported diagnoses can also be asked in surveys. The etiology – i.e., causes of diseases – differs between various conditions. Thus data on diseases allow causes specific to particular diseases to be examined.

THE DOMAINS OF SOCIAL STRATIFICATION

The production of health and illness across the various domains is multi-etiological; that is, the factors contributing to health are manifold. Genetic and constitutional factors play their role but they are not the focus in this sociological analysis. Age and sex/gender are both biologically as well as socially constructed since our social roles and positions are strongly affected by chronological age and the phase of life course as well as biological sex and socially constructed gender. These, together with ethnicity, are necessary background variables in medical sociology. Further key social determinants of health exert their influence at varying causal distance. Proximal factors are closest and include lifestyles and behaviors, such as smoking, drinking, eating, and exercising. Mid-range factors include social and family relationships and social support rendered by them. Distal factors are causally most distant and include people's living and working conditions as well as social structures and social stratification (Dahlgren and Whitehead 1991). All these factors bear significance for the analyses of health and health inequalities. In particular, lifestyles and behaviors, social relations, and living and working conditions are typically unequally distributed between individuals and groups, providing potential reasons for the production of socioeconomic inequalities in health. Age and gender need to be taken into account in any analysis of health.

In the examination of health and social stratification, a major focus is on distal factors, in particular social structural factors, as determinants of health. As a very basic sociological construct, social stratification is about the social structure of society and how people are attached to that structure; that is, what is their socioeconomic position (Liberatos, Link, and Kelsey 1988; Lynch and Kaplan 2000). Socioeconomic positions differ from each other on the basis of access to power, prestige, and status as well as wealth and other resources. A person's socioeconomic position is the key source of inequality, including health, in contemporary societies (Cockerham 2007).

There are two main traditions of social stratification, each of which is attached to two seminal figures in sociological theory: Karl Marx and Max Weber. At the risk of oversimplification, a brief overview is made here to their basic ideas of social stratification. For Marx, production relations, exploitation, and economic inequality gave rise to two antagonistic social classes, the propertied bourgeoisie and the propertyless working class or proletariat. The role of intermediate "middle classes", including the intelligentsia is much more unclear in the Marxist analysis of stratification. For Weber, economic inequalities emerged in the consumption and labor markets from class differences in resources and opportunities. These opportunities or life chances emerge from income and education as well as lifestyles and status. Weber identified several white-collar classes and the working class. Both traditions have had strong influences on the theoretization of social class and stratification in general sociology as well as empirical sociological analysis, not least in medical sociology. The Marxist tradition has had far-reaching influences on later examinations of inequalities through its emphasis on material and work-related factors, as exemplified by the contrast between manual workers and non-manual employees. The Weberian tradition has probably had even more influence on the examination of hierarchical inequalities by resources, such as education, occupation, and income (Cockerham 2007; Lynch and Kaplan 2000).

Social stratification is typically assumed to be hierarchical, but it may also contain qualitative elements. This may be the case for occupational classifications that qualitatively distinguish between farmers, entrepreneurs, and employees. Differences between upper and lower professionals or white-collar employees as well as non-manual employees and manual workers can be regarded as hierarchical. Many stratification schemes are fully hierarchical and form ordinal scales, such as those based on amount of prestige, income, or education. Influences from the two class traditions are typically mixed in many later socioeconomic classifications.

A structural perspective to stratification considers positions across the full range of the social ladder and arranges positions along a hierarchy from the top through intermediate to bottom positions (Graham 2007). Thus, systematic inequalities are assumed from those at the bottom of the ladder to the top with the level of health following the order of the hierarchical socioeconomic positions. An alternative marginal perspective assumes that only the worst-off differ from other groups. Such a perspective would predict that only the most disadvantaged, such as poor or excluded people, have poorer health than the other groups, which share a similar level of health (Najman 1993). A threshold perspective is closely related to the marginal one. It predicts that health inequalities can be found under or above a threshold. This is exemplified by Figure 4.1, where the poorest countries showed differences in life expectancy by affluence, whereas among the richest countries these differences were non-existent. Similarly, a threshold might be found for income or for education, and it has been suggested that the amount of money available up to a certain level contributes to people's well-being, but an additional increase of money after that level may have no impact (Warr 1987).

Whether a structural, marginal, or threshold perspective is valid for an examination of health inequalities cannot be resolved a priori. Also, time periods and countries are likely to differ from one another. Furthermore, different stratification schemes and criteria can be used. As social structures change and new social divisions emerge, it is important to consider multiple domains of socioeconomic position and also emerging novel dimensions of stratification. This will also help respond to the challenges suggested by late modernist social theorizing on the "death of class" (Scambler and Higgs 1999).

There are several domains of social stratification, and they have been applied in empirical analyses of health inequalities. The following review focuses on three key structural domains of social stratification classifying people across the whole social ladder, that is, occupation, education, and income. As social stratification is a comprehensive concept, and the three more or less interrelated domains only represent the key ones, they also need to be considered together and further complemented.

Occupation

Employment status is closely related to social stratification by occupation, and it divides people into those gainfully employed or non-employed. Employed people can be employees or self-employed. The non-employed include unemployed, those doing housework, disabled or retired, and full-time students. Being non-employed may increase the risk of poor health, but employment status is subject to reverse causality as those with poor health may drift out of the labor market into non-employment (Arber 1997). The non-employed typically have poorer health than the employed, and the reverse causality is called the "healthy worker effect" (Manderbacka, Lahelma, and Rahkonen 2001).

Occupational social class divisions are very basic measures of social stratification. They attach people by their current occupation to the social structure. The individual approach uses a person's own occupation (Arber 1997). For the non-employed, their last occupation can be used. However, some people may never have been employed and have no past occupation. It has been typical in many countries for a substantial proportion of women to remain outside paid employment throughout their lives. In such cases the conventional approach can be used, and the person's missing occupational position can be substituted by his or her partner's occupation.

The benefits of occupational classification schemes include links to traditional macro-sociological class divisions as presented by classical sociologists. A drawback is that occupational classifications are only well suited to those who are employed. A gender bias is likely depending on the proportion of women who are non-employed. Classifications may also be more detailed for male-dominated than female-dominated jobs. Occupational structures change over time and differ between countries, and this complicates comparisons. For example, farmers currently form small groups only in affluent countries, whereas some decades ago they may still have been substantial groups.

Socioeconomic classifications within the occupational domain are typically based on Weberian principles and distinguish between several classes, for example: the

Table 4.1 The Erikson–Goldthorpe occupational class schema (EGP)

I	Professionals, administrators, and managers: higher-grade
II	Professionals, administrators, and managers: lower-grade and higher-grade technicians
IIIa	Routine non-manual employees: higher-grade
IIIb	Routine non-manual employees: lower-grade
IVabc	Small proprietors and employers, self-employed workers
V	Lower-grade technicians, supervisors of manual workers
VI	Skilled manual workers
VII	Non-skilled manual workers

Source: Goldthorpe 2000.

upper class, including wealthy top managers and professionals; the upper middle class, including affluent managers and professionals; the lower middle class, including nurses and office employees; the working class, including skilled and semi-skilled manual workers; and the lower class, including unskilled workers and unemployed people. This kind of classification is used in many countries and is followed by many medical sociologists in the United States (Cockerham 2007). The British Registrar General's hierarchical occupational classification by Stevenson has been used in numerous British studies since the 1920s. An example of a neo-Marxist classification is that by US scholar Eric Olin Wright (1985) based on exploitation and organizational assets. Another classification also used in health research is the Erikson–Goldthorpe (EGP) class schema. It can be said to contain ingredients from the Marxist tradition in its emphasis on work and from the Weberian tradition in its emphasis on hierarchies based on markets and resources (Erikson and Goldthorpe 1993; Goldthorpe 2000). Table 4.1 presents the seven-class version of the Erikson–Goldthorpe classification.

Education

Education as a domain of social stratification reflects people's socioeconomic position in a broad manner and is related to their material and non-material resources. Classifications of educational attainment have been used in many countries, and in the United States education has traditionally been the most common socioeconomic indicator in health research (Krieger et al. 1997). The significance of education in many countries may even increase in competitive societies that struggle for a highly qualified labor force. Education can be measured using the highest passed examination or years of completed education. Classifications are many, but they often distinguish between basic education, secondary and/or vocational education, and higher education (Graham 2007).

Less structural educational classifications have some advantages over occupational classifications. Each individual can be allocated to the educational hierarchy irrespective of his or her employment status. Education is typically achieved by early adulthood and remains broadly stable across the later life course. Education is equally suitable for women and men. The amount of completed education forms an ordinal scale. Also, while education is likely to influence health, it is unlikely that adult poor health would influence education. Education is better comparable across countries than occupation (Valkonen 1989). The drawback of education is that educational structures have strongly changed over time. Difficulties with the use of education are caused by this skewness, which varies across birth cohorts and countries. The distribution of education is particularly skewed for the oldest cohorts, large segments of which have completed basic education only. Education by its very nature provides people with knowledge and qualifications. Therefore, education shapes people's health consciousness and health behaviors, and through these affects their health and illness.

Income

Income is the third main domain of social stratification. It most clearly indicates material resources and the availability of money (Graham 2007; Krieger et al. 1997). Gross and net income can be measured. Gross income can be taken as an indicator of individual socioeconomic position, whereas net income more closely indicates available resources. As many people live in couples and families, household income is a more accurate measure of their available resources than individual income. Usually, income is used to allocate people across the whole social ladder, but also marginal approaches can be used to distinguish poor people. Classifications use absolute sums of income as well as relative income groups, such as quintiles or deciles.

The main advantage of income measures is that in principle they allow accurate measurement across an ordinal scale. The main drawback is that causal relationships may be difficult to establish. A person's income may contaminate his or her own health since, on the one hand, low income is likely to contribute to ill health, and on the other hand, ill health is equally likely to contribute to lowered incomes. The latter occurs when people with poor health drift to less well-paid jobs or into non-employment. Usually, the non-employed have lower incomes. For example, women doing housework lack their own income. The measurement of income is often difficult since self-reports are inaccurate, and people may refuse to report on their incomes. In some cases income information is available from national taxation registers, which are comprehensive and reliable sources (Martikainen et al. 2001).

In addition to individual or household income, the association between income distribution and health has been examined in many countries, including the United States (Kawachi and Kennedy 1999; Wilkinson and Pickett 2006). It is argued that an individual's relative position in the income distribution, not the absolute amount of money available, contributes to poor health and mortality through lack of cohesion and stress. However, evidence is inconsistent and instead of income inequality, individual or household income is likely to be the key income-based determinant of health (Cockerham 2007; Mackenbach 2002).

Interrelationships

In addition to the three key *intra*generational domains of social stratification presented above, there are additional intragenerational and further *inter*generational domains of social stratification which together influence production of health and illness. Additional intragenerational domains include childhood and adulthood economic conditions, which provide complementary socioeconomic information over the life course (Kestilä et al. 2005). Wealth is rarely considered but is important to stratification. It can be approximated by housing but also the number of cars has been used (Krieger et al. 1997; Laaksonen et al. 2008). Further intergenerational domains include parental socioeconomic position, which through social mobility contributes to a person's own position. For example, mother's and father's education affects their children's education and through that subsequent occupational class and income (Laaksonen et al. 2005a).

Although the issue of health and social stratification has typically been examined by relying on one particular socioeconomic domain or indicator at a time, the intra- and intergenerational domains are typically interrelated. This is understandable since social stratification is a comprehensive umbrella concept, and various domains and indicators are assumed to be included under it. Thus, interrelationships and pathways between different domains and indicators of socioeconomic position can be assumed and have also been confirmed (Dahl 1994; Laaksonen et al. 2005a; Lahelma et al. 2004; Martikainen, Blomgren, and Valkonen 2007).

Figure 4.2 schematically presents some of the main interrelationships and pathways between the domains of social stratification to be considered in the production of health inequalities. Thus, even before own socioeconomic position, the socioeconomic position of a person's origin – that is, his or her parents' position – influences the position of destination, the individual's own achieved socioeconomic position. A temporal order among the key domains can be assumed. Education is typically acquired first over the life course, that is, by early adulthood. Next, education contributes to the qualifications needed in the labor market and directs people to occupations that can be hierarchically arranged into occupational classes. Finally, most people's income derives mainly from pay for work done outside the home; thus, occupational class position strongly contributes to income level. Parents' socioeconomic position and their own income over the life course contribute to the wealth of people and their households.

The interrelationships and pathways among key adult domains of social stratification suggest that none of them can be preferred over another. Not only do the domains compete with one another for being the "best," but each domain and indicator in part reflects the common conceptual contents of the comprehensive concept of socioeconomic position. In addition, each domain reflects conceptual contents specific to that domain only (Braveman et al. 2005; Liberatos et al. 1988;

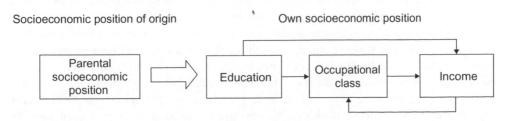

Figure 4.2 Pathways between domains of social stratification.

Lynch and Kaplan 2000). Recognizing the basic multidimensional nature of socio-economic position allows us to proceed from simple to complex multidimensional models in the production of health inequalities through several interrelated domains of social stratification (Laaksonen et al. 2005a; Lahelma et al. 2004; Martikainen et al. 2007).

EXPLANATIONS AND CAUSES

Much of the work done on health and social stratification is descriptive, showing us that there are inequalities, for example, in total mortality or self-rated health by education, occupation, or income. The pathways presented in Figure 4.2 already take steps toward explanations as we assume that there are mutual influences from the domains of stratification to poor health. We can thus ask to what extent education will have direct influences on health, or whether its influences are mediated through occupational class, or whether the influences of income on health are direct and independent, or whether they can be explained by preceding occupational class and/or education. But we can also ask whether the associations might under certain conditions be the reverse; that is, whether poor health might contribute to socioeconomic position such as lower income and sometimes lead to non-employment. The ultimate aim of all research is to deepen our understanding and provide explanations for the studied phenomena. Thus, we need to proceed further from simple descriptive analyses to more complex pathway analyses and to explanatory analyses, asking what are the reasons for the inequalities in health that have been found.

There are several types of explanation for health inequalities partly identified already in the earlier phases of the research tradition. The Black Report (Townsend and Davidson 1982) presented a typology including four main explanations: (1) artifact, (2) natural or social selection, (3) materialist or structuralist, and (4) cultural or behavioral explanation. These types have been further developed by Sally Macintyre (1997), who emphasized that the explanations are not necessarily mutually exclusive. She distinguished between "hard" and "soft" versions of the types of explanation, as presented in Table 4.2.

The artifact explanation in its hard version suggests that the observed association between socioeconomic position and health is spurious and nonexistent due to measurement errors of the studied variables. A soft version recognizes that the measurement errors do not fully produce the observed inequalities in health, but nevertheless may contribute to the magnitude. An example of this is the numerator/denominator problem discussed in Britain, since census data and death certificates are not linked at the individual level, and data from different sources such as census data and death certificates may not match with each other.

Natural or social selection explanations are related to the direction of causality. The hard version of this explanation implies that the association between socioeconomic position and health is a real one, but that health directly determines socioeconomic position rather than the other way round. People are recruited to social classes on the basis of their health and, therefore, people with poor health end up in low socioeconomic positions. According to the soft version, recruitment to socioeconomic positions is not fully determined by health-related selection, but

Table 4.2 Types of explanations for health inequalities

	"Hard" version	*"Soft" version*
Artifact	No relation between class and mortality; purely an artifact of measurement	Magnitude of observed class gradients will depend on the measurement of both class and health
Natural/social selection	Health determines class position, therefore class gradients are morally neutral and "explained away"	Health can contribute to achieved class position and help to explain observed gradients
Materialist/structural	Material, physical, conditions of life associated with the class structure are the complete explanation for class gradients in health	Physical and psychosocial features associated with the class structure influence health and contribute to observed gradients
Cultural/behavioral	Health-damaging behaviors freely chosen by individuals in different social classes explain away social class gradients	Health-damaging behaviors are differentially distributed across social classes and contribute to observed gradients

Source: Macintyre 1997.

nevertheless selective entry into socioeconomic positions can contribute to the production of health inequalities in some cases. For example, illness in childhood may influence school performance and through this contribute to adult socioeconomic position, or those with illness in adulthood may be excluded from higher positions and even from the labor market. Similar indirect selection may also take place if tall people are recruited to higher positions, and height is a marker of health as well. Thus, the soft versions of selection may indicate discrimination of people in important arenas of life.

Materialist or structuralist explanations are often sought in medical sociological research on health inequalities. According to the hard version, education and occupational class together with income and wealth determine people's physical and material living and working conditions, and these produce an unequal distribution of health in the population. According to the soft version, living conditions determined by socioeconomic position include additional factors such as non-material resources, qualifications, values, and psychosocial factors. In this way, the soft version takes into account social and cultural capital available to people, to which education in particular contributes.

Cultural/behavioral explanations in the hard version imply that observed health inequalities can be fully explained by health-damaging behaviors, such as smoking, drinking, lack of exercise, or poor diet. The soft version suggests that health-damaging behaviors may be unequally distributed across socioeconomic positions and to a greater or lesser extent contribute to health inequalities. Smoking, for example, is more prevalent among lower positions and this contributes to a range of health problems with an unequal distribution. Thus, behavioral explanations are potentially important because it is not only health outcomes but also health behaviors that are shaped by social stratification.

The idea of a typology of explanations for health inequalities should not cast the different explanations against one another. Rather, unnecessary controversies among explanations should be avoided. For example, it is not a fruitful starting point to ask whether health inequalities are caused by material living conditions *or* by health-damaging behaviors. An exclusive individualist interpretation of the influence of health behaviors easily leads to blaming individuals themselves for health-damaging behaviors, when the task is to understand the social and economic processes leading to such behaviors. Sticking instead exclusively to macro-structural and material living conditions may omit other potentially important simultaneous influences and overlook the social production of behavioral processes behind health inequalities. Another controversy concerns the possibility of bidirectional causality between socioeconomic position and health. Looking only at one direction overlooks either the contribution of adverse socioeconomic circumstances to health, or social exclusion and discrimination taking place due to ill health. A third controversy is that between absolute living conditions of individuals per se and relative socioeconomic position as determinants of health inequalities. An exclusive emphasis on absolute living conditions, such as the amount of money available, overlooks the potential significance of relative inequalities, whereas an exclusively relative emphasis overlooks the contribution of absolute scarcity of resources to health inequalities.

Thus, in most cases the hard explanations for health inequalities are likely to be fundamentalist given that there is a broad variety of potential determinants. Theoretical frameworks as well as the available evidence suggest that accepting the multi-etiological nature of health inequalities is an important starting point. The production of health inequalities is a very complex process, ranging from parental and early life influences to multiple adult influences and to social consequences of ill health, and finally to death. Additionally, age, gender, ethnicity, and other variables further shape these processes. Following only one explanation runs the risk of obscuring the richness and complexity of the area of health and social stratification. While the typology of the four explanations indentifies important areas and suggests where explanations need to be sought, the soft version suggests that broad frameworks are useful and alternative hypotheses need to be formulated and tested against one another.

THE PATTERNING OF HEALTH BY SOCIOECONOMIC POSITION

The Black Report (Townsend and Davidson 1982) provided the first summary of health inequalities up to the late 1970s. After that, evidence has accumulated showing that health inequalities by socioeconomic position exist all over the developed world and also in poorer countries (Macintyre 1997; Mackenbach et al. 2008; Marmot 2005). Much of the evidence is on relative inequalities, for example on the risk of ill health or death among manual workers compared to white-collar employees. Absolute inequalities, in turn, indicate the absolute amount of cases of ill health or death in the compared groups. Both measures are important and health policies in particular aim to influence absolute inequalities.

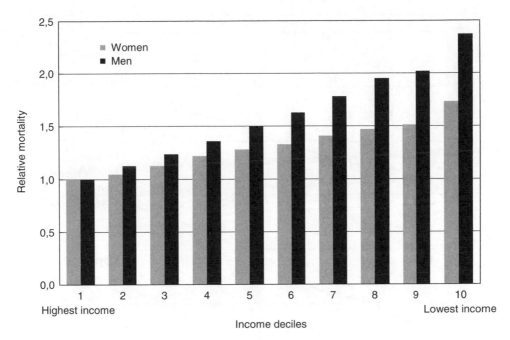

Figure 4.3 Relative differences in mortality by income deciles.
Source: Martikainen et al. 2001.

The review that follows raises some examples of current analyses of health inequalities to highlight the patterning of health by social stratification. We start by examining the patterning of mortality by income and make use of a study based on large and reliable population register data representing the Finnish adult population (Martikainen et al. 2001). Figure 4.3 summarizes relative inequalities in mortality by income deciles among women as well as men.

Inequalities in mortality by income are stark in Finland, which is an affluent welfare state with internationally small income inequalities. There is a linear gradient with higher mortality towards the lower income deciles. Similar inequalities can be found for both women and men, although the gradient for men is steeper. For further domains of socioeconomic position, education or occupational class inequalities in Finland show very similar gradients (Martikainen et al. 2007). There are similar inequalities for the main causes of death. Inequalities for cardiovascular diseases and lung cancer as well as accidents and violence are particularly large (Valkonen et al. 2000). In the United States, mortality shows similarly clear inequalities by education and income among both women and men (Backlund, Sorlie, and Johnson 1999; Mackenbach et al. 1999).

In addition to mortality, inequalities can be found for the subjective, functional, and medical domains of health, covering conditions from serious diseases to minor symptoms (Lahelma et al. 2005). Inequalities in self-rated health are equally found by the key domains of social stratification, education, occupational class, and income (Laaksonen et al. 2005a). Similar findings are available from many countries and the US evidence also confirms large inequalities in self-rated health by education and income, with further variation between the states (Braveman et al. 2005;

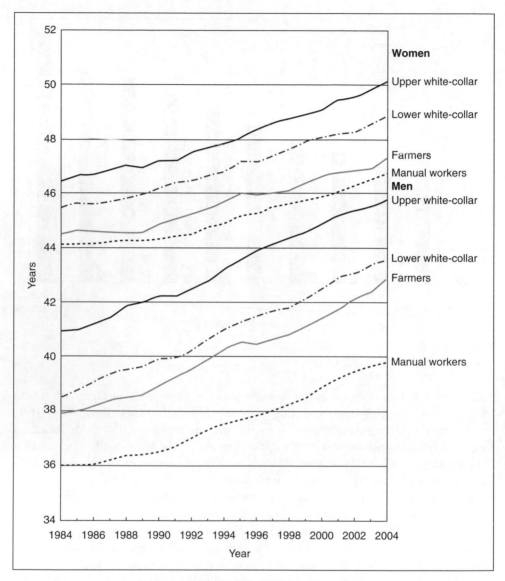

Figure 4.4 Life expectancy at 35 by occupational class among Finnish women and men, 1980–2005.
Source: Valkonen et al. 2009.

Subramanian, Kawachi, and Kennedy 2001). For severe mental disorders, socioeconomic inequalities are as clear as for physical health, as exemplified by evidence from the United States (Kessler et al. 1994). However, evidence from European countries would suggest that for common mental disorders, inequalities by the key indicators of socioeconomic position may be less universal (Laaksonen et al. 2007).

It is important to know whether health inequalities are widening or narrowing over time. Finnish population registry data from the early 1980s to mid-2000s provide a convincing example of trends in occupational class inequalities in life expectancy at 35 years (Valkonen et al. 2009). As shown by Figure 4.4, there is a stark linear occupational class gradient in mortality which is steeper for men than for women. All occupational classes have increased their life expectancy over time, but the upper classes have benefited more than the lower classes from the increase. Thus, inequalities in life expectancy have not only remained but have also widened, among both men and women. The trends in health inequalities may vary between countries, periods, domain of health, and socioeconomic position. However, the available evidence suggests that health inequalities are universally persistent. Thus, in the United States as well, inequalities in mortality by income among both women and men are clear, and they have shown widening trends. The mechanism in the United States has been similar to that found in Finland; that is, the higher-income groups benefit more than the lower-income groups from the declining mortality trends (Schalick et al. 2000). There are many more examples of widening inequalities, but narrowing inequalities have not been reported (Mackenbach et al. 2003; Kunst et al. 2005).

It has been emphasized that socioeconomic position is a broad comprehensive construct and we need to simultaneously consider several of its domains to be able to detect interrelationships and pathways in the production of health inequalities. Analyses have found examples of such pathways, which go, for example, from parental education to own education to health. Another pathway suggests that inequalities in health by income may be explained by preceding occupational class and education (Laaksonen et al. 2005a; Lahelma et al. 2004).

Analyses using broad frameworks and simultaneously testing several types of explanations for health inequalities are so far rare. However, some studies have compared the main types of explanations, such as material, behavioral, and psychosocial factors, and their results are illuminating. The strongest explanations have been provided by material living conditions, physical working conditions, and health behaviors. Explanations provided by psychosocial factors such as work stress, in turn, tend to be smaller or nonexistent, sometimes even reverse (Laaksonen et al. 2005b; Van Lenthe et al. 2002; Van Oort, Van Lenthe, and Mackenbach 2005).

The above examples confirm health inequalities across key domains of socioeconomic position as well as key domains of health and mortality. However, the data presented are exemplary from a couple of countries, such as Finland and the United States. They cannot yet be generalized without qualification. Similarities and dissimilarities among countries are likely. The next section examines comparative research on health inequalities.

THE INTERNATIONAL EVIDENCE

International comparisons allow for testing whether socioeconomic inequalities in ill health and mortality exist across different countries, whether the patterning of inequalities in health is similar, and whether the size of inequalities varies between countries. A number of comparisons have been made, but the picture emerging from these is still patchy and at best covers Western European countries, with some comparisons to the United States.

The first broad comparison of inequalities in mortality and self-rated health from the 1980s showed inequalities in 11 Western European countries (Mackenbach et al. 1997). Although country differences were not very large for male mortality by occupational class, the order of countries nevertheless was unexpected. The Nordic European welfare states, which emphasize egalitarian policies, tend to have larger inequalities than most other Western European countries. Educational inequalities for self-rated health were equally large in the Nordic countries. The unexpected patterning of both mortality and morbidity raised much discussion, but the reasons still remain open. While the picture was based on relative inequalities, it may be partly different from that provided by absolute inequalities.

Following up trends in inequalities in mortality and self-rated health in Western Europe from the 1980s to the 1990s largely confirms the earlier patterning. However, relative inequalities in mortality by education and occupational class among women as well as men showed a widening trend, although absolute inequalities remained mostly stable (Mackenbach et al. 2003). Corresponding trends in self-rated health by education also showed that relative inequalities had largely remained among both women and men, with some countries showing a widening and some others a stable development (Kunst et al. 2005).

A subsequent update from the turn of the millennium adds to the previous picture since as many as 22 countries from Western and additionally Eastern Europe could be compared (Mackenbach et al. 2008). Country differences in the magnitude of relative inequalities in mortality in Western Europe have remained broadly similar, but the inclusion of Eastern European countries produces new features in the earlier picture. The East–West mortality divide is striking as most Eastern European and Baltic countries have very large inequalities compared to the Western European countries. Inequalities in self-rated health by education were still large in the Nordic countries, but in particular among women. Also, some Eastern European countries had very large inequalities in self-rated health, but so did some Western European countries. Potential reasons for the observed inequalities in mortality could be suggested. The large Eastern European inequalities in mortality can at least partly be attributed to causes of death related to smoking or drinking, or being preventable through medical care.

Some studies have compared Western European countries with the United States, although they may add less than expected to the international picture. Thus, relative inequalities in mortality by education among US women and men are largely at a similar level with Western European countries (Mackenbach et al. 1999). Cardiovascular disease mortality by occupational class equally shows that inequalities in the United States correspond to average Western European inequalities (Mackenbach et al. 2000). A two-country comparison of mortality by education and income between Finland and the United States confirms clear inequalities of similar magnitude in both countries among women as well as men (Elo, Martikainen, and Smith 2006). In these two countries, inequalities by education were linear but inequalities by income were curvilinear, suggesting that the income–mortality association was particularly strong at the lower end of the income distribution. Some clues for explanation were received implying that being employed and married narrowed the inequalities. We lack comparisons for further domains of health including the United States. However, for mortality our current knowledge supports the pattern and magnitude of inequalities in the United States being comparable to those in Western European countries.

The comparative picture on health inequalities is still very incomplete and comparative studies face particular challenges. These concern reliability and comparability of data, but also interpretations of disparities between countries differing in history, culture, and social structures (Mackenbach et al. 2008). All this casts much uncertainty on results from the existing comparative studies. Nevertheless, expanding the coverage of countries has repeatedly strengthened the universal nature of health inequalities, and there is no country that would lack substantial inequalities in health. Comparisons also suggest that there are differences in health inequalities among affluent Western countries, but at least for mortality the country differences are unlikely to be very large. It remains a puzzling issue that health inequalities in the relatively egalitarian Nordic welfare states are not smaller than elsewhere (Dahl et al. 2006). However, many Eastern European countries have very large inequalities in mortality. Inequalities in self-rated health also show a large variation in magnitude, with some Western and some Eastern European countries having very large inequalities. What is most alarming is that health inequalities across countries are very persistent and show a widening or stable development over time.

POLICY AND FUTURE PERSPECTIVES

From its early beginnings the examination of health inequalities has proceeded to systematic mapping and explanatory analyses searching for reasons for existing inequalities in mortality and morbidity. National as well as international studies confirm the persistence and universal nature of health inequalities. Thus, health inequalities provide a major future challenge for medical sociological analysis as well as policies and interventions. What is clear from the analyses on health inequalities is that social stratification continues to matter a lot for health. Even more than that, socioeconomic position is the most powerful structural determinant of health and survival (Cockerham 2007).

Health inequalities also provide a major future challenge for health and welfare policies. Large inequalities in health are unfair and unjust (Braveman and Gruskin 2003), and as such should be efficiently tackled. Additionally, health in the lower socioeconomic positions is so much worse than in the higher positions that this posits serious obstacles for the positive development of overall population health. To enhance both social justice and the level of public health calls for efficient health and welfare policies to reduce health inequalities.

In order to proceed from pure descriptions, medical sociological analysis of health inequalities should aim at a deeper understanding of the production of health inequalities. This is important for scientific progress, but it is equally important for evidence-based policies and interventions to reduce health inequalities (Mackenbach and Bakker 2002). Comparing the relative importance of explanations for health inequalities suggests that the key causes include such distal factors as material living conditions and physical working conditions as well as such proximal factors as health behaviors, in particular smoking and in many countries drinking as well (Laaksonen et al. 2005b; Van Lenthe et al. 2002, Van Oort et al. 2005). Further potential explanations are needed and, for example, early living conditions (Kestilä et al. 2005), wealth, and housing have thus far been little studied (Laaksonen et al. 2008).

The explanations suggested by existing research are still limited, but they are likely to have strong contributions to health inequalities at least in affluent Western countries. As such they also suggest what tools are likely to be efficient in reducing health inequalities. It is a key task to be able to tackle health inequalities, first by stopping the widening of inequalities, and second by narrowing the inequalities so that those with worst health benefit most.

Finally, we need to consider the global context of health inequalities. This has been amply advocated by the World Health Organization Commission on Social Determinants of Health led by Sir Michael Marmot in its final report from 2008 (WHO 2008). This commission had a global task, and its work paves the way for narrowing the health gap between countries and within countries over the next generation. The measures suggested include improving daily living conditions as well as tackling the inequitable distributions of power, money, and resources, in other words, the structural drivers of those conditions globally, nationally, and locally.

References

Arber, Sara. 1997. "Insights about the Non-Employed, Class and Health: Evidence from the General Household Survey." Pp. 78–92 in D. Rose and K. O'Reilly (eds.), *Constructing Classes: Towards a New Social Classification for the UK*. Swindon: Office for National Statistics.

Backlund, Eric, Paul Sorlie, and Norman Johnson. 1999. "A Comparison of the Relationships of Education and Income with Mortality: The National Longitudinal Mortality Study." *Social Science and Medicine* 49: 1373–84.

Bartley, Mel. 2004. *Health Inequality*. Cambridge: Polity Press.

Blaxter, Mildred. 1989. "A Comparison of Measures of Inequality in Morbidity." Pp. 199–230 in A. J. Fox (ed.), *Health Inequalities in European Countries*. Aldershot: Gower.

Blaxter, Mildred. 1997. "Whose Fault Is It? People's Own Conceptions of the Reasons for Health Inequalities." *Social Science and Medicine* 44: 747–56.

Bowling, Ann. 1991. *Measuring Health: A Review of Quality of Life Measurement Scales*. Buckingham: Open University Press.

Bowling, Ann. 1995. *Measuring Disease: A Review of Disease-Specific Quality of Life Measurement Scales*. Buckingham: Open University Press.

Braveman, Paula, Catherine Cubbin, Susan Egerter, Sekai Chideya, Kristen Marchi, Marilyn Metzler, and Samuel Posner 2005. "Socioeconomic Status in Health Research: One Size Does Not Fit All." *Journal of the American Medical Association* 294: 2879–88.

Braveman, Paula and Sofia Gruskin. 2003. "Defining Equity in Health." *Journal of Epidemiology and Community Health* 57: 254–8.

Claus, Lisbeth. 1983. "The Development of Medical Sociology in Europe." *Social Science and Medicine* 17: 1591–7.

Cockerham, William. 2007. *Social Causes of Health and Disease*. Cambridge: Polity Press.

Dahl, Espen. 1994. "Social Inequalities in Health: The Significance of Occupational Status, Education and Income – Results from a Norwegian Survey." *Sociology of Health and Illness* 16: 644–67.

Dahl, Espen, Johan Fritzell, Eero Lahelma, Pekka Martikainen, Anton Kunst, and Johan Mackenbach. 2006. "Welfare State Regimes and Health Inequalities." Pp. 193–222 in J. Siegrist and M. Marmot (eds.), *Social Inequalities in Health: New Evidence and Policy Implications*. Oxford: Oxford University Press.

Dahlgren, Göran and Margaret Whitehead. 1991. *Policies and Strategies to Promote Social Equity in Health*. Stockholm: Institute of Future Studies.

Davey Smith, George, Mel Bartley, and David Blane. 1990. "The Black Report on Socio-Economic Inequalities in Health 10 Years on." *British Medical Journal* 301: 373–77.

Deaton, Angus. 2003. "Health, Inequality, and Economic Development." *Journal of Economic Literature* 41: 113–58.

Durkheim, Emile. 1897. *Le Suicide: Etude de Sociologie*. Paris: Les Presses Universitaires de France.

Elo, Irma, Pekka Martikainen, and Kirsten Smith. 2006. "Socioeconomic Differentials in Mortality in Finland and the United States: The Role of Education and Income." *European Journal of Population* 22: 179–203.

Erikson, Robert and John Goldthorpe. 1993. *The Constant Flux: A Study of Class Mobility in Industrial Societies*. Oxford: Clarendon Press.

Fritzell, Johan and Olle Lundberg. 2005. "Fighting Inequalities in Health and Income: One Important Road to Welfare and Social Development." Pp. 164–85 in O. Kangas and J. Palme (eds.), *Social Policy and Economic Development in the Nordic Countries*. Basingstoke: Palgrave.

Galobardes, Bruna, Mary Shaw, Debbie Lawlor, John Lynch, and George Davey Smith. 2006a. "Indicators of Socioeconomic Position (Part 1)." *Journal of Epidemiology and Community Health* 60: 7–12.

Galobardes, Bruna, Mary Shaw, Debbie Lawlor, John Lynch, and George Davey Smith. 2006b. "Indicators of Socioeconomic Position (Part 2)." *Journal of Epidemiology and Community Health* 60: 95–101.

Gerhardt, Uta. 1989. *Ideas about Illness: An Intellectual and Political History of Medical Sociology*. London: Macmillan.

Goldthorpe, John. 2000. *On Sociology: Numbers, Narratives, and the Integration of Research and Theory*. Oxford: Oxford University Press.

Graham, Hilary. 2007. *Unequal Lives: Health and Socioeconomic Inequalities*. Maidenhead: Open University Press.

Hamlin, Christopher. 1995. "Could You Starve to Death in England in 1839? The Chadwick–Farr Controversy and the Loss of the Social in Public Health." *American Journal of Public Health* 85: 856–66.

Heistaro, Sami, Pekka Jousilahti, Eero Lahelma, Erkki Vartiainen, and Pekka Puska. 2001. "Self-Rated Health and Mortality: A Long-Term Prospective Study in Eastern Finland." *Journal of Epidemiology and Community Health* 55: 227–32.

Kadushin, Charles. 1964. "Social Class and the Experience of Ill Health." *Sociological Inquiry* 34: 67–80.

Kawachi Ichiro and Bruce Kennedy. 1999. "Income Inequality and Health: Pathways and Mechanisms." *Health Services Research* 34: 215–27.

Kessler, Ronald, Katherine McGonagle, Shanyang Zhao, Christopher Nelson, Michael Hughes, Suzann Eshleman, Hans-Ulrich Wittchen, and Kenneth Kendler. 1994.

"Lifetime and 12-Month Prevalence of DSM-III-R Psychiatric Disorders in the United States: Results from the National Comorbidity Survey." *Archives of General Psychiatry* 51: 8–19.

Kestilä, Laura, Seppo Koskinen, Tuija Martelin, Ossi Rahkonen, Tiina Pensola, Hillevi Aro, and Arpo Aromaa. 2005. "Determinants of Health in Early Adulthood: What Is the Role of Parental Education, Childhood Adversities and Own Education?" *European Journal of Public Health* 16: 305–14.

Krieger, Nancy and Elizabeth Fee. 1996. "Measuring Social Inequalities in Health in the United States: An Historical Review, 1900–1950." *International Journal of Health Services* 26: 391–418.

Krieger, Nancy, David Williams, and Nancy Moss. 1997. "Measuring Social Class in US Public Health Research." *Annual Review of Public Health* 18: 341–78.

Kunst, Anton, Vivian Bos, Eero Lahelma, Mel Bartley, Inge Lissau, Enrique Regidor, Andreas Mielck, Mario Cardano, Jetty A. A. Dalstra, José Geurts, Uwe Helmert, Carin Lennartsson, Jorun Ramm, Teresa Spadea, Willibald Stronegger, and Johan Mackenbach. 2005. "Trends in Socioeconomic Inequalities in Self-Assessed Health in 10 European Countries." *International Journal of Epidemiology* 34: 295–305.

Laaksonen, Elina, Pekka Martikainen, Eero Lahelma, Tea Lallukka, Tarani Chandola, Jenny Head, and Michael Marmot. 2007. "Socioeconomic Circumstances and Common Mental Disorders among Finnish and British Public Sector Employees." *International Journal of Epidemiology* 34: 776–86.

Laaksonen, Mikko, Pekka Martikainen, Elina Nihtilä, Ossi Rahkonen, and Eero Lahelma. 2008. "Home Ownership and Mortality: A Register-Based Follow-Up Study of 300,000 Finns." *Journal of Epidemiology and Community* 62: 293–7.

Laaksonen, Mikko, Ossi Rahkonen, Pekka Martikainen, and Eero Lahelma. 2005a. "Socioeconomic Position and Self-Rated Health: The Contribution of Childhood Socioeconomic Environment, Adult Socioeconomic Status, and Material Resources." *American Journal of Public Health* 95: 1403–9.

Laaksonen, Mikko, Eva Roos, Ossi Rahkonen, Pekka Martikainen, and Euro Lahelma. 2005b. "Influence of Material and Behavioural Factors on Occupational Class Differences in Health." *Journal of Epidemiology and Community Health* 59: 163–9.

Lahelma, Eero, Antti Karisto, and Ossi Rahkonen. 1996. "Analysing Inequalities: The Tradition of Socioeconomic Health Research in Finland." *European Journal of Public Health* 6: 87–93.

Lahelma, Eero, Pekka Martikainen, Mikko Laaksonen, and Akseli Aittomäki. 2004. "Pathways Between Socioeconomic Determinants of Health." *Journal of Epidemiology and Community Health* 58: 327–32.

Lahelma, Eero, Pekka Martikainen, Ossi Rahkonen, Eva Roos, and Peppiina Saastamoinen. 2005. "Occupational Class Inequalities across Key Domains of Health: Results from the Helsinki Health Study." *European Journal of Public Health* 15: 504–10.

Lee, David and Brian Turner. 1996. "Introduction: Myths of Classlessness and the Death of Class Analysis." Pp. 1–25 in D. J. Lee and B. S. Turner (eds.), *Conflicts about Class: Debating Inequality in Late Industrialism*. London: Longman.

Liberatos, Penny, Bruce Link, and Jennifer Kelsey. 1988. "The Measurement of Social Class in Epidemiology." *Epidemiological Review* 10: 87–121.

Lynch, John and George Kaplan. 2000. "Socioeconomic Position." Pp. 13–35 in L. Berkman and Kawachi Ichiro (eds.), *Social Epidemiology*. New York: Oxford University Press.

Macintyre, Sally. 1997. "The Black Report and Beyond: What Are the Issues?" *Social Science and Medicine* 44: 723–45.

Mackenbach, Johan. 2002. "Income Inequality and Population Health." *British Medical Journal* 324: 1–2.

Mackenbach, Johan and Martijntje Bakker (eds.). 2002. *Reducing Inequalities in Health: A European Perspective*. London: Routledge.

Mackenbach, Johan, Vivian Bos, Otto Andersen, Mario Cardano, Giuseppe Costa, Seeromanie Harding, Alison Reid, Örjan Hemström, Tapani Valkonen, and Anton Kunst. 2003. "Widening Socioeconomic Inequalities in Mortality in Six Western European Countries." *International Journal of Epidemiology* 32: 830–7.

Mackenbach, Johan, Adriënne Cavelaars, Anton Kunst, Feikje Groenhof, and the EU Working Group on Socioeconomic Inequalities in Health. 2000. "Socioeconomic Inequalities in Cardiovascular Disease Mortality: An International Study." *European Heart Journal* 21: 1141–51.

Mackenbach, Johan, Anton Kunst, Adriënne Cavelaars, Feikje Groenhof, Jose Geurts, and the EU Working Group on Socioeconomic Inequalities in Health. 1997. "Socioeconomic Inequalities in Morbidity and Mortality in Western Europe." *Lancet* 349: 1655–9.

Mackenbach, Johan, Anton Kunst, Feikje Groenhof, Jens-Kristian Borgan, Giuseppe Costa, Fabrizio Faggiano, Peter Józan, Mall Leinsalu, Pekka Martikainen, Jitka Rychtarikova, and Tapani Valkonen. 1999. "Socioeconomic Inequalities in Mortality Among Women and Among Men: An International Study." *American Journal of Public Health* 89: 1800–6.

Mackenbach, Johan, Irina Stirbu, Albert-Jan Roskam, Maartje Schaap, Gwenn Menvielle, Mall Leinsalu, and Anton Kunst for the EU Working Group on Socioeconomic Inequalities in Health. 2008. "Socioeconomic Inequalities in Health in 22 European Countries." *New England Journal of Medicine* 358. 2468–81.

Manderbacka, Kristiina. 1998. "Examining What Self-Rated Health Question is Understood to Mean by Respondents." *Scandinavian Journal of Social Medicine* 26: 145–53.

Manderbacka, Kristiina, Eero Lahelma, and Ossi Rahkonen. 2001. "Structural Changes and Social Inequalities in Health in Finland, 1986–1994." *Scandinavian Journal of Social Medicine*, Supplement 55: 41–54.

Marmot, Michael. 2005. "Social Determinants of Health Inequalities." *Lancet* 365: 1099–104.

Martikainen, Pekka, Jenni Blomgren, and Tapani Valkonen. 2007. "Change in the Total and Independent Effects of Education and Occupational Social Class on Mortality: Analyses of All Finnish Men and Women in the Period 1971–2000." *Journal of Epidemiology and Community* 61: 499–505.

Martikainen, Pekka, Pia Mäkelä, Seppo Koskinen, and Tapani Valkonen. 2001. "Income Differences in Mortality: A Register-Based Follow-Up Study of Three Million Men and Women." *International Journal of Epidemiology* 30: 1397–1405.

Najman, Jake. 1993. "Health and Poverty: Past, Present and Prospects for the Future." *Social Science and Medicine* 36: 157–66.

Rosen, George. 1993. *A History of Public Health*, expanded edition. Baltimore: Johns Hopkins University Press.

Scambler, Graham and Paul Higgs. 1999. "Stratification, Class and Health: Class Relations and Health Inequalities in High Modernity." *Sociology* 33: 275–96.

Schalick, Lisa, Wilbur Hadden, Elsie Pamuk, Vicente Navarro, and Gregory Pappas. 2000. "The Widening Gap in Death Rates among Income Groups in the United States for 1967–1986." *International Journal of Health Services* 30: 13–26.

Subramanian, S. V., Kawachi Ichiro, and Bruce Kennedy. 2001. "Does the State You Live in Make a Difference? Multilevel Analysis of Self-Rated Health in the US." *Social Science and Medicine* 53: 9–19.

Totman, Richard. 1979. *Social Causes of Illness*. New York: Pantheon Books.

Townsend, Peter and Nick Davidson. 1982. *Inequalities in Health: The Black Report*. London: Penguin.

Townsend, Peter, Nick Davidson, and Margaret Whitehead. 1990. *Inequalities in Health: The Black Report and the Health Divide*. London: Penguin.

Valkonen, Tapani. 1989. "Adult Mortality and Level of Education: A Comparison of Six Countries." Pp. 142–60 in A. J. Fox (ed.), *Health Inequalities in European Countries*. Aldershot: Gower.

Valkonen, Tapani, Hilkka Ahonen, Pekka Martikainen, and Hanna Remes. 2009. "Socioeconomic Differences in Mortality." Pp. 40–60 in H. Palosuo, S. Koskinen, E. Lahelma et al. (eds.), *Health Inequalities in Finland: Trends in Socioeconomic Health Differences 1980–2005*. Helsinki: Publications of the Ministry of Social Affairs and Health 2009: 9.

Valkonen, Tapani, Pekka Martikainen, Marika Jalovaara, Seppo Koskinen, Tuija Martelin, and Pia Mäkelä. 2000. "Changes in Socioeconomic Inequalities in Mortality During an Economic Boom and Recession among Middle-Aged Men and Women in Finland." *European Journal of Public Health* 10: 274–80.

Van Lenthe, Frank, Evelien Gevers, Inez Joung, Hans Bosma, and Johan Mackenbach. 2002. "Material and Behavioral Factors in the Explanation of Educational Differences in the Incidence of Acute Myocardial Infarction: The Globe Study." *Annals of Epidemiology* 12: 535–42.

Van Oort, Floor, Frank Van Lenthe, and Johan Mackenbach. 2005. "Material, Psychosocial, and Behavioural Factors in the Explanation of Educational Differences in Mortality in the Netherlands." *Journal of Epidemiology and Community Health* 59: 214–20.

Warr, Peter. 1987. *Work, Unemployment and Mental Health*. Oxford: Oxford University Press.

Whitehead, Margaret. 1992. "Concepts and Principles of Equity in Health." *International Journal of Health Services* 22: 429–45.

Whitehead, Margaret. 1997. "Life and Death over the Millennium." Pp. 7–28 in F. Drever and M. Whitehead (eds.), *Health Inequalities: Decennial Supplement*. Office for National Statistics Series DS, No. 15. London: HMSO.

WHO. 1985. *Targets for Health for All*. Copenhagen: World Health Organization, Regional Office for Europe.

WHO. 2008. *Closing the Gap in a Generation: Health Equity Through Action on the Social Determinants of Health. Final Report of the Commission on Social Determinants of Health*. Geneva: World Health Organization.

Wilkinson, Richard and Kate Pickett. 2006. "Income Inequality and Population Health: A Review and Explanation of the Evidence." *Social Science and Medicine* 62: 1768–84.

Wright, Eric Olin. 1985. *Classes*. London: Verso.

5

Health Status and Gender

ELLEN ANNANDALE

Although the social relations of gender find different expression in various national and local contexts, they are a potent explanation for the sometimes far-reaching differences in the health of men and women, boys and girls around the world. Thus, as Sen and Östlin (2008: 1) relate, "gender inequality damages the health of millions of girls and women across the globe." Boys and men do not escape the negative effects of gender inequality, however, for despite the privileges they habitually enjoy, expectations of masculinity often convert into behaviors that are a risk to health and longevity.

The purpose of this chapter is to highlight the complexity of gender-related social change and its relationship to health and illness. In so doing, it aims to inject a more dynamic perspective into analyses of "gender and health" than has been the case in research that relies on rather static conceptualizations of health and the social roles and statuses of men and women in particular times and places. By taking a broadly historical and to some extent comparative approach, the discussion also attempts to move away from analyses of gender and health which begin from the simple standpoint of men and women as two opposed biological and/or social groups who inevitably have more in common with each other than with the "opposite" sex or gender. The chapter begins by outlining why such an approach is more possible now than when gender and health research took off in the 1970s. It then charts international variations in the extent of male/female differences in life expectancy. This is followed by an analysis of changing patterns of mortality and morbidity amongst men and women in selected national contexts and a reflection on how they might be explained. In this discussion, the changing lives of men and women must be considered, particularly as they relate to longevity and the incidence of certain health conditions.

FROM "WOMEN'S HEALTH" TO "GENDER AND HEALTH"

Our ability to fashion a more dynamic and "gender-inclusive" approach to gender and health has been made possible by recent shifts in how both sociologists and members of society think about the health and social circumstances of men and women. Gender and health used to be synonymous with women's health. This association took root in the late 1960s and early 1970s when feminist social scientists and health activists in the United States and beyond sought to demonstrate that women's higher prevalence of ill health is socially constructed rather than, as had conventionally been believed, biologically given (Annandale 2009; Annandale and Riska 2009; Morgen 2002). A central plank of this argument was the distinction between biological sex and social gender. Feminists were deeply aware that health was a lens into the wider social oppression of women through the body. Thus in the mid-1980s, Olesen and Lewin (1985: 19) remarked that the examination of health "permits the revelation of most of the elements of western cultures which bear most directly on the construction of gender and its consequences for women, men, and the larger social order." Foregrounding the economic and social consequences of patriarchy did, of course, make male domains such as the state and health systems, as well as the attitudes and actions of individual men (in work, in the family, in health care, and so on), essential components of any analysis of women's health. However, from the perspective of men's *own* health, the male body and male health practices remained resolutely gender blind until quite recently (Arber and Thomas 2001; Riska 2004).

It has been pointed out with increasing force since around the mid-1990s that while the conceptualization of human health "using the (white, middle-class) male as the norm (the 'universal man')" ignores the possibility that the socially and biologically embodied experience of women may differ from that of men, "less attention has been paid to the way that this tacit but widespread notion of the 'universal man' has led to the construction of men as a homogeneous group and to a 'gender-neutral' conceptualization of men's health" (Emslie and Hunt 2009: 156–7). Once the scourge only of women's health, patriarchy is now the recognized source for many of men's health problems (Annandale 2009; Lohan 2007; Stanistreet, Bambra, and Scott-Samuel 2005). In many Western countries, this shift has been driven by concerns about a "crisis of masculinity" following economic restructuring, rising unemployment for some social groups of men, and women's advances in the spheres of education and work. Health is becoming increasingly "feminized" as the "male outlook on life" is more and more equated with ill health (Lee and Frayn 2008: 115). Alongside the demise of "women's studies" as it has been replaced by "gender studies" and "men's studies" in many universities (Hemmings 2006), these developments help to explain the quite rapid growth of the academic and activist arms of the "men's health movement" from the mid-1990s. Organizations such as the UK-based Men's Health Forum, the European Men's Health Forum, and a wealth of similar organizations in other parts of the world including the United States and Australia have mushroomed since the mid-1990s. For example, the First Asian Pacific International Society for Men's Health Symposium took place in Shanghai in 2006.

It is instructive to note that, while interest in men's health has risen, Western feminist academic interest in matters of health has declined (Annandale 2009; Kuhlmann and Babitsch 2002). The push for female-controlled alternatives to conventional male-controlled health care, particularly for reproductive health, that dominated the feminist agenda in the 1970s and early 1980s has also diminished (see Morgen 2002; Weisman 1998). As Kuhlmann (2009) points out, there are forceful international drivers for the conversion of gender inequality from a "women's problem" to a "societal concern." Stimulated by the activities of international organizations such as the Council of Europe (2008), the World Health Organization (WHO Europe 2001), and the United Nations (2002), gender mainstreaming and gender-sensitive approaches are gaining currency in many national contexts (Doyal 2006; Jonsson et al. 2006; Standing 1997). Of course, health care itself has changed in major ways since the 1970s, becoming progressively more commercialized and market-driven around the world (for a general discussion, see Henderson and Petersen 2002). Thus, with reference to the United States, it has been argued that the original meaning and purpose of the "key feminist concepts of women-centered care and empowerment" are increasingly being distorted and turned into high-tech vehicles for profit maximization by "women's health centers" located in corporate for-profit hospitals (Thomas and Zimmerman 2007: 359). This has occurred alongside the rise of "gender-specific" medicine, a movement which shifts attention away from so-called "old school" views of women's health as a limited feminist or "boutique" issue towards a new science which, as one of its advocates puts it, "embraces the entire organism and includes men as well as women within its remit" (Legato 2003, 2006: 16).

The branching out of the roots of gender and health to include men is not without tensions. As Lagro-Janssen (2007: 13) explains, "now that men are focusing attention on the disadvantages of being male in terms of danger to health, the danger arises that there will be a competition for public interest and sympathy between men and women: who is the worst off?" and a related competition for resources. For example, Kurz (2004) argues that social, economic, and ideological changes are affecting men much more than women, a phenomenon which Meryn (2004) dubs "societal syndrome." Moreover, if our concern becomes appreciating men's problems, then this can neglect men as part of the problem in relation to women's health, something which is especially important in parts of the world where marked inequalities in access to power and resources render women vulnerable to conditions such as HIV and the mental and physical health consequences of interpersonal violence (Garcia-Moreno 2002; Mantell et al. 2006). However, there is also a positive side: The more inclusive approach to gender and health encourages us to question assumptions that particular health problems *belong* to either men (e.g., heart disease, workplace stress) or to women (e.g., postnatal depression, anorexia, and other weight problems) (Annandale et al. 2007; Lee and Frayn 2008). It prompts us to think about the experience of health, illness, and health care as at least potentially cross-cutting what are still commonly constructed as given divides of biological sex and social gender in complex and often contested ways (Annandale and Clark 1996). This is explored in the next section of the chapter by looking at differences in mortality and morbidity in the international context and how they have changed over time.

MALE/FEMALE LONGEVITY DIFFERENTIALS

For many people in the early twenty-first-century world, women's longer life expectancy is pretty much an accepted fact of life. This is borne out for average life

Table 5.1 Life expectancy at birth in selected WHO member states, 2006

Country	Life expectancy at birth (years)	
	Males	Females
Australia	79	84
Finland	76	83
France	77	84
United Kingdom	77	84
United States of America	75	80
Russian Federation	60	73
Hungary	69	78
Bulgaria	69	76
Bangladesh	63	63
Zimbabwe	44	43
Rwanda	51	53
United Republic of Tanzania	50	51
Iraq	48	67

Source: Mortality of Burden of Disease (World Health Organization 2008).

expectancy in 2006 for virtually every World Health Organization (WHO) member state shown in Table 5.1. However, the *extent* of women's greater longevity varies considerably: from just one or two years in Zimbabwe and in the United Republic of Tanzania, to 13 years in the Russian Federation and a massive 19 years in war-torn Iraq, where many men have been engaged in deadly armed conflict. There are also palpable differences in longevity between men and between women across nations. Thus, in Zimbabwe men and women alike can expect on average to die before they reach their mid-40s, while their counterparts in Australia can expect to live to their late 70s and early 80s. Healthy life expectancies paint an even starker picture: While Australian men and women can anticipate living healthy lives into their early 70s, the equivalent decade for Zimbabwean men and women is the early 30s (WHO 2008; see also McMichael et al. 2004). We can also see that, generally speaking, the life expectancy of *men* in the Western countries of Australia, Finland, France, the UK, and the USA bears more similarity to that of *women* in Eastern Europe than it does to their compatriots in the West.

These cross-country differentials also signal that, while women may enjoy some biological advantages in relation to longevity, this can easily be overridden by the circumstances of their lives. As Amartya Sen (1992, 2003) discusses, in Europe and North America women outnumber men. Thus, the ratio of women to men exceeds 1.05 in the UK, France, and the USA. Yet in many "third world" countries, especially Asia and North Africa, the female : male ratio is as low as 0.90 or below. About 5 percent more boys than girls are born around the world. Yet "women are hardier than men and, given similar care, survive better at all ages – including in utero" (Sen 1992: 587). On this basis, Sen concludes that millions of women are "missing" around the world, particularly in China and India. He concludes that sex-specific abortion (female feticide), the neglect of female health, and poor nutrition in infancy provide the major explanations for their absence (Sen 1992, 2003). Thus "social factors can overrule or even negate biological propensities" (Baunach 2003: 332). Such factors operate across the lifespan, be it short or long, and often result in higher prevalence of illnesses for girls and women, even if they do not necessarily culminate in their earlier death (Sen and Östlin 2007).

Since the data in Table 5.1 relate to 2006, they are simply a snapshot in recent time. Significant gender-related changes have been taking place globally since the last quarter of the twentieth century. In different parts of the world, and within different countries, extremely complex and multifaceted patterns of similarity and difference, equality and inequality are emerging from the ferment of gender-related change, and these are reflected in new configurations of mortality and morbidity as well as in how health care is provided. While these are not easily summarized, several broad global trends can be highlighted.

Changes in life expectancy in the West: A reducing gap

The hundred or so years from roughly the 1880s to around the 1970s were a period of gradually increasing female longevity advantage in much of the West. Thus, in England and Wales, the number of extra years, on average, that a female might expect to live at birth compared to a male rose from around 2.0 years for those born in 1841, to 3.6 years for those born in 1910, 4.4 years for those born in 1950, and peaked at 6.9 years for those born in 1969 (Office for National Statistics 2007; Yuen 2005). In the USA, females born in 1900 could expect to live, on average, 2.0 years longer than their male counterparts. This rose to 5.5 years for those born in 1950, to reach a sizable 7.6 years for those born in 1970 (National Center for Health Statistics 2007). The longevity advantage grew from 3.6 years for Australian females, and from about 3 years for Canadian females who were born at the start of the twentieth century, to a projected 7.0 and 7.1 years respectively for those born in the early 1980s (Australian Institute of Health and Welfare 2006; Statistics Canada 2001).

However, the late 1960s and early 1970s marked an historical peak as this female longevity advantage began to be chipped away during the last quarter of the twentieth century. While life expectancy at birth continues to grow for both males and for females, as we can see in Table 5.2, the *gap* between them has been reducing. Table 5.3 gives statistics for "residual life expectancy," that is, "life left" at different ages using the example of Sweden, a particularly interesting case given the long history of gender equity policies in the country. Here we can see that both males and females have gained over the period 1980 to 2003, and that this has occurred at each selected point in the life course (birth, age 45, and age 65). But alongside this, we see a reducing female/male gap. This can be seen in the differences along the bottom row of the table, which are greater in 1980 than in 2003. Interestingly, as the table also shows, this narrowing gap is related to larger *male gains* at all age points. This point is fairly generalizable. In the USA, for example, men gained 3 years of average life expectancy between 1990 and 2004, while women gained just one (National Center for Health Statistics 2007). Turning to Europe: The life expectancy of Western European men as a whole increased by 6.5 percent, while that of women increased by 3.5 percent between 1980 and 2003 (White and Cash 2004).

Table 5.2 The life expectancy gap 1980 and 2002 in the West

Country	1980	2002
UK	6.0	4.7
USA	7.4	5.4
Sweden	6.0	4.4
Finland	8.5	6.6
France	8.1	7.4
Iceland	6.5	3.9
Australia (1980–2)	7.0	4.9

Source: Australian Institute of Health and Welfare (2006); Council of Europe (2005), T4.3, T4.6; Gjonça et al. (2005).

Table 5.3 Residual life expectancy at selected ages (Sweden)

Year	At birth			Age 45			Age 65		
	M	F	*diff.*	M	F	*diff.*	M	F	*diff.*
1980	72.8	78.8	**6.0**	30.4	35.4	**5.0**	14.3	17.9	**3.6**
1990	74.8	80.4	**5.6**	32.0	36.8	**4.8**	15.3	19.0	**3.7**
2003	77.9	82.4	**4.5**	34.4	38.4	**4.0**	17.0	20.3	**3.3**
Over period	**5.1**	**3.6**		**4.0**	**3.0**		**2.7**	**2.4**	

Source: Council of Europe (2005), T4.3, T4.4, T4.6.

Data from 14 European countries show that, between 1995 and 2003, life expectancy at birth rose on average by three months a year for men, compared to two months a year for women (European Health Expectancy Monitoring Unit 2005).

Generally speaking, *healthy* life expectancy falls as life expectancy increases, reflecting the burden of illness that often accompanies aging, especially older age. So, although on average women still live longer than men, generally their extra years are not spent in good health. As men's life expectancy increases, we might expect them to follow suit. It is therefore noteworthy that research from the Netherlands has found that men's overall life expectancy not only *grew more* than women's between 1989 and 2000, but also was accompanied by greater gains in *healthy* life expectancy (Perenboom et al. 2005). Bird and Rieker (2008) report a similar trend for the USA. Although it is too soon to come to any firm conclusions, it will be interesting to see whether or not a gap in *healthy* life expectancy favoring men emerges in future years.

Changes in life expectancy in Eastern Europe: An increasing gap

The decline in life expectancy in the former Soviet Union and Eastern Europe has been "one of the most significant developments in world health" since the late twentieth century (Cockerham 1999: 1), making Eastern Europe a natural laboratory within which to observe just how swiftly economic and social change is marked on the body through changes in health. In the region – which, it should be noted,

Table 5.4 The life expectancy gap 1980 and 2002, Eastern Europe

	1980	2002
Russian Federation	11.6	13.0
Hungary	7.2	9.0

Source: Figures for 1980 from Gjonça et al. (2005); figures for 2002 from Council of Europe (2005), T4.6.

is quite diverse – life expectancy is lowest for men in Russia, Kazakhstan, and Turkmenistan at around 59 years in 2002. Kazakhstan and Turkmenistan also have the lowest life expectancies for women at between 66 and 67 years (Nolte, McKee, and Gilmore 2005). This means that in these regions men can on average expect to live about 20 years less, and women about 15 years less, than men and women in Sweden (Nolte et al. 2005).

Much like their counterparts in the West, the women of Eastern Europe have longer average life expectancies than men. However, as shown in Table 5.4, in contrast to the Western countries, the *gap* in life expectancy between men and women has *increased* in a number of countries of Eastern Europe. In the Russian Federation, where this is most marked, the increasing gap can largely be explained by the swifter decline in male life expectancy since the mid-1980s (female life expectancy has been more stable, and relatively high). In Hungary, the increasing gap is less marked and, similary to the experience of the Russian Federation, has been accompanied by gradually rising life expectancy for both males and females, though females have gained more years than men have over the period (Gjonça et al. 2005). Thus it is clear that men have been especially vulnerable in these transition countries (Chenet 2000; Nolte et al. 2005). This is somewhat of a contrast to the West where, as we have seen, although men's average life expectancies are still lower than women's, they have been "gaining" more years recently.

The complexity of gender inequality, longevity, and health

These international comparisons relate to only some parts of the world, but they are nonetheless instructive because they draw our attention to the sensitivity of health to social change, often over relatively short periods, and to the variable impacts of such change on men and women. However, it needs to be borne in mind that the data we have been looking at are average life expectancies which inevitably conceal often large socioeconomic inequalities that exist between people in most countries, differences which are themselves related to gender inequalities. As Iyer, Sen, and Östlin (2008: 13) explain, "different axes of social power relations, such as gender and class, are interrelated, not as additive but as interacting processes." As these authors continue, while the research tells us that, despite their greater life expectancy, women tend to report more ailments than men, there is relatively little research which looks at whether differentials are similar (or not) in different socioeconomic groups. Research which looks at gender and socioeconomic status as intersecting influences on health is especially limited (Iyer et al. 2008). In resource-poor countries in particular, access to material and non-material resources is highly associated with gender. Thus, 70 percent of the world's poor are women (Sen, Asha, and Östlin 2002). Discrimination at the household level, particularly in relation to access to food, is especially important (Payne 2006; United Nations 2003). The growth of poverty in Russia, for example, has hit women as well as men, and elderly women in female-headed households have especially suffered (United Nations 2003). Laurent Chenet (2000: 203) reports that, even though women in Moscow live longer than men on average, and as a whole their mortality rates are lower than men's, women in lower socioeconomic status have higher mortality rates than their male equivalents for a number of causes, suggesting that women have "suffered disproportionately" from the transition.

Thus, the relationship between gender and health in different national contexts defies easy summary. Very broadly speaking, changes that are taking place in the West, such as the reducing gender gap in longevity, are increasingly addressed through the lens of *gender convergence*, or as more popularly conceived, "men becoming more like women and women becoming more like men." By contrast, for Russia and some other countries of Eastern Europe, *gender divergence* seems to be a more apt summary of the health experiences of men and women at the present time. The next section of the chapter briefly considers the issues of gender convergence and divergence in health and why they may be occurring, focusing in particular on health-related behaviors in their social structural context.

"GENDER CONVERGENCE" AND "GENDER DIVERGENCE" IN HEALTH AND HEALTH-RELATED BEHAVIORS

The explanation for the changes in the longevity gap in affluent Western nations has been sought in factors such as changing employment patterns and educational achievement levels, family structures, gender-related attitudes, and an apparent convergence in the "lifestyles" of men and women. The so-called "women's emancipation thesis," whereby "the changing roles of women and a general liberalisation of norms concerning women's behaviour have resulted in decreasing gender differences in mortality" (Waldron 2000: 152), has been important to debate. Thus, the popular and, to some extent, academic accent has been on changes amongst women. I have written elsewhere of how the gender landscapes of late modernity in the affluent West have thrown up new subjectivities that are fracturing the traditional binary social script of male/female biological and social difference in favor of more fluid identities which cross-cut erstwhile divides. I have suggested that, while there remain heavy brakes on how far men and women can stray from the culturally defined *masculine* and *feminine* without threatening their identities, "destabilised 'sex' and 'gender' identities have become an indispensable condition for the cross-marketing of products and lifestyles previously identified more readily with either men or women, such as cigarettes, alcohol and cosmetic surgery, with dubious or nebulous benefits to health and well-being" (Annandale 2009: 118).

There is a lag effect whereby so-called health behaviors, such as cigarette smoking and alcohol consumption, although initiated 20 or so years earlier in life, later manifest as some of the major causes of death, such as some forms of cancer and coronary heart disease (CHD). Thus, it is interesting to reflect here on gender-related changes in such behaviors over recent years.

Cigarette smoking is still responsible for more deaths amongst men than women around the world. However, smoking rates have been declining in many affluent Western countries since the last quarter of the twentieth century, and this decline has been much more marked amongst men than amongst women, with the difference in smoking prevalence having all but disappeared in some. Taking the UK as an illustration, over 50 percent of men smoked in 1974, while only about 28 percent smoked in 2002. For women, about 40 percent smoked in 1974 and 24 percent in 2002, reflecting a much less significant drop (Office for National Statistics 2006). Data for Canada show that, while 61 percent of men smoked in 1965, only 25 percent did so by 2001. The equivalent figures for women were 38 percent and 21 percent (Canadian Institute for Health Information 2003).

Alcohol consumption above daily recommended rates, and especially "binge drinking," is indirectly associated with CHD (Unal, Critchley, and Capewell 2004). Despite what we might be led to believe from the moral panic over young women's drinking, cross-nationally, men still consume considerably more alcohol than women (Bird and Rieker 2008; Payne 2006). In the UK, for example, in 2006, 40 percent of men and one third of women reported exceeding the recommended daily amount of alcohol on at least one day (Office for National Statistics 2008). However, although males generally consume more alcohol than females, the percentage of men consuming more than the recommended weekly level in Britain has remained more or less stable since the mid-1990s, while consumption above recommended levels has increased by over 50 percent amongst women (General Household Survey, cited by Petersen et al. 2005). By way of further illustration, although comparatively speaking levels of alcohol consumption are relatively low in Sweden, consumption has been rising. There too men still drink more than women, but there has been "convergence between sexes, at least in urban areas" in recent years (Helmersson Bergmark 2004: 297). Alcohol-related death rates have increased significantly in many affluent Western countries in recent years. Much of the increase since the early 1990s in the UK, for instance, is attributable to male deaths, with the gap between males and females widening over the period to reach 18.3 deaths per 100,000 for men and 8.8 deaths per 100,000 for women in 2006 (Office for National Statistics 2008).

The major causes of death in many societies are circulatory disease (including heart disease and stroke) and cancer. Although, generally speaking, men start and end with higher rates, the decrease in deaths from circulatory disease generally and from cardiovascular disease (CVD) has been less pronounced amongst women than men since the 1970s. For example, the age-standardized death rate for circulatory disease for British men reduced from 6,900 per million in 1971 to 2,600 per million in 2005. The equivalent figures for women were 4,300 per million and 1,700 per million (Office for National Statistics 2007). For CHD specifically, the decline in deaths in the UK has been slower for younger ages and, again, especially amongst women (Petersen et al. 2005).

Overall cancer mortality rates have changed relatively little over the last 30 or so years in many affluent nations. However, again to take the UK as an illustration, male deaths peaked in the mid-1980s at 2,900 per million and then fell to 2,200 per million by 2005. By contrast, female death rates peaked in the late 1980s, at 1,900 per million, and then gradually fell to 1,600 per million by 2005 (Office for National Statistics 2007). These overall rates conceal variations in trends for different kinds of cancer. Most notable in this respect is lung cancer. Although both incidence and mortality rates are higher for men than women worldwide (Payne 2005), the timing of peaks and troughs is quite different and varies across countries. For men in Britain, both incidence and mortality rose enormously from the mid-twentieth century through to the early 1980s and thereafter began to fall, with a decrease of around 40 percent between the mid-1970s and 2001. Incidence and mortality for women meanwhile has lagged about 20 years behind and plateaued as recently as the mid-1990s, with an increase of about 80 percent over the same period (Office for National Statistics 2006, 2007). In the USA, lung cancer accounted for only 3 percent of all female cancer deaths in 1950; by 2000, this had risen to 25 percent (Department of Health and Human Services 2001). The experiences of particular age-cohorts are also important. In the UK, for example, current male improvements are noticeable after the age of 50 and before the age of 70 (Gjonça et al. 2005). Broadly speaking, women at highest risk of lung cancer over recent years were born in the 1920s and 1930s, around the time that social impediments to women's smoking began to loosen. The cohort effect in smoking is likely to be a significant contributor to the narrowing longevity gap from around the 1970s, since by this time women born in the 1920s would be around 60 years old and already subject to the negative effects of smoking. Male smoking rates and lung cancer deaths were already declining by this time. Moreover, the smoking epidemic within a country tends to go though stages, beginning with men in higher socioeconomic status groups, followed by women in the same strata, then spreading to men, and then to women, in lower socioeconomic groups. The particular timing of this process in Western countries means that the burden is now increasingly borne by women in lower socioeconomic groups and that it is associated with multiple disadvantage (Harman et al. 2006).

What do these trends tell us in terms of "gender convergence"? Generally speaking, we can see that while men are still worse off than women, incidence and mortality of these major diseases seem to be improving at a faster pace for men than for women in the West, thereby contributing to their overall "catch-up" in life expectancy and reduction in the longevity gap discussed earlier. The complex etiology of many major diseases such as heart disease and many cancers makes it difficult to draw one-to-one associations with social factors. Women and men appear to have different biological vulnerabilities to heart disease and cancer related to underlying genetic, hormonal, and metabolic differences. For instance, for lung cancer there is some as yet poorly understood evidence that differences in gene expression increase women's risk of lung cancer at the same level of smoking (Payne 2001). Women also seem more biologically vulnerable to health damage from alcohol. Women reach higher blood alcohol levels than men while consuming similar weight-adjusted amounts of alcohol, suggesting that men and women metabolize alcohol differently (Bird and Rieker 2008). Even though these biological factors need to be taken into account, they do not negate the likelihood that changes in life expectancy and in particular causes of death are significantly related to changes in gender expectations at the societal level.

Women and men do not, of course, live their lives through a neatly packaged set of behaviors that are either "risky" or "not risky" for their health; things are much more complicated than this (Bird and Rieker 2008). The problem, however is that it is very difficult to draw definitive links from "health and lifestyles" to patterns of morbidity and mortality since their social etiology is highly complex. It has long been noted that women's higher levels of "health consciousness" associated with an attentiveness to the reproductive body (e.g., menstruation and pregnancy) and responsibility for the care of children and partners may contribute to improved health. This has prompted commentators on men's health to propose that men cutting back on health-damaging behaviors like cigarette smoking, lower exposure to risks on the road and at work, and so on, may contribute to "convergence" (e.g., Vallin, Meslé, and Valkonen 2001). At the same time, women's greater longevity as well as lower age-specific incidence of many major diseases and their health consciousness have been used as benchmarks against which men's (poorer) health can be understood. Thus men's shorter life expectancy can only really be framed as "premature death" and their higher age-related incidence of major diseases such as CHD framed as "excess" (see, e.g., Meryn 2005; White and Cash 2004) when compared to women's longer average life expectancy and/or lower incidence of diseases.

Is masculinity a danger to health?

This way of thinking is quite understandable in the context of the binary approach to sex and gender that, despite changes in gender-related attitudes and behaviors amongst (some groups of) men and women, still drives our thinking (as the discussion in this chapter itself reflects). Since women's use of health care tends to be higher than men's, this directs researchers to focus on men's relative failure to seek help. Thus, it has been pointed out that norms of stoicism and control associated with traditional hegemonic masculinity can deter men from seeking care, since entry into health care risks lapsing into the more passive, and female-defined, sick role traditionally associated with weakness (see, e.g., Addis and Mahalik 2003; White 2002). However, there is relatively little research that directly compares men's and women's responses to common or shared symptoms or health-related concerns, heart disease being a notable exception. The result is that research may be drawing attention to "gendered experiences" to the neglect of health-seeking experiences that men and women hold in common, as well as drawing attention away from what may be significant variations within men and within women as groups (Annandale et al. 2007). Thus, norms of *masculinity* do not just affect men. In the popular sphere, most notably in the media (see Day, Gough, and McFadden 2004), women – and young women especially – are often castigated for "aping men" in their behaviors, cigarette smoking and binge drinking being cases in point. Certainly, many young women in the West and beyond have been released from the shackles of the binary social scripts that bound their grandmothers, even mothers, to hearth and home, though their counterparts in less developed nations have not been so fortunate. Yet, as Archer Mann and Huffman (2005: 70–1) relate, personal narratives tell of the "contradictions, uncertainties, and dilemmas they face in their everyday lives." Equally, male masculinity is fragmented; it can, for example, be hegemonic, subordinated, marginalized, and complicit in form (Connell 1995). As Sabo and Gordon (1995: 10) explained some time ago now, "all men are not alike, nor do all male groups share the same stakes in the gender order. At any given historical moment, there are competing masculinities – some hegemonic, some marginalised, and some stigmatised – each with their respective structural, psycho-logical and cultural moorings" (see also Robertson 2007).

It is hegemonic masculinity in particular that has been associated with risks to men's health and to premature death (Courtenay 2000). The problems that hege-monic masculinity can bring for men can be drawn upon to account for the "crisis of masculinity" in Soviet Russia since the 1970s, as well as for men's difficulties in adapting to rapid social change since the 1990s. According to Pietilä and Rytkönen (2008: 1073), health-damaging practices of Russian men can be seen as " 'compen-satory behaviours' for men's marginalisation where ultra-masculine practices and behaviours are used to compensate for a perceived subordinate position of men." Their interview-based research conducted in St. Petersburg shows that men and women alike tended to attribute men's decreasing life expectancy to the structural conditions and life-chances in Russian society, such as stress related to the struggle for money in an insecure market and the inability to fulfill the traditional breadwin-ner role. Although women experienced similar labor market insecurity, they were felt to be protected from the worst consequences of this because they had the "natural resort" of the home and family. Heavy alcohol consumption amongst men was seen as a culturally embedded practice that was a "more or less inevitable consequence of daily difficulties and frustration" (Pietilä and Rytkönen 2008: 1078). Yet, as Hinote, Cockerham, and Abbott (2009) explore, the higher burden of pre-mature morbidity amongst men has tended to mean that women have been over-looked. Their research on eight former Soviet states shows that, although alcohol consumption has not been particularly common amongst women, trends are chang-ing. They relate that, with the collapse of Soviet communism, many, often younger, females may be adopting behaviors such as higher levels of alcohol consumption "either as a personal statement against a formerly masculine-dominated social system or against the traditionalist Soviet order, or as a way of exercising agency or individual choice in an increasingly uncertain time" (Hinote et al. 2009: 1260).

CONCLUSION

The chapter has highlighted that social relations of gender have a forceful impact on health and illness around the world, even though the forms that they take are varied and changing. Thus, even though women still on average tend to live longer than men and to experience lower age-specific incidences of major diseases, resting at this conclusion fails to do justice to the complex patterns of convergence and divergence that are taking place in particular countries and parts of the world in response to socioeconomic changes that are leading men and women to think and act differently in relation to health and health-related behaviors. As stated at the start of the chapter, it used to be the case that gender and health meant women's health. The remit of gender and health research has now been extended to include men and now much better appreciates differences within men and within women, such as those related to socioeconomic status, age, and ethnicity (which it has not been possible to discuss here). But truly gender comparative research still remains rare, with data on major mortality and life expectancy – the focus of this chapter – amongst the exceptions when looking at the international context. It can be hoped that as the research remit continues to evolve, our understanding of the relationship between health status and gender will be extended even further.

References

Addis, Michael E. and James R. Mahalik. 2003. "Men, Masculinity, and the Contexts of Help Seeking." *American Psychologist* 58: 5–14.

Annandale, Ellen. 2009. *Women's Health and Social Change*. London: Routledge.

Annandale, Ellen and Judith Clark. 1996. "What is Gender? Feminist Theory and the Sociology of Human Reproduction." *Sociology of Health and Illness* 18(1): 17–44.

Annandale, Ellen, Janet Harvey, Debbie Cavers, and Mary Dixon-Woods. 2007. "Gender and Access to Healthcare in the UK: A Critical Interpretive Synthesis of the Literature." *Evidence and Policy* 3(4): 463–86.

Annandale, Ellen and Elianne Riska. 2009. "Editorial Introduction. New Connections: Towards a Gender-Inclusive Approach to Women's and Men's Health." *Current Sociology Monograph* 57(2): 123–33.

Archer, Sara and Hilary Thomas. 2001. "From Women's Health to a Gender Analysis of Health." Pp. 94–123 In W. C. Cockerham (ed.), *The Blackwell Companion to Medical Sociology*. Oxford: Blackwell.

Archer Mann, Susan and Douglas J. Huffman. 2005. "The Decentering of Second Wave Feminism and the Rise of the Third Wave." *Science and Society* 69(1): 56–91.

Australian Institute of Health and Welfare. 2006. *Australia's Health 2006* Canberra: AIHW.

Baunach, Dawn Michelle. 2003. "Gender, Mortality, and Corporeal Inequality." *Sociological Spectrum* 23: 331–58.

Bird, Chloe and Patricia Rieker. 2008. *Gender and Health: The Effects of Constrained Choices and Social Policies*. Cambridge: Cambridge University Press.

Canadian Institute for Health Information. 2003. *Women's Health Surveillance Report*. Ottawa: Canadian Institute for Health Information.

Chenet, Laurent. 2000. "Gender and Socio-Economic Inequalities in Mortality in Central and Eastern Europe." Pp. 182–210 in Ellen Annandale and Kate Hunt (eds.), *Gender Inequalities in Health*. Buckingham: Open University Press.

Cockerham, William C. 1999. *Health and Social Change in Russia and Eastern Europe*. London: Routledge.

Connell, Robert. 1995. *Masculinities*. Cambridge: Polity Press.

Council of Europe. 2005. *Recent Demographic Developments in Europe 2004*. Strasbourg: Council of Europe.

Council of Europe. 2008. *Recommendation CM/Rec(2008)1 of the Committee of Ministers to Member States on the Inclusion of Gender Differences in Health Policy*. Retrieved November 20, 2008 (wcd.coe.int/ViewDoc.jsp?id=1241743&Site=CM&BackColorInternet=9999CC&Back%20ColorIntranet=FFBB55&BackColorLogged=FFAC75).

Courtenay, Will. 2000. "Constructions of Masculinity and Their Influence on Men's Well-Being: A Theory of Gender and Health." *Social Science and Medicine* 50(10): 1385–401.

Day, Katy, Brendan Gough, and Majella McFadden. 2004. "'Warning! Alcohol Can Seriously Damage Your Health': A Discourse Analysis of Recent British Newspaper Coverage of Women and Drinking." *Feminist Media Studies* 4(2): 166–83.

Department of Health and Human Services. 2001. *Women and Smoking*. Rockville, Maryland: *DHSS*.

Doyal, Lesley. 2006. "Sex, Gender and Medicine." Pp. 146–61 in David Kelleher, Jonathan Gabe, and Gareth Williams (eds.), *Challenging Medicine*, 2nd edition. London: Routledge.

Emslie, Carol and Kate Hunt. 2009. "Men, Masculinities and Heart Disease: A Systematic Review of the Qualitative Literature." Pp. 155–200 in Ellen Annandale and Elianne Riska (eds.), "Towards a Gender-Inclusive Approach to Women's and Men's Health." *Current Sociology Monograph* 57(2).

European Health Expectancy Monitoring Unit. 2005. *Are We Living Longer, Healthier Lives in the EU?* Montpellier: EHEMU Technical Report 2.

Garcia-Moreno, Claudia. 2002. "Violence Against Women: Consolidating a Public Health Agenda." Pp. 111–42 in G. Sen, A. George, and P. Östlin (eds.), *Engendering International Health*. Cambridge, MA: MIT Press.

Gjonça, Arjan, Cecilia Tomassini, Barbara Toson, and Steve Smallwood. 2005. "Sex Differences in Mortality, a Comparison of the United Kingdom and Other Developed Countries." *Health Statistics Quarterly* 26: 6–16.

Harman, Juliet, Hilary Graham, Brian Frances, Hazel Inskip, and the SWS Study Group. 2006. "Socioeconomic Gradients in Smoking Among Young Women: A British Survey." *Social Science and Medicine* 63(11): 2791–800.

Helmersson Bergmark, Karin. 2004. "Gender Roles, Family, and Drinking: Women at the Crossroads of Drinking Cultures." *Journal of Family History* 29(3): 293–307.

Hemmings, Clare. 2006. "The Life and Times and Academic Feminism." Pp. 13–34 in K. Davis, M. Evans, and J. Lorber (eds.), *Handbook of Gender and Women's Studies*. London: Sage.

Henderson, Sara and Alan Petersen (eds.). 2002. *Consuming Health: The Commodification of Health Care*. London: Routledge.

Hinote, Brian P., William C. Cockerham, and Pamela Abbott. 2009. "The Spectre of Post-Communism: Women and Alcohol in Eight Post-Soviet States." *Social Science and Medicine* 68(7): 1254–62.

Iyer, Aditi, Gita Sen, and Piroska Östlin. 2008. "The Intersections of Gender and Class in Health Status and Health Care." *Global Public Health* 3(S1): 13–24.

Jonsson, Pia Maria, Ingrid Schmidt, Vibeke Sparring, and Göran Tomson. 2006. "Gender Equity in Health Care in Sweden: Minor Improvements Since the 1990s." *Health Policy* 77: 24–36.

Kuhlmann, Ellen. 2009. "From Women's Health to Gender Mainstreaming and Back Again." Pp. 135–54 in Ellen Annandale and Elianne Riska (eds.), "Towards a Gender-Inclusive Approach to Women's and Men's Health." *Current Sociology Monograph* 57(2).

Kuhlmann, Ellen and Birgit Babitsch. 2002. "Bodies, Health and Gender: Bridging Feminist Theories and Women's Health." *Women's Studies International Forum* 25(4): 433–42.

Lagro-Janssen, Toine. 2007. "Sex, Gender and Health: Developments in Research." *European Journal of Women's Studies* 14(1): 9–20.

Lee, Ellie and Elizabeth Frayn. 2008. "The 'Feminization' of Health." Pp. 115–33 in David Wainwright (ed.), *A Sociology of Health*. London: Sage.

Legato, Marianne. 2003. "Beyond Women's Health: The New Discipline of Gender-Specific Medicine." *Medical Clinics of North America* 87: 917–37.

Legato, Marianne. 2006. "Foreword to World Congress on Gender-Specific Medicine, Berlin 2006." *Gender Medicine* 3(1): S16.

Lohan, Maria. 2007. "How Might We Understand Men's Health Better? Integrating Explanations From Critical Studies on Men and Inequalities in Health." *Social Science and Medicine* 65(3): 493–504.

Mantell, Joanna, Landon Myer, Alex Carbollo-Diéguez, Zena Stein, Neetha Morar, and Polly Harrison. 2006. "The Promises and Limitations of Female-Initiated Methods of HIV/STI Protection." *Social Science and Medicine* 63(8): 1998–2009.

McMichael, Anthony J., Martin KcKee, Vladimir Shkolnikov, and Tapani Valkonen. 2004. "Morality Trends and Setbacks: Global Convergence or Divergence." *Lancet* 363(9415): 1155–9.

Meryn, Siegfried. 2004. "Gender Quo Vadis: The 21st Century Female Century?" *Journal of Men's Health and Gender* 1(1): 3–7.

Meryn, Siegfried. 2005. "Men's Health 2005: A Small Step for Mankind." *Journal of Men's Health and Gender* 2(4): 389–90.

Morgen, Sandra. 2002. *Into Our Own Hands: The Women's Health Movement in the United States, 1969–1990*. London: Rutgers University Press.

National Center for Health Statistics. 2007. *Health, United States, 2007*. Hyattsville, MD: National Center for Health Statistics.

Nolte, Ellen, Martin McKee, and Anna Gilmore. 2005. "Morbidity and Mortality in the Transition Countries of Europe." Pp. 153–76 in M. Macura, A. L. MacDonald, and W. Haug (eds.), *The New Demographic Regime: Population Challenges and Policy Responses* Geneva: United Nations.

Office for National Statistics. 2006. *Focus on Health*. London: The Stationery Office.

Office for National Statistics. 2007. *Social Trends 37*. London: The Stationery Office.

Office for National Statistics. 2008. *Social Trends 38*. London: The Stationery Office.

Olesen, Virginia and Ellen Lewin. 1985. "Women, Health, and Healing." Pp. 1–24 in E. Lewin and V. Olesen (eds.), *Women, Health, and Healing*. London: Tavistock.

Payne, Sarah. 2001. " 'Smoke Like a Man, Die Like a Man?': A Review of the Relationship Between Gender, Sex and Lung Cancer." *Social Science and Medicine* 53(8): 1067–80.

Payne, Sarah. 2005. *Gender in Lung Cancer and Smoking Research*. Geneva: World Health Organization.

Payne, Sarah. 2006. *The Health of Men and Women*. Cambridge: Polity Press.

Perenboom, R., L. van Herten, H. Boshuizen, and G. van den Bos. 2005. "Life Expectancy Without Chronic Morbidity: Trends in Gender and Socioeconomic Disparities." *Public Health Reports* 120(1): 46–54.

Petersen, Sophie, Viv Peto, Peter Scarborough, and Mike Rayner. 2005. *Coronary Heart Disease Statistics 2005 Edition*. London: British Heart Foundation.

Pietilä, Ilkka and Marja Rytkönen. 2008. " 'Health Is Not a Man's Domain': Lay Accounts of Gender Difference in Life-Expectancy in Russia." *Sociology of Health and Illness* 30(7): 1070–83.

Riska, Elianne. 2004. *Masculinity and Health: Coronary Heart Disease in Medical and Public Discourse*. Oxford: Rowman and Littlefield.

Robertson, Steve. 2007. *Understanding Men's Health: Masculinities, Identity and Well-Being*. Maidenhead: Open University Press/McGraw-Hill.

Rutz, Wolfgang. 2004. "Men's Health on the European WHO Agenda." *Journal of Men's Health and Gender* 1(1): 22–5.

Sabo, Donald and David Gordon. 1995. "Rethinking Men's Health and Illness." Pp. 1–21 in D. Sabo and D. Gordon (eds.), *Men's Health and Illness: Gender, Power and the Body*. London: Sage.

Sen, Amartya. 1992. "Missing Women: Social Inequality Outweighs Women's Survival Advantage in Asia and North Africa." *British Medical Journal* 304(March 7): 587–8.

Sen, Amartya. 2003. "Missing Women – Revisited." *British Medical Journal* 327(December 6): 1297–8.

Sen, Gita, George Asha, and Piroska Östlin. 2002. "Engendering Health Equity: A Review of Research and Policy." Pp. 1–33 in G. Sen, A. George, and P. Östlin (eds.), *Engendering International Health*. Cambridge, MA: MIT Press.

Sen, Gita and Piroska Östlin. 2007. *Unequal, Unfair, Ineffective and Inefficient. Gender Inequity in Health: Why It Exists and How We Can Change It*. Final report to the WHO Commission on Social Determinants of Health. Retrieved November 20, 2008 (www.who.int/social_determinants/knowledge_networks/final_reports/en/index.html).

Sen, Gita and Piroska Östlin. 2008. "Gender Inequity and Health: Why It Exists and How We Can Change It." *Global Public Health* 3(S1): 1–12.

Standing, Hilary. 1997. "Gender and Equity in Health Sector Reform Programmes: A Review." *Health Policy and Planning* 12(1): 1–12.

Stanistreet, Debbie, Clare Bambra, and Alex Scott-Samuel. 2005. "Is Patriarchy the Source of Men's Higher Mortality?" *Journal of Epidemiology and Community Health* 59(10): 873–6.

Statistics Canada. 2001. "Death – Shifting Trends." *Health Reports* 12(3): 41–6.

Thomas, Jan E. and Mary K. Zimmerman. 2007. "Feminism and Profit in American Hospitals: The Corporate Construction of Women's Health Centers." *Gender and Society* 21(3): 359–83.

Unal, Belgin, Julia Alison Critchley, and Simon Capewell. 2004. "Modelling the Decline in Coronary Heart Disease Deaths in England and Wales, 1981–2000: Comparing Contributions from Primary Prevention and Secondary Prevention." *Circulation* 109(9): 1101–7.

United Nations. 2002. *Gender Mainstreaming: An Overview*. New York: United Nations, Office of the Social Advisor on Gender Issues and Advancement of Women.

United Nations. 2003. *Human Development Report 2003*. Oxford: Oxford University Press.

Vallin, Jacques, France Meslé, and Tapani Valkonen. 2001. *Trends in Mortality and Differential Mortality*. Strasbourg: Council of Europe Publishing.

Waldron, Ingrid. 2000. "Trends in Gender Differences in Mortality: Relationships to Changing Gender Differences in Behaviour and Other Causal Factors." Pp. 150–81 in Ellen Annandale and Kate Hunt (eds.), *Gender Inequalities in Health*. Buckingham: Open University Press.

Weisman, Carol. 1998. *Women's Health Care: Activist Traditions and Institutional Change*. Baltimore: Johns Hopkins University Press.

White, Alan and Keith Cash. 2004. "The State of Men's Health in Europe." *Journal of Men's Health and Gender* 1(1): 60–6.

White, Rob. 2002. "Social and Political Aspects of Men's Health." *Health* 6: 267–85.

World Health Organization Europe. 2001. *Mainstreaming Gender Equity in Health: Madrid Statement*. Copenhagen: WHO Europe.

World Health Organization. 2008. *World Health Statistics 2008: Global Health Indicators* (www.who.int/whosis/whostat/EN_WHS08_Table1_Mort.pdf).

Yuen, Peter. 2005. *Compendium of Health Statistics 2005–2006*. London: Office of Health Economics.

6

Health, Ethnicity, and Race

Hannah Bradby and James Y. Nazroo

This chapter explores the relationship between ethnicity, race, and health, drawing on sociological evidence from the UK and the US. Insights from quantitative traditions of research into health inequalities and from qualitative work on meanings and experience are used to consider how understandings have developed over the past two decades.

The chapter falls into seven sections. We start with a consideration of what *race* and *ethnicity* mean in US and UK contexts and interrogate the role of *slavery* and *empire* in *migration*; we then discuss how *culture* became a key issue in debates on the ways in which ethnicity and race relate to health and health experiences. Second, we consider the ways in which ethnic and racial categories are used in official data in the US and UK, which leads into the third section summarizing the patterns of stratification of health outcomes from UK and US published sources. Fourth, we assess what these data tell us about inequalities in health and critique the development of crude explanatory models. Fifth, we evaluate the evidence on how ethnicity influences the use and experience of health services, including the role that culture plays. Sixth, we touch on the relationship between migration, ethnicity, and health work, considering how the transglobal processes that brought about the creation of ethnic minority groups in Anglophone countries have also staffed the health care industry. Finally, we return to the theoretical treatment of this topic to consider whether, given our critique of existing data, the sociological problematic has been adequately described.

Defining the Terms of the Discussion: What Do "Ethnicity" and "Race" Mean?

Ethnicity and race are difficult concepts to discuss with precision, since their meanings are highly charged politically, have been subject to change over recent history, and, like many sociological concepts, have a scientific as well as popular usage, and the two do not always coincide. Furthermore, there are subtle but significant differences in the uses of these terms in different social settings; thus, discussing ethnicity or race in the US can have different implications compared with their discussion in the UK. Some of the contrasts between the UK and the US can be understood in terms of the history of empire and colonization, the role of institutionalized slavery, migration, and their implications for the construction of the social problem of ethnic and racial difference in contemporary society.

Slavery and migration

Britain was involved in the Atlantic slave trade and benefited economically from it. While some migration from overseas colonies occurred as a result, the UK was not a major destination for slave labor and slavery was not institutionalized in the UK. Although slavery has been illegal in the US since the second half of the nineteenth century, its influence persists in terms of the current meaning of race and it has played an important role in determining current lines of social stratification. Much of the early press interest in Barack Obama's presidential campaign focused on his Black father being a Kenyan national (rather than an African American descended from slaves) and the identification of slave owners among his White mother's ancestors. The lack of slave ancestors had been identified as potentially reducing Obama's ability to attract Black votes on which Democrat candidates rely, although post-election celebrations indicate how he has become identified as a symbol of "Black America."

The system of indentured and slave labor was responsible for the transport of large numbers of people from West Africa to the US – estimates vary from 9 to 20 million – as well as smaller numbers from Scotland, Ireland, England, and Germany. The majority of Black slaves were used in agricultural work in the Southern States, a fact that is reflected in the greater proportion of African Americans in the South compared with the North that persists today. Migration over the past four centuries accounts for the presence of almost all of the US population, with the exception of about 2 percent who are descendants of indigent populations. The US is a land of migrants where old historical allegiances were abandoned in the construction and celebration of the "new world," yet "melting pot" multiculturalism has tended to include European, and especially Protestant, immigrants and exclude Africans and Native Americans. Indeed, while migrant status is a central symbol of US national character, the extent to which the most recent immigrants from Asia and Latin America will be assimilated remains to be seen.

Empire and migration

While the British Isles have long received immigrants, particularly in urban, maritime centers, mass migration of non-White groups to the UK occurred after World War II (1939–45) when British colonials were invited to make good the labor shortage in the "mother country." The character of migration to the UK has been shaped by the legacy of its empire, a massive global power in the nineteenth century, which transmitted cultural and linguistic influence overseas so that labor migrants were familiar with the English language and aspects of British culture. While racist atti-

tudes and practices shaped the experience of many immigrants to the UK, discrimination was neither ensured nor prevented through legal statute. The White
British ethnic majority sees itself as non-immigrant, or assumes origins traceable to
Norman immigration ten centuries ago. The attitude to immigrants, particularly in
the 1950s and 1960s, was "assimilationist"; where immigrants were welcomed or
tolerated, there was an assumption that they would wish to become "British" and
integrate into the ethnic majority population. Imperial British history has contributed to an assumption that "Britishness," with its particular blend of individualism,
establishment Christianity, and phlegmatism, would be embraced as a superior way
of life by immigrants and their descendants. The rejection of, or exclusion from,
aspects of British life by immigrants was interpreted as the failure of minorities to
assimilate. Multicultural social and educational policies that acknowledged, celebrated, and maintained features of a range of different ethnic and religious identities
were introduced in the 1990s to promote integration, if not assimilation. Ongoing
marginalization of ethnic minority groups, interpreted as a form of separatism and
hence at the root of racial tensions, has raised serious questions about the "failure"
of multiculturalism and the place of minorities in the British population. Minority
culture has thus been regularly pathologized as problematic in preventing assimilation, and culture (like ethnicity) has been identified as something that minorities
have, but the mainstream majority does not.

Culture

The role allocated to culture as a marker and a cause of ethnic or racial difference
can be contrasted between the US and UK. In the US, residential segregation underpins many other aspects of racialized inequality (Massey and Denton 1993), whereas
in the UK, the extent to which inequality can be characterized as segregation continues to be debated (McCulloch 2007) and cultural difference carries more weight
as both explanation and cause.

The plurality of a melting pot of culture as a rhetorical ideal (if not a lived norm)
in the US, the Atlantic slave trade, and the internal movement of slaves west during
the "second passage" effectively destroyed the cultural patterns of the enslaved.
Discrimination against people of African origin in the US has not focused on the
content of minority culture, but rather has relied on biologically justified racism.
This discrimination resembles divisions of class in the British context, where an
assumption about the inherent nature of difference between groups is deep-seated
and difficult to challenge. The UK pattern of cultural difference justifying discrimination assumes, as described, that minorities could and should change their culture
in favor of the majority. This ignores the important role that culture may play in
people's identity. Although it cannot be assumed, elements of culture, such as religion and/or marriage practices, can have overwhelming importance for people's
sense of themselves.

Unfortunately, in the analysis of inequality, rather than informing an appropriately complex view of cultural identity, a focus on culture has regularly diverted
attention from structural inequalities. When culture comes to be seen as a feature
of the minority rather than the majority, it can be used as a euphemism for referring
to a problematic deviation from the majority, such that culture becomes no more

than "a tool for blaming black people within popular ideology and in research" (Donovan 1986: 45). As a result, minorities are seen as the authors of their own disadvantage and culture comes to be identified as a cause.

Much of the evidence for inequalities in health within and between ethnic groups comes from official data sets and large-scale surveys in the US and the UK. Using a "complicated view of culture" as part of a definition of ethnicity in social surveys presents particular challenges (Bradby 2003), which means that simplified proxies are inevitably employed. We discuss these proxies and the data that they have generated next.

OFFICIAL DATA ON ETHNIC AND RACIAL CATEGORIES

The use of ethnic and racial categories in official data in the US and the UK and the changes in usage over time have been described elsewhere (Nazroo and Williams 2005). Racialized categories have been deployed in the US since the first census in 1790, whereas ethnic categories have only been used in the last two UK censuses (1991 and 2001). In both the US and the UK, the classification system has changed from census to census to reflect both changing patterns of migration and the development of ideas about racialized difference. In the US, alterations to the legal status of racialized groups have been key, as for instance with the disappearance of slave as a category of enumeration between the censuses of 1860 and 1870, following the abolition of slavery in the intervening years.

The terms *ethnic* and *racial* are sometimes used as synonyms, but they are used in distinct ways in official data. UK data only report on ethnicity and there are no racial classifications, whereas US data use both racial and ethnic classifications. The distinction between race and ethnicity is based on convention rather than theoretical or empirical data and cannot be justified except through the historical development of categories.

US official data

Racial classifications were crucial for administering the system of slavery and, subsequently, racial segregation, including the prohibition on interracial marriage. Historically, the legal distinction between the free and the slave, and then between subjugated Black and subordinating White, distinguished unambiguously between Black and White, preserving privileged White access to property, education, employment, housing, and other resources. The illegality of intermarriage coexisted with sexual unions (often exploitative of the enslaved) producing a substantial mixed population, while White privilege created a strong incentive for light-skinned people of mixed origins to pass as White. First documented in the 1850 census, people with Black and White parents were formally treated as Black according to the "one drop rule," whereby membership of the White race was limited to those without any Black ancestors. The Black–White line was thus preserved in law, in race theory, and in popular culture, but not in the genealogical legacies of the population (Perlmann and Waters 2002: 5).

The system of racial classification operating for Native Americans and Hispanic Americans relies on another logic, since this group was not subject to institutionalized slavery. Tribal membership was defined for official purposes by the proportion of an individual's ancestors who were tribal members (with the proportion required for membership differing between tribes), plus recognition of that individual as a member of the tribe by other tribe members. The rules for Hispanic Americans, descended from very mixed populations in Latin America, differed again and have been constituted as a separate category through the use of a Spanish language question in the US census (Perlmann and Waters 2002: 6).

Racial classification of Black, White, Native, and Hispanic Americans has played a key role in defining the structural and symbolic aspects of the American population. The role that ethnicity has played is of interest because of the way that it has reinforced White advantage. Ethnicity is similar to race in that it is often assigned involuntarily through heredity, although for White minorities its expression is voluntaristic. Thus, for this group there may be a considerable degree of choice both in the ethnic group with which one aligns oneself and how this allegiance is manifest: Italian ancestry, for instance, is popular and regularly claimed, whereas Scottish ancestry is not (Waters 1990: 34). The consumption of special foods and the celebration of particular holidays offer White Americans an ethnic identity and mark belonging to a community, but a highly individualized personal choice over the adoption of these practices is retained (Waters 1990: 151). Ethnicity generally operates as both a resource and a liability (Jenkins 1995), yet for White minorities little effort is put into sustaining group cohesion and if sexist, racist, clannish, and narrow-minded aspects related to ethnicity are encountered, the voluntary nature of participation means that they can abandon their liability. This is the crucial difference between race and ethnicity: for suburban Whites, ethnicity lacks social costs, provides enjoyment, and is chosen voluntarily, none of which is true for non-White Americans (Waters 1990).

Racial minorities cannot exercise choice in the same way as "ethnics" (Waters 1990: 158), particularly White ethnics. If one's ethnicity is a voluntaristic, personal matter it can be difficult to see that other groups are subject to political, societal forces that are not a matter of individual choice. White European immigrants (certain exclusions for Italians and Irish notwithstanding) have never faced the systematic legal and official discrimination experienced by Blacks, Hispanics, and Asians in America (Waters 1990: 164). Ethnic identification for White Americans is so voluntaristic and so unaccompanied by discrimination or prejudice that in due course White groups may no longer exist: As the time since migration extends, and assuming high rates of intermarriage persist, there will no longer be White enclaves where the individuals have a distinct cultural or genetic profile. Paradoxically, Americans who emphasize, for instance, their Italian or Irish ethnicity continue to think of both ethnicity and race as biologically rooted and persistently ascribe identities to others, especially those based on skin color. White minorities can enjoy the voluntary aspects of ethnic traditions, but because ethnic and racialized divisions are thought of as equivalent, the rise of White suburban ethnic identification has had an exacerbating effect on racial tensions (Waters 1990: 167).

UK official data

Until the 1991 census, country of birth was typically used in UK official statistics to identify ethnicity or race, with the clear implication that racial and ethnic minorities were "foreign," despite the majority also being British citizens. As post-World War II migration became more distant, the inadequacies of this approach for identifying growing numbers of UK-born minorities became increasingly obvious, and a question about ethnic identity was introduced in the 1991 census. The question was updated for the 2001 census (and will be updated again for the 2011 census), with respondents asked to select a category that best describes their ethnic identity from a list. The question varied very slightly across the countries of the UK, with the following categories used in England and Wales:

- **White** – British or Irish or Any Other White background (write in)
- **Mixed** – White and Black Caribbean or White and Black African or White and Asian or Any Other Mixed background (write in)
- **Asian** or **Asian British** – Indian or Pakistani or Bangladeshi or Any Other Asian background (write in)
- **Black** or **Black British** – Caribbean or African or Any Other Black background (write in)
- **Chinese** or **other ethnic group** – Chinese or Any Other (write in)

Respondents were expected to select a single main category that applied to them (the first descriptor for each bullet point, shown in bold above), and then to choose a subcategory from the options that follow. This official categorization of a diverse population has no historical legal definition on which to draw and compounds a number of aspects of ethnicity pertinent to UK race relations, including nationality, country of birth, geographical origin, and skin color. Notable here is how the "Mixed" and "White Irish" categories emerged between the 1991 and 2001 censuses in response to both popular and policy concerns. Inevitably, this form of classification contains compromises, for example all individuals from sub-Saharan Africa are covered by a single category, as are all those claiming an Indian identity. Such compromises also reflect the ways in which ethnicity is conceptualized and the dimensions of an ethnic identity that *are* perceived to be of policy importance. For example, a question on religious identity was included in the 2001 England and Wales census for the first time, as religion became increasingly significant on the public policy agenda.

The lack of institutionalized racial categories in the UK means that classifications inevitably reflect powerfully felt racialized folk typologies that both constrain and inform people's identities. Conceiving a classification that usefully captures the experience of identity without promoting the essentializing of difference has proved difficult. Recent critiques of the homogenizing assumptions of pan-ethnic classifications (for example, Zsembik and Fennel 2005) suggest that lessons from previous work have not been learned.

In the next section we describe, in general terms, the patterning of ethnic/racial disparities in health and point to the implications of crude quantitative classificatory schemes for explanatory models. Arguably, the use of broad classifications as proxies for ethnic or cultural group has hindered the development of sophisticated explanatory models for inequalities in health and allowed the persistence of crude stereotyped explanations (Nazroo and Williams 2005: 239).

INEQUALITIES IN HEALTH IN THE US AND UK

Differences in health across ethnic groups, in terms of both morbidity (the presence of illness and disease) and mortality, have been repeatedly documented in the UK (Erens, Primatesta, and Prior 2001; Harding and Maxwell 1997; Marmot et al. 1984) and the US (Davey Smith et al. 1998; Sorlie, Backlund, and Keller 1995; Sorlie et al. 1992; Williams 2001). Health is, of course, a multidimensional and complex concept (Blaxter 1990), yet in statistics it is often reduced to death and/or specific disease categories (such as coronary heart disease, hypertension, or diabetes). In the UK, mortality data are not available by ethnic group, but country of birth is recorded on death certificates and mortality rates have been published by country of birth using data around the 1971, 1981, and 1991 censuses and, to a more limited extent, the 2001 census. Given the relatively recent mass migration to the UK, analyses of mortality by country of birth are typically taken to indicate *ethnic* inequalities in health. Analyses around the 1991 census showed marked variation in mortality rates by country of birth and gender (Harding and Maxwell 1997):

- Men born in the Caribbean had low mortality rates overall, and particularly low mortality rates for coronary heart disease, but high rates of mortality from stroke, as did women born in the Caribbean.
- This high mortality rate from stroke and low mortality rate from coronary heart disease was also found among those born in West/South Africa, who also had a high overall mortality rate.
- Men and women born in the Indian subcontinent and East Africa (presumed to be South Asian migrants) had high rates of death from coronary heart disease, with the highest rates found among those born in Bangladesh.
- Those born in the Indian subcontinent also had high mortality rates from stroke.
- Those born in Ireland had high mortality rates for most diseases.
- On the whole, the non-White migrant groups had lower mortality rates from respiratory disease and lung cancer.
- There were very high death rates among non-White migrants for conditions relating to diabetes.

Despite being statistically robust, these findings, based as they are on country of birth, cannot be extrapolated unproblematically to ethnic categories. The most obvious problem is that the experience of UK-born ethnic minority people, which is likely to differ from migrants, is ignored.

Although the UK does not record mortality data by ethnicity, there has been a growth in data on ethnic differences in morbidity over the last two decades. While these contradict the immigrant mortality data in some respects (Nazroo 2001), the patterns are basically similar. For example, findings from the 1999 Health Survey for England (Erens et al. 2001) on ethnic differences in self-reported general health showed considerable heterogeneity in experience, with the non-White groups having a variably increased risk of poor health compared with the White groups. Most notable, perhaps, was the wide variation for the three South Asian groups identified, with Indians having better health than Pakistanis, who had better health than Bangladeshis.

In the US, there is a similar heterogeneity of outcomes across racial groups (Nazroo and Williams 2005; Sorlie et al. 1995). Mortality rates for non-Hispanic Black people are more than twice as high as those for non-Hispanic White people until early old age, when the gap begins to narrow. A similar pattern is found for Native Americans, though differences are smaller at younger ages, and the improvement relative to non-Hispanic White people at older ages is clearer. Mortality rates for Hispanic people are generally lower than those of non-Hispanic Whites, though the differences are small at younger ages. Rates for Asian/Pacific Islanders are uniformly lower than those for non-Hispanic Whites.

The favorable position of Hispanic people, given their relatively poor socio-economic position, has generated considerable research interest. It has been suggested that these findings reflect: a "protective" Hispanic culture; health selection, whereby only the healthiest migrate to the US; and/or poor data quality, with undercoverage of denominators and inaccuracies in the reporting of numerators (see Nazroo and Williams 2005 for a review). Indeed, there are important limitations linked to the quality of these mortality data for all groups. The numerator for the officially reported death rates in the United States comes from death certificates, and it is estimated that officials who record racial and ethnic status on the death certificate misclassify as many as 26 percent of self-identified American Indians, 18 percent of Asians and Pacific Islanders, and 10 percent of Hispanics, with misclassifications largely allocated to White/non-Hispanic categories (Sorlie et al. 1992). This undercount in the numerator suppresses the death rates for the minority groups and slightly inflates the death rates for non-Hispanic Whites.

In both the US and the UK, problems with the denominator can also affect the quality of mortality statistics. Census data are used to calculate the denominators for mortality rates and a denominator that has an undercount inflates the obtained rate in exact proportion to the undercount. Although the overall undercount for the US and UK populations is relatively small, it is much higher for non-Whites. For example, in the US, an evaluation based on demographic analysis suggests that there is a net census undercount of 11–13 percent for Black males between the ages of 25 and 64 (National Center for Health Statistics 1994). Thus, all of the officially reported morbidity and mortality rates for African American males in these age groups are potentially 11–13 percent too high.

The heterogeneity found in mortality and morbidity rates parallels the heterogeneity in migration, settlement, and socioeconomic experiences. There is a need to reflect the diversity of experience in data collection, making efforts to contact an appropriate range of people, while remaining aware of, and sensitive to, potential ethnic differences within groups since we cannot assume that all Pacific Islanders, or all Hispanics, or all South Asians are equivalent.

EXPLAINING ETHNIC/RACIAL INEQUALITIES IN HEALTH

How can we make sense of the data showing differences in health across these broad race/ethnic groups? There is a strong temptation to read meaning directly into the categories the statistical data provide. Just as we might say that Pakistani men have high rates of unemployment, or Black American families are more likely to be headed by a single parent, so we might say that Bangladeshi people have poor health. It is then straightforward to go from this simple assertion to seeking an explanation for poor health in the nature of what it is to be (in this example) Bangladeshi. The impulse to resort to explanation based on an understanding of a reified category, stripped of contextual meaning and stereotyped, is strong. Just as we might seek explanations for higher rates of single parenthood in Black cultures, we can seek explanations for high rates of illness or disease in the cultures of the ethnic categories associated with these higher rates. Culture and genetics become all the more compelling as an explanatory variable for minority group difference when we see a diversity of outcomes across ethnic groups or across disease categories. So, if Pakistani people have high rates of heart disease, but Caribbean people do not, how can this be explained on the basis of an ethnic socioeconomic disadvantage? And if the low rates of respiratory illness and lung cancer among Pakistani people can be explained as a consequence of low rates of smoking, cannot "their" high rates of cardiovascular disease be similarly explained as a consequence of cultural traits?

If we are to develop adequate explanatory models for ethnic differences in health, we have to consider how the categories we use reflect heterogeneous social identities and how they relate to wider social and economic inequalities. In the UK, there has been a long tradition of investigating inequalities in health associated with factors such as class, residential area (for example, see the collection in Gordon et al. 1999), and gender (Annandale and Hunt 1999), producing strong evidence that these health disparities are a consequence of socioeconomic inequalities (Marmot and Wilkinson 2005). In the main, this work has not informed investigations of ethnic inequalities in health. This disjunction in the conceptual development of explanations of health inequalities is perhaps due to the impact of Marmot and colleagues' (1984) study of immigrant mortality rates. Published shortly after the Black Report had put socioeconomic inequalities in health on the research agenda (Townsend and Davidson 1982), this study used the combination of British census and death certificate data to explore the relationship between country of birth and mortality rates (Marmot et al. 1984). A central finding was that there was no relationship between occupational class and mortality for immigrant groups, even though there was a clear relationship for those born in the UK. It was concluded that differences in socioeconomic position could not explain the higher mortality rates found in some migrant groups in the UK (Marmot et al. 1984).

From 1984, it took more than a decade for socioeconomic position to reappear in published UK data exploring the relationship between ethnicity and health. Conclusions drawn from analysis of immigrant mortality data did not appear to support a socioeconomic explanation for the different rates of mortality across immigrant and non-immigrant groups (Harding and Maxwell 1997). However, work on morbidity suggested that socioeconomic factors made a major contribution to ethnic differences in health (Nazroo 1997). Some continued to claim that socioeconomic inequalities make a minimal, or nonexistent, contribution to ethnic inequalities in health (Wild and McKeigue 1997). Such denials of the relevance of socioeconomic inequalities to ethnic inequalities in health can be interrogated first by considering the limitations of quantitative empirical models. The sociological significance of ethnicity, ethnic relations, and ethnic identity cannot be captured in ethnic classifications. The role played by local and historical context, generation and period since migration, and so forth, is difficult to encapsulate in the proxies used, and is easily ignored when using crudely quantified categories that result in ethnicity being operationalized in fixed and reified terms. Furthermore, there is a lamentable lack of good, or often any, data on economic position in health studies, let alone data that can deal with other elements of social disadvantage faced by ethnic minority groups, such as inequalities related to geography and experiences of racial discrimination and harassment.

Despite the limitations of the data, there is an emerging consensus that a socioeconomic patterning of health is present within ethnic groups in developed countries. Analysis of the US Multiple Risk Factor Intervention Trial (MRFIT) data showed that all causes of mortality rates over its 16-year follow-up period had a very clear relationship to median income in the area of residence of respondents for both Black and White men. Mortality rates increased with decreasing income, resulting in a twofold difference in mortality rates between those in the top ($27,500 or higher) and those in the bottom (less than $10,000) annual income bands for both Black and White men (Davey Smith et al. 1998). Similarly, in data from England, rates of reporting fair or bad general health by household income show a clear relationship between reported general health and income for each of several ethnic groups included (Nazroo 2003). These analyses point to heterogeneity within broad ethnic groupings in health: for example, Black Americans in better socioeconomic positions have better health. There is nothing inevitable, or inherent, in the link between being Black American or being British Bangladeshi and a greater risk of mortality and morbidity. There is an urgent need to move beyond explanations that appeal to, and further cement, assumptions of essentialized and fixed ethnic or race effects.

If socioeconomic position is related to health within groups, it seems probable that inequalities in socioeconomic position across ethnic groups might be related to ethnic inequalities in health. Here the interpretation of data becomes more contentious. In most analyses, once adjustments for socioeconomic position have been made, there is a clear and often large reduction in risk for ethnic/racial minority groups. For example, analysis of the US MRFIT data showed that standardizing for mean household income in area of residence greatly reduced the relative risk for all causes of mortality of Black compared with White men – it dropped from 1.47 to 1.19, thereby statistically explaining about two thirds of the elevated mortality risk among Black men with this income measure (Davey Smith et al. 1998). Nevertheless, in such analyses, for most groups and for most health outcomes, differences remain once the adjustment for the socioeconomic indicator has been made. Here again, it is important to recognize the limitations of such quantitative models. The process of standardizing for socioeconomic position when making comparisons across groups assumes that all necessary factors are accounted for by the measures available (Kaufman, Cooper, and McGee 1997; Kaufman et al. 1998). Evidence from the UK indicates this assumption may be fallacious. An analysis of ethnic differences in income within class groups showed that, within each class group, ethnic minority people had a smaller income than White people (Nazroo 2001). Indeed, for the poorest group – Pakistani and Bangladeshi people – differences were twofold and equivalent in size to the difference between the richest and poorest class groups in the White population. Similar findings have been reported in the US. For example, within occupational groups, White people have higher incomes than Black people; once below the poverty line, Black people are more likely to remain in this situation than White people, and, within income strata, Black people have considerably lower wealth levels than White people and are less likely to be home owners (Oliver and Shapiro 1995). The implication of this is clear: Using either single or crude indicators of socioeconomic position does not "control out" the impact of socioeconomic position. Within any given level of a particular socioeconomic measure, the circumstances of minority people are less favorable than those of White people. Nevertheless, research typically presents data that are "standardized" for socioeconomic position, allowing both the author and reader to mistakenly assume that all that is left is an ethnic/race effect, often attributed to "cultural" or "genetic" difference.

In addition, these kinds of analyses reflect current socioeconomic position only, since data assessing the effect of the life course and other forms of social disadvantage are not included. In fact, in the US, research on the links between health and experiences of racism and discrimination (crucial as a form of social disadvantage) has shown a relationship between self-reported experiences of racial harassment and a greater likelihood of reporting various measures of ill health, including hypertension, psychological distress, poorer self rated health, and days spent unwell in bed (Krieger 2000; Krieger and Sidney 1996; Williams, Neighbors, and Jackson 2003). In the UK, analyses have shown a relationship between reports of experiences of racial harassment, perceptions of racial discrimination, and being fearful of racism and a range of physical and mental health outcomes across ethnic groups (Karlsen and Nazroo 2002a, 2002b, 2004; Karlsen et al. 2005).

EXPERIENCE AND USE OF HEALTH SERVICES

The quality of experience when using health services is a matter of social justice, regardless of resultant health outcomes. In addition to offering an equitable service, health professionals should play a role in ameliorating existing inequalities, whereas in practice, existing ethnic/racial inequalities in health may be aggravated by inequity in access to good quality services. In the US, ethnic/racial inequalities in access to and quality of health care have been repeatedly documented, with inequalities that are consistent across a range of outcomes and types of providers. An Institute of Medicine (IOM) study, requested by Congress, identified ethnic/racial differences in health care insurance status as a key determinant of these inequalities (Smedley, Stith, and Nelson 2003). However, the primary focus of the IOM study was on non-access-related factors and the authors noted that while inequalities diminish significantly when insurance status and socioeconomic factors are controlled, some typically remain. Suggested explanations for the remaining inequalities included:

characteristics of institutions (such as language barriers and time pressures on physicians); behaviors of practitioners (such as prejudice against or uncertainty with ethnic/racial minorities); and behaviors of patients (such as non-compliance and delay in seeking care) (Smedley et al. 2003).

The IOM report also noted that the studies of ethnic/racial inequalities in health care that controlled for insurance status had only done so at a crude level, without accounting for the ethnic/racial differences in the extent of coverage provided (Smedley et al. 2003). Thus, minorities are likely to have less comprehensive coverage than White Americans and, consequently, to have a more limited choice of providers, health care settings, and types of services. This confirms the point that ethnic inequalities in health are driven by socioeconomic inequalities. One way of testing whether differences in health care insurance coverage explain inequalities in health care is to examine the extent of ethnic/racial inequalities in health care systems with more comprehensive access. Studies of health care provided by the US military do support the possibility that universal access to health care eliminates the inequalities found in other systems (Smedley et al. 2003).

The publicly funded British National Health Service (NHS) provides (almost) free and universal access to health care, so one might expect ethnic inequalities in access to quality health care to be minimal, or at least smaller than those in the US. However, the benefits of universal access may be offset by the existence of widespread institutional racism in UK public services. Insofar as there is evidence from the UK, it supports the possibility that inequalities in access to health care are not present, but there are inequalities in the quality of care received, supportive of an institutional racism hypothesis. So, UK studies have shown that ethnic minority people on the whole make greater use of primary health care services than White people (with Chinese people being the exception) (Erens et al. 2001), even when adjustments are made for self-reported morbidity (Nazroo 1997). However, this does not appear to be reflected in greater use of secondary care services (Nazroo 1997), and there are suggestions that the quality of service received by ethnic minorities is poorer. For example, in primary care, ethnic minorities are more likely to be dissatisfied with various aspects of the care received, to wait longer for an appointment, and to face language barriers during the consultation (Nazroo 1997).

The evidence from the UK does, then, support the possibility of institutional racism, indicating that regardless of individual professionals' intentions, health services have discriminatory effects. The concept of institutional racism remains contested, not least by medical professionals, and the mechanisms through which organizational processes discriminate are difficult to describe and therefore to reform. Health services operate in the context of broader social and economic processes and understanding institutional racism is a crucial element of tackling persistent inequalities at a time when overt racism in public services is proscribed and relatively rare.

These issues have perhaps been most intensively debated in the mental health field, where symptomatic expression is core to diagnostic processes and where there is a large literature querying the cross-cultural validity of psychiatric diagnostic practices. The concern is that members of different ethnic groups will have different symptomatic experiences when mentally ill, because of cultural differences in the idioms used to express mental distress. For example, it has been suggested that South

Asian people in the UK may experience particular "culture-bound" syndromes: that is, a cluster of symptoms that is restricted to a particular culture, such as *sinking heart* (Krause 1989), which consequently may not be identified as mentally ill by standard diagnostic practices and research instruments. Kleinman (1987) argues that the different idioms for expressing mental distress in different cultures allows for a "category fallacy," where the use of a category of illness that was developed in one cultural group fails to identify ill people in another cultural group, because it lacks coherence in that culture. While the Western category of depression is treated as if it were universal, the idioms of mental distress in a non-Western group may be sufficiently different for Western diagnostic practices to fail. Indeed, it has been argued that Western depression amounts to a culturally specific diagnosis (Jadhav 1996).

Small-scale empirical work with British Pakistanis has identified an expression of mental distress described as "thinking too much in my heart" (Fenton and Sadiq-Sangster 1996). While this was found to correlate strongly with the expression of most of the standard Western symptoms of depression, some of these standard symptoms were not present (those relating to a loss of meaning in life and self-worth), suggesting that the form that the disease took was different. Fenton and Sadiq-Sangster point out that "thinking too much in my heart" was not only a symptom but the core experience of the illness, raising the possibility that there were more fundamental differences between this illness and depression. Nazroo and O'Connor (2002) found similar differences, but also important commonalities, indicating that cultural differences may not lie in broader constructs of mental illness but in the detail of the idioms used to express distress. Qualitative analysis of accounts of mental distress demonstrates that people of Pakistani origin living in the UK show considerable fluency across different symbolic domains and refutes the suggestion that culture-bound metaphors or similes might determine patterns of help-seeking and health care use (Mallinson and Popay 2007).

Ethnic minority cultural practices and religious beliefs can prompt particular health behaviors but, as with the ethnic majority, minorities' non-medical practices tend to be used alongside medical advice which is attributed considerable respect (Bradby 1997). In considering the effect of culture on health service use by ethnic minorities, the culture of the health service providers and the organizational culture should be considered. A major barrier to getting access to good quality health care is the lack of common language between patient and staff. Greenhalgh, Voisey, and Robb (2007) show how organizational features of a sample of general practices in London influenced whether interpretation services were available.

MIGRANT AND MINORITY STAFF IN THE HEALTH SERVICES

In both the US and the UK, migrants have filled crucial labor shortages, thereby maintaining health services. For those migrants who are also from a minority, the experience of discrimination is routine and this is true of low-paid staff doing cleaning or catering work as well as skilled medical migrants. From the US, there is evidence that White patients treated by White doctors are less likely to report medical errors than White patients treated by non-White doctors. In a nationally representative data set, the likelihood of reporting medical error does not vary among non-White patients according to their ethnic or racial concordance with the physician (Stepanikova 2006: 3065). The systematically lower status of non-White doctors compared with White doctors is the explanation offered for White patients' greater preparedness to report medical error. This echoes the suggestion that the class position of the skilled migrant doctors who have maintained the NHS in the UK has been mediated by discrimination, leaving them in a "pariah" position compared with other doctors (Kyriakides and Virdee 2003: 296).

Wealthy nations continue to attract qualified, skilled medical practitioners from poorer countries, who can ill afford to lose them. The ethics of global medical migration are fraught, involving as they do issues around the freedom of movement, equal opportunities to employment, and the regulation of health care markets, but the injustice of wealthy populations profiting from the education provided by poor populations is inescapable.

CONCLUSION

The conditions leading to health and to illness, the experience of illness, and the seeking of health care are all, in a sociological analysis, best understood as a dimension and a product of social relations. The ways in which ethnicity and racism play out in the social relations of health, illness, and health care are both complex and, at times, subtle. As an identity which is both self-ascribed and imposed by others, ethnicity or race comes into play differentially according to actors' own choices, and is dependent on the context in which those choices are exercised. Individual identities reflect structural dimensions of society, with individuals' range of choices being differentially constrained. Both structural and identity aspects of ethnicity and race develop over time, so being a Muslim or Polish carry different meanings now compared with 50 years ago, in the US as well as the UK. Slavery is identified as being an important context for understanding racial categories in the US and the resonance of empire is highly relevant to ethnicity in the UK.

The terminology of quantitative analysis can give the misleading impression that the effects of race or ethnicity on health can be controlled for. Understanding social relations to be racialized implies that structure and identity are inflected by race and there is no means of stepping outside or beyond this process: There is no "un-raced" body, just as there is no body free of gender. The demonstrably false assumption that socioeconomic status can be controlled for in statistical models has led to interpretations that attribute health disparities to the racial or ethnic character of the minority population. *Culture*, particularly in the UK context, has become a euphemism for "problematic difference," which in its usage is difficult to distinguish from biologically determined race talk. Thus, the health deficits of minority ethnic or racial groups have all too frequently been understood as the direct effect of the content of the minority culture, and the effects of racism, poverty, and other exclusions are lost from view.

Despite its abuse, culture needs to be retained as an analytic term, given its immense importance for identity, but, as has been noted, it needs to be adequately complicated (Bradby 2003; Hillier and Kelleher 1996). Culture should be understood as a property of organizations, as well as of individuals, if the effects of institutional racism are to be mapped, and the interactions of minority and majority practices must be given equal consideration in an effort to understand culture through the life course.

References

Annandale, Ellen and Kate Hunt (eds.). 1999. *Gender Inequalities in Health*. Buckingham: Open University Press.

Blaxter, Mildred. 1990. *Health and Lifestyles*. London: Tavistock/Routledge.

Bradby, Hannah. 1997. "Health, Heating and Heart Attacks: Glaswegian Punjabi Women's Thinking About Everyday Food." Pp. 211–33 in P. Caplan (ed.), *Food Health and Identity*. London: Routledge.

Bradby, Hannah. 2003. "Describing Ethnicity in Health Research." *Ethnicity and Health* 8(1): 5–13.

Davey Smith, George, James D. Neaton, Deborah Wentworth, Rose Stamler, and Jeremiah Stamler. 1998. "Mortality Differences Between Black and White Men in the USA: Contribution of Income and Other Risk Factors Among Men Screened for the MRFIT." *Lancet* 351: 934–9.

Donovan, Jenny. 1986. *We Don't Buy Sickness, It Just Comes: Health, Illness and Health Care in the Lives of Black People in England*. Aldershot: Gower.

Erens, Bob, Paola Primatesta, and Gillian Prior. 2001. *Health Survey for England 1999: The Health of Minority Ethnic Groups*. London: The Stationery Office.

Fenton, Steve and Azra Sadiq Sangster. 1996. "Culture, Relativism and the Expression of Mental Distress: South Asian Women in Britain." *Sociology of Health and Illness* 2: 66–85.

Gordon, David, Mary Shaw, Danny Dorling, and George Davey Smith (eds.). 1999. *Inequalities in Health: The Evidence Presented to the Independent Inquiry into Inequalities in Health, Chaired by Sir Donald Acheson*. Bristol: Policy Press.

Greenhalgh, Trisha, Christopher Voisey, and Nadia Robb. 2007. "Interpreted Consultations as 'Business as Usual'? An Analysis of Organisational Routines in General Practices." *Sociology of Health and Illness* 29(6): 931–54.

Harding, Seeromanie and Rory Maxwell. 1997. "Differences in the Mortality of Migrants." Pp. in F. Drever and M. Whitehead (eds.), *Health Inequalities: Decennial Supplement Series DS no. 15*. London: The Stationery Office.

Hillier, Sheila and David Kelleher. 1996. "Culture, Ethnicity and the Politics of Health." Pp. 1–10 in David Kelleher and Sheila Hillier (eds.), *Researching Cultural Differences in Health*. London: Routledge.

Jadhav, Shushrut. 1996. "The Cultural Origins of Western Depression." *International Journal of Social Psychiatry* 42(4): 269–86.

Jenkins, Richard. 1995. "Rethinking Ethnicity." *Ethnic and Racial Studies* 17(2): 197–224.

Karlsen, Saffron and James Y. Nazroo. 2002a. "Agency and Structure: The Impact of Ethnic Identity and Racism on the Health of Ethnic Minority People." *Sociology of Health and Illness* 24: 1–20.

Karlsen, Saffron and James Y. Nazroo. 2002b. "The Relationship Between Racial Discrimination, Social Class and Health Among Ethnic Minority Groups." *American Journal of Public Health* 92: 624–31.

Karlsen, Saffron and James Y. Nazroo. 2004. "Fear of Racism and Health." *Journal of Epidemiology and Community Health* 58: 1017–18.

Karlsen, Saffron, James Y. Nazroo, Kwame McKenzie, Kam Bhui, and Scott Weich. 2005. "Racism, Psychosis and Common Mental Disorder Among Ethnic Minority Groups in England." *Psychological Medicine* 35(12): 1795–1803.

Kaufman, Joy S., R. S. Cooper, and D. L. McGee. 1997. "Socioeconomic Status and Health in Blacks and Whites: The Problem of Residual Confounding and the Resiliency of Race." *Epidemiology* 8(6): 621–8.

Kaufman, Joy S., A. E. Long, Y. Liao, R. S. Cooper, and D. L. McGee. 1998. "The Relation Between Income and Mortality in US Blacks and Whites." *Epidemiology* 9(2): 147–55.

Kleinman, Arthur. 1987. "Anthropology and Psychiatry: The Role of Culture in Cross-Cultural Research on Illness." *British Journal of Psychiatry* 151: 447–54.

Krause, Inga-Britt. 1989. "Sinking Heart: A Punjabi Communication of Distress." *Social Science and Medicine* 29(4): 563–75.

Krieger, Nancy. 2000. "Discrimination and Health." Pp. 36–75 in Lisa F. Berkman and Kawachi Ichiro (eds.), *Social Epidemiology*. Oxford: Oxford University Press.

Krieger, Nancy and Stephen Sidney. 1996. "Racial Discrimination and Blood Pressure: The CARDIA Study of Young Black and White Adults." *American Journal of Public Health* 86(10): 1370–8.

Kyriakides, Christopher and Satnam Virdee. 2003. "Migrant Labour, Racism and the British National Health Service." *Ethnicity and Health* 8(4): 283–305.

Mallinson, Sara and Jennie Popay. 2007. "Describing Depression: Ethnicity and the Use of Somatic Imagery in Accounts of Mental Distress." *Sociology of Health and Illness* 29(6): 857–71.

Marmot, Michael G., Abraham M. Adelstein, L. Bulusu, and OPCS. 1984. *Immigrant Mortality in England and Wales 1970–78: Causes of Death by Country of Birth*. London: HMSO.

Marmot, Michael and Richard G. Wilkinson (eds.). 2005. *Social Determinants of Health*, 2nd edition. Oxford: Oxford University Press.

Massey, Douglas S. and Nancy A. Denton 1993. *American Apartheid: Segregation and the Making of the Underclass*. Cambridge, MA: Harvard University Press.

McCulloch, Andrew. 2007. "The Changing Structure of Ethnic Diversity and Segregation in England, 1991–2001." *Environment and Planning* 39(4): 909–27.

National Center for Health Statistics (NCHS). 1994. *Vital Statistics of the United States, 1990. Vol. 2: Mortality, Part A*. Washington, DC: Public Health Service.

Nazroo, James Y. 1997. *The Health of Britain's Ethnic Minorities: Findings From a National Survey*. London: Policy Studies Institute.

Nazroo, James Y. 2001. *Ethnicity, Class and Health*. London: Policy Studies Institute.

Nazroo, James Y. 2003. "The Structuring of Ethnic Inequalities in Health: Economic Position, Racial Discrimination and Racism." *American Journal of Public Health* 93(2): 277–84.

Nazroo, James Y. and William O'Connor. 2002. "Idioms of Mental Distress." Pp. 29–39 in W. O. Connor and J. Nazroo (eds.), *Ethnic Differences in the Context and Experience of Psychiatric Illness: A Qualitative Study*. London: The Stationery Office.

Nazroo, James Y. and David R. Williams. 2005. "The Social Determination of Ethnic/Racial Inequalities in Health." Pp. 238–66 in M. Marmot and R. G. Wilkinson (eds.), *Social Determinants of Health*, 2nd edition. Oxford: Oxford University Press.

Oliver, Melvin L. and Thomas M. Shapiro. 1995. *Black Wealth/White Wealth: A New Perspective on Racial Inequality*. New York: Routledge.

Perlmann, Joel and Mary C. Waters. 2002. "Introduction." Pp. 1–30 in J. Perlmann and M. C. Waters (eds.), *The New Race Question: How the Census Counts Multiracial Individuals*. New York: Russell Sage Foundation.

Smedley, Brian D., Adrienne Y. Stith, and Alan R. Nelson (eds.). 2003. *Unequal Treatment: Confronting Racial and Ethnic Disparities in Health Care*. Washington: Institute of Medicine of the National Academies.

Sorlie, Paul D., Eric Backlund, and J. Keller. 1995. "US Mortality by Economic, Demographic and Social Characteristics: The National Longitudinal Mortality Study." *American Journal of Public Health* 85: 949–56.

Sorlie, Paul, Eugene Rogot, Roger Anderson, Norman J. Johnson, and Eric Backlund. 1992. "Black–White Mortality Differences by Family Income." *Lancet* 340: 346–50.

Stepanikova, Irena. 2006. "Patient–Physician Racial and Ethnic Concordance and Perceived Medical Errors." *Social Science and Medicine* 63: 3060–6.

Townsend, Peter and Nick Davidson. 1982. *Inequalities in Health: The Black Report*. London: Penguin.

Waters, Mary C. 1990. *Ethnic Options: Choosing Identities in America*. Berkeley: University of California Press.

Wild, Sarah and Paul McKeigue. 1997. "Cross-Sectional Analysis of Mortality by Country of Birth in England and Wales." *British Medical Journal* 314: 705–10.

Williams, David R. 2001. "Racial Variations in Adult Health Status: Patterns, Paradoxes and Prospects." Pp. 371–410 in N. J. Smelser, W. J. Wilson, and F. Mitchell (eds.), *America Becoming: Racial Trends and Their Consequences*. Washington, DC: National Academy Press.

Williams, David R., Harold W. Neighbors, and James S. Jackson. 2003. "Racial/Ethnic Discrimination and Health: Findings From Community Studies." *American Journal of Public Health* 93(2): 200–8.

Zsembik, Barbara A. and Dana Fennel. 2005. "Ethnic Variation in Health and the Determinants of Health Among Latinos." *Social Science and Medicine* 61: 53–63.

Part III

Health and Social Relationships

7

Health and Religion

ELLEN L. IDLER

The relationship between religion and health may be thought of in two distinct ways that are of equal interest to medical sociology. Religion or, more properly, religions make up an array of social institutions found in all human societies; these institutions may have simple or complex social structures, but all have elaborated belief systems and symbols, rituals, or practices that evoke a connection with a state that transcends daily life. Similarly, medicine may properly be thought of in the plural sense; it takes on some institutionalized form in every society in response to the universal human problem of illness, and it similarly carries the weight of an institution that addresses ultimate issues of life and death. The first of the two distinct forms of the relationship of these two major institutions is the sense in which religion is a factor in the social environment that to some extent determines the health of populations. We might refer to this as religion's role in social epidemiology and public health. The second is religion's role in the practice and organization of medicine; in the lives of patients, their families and social networks, health professionals, and the institutions in which they interact.

In this chapter we will examine: (1) the deep roots of this area of research in the origins of the discipline of sociology itself; (2) an overview of research in the area of the sociology of religion and health with particular attention to the dominant conceptualizations and study designs; (3) the evidence for a number of mediating pathways linking religion to health; (4) the social forces of support, control, and selection; (5) evidence for cumulative effects of religion on health over the life course; (6) religious practices and coping among ill and vulnerable populations; (7) the potential for harm in this relationship; (8) controversies over the research; (9) religion's role in social innovations for providing care; (10) a view of the international research in the area; and (11) some emerging areas of research that seem especially interesting. The emphasis in each of the following sections is placed on seminal articles in the field, published reviews of the empirical evidence, and significant recent studies.

DEEP ROOTS OF HEALTH AND RELIGION RESEARCH IN THE ORIGINS OF THE DISCIPLINE

Health and religion research begins at the very beginning of the history of the social sciences, in both theory and empirical research. In 1897, Emile Durkheim, son of a French rabbi, showed that the putatively isolated and individualistic act of suicide was, in fact, not random but could be systematically linked to specific characteristics of societies. His analysis of vital statistics for nations and regions in Western Europe demonstrated that mortality from suicide varied dramatically and predictably with certain social characteristics, among them the predominance of one religion or another. His well-known finding that suicide rates were lower in areas with predominantly Catholic and Jewish populations compared with largely Protestant areas led Durkheim to characterize types of suicides (*anomic* and *egoistic*) that were on the rise in modern societies. The encouragement, in Protestantism, of free inquiry, and the loosening of the bonds of authority of the church, left individuals without a "sufficiently intense collective life" (Durkheim 1951 [1897]: 170) to protect them from the normlessness of modern society. Religion and other social institutions that regulated or constrained the behavior and desires of individual members, and that also provided them with integrative and socially supportive relationships, effectively protected their members from committing the desperate act of suicide.

A second, later work of Durkheim is also relevant to thinking about health, religion, and society. In *Elementary Forms of the Religious Life* (1965 [1915]), Durkheim elaborated the distinction between the sacred and the profane, a distinction that is identified and maintained by religions. This fundamental category of classification carries with it profound moral meaning that is applied to the ways in which members of a society and a religious tradition perceive such basic phenomena as time and space. Anthropologist Mary Douglas (1966) has related these concepts of the sacred and the profane to her observations of practices regarding beliefs about purity and danger; one important theme emerging from both Durkheim and Douglas is the essential function of these beliefs for the maintenance of the identity and boundaries of the social group, boundaries that may be drawn on the basis of religious beliefs and practices, and that are maintained by social control and sanctions. The ability of religious groups to constrain behavior in critical areas such as diet, sexuality, work and rest, the care of children and the elderly, and practices of burial or cremation of the dead carries public health consequences, intended or not.

In the United States at about the same time as Durkheim, the connection between religion and health was being made in a very different way by the Social Gospel movement, a group of progressive Protestant theologians and activists who were active in public health, labor reform, education, and the general improvement of the lives of the poor. Most often associated with the organization called the Brotherhood of the Kingdom, and the writings of Walter Rauschenbusch, a New York Baptist clergyman and professor of theology, the Social Gospel movement sought to bring a radical view of Christian ethics to problems caused by industrialization, chief among them poverty. In an 1897 paper in the *American Journal of Sociology*, Rauschenbusch writes: "In the measure in which the people are drained of their strength by excessive hours of labor, and by poor ventilation, insufficient noonday rest, etc., in that measure the churches are robbed of their workers. ... To men in Chicago, the heavens do not declare the glory of God because they are covered with smoke" (1897: 25, 29). Liberal Protestantism was also a strong influence among the early Chicago School sociologists; in his history of medical sociology, Bloom notes that Albion Small and W. I. Thomas were both sons of Congregational ministers, and that the late nineteenth century saw a "displacement of personnel from the clergy to the academy" (Bloom 2002: 66).

Within public health, in the early twentieth century, there were also strong moral impulses, even in the most scientifically advanced university medical schools. Note the implicit social activism in the words of Charles-Edward Avery Winslow, bacteriologist and professor at the University of Chicago, Massachusetts Institute of Technology, the League of Nations, and the founder of Yale's schools of public health and nursing:

> Public health is the science and the art of preventing disease, prolonging life, and promoting physical health and efficiency through: organized community efforts for the sanitation of the environment, the control of community infections, the education of the individual in principles and personal hygiene, the organization of medical and nursing services for early diagnosis and preventive treatment of disease, and the development of the social machinery which will ensure to every individual a standard of living adequate for the maintenance of health; organizing these benefits in such a fashion as to enable every citizen to realize his birthright of health and longevity (Winslow, 1920, Yale University Medical School, Department of Epidemiology and Public Health mural)

Winslow makes the connection between religion and public health quite directly in the entry for "Public Health" in the original *Encyclopaedia of the Social Sciences*, when he writes in his very first sentence: "The earliest examples of practices designed to promote the public health are to be found, among primitive peoples, inextricably mingled with the ritual of religion" (Winslow 1935). Winslow was known for his studies of the decline in infectious disease mortality. In his authoritative account of public health in the 1930s, he draws attention to early quarantine efforts in ancient Persia and among the Biblical Hebrews, not because they were intended as effective public health practices, but because they were motivated by religious beliefs, and only secondarily had an impact on public health. The burial of the dead, the separation of lepers from the community, or the ritualistic preparation of meat for consumption, are but a few of the examples of early practices carried out for religious reasons that had such unintended consequences.

With this brief sketch of religion, public health, and social movements of the early twentieth century, we see an intriguing prefiguring of the current paradigms for understanding the larger role of society in determining the health of populations. In one line of thought, Durkheim's positing of social integration as the primary force tying individuals to society, preventing alienation, and hence death by suicide, is carried on today in the tradition of research on social support and the importance of close social ties in preserving health. In a second view, the social gospel tradition has its present-day manifestation in research on the influential role of disadvantage and social inequality in health, both within and between societies. A third tradition of research emphasizes religious groups' beliefs, enacted social control, selection, and in-group, out-group mechanisms for maintaining health-relevant behaviors. In sum, although religion has been somewhat peripheral in medical sociology in understanding social forces in health, its early articulations raised issues that have remained central to debates to the present day.

MEASURING HEALTH, MEASURING RELIGION

Despite these promising late nineteenth-century beginnings, the consideration of religion was largely absent from social scientific work in health until the last decades of the twentieth century. Then, beginning in the 1970s, studies began to appear that showed substantially lower rates of all-cause mortality, as well as cardiovascular and cancer mortality, for highly observant sectarian groups, especially Seventh-Day Adventists, Mormons, and the Amish in the US, Norway, and the Netherlands, when compared with standard populations (reviewed in Jarvis and Northcott 1987). For example, Phillips and colleagues (1980), in a 17-year study of California Seventh-Day Adventists (SDA), found that deaths from all causes among SDA males were 34 percent lower, and deaths among SDA females were 12 percent lower than those of Californians as a whole. The authors concluded that "one or more components of the typical SDA lifestyle are protective for these diseases" (Phillips et al. 1980: 310). Recently, a 24-year follow-up study found a 55 percent lower standardized mortality ratio (SMR) for religiously active Mormon males, and a 45 percent lower SMR for females, compared to a nationally representative sample of respondents to the 1987 National Health Interview Study (Enstrom and Breslow 2008).

Research on differential rates of suicide by religious affiliation has continued to appear, with generally consistent support for Durkheim's original findings (Pescosolido and Georgianna 1989; Stack 2000). Group-level studies such as these form a distinctive body of research that derives directly from Durkheim's original methods but is ultimately bound by the same limitations. The first is the well-known ecological fallacy, that high rates for some phenomenon in a diverse society may not always reflect the (assumed) positive correlation between the phenomenon and the majority group. A second, more subtle limitation is that different rates between a religious group and the standard population simply capture the holistic "lifestyle" of the religious group; any separate, individual-level mediators of the association between religion and health cannot be identified, because individual-level data are not available. Third, and most importantly, selection into such highly observant, regulated, and disciplined religious groups can never be cleanly separated from causal processes that may take place during membership.

In 1979, however, the Alameda County Study appeared (Berkman and Syme 1979), which demonstrated a strong, dose-response association of social network ties (among them religious group affiliation) with all-cause mortality. Here the measurement was at the level of the individual rather than the group. Alameda County was quickly followed by similar findings from large longitudinal population studies in Tecumseh County, Michigan, and Evans County, Georgia. In each study, social ties (including ties to religious congregations) were associated with lower mortality risks (House, Landis, and Umberson 1988). In addition to their focus on individual-level measurement, these studies were important for creating a new view of the role of the social environment in health. Until this time, the social environment, long a member of the epidemiological agent–host–environment triad of disease causation, had primarily been thought of as having a negative impact on health. Social environments had until that time been conceptualized primarily as synonymous with stress, poverty, urban crowding, exploitative working conditions, or the time pressures of modern life. Durkheim's anomic Protestants with their higher rates of suicide, and the highly traditional, even anti-modern (in the case of the Amish) religious groups with their lower mortality rates, underscored this fundamentally threatening view of the role of modern society in health. What the social network studies opened for consideration was the possibility that the social environment might also provide positive or protective factors in health. In these initial studies, ties to religious congregations were simply one among many types of available social ties that individuals could call on to prevent social isolation and provide social support.

Since the initial social network studies, a substantial amount of research focusing specifically on religion as a mortality risk factor has appeared, most showing a moderately large and significant protective effect, even after adjustments for possible selection factors, confounders, and mediators. A number of extensive reviews have appeared, including those of Koenig, McCullough, and Larson (2001), Powell, Shahabi, and Thoresen (2003), and Hummer et al. (2004). A meta-analysis of studies of religious involvement and mortality conducted on 42 independent samples found an overall odds ratio of 1.29 (95 percent C.I. 1.20–1.39) for the association of lower levels of religious involvement with higher mortality from all causes (McCullough et al. 2000). One recent study, with a US national cohort of those aged 40 and older ($N = 8,450$) and a nine-year follow-up, found the hazard of all-cause mortality for those who attended religious services more than weekly was 30 percent lower than for those who never attended (Gillum et al. 2008).

Probability samples with an individual level of measurement represent general populations with their natural heterogeneity in religious behaviors and beliefs; the association at the individual level means that the religious involvement of any single individual is tied to his/her own risk of mortality. Like the social network studies, these mortality follow-up studies were by definition longitudinal, and they provide strong adjustment for the prior health status of respondents at the start of the study. Particularly when measurement of the religion variable is limited to the indicator of attendance at religious services, as it has been in many of the mortality studies, a well-designed health status assessment at baseline is critical; the selection bias of healthier members of the population being physically capable of attending religious services more frequently, while simultaneously being at lower risk of mortality, is an obvious risk to the validity of these studies. Additional important selectivity variables included in these analyses include age, sex, socioeconomic status, education, ethnicity, and marital status, as religious participation is generally higher for women, married couples, Blacks, older people, and those with higher education and income.

Despite the apparent consistency of the findings regarding religious attendance and mortality, it is frequently observed that methodological problems limit the fuller understanding of the underlying processes. A chief criticism is that most analyses usually contain only one indicator of religiousness, attendance at religious services, an unsatisfactorily crude level of measurement for a multidimensional and highly complex set of practices, beliefs, and institutions. In their review of the evidence, Powell et al. (2003: 36) find that when some measure of private religious feelings or practices is also studied, attendance is usually the measure with larger protective effects than the more subjective or "intrinsic" dimensions of religiousness and spirituality; they conclude that "In healthy participants, there is a strong, consistent, prospective, and often graded reduction in risk of mortality in church/service attenders," but on the other hand that "evidence fails to support a link between depth of religiousness and physical health." A number of reviews conclude that better measurement of the multiple dimensions of religiousness is clearly necessary before a larger understanding of explanatory mechanisms can be gained (Egbert, Mickley, and Coeling 2004; Hill and Pargament 2003; Idler et al. 2003). Some recent studies exploring multiple dimensions of religiousness and multiple dimensions of health show a complex cross-sectional picture of associations that may differ for males and females (Maselko and Kubzansky 2006; Ostbye et al. 2006). Ironically, more attention has been given to the development of new measures for subjective religious/spiritual states (intrinsic religiousness) and less attention has been given to understanding aspects of public religiousness involvement, particularly the experience of worship services (Idler et al. 2009).

MEDIATING PATHWAYS: RISK BEHAVIORS, SOCIAL SUPPORT NETWORKS, AND BIOLOGY

Religious group membership and participation channels human behaviors in numerous ways that are relevant to health. An early observation of this broad effect on ways of living was made by health economist Victor Fuchs (1974: 52–5) as he noted the striking differences in infant, child, adolescent, and adult mortality rates in the two adjacent states of Utah and Nevada. Many relevant characteristics – including population density, climate, health care, income, and education levels – were quite similar in the two states, and any advantage went to Nevada. And yet death rates in Nevada for males aged 40–9 were 54 percent higher, and for females 69 percent higher, than in Utah. Deaths due to cirrhosis of the liver and cancer of the respiratory system were 111 percent and 296 percent higher. Fuchs attributes the dramatic differences to the "different life-styles" of the residents of the two states; Utah's population is 70 percent abstinent, non-smoking Mormons who "in general lead stable, quiet lives" with high marriage and fertility rates, and low divorce rates.

Health-risk behaviors

Although most religious groups do not have specific teachings regarding many of the behavioral risk factors implicated in leading risk-factor models for cardiovascular disease, cancer, and diabetes, an increasing number of large, representative, population-based studies show a consistent pattern of higher levels of religious participation being associated with lower levels of a number of risk behaviors, including smoking, alcohol and drug use, lack of physical activity, risky sexual practices, and high-fat diet. Rates for prevalence of, and more importantly initiation of, cigarette smoking are significantly lower not only among sectarian religious groups (e.g., Ferketich et al. 2008), but also among individuals in heterogeneous religious communities who attend religious services regularly (Timberlake et al. 2006). Moreover, data from the Alameda County study show that frequent religious attenders who *did* smoke at baseline were more likely than those who did not attend to *quit* smoking during follow-up, and thus reduce their already lower mortality risk (Strawbridge et al. 1997).

Findings from the 2000 National Alcohol Survey showed that religious preference and religiosity were strongly associated with abstinence from alcohol, and were also associated with moderate (as opposed to heavy) drinking (Michalak, Trocki, and Bond 2007). Alcohol risk reduction has especially been linked to religious affiliation groups who differentiate themselves from dominant cultural norms (Haber and Jacob 2007). The 2001–3 National Comorbidity Survey Replication (NCS-R) found that religious affiliation and religiosity were associated robustly with less use of alcohol and tobacco, but also with lower extra-medical use of psychoactive drugs, cannabis, and cocaine (Degenhardt et al. 2007). With respect to sexual activities, recent studies show fewer sexual partners and less high-risk sexual activity among Catholic and more highly religious people with HIV compared with less observant non-Catholics (Galvan et al. 2007) and higher levels of sexual infidelity during a 12-month period were found among the less religious (Whisman, Gordon, and Chatav 2007).

Religiousness has been associated with positive health behaviors as well, not only the avoidance of negative ones. In the Third National Health and Nutrition Examination Survey (NHANES), older women (but not men) who were weekly attenders at religious services and had no mobility limitations were significantly more likely to engage in physical activity and exercise compared with less frequent attenders (Gillum 2006). Higher levels of religious observance in a national sample were also positively related to increased use of preventive health care, including mammograms, Pap smears, and breast self-exams (Benjamins and Brown 2004). The picture regarding diet and overweight is less clear. Analysis of data from the National Survey of Midlife Development in the United States (MIDUS) showed that, relative to their actual weight, more religious men and women tended to underestimate their reported weight, with the exception of Jewish women, who overestimated their weight; there were no differences by religiousness in intentional weight control behavior during the previous 12 months (Kim 2007). Dietary data from the Third NHANES showed higher levels of fish consumption for more religious respondents, but no significant differences by religious attendance for serum lipids or fat in the diet (Obisesan et al. 2006). Thus, with the exception of diet and weight-related behaviors, there is considerable evidence linking religiousness to numerous low-risk behaviors with well-understood effects on health and mortality. Religion appears to place constraints on behaviors that are sensation-seeking, self-stimulating, and that increase risk to self and others; this results in lowered risks for lifestyle-related causes of death. Risk behaviors that have been associated with religiousness are precisely those for which the mortality risks, across the most prevalent causes of death, have been best established.

Social networks and support

A second potential causal pathway by which religious involvement may have an impact on health is through the social network ties that are made available and maintained, primarily through local congregations. As we have noted, the study of religion and health at the individual level derived directly from the larger study of social networks and health in Alameda County and elsewhere. Belonging to a religious congregation would, logically, increase the number of social ties available to a person, increasing this number additively. But religious social ties may also increase total ties multiplicatively, if those ties link the individual to other charitable and community organizations (Lodi-Smith and Roberts 2007; McIntosh, Sykes, and Kubena 2002). Religious congregation members, in fact, report having larger social networks of both friends and relatives, and also more social support from them, compared with non-attenders (Ellison and George 1994). Moreover, congregation ties have distinct qualities that promote social capital among members: Evidence from the National Longitudinal Study of Adolescent Health (Add Health) found that religious attendance promotes stronger intergenerational ties, friendship networks with higher levels of education, and more extracurricular activities (Glanville, Sikkink, and Hernández 2008). For several reasons, religious congregations may serve as centers of particularly effective social support for elderly persons, many of whom live in age-segregated environments and for whom the intergenerational nature of the religious institution may provide rare but welcome contacts with children and young people. Congregations offer a mix of strong and weak ties, and can thus offer a broad range of both emotional and more practical, instrumental supports. Congregations of all major faiths share values and beliefs about the importance of helping others who are less fortunate and also provide organizational structure for mounting such efforts. Religious institutions provide both support to members and opportunities to help others in need, and reciprocal or bidirectional social support may be the most beneficial. Finally, as a corollary of this, members of religious groups who have served others in the past, and who have seen others receiving help, have reason to anticipate support in the future in the event of need, and anticipated support has been associated with better health (Krause 2006). Most of the literature in this area emphasizes the "helping hand" or social support functions of religion, one arm of the Durkheimian theory for how society promotes health. In the following section, we also examine the equally important social regulation and control functions.

Biological pathways

Religious rituals, as Durkheim and Douglas point out, have the cognitive function of separating the sacred from the profane in time and space, and ritual acts also inevitably involve the physical body. Participation in worship services may evoke all of the five senses, through the smell of incense, the sound of singing, the grasp of another's hand, the visual beauty of art and architecture, the taste of wine and bread. Moreover, the patterns of prayer postures, periods of meditation and contemplation, and regulation of respiration and heart rate engaged in while singing or praying simultaneously with others may provide physiological benefits about which relatively little is known. One interesting study compared the effect of rosary prayer and yoga mantras on autonomic cardiovascular rhythms, finding that both practices significantly increased favorable cardiovascular rhythms (Bernardi et al. 2001). A large, population-based study in the US found that more frequent attendance at religious services was associated with lower adjusted hypertension prevalence and lower blood pressure (Gillum and Ingram 2006). A third study found weekly service attendance was associated with lower total allostatic load in women, but not in men (Maselko et al. 2007). A review of the evidence regarding biological processes concluded that the available evidence is limited but consistent with the hypothesis that cardiovascular, neuroendocrine, and immune function processes may all be linked to religiousness/spirituality (Seeman, Dubin and Seeman 2003). The authors conclude that the strongest evidence links frequent religious attendance to lower blood pressure.

Individual-level population-based studies of religiousness and health outcomes, especially mortality, have generally included measures of some set of (behavioral and/or social) mediating variables (e.g., Hummer et al. 2004; Strawbridge et al. 1997). In most cases religious involvement is associated with better health practices and with higher levels of social support, and these known behavioral and psychosocial risk factors explain some portion (but not all) of the effect of religiousness on later health outcomes. In other words, some of the effect of religiousness on mortality is explained because it reduces the known health risks of poor health practices and social isolation, which are less frequently found among more religious participants. In sum, in studies of healthy populations, religion (conventionally operationalized as attendance at religious services) appears to be related to a lower risk of mortality after adjustment for known confounders and selectivity variables, with the effect partly explained by existing explanatory mechanisms and partly independent of them. However, the number of large and well-controlled studies is relatively few, the measurement of the religion variable is unsophisticated, the research has been largely done in US populations with primarily Judeo-Christian beliefs, and there are other explanatory mechanisms that should be tested.

THREE SOCIAL FORCES: SOCIAL SUPPORT, SOCIAL CONTROL, AND SELECTION

Research on the mediating pathways linking religion to health has tended to emphasize the social support and integration functions of religious groups in their provision of emotional and instrumental support, information, encouragement, and the availability of strong-tie intimate confidants as well as weak-tie potential employers. However, Durkheim's "sufficiently intense collective life" was made up not only of the "helping hand" functions of social integration but also of the constraining and potentially punitive forces of social control and regulation, where the metaphorical hand may be giving a warning, a restraint, or even a slap.

Although it has been given less attention, the social control functions of religion may be just as, or even more important than, the kindlier support functions in affecting health (Idler 2004). Social groups, and especially religious groups, submerge the interests of the individual beneath the group's interest. Powerful religious institutions, through their teachings, examples, and social pressure, can compel considerable self-sacrifice of time and resources in the service of others, for which there is some evidence of benefit to the providers themselves (Krause, Herzog, and Baker 1992; Steffen and Masters 2005). Religious groups' social control promotes prosocial, ethical, other-directed behavior, but also may extend to prohibiting mildly self-stimulating practices such as moderate alcohol or caffeine consumption, as well as to the obvious injunctions against more self-indulgent practices such as drug abuse or extra-marital sexual activity. In each case, the well-being and preservation of the group takes precedence over the desires and proclivities of individuals. Conformity with these social proscriptions marks an individual as a member in good standing of the group, an insider (Chawla et al. 2007). Violating social norms, particularly in religious groups, leads in extreme cases to severance of the individual's tie to the community (excommunication) and the surrendering of the privileges of membership, including access to the group's social support and integration functions. Thus the purity and sacredness of the group – and, one might even say, its "health" – are maintained through the expulsion of individuals who cannot conform to its dictates.

This mechanism of social control, with its potential consequences of separation of the individual from the group, raises the third important social force – selection. Implications of the process of selection into and out of religious groups have been underappreciated by most research in religion and health. Although Fuchs (1974) recognized in his early observations on Utah and Nevada that many individuals selected themselves out of the ascetic Mormon lifestyle, religion and health research does not frequently remind us that, in the United States at least, religious group membership is a matter of choice, and continued participation is voluntary. Highly observant members of religious groups are self-selected into their social settings, and remain there, willingly subject to the sometimes severe social constraints that are required for continued membership in good standing. Thus, the more frequently noted consideration of the selection of healthier individuals into high-attendance groups because ill or disabled individuals are less physically capable of attendance is only the most obvious source of potential confounding due to selection processes. Selection processes are the reason why causal arguments about the relationship between religion and health can never be a complete explanation.

Cumulative Effects over the Life Course

Whether through social support, social control, or selection, however, the role of religion appears to have an accumulating effect over the life course. A large number of studies examine the impact of religiousness on adolescent health risk and health-protective behaviors (reviewed in Rew and Wong 2006), particularly among vulnerable or disadvantaged youth including adolescents in foster care (Scott et al. 2006), Latino adolescents (Livaudais et al. 2007), and young people at risk of violence (Schreck, Burek, and Clark-Miller 2007). Large, nationally representative data sets such as the National Longitudinal Study of Adolescent Health (Add Health) and the Monitoring the Future Study find that more frequent attenders, and those who thought religion was important in their lives, had lower rates of smoking, alcohol and marijuana use, carrying weapons, getting into fights, driving while drinking, and lower rates of sexual intercourse. They also had higher rates of positive health practices such as seatbelt use, and eating fruits, vegetables, and breakfast (Nonnemaker, McNeely, and Blum 2003; Wallace and Forman 1998).

Religious involvement among adolescents that lowers many behavioral health risks is especially important because it represents a lowering of premature mortality risks such as drunk driving and violence, as well as lifetime risks for the onset of behaviors such as smoking and alcohol abuse, which are most likely to begin in adolescence. The cumulative impact of early-onset drinking is demonstrated by Masten et al. (2008) in their follow-up of data from the Monitoring the Future Study: Heavy teen drinkers are 4.5 times more likely to have alcohol problems as adults, are less likely to finish college, to form close relationships as adults, and are more likely to have mental health disorders and low-paying jobs. A notable study finding a cumulative impact of early religious involvement on later health showed that Norwegian Seventh-Day Adventist men and women who joined the church as children or adolescents had quite low standardized mortality ratios (SMRs) of just 69 and 59 (compared to the population reference level of 100); those who joined at ages 19 to 34 had higher SMRs of 72 and 87; and those who joined after age 34 had higher still SMRs of 89 and 103, much closer to those of the population as a whole (Fønnebø 1992), showing the much greater health benefit for Seventh-Day Adventists of early entry into the church. Lifelong religious observance, then, appears to be associated with greater health benefits because it is associated with some of the primary mediating or causal pathways that have particularly salient cumulative effects. This phenomenon is especially borne out in the long lives of men and women who join religious orders as adolescents (Snowdon 2001; Stein 1992).

ILLNESS AND THE SEARCH FOR HEALING, COMFORT, AND MEANING

A large proportion of the research on religion and health has taken as its starting point, not the *unintended* health consequences of the religious practices of healthy, population-based samples, but religious beliefs and practices that are engaged in by patients and families as a direct result of illness. This situation posits a potentially different time-ordering and a different motivation for participation. Religious involvement in patient samples in response to illness is undertaken in the pursuit of physical healing sometimes, but also for the purpose of seeking comfort, under-standing, and strength for coping with experiences of suffering. At the social level, religious groups offer both spiritual and tangible support to the sick, including prayers and reassuring rituals, but also practical help with meals, transportation, child care, and even financial assistance.

There is disease-specific research on HIV-1 (reviewed in Ironson and Hayward 2008; Pargament 2004), heart disease (Ai et al. 2006; Koenig 2007b), and cancer (reviewed in Thune-Boyle et al. 2006; Weaver and Flannelly 2004). Such studies frequently find *higher* levels of religious involvement among those suffering from serious illness compared to those who are healthier, a quite different correlational direction from those discussed in previous sections of this chapter. For example, the

2003 Complementary and Alternative Medicine supplement to the 2001 California Health Interview Survey found that cancer survivors and those with other chronic illness were more likely than those with no disease to use religious/spiritual prayer and healing practices, although they were not more likely to identify themselves as religious/spiritual (Ambs et al. 2007); and the 65-year Study of Adult Development found Harvard graduates with major depression or multiple negative life events twice as likely to show high religious involvement as those with less "stress" (Vaillant et al. 2008).

Research on the effects of religious coping with serious physical illness has most often taken indicators of quality of life and emotional well-being as outcomes. A frequent finding is that, among patients with serious illness or functional disability, religious involvement mitigates affective consequences, often measured as symptoms of depression. For example, hospitalized inpatients also diagnosed with depression were found to be less religiously involved than those with equally serious illness but less depression (Koenig 2007b); African-Americans with functional difficulties and low spirituality were found to have significantly more depressive symptoms than those with higher levels of spirituality (Gitlin et al. 2007); and new functional limitations were associated with lower levels of personal growth and higher levels of depressive symptoms in the National Survey of Families and Households, except among those who continuously participated in religious groups (Greenfield and Marks 2007). Religious involvement among informal caregivers for the seriously ill and disabled has also been studied; a recent review finds mixed associations between religion/spirituality and well-being, although study quality is uneven (Hebert et al. 2006). One well-designed study found higher levels of religiousness associated with fewer depressive symptoms in current caregivers, and with less complicated grief in the bereaved (Hebert, Dang, and Schulz 2007).

Classical sociological theories of religion again anticipate these functions of religion in health. Max Weber's concept of theodicy describes the ability of religious language to articulate experiences of suffering, to give them language and meaning (Weber 1964 [1922]). Religious individuals can draw on the experiences of fellow believers or the stories of their faith to put their own lives into a larger context, to find models in others who have faced similar circumstances, to reduce fear, or to gain hope for the future. Religious ritual practices for mourning or for healing can assist individuals in making transitions to new life stages in which adaptation to loss is required. Qualitative studies show that religious coping strategies appear prominently in the meaning-making repertoires of individuals faced with their own serious illness or the illness or death of a loved one, situations over which the individual has little direct control and which may lack clear explanations, or challenge beliefs that the world is just (Elliott, Gessert, and Peden-McAlpine 2007; Gerdner, Tripp-Reimer, and Simpson 2007; Ka'opua, Gotay, and Boehm 2007). In contrast to the population studies described above, in which attendance at worship services was the dimension of religious involvement that most predicted later health outcomes, studies of religious coping frequently find that subjective religious beliefs, or non-organizational forms of religious practice such as private prayer, play an important role.

Religious beliefs and practices may be especially salient in the concerns of caregivers, clinicians, and individuals themselves at the end of life, from the perspective of both meaning-making and decision-making (Balboni et al. 2007; Grodin 1993; Hebert et al. 2008). Daaleman et al. (2008) found, in a study of family members of patients who died in 100 long-term care facilities in four eastern states, that most decedents had received spiritual care in their institutions, and that those who did were perceived by family members to have had better end-of-life care overall. The influence of religious beliefs and traditions on end-of-life treatment preferences was shown to be quite strong in a large study of end-of-life decisions in European intensive care units where withholding treatment, withdrawing treatment, and discussing treatment decisions with families varied substantially by the religious affiliation of the physician (Sprung et al. 2007). Particularly for African-Americans (Johnson, Elbert-Avila, and Tulsky 2005), higher levels of patient religiousness have been shown to be associated with the desire for continuing aggressive medical intervention rather than shifting to palliative care.

There is also some evidence that the observance of religious holidays may alter the timing of death. Beginning with Phillips' original analysis of the timing of death around ceremonial occasions (Phillips and Feldman 1973), studies in both Jewish and Christian populations have observed a higher probability of death after the holiday than before, permitting the celebration of a last sacred ritual among those who were already near the end of life (Anson and Anson 2001; Idler and Kasl 1992). Following the death, in the period of mourning and after, religiousness on the part of the bereaved has been linked to generally positive adjustment outcomes (Hebert et al. 2007; Wortmann and Park 2008). In sum, religious traditions offer frameworks of meaning built on symbols, rituals, and liturgies for making sense of the painful, threatening, and ultimate experiences of illness and dying. There is evidence that these frameworks are sought out, that they may affect behavior in critical decisions, and that they may provide benefits in the form of quality of life and emotional adjustment.

THE POTENTIAL FOR HARM

Durkheim's original formulation of the relationship between religion and health clearly included the potential for harm (Durkheim 1951 [1987]). While a certain level of intensity of "collective life" was necessary and desirable, excessive amounts of social control could lead to what he called *altruistic* suicide: "If ... excessive individuation leads to suicide, insufficient individuation has the same effects. When man has become detached from society, he encounters less resistance to suicide in himself, and he does so likewise when social integration is too strong" (1951: 217). And he gives the example of precisely an excess of *religious* control leading to suicide: the Hindu custom of suicide by widows following the deaths of their husbands. Mass suicides of members of religious cults in Jonestown, Waco, and Heaven's Gate are recent examples of the phenomenon (Dein and Littlewood 2005). More mild examples of the negative impact of religion on health would include: the tendency of those with fatalistic religious beliefs to make less use of health services and to engage in fewer positive health behaviors (Franklin et al. 2007); the effects of negative social interaction within congregations (Krause, Ellison, and Wulff 1998); the intolerant attitudes of conservative religious groups towards sexual or other minority groups (Rostosky, Danner, and Riggle 2007); and religious struggle with such issues as sin or anger at God among seriously ill patients (Pargament et al. 2001; Sherman et al. 2005). Such beliefs may appear deviant or illogical to researchers or to health care personnel, but given their theoretical and empirical potential for influencing behavior and having an effect on outcomes, they should be included in research design and analysis.

CONTEMPORARY CONTROVERSIES

Beginning in 1999 with editorials in the British medical journal *Lancet* and the *New England Journal of Medicine*, a critical or skeptical perspective of research on religion and health has developed (Sloan, Bagiella, and Powell 1999; Sloan et al. 2000), receiving considerable attention in major medical journals and the news media. This critique has contended that there is inconsistency in the measures and findings in the research on religion and health, that there is a failure to control for confounding variables, a failure to adjust significance levels for multiple comparisons, and most importantly, that there are ethical problems in drawing clinical practice implications (for individuals) from what is primarily epidemiological research (based on groups). The purview of this critique is both wider in some ways and narrower than the topics covered in the present chapter on the sociology of religion and health. For example, Sloan and Bagiella argue that studies concerning the total cholesterol levels of Seventh-Day Adventists when compared with non-SDA populations are not relevant to the study of religious involvement and health because "most denomination studies have been conducted to take advantage of denominational differences in genetic endowment, health behaviors, or ethnicity" (Sloan and Bagiella 2002: 15). The critique further contends that plausible links between religious involvement and health that have been discussed here as mediating pathways (health behaviors, social support, and social control) are merely confounders of the association, and to the extent that they diminish or eliminate the unadjusted association between religion and health, they rule it out. From a sociological standpoint, however, the subject matter of the latent consequences of behaviors, social norms and control, and the relationship between beliefs and actions, particularly in sectarian religious groups where these social forces are most obviously at work, are quite relevant to the larger picture of religion and health. It would seem that religion's relationship, in sectarian and mainstream denominations alike, to an impressive number of health-relevant behaviors that serve as mediators of the overall relationship should make it *more* important scientifically as a fundamental cause in understanding human health, not less important.

The critique is, on the other hand, somewhat more expansive than this chapter in its concerns about the clinical implications of the research. One particular focus of the critique has been on a series of intercessory prayer studies (Astin, Harkness, and Ernst 2000; Masters, Spielmans, and Goodson 2006) that are often used as justification for introducing prayer or other "spiritual interventions" into the clinical practice setting, especially in physician–patient interactions (Mueller, Plevak, and Rummans 2001). The evaluation of intercessory prayer and distant healing studies, where the study design is explicitly intended to eliminate any influence of social support (individual patients are chosen randomly to be prayed for by other individuals who do not know them, from a remote location), and recommendations for improving care in clinical practice, are both well beyond the scope of this chapter or the expertise of this author. Thus we note that there is cultural controversy in the field over methods and findings, and particularly over the implications that some researchers have drawn from them.

RELIGIOUSLY INSPIRED INNOVATIVE INSTITUTIONS IN HEALTH

Religion has played an additional role in health to which less attention has been paid, and that is as the originator of new forms of social organization for the care of the ill, the disabled, the frail elderly, and the dying. There are a surprising number of examples of such *de novo* institutions in the area of religiously based care for disabled, aging, and end-of-life populations. Moreover, in some cases the models have "caught on" and been rapidly reproduced, sometimes in secular forms.

The first home for the aged in the United States, the Indigent Widows' and Single Women's Society, was founded in 1817 by two Quaker women who had been shocked to find elderly, formerly middle-class women living in the Philadelphia Almshouse (Haber and Gratton 1994). Its founders maintained a nonsectarian home-like atmosphere, with private or semi-private rooms, communal meals, medical care, organized outings, and a clean and wholesome environment. Although the residents were cared for until they died, care was not provided for the insane or senile. By the end of the nineteenth century, there were many such homes in Philadelphia, most of them established and supported by religious congregations, including the Presbyterians, Methodists, Lutherans, Baptists, and Jews, and providing care primarily to their own church members. Perceptions of specialized need resulted in institutions providing care to aged couples, single men, and former slaves (Haber 1977). By the mid-twentieth century a report for the National Association of Social Workers estimated that 40 percent of homes for the aged in the US were under the auspices of religious groups (Tibbitts, cited in Maves 1960). Some homes were offering services that would be considered innovative even today, including the Home for Aged and Infirm Hebrews in New York City, which offered nursing care, independent-living apartments, a community center for non-residents, and a training program in geriatric medicine (Maves 1960).

Beginning in the 1960s, the development of residential care for the elderly took a new turn, as continuing care retirement communities (CCRC) were established by religious groups; some of the earliest include Foulkeways at Gwynedd (Pennsylvania) started by the Quakers, Glacier Hills in Ann Arbor (Michigan) begun by the Lutherans, and Moravian Manor in Lititz (Pennsylvania), begun by the Moravian Church. This entirely new form of care has emerged in the US in the late twentieth century in response to the fragmented array of services available to the aging. It is structured around a contract, which requires from the resident a high initial entrance fee, in many cases amounting to all or almost all of a resident's estate, and continuing monthly fees; in return the CCRC provides all levels of care from independent living to end-of-life care, within the community, for the rest of the resident's life (Stone 2008). While some CCRCs developed from previously established, often church-related old age homes, the model bears strong resemblance to religious social organizations with a basis in communal property: the ancient Essenes, the modern kibbutz movement, the Shakers.

L'Arche is an international network of permanent, communal homes for individuals with developmental disabilities living together with those who assist them. The first L'Arche home was begun in 1964, in Trosly-Breuil, France; the name "L'Arche" means Ark, as in Noah's Ark, a place of safety and refuge. The founder, Jean Vanier, was inspired by a Dominican priest to take two developmentally disabled men into his home. Today L'Arche homes and day centers can be found in 130 other communities around the world (www.larche.org/). These faith-based communities foster an ethic of egalitarianism in what would otherwise, even in caregiving institutions, be highly unequal relationships; as the L'Arche Charter (1993) says: "In a divided world, L'Arche wants to be a sign of hope. Its communities, founded on covenant relationships between people of differing intellectual capacity, social origin, religion and culture, seek to be signs of unity, faithfulness and reconciliation."

The modern hospice institution for care of the dying began in England in the 1960s; it was modeled after ancient and medieval Christian institutions for the care of travelers, the sick, and the dying. Dame Cicely Saunders – nurse, physician, and writer – founded St. Christopher's Hospice in Sydenham, England, in 1967. Her vision for a new institution to care for the dying combined the meditative tranquility of the medieval monastery with the scientifically informed pain control of the modern hospital; the goal of hospice care was to allow dying patients to be conscious and comfortable, and surrounded by family and significant others (Saunders and Clark 2006). These elements of hospice care have influenced care for the dying in institutions outside of hospice care as well; the spiritual concerns of patients are more prominent in the field of palliative medicine than in other medical specialties (Puchalski et al. 2003).

Two final examples of innovative programs in religion and health are congregation-based. The first is the Parish Nurse Movement, begun in 1984 by Granger Westburg, a Lutheran pastor, chaplain, and professor of theology. Originally a program of the Park Ridge, Illinois, Lutheran General Hospital and six local congregations, it is now a worldwide ecumenical movement to bring the resources of the health care system directly to members of congregations. Parish nurses may be volunteer or paid, but take on formal responsibilities for health promotion and disease prevention in the congregation (Buijs and Olson 2001). A second example of congregationally located health programs is the Interfaith Health Program of the Robert Wood Johnson Foundation and the Carter Center, which have funded hundreds of health promotion programs in local congregations around the country (Cantor 1996). One survey of congregational health ministries found that such programs delievered a wide array of health promotion and disease prevention programs with a minimal amount of resources (Catanzaro et al. 2007).

From a sociological point of view the level of social inventiveness in these examples is quite remarkable. Social institutions evolve and change over time in response to changing needs in society, but it is rather rare that entirely new forms are started with little precedent and then establish themselves successfully. The role of single, inspired individuals in the history of these institutions is clear, but the influence of religious and ethical ideals and the models of historical religious institutions is also evident.

INTERNATIONAL RESEARCH

Participation in organized religious groups and self-reported individual levels of religiousness are much higher in the United States than in other Western industrialized nations. Not surprisingly, then, much of the research on religion and health has been conducted in the US. However, there is recent research in many of the areas already covered in this review with, by and large, similar findings to comparable studies in US populations.

Religious involvement is associated with survival in recent studies from Denmark (La Cour, Avlund, and Schultz-Larsen 2006), Taiwan (Yeager et al. 2006), and China (Zhang 2008), and in each case it was religious participation, rather than more subjective dimensions of religiousness, that was associated with the lower hazard of mortality. Associations of religiousness with the primary proposed mediators discussed earlier again show similar findings. Weekly attendance at services was associated with lower rates of smoking in pregnant Australian women (Agrawal et al. 2008). A review of gender differences in alcohol use, with a focus on developing countries, found religiosity was associated with lower levels of alcohol use by both men and women (Kerr Correa et al. 2007). A study of adolescent drug use in Mexico City found more religious adolescents were less likely to have been exposed to drug use opportunities, and were consequently less likely to have used drugs themselves (Benjet et al. 2007); and, also in Mexico, Benjamins (2007) found religious salience and attendance were associated with more frequent use of preventive health services. In general, these findings mirror those from the United States.

As in Durkheim's work, there is international research interest in the relative health of different faith groups. In Northern Ireland, Church of Ireland members were found to have the highest mortality rates when compared with Catholics, Protestants, Methodists, other Christians, and other (not stated) (O'Reilly and Rosato 2008). Christians, by comparison with Muslims or other religious groups in Tanzania, had higher alcohol abuse rates (Mitsunaga and Larsen 2008); and Christians were found to make more use of maternal and child health services in Ghana when compared with Muslim and traditional women (Gyimah, Takyi, and Addai 2006), resulting in lower infant mortality (Gyimah 2007). Particularly in Africa, there is an attempt to implement HIV prevention efforts through local congregations (Allen et al. 2007).

This brief list of comparable studies, however, merely applies the US paradigm to the international context. A more complete account of international research on religion and health would require an ambitious effort to describe the epidemiology of religious practices such as dietary regulations, the anthropology of religious healing in the major faith traditions around the world, and the history of churches' and religious non-governmental organizations' efforts to improve health in poor and developing countries, far beyond the scope of this chapter.

Future Directions

Despite its background in the classical traditions of the sociology of religion and public health, the field of research in religion and health remained mostly unexplored until it began growing quite rapidly in the 1990s, especially in the US, where levels of interest and participation in religion are generally higher than in Europe. One may anticipate further growth in this field, as the measurement and conceptualization of the relevant domains of religiousness and spirituality improve, and as the population ages and the prevalence of chronic illness increases.

One area in which interest is likely to grow in the future includes the role of religion in mind–body medicine and complementary and alternative medicine; these areas of research have tended to remain quite separate, although there is evidence that individuals themselves integrate these more traditional and less traditional practices (Tindle et al. 2005; Wade et al. 2008).

Another area of considerable current research interest where religion has played a relatively underappreciated role to date has been in the importance of social context, neighborhood-level analyses, and community social capital. One analysis of data from the Israel Longitudinal Mortality Study finds that mortality rates were lower for men and women living in religiously affiliated statistical areas when compared with non-affiliated areas (Jaffe et al. 2005). A second study shows that the proportion of community social capital that is attributable to religious groups is strongly associated with lower smoking rates (Brown et al. 2006). A third study showed a significant inverse relationship between the number of churches per capita in US communities and their rates of mental disorders and substance use (Stockdale et al. 2007). This "new" topic makes a complete circle, back to the Durkheimian origins of the field and analyses at the societal level.

To conclude, we return to the distinction with which we began this chapter. In the first view of religion and public health, religious participation, through a variety of mechanisms, appears to improve the health of populations. In the second, religion to some extent shapes social institutions involved in the intersection when illness occurs: Religious institutions provide formal and informal care for the sick, sometimes in innovative ways, and health care institutions are shaped by the religious views of patients and practitioners. Looking forward, we may see the first having implications for the second. If religion has a differential impact on survival of individuals in populations according to their level of participation, that means that the life expectancy of more religious individuals will be longer than that of less religious individuals. Religious institutions at the local level of congregations will accumulate ever larger numbers of aging individuals in this process of mortality selection. As social institutions, they will be obligated to provide more care for their members who require it. The history of social innovation in providing care for the aging that has already been seen suggests a good fit between need and resources to meet it.

In a relatively brief period, social research on religion and health has developed a complex structure and body of findings. With improvements in measurement and study design, with a broadened view of the relevant areas of study, and with interdisciplinary efforts combining medicine, public health, and the social sciences, it promises to give us a window on fundamental determinants of individual well-being, on the larger field of medical sociology, and on these two major social institutions themselves.

References

Agrawal, Arpana, Valerie S. Knopik, Michele L. Pergadia, Mary Waldron, Kathleen K. Bucholz, Nicholas G. Martin, Andrew C. Heath, and Pamela A. Madden. 2008. "Correlates of Cigarette Smoking during Pregnancy and its Genetic and Environmental Overlap with Nicotine Dependence." *Nicotine and Tobacco Research* 10: 567–78.

Ai, Amy L., Christopher Peterson, Terrence N. Tice, Willard Rodgers, E. Mitchell Seymour, and Steven F. Bolling. 2006. "Differential Effects of Faith-Based Coping on Physical and Mental Fatigue in Middle-Aged and Older Cardiac Patients." *International Journal of Psychiatry in Medicine* 36: 351–65.

Allen, Susan, Etienne Karita, Elwyn Chomba, David L. Roth, Joseph Telfair, Isaac Zulu, Leslie Clark, Nzali Kancheya, Martha Conkling, Rob Stephenson, Brigitta Bekan, Katherine Kimbrell, Steven Dunham, Faith Henderson, Moses Sinkala, Michel Carael, and Alan Haworth. 2007. "Promotion of Couples' Voluntary Counseling and Testing for HIV through Influential Networks in Two African Capital Cities." *BMC Public Health* 7: 349.

Ambs, A. H., M. F. Smith, M. S. Goldstein, A. F. Hsiao, and R. Ballard-Barbash. 2007. "Religious and Spiritual Practices and Identification among Individuals Living with Cancer and Other Chronic Disease." *Journal of the Society for Integrative Oncology* 5: 53–60.

Anson, Jon and Ofra Anson. 2001. "Death Rests a While: Holy Day and Sabbath Effects on Jewish Mortality in Israel." *Social Science and Medicine* 52: 83–97.

Astin, John A., Elaine Harkness, and Edzard Ernst. 2000. "The Efficacy of 'Distant Healing': A Systematic Review of Randomized Trials." *Annals of Internal Medicine* 132: 903–10.

Balboni, Tracy A., Lauren C. Vanderwerker, Susan D. Block, M. Elizabeth Paulk, Christopher S. Lathan, John R. Peteet, and Holly G. Prigerson. 2007. "Religiousness and Spiritual Support among Advanced Cancer Patients and Associations with End-of-Life Treatment Preferences and Quality of Life." *Journal of Clinical Oncology* 25: 555–60.

Benjamins, Maureen R. 2007. "Predictors of Preventive Health Care Use among Middle-Aged and Older Adults in Mexico: The Role of Religion." *Journal of Cross-Cultural Gerontology* 22: 221–34.

Benjamins, Maureen R. and Carolyn Brown. 2004. "Religion and Preventative Health Care Utilization among the Elderly." *Social Science and Medicine* 58: 109–18.

Benjet, Corina, Guilherme Borges, Maria Elena Medina-Mora, Jeronimo Blanco, Joaquin Zambrano, Ricardo Orozco, Clara Fleiz, and Estela Rojas. 2007. "Drug Use Opportunities and the Transition to Drug Use among Adolescents from the Mexico City Metropolitan Area." *Drug and Alcohol Dependence* 90: 128–34.

Berkman, Lisa F. and Leonard S. Syme. 1979. "Social Networks, Host Resistance, and Mortality." *American Journal of Epidemiology* 109: 186–204.

Bernardi, Luciano, Peter Sleight, Gabriele Bandinelli, Simone Cencetti, Lamberto Fattorini, Johanna Wdowczyc-Szulc, and Alfonso Lagi. 2001. "Effect of Rosary Prayer and Yoga Mantras on Autonomic Cardiovascular Rhythms: Comparative Study." *British Medical Journal* 323: 1446–9.

Bloom, Samuel W. 2002. *The Word as Scalpel: A History of Medical Sociology*. New York: Oxford University Press.

Brown, Timothy, Richard M. Scheffler, Sukyong Seo, and Mary Reed. 2006. "The Empirical Relationship between Community Social Capital and the Demand for Cigarettes." *Health Economics* 15: 1159–72.

Buijs, Rosanne and Joanne Olson. 2001. "Parish Nurses Influencing Determinants of Health." *Journal of Community Health Nursing* 18: 13–23.

Cantor, Carla. 1996. "Mobilizing Faith into Health Care Activities." *Advances: The Quarterly Newsletter of the Robert Wood Johnson Foundation* 3: 1, 10.

Catanzaro, Ana Maria, Keith G. Meador, Harold G. Koenig, Margaratha Kuchibhatla, and Elizabeth C. Clipp. 2007. "Congregational Health Ministries: A National Study of Pastors' Views." *Public Health Nursing* 24: 6–17.

Chawla, N., C. Neighbors, M. A. Lewis, C. M. Lee, and M. E. Larimer. 2007. "Attitudes and Perceived Approval of Drinking as Mediators of the Relationship Between the Importance of Religion and Alcohol Use." *Journal of Studies on Alcohol* 68: 410–18.

Daaleman, Timothy P., Christianna S. Williams, V. Lee Hamilton, and Sheryl Zimmerman. 2008. "Spiritual Care at the End of Life in Long-Term Care." *Medical Care* 46: 85–91.

Degenhardt, Louisa, Wai Tat Chiu, Nancy Sampson, Ronald C. Kessler, and James D. Anthony. 2007. "Epidemiological Patterns of Extra-Medical Drug Use in the United States: Evidence from the National Comorbidity Survey Replication, 2001–2003." *Drug and Alcohol Dependence* 90: 210–23.

Dein, Simon and Roland Littlewood. 2005. "Apocalyptic Suicide: From a Pathological to an Eschatological Interpretation." *International Journal of Social Psychiatry* 51: 198–210.

Douglas, Mary. 1966. *Purity and Danger: An Analysis of Concepts of Pollution and Tabu*. London: Routledge.

Durkheim, Emile. 1951 [1897]. *Suicide: A Study in Sociology*, translated by John Spaulding and George Simpson. New York: Free Press.

Durkheim, Emile. 1965 [1915]. *The Elementary Forms of the Religious Life*, translated by Joseph Ward Swain. New York: Free Press.

Egbert, Nichole, Jacqueline Mickley, and Harriet Coeling. 2004. "A Review and Application of Social Scientific Measures of Religiosity and Spirituality: Assessing a Missing Component in Health Communication Research." *Health Communication* 16: 7–27.

Elliott, Barbara A., Charles E. Gessert, and Cynthia Peden-McAlpine. 2007. "Decision Making by Families of Older Adults with Advanced Cognitive Impairment: Spirituality and Meaning." *Journal of Gerontological Nursing* 33: 49–55.

Ellison, Christopher E. and Linda K. George. 1994. "Religious Involvement, Social Ties, and Social Support in a Southeastern Community." *Journal for the Scientific Study of Religion* 33: 46–61.

Enstrom, James E. and Lester Breslow. 2008. "Lifestyle and Reduced Mortality among Active California Mormons, 1980–2004." *Preventive Medicine* 46: 133–6.

Ferketich, Amy K., Mira L. Katz, Ross M. Kauffman, Electra D. Paskett, Stanley Lemeshow, Judith A. Westman, Steven K. Clinton, Clara D. Bloomfield, and Mary Ellen Wewers. 2008. "Tobacco Use among the Amish in Holmes County, Ohio." *Journal of Rural Health* 24: 84–90.

Fønnebø, Vinjar. 1992. "Mortality in Norwegian Seventh-Day Adventists 1962–1986." *Journal of Clinical Epidemiology* 45: 157–67.

Franklin, Monica D., David G. Schlundt, Linda H. McClellan, Tunu Kinebrew, Jylana Sheats, Rhonda Belue, Anne Brown, Dorlisa Smikes, Kushal Patel, and Margaret Hargreaves. 2007. "Religious Fatalism and its Association with Health Behaviors and Outcomes." *American Journal of Health Behavior* 31: 563–72.

Fuchs, Victor F. 1974. *Who Shall Live? Health, Economics, and Social Choice*. New York: Basic Books.

Galvan, Frank H., Rebecca L. Collins, David E. Kanouse, Philip Pantoja, and Daniela Golinelli. 2007. "Religiosity, Denominational Affiliation and Sexual Behaviors among People with HIV in the United States." *Journal of Sex Research* 44: 49–58.

Gerdner, Linda A., Toni Tripp-Reimer, and Helen C. Simpson. 2007. "Hard Lives, God's Help, and Struggling Through: Caregiving in Arkansas Delta." *Journal of Cross-Cultural Gerontology* 22: 355–74.

Gillum, R. Frank. 2006. "Frequency of Attendance at Religious Services and Leisure-Time Physical Activity in American Women and Men: The Third National Health and Nutrition Examination Survey." *Annals of Behavioral Medicine* 31: 30–5.

Gillum, R. Frank and Deborah D. Ingram. 2006. "Frequency of Attendance at Religious Services, Hypertension, and Blood Pressure: The Third National Health and Nutrition Examination Survey." *Psychosomatic Medicine* 68: 382–5.

Gillum, R. Frank, Dana E. King, Thomas O. Obisesan, and Harold G. Koenig. 2008. "Frequency of Attendance at Religious Services and Mortality in a US National Cohort." *Annals of Epidemiology* 18: 124–9.

Gitlin, Laura N., Walter W. Hauck, Marie P. Dennis, and Richard Schulz. 2007. "Depressive Symptoms in Older African-American and White Adults with Functional Difficulties: The Role of Control Strategies." *Journal of the American Geriatrics Society* 55. 1027–30.

Glanville, Jennifer L., David Sikkink, and Edwin I. Hernández. 2008. "Religious Involvement and Educational Outcomes: The Role of Social Capital and Extracurricular Participation." *Sociological Quarterly* 49: 105–37.

Greenfield, Emily A. and Nadine Marks. 2007. "Continuous Participation in Voluntary Groups as a Protective Factor for the Psychological Well-Being of Adults who Develop Functional Limitations: Evidence from the National Survey of Families and Households." *Journal of Gerontology: Social Sciences* 62: S60–8.

Grodin, Michael A. 1993. "Religious Advance Directives: The Convergence of Law, Religion, Medicine, and Public Health." *American Journal of Public Health* 83: 899–903.

Gyimah, Stephen Obeng. 2007. "What has Faith Got to Do With It? Religion and Child Survival in Ghana." *Journal of Biosocial Science* 39: 923–37.

Gyimah, Stephen Obeng, Baffour K. Takyi, and Isaac Addai. 2006. "Challenges to the Reproductive-Health Needs of African Women: On Religion and Maternal Health Utilization in Ghana." *Social Science and Medicine* 62: 2930–44.

Haber, Carole. 1977. "The Old Folks at Home: The Development of Institutionalized Care for the Aged in Nineteenth-Century Philadelphia." *Pennsylvania Magazine of History and Biography* 101: 240–57.

Haber, Carole and Brian Gratton. 1994. *Old Age and the Search for Security*. Bloomington: Indiana University Press.

Haber, Jon R. and Theodore Jacob. 2007. "Alcoholism Risk Moderation by a Socio-Religious Dimension." *Journal of Studies on Alcohol* 68: 912–22.

Hebert, Randy S., Qianyu Dang, and Richard Schulz. 2007. "Religious Beliefs and Practices are Associated with Better Mental Health in Family Caregivers of Patients with

Dementia: Findings from the REACH Study." *American Journal of Geriatric Psychiatry* 15: 292–300.

Hebert, Randy S., Richard Schulz, Valire Copeland, and Robert M. Arnold. 2008. "What Questions do Family Caregivers Want to Discuss with Health Care Providers in Order to Prepare for the Death of a Loved One? An Ethnographic Study of Caregivers of Patients at End of Life." *Journal of Palliative Medicine* 11: 476–83.

Hebert, Randy S., E. Weinstein, Lynn M. Martire, and Richard Schulz. 2006. "Religion, Spirituality and the Well-Being of Informal Caregivers: A Review, Critique, and Research Prospectus." *Aging and Mental Health* 10: 497–520.

Hill, Peter C. and Kenneth I. Pargament. 2003. "Advances in the Conceptualization and Measurement of Religion and Spirituality: Implications for Physical and Mental Health Research." *American Psychologist* 58: 64–74.

House, James S., Karl Landis, and Debra Umberson. 1988. "Social Relationships and Health." *Science* 241: 540–5.

Hummer, Robert A., Christopher G. Ellison, Richard G. Rogers, Benjamin E. Moulton, and Ron R. Romero. 2004. "Religious Involvement and Adult Mortality in the United States: Review and Perspective." *Southern Medical Journal* 97: 1223–30.

Idler, Ellen. 2004. "Religious Observance and Health: Theory and Research." Pp. 20–43 in K. Warner Schaie, Neal Krause, and Alan Booth (eds.), *Religious Influences on Health and Well-Being of the Elderly*. New York: Springer.

Idler, Ellen, Richard J. Contrada, David A. Boulifard, Erich W. Labouvie, Yung Chen, and Tyrone J. Krause. 2009. "Looking in the Black Box of 'Attendance at Services': Exploring an Old Dimension for Religion and Health Research." *International Journal for the Psychology of Religion* 19: 1–20.

Idler, Ellen, Christopher Ellison, Linda George, Neal Krause, Marcia Ory, Kenneth Pargament, Lynda Powell, David Williams, and Lynn Underwood. 2003. "Measuring Multiple Dimensions of Religion and Spirituality for Health Research: Conceptual Background and Findings from the 1998 General Social Survey." *Research on Aging* 25: 327–65.

Idler, Ellen and Stanislav Kasl. 1992. "Religion, Disability, Depression, and the Timing of Death." *American Journal of Sociology* 97: 1052–79.

Ironson, Gail and H'sien Hayward. 2008. "Do Positive Psychosocial Factors Predict Disease Progression in HIV-1? A Review of the Evidence." *Psychosomatic Medicine* 70: 546–54.

Jaffe, Dena H., Zvi Eisenbach, Yehuda D. Neumark, and Orly Manor. 2005. "Does Living in a Religiously Affiliated Neighborhood Lower Mortality?" *Annals of Epidemiology* 15: 804–10.

Jarvis, George K. and Herbert C. Northcott. 1987. "Religion and Differences in Morbidity and Mortality." *Social Science and Medicine* 25: 813–24.

Johnson, Kimberly S., Katja I. Elbert-Avila, and James A. Tulsky. 2005. "The Influence of Spiritual Beliefs and Practices on the Treatment Preferences of African Americans: A Review of the Literature." *Journal of the American Geriatrics Society* 53: 711–19.

Ka'opua, Lana Sue, Carolyn C. Gotay, and Patricia S. Boehm. 2007. "Spiritually Based Resources in Adaptation to Long-Term Prostate Cancer Survival: Perspectives of Elderly Wives." *Health and Social Work* 32: 29–39.

Kark, Jeremy D., Galia Shemi, Yechiel Friedlander, Oz Martin, Orly Manor, and S. Blondheim. 1996. "Does Religious Observance Promote Health? Mortality in Secular vs. Religious Kibbutzim in Israel." *American Journal of Public Health* 86: 341–6.

Kerr-Correa, Florence, Thais Zamudio Igami, Vivian Hiroce, and Adriana Marcassa Tucci. 2007. "Patterns of Alcohol Use between Genders: A Cross-Cultural Evaluation." *Journal of Affective Disorders* 102: 265–75.

Kim, Karen H. 2007. "Religion, Weight Perception, and Weight Control Behavior." *Eating Behaviors* 8: 121–31.

Koenig, Harold G. 2007a. "Religion and Depression in Older Medical Inpatients." *American Journal of Geriatric Psychiatry* 15: 282–91.

Koenig, Harold G. 2007b. "Religion and Remission of Depression in Medical Inpatients with Heart Failure/Pulmonary Disease." *Journal of Nervous and Mental Disease* 195: 389–95.

Koenig, Harold G., Michael E. McCullough, and David B. Larson. 2001. *Handbook of Religion and Health*. New York: Oxford University Press.

Krause, Neal. 2006. "Church-Based Social Support and Change in Health over Time." *Review of Religious Research* 48: 125–40.

Krause, Neal, Christopher G. Ellison, and Keith M. Wulff. 1998. "Church-Based Emotional Support, Negative Interaction, and Psychological Well-Being: Findings from a National Sample of Presbyterians." *Journal for the Scientific Study of Religion* 37: 725–41.

Krause, Neal, A. Regula Herzog, and Elizabeth Baker. 1992. "Providing Support to Others and Well-Being in Later Life." *Journals of Gerontology: Psychological Sciences* 47: 300–11.

L'Arche. 1993. "Charter of the Communities of L'Arche." General Assembly of the Cap Rouge, Province of Quebec. Retrieved February 10, 2009 (www.larche.ca/en/members/vision_future/larche_charter/charter communities of larche.pdf).

La Cour, Peter, Kirsten Avlund, and Kirsten Schultz-Larsen. 2006. "Religion and Survival in a Secular Region: A Twenty-Year Follow-Up of 734 Danish Adults Born in 1914." *Social Science and Medicine* 62: 157–64.

Livaudais, Jennifer C., Anna Napoles-Springer, Susan Stewart, and Celia Patricia Kaplan. 2007. "Understanding Latino Adolescent Risk Behaviors: Parental and Peer Influences." *Ethnicity and Disease* 17: 298–304.

Lodi-Smith, Jennifer and Brent W. Roberts. 2007. "Social Investment and Personality: A Meta-Analysis of the Relationship of Personality Traits to Investment in Work, Family, Religion, and Volunteerism." *Personality and Social Psychology Review* 11: 68–86.

Maselko, Joanna and Laura D. Kubzansky. 2006. "Gender Differences in Religious Practices, Spiritual Experiences and Health: Results from the US General Social Survey." *Social Science and Medicine* 62: 2848–60.

Maselko, Joanna, Laura Kubzansky, Kawachi Ichiro, Teresa Seeman, and Lisa Berkman. 2007. "Religious Service Attendance and Allostatic Load among High-Functioning Elderly." *Psychosomatic Medicine* 69: 464–72.

Masten, Ann S., Vivian B. Faden, Robert A. Zucker, and Linda P. Spear. 2008. "Underage Drinking: A Developmental Framework." *Pediatrics* 121 Suppl: S235–51.

Masters, Kevin S., Glen I. Spielmans, and Jason T. Goodson. 2006. "Are There Demonstrable Effects of Distant Intercessory Prayer? A Meta-Analytic Review." *Annals of Behavioral Medicine* 32: 21–6.

Maves, Paul B. 1960. "Aging, Religion, and the Church." Pp. 698–749 in Clark Tibbitts (ed.), *Handbook of Social Gerontology*. Chicago: University of Chicago Press.

McCullough, Michael E., William T. Hoyt, David B. Larson, Harold G. Koenig, and Carl Thoresen. 2000. "Religious Involvement and Mortality: A Meta-Analytic Review." *Health Psychology* 19: 211–22.

McIntosh, William A., Dianne Sykes, and Karen S. Kubena. 2002. "Religion and Community among the Elderly: The Relationship between the Religious and Secular Characteristics of their Social Networks." *Review of Religious Research* 44: 109–25.

Michalak, Laurence, Karen Trocki, and Jason Bond. 2007. "Religion and Alcohol in the US National Alcohol Survey: How Important is Religion for Abstention and Drinking?" *Drug and Alcohol Dependence* 87: 268–80.

Mitsunaga, Tisha and Ulla Larsen. 2008. "Prevalence of and Risk Factors Associated with Alcohol Abuse in Moshi, Northern Tanzania." *Journal of Biosocial Science* 40: 379–99.

Mueller, Paul S., David J. Plevak, and Teresa A. Rummans. 2001. "Religious Involvement, Spirituality, and Medicine: Implications for Clinical Practice." *Mayo Clinic Proceedings* 76: 1225–35.

Nonnemaker, James M., Clea A. McNeely, and Robert W. Blum. 2003. "Public and Private Domains of Religiosity and Adolescent Health Risk Behaviors: Evidence from the National Longitudinal Study of Adolescent Health." *Social Science and Medicine* 57: 2049–54.

Obisesan, Thomas, Ivor Livingston, Harold D. Trulear, and Frank Gillum. 2006. "Frequency of Attendance at Religious Services, Cardiovascular Disease, Metabolic Risk Factors, and Dietary Intake in Americans: An Age-Stratified Exploratory Analysis." *International Journal of Psychiatry in Medicine* 36: 435–48.

O'Reilly, Dermot and Michael Rosato. 2008. "Religious Affiliation and Mortality in Northern Ireland: Beyond Catholic and Protestant." *Social Science and Medicine* 66: 1637–45.

Ostbye, Truls, Katrina M. Krause, Maria C. Norton, JoAnn Tschanz, Linda Sanders, Kathleen Hayden, Carl Pieper, Kathleen A. Welsh-Bohmer, and Cache County Investigators. 2006. "Ten Dimensions of Health and Their Relationships with Overall Self-Reported Health and Survival in a Predominantly Religiously Active Elderly Population: The Cache County Memory Study." *Journal of the American Geriatrics Society* 54: 199–209.

Pargament, Kenneth I. 1997. *The Psychology of Religion and Coping*. New York: Guilford Press.

Pargament, Kenneth I. 2004. "Religion and HIV: A Review of the Literature and Clinical Implications." *Southern Medical Journal* 97: 1201–9.

Pargament, Kenneth I., Harold G. Koenig, Nalini Tarakeshwar, and June Hahn. 2001. "Religious Struggle as a Predictor of Mortality among Medically Ill Elderly Patients." *Archives of Internal Medicine* 161: 1881–5.

Pescosolido, Bernice and Sharon Georgianna. 1989. "Durkheim, Suicide, and Religion: Toward a Network Theory of Suicide." *American Sociological Review* 54: 33–48.

Phillips, David and Kenneth Feldman. 1973. "A Dip in Deaths before Ceremonial Occasions: Some New Relationships between Social Integration and Mortality." *American Sociological Review* 38: 678–96.

Phillips, Roland L., Jan W. Kuzma, W. Lawrence Beeson, and Terry Lotz. 1980. "Influence of Selection versus Lifestyle on Risk of Fatal Cancer and Cardiovascular Disease Among Seventh Day Adventists." *American Journal of Epidemiology* 112: 296–314.

Powell, Lynda H., Leila Shahabi, and Carl E. Thoresen. 2003. "Religion and Spirituality: Linkages to Physical Health." *American Psychologist* 58: 36–52.

Puchalski, Christina M., Shelley Dean Kilpatrick, Michael E. McCullough, and David B. Larson. 2003. "A Systematic Review of Spiritual and Religious Variables in *Palliative*

Medicine, American Journal of Hospice and Palliative Care, Hospice Journal, Journal of Palliative Care, and *Journal of Pain and Symptom Management.*" *Palliative and Supportive Care* 1: 7–13.

Rauschenbusch, Walter. 1897. "The Stake of the Church in the Social Movement." *American Journal of Sociology* 3: 18–30.

Rew, Lynn and Y. Joel Wong. 2006. "A Systematic Review of Associations among Religiosity/Spirituality and Adolescent Health Attitudes and Behaviors." *Journal of Adolescent Health* 38: 433–42.

Rostosky, Sharon S., Fred Danner, and Ellen D. Riggle. 2007. "Is Religiosity a Protective Factor against Substance Use in Young Adulthood? Only if You're Straight!" *Journal of Adolescent Health* 40: 440–7.

Saunders, Cicely and David Clark. 2006. *Cicely Saunders: Selected Writings 1958–2004.* Oxford: Oxford University Press.

Schreck, Christopher J., Melissa W. Burek, and Jason Clark-Miller. 2007. "He Sends Rain upon the Wicked: A Panel Study of the Influence of Religiosity on Violent Victimization." *Journal of Interpersonal Violence* 22: 872–93.

Scott, Lionel D., Michelle R. Munson, J. Curtis McMillen, and Marcia T. Ollie. 2006. "Religious Involvement and Its Association to Risk Behaviors among Older Youth in Foster Care." *American Journal of Community Psychology* 38: 223–36.

Seeman, Teresa E., Linda F. Dubin, and Melvin Seeman. 2003. "Religiosity/Spirituality and Health: A Critical Review of the Evidence for Biological Pathways." *American Psychologist* 58: 53–63.

Sherman, Allen C., Stephanie Simonton, Umaira Latif, Rebecca Spohn, and Guido Tricot. 2005. "Religious Struggle and Religious Comfort in Response to Illness: Health Outcomes among Stem Cell Transplant Patients." *Journal of Behavioral Medicine* 28: 359–67.

Sloan, Richard P. and Emilia Bagiella. 2002. "Claims about Religious Involvement and Health Outcomes." *Annals of Behavioral Medicine* 24: 14–21.

Sloan, Richard P., Emilia Bagiella, and Tia Powell. 1999. "Religion, Spirituality, and Medicine." *Lancet* 353: 664–7.

Sloan, Richard P., Emilia Bagiella, Larry VandeCreek, Margot Hover, Carlo Casalone, Trudi Jinpu Hirsch, Ralph Kreger, and Peter Poulos. 2000. "Should Physicians Prescribe Religious Activities?" *New England Journal of Medicine* 342: 1913–16.

Snowdon, David. 2001. *Aging with Grace: What the Nun Study Teaches Us about Leading Longer, Healthier, and More Meaningful Lives.* New York: Bantam Books.

Sprung, Charles L., Paulo Maia, Hans-Henrik Bulow, Bara Ricou, Apostolos Armaganidis, Mario Baras, Elisabet Wennberg, Konrad Reinhardt, Simon L. Fries, George Dietmar R. Nakos, Lambertius G. Thijs, and the Ethicus Study Group. 2007. "The Importance of Religious Affiliation and Culture on End-of-Life Decisions in European Intensive Care Units." *Intensive Care Medicine* 33: 1732–9.

Stack, Stephen. 2000. "Suicide: A 15-Year Review of the Sociological Literature. Part II: Modernization and Social Integration Perspectives." *Suicide and Life-Threatening Behavior* 30: 163–76.

Steffen, Patrick R. and Kevin S. Masters. 2005. "Does Compassion Mediate the Intrinsic Religion–Health Relationship?" *Annals of Behavioral Medicine* 30: 217–24.

Stein, Stephen J. 1992. *The Shaker Experience in America.* New Haven: Yale University Press.

Stockdale, Susan E., Kenneth B. Wells, Lingqi Tang, Thomas R. Belin, Lily Zhang, and Cathy D. Sherbourne. 2007. "The Importance of Social Context: Neighborhood Stressors,

Stress-Buffering Mechanisms, and Alcohol, Drug, and Mental Health Disorders." *Social Science and Medicine* 65: 1867–81.

Stone, Robyn. 2008. "Continuing Care Retirement Communities." Pp. 163–5 in Elizabeth A. Capezuti, Eugenia L. Siegler, and Mathy D. Mezey (eds.), *The Encyclopedia of Elder Care*, 2nd edition. New York: Springer.

Strawbridge, William J., Richard D. Cohen, Sarah J. Shema, and George Kaplan. 1997. "Frequent Attendance at Religious Services and Mortality over 28 Years." *American Journal of Public Health* 87: 957–61.

Thune-Boyle, Ingela C., Jan A. Stygall, Mohammed R. Keshtgar, and Stanton P. Newman. 2006. "Do Religious/Spirituality Coping Strategies Affect Illness Adjustment in Patients with Cancer? A Systematic Review of the Literature." *Social Science and Medicine* 63: 151–64.

Timberlake, David S., Soo Hyun Rhee, Brett C. Haberstick, Christian Hopfer, Marissa Ehringer, Jeffrey M. Lessem, Andrew Smolen, and John K. Hewitt. 2006. "The Moderating Effects of Religiosity on the Genetic and Environmental Determinants of Smoking Initiation." *Nicotine and Tobacco Research* 8: 123–33.

Tindle, Hilary A., Peter Wolsko, Roger B. Davis, David M. Eisenberg, Russell S. Phillips, and Ellen P. McCarthy. 2005. "Factors Associated with the Use of Mind Body Therapies among United States Adults with Musculoskeletal Pain." *Complementary Therapies in Medicine* 13: 155–64.

Vaillant, George, Janice Templeton, Monica Ardelt, and Stephanie E. Meyer. 2008. "The Natural History of Male Mental Health: Health and Religious Involvement." *Social Science and Medicine* 66: 221–31.

Wade, Christina, Maria Chao, Fredi Kronenberg, Linda Cushman, and Debra Kalmuss. 2008. "Medical Pluralism among American Women: Results of a National Survey." *Journal of Women's Health* 17: 829–40.

Wallace, John M. and Tyrone Forman. 1998. "Religion's Role in Promoting Health and Reducing Risk among American Youth." *Health Education and Behavior* 25: 721–41.

Weaver, Andrew J. and Kevin J. Flannelly. 2004. "The Role of Religion/Spirituality for Cancer Patients and Their Caregivers." *Southern Medical Journal* 97: 1210–14.

Weber, Max. 1964 [1922]. *The Sociology of Religion*. Boston: Beacon Press.

Whisman, Mark A., Kristina C. Gordon, and Yael Chatav. 2007. "Predicting Sexual Infidelity in a Population-Based Sample of Married Individuals." *Journal of Family Psychology* 21: 320–4.

Winslow, Charles-Edward Amory. 1935. "Public Health." Pp. 646–57 in Edwin R. A. Seligman (ed.), *Encylopaedia of the Social Sciences*. New York: Macmillan.

Wortmann, Jennifer H. and Crystal L. Park. 2008. "Religion and Spirituality in Adjustment following Bereavement: An Integrative Review." *Death Studies* 32: 703–36.

Yeager, D. M., Dana A. Glei, Melanie Au, Hui-Sheng Lin, Richard P. Sloan, and Maxine Weinstein. 2006. "Religious Involvement and Health Outcomes among Older Persons in Taiwan." *Social Science and Medicine* 63: 2228–41.

Zhang, Wei. 2008. "Religious Participation and Mortality Risk among the Oldest Old in China." *Journal of Gerontology: Social Sciences* 63B: S293–7.

8

Health Lifestyles

Bringing Structure Back*

WILLIAM C. COCKERHAM

In past historical periods, people more or less took their health for granted. That is, they were either healthy or unhealthy and that simply was the way life had turned out for them. But this situation has changed dramatically (Crawford 1984). Health today has become viewed as an achievement – something that people are supposed to work at to enhance their quality of life or risk chronic illness and premature death if they do not (Clarke et al. 2003). The primary mechanism by which health is manufactured or undermined in contemporary society is through health-related lifestyles. Most individuals begin life healthy, but their living conditions and the lifestyle practices associated with these conditions impact on their prospects for a healthy life over the course of their lives and personal efforts are typically required to maintain their health. Consequently, the study of health lifestyles is emerging as a relatively new and important area of research in medical sociology that will be discussed in this chapter.

Health lifestyles can be defined as collective patterns of health-related behavior based on choices from options available to people according to their life chances (Cockerham 2000a, 2007a). This definition incorporates the dialectical relationship between life choices and life chances proposed by Weber in his lifestyle concept (1978: 926–39 [1922: 531–9]). Health lifestyle choices, as is the case for other types of lifestyles, are voluntary, but life chances – which primarily represent class position – either empower or constrain choices as choices and chances work off each other in tandem to determine behavioral outcomes. In a Weberian context, life choices are a proxy for the exercise of agency and life chances are a form of structure.

Sociologists have been slow to recognize the importance of lifestyles on behavior and ultimately on health. One reason may have been the influence of Thorstein Veblen's (1994 [1899]) classic, the *Theory of the Leisure Class*, which affixed the term "lifestyle" to the upper class. We now know, as Giddens (1991: 6) pointed

*This is a revised and updated version of a paper that appeared as "Health Lifestyle Theory and the Convergence of Agency and Structure" in the *Journal of Health and Social Behavior* 46 (2005): 41–57 and as a chapter in *Social Causes of Health and Disease* (Polity Press, 2007).

out, that it would be a major error to suppose that lifestyles are confined to those in more privileged material circumstances. Everyone has a lifestyle, even the poorest of the poor. Moreover, as Giddens (1991), Turner (1992), and others (Clarke et al. 2003) have concluded, lifestyle options have now become integrated with bodily regimens or routines. People in advanced societies have normatively been assigned greater responsibility for their health and even the design of their own bodies. The consequence for individuals is facing varying degrees of stigma at the hands of the wider community and the social devaluation that accompanies it if they do not work at being healthy and/orappear healthy for their age.

According to Cockerham (2005, 2007a), this circumstance originates from changes in (1) disease patterns, (2) modernity, and (3) social identities. The first change is the twentieth-century epidemiological transition from acute to chronic illnesses as the major cause of death throughout most of the world. Chronic diseases – namely, heart disease, cancer, stroke, diabetes, and the like – cannot be cured by medical treatment, and health lifestyle practices, such as smoking, alcohol and drug abuse, eating high-fat foods, and unprotected sex in the case of sexually transmitted diseases, can cause health problems and end life prematurely. The result has been greater public awareness that medicine is not the automatic answer to all health situations (Crawford 1984). Unhealthy lifestyle practices like smoking can cause lung cancer and the afflicted person is likely to die from it regardless of what a doctor may do to forestall the eventuality. The realization that this is a certainty carries with it the revelation that the responsibility for one's health ultimately falls on oneself through healthy living. Greater personal responsibility means that achieving a healthy lifestyle has become more of a life or (time of) death option.

The second change is the current era of late modern social alterations creating a new form of modernity (Bauman 1999; Giddens 1991). While notions of an absolute break with the past modernity associated with the industrial age are unconvincing, it is nevertheless clear that society is in a transition to a new social form (Pescosolido and Rubin 2000). This is seen in the new world order evolving out of the collapse of Soviet-style socialism, the rise of China as the leading world manufacturing center for light consumer goods, the expanding multiculturalization of Europe and North America, the rise of cultural and gender politics, the multiplicity of family forms, changing patterns of social stratification, and the increasing use of knowledge as a commodity.

Late modern changes extend to health matters as well. Major examples are the continued decline in the status and professional authority of physicians through lessened control over the medical marketplace and the growing feminization of the medical profession. We also see greater movement toward the mutual participation model of the physician–patient relationship in which the patient has a greater share in the decision-making about his or her medical care. This circumstance has accelerated with the advent of Internet medicine and the extensive diffusion of medical information in the public domain (Hardey 1999). In the still-emerging late modern society, where traditional industrial age centers of power and authority such as medicine are weakening, adopting a healthy lifestyle accords people greater control over their health and longevity.

The third change is movement in late modernity toward an adjustment in the primary locus of social identity. Previously, work or occupation largely determined social class position and a person's way of life. Beginning in the second half of the twentieth century, lifestyle consumer habits have been increasingly experienced in advanced societies as a primary source of social identification (Bauman 1992; Crompton 2007; Giddens 1991). That is, what people consume, wear, and use reflects who they are. This situation was made possible by the rise in economic productivity promoting a general improvement in living standards and purchasing power after World War II. The easier acquisition of basic material needs allowed styles of consumption to supersede occupation for signaling social similarities and distinctions for many people (Crompton 2007).

Scott (1996), for example, found years ago that the lifestyles of manual workers in Britain have been altered, with major implications for class identification. He observes that social distinctions within the working class are determined more by consumption patterns than relationships to the means of production. Affluent workers aspired to higher living standards and greater purchasing power, but they did not see this as a way of attaining middle-class status. "Their principal status concerns," states Scott (1996: 238), "were those of maintaining their position above 'rough' and relatively improverished manual workers and of securing their own standing in what they saw as a social hierarchy defined in purely monetary, consumption terms."

Therefore, as Crompton (2007) points out, the claim that lifestyles have become more significant in class formation and social identification needs to be taken seriously. She (Crompton 2007: 97) observes that in addition to the role of specific lifestyles in the reproduction of established groups, lifestyles in the broader sense may be seen as contributing to the emergence of newly differentiated groups and providing new focuses for the expression of interests and concerns. This conclusion is consistent with Giddens' (1991) assertion that lifestyles not only fulfill utilitarian needs, but additionally express a person's self-identity. Giddens (1991: 81) explains it this way:

> The notion of lifestyle sounds somewhat trivial because it is so often thought of solely in terms of superficial consumerism: lifestyles as suggested by glossy magazines and advertising images. But there is something much more fundamental going on than such a conception suggests: in conditions of high modernity, we all not only follow lifestyles, but in an important sense are forced to do so – we have no choice but to choose. A lifestyle can be defined as a more or less integrated set of practices which an individual embraces, not only because such practices fulfill utilitarian needs, but because they give material form to a particular narrative of self-identity.

An important lifestyle configuration and the accompanying social marker are those practices affecting health and the distinctions they also contribute to differences in social identities (Annandale 1998). Bourdieu (1984) furnishes us with an example in noting the distinctions between social classes in France with respect to differing tastes in foods (hearty vs. tasty, light, and low in calories) and sports (wrestling and boxing vs. sailing and tennis). The link between lifestyles and social identity signals the growing importance of lifestyles in the analysis of social life. There have been suggestions that lifestyles are a stronger measure of social position than class as class boundaries become less distinct and lifestyles better express differences between class groupings. However, enough evidence has not yet accumulated to show that this is indeed the case. Class today remains a powerful social variable. Nevertheless, as Giddens (1991: 5) concludes, the lifestyle concept has taken on a particular significance in understanding contemporary social life. It has also taken on particular significance with respect to health.

THE AGENCY–STRUCTURE DEBATE

The theoretical conceptualization of health lifestyles, however, is affected by the agency–structure debate. The relative contributions of agency and structure in influencing social behavior have been *the* central sociological question since the beginning of the discipline. As Archer (1995: 1) explains: "the vexatious task of understanding the linkage between 'structure and agency' will always retain this centrality because it derives from what society intrinsically is." However, medical sociologists have paid little attention to the agency–structure debate, although it is clearly relevant to theoretical discussions of health and lifestyles (Pescosolido, McLeod, and Alegría 2000; S. Williams 1995). When applied to health lifestyles, the question becomes whether the decisions people make with respect to food, exercise, smoking, and the like are largely a matter of individual choice or are principally molded by structural variables such as social class position and gender.

It is crucial in analyzing any exercise of *agency* that the actor could have acted otherwise in a particular situation if he or she had chosen to do so (Bhaskar 1998). Emirbayer and Mische (1998) suggest, accordingly, that human agency consists of three different elements: (1) *iteration* (the selective reactivation of past patterns of thought and action), (2) *projectivity* (the imaginative generation of possible future trajectories of action in which structures of thought and action may be creatively reconfigured), and (3) *practical evaluation* (the capacity to make practical and normative judgments among alternative possibilities). Agency can thus be considered a process in which individuals recall their past, imagine their future actions, critically evaluate their present circumstances, and choose their behavior based upon their assessment of the situation.

William Sewell (1992: 19) provides a definition of *structures* as "sets of mutually sustaining schemas and resources that empower or constrain social action and tend to be reproduced by that social action." Schemas are transposable rules or procedures applied to the enactment of social life. Resources are of two types, either human (e.g., physical strength, dexterity, knowledge) or non-human (naturally occurring or manufactured) that can be used to enhance or maintain power. Sewell equates resources with the power to influence action consistent with Giddens' (1984) notion of the duality of structure as both constraining and enabling. This duality, while correct, nonetheless contains a contradiction. The enabling function suggests resources increase the range and style of options from which the actor can choose, but constraint means that resources invariably limit choices to what is possible.

Although agency theorists maintain that agency will never be completely determined by structure, it is also clear that "there is no hypothetical moment in which agency actually gets 'free' of structure; it is not, in other words, some pure Kantian transcendental free will" (Emirbayer and Mische 1998:1004). This is because, as

Bauman (1999) observes, individual choices in *all* circumstances are confined by two sets of constraints: (1) choosing from among what is available and (2) social roles or codes telling the individual the rank order and appropriateness of preferences. People do have the capability to act independently of the social structures in their lives, but the occasions on which they do so appear to be rare.

MAX WEBER: BRINGING BACK STRUCTURE

Much of what we know about lifestyles has its theoretical origins in the early twentieth-century work of Max Weber (1978 [1922]). Weber's conceptualization of the dialectical interplay between life choices and life chances as the two basic components of lifestyles seems to accord a dominant role to choice. People have needs, goals, identities, and desires that they match against their chances and probabilities for acquiring; they then select a lifestyle based on their assessments and the reality of their circumstances (Cockerham, Rütten, and Abel 1997: 325). Even though this concept and others by Weber reflect an individualist and agency-oriented outlook, serious Weberian scholars recognize he did not view patterns of social action as the uncoordinated practices of disconnected individuals (Alexander 1983; Kalberg 1994; Mommsen 1989; Ringer 2004). Instead, he saw social action in terms of regularities and uniformities repeated by numerous actors over time. As Kalberg (1994: 30) explains, the manner in which the natural random flow of action is transformed into regularities constitutes one of Weber's most basic and central themes. His focus was not on the way in which people act individually but together.

According to Ringer (2004), Weber never abandoned his commitment to the rational individual as key to understanding social action; however, his theory of action extended well beyond this foundation. Ringer (2004: 178) states:

> From 1910 on, Weber explicitly distinguished the work of the sociologist from that of the historian. He thought it possible to detect "regularities" in the realm of social action, cases in which similar "meanings" lead to similar "progressions" of behavior. Sociology, he argued, is concerned with such "types" of progressions, ... [and] develops ... typological concepts and seeks general rules about events.

Consequently, the bridge from agency to structure for Weber was his construction of "ideal types" that were conceptual entities existing beyond the individual, such as his model of bureaucracy or conceptualizations of macro-level processes like the spread of formal rationality in Western society (Kalberg 1994). Ideal types represented a progression from individuals to structures that allowed him to make general statements about collective patterns of social behavior. For example, in *The Protestant Ethic and the Spirit of Capitalism* (1958), Weber emphasized macro-structure in an essentially "top-down" fashion by showing how social institutions (Calvinist religion) and widespread belief systems (the spirit of capitalism) were powerful forces in shaping the thoughts and behavior of individuals (Sibeon 2004). As Weber (1958: 55) states: "In order that a manner of life well adapted to the peculiarities of capitalism ... could come to dominate others, it had to originate somewhere, and not in isolated individuals alone, but as a way of life common to whole groups of men."

Therefore, Weber's approach to social action does not favor the individual to the neglect of external conditions; rather, it is multidimensional, which is one of his great strengths as a theorist. Alexander (1983: 55) discusses "normative force as the other major environment of the individual act" and details Weber's multidimensional perspective in his early writings, his retreat from multidimensionality, and his return to it as a mature scholar. Mommsen (1989), like Alexander, Kalberg, and Ringer, also credits Weber with a multidimensional approach to social action. Mommsen (1989: 151) finds that even though Weber emphasized innovative deeds of individuals, he repeatedly pointed out that social processes are largely determined by rigid institutional structures and that individuals are usually helpless against them because, as a rule, their life-conduct is largely determined by them since their economic interests require adaptation and conformity with the social order. Mommsen (1989: 150) says this about Weber's view of social action:

> He persistently emphasized the key role played by individual action.... Yet at the same time he argued again and again that the life-conduct of individuals is largely determined by socio-economic conditions beyond their control; the average person at any rate has little choice other than to adapt his or her life-conduct to the prevailing social and economic circumstances; conformity to given conditions and traditions is likely to be the individual's normal reaction.

However, when we consider Weber's influence on conceptualizing health lifestyles, we find that conditions external to the individual like norms, life chances, and other structural dimensions are often submerged in relation to the more powerful role for agency or choice (Cockerham 2007a). According to Frohlich, Corin, and Potvin (2001: 782): "When lifestyle is currently discussed within the socio-medical discourse, there is a decided tendency for it to be used in reference to individual behavioural patterns that affect disease status," thereby neglecting its collective (structural) characteristics. Such studies depict health lifestyles as individually constructed forms of behaviors. This type of approach is an example of Archer's (1995) notion of "upwards conflation" in which individuals are seen as exercising power in a one-way, upwards fashion in society that seems incapable of acting back to influence them.

Sociological concepts reflecting literally all theories of social life attest to the fact that *something* (namely structure) exists beyond the individual to give rise to customary patterns of behavior. These concepts range from Durkheim's (1950 [1895]: 13) notion of social facts as "every way of acting, fixed or not, capable of exercising on the individual an external constraint" to Mead's (1934: 155) view of the "generalized other" as the organized attitudes of the whole community and the social process through which "the community exercises control over the conduct of its individual members."

Structural influences on health lifestyle practices are seen, for example, in the studies of Andrée Demers and her colleagues in Canada on alcohol consumption by married women (Demers, Bisson, and Palluy 1999) and university students (Demers et al. 2002). This research shows that the social relationships of the people drinking and the social context of the drinking situation have substantial effects on alcohol intake and drinking behavior. Married women, for example, were found to adopt the same drinking patterns of their husbands, unless they were in an older age group or had children. The happier the couple were together, the greater the convergence in drinking. The alcohol intake of university students varied with the drinking situation. That is, why, where, when, and with whom students drank had an important effect on how much alcohol they consumed. Thus the drinking situation shaped their drinking. "It is apparent from our findings," state Demers et al. (2002: 422), "that the individual cannot be conceptualized as an autonomous actor making self-governing decisions in a social vacuum."

Another example of structural influences on health lifestyles is the antismoking campaign in the United States. For over 20 years, massive efforts were made to reduce cigarette smoking through educational programs on the hazards of smoking. "These individual approaches to the cessation of smoking encouraged many to stop," conclude Sweat and Denison (1995: S252), "however, not until smoking was banned in many public places did the prevalence of smoking significantly decline." This ban had the effect of labeling smokers as social outcasts and deviants. Antismoking laws, social isolation, and stigma significantly increased smoking cessation "far beyond the results of purely individualistic approaches" (Sweat and Denison 1995: S252).

Whereas these studies show structural influences have a significant effect on health lifestyles, there are situations in which structure can be so overwhelming that agency is rendered inert. Gareth Williams (2003) reports on the high mortality of a group of Welsh coal miners in the 1930s. These were men "unsung in any chronicle of existence" (cited in Williams 2003: 145). Their lives were severely curtailed by their punishing work and diet of beggars. However, the unremitting toll of childbirth and domestic labor impaired the health and shortened the lives of the women as much as or more than that of the men. The weight of structural conditions was so heavy that individual capabilities and capacities were ineffective. This situation, comments Williams (2003: 146); "provides a salutary reminder of the way in which the balance between agency, context, and structure is itself highly determined by structural forces."

In more recent research investigating contemporary social conditions in a working-class neighborhood in a city in northwest England, Williams observes that the influence of structure on agency in relation to health lifestyles is still heavy-handed. He finds that assuming people have the freedom to make healthy choices is out of line with what many people experience as real possibilities in their everyday lives. "The respondents," concludes Williams (2003: 147), "understood the behavioural risk factors that made ill-health more likely and for which they were, in a limited sense, responsible, but they were also aware that the risks they faced were part of social conditions that they could do little to change."

Any theory of health lifestyles needs to account for both agency and structure. The remainder of this chapter will consider the author's (Cockerham 2005, 2007a) health lifestyle paradigm. While agency is important, it will be argued that structural conditions can act back on individuals and configure their lifestyle patterns in particular ways. Agency allows them to reject or modify these patterns, but structure limits the options that are available and shapes the decisions that are made.

A HEALTH LIFESTYLES MODEL

Weber associated lifestyles not with individuals but with status groups, thereby treating them as a collective social phenomenon. Weber maintained that status groups are aggregates of people with similar status and class backgrounds, and they originate through a sharing of similar lifestyles. People who wish to be part of a particular status group are required to adopt the appropriate lifestyle. Status groups are stratified according to their patterns of consumption. These patterns not only establish differences between groups, but they also *express* differences that are already in place (Bourdieu 1984). Health lifestyles are a form of consumption in that the health that is produced is used for something, such as a longer life, work, or enhanced enjoyment of one's physical being (Cockerham 2000a; d'Houtaud and Field 1984). Moreover, health lifestyles are supported by an extensive health products industry of goods and services (e.g., running shoes, sports clothing, diet plans and vitamin supplements, health foods, health club and spa memberships) promoting consumption as an inherent component of participation.

Additionally, as David Gochman (1997) points out, positive health lifestyle behaviors are the opposite of risk behaviors. Good nutrition, for example, is the reverse of bad nutrition. The binary nature of health lifestyle practices means that the outcome generated from the interplay of choices and chances has either positive or negative effects on health. Gochman also observes that health lifestyles are intended to avoid risk in general and are oriented toward achieving or maintaining overall health and fitness.

However, while the term health lifestyle is meant to encompass a general way of healthy living, there has been discussion over whether or not there is an overall "health lifestyle." The best evidence suggests that for many people their health lifestyle can be characterized as either generally positive or negative. A study of US Navy personnel found, for example, that positive health behaviors clustered along two dimensions, one promoting wellness and the other avoiding risk (Vickers, Conway, and Hervig 1990). Other research from Finland provides strong evidence that health practices are related, with people who behave unhealthily in one respect doing so in others and vice versa (Laaksonen, Prättälä, and Lahelma 2002). Smoking had the strongest and most consistent association with other unhealthy lifestyle practices in that people who smoked were also likely to drink, have poor food habits, and not exercise. Multiple unhealthy practices were most common among lower socioeconomic groups. A significant body of research attaches the most positive health lifestyle practices to higher social strata and women, the most negative to lower strata and men (Blaxter 1990; Cockerham 2000a, 2005, 2007a; Grzywacz and Marks 2001; Link and Phelan 2000).

It therefore appears that health lifestyles are not the uncoordinated behaviors of disconnected individuals, but are personal routines that merge into an aggregate form representative of specific groups and classes. While definitions and a general concept of health lifestyles exist in the literature, it is time that a theoretical paradigm is also available. This paradigm is presented in Figure 8.1. The arrows between boxes indicate hypothesized causal relationships.

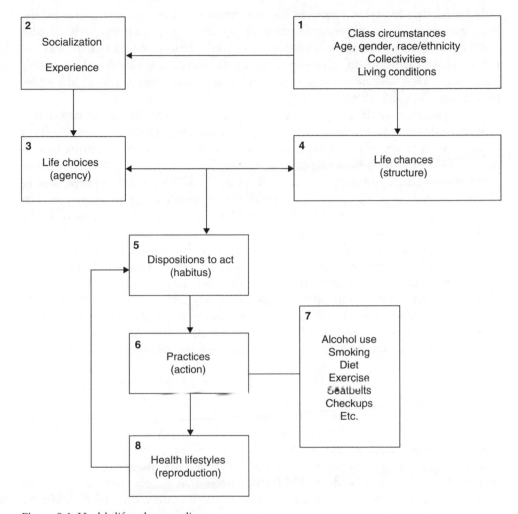

Figure 8.1 Health lifestyles paradigm.

Beginning with box 1, in the top right-hand corner of Figure 8.1, four categories of structural variables are listed that have the capacity to shape health lifestyles: (1) class circumstances, (2) age, gender, and race/ethnicity, (3) collectivities, and (4) living conditions. Each of these categories is suggested by a review of the research literature.

Class circumstances

The first category of structural variables is class circumstances, which is likely the most important influence on lifestyle forms. The close connection between class and lifestyles has been observed since the nineteenth century (Veblen 1994 [1899]). However, it remained for Weber (1978 [1922]) to produce the most insightful account of the link between lifestyles and socioeconomic status. Weber (1946) not only found that lifestyles expressed distinct differences between status groups and their adoption was a necessary feature of upward social mobility, but he also observed that powerful social strata were "social carriers" of particular ways of living. These carrier strata were important causal forces in their own right as they transmitted class-specific norms, values, religious ethics, and ways of life across generations (Kalberg 1994).

The seminal study detailing class as the most decisive variable in the determination of health lifestyles is Bourdieu's (1984) *Distinction*, which included a survey of differences in sports preferences and eating habits between French professionals (upper-middle class) and the working class. Bourdieu found the working class to be more attentive to maintaining the strength of the male body than its shape, and to favor food that is both cheap and nutritious; in contrast, the professional class prefers food that is tasty, healthy, light, and low in calories. As for leisure sports such as sailing, skiing, golf, tennis, and horseback riding, Bourdieu noted that the working class faces not only economic barriers, but also social barriers in the form of hidden entry requirements of family tradition, obligatory dress and behavior, and early socialization. Also these sports are usually practiced in exclusive locations with chosen partners and require investments of money, time, and training that the working class lacks. The working class, in contrast, opts for sports that are popular with the general public and equally accessible to all classes. These are sports like football (soccer), wrestling, and boxing that feature strength, endurance, and violence.

Thus, Bourdieu formulated the notion of "distance from necessity" that emerges as a key explanation of class differences in lifestyles. He points out that the more distant a person is from having to forage for economic necessity, the greater the freedom and time that person has to develop and refine personal tastes in line with a more privileged class status. Lower social strata, in turn, tend to adopt the tastes consistent with their class position, in which acquiring items of necessity is paramount. For example, Bourdieu (1984: 177) notes that as one rises in the social hierarchy, the proportion of income spent on food diminishes, or that within the food budget, the proportion spent on heavy, fattening foods, which are also cheap – pasta, potatoes, beans, bacon, and pork – declines, as does that spent on wine, whereas an increasing proportion is spent on leaner, lighter, non-fattening foods and especially fresh fruits and vegetables.

Bourdieu finds that social classes not dominated by the ordinary interests and urgencies of making a daily living claim superiority in social and cultural tastes over those who have only fundamental levels of material well-being. "As the objective distance from necessity grows," states Bourdieu (1984: 55), "life-style increasingly becomes the product of what Weber calls a 'stylization of life,' a systematic commitment which orients and organizes the most diverse practices – the choice of a vintage or a cheese or the decoration of a holiday home in the country." The greater the social distance, the greater the refinement of practices. The relevance of the distance from necessity concept is seen in health lifestyles where classes higher on the social scale have the time and resources to adopt the healthiest practices.

In a similar fashion, research in France by d'Houtaud and Field (1984) found that different classes also value health in different ways. Health was conceptualized as something to be cultivated for increased vitality and the enjoyment of life among the upper and middle classes, and for the capability to continue to work for the classes below them. For those closest to necessity, being unhealthy meant being unable to work and secure those necessities; however, for those whose resources placed them beyond the range of basic necessity, being unhealthy meant less enjoyment out of life. In sum, lower socioeconomic status (SES) persons viewed health largely as a means to an end (to be able to work), while higher SES persons regarded health as an end in itself (vitality).

In Britain, Blaxter (1990) found important differences in health lifestyles persisted between the various social classes, with the upper and middle classes taking better care of their health than the working and lower classes. Of course, not everyone in the lower class has an unhealthy lifestyle, nor does everyone in the upper class live in a healthy manner. There are variations within classes. However, as Blaxter's data show, major distinctions *between* classes are readily apparent. Smoking was by far the most prevalent among male blue-collar workers in industrial areas, along with heavy alcohol consumption. More frequent drinking, but in lower quantities, was found among higher-status males. Sports participation and good dietary habits were also significantly more common at the upper end of the social scale.

Blaxter concluded that socioeconomic circumstances and the living environment determined the extent to which health lifestyles were practiced effectively. This is an important finding in that it shows the structural conditions of people's lives make it probable or improbable that they can achieve a positive health lifestyle. As Blaxter (1990: 216) puts it: "If circumstances are good, 'healthy' behaviour appears to have a strong influence on health. If they are bad, then behaviours make rather little difference." Consequently, living a healthy lifestyle was not simply a matter of individual choice, but to a large extent depended upon a person's social and material environment for its success.

Other research in Britain has also identified major distinctions in health lifestyles between the various classes, with less positive lifestyles practiced the lower the rung a person occupies on the social ladder (Jarvis and Wardle 1999; Reid 1998). A decline in smoking, for instance, was far greater among the affluent, but very little change was observed among the British poor (Jarvis and Wardle 1999). In the United States, the poor have likewise been found to be especially disadvantaged with respect to positive health lifestyles compared to other social classes. The lower class shows the highest levels of cigarette consumption, unhealthy eating and drinking, and less participation in exercise in adulthood (Carpiano, Link, and Phelan 2008; Grzywacz and Marks 2001; Snead and Cockerham 2002; Wickrama et al. 1999).

Elsewhere, in Russia, negative health lifestyles – featuring heavy alcohol consumption and binge drinking, smoking, high-fat diets, and an absence of exercise – instigated a mortality crisis among middle-age, working-class men that has lasted since the mid-1960s (Cockerham 1999, 2000b, 2006, 2007b; Cockerham, Snead, and DeWaal 2002; Dmitrieva 2005; Van Gundy et al. 2005). Class plays a decisive role in this ongoing problem, as the Russian middle class – the usual social carrier of positive health lifestyles – remains underdeveloped (Shankina 2004), leaving the much larger and more influential working class with its heavy drinking and smoking norms as the most influential class in health matters (Cockerham 2006, 2007b).

Overall, the lifestyles of the upper and upper-middle classes are the healthiest. Virtually every study confirms this. These classes have the highest participation in leisure-time sports and exercise, healthier diets, moderate drinking, little smoking, more physical checkups by physicians, and greater opportunities for rest, relaxation, and coping successfully with stress (Blaxter 1990; Grzywacz and Marks 2001; Jarvis and Wardle 1999; Robert and House 2000; Snead and Cockerham 2002). The upper and upper-middle classes are also the first to have knowledge of new health risks and, because of greater resources, are most able to adopt new health strategies and practices (Link and Phelan 2000). The advantaged classes are able to move in a more fluid fashion to embrace new health behaviors, such as adopting low-cholesterol and low-carbohydrate diets. Advantaged classes were able to reduce their risk of heart disease in the United States (which at one time was high relative to the lower class) so that lower-class individuals are now at greater risk. While education is obviously a critical factor, it is, as noted, only one feature of the broader dimension of class membership that enables members of higher social strata to be healthier over the life course. The other factors are income that provides them with the financial resources to live a healthy life and occupational status that provides them with high self-esteem and sense of responsibility.

Although capitalism is inherently a system of inequality, the paradox is that it has clearly been compatible with major improvements in overall standards of living and health. Today in most advanced countries traditional health indicators such as life expectancy and infant mortality have never been better. Communicable diseases that used to take the lives of young and middle-age people have been severely diminished or curtailed, as in the case of smallpox and polio. Additional advances in medical care like organ transplants have saved lives, progress in reproductive health has improved fertility, and other measures like hip replacementsand surgery for cataracts have enhanced the quality of some people's lives. In the process, the health and longevity of all socioeconomic groups has improved, even though the gap between the top and bottom of society not only persists, but in some cases – like in Britain – has even increased. "General health improvement," states Michael Bury (2005: 24), "can therefore occur alongside persisting and even widening inequalities."When it comes to health lifestyles, the advantage likewise accrues to higher social strata.

Age, gender, and race/ethnicity

Weber did not consider other stratification variables such as age, gender, and race/ethnicity, yet contemporary empirical studies show that these variables influence health lifestyles. Age affects health lifestyles because people tend to take better care of their health as they grow older by being more careful about the food they eat, resting and relaxing more, and either reducing or abstaining from alcohol use and smoking (Backett and Davison 1995). Exercise, however, is one major health lifestyle activity that declines and is often lost with advancing age (Grzywacz and Marks 2001). Yet we know that class can intersect with age to produce further differences in lifestyle practices within age groups, as seen in teenage smoking, which appears significantly more among the lower strata than the middle and upper (Jarvis and Wardle 1999).

Gender is a highly significant variable in that women eat more healthy foods, drink less alcohol, smoke less, visit doctors more often for preventive care, wear seatbelts more frequently when they drive, and, with the exception of exercise, have healthier lifestyles overall than men (Abel et al. 1999; Blaxter 1990; Cockerham 2000a, 2000b; Grzywacz and Marks 2001; Roos et al. 1998). Furthermore, in adolescence males tend to adopt the health lifestyles of their fathers and females those of their mothers, thereby setting the parameters for the transmission of gender-specific health practices into adulthood (Wickrama et al. 1999).

Whereas gender is a strong predictor of health lifestyle practices, its effects can also be moderated by class distinctions, as people higher on the social scale, regardless of gender, eat healthier diets, smoke less, and participate more in leisure-time exercise (Adonis and Pollard 1997; Blaxter 1990; Reid 1998). This is seen in research in Britain on the food preferences of middle-class and working-class women (Calnan 1997) and in the United States where lower-class women were exceedingly less likely to exercise (other than housework) than higher-strata women and men (Ford et al. 1991).

Race and ethnicity are presumed to be important, but there is a paucity of research directly comparing the health lifestyles of different racial and ethnic groups. Black–White comparisons in the United States show that Whites often drink alcohol, smoke, exercise, and practice weight control more than Blacks (George and Johnson 2001; Grzywacz and Marks 2001; Johnson and Hoffman 2000; Lindquist, Cockerham, and Hwang 1999; Pampel 2008), but the differences have not been fully documented. There is evidence that exercise declines more steeply for Blacks than Whites across the course of adulthood, yet this pattern may be caused by Blacks having more functional health problems and living in less safe neighborhoods (Grzywacz and Marks 2001). The risk of victimization in an unsafe neighborhood can significantly undermine the motivation to engage in outdoor exercise. Most studies on health and race, however, address levels of morbidity and mortality rather than specific health practices. These studies often suggest that racial disparities in health are largely but not exclusively determined by class position, with disadvantaged socioeconomic circumstances and the adverse life experiences associated with them promoting poor health (Robert and House 2000; Smaje 2000).

Research is also needed that investigates the relationship between health lifestyles and different ethnic groups, including how to best conceptualize and measure ethnicity. Existing studies of ethnicity, like those of race, have focused more on overall health profiles than health lifestyles. Nevertheless, some of these studies are instructive, as seen in research by Karlsen and Nazroo (2002) on the respective influences of agency and structure on the health of ethnic minorities in Great Britain. The sample for this study consisted of people of Pakistani, Bangladeshi, Indian, and African-Asian ethnic heritage. Ethnic identity was considered a consequence of agency, even though it is subject to external influences, because a person's identity is self-constructed and internally defined by the individual. "However, our findings suggest," state Karlsen and Nazroo (2002: 18), "that ethnicity as identity does not appear to influence health; rather ethnicity as structure – both in terms of racialisation [discrimination/harassment] and class experience – is strongly associated with health for ethnic minority people living in Britain." When it comes to health lifestyles, the effects of race and ethnicity may indeed reside more powerfully in structure than agency, as social discrimination and working/lower-class experiences had greater effects on health than personal identities.

Collectivities

Collectivities are collections of actors linked together through particular social relationships, such as kinship, work, religion, and politics. Their shared norms, values, ideals, and social perspectives constitute intersubjective "thought communities" beyond individual subjectivity that reflect a particular collective world view (Zerubavel 1997). The notion of thought communities is akin to Mead's (1934) concept of the generalized other in that both are abstractions of the perspectives of social collectivities or groups that enter into the thinking of the individual. While people may accept, reject, or ignore the normative guidance rendered, collective views are nevertheless likely to be taken into account when choosing a course of action (Berger and Luckmann 1967). Weber (1978 [1922]) notes that concepts of collective entities have meaning in the minds of individuals, partly as something actually existing and partly as something with normative authority. "Actors," states Weber (1978 [1922]: 14), "thus in part orient their action to them, and in this role such ideas have a powerful, often a decisive, causal influence on the course of action of real individuals."

Religion and ideology are examples of collective perspectives that have implications for health lifestyles. This is seen in the usual preference of highly religious persons and groups for positive health lifestyles since their beliefs invariably promote healthy living in the form of good nutrition, exercise, and personal hygiene, while discouraging alcohol use and smoking cigarettes (Brown et al. 2001; Hill et al. 2007). However, the full extent of the relationship between religiosity and health lifestyles is not known because of a lack of relevant studies. This is an important area that needs further research.

Little is also known about ideology and health lifestyles. Research on the effects of the socialist heritage in contemporary Russia shows that pro-socialists (those who are in favor of a return to state socialism as it was before Gorbachev) have less healthy lifestyles than anti-socialists, even though neither group demonstrated exceptionally positive health practices (Cockerham et al. 2002). Pro-socialists had a particularly passive approach to health lifestyles that seemed leftover from Soviet times. The choices of individuals in Soviet society were confined to a single social and political ideology (communism) and expected to conform to it. When a person got sick, the state was responsible for taking care of that person as a benefit of state socialism. Individual incentives in health matters were encouraged. Thus it could be argued that communism was bad for one's health as it failed to promote healthy lifestyles practices. However, the extent to which ideology generally affects health lifestyles beyond this example has not been determined.

Surprisingly, there is also little research on family and kinship group influences concerning health lifestyles, although we know from K. A. S. Wickrama and his colleagues (1999) in the United States that such influence can be strong. The family typically influences how a particular person perceives his or her health situation (Cockerham 2007a). Most individuals are born into a family of significant others – significant because they provide the child with a specific social identity. This identity includes not only an appraisal of physical and intellectual characteristics, but also knowledge about the family's social and medical history. In addition to learning the family's social status, perspective, and cultural orientation, the child learns about the health threats most common for the family and the measures needed to cope with them. As the child becomes older and takes as his or her own the values and attitudes of the immediate family, community, and wider society as presented through the mediating influence of the family, the child is considered properly socialized in that he or she behaves in accordance with group-approved rules.

While children can either accept or reject the social perspective put forth by their family as representative of their own social reality, the reality presented to them in the process of primary socialization is set by adults who determine both what information is provided and assessments of the validity of opposing viewpoints. Although children are not necessarily passive in the socialization experience, what is important is that they have no choice in the selection of their significant others so that identification with them is quasi-automatic (Berger and Luckmann 1967). This further means that children's internalization of their family's interpretation of social reality is quasi-inevitable. Although the initial social world presented to children by their significant others may be weakened by later social relationships and views, it can nonetheless be a lasting influence. Parental influence, for example, has been found to be the most important and persistent influence on the preventive health beliefs of their children and significant in shaping their health lifestyles (Wickrama et al. 1999).

Living conditions

Living conditions are a category of structural variables pertaining to differences in the quality of housing and access to basic utilities (e.g., electricity, gas, heating, sewers, indoor plumbing, safe piped water, hot water), neighborhood facilities (e.g., grocery stores, parks, recreation), and personal safety. To date there has been little research linking living conditions to health lifestyles, but the connection is important. As noted, Blaxter (1990) found in her nationwide British survey that the conditions within which a person lives have important implications for health-related behavior. Health lifestyles were most effective in positive circumstances and least effective under negative living conditions. In the United States, living in disadvantaged neighborhoods has been associated with a less positive health status (Browning and Cagney 2002, 2003) and increased peer drinking that is further associated with increased adolescent alcohol use (Chuang et al. 2005). Other research, as also previously noted, shows that living in less safe neighborhoods significantly contributes to the low participation of adult Blacks in vigorous outdoor exercise (Grzywacz and Marks 2001). Consequently, living conditions can constrain or enhance health lifestyles.

Socialization and experience

Class circumstances and the other variables shown in box 1 of Figure 8.1 provide the social context for socialization and experience as depicted by the arrow leading to box 2.

This is consistent with Bourdieu's (1977) view that dispositions to act in particular ways are constructed through socialization and experience, with class position providing the social context for this process. The present model, however, adds the additional structural categories – age, gender, race/ethnicity, collectivities, and living conditions – depicted in box 1, since they may also influence the social environment within which socialization and experience occur.

Whereas primary socialization represents the imposition of society's norms and values on the individual by significant others and secondary socialization results from later training, experience is the learned outcome of day-to-day activities that comes about through social interaction and the practical exercise of agency. It is through both socialization and experience that the person or actor acquires reflexive awareness and the capacity to perform agency, but experience – with respect to life choices – provides the essential basis for agency's practical and evaluative dimensions to evolve over time. This is especially the case as people confront new social situations and conditions.

Life choices (agency)

Figure 8.1 shows that socialization and experience (box 2) provides the capacity for life choices (agency) depicted in box 3. As previously noted, the term "life choices" was introduced by Weber as one of the two major components of lifestyles (the other is life chances) and refers to the self-direction of one's behavior. It is an English-language translation of *Lebensführung*, which in German literally means conducting or managing one's life. Life choices are a process of agency by which individuals critically evaluate and choose their course of action. Weber's notion of life choices differs from rational choice theory in that it accounts for both means–ends rationality and the interpretive process whereby the potential outcomes of choices are imagined, evaluated, and reconstructed in the mind (Emirbayer and Mische 1998). Weber (1946) maintained that individuals have the capacity to interpret their situation, make deliberate choices, and attach subjective meaning to their actions. All social action in his view takes place in contexts that imply both constraints and opportunities, with the actor's interpretive understanding (*Verstehen*) of the situation guiding behavioral choices (Kalberg 1994).

Life chances (structure)

Class circumstances and to a lesser degree the other variables in box 1 constitute life chances (structure) shown in box 4. Life chances are the other major component of lifestyles in Weber's model. Weber was ambiguous about what he meant by life chances, but the term is usually associated with the advantages and disadvantages of relative class situations. Dahrendorf (1979: 73) finds that the best meaning of life chances in Weber's work is the "crystallized probability of finding satisfaction for interests, wants and needs, thus the probability of the occurrence of events which bring about such satisfaction." Consequently, the higher a person's position in a class hierarchy, the better the person's life chances or probabilities for finding satisfaction and vice versa. Dahrendorf (1979: 65) adds the following clarification: "for Weber, the probability of sequences of action postulated in the concept of chance is not merely an observed and thus calculable probability, but is a probability which is invariably anchored in structural conditions." Thus a person's probabilities for satisfaction that constitute his or her life chances are based on the structural conditions in their life, especially their class position. Weber's thesis is that chance is socially determined and social structure is an arrangement of chances. Therefore, life chances represent the influence of structure in Weber's *œuvre* and this paradigm.

Choice and chance interplay

The arrows in Figure 8.1 indicate the dialectical interplay between life choices (box 3) and life chances (box 4). This interaction is Weber's most important contribution to conceptualizing lifestyle construction (Cockerham, Abel, and Lüschen 1993; Cockerham et al. 1997). Choices and chances operate in tandem to determine a distinction lifestyle for individuals, groups, and classes. Life chances (structure) either constrain or enable choices (agency); agency is not passive in this process, however. As Archer (2003) explains, whether or not constraints and enablements are exercised as causal powers is based on agency choosing the practices to be activated. "Constraints," says Archer (2003: 4), "require something to constrain, and enablements something to enable." Consequently, people have to consider a course of action if their actions are to be either constrained or enabled. People therefore align their goals, needs, and desires with their probabilities for realizing them and choose a lifestyle according to their assessments of the reality of their resources and class circumstances. Unrealistic choices are not likely to succeed or be selected, while realistic choices are based upon what is structurally possible.

In this context, choices and chances are not only connected dialectically, they are also analytically distinct. As Archer (1998: 369) points out: "Because the emergent properties of structures and the actual experiences of agents are not synchronized (due to the very nature of society as an open system), then there will always be the inescapable need for a two-part account." Weber provides such a framework. He conceptualizes choice and chance as separate components in the activation and conduct of a lifestyle and merges the different functions of agency and structure without either losing their distinctiveness.

Dispositions to act (habitus)

Figure 8.1 shows that the interaction of life choices and life chances produces individual dispositions toward action (box 5). These dispositions constitute a habitus. The notion of habitus originates with Edmund Husserl (1989 [1952]: 266–93), who used the term to describe habitual action that is intuitively followed and anticipated. The concept has been expanded by Bourdieu (1977: 72–95) to serve as his core explanation for the agency–structure relationship in lifestyle dispositions (Bourdieu 1984: 169–225). Bourdieu (1990: 53) defines habitus as "systems of durable, transposable dispositions, structured structures predisposed to operate as structuring structures, that is, as principles which generate and organize practices and representations that can be objectively adapted to their outcomes without presupposing a conscious aiming at ends or an express mastery of the operations necessary in order to attain them." Put another way, the habitus serves as a cognitive map or set of perceptions in the mind that routinely guides and evaluates a person's choices and options. It provides enduring dispositions toward acting deemed appropriate by a person in particular social situations and settings. Included are dispositions that can be carried out even without giving them a great deal of thought in advance. They are simply habitual ways of acting when performing routine tasks.

The influence of exterior social structures and conditions is incorporated into the habitus, as well as the individual's own inclinations, preferences, and interpretations. The dispositions that result not only reflect established normative patterns of social behavior, but they also encompass action that is habitual and even intuitive. Through selective perception, the habitus molds aspirations and expectations into "categories of the probable" that impose perceptual boundaries on dispositions and the potential for action. "As an acquired system of generative schemes," observes Bourdieu (1990: 55), "the *habitus* makes possible the free production of all the thoughts, perceptions, actions, inherent in the particular conditions of its production – and only those."

When Bourdieu speaks of the internalization of class conditions and their transformation into personal dispositions toward action, he is describing conditions similar to Weber's concept of life chances that determine materially, socially, and culturally what is probable, possible, or impossible for a member of a particular social class or group (Swartz 1997: 104). Individuals who internalize similar life chances share the same habitus because, as Bourdieu (1977: 85) explains, they are more likely to have similar shared experiences: "Though it is impossible for *all* members of the same class (or even two of them) to have the same experiences, in the same order, it is certain that each member of the same class is more likely than any member of another class to have been confronted with the situations most frequent for members of that class." As a result, there is a high degree of affinity in health lifestyle choices among members of the same class. Bourdieu maintains that while they may depart from class standards, personal styles are never more than a deviation from a style of a class that relates back to the common style by its difference.

Even though Bourdieu allows agency some autonomy (e.g., agents are determined only to the extent they determine themselves), his emphasis on structure with respect to routine operations of the habitus clearly delineates a lesser role for agency than the individualist approach to health lifestyles. Some have argued that Bourdieu strips agency of much of its critical reflexive character (Bohman 1999). Bryan Turner and Stephen Wainwright (2003: 273), however, disagree and find that Bourdieu gives "full recognition" to "agency through his notions of strategy and practices," while illustrating the powerful role of institutions and resources "in shaping, constraining, and producing human agency." Simon Williams (1995) also defends Bourdieu by pointing out that choice is not precluded by the habitus, and he is able to account for the relative durability of different forms of lifestyles among the social classes. As the concept of the habitus is not original to Bourdieu, even though he revitalized it, his lasting contribution may in fact be his analysis of the importance of differential and durable tastes and lifestyles that distinguish the social classes from one another.

It can also be argued that the *process* of experience rescues Bourdieu's concept of habitus from the charge of downward conflation. Through experience, agency acquires new information and rationales for prompting creativity and change by way of the habitus. As Bourdieu (Bourdieu and Wacquant 1992: 133) explains, even though experiences confirm habitus, since there is a high probability that most people encounter circumstances that are consistent with those that originally fashioned it, the habitus nevertheless "is an *open system of dispositions* that is constantly subjected to experiences, and therefore constantly affected by them in a way that reinforces or modifies its structures." Thus the habitus can be creative and initiate changes in dispositions, although this potential is not stressed in Bourdieu's work.

Bourdieu calls for the abandonment of theories that explicitly or implicitly treat people as mere bearers (*Trägers*) of structure. Yet he also maintains that the rejection of mechanistic theories of behavior does not imply that we should bestow on some creative free will the exclusive power to generally constitute the meanings of situations and determine the intentions of others. The dispositions generated by the habitus tend to be compatible with the behavioral parameters set by the wider society; therefore, usual and practical modes of behaving – not unpredictable novelty – typically prevail. Consequently, Bourdieu emphasizes structure more than agency even though he accords agency the capacity to direct behavior when motivated; otherwise, his perspective largely accounts for routine behaviors that people enact without having to analyze or even think much about unless deeper attention is required.

Completing the model

Figure 8.1 shows that dispositions (box 5) produce practices (action) that are represented in box 6. The practices that result from the habitus can be based on deliberate calculations, habits, or intuition. Bourdieu (1984) helps us to realize that practices linked to health lifestyles can be so integrated into routine behavioral repertoires that they can be acted out more or less unthinkingly once established in the habitus. Bourdieu observes that people tend to adopt generalized strategies (a sense of the game) oriented toward practical ends in routine situations that they can habitually follow without stopping to analyze them. As a routinized feature of everyday life, it is therefore appropriate to view health lifestyles as guided more by a practicalthan an abstract logic (S. Williams 1995).

The four most common practices measured in studies of health lifestyles are alcohol use, smoking, diet, and exercise. These are shown in box 7 along with other practices such as physical checkups by physicians and automobile seatbelt use that comprise other typical forms of action or not taken. The practices themselves may be positive or negative, but they nonetheless comprise a person's overall pattern of health lifestyles as represented in box 8. It is important to note that these practices sometimes have a complexity of their own. Smoking tobacco in any form is negative, but moderate alcohol use (preferably red wine) reduces the risk of heart disease more so than heavy drinking (which promotes it) and abstinence (Klatsky 1999). In the United States, moderate drinking is considered to be the equivalent of one to two glasses of wine a day, while in Britain low consumption of one to two glasses five days a week is recommended. Eating fresh fruits and vegetables is positive, but consuming meat can be either positive or negative depending on how it is cooked and its fat content. Relatively vigorous leisure-time exercise has more health benefits than physical activity at work because the latter is subject to stress from job demands and time schedules, while walking and other everyday forms of exercise have some value (Dunn et al. 1999). However, measures of leisure-time exercise may not fully represent the physical activities of women who take care of children and do housework (Ainsworth 2000). It is therefore necessary that researchers take the multifaceted features of health lifestyle practices into account when analyzing them.

Action (or inaction) with respect to a particular health practice leads to its reproduction, modification, or nullification by the habitus through a feedback process. This is seen in Figure 8.1 by the arrow showing movement from box 8 back to box 5. This is consistent with Bourdieu's (1977, 1984) assertion that when dispositions are acted upon they tend to produce or modify the habitus from which they are derived. As conceptualized by Bourdieu, the habitus is the centerpiece of the health lifestyle model.

CONCLUSION

A central theme of this chapter is that the individualistic paradigm of health lifestyles is too narrow and unrealistic because it fails to consider structural influences on health lifestyle choices. In order to correct this course and formulate a theory where none previously existed, a health lifestyle model is presented here that accords structure a role that is consistent with its influence in the empirical world. There are times when structure outweighs but does not negate agency and other times when structure overwhelms agency, and these situations need to be included in concepts explaining health lifestyle practices. A macrosocial orientation does not mean that action is structurally predetermined; rather, it recognizes that social structures influence the thoughts, decisions, and actions of individuals (Sibeon 2004).

The theoretical model presented here is strongly influenced by Weber and Bourdieu. Although Bourdieu, in particular, has his critics, his notion of habitus nevertheless represents a novel and logical conceptualization of the internalization of external structures in the mind and perceptual processes of the individual. The result is a registry of dispositions to act in ways that are practical and usually consistent with the socially approved behavioral pathways of the larger social order or some class or group therein. Deviant behavior, of course, is an exception.

This model of health lifestyles states that four categories of (1) structural variables, namely (a) class circumstances, (b) age, gender, and race/ethnicity, (c) collectivities, and (d) living conditions, provide the social context for (2) socialization and experience that influence (3) life choices (agency). These structural variables also collectively constitute (4) life chances (structure). Choices and chances interact and commission the formation of (5) dispositions to act (habitus), leading to (6) practices (action), involving (7) alcohol use, smoking, diets, and other health-related actions. Health practices constitute patterns of (8) health lifestyles whose reenactment results in their reproduction (or modification) through feedback to the habitus. This theory is an initial representation of the health lifestyle phenomenon and is subject to verification, change, or rejection through future empirical application. It is a beginning for theoretical formulations concerning a major aspect of day-to-day social behavior for which no other theory now exists. Moreover, it moves beyond current theoretical trends reflecting methodological individualism to bring considerations of structure consistent with the reality of everyday life back into the conceptual focus of theory in medical sociology. Finally, it shows that structure has a direct causal effect on health through lifestyle practices.

References

Abel, Thomas, Esther Walter, Steffen Niemann, and Rolf Weitkunat. 1999. "The Berne–Munich Lifestyle Panel." *Sozial und Präventivmedizin* 44: 91–106.

Adonis, Andrew and Stephen Pollard. 1997. *A Class Act: The Myth of Britain's Classless Society*. London: Penguin.

Ainsworth, Barbara E. 2000. "Issues in the Assessment of Physical Activity in Women." *Research Quarterly for Exercise and Sport* 71: 37–50.

Alexander, Jeffrey C. 1983. *Theoretical Logic in Sociology. Vol. 3: The Classical Attempt at Theoretical Synthesis: Max Weber*. Berkeley: University of California Press.

Annandale, Ellen. 1998. *The Sociology of Health and Medicine: A Critical Introduction*. Cambridge: Polity Press.

Archer, Margaret S. 1995. *Realist Social Theory: The Morphogenetic Approach*. Cambridge: Cambridge University Press.

Archer, Margaret S. 1998. "Realism and Morphogenesis." Pp. 356–81 in M. Archer, R. Bhaskar, A. Collier, T. Lawson, and A. Norrie (eds.), *Critical Realism*. London: Routledge.

Archer, Margaret S. 2003. *Structure, Agency, and the Internal Conversation*. Cambridge: Cambridge University Press.

Backett, Kathryn C. and Charlie Davison. 1995. "Lifecourse and Lifestyle: The Social and Cultural Location of Health Behaviours." *Social Science and Medicine* 40: 629–38.

Bauman, Zygmunt. 1992. *Intimations of Postmodernity*. London: Routledge.

Bauman, Zygmunt. 1999. *In Search of Politics*. Stanford: Stanford University Press.

Berger, Peter L. and Thomas Luckmann. 1967. *The Social Construction of Reality*. New York: Anchor.

Bhaskar, Roy. 1998. *The Possibility of Naturalism: A Philosophical Critique of the Contemporary Human Sciences*. London: Routledge.

Blaxter, Mildred. 1990. *Health Lifestyles*. London: Routledge.

Bohman, James. 1999. "Practical Reason and Cultural Constraint: Agency in Bourdieu's Theory of Practice." Pp. 129–52 in R. Schusterman (ed.), *Bourdieu:A Critical Reader*. Oxford: Blackwell.

Bourdieu, Pierre. 1977. *Outline of a Theory of Practice*, translated by R. Nice. Cambridge: Polity Press.

Bourdieu, Pierre. 1984. *Distinction*, translated by R. Nice. Cambridge, MA: Harvard University Press.

Bourdieu, Pierre. 1990. *The Logic of Practice*, translated by R. Nice. Stanford: Stanford University Press.

Bourdieu, Pierre and Loïc Wacquant. 1992. *An Invitation to Reflexive Sociology*. Cambridge: Polity Press.

Brown, Tamara L., Gregory S. Parks, Rick S. Zimmerman, and Clarenda M. Phillips. 2001. "The Role of Religion in Predicting Adolescent Alcohol Use and Problem Drinking." *Journal of Studies on Alcohol* 65: 696–706.

Browning, Christopher R. and Kathleen A. Cagney. 2002. "Neighborhood Structural Disadvantage: Collective Efficacy and Self-Rated Health in a Physical Setting." *Journal of Health and Social Behavior* 43: 383–99.

Browning, Christopher R. and Kathleen A. Cagney. 2003. "Moving Beyond Poverty: Neighborhood Structure, Social Processes, and Health." *Journal of Health and Social Behavior* 44: 552–71.

Bury, Michael. 2005. *Health and Illness*. Cambridge: Polity Press.

Calnan, Michael. 1997. *Health and Illness: The Lay Perspective*. London: Tavistock.

Carpiano, Richard, Bruce G. Link, and Jo C. Phelan. 2008. "Social Inequality and Health: Future Directions for the Fundamental Cause Explanation." Pp. 232–63 in Annette Lareau and Dalton Conley (eds.), *Social Class: How Does It Work?* New York: Russell Sage.

Chuang, Ying-Chih, Susan T. Enett, Karl E. Bauman, and Vangie A. Foshee. 2005. "Neighborhood Influences on Adolescent Cigarette and Alcohol Use: Mediating Effects Through Parent and Peer Behaviors." *Journal of Health and Social Behavior* 46: 187–204.

Clarke, Adele E., Janet K. Shim, Laura Mamo, Jennifer Ruth Fosket, and Jennifer R. Fishman. 2003. "Biomedicalization: Technoscientific Transformations of Health, Illness, and US Biomedicine." *American Sociological Review* 68: 248–58.

Cockerham, William C. 1999. *Health and Social Change in Russia and Eastern Europe*. London: Routledge.

Cockerham, William C. 2000a. "The Sociology of Health Behavior and Health Lifestyles." Pp. 159–72 in C. Bird, P. Conrad, and A. Fremont (eds.), *Handbook of Medical Sociology*, 5th edition. Upper Saddle River, NJ: Prentice-Hall.

Cockerham, William C. 2000b. "Health Lifestyles in Russia." *Social Science and Medicine* 51: 1313–24.

Cockerham, William C. 2005. "Health Lifestyle Theory and the Convergence of Agency and Structure." *Journal of Health and Social Behavior* 46: 51–67.

Cockerham, William C. 2006. "Class Matters: Health Lifestyles in Post-Soviet Russia." *Harvard International Review* (Spring): 42–5.

Cockerham, William C. 2007a. *Social Causes of Health and Disease*. Cambridge: Polity Press.

Cockerham, William C. 2007b. "Health Lifestyles and the Absence of the Russian Middle Class." *Sociology of Health and Illness* 29: 457–73.

Cockerham, William C., Thomas Abel, and Günther Lüschen. 1993. "Max Weber, Formal Rationality, and Health Lifestyles." *Sociological Quarterly* 34: 413–25.

Cockerham, William C., Alfred Rütten, and Thomas Abel. 1997. "Conceptualizing Health Lifestyles: Moving Beyond Weber." *Sociological Quarterly* 38: 321–42.

Cockerham, William C., M. Christine Snead, and Derek F. DeWaal. 2002. "Health Lifestyles in Russia and the Socialist Heritage." *Journal of Health and Social Behavior* 43: 42–55.

Crawford, Robert. 1984. "A Cultural Account of Health: Control, Release, and the Social-Body." Pp. 60–103 in J. McKinley (ed.), *Issues in the Political Economy of Health Care*. New York: Tavistock.

Crompton, Rosemary. 2007. *Class and Stratification*, 3rd edition. Cambridge: Polity Press.

Dahrendorf, Ralf. 1979. *Life Chances*. Chicago: University of Chicago Press.

Demers, Andrée, Jocelyn Bisson, and Jézabelle Palluy. 1999. "Wives' Convergence with Their Husbands' Alcohol Use: Social Conditions as Mediators." *Journal of Studies of Alcohol* 60: 368–77.

Demers, Andrée, Sylvia Kairouz, Edward M. Adlaf, Louis Glickman, Brenda Newton-Taylor, and Alain Marchand. 2002. "Multilevel Analysis of Situational Drinking Among Canadian Undergraduates." *Social Science and Medicine* 48: 1221–35.

d'Houtaud, A. and Mark G. Field. 1984. "The Image of Health: Variations in Perception by Social Class in a French Population." *Sociology of Health and Illness* 6: 30–59.

Dmitrieva, Elena. 2005. "The Russian Health Care Experiment: Transition of the Health Care System and Rethinking the Sociology of Medicine." Pp. 320–33 in W. Cockerham (ed.), *The Blackwell Companion to Medical Sociology*. Oxford: Blackwell.

Dunn, Andrea L., Bess H. Marcus, James B. Kampert, Melissa E. Garcia, Harold W. Kohl III, and Steven N. Blair. 1999. "Comparison of Lifestyle and Structural Interventions to Increase Physical Activity and Cardiovascular Fitness." *Journal of the American Medical Association* 281: 327–34.

Durkheim, Emile. 1950 [1895]. *The Rules of Sociological Method*. New York: Free Press.

Emirbayer, Mustafa and Ann Mische. 1998. "What is Agency?" *American Journal of Sociology* 103: 962–1023.

Ford, Earl S., Robert K. Merritt, Gregory W. Heath, Kenneth E. Powell, Richard A. Washburn, Andrea Kriska, and Gwendolyn Halle. 1991. "Physical Activity in Lower and Higher Socioeconomic Status Populations." *American Journal of Epidemiology* 133: 1246–56.

Frohlich, Katherine L., Ellen Corin, and Louise Potvin. 2001. "A Theoretical Proposal for the Relationship Between Context and Disease." *Sociology of Health and Illness* 23: 776–97.

George, Valerie A. and Paulette Johnson. 2001. "Weight Loss Behaviors and Smoking in College Students of Diverse Ethnicity." *American Journal of Health Behavior* 25: 115–24.

Giddens, Anthony. 1984. *The Constitution of Society: Outline of a Theory of Structuration*. Berkeley: University of California Press.

Giddens, Anthony. 1991. *Modernity and Self-Identity*. Stanford: Stanford University Press.

Gochman, David S. 1997. "Health Behavior Research, Cognate Disciplines, Future Identity, and an Organizing Matrix: An Integration of Perspectives." Pp. 395–425 in D. Gochman (ed.), *Handbook of Health Behavior*, vol.4. New York: Plenum.

Grzywacz, Joseph G. and Nadine F. Marks. 2001. "Social Inequalities and Exercise During Adulthood: Toward an Ecological Perspective." *Journal of Health and Social Behavior* 42: 202–20.

Hardey, Michael. 1999. "Doctor in the House: The Internet as a Source of Lay Knowledge and the Challenge to Expertise." *Sociology of Health and Illness* 21: 820–35.

Hill, Terrence D., Christopher G. Ellison, Amy M. Burdette, and Marc A. Musick. 2007. "Religious Involvement and Healthy Lifestyles: Evidence from a Survey of Texas Adults." *Annals of Behavioral Medicine* 34: 217–22.

Husserl, Edmund. 1989 [1952]. *Ideas Pertaining to a Pure Phenomenology and to a Phenomenological Philosophy*, translated by R. Rojecwicz and A. Schuwer. London: Kluwer Academic.

Jarvis, Martin and Jane Wardle. 1999. "Social Patterning of Individual Health Behaviours." Pp. 240–55 in M. Marmot and R. Wilkinson (eds.), *Social Determinants of Health*. Oxford: Oxford University Press.

Johnson, Robert A. and John P. Hoffman. 2000. "Adolescent Cigarette Smoking in the US Racial/Ethnic Subgroups: Findings from the National Education Longitudinal Study." *Journal of Health and Social Behavior* 41: 392–407.

Kalberg, Stephen. 1994. *Max Weber's Comparative Historical Sociology*. Chicago: University of Chicago.

Karlsen, S. and J. Y. Nazroo. 2002. "Agency and Structure: TheImpact of Ethnic Identity and Racism on the Health of Ethnic Minority People." *Social Health and Illness* 24: 1–20.

Klatsky, Arthur L. 1999. "Moderate Drinking and Reduced Risk of Heart Disease." *Alcohol Research and Health* 23: 15–23.

Laaksonen, Kikko, Ritva Prättälä, and Eero Lahelma. 2002. "Sociodemographic Determinants of Multiple Unhealthy Behaviours." *Scandinavian Journal of Public Health* 30: 1–7.

Lindquist, Christine, William C. Cockerham, and Sean-Shong Hwang. 1999. "Drinking Patterns in the American Deep South." *Journal of Studies on Alcohol* 60: 663–6.

Link, Bruce G. and Jo Phelan. 2000. "Evaluating the Fundamental Cause Explanation for Social Disparities in Health." Pp. 33–46 in C. Bird, P. Conrad, and A. Fremont (eds.), *The Handbook of Medical Sociology*, 5th edition. Upper Saddle River, NJ: Prentice-Hall.

Mead, George H. 1934. *Mind, Self, and Society*. Chicago: University of Chicago Press.

Mommsen, Wolfgang J. 1989. *The Political and Social Theory of Max Weber*. Cambridge: Polity Press.

Pampel, Fred C. 2008. "Racial Convergence to Cigarette Use from Adolescence to the Mid-Thirties." *Journal of Health and Social Behavior* 49: 484–98.

Pescosolido, Bernice A., Jane McLeod, and Margarita Alegría. 2000. "Confronting the Second Contract: The Place of Medical Sociology in Research and Policy for the Twenty-First Century." Pp. 411–26 in C. Bird, P. Conrad, and A. Fremont (eds.), *The Handbook of Medical Sociology*, 5th edition. Upper Saddle River, NJ: Prentice-Hall.

Pescosolido, Bernice A. and Beth A. Rubin. 2000. "The Web of Group Affiliations Revisited: Social Life, Postmodernism, and Sociology." *American Sociological Review* 65: 52–76.

Reid, Ivan. 1998. *Class in Britain*. Cambridge: Polity Press.

Ringer, Fritz. 2004. *Max Weber: An Intellectual Biography*. Chicago: University of Chicago Press.

Robert, Stephanie A. and James S. House. 2000. "Socioeconomic Inequalities in Health: An Enduring Sociological Problem." Pp. 79–97 in C. Bird, P. Conrad, and A. Fremont (eds.), *The Handbook of Medical Sociology*, 5th edition. Upper Saddle River, NJ: Prentice-Hall.

Roos, Eva, Eero Lahelma, Mikko Virtanen, Ritva Prättälä, and Pirjo Pietinen. 1998. "Gender, Socioeconomic Status and Family Status as Determinants of Food Behavior." *Social Science and Medicine* 46: 1519–29.

Scott, John. 1996. *Stratification and Power: Structures of Class, Status, and Command*. Cambridge: Polity Press.

Sewell, William H. 1992. "A Theory of Structure: Duality, Agency, and Transformation." *American Journal of Sociology* 98: 1–29.

Shankina, A. I. 2004. "The Middle Class in Russia: Hunting Nessie." *Russian SocialScience Review* 45: 26–41.

Sibeon, Roger. 2004. *Rethinking Social Theory*. London: Sage.

Smaje, Chris. 2000. "Race, Ethnicity, and Health." Pp. 114–28 in C. Bird, P. Conrad, and A. Fremont (eds.), *The Handbook of Medical Sociology*, 5th edition. Upper Saddle River, NJ: Prentice-Hall.

Snead, M. Christine and William C. Cockerham. 2002. "Health Lifestyles and Social Class in the Deep South." *Research in the Sociology of Health Care* 20: 107–22.

Swartz, David. 1997. *Culture and Power: The Sociology of Pierre Bourdieu.* Chicago: University of Chicago Press.

Sweat, Michael D. and Julie A. Denison. 1995. "Reducing HIV Incidence in Developing Countries with Structural and Environmental Interventions." *AIDS* 9: S251–7.

Turner, Bryan S. 1992. *Regulating Bodies: Essays in Medical Sociology.* London: Routledge.

Turner, Bryan S. and Steven P. Wainwright. 2003. "Corps de Ballet: The Case of the Injured Dancer." *Sociology of Health and Illness* 25: 269–88.

Van Gundy, Karen, Scott Schieman, Margaret S. Kelley, and Cesar J. Rebellion. 2005. "Gender Role Orientations and Alcohol Use among Moscow and Toronto Adults." *Social Science and Medicine* 61: 2317–30.

Veblen, Thorstein. 1994 [1899]. *Theory of the Leisure Class.* New York: Dover.

Vickers, Ross R., Terry L. Conway, and Linda K. Hervig. 1990. "Demonstration of Replicable Dimensions of Health Behaviors." *Preventive Medicine* 19: 377–401.

Weber, Max. 1946. *From Max Weber: Essays in Sociology,* translated and edited by Hans H. Gerth and C. Wright Mills. New York: Oxford University Press.

Weber, Max. 1958. *The Protestant Ethic and the Spirit of Capitalism,* translated by T. Parsons. New York: Free Press.

Weber, Max. 1978 [1922]. *Economy and Society,* 2 vols., translated and edited by G. Roth and C. Wittich. Berkeley: University of California Press.

Wickrama, K. A. S., Rand D. Conger, Lora Ebert Wallace, and Glen H. Elder, Jr. 1999. "The Intergenerational Transmission of Health-Risk Behaviors: Adolescent Lifestyles and Gender Moderating Effects." *Journal of Health and Social Behavior* 40: 258–72.

Williams, Gareth. 2003. "The Determinants of Health: Structure, Context and Agency." *Sociology of Health and Illness* 25: 131–54.

Williams, Simon J. 1995. "Theorising Class, Health and Lifestyles: Can Bourdieu Help Us?" *Sociology of Health and Illness* 25: 131–54.

Zerubavel, Eviatar. 1997. *Social Mindscapes.* Cambridge, MA: Harvard University Press.

9

Social Capital and Health

LIJUN SONG, JOONMO SON, AND NAN LIN

INTRODUCTION

An old axiom states that it is not what you know, but who you know (with who you know being a form of social capital). The idea of social capital has a long history in the social sciences. Scholars with disparate theoretical perspectives, however, debate its intellectual origins (for reviews, see Islam et al. 2006; Macinko and Starfield 2001). Some quote classic sociological predecessors, including Emile Durkheim, Talcott Parsons, Karl Marx, Frederick Engels, Max Weber, and Georg Simmel, for their insights into this concept (Portes and Sensenbrenner 1993). Some attribute this idea to the legacy of economists, such as David Hume, Edmund Burke, and Adam Smith (Woolcock 1998). Others identify the philosophy of John Dewey as the central source of social capital (Farr 2004). As Putnam (2000) finds, the term social capital itself first appeared in a 1916 article by Lyda Judson Hanifan on a rural school community center (Hanifan 1916).

Despite competing claims to its nativity, social capital has grown to become a popular paradigm in multidisciplinary research during the last two decades. A search of the Social Sciences Citation Index for articles with "social capital" in their topics depicts the explosively growing trajectory from the 1990s. On average, there were fewer than four such articles per year from 1956 to 1989, while the annual number increased to 145 in the 1990s and dramatically jumped to 565 from 2000 to 2008. As is the case with new concepts in social sciences, social capital has triggered extensive debates. There is lack of consensus on its definition, which inevitably results in controversial operationalizations, divergent measurements, disparate mechanisms, mixed empirical evidence, various implications, and arduous challenges. The key figures who popularized this concept and stimulated its theoretical development during the 1980s and the early 1990s include three sociologists, Pierre Bourdieu (1986 [1983]), Nan Lin (1982, 2001a), and James S. Coleman (1988, 1990), and one political scientist, Robert D. Putnam (1993, 2000).

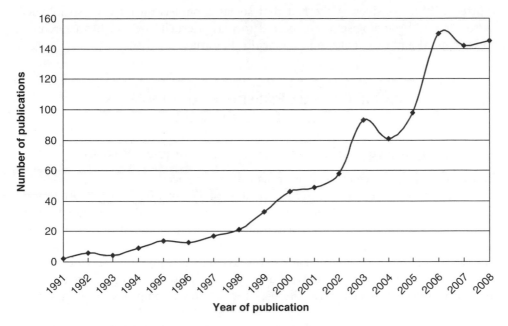

Figure 9.1 Articles with "social capital" and "health" in their topics: Social Sciences Citation Index (as of December 20, 2008).

As in other fields, social capital as a theoretical tool has easily gained burgeoning acceptance in the health sciences. For instance, another search of the Social Sciences Citation Index for articles with "social capital" and "health" in their topics showed an accelerating popularity from the early 1990s (Figure 9.1). There were only two such articles in 1991. But the number rose to 93 in 2003, further jumped to 150 in 2006, and remained above 140 in 2007 and 2008. Indeed, edited books on social capital and health have appeared in the last couple of years (e.g., Kawachi, Subramanian, and Kim 2008a; McKenzie and Harpham 2006). A few reviews have surveyed the associations of social capital with various health-related outcomes across cultures and societies (e.g., Almedom 2005; Cockerham 2007; De Silva et al. 2005; Hawe and Shiell 2000; Islam et al. 2006; Kawachi 1999; Macinko and Starfield 2001; Muntaner, Lynch, and Davey Smith 2001; Shortt 2004; Whitley and McKenzie 2005). Despite the substantial development of this literature, Putnam's notion of social capital absorbed by public health researchers has dominated the field. The original contributions of alternative sociological theories have thus been understated.

In this chapter, we do not aim to reconcile different approaches to social capital. Instead, our goal is to highlight social capital as a significant social antecedent of health from a sociological perspective. We begin with the introduction of social capital concepts advanced by Bourdieu, Lin, Coleman, and Putnam. We then turn to the theoretical extension and empirical application of these four perspectives to the social production of health. We conclude with a discussion of issues and future research directions. Social capital is one of the most acknowledged contributions from sociology to social science and public discourse during the last two decades

(Portes 1998). Considering the fact that social capital is an intrinsic sociological factor, medical sociologists are expected to play a crucial role in further refining social capital and its extension in the health literature.

SOCIAL CAPITAL: EMBEDDED RESOURCES IN SOCIAL RELATIONSHIPS

Bourdieu: Exclusive resources from durable networks

Bourdieu is the pioneer in the conceptualization of social capital in sociology. He introduced this concept in his French version of *Distinction* in 1979 (Adam and Rončević 2003; Bourdieu 1984). His theory on social capital was originally published in French in 1983, and translated into English for the first time in 1986. He distinguished social capital from its sources and returns in the forms of other types of capital at the individual level. He also discussed its cross-context network embeddedness and its exclusive nature. He did not explicitly discuss its operationalizations and measurements, which paves the way for debates in empirical applications of his work.

Bourdieu was concerned with fundamental causes of social stratification. He contended that it is the unequal distribution and accumulation of capital that accounts for the production and reproduction of social structure. Capital is "accumulated labor" allowing its possessors to "appropriate social energy in the form of reified or living labor" (Bourdieu 1986 [1983]: 241). It has three essential forms: economic, cultural, and social (Bourdieu 1986 [1983]: 242–8). The first two forms are personally owned. Economic capital is material goods invested in mercantile relationships for monetary profits. Cultural capital consists of three subforms: the embodied state (i.e., the cultivation process), the objectified state (i.e., cultural goods), and the institutionalized state (i.e., educational credentials).

In contrast, social capital is embedded in networks of social relationships. It is "the aggregate of the actual or potential resources which are linked to possession of a durable network of more or less institutionalized relationships of mutual acquaintance and recognition – or in other words, to membership in a group – which provides each of its members with the backing of the collectivity-owned capital, a 'credential' which entitles them to credit, in the various senses of the word" (Bourdieu 1986 [1983]: 248–9). The volume of social capital to which an individual has access depends on two elements: "the size of the network of connections he can effectively mobilize" and "the volume of the capital (economic, culture or symbolic) possessed in his own right by each of those to whom he is connected" (Bourdieu 1986 [1983]: 249). Since Bourdieu does not further discuss measurements of social capital, these two elements can serve as proxy indicators of social capital in his work.

Sources and returns of social capital are other forms of capital. The foundation of capital reproduction, and thus stratification reproduction, is the convertibility of capital (Bourdieu 1986 [1983]: 249–55). Economic capital, the root of other forms of capital, creates cultural and social capital. In turn, social capital generates economic capital (i.e., material profits such as services) and cultural capital (i.e., symbolic profits from being associated with prestigious groups). Despite such convertibility, social capital exerts its unique effects independently from other forms of capital. "These effects, in which spontaneous sociology readily perceives the work of 'connections,' are particularly visible in all cases in which different individuals obtain very unequal profits from virtually equivalent (economic or cultural) capital, depending on the extent to which they can mobilize by proxy the capital of a group (a family, the alumni of an elite school, a select club, the aristocracy, etc.) that is more or less constituted as such and more or less rich in capital" (Bourdieu 1986 [1983]: 256).

Networks of relationships spread across multiple contexts. They are "based on indissolubly material and symbolic exchanges" and "partially irreducible to objective relations of proximity in physical (geographical) space or even in economic and social space" (Bourdieu 1986 [1983]: 249). Networks of relationships are the consequence of purposive "investment strategies, individual or collective, consciously or unconsciously aimed at establishing or reproducing social relationships that are directly usable in the short or long term" (Bourdieu 1986 [1983]: 249). Social exclusion is one of these strategies. Social institutions legitimate and motivate within-group exchanges between homogeneous members, and exclude members whose mistakes threaten group interests (Bourdieu 1986 [1983]: 249–51).

Lin: Resources embedded in social networks

Lin's book on social capital appeared in 2001, providing a fully developed theoretical scheme (Lin 2001a). His theory builds upon the social resources theory that he and colleagues gradually developed in the late 1970s and early 1980s (Lin 1982; Lin, Dayton, and Greenwald 1978; Lin, Ensel, and Vaughn 1981). His framework is rooted in classic sociological traditions. He differentiated two types of social capital from its structural and networking sources at the micro- and meso-levels, its mechanisms, and its instrumental and expressive returns. He also offered an empirically falsifiable operationalization and measurement instrument of social capital.

Social capital is, according to Lin, "resources embedded in a social structure that are accessed and/or mobilized in purposive actions" (2001a: 29). This definition is grounded in the classic tradition of personal capital theories (e.g., Marx's capital, human capital, cultural capital). Personal capital is resources under the control of individuals themselves. Social capital is assets possessed by an individual's network members. In a presumed hierarchical social structure in the shape of a pyramid, resource allocation depends on structural positions. The amount of social capital hinges in general upon structural positions of other members in social networks, including networks in cyberspace.

Lin distinguished two types of social capital: contact resources and network resources (Lin 2001b). The former refers to resources from network members that individuals actually mobilize in their own purposive actions, and is indicated by resources (e.g., socioeconomic attributes) of contacts that individuals use in purposive actions. The latter corresponds to resources available from network members to whom individuals have access. To capture network resources, Lin and colleagues developed a position generator to map positional networks (Lin and Dumin 1986; Lin, Fu, and Hsung 2001), which are not constrained by tie strength, geographical location, content, and homogeneity (Lin 2008; Lin et al.

2001). This instrument asks respondents to identify their contacts associated with a representative sample of occupational positions salient in a society. If respondents know several people in that type of position, they are usually asked to name the one that occurs to them first. Three social capital indices are usually created based on the quantity, quality, and diversity of accessed positions: extensity, upper reachability, and range. Extensity is the total number of positions in which respondents identify one contact; this estimates the quantity of social capital. Upper reachability is the highest prestige score of occupations to which respondents have access; it predicts the quality of social capital. Range is the difference between the highest and lowest prestige scores of occupations to which respondents have access, a reflection of the diversity of social capital. These social capital indices are consistent with Bourdieu's elements of social capital: network size and network members' personal capital.

Network resources can also be derived from two other network instruments: the name generator and the resource generator. The name generator maps personal networks (McCallister and Fischer 1978). It asks respondents to name a fixed number of contacts (usually five) with whom they discuss important matters (Burt 1984). Similar to the position generator, it may calculate social capital, for example, based on socioeconomic attributes of named contacts. The resource generator (Snijders 1999; Van der Gaag and Snijders 2005) directly maps resource networks. It asks respondents to identify contacts associated with a fixed list of useful and concrete social resources across multiple life domains. It measures social capital as the sum score of access to all different resources. The position generator proves to be generalized across societies due to its association with the occupational structures common in modern societies; it is more flexible, useful, and efficient in describing access to social capital than the name generator and the resource generator (Lin 1999; Song and Lin 2009; Van der Gaag, et al. 2008).

Social capital stems from two sources: structural and networking (Lin 2001a). Structural sources include an individual's earlier hierarchical roles or positions, both ascribed (e.g., gender, race, family origins) and achieved (e.g., prior socioeconomic status). The higher the previous social position, the greater the chance of access to social capital. Networking sources consist of tie strength and network location. Weak ties and closeness to social bridge in social networks create more social capital (Burt 1992; Granovetter 1973). Lin (2001a) criticizes Bourdieu's and Coleman's argument on exclusive or closed networks because it ignores these networking properties. Besides, collective assets such as trust and norms can either foster or restrict the access to social capital.

Social capital exerts both main and moderating effects (Lin 2001a). It generates instrumental (e.g., wealth, power, and reputation) and expressive (e.g., health and life satisfaction) returns through four mechanisms: providing information, exerting influence, acting as social credentials, and reinforcing group identity and recognition (Lin 2001a). This effect interplays with tie strength. Social capital derived from weak ties creates more instrumental returns, while social capital embedded in strong ties produces more expressive returns. Also, instrumental returns and expressive returns fortify each other.

Lin's initial efforts were geared more toward an individual-level analysis. Recently, he extended his original theory to the macro-level (Lin 2008). He defined two forms of social capital for a collectivity. Internal social capital is resources provided by members within a collectivity (i.e., associations, organizations, communities, regions, or nation-states), and external social capital refers to resources accessible from other collectivities with which the focal collectivity is networked.

Coleman: Functional social-structural resources

It is Coleman's (1988) systematic examination of social capital and its role in the creation of human capital that called multidisciplinary attention to this term. Then, in his masterwork on *Foundations of Social Theory* (1990), Coleman devoted one chapter to analyzing social capital, including its functionalist definition, multiple operationalizations, and structural sources at the meso- and macro-levels. He also emphasized its positive functions and returns at the collective level.

Coleman conceptualized social capital as functional "social-structural resources" derived from structures of social relations: "Social capital is defined by its function. It is not a single entity, but a variety of different entities having two characteristics in common: They all consist of some aspect of a social structure, and they facilitate certain actions of individuals who are within that structure. Like other forms of capital, social capital is productive, making possible the achievement of certain ends that would not be attainable in its absence" (Coleman 1990: 302). He justified such a broad conception by its utility in explaining multiple outcomes and bridging the micro- and macro-levels.

A catch-all definition inevitably opens the door to multiple operationalizations. Coleman (1990) proposed six forms of social capital that facilitate actions: (1) obligations, expectations of reciprocity, and trustworthiness (i.e., individuals do things for each other and trust each other to reciprocate in the future), (2) information potential from social relations, (3) norms (in particular "a prescriptive norm ... that one should forgo self-interests to act in the interests of the collectivity" [1990: 311]) and effective sanctions, (4) authority relations (i.e., transferrable rights of control between individuals) that can solve common problems, (5) appropriable social organizations (i.e., organizations whose resources benefit their participants), and (6) intentional organizations (i.e., organizations whose resources not only benefit their participants but also the public). His operationalization equates social capital with its sources (e.g., organizations) and returns (e.g., information) (Portes 1998). Coleman did not offer specific measurements for each form. He was actually hesitant about the value of social capital as a quantifiable concept (Coleman 1990). In his work on the association of social capital with dropout rates (Coleman 1988), he measured social capital within the family as the presence of parents, the number of siblings, and mother's expectation for child's education, and he quantified social capital in the community based upon the presence of religiously based high schools and the frequency of students' religious attendance.

Coleman (1990: 318–21) also discussed five macro-level structural preconditions for the quantity of social capital: network closure, stability of social structure, collectivist ideology, affluence, and government support. The first three conditions have positive associations with social capital, although extreme network closure could damage social capital instead. The last two conditions decrease social capital, by increasing interpersonal independence and decreasing the maintenance of social relationships.

Coleman held that social capital functions in both positive and negative directions – and at both individual and collective levels. But he obviously emphasized the positive functions of various forms of social capital for the collective, while admitting some forms of social capital such as norms could also constrict some actions (1990: 311). Also, in contrast with financial (i.e., money), physical (i.e., material objects), and human (i.e., skills and knowledge) capital that can only be privately owned, Coleman (1990) argued social capital is not a private property of individual beneficiaries but a property of social structure. It favors not only purposive investors in a structure, but also all the members of that structure, as a public good. Coleman's (1988) empirical research focuses on the positive role of social capital in educational attainment. He only briefly illuminated the importance of social capital in the health care process, mentioning that the lack of social capital (i.e., trust) between patients and physicians increases costs of – and decreases access to – medical care (Coleman 1990).

Putnam: Facilitating features of social organization

Putnam's work on social capital and its association with democracy appeared in 1993. It is his 1995 article, "Bowling Alone," and its expansion into a book of the same main title in 2000 that popularized the term social capital beyond the academic community, making it a part of public discourse. Drawing on Coleman's work, Putnam proposed a functionalist definition and mixed operationalizations and a state-level social capital index. He distinguished two types of social capital and emphasized positive returns of social capital as a public good. He analyzed macro-level structural sources and returns of social capital.

In his earlier functionalist definition, social capital refers to "features of social organization, such as trust, norms and networks that can improve the efficiency of society by facilitating coordinated actions" (Putnam 1993: 167). In his later definition of social capital as "connections among individuals – social networks and the norms of reciprocity and trustworthiness that arise from them" (Putnam 2000: 19), he tended to emphasize the causal directions between different components of social capital. Formal social connections include memberships and participation in formal organizations and activities such as political, educational, recreational, religious, and professional organizations and activities, and connections in the workplace. Informal social connections refer to participation with family, friends, and neighbors in informal social and leisure activities. Networks of social connections increase productivity of individuals and reinforce norms of reciprocity. Similar to Coleman's explanation, the norms of generalized reciprocity mean that "I'll do this for you without expecting anything specific back from you in the confident expectation that someone else will do something for me down the road" (Putnam 2000: 21). The norms of reciprocity as a community asset increase efficiency. Honesty and social trust (i.e., trust in other people) lubricate social life. Like Coleman, Putnam (2000: 137) equated social capital with networks, reciprocity, honesty, and social trust, leaving their causal relations for future research. Besides, he included other consequences of networks such as altruism, volunteering, and philanthropy as alternative indicators of social capital. Putnam also developed a state-level social capital index, containing 14 items covering areas such as community organizational life, engagement in public affairs, community volunteerism, informal sociability, and social trust (Putnam 2000).

Putnam (2000) distinguishes two subtypes of social capital: bonding and bridging. Bonding social capital exists in relationships connecting homogeneous individuals, while bridging social capital lies in connections linking heterogeneous persons. Also, bonding social capital works for enhancing within-group reciprocity and solidarity, while bridging social capital helps obtain goods from outside groups. Putnam emphasized the positive functions of both types of social capital, while admitting that bonding social capital may lead to between-group enmity. This typology has been critiqued from a strict social network perspective since bonding and bridging are properties of social networks instead of social capital (Lin 2008).

Putnam emphasized positive functions of social capital at two levels: individual and collective. Social capital is both a "private good" and a "public good" (Putnam 2000: 20). One's investment in social capital not only benefits oneself, but also spills over to others. Putnam recognized that functions of social capital are sometimes negative for those outside of a given network if social capital is used for antisocial purposes, even while generally positive for those within that network.

Putnam reported an overall decline of social capital in American society based on his preliminary bivariate correlation analyses. He attributed that decline to multiple macro-level factors, such as pressures of time and money, residential mobility and sprawl, electronic entertainment, and generational change (Putnam 2000). He highlighted the potential of small groups, social movements, and telecommunications including the Internet to offset that decline. He discussed positive associations of social capital with education and children's welfare, neighborhood safety and productivity, economic development, health and happiness, democracy, and tolerance and equality. Drawing on previous research on network-based concepts such as social integration, social cohesion, and health, Putnam argued for health returns to social capital without explicitly distinguishing social capital from those concepts. He reported only correlations of social capital at the state level with public health and mortality, and of social connections at the individual level with happiness (Putnam 2000). It is other researchers who have systematically theorized and testified to the health effect of social capital using advanced analysis techniques, as described in the next section.

To summarize, all four of the aforementioned scholars agreed that social capital contains resources derived from social networks and social structures, and that it operates effectively net of personal capital such as economic capital, human capital, and cultural capital (Lin 2001a). However, their definitions and operationalizations diverge from one another. We distinguish two schools.[1] Bourdieu and Lin exemplify a network-based approach. They defined social capital as a relational asset available to individuals. Their approach is more refined, distinguishing social capital from its antecedents and yields for individuals from a conflict perspective (Adam and Rončević 2003; Portes 1998). They discussed the interplay between personal and social capital. They asserted that networks are preconditions of social capital and exist across multiple contexts. Lin developed a strict methodological instrument to measure social capital embedded in social networks. Bourdieu did not discuss measurements, but his proposed elements of social capital (i.e., network size, personal capital of network members) are consistent with social capital indices derived from the position generator. One major difference between Bourdieu and Lin is in the creation process of social capital. Bourdieu valued network closure while Lin emphasized network bridging. In addition, Lin specified collective assets such as trust and norms as sources instead of elements of social capital, as in the work of Coleman and Putnam.

Coleman and Putnam represented a normative approach in the sense that both underlined moral norms such as trust and reciprocity as forms of social capital. They emphasized the benefits of social capital as a collective asset or public good from a functionalist perspective. Their concept and operationalization of social capital mingle social capital with its sources and outcomes. One major distinction between Coleman and Putnam exists in their causal arguments on social networks. Coleman used networks as sources of social capital, while Putnam subsumed networks under the umbrella of social capital. Unlike Lin, Putnam did not directly map social networks. His proposed indicators reflect social integration, an antecedent of social networks. Next, we review theoretical and empirical applications of each framework in the health literature.

SOCIAL CAPITAL AND HEALTH: THEORETICAL DEVELOPMENT AND EMPIRICAL EVIDENCE

Bourdieu: Incomplete application

Unlike his well-known concept of cultural capital, Bourdieu's notion of social capital received limited attention in the literature. Its theoretical utility for health was recognized only recently. Its quantitative and qualitative applications raised debates, primarily because Bourdieu did not explicitly measure social capital. Ziersch and colleagues (2005) extend Bourdieu's conceptualization to health in Adelaide, Australia. They argue that Bourdieu's work is valuable for individual-level inequality research, in contrast with Putnam's focus on the collective-level social capital as a public good (Ziersch et al. 2005), and is helpful for distinguishing sources and consequences of social capital (Ziersch 2005). Ziersch and colleagues (2005) use five indicators of neighborhood-based social capital: neighborhood connections, neighborhood trust, reciprocity, neighborhood safety, and local civic action. These researchers find that neighborhood safety explains physical health, and neighborhood safety and neighborhood connections predict mental health. Ziersch (2005) distinguishes social capital infrastructure from social capital resources. She uses three measurements for the former (i.e., informal networks, formal networks, and values such as trust, reciprocity, and safety), and four measurements for the latter (i.e., help, acceptance, civic actions, and control). Among these measurements, values, informal networks, help, and control are – either directly or indirectly – positively associated with mental health, but none are associated with physical health.

Carpiano (2006) constructs a Bourdieu-based conceptual model of neighborhood social capital for health. Influenced by Portes (1998), he states that Bourdieu's work helps distinguish social capital from its sources and outcomes. He suggests that, from a sociological perspective, we should use social capital exclusively for network resources as Bourdieu conceived, and that Putnam's notion of social capital based on social cohesion should be seen as a precondition of social capital. He makes efforts to distinguish social capital from its sources (e.g., neighborhood socioeconomic conditions, social cohesion) and outcomes as well. He uses connectedness and values such as trust and familiarity to indicate Putnam's social cohesion. He uses four measures to indicate Bourdieu's social capital, including neighborhood organization participation, informal social control, social support, and social leverage (i.e., neighbors ask each other for advice). He also adds neighborhood attachment in his model, which is hypothesized to moderate the social capital effect. His two empirical studies analyze Los Angeles Family and Neighborhood Survey data. In one study on adults (Carpiano 2007), he finds unexpected positive associations of social support with daily smoking and binge drinking, negative association of social leverage with daily smoking, negative association of informal social control with binge drinking, and no associations of either social capital indicator with perceived health. He also shows evidence that neighborhood attachment interacts positively with informal social control and negatively with neighborhood organization participation for perceived health. In another study on female caregivers (Carpiano 2008), he reports an unexpected positive association of social support with daily smoking, negative association of social leverage with daily smoking, and positive association of neighborhood organization participation with perceived health. Neighborhood attachment interplays negatively with social leverage for perceived health and with informal social control for daily smoking.

Stephens (2008) points out that Bourdieu's work advances our understanding of health inequality in broader social connections beyond neighborhoods, in interrelationships of economic, cultural, and social capital, and in the social exclusion process. She credits the above quantitative applications for their efforts to disentangle sources and outcomes of social capital. She further criticizes them for constraining attention to geographical locations and measuring social capital as existing concepts using secondary data. She employs a qualitative method to document social connections in three neighborhoods in New Zealand and reports evidence for the existence of social networks beyond geographical community. She shows that personal and community capital is convertible to social networks. Interviewees from different individual and community socioeconomic backgrounds had different social connections for different needs. She also finds evidence for health-relevant returns to social capital when some interviewees participated in voluntary groups in order to offset the loss of services including health services. Stephens (2008) takes an extreme position that social capital cannot be quantified at the individual level.

Lin: Limited but consistent evidence

The concept of social capital developed by Lin helped produce substantial studies on status attainment. The impact of prior social positions on social capital, as well as the effect of social capital on socioeconomic well-being, have been well documented across societies (for a review, see Lin 1999). Health returns to social capital, though, have received less attention. Nonetheless, available studies report consistent findings of the effect of social capital. Social capital is proposed to be associated positively with health, both directly and indirectly. Four mechanisms, conceptualized primarily for instrumental returns, are applicable to health outcomes (Song and Lin 2009). First, social capital brings valuable health information. Also, network members' resources, such as power and authority, exert influence on health in the same way that individually possessed power and social ordering affect health policies, control health information, and moderate exposure and vulnerability to health risks. Next, social capital acts as social credentials. A case study shows that the care and attitudes of hospital staff changed dramatically for a Black woman near death after her ex-husband, a physician, advocated on her behalf (Abrums 2000). Finally, social capital reinforces group identity and generates emotional support.

Also, social capital may interplay with personal capital with two possibilities (Song and Lin 2009). One hypothesis is the compensation effect proposition. Individuals lacking personal capital are more motivated to resort to social capital, and thus receive more health benefits from social capital. An alternative hypothesis is the cumulative advantage proposition. Individuals with more personal capital are more able to successfully mobilize social capital, thus receiving more health resources from social capital.

Three quantitative studies testify to the health returns for social capital. Acock and Hurlbert (1993), for example, analyze 1985 General Social Survey data. They use the name generator and calculate the mean educational level of named contacts to indicate social capital. They find that social capital enhances life satisfaction and reduces anomie. Webber and Huxley (2007) adapt the resource generator originally developed in the Netherlands to construct a 27-item resource generator for UK respondents. These items form one scale and also reflect four subscales, including domestic resources, expert advice, personal skills, and problem-solving resources. That scale, as well as two other subscales such as domestic resources and personal skills, is negatively associated with mental disorder. Song and Lin (2009) use the 1997 Taiwan Social Change Survey data, an island-wide stratified probability sample of adults in Taiwan. They derive social capital from two name generators and one position generator. One name generator asked respondents to name at most five contacts with whom they had communicated in the last year to discuss worries and personal problems, and the other respondents to name at most five contacts that they reached for actual help or information in the last year when encountering difficulties in life. The position generator listed a sample of 15 ordered occupational positions salient in Taiwan, ranging from housemaids/cleaning workers up to physicians. Social capital (a factor score derived from extensity, upper reachability, and range) measured through the position generator instead of the name generators reduces depression and enhances self-reported health net of social support and personal capital. Also, social capital interacts with education. It decreases depression to a greater degree for those with less education, which supports the compensation effect hypothesis.

Social capital embedded in electronic networks also receives attention nowadays. For example, Drentea and Moren-Cross (2005) employ a mixed-method approach to study a mothering board on a website for parents. As they report, social capital embedded in online mothers' networks may influence mothers' and their children's health indirectly by providing emotional support and instrumental support such as informal health information sharing.

Coleman: Neighborhood efficacy

Coleman's social capital has been broadly applied to educational attainment, but not to health outcomes. Sociologist Sampson and colleagues have contributed explicitly to extending Coleman's work by developing a neighborhood-level collective efficacy theory (Sampson, Morenoff, and Earls 1999; Sampson et al. 1997). Collective efficacy is a social good and meets collective needs. It is the degree of neighbors' mutual trust and willingness to intervene in social control for the common good. It thus redefines social capital as shared expectations for action among neighbors. It includes: informal social control (i.e., neighbors are counted on to intervene), social cohesion (i.e., neighborhood is close-knit; neighbors help each other, get along with each other, and share values), and trust (i.e., neighbors can be trusted). Individual responses to these elements are aggregated to the neighborhood level to indicate collective efficacy. Collective efficacy is characterized by spatial dynamics. In other words, collective efficacy from surrounding neighborhoods positively influences that within focal neighborhoods.

Collective efficacy is expected to influence individuals' health by depressing health risks in neighborhoods, creating stress buffers such as social support and safety nets, and maintaining and achieving health-relevant resources such as educational, clinical, and housing resources (Drukker et al. 2005). Three studies have examined collective efficacy theory. All of them target the youth population, but report mixed empirical evidence. Drukker and colleagues (2003) analyze data on children of about 11 or 12 years old who attended one level of the primary school in Maastricht, the Netherlands. Their multilevel regression analysis shows that net of neighborhood socioeconomic status, informal social control is positively associated with children's mental health but not with their general health, while social cohesion and trust are not associated with both outcomes. In order to explore collective efficacy theory across societies, Drukker and colleagues (2005) continue to use the same data in Maastricht, and include additional community survey data on children aged 12 in Chicago. Their multilevel analysis implies that informal social control – and social cohesion and trust – increase adolescents' perceived health for the Dutch sample and the Hispanic subsample in the United States but not for the non-Hispanic subsample. Van der Linden and colleagues (2003) examine data on 56 children utilizing the mental health service and 206 children not using that service in Maastricht, the Netherlands. Their multilevel regression analysis reports that neither informal social control, nor social cohesion and trust, predict children's mental health service use; but social cohesion and trust offset the effect of neighborhood socioeconomic deprivation on that type of service use.

Putnam: Expansive and diverse applications

Kawachi and colleagues first applied Putnam's social capital, exploring its association with mortality in 1997 (Moore et al. 2005). A huge multidisciplinary literature has emerged since then. Social capital has been divided into different dimensions: structural and cognitive (Bain and Hicks 1998). Structural social capital includes formal and informal social connections, and cognitive social capital involves trust and norms of reciprocity. Social capital has also been measured at multiple levels.

Its individual-level measurement reflects individual social capital, which exerts a compositional effect, and their higher-level measurement, usually as the aggregation of individual responses at the community, state, and even country level, indicates ecological social capital, which has a contextual impact (De Silva et al. 2007; Macintyre and Ellaway 2000).

Different mechanisms have been proposed to link multiple levels of social capital to health (Kawachi 1999; Kawachi et al. 2008b; Kawachi, Kennedy, and Glass 1999; Kawachi, Kennedy, and Wilkinson 1999). Social capital functions at an individual level through the supply of social support, the impact of social influence (i.e., the maintenance of healthy norms, the promotion of health behaviors), social engagement, and physiological and biological mechanisms. Social capital operates at the neighborhood levels through the process of informal social control, the maintenance of healthy norms, the promotion of health behaviors, the enhancement of services and facilities, collective socialization, and the supply of social support. Social capital at the state level protects health through egalitarianism-oriented political participation and policy making.

Apart from its direct path to health, social capital, in particular ecological social capital, may also operate as one mechanism linking income inequality to health. Wilkinson (1996, 1999) proposes that social capital, reflecting underlying psychosocial risk factors, significantly mediates the negative association between income inequality and health. His opponents (Lynch et al. 2000a; Lynch et al. 2000b; Muntaner and Lynch 1999) criticize him for ignoring other sociological models of stratification such as class relations and class formation, and for overstating subjective consequences of inequality while downplaying structural sources of inequality. Their neo-material model argues that health inequality is rooted in the material world where income inequality represents only one factor.

A huge literature has examined the linkages of multiple forms of social capital as Putnam conceives it to various health and well-being outcomes such as life expectancy, mortality, physical health, mental health, health behavior, health care and services, health information, and life satisfaction among diverse populations of adolescents, adults, and the elderly across levels of social capital, cultures, and societies. Their popularity is probably because of their political implications and quick measurements in secondary data (Foley and Edwards 1999). An extensive review of that literature is beyond the scope of this chapter.[2] We are only able to illustrate the extensiveness of this empirical literature. In brief, the empirical results are mixed, varying with forms and levels of social capital, outcomes, units of analysis, data sources, research populations, and societies.

At the individual level, some studies find consistent evidence on various health-relevant outcomes across societies. An instrumental analysis of the 2006 Social Capital Community Survey data in the United States finds that all five social capital indicators (i.e., social trust, associational involvement, organized interaction, informal socializing, and volunteer activity) can enhance self-reported health (Schultz, O'Brien, and Tadesse 2008). A study of data from the National Survey on Drug Use and Health in the United States reports a negative association between group participation and adolescent alcohol or drug use (Winstanley et al. 2008). Another study of data from six communities in the United States shows that civic participation, especially in organizations providing health information, leads to more cardiovascular disease health messages (Viswanath, Steele, and Finnegan 2006). Another study of the 2003 Health Survey for England finds that civic participation, social trust, perceived social support, and reciprocity lead to better self-reported health (Petrou and Kupek 2008). In Sweden, two studies of community survey data respectively show that civic participation increases leisure-time physical activity and that trust protects self-reported psychological health (Lindström 2008; Lindström, Hanson, and Östergren 2001).

Some studies find mixed evidence. A two-wave prospective panel study of a national representative sample in the US reports that trust in neighbors rather than civic participation decreases major depression (Fujiwara and Kawachi 2008a). A fixed-effect analysis of adult twins in the United States (Fujiwara and Kawachi 2008b) measures four social capital variables, namely, social trust, sense of belonging, volunteering, and community participation, and examines four outcomes, namely, perceived physical health, perceived mental health, number of depressive symptoms, and major depression. For both dizygotic and monozygotic twins, perceived physical health is positively associated with social trust. For dizygotic twins, number of depressive symptoms is negatively related to sense of belonging and community participation, and perceived mental health is positively associated with sense of belonging.

In Canada, a study of community survey data (Veenstra et al. 2005) shows that voluntary participation is predictive of overweight status but not of self-rated health, emotional distress, and chronic illness. Also, religious participation enhances self-rated health while secular participation enhances self-rated health only for the elderly (Veenstra 2000). In Sweden, a study of community survey data on adolescents finds that social trust and social participation are associated with smoking and illicit drug use but not with binge drinking (Lundborg 2005). In Finland, a study of data from a national survey reports that social trust predicts good psychological health for both gender groups and self-reported health only for women, while social participation and social contacts do not explain both outcomes (Nyqvist et al. 2008). Another study of community survey data in Cali, Colombia, reports no associations of four social capital indicators (i.e., informal social control, social cohesion, civic participation, and trust in neighbors) with mental health among the youth population aged 15–25 (Harpham, Grant, and Rodriguez 2004).

Studies on ecological social capital also report mixed evidence. At the community level, for example, Lochner and colleagues (2003) use data from the 1995 Community Survey of the Project on Human Development in Chicago Neighborhoods to measure three components of neighborhood social capital: civic participation (i.e., the average per capita membership of voluntary participation by neighborhood), trust (i.e., the proportion of residents who think people in the neighborhood can be trusted), and reciprocity (i.e., the proportion of residents who think people are willing to help neighbors). As their hierarchical analysis shows, civic participation predicts all-cause and other-cause death rates for all race–sex groups and heart disease death rates only for Whites. Trust explains all-cause death rates for all race–sex groups except for Black men, heart disease death rates only for White women and men, and other-cause death rates for all race–sex groups except for Black women. Reciprocity is relevant to all-cause death rates and other-cause death rates for all race–sex groups except for Black women, and heart disease death rates only for White men. None were associated with cancer death rates.

At the neighborhood level, one study on live births in Chicago measures social capital as the combination of reciprocal exchange and local voluntary participation, both of which are aggregated to the neighborhood level (Morenoff 2003). Neighborhood internal social capital protects birth weight and mediates the effect of neighborhood poverty and residential mobility. Also, social capital from surrounding neighborhoods predicts birth weight, and such protection is stronger for focal neighborhoods with more internal social capital. Studies of national survey data in the United States show that college students' average volunteering time at the campus level decreases their alcohol or drug use (Weitzman and Chen 2005; Weitzman and Kawachi 2000). At the state level in the United States, one study of 39 states (Kawachi, Kennedy, and Glass 1999) finds that all three social capital indicators are associated with individuals' self-reported health, including civic engagement (i.e., per capita membership of voluntary associations in each state), trust (i.e., the percentage of residents who think most people can not be trusted), and reciprocity (i.e., the percentage of residents who think most people look out for themselves). Some studies of 48 states imply that Putnam's state-level index predicts individual self-reported health but not sexually transmitted diseases (Mellor and Milyo 2005; Semaan et al. 2007).

The debate on the mediating role of social capital in the association of income inequality with health also triggers studies on ecological social capital. Some studies support the mediating effect hypothesis. At the state level, in a study of 39 US states (Kawachi et al. 1997), both per capita group membership and lack of social trust are associated with both income inequality and total mortality. In another study of 48 US states (Weaver and Rivello 2006–7), mortality rates are associated with the state-level Putnam index but not with three income inequality indicators. Some studies disconfirm the mediating hypothesis. In one study of 16 wealthy countries (Muntaner et al. 2002), cause-specific mortality is associated more strongly with economic inequality and working-class power than with social capital. In another study of 19 countries (Kennelly, O'Shea, and Garvey 2003), social trust, membership in organizations, and volunteering exert no significant effects on population health, including life expectancy, infant mortality, and perinatal mortality, while per capita income and the proportion of health expenditure financed by the government are associated with better population health. In another analysis of 23 rich and poor countries (Lindström and Lindström 2006), social trust does not explain population health such as adult mortality rate, life expectancy, and infant mortality rate for poor, rich, or all 23 countries. While the Gini index predicts infant mortality rate for rich countries, gross national product per capita explains life expectancy for all countries, and the Gini index and gross national product per capita are relevant to infant mortality rates for poor countries. One study of 45 countries (Mansyur et al. 2008) further shows that whether country-level social capital (i.e., social network density, societal trust) and income inequality (i.e., GNP, Gini index) influence self-reported health depends on the countries included.

There are also studies on multilevel social capital. For example, one study based on data from 40 US communities in the 2000 Social Capital Community Benchmark Survey (Kim, Subramanian, and Kawachi 2006) measures six individual-level social capital indicators, including formal bond (i.e., formal involvement in homogeneous groups), trust in own racial/ethnic groups, formal bridge (i.e., formal involvement in heterogeneous groups), informal bridge (i.e., interaction outside one's own racial/ethnic groups), diversity (i.e., diversity of friendships), and social trust. It combines and aggregates the first two indicators to the community level as community bonding social capital, and the next three indicators to the community level as community bridging social capital. As it reports, three individual-level social capital indicators such as formal bonding, trust in own racial/ethnic groups, and social trust are positively associated with self-reported health, and community bonding social capital instead of community bridging social capital exerts a modest effect on self-reported health. One study of 45 countries (Mansyur et al. 2008) finds individual voluntary participation and social trust have a positive effect on individual self-reported health, while the significance of national voluntary participation and trust depends on the countries included. Another study of 22 European countries (Poortinga 2006) shows that individual instead of national civic participation and social trust predict individual self-rated health. Also, the effect of individual participation and social trust is stronger in countries with higher national civic participation and social trust. In addition, two studies of four developing countries (Peru, Ethiopia, Vietnam, and India) report that whether individual participation and its community aggregation contribute to the mental health of mothers of a 1-year-old child and child nutritional status varies with societies (De Silva and Harpham 2007; De Silva et al. 2007).

ISSUES AND FUTURE DIRECTIONS

As this review suggests, social capital has opened up a burgeoning multidisciplinary health research literature across societies during the last two decades. Four scholars – Bourdieu, Lin, Coleman, and Putnam – have contributed to the theoretical construction of social capital from different perspectives. Among them, Putnam's notion has captured most attention in the health literature with the effort of public health researchers, while the value of other sociological theories has been under-studied. To extend Woolcock's (1998) statement, the popularity of social capital may contribute to driving sociologists into multidisciplinary discourse on public and individual health issues. Sociologists may contribute greatly to increasing the understanding of the relationship between social capital and health by responding to the following four queries.

What is the added value of social capital? In other words, can we integrate social capital into the previous health literature? The integration requires us to examine the distinctions and associations between social capital and other established social antecedents of health. Putnam, Coleman, Sampson, and other scholars tend to equate social capital with other relationship-based concepts such as social networks, social integration, social cohesion, and social support (e.g., Carpiano 2006; Putnam 2000, 2004; Sampson et al. 1997; Szreter and Woolcock 2004; Ziersch et al. 2005). Such equalization pours old wine into new bottles (Kawachi et al. 2004) and endangers the added theoretical value of social capital (Lin 2001a; Portes 1998). Also as mentioned earlier, the 14 items in the Putnam index do not statistically reflect one single latent factor (Kim and Kawachi 2007; Kim et al. 2006). In contrast, Lin's definitions and specifications of social capital allow us to distinguish these relevant concepts (Song and Lin 2009). A social network is "a specific set of linkages among a defined set of persons, with the additional property that the characteristics of these linkages as a whole may be used to interpret the social behavior of the persons involved" (Mitchell 1969: 2). Social networks are one of the most distinct social antecedents of health status (for reviews, see Berkman et al. 2000; House, Landis, and Umberson 1988; Lin and Peek 1999; Pescosolido and Levy 2002; Smith and Christakis 2008). The notion of social networks is not a theory but a perspective (Mitchell 1974). Specific theories are derived from the social network perspective to interpret mechanisms through which social networks function to impact health (Berkman et al. 2000; Lin and Peek 1999; Pescosolido 2007), including social integration, social cohesion, and social support as well as social capital. Social integration is the extent of participation in social networks, indicated by active engagement in social roles and social activities, and cognitive identification with network members (Brissette, Cohen, and Seeman 2000). Social cohesion is the degree of social bonds and social equality within social networks, indicated by trust, reciprocity, and the lack of social conflict (Kawachi and Berkman 2000). We trace these two ideas back to the 1897 book on suicide by the founder of modern sociology, Emile Durkheim (1951 [1897]) (Turner 2003).

Social support is the assistance from social networks, indicated by the quantity and quality of perceived or received help from network members (Lakey and Cohen 2000; Pearlin 1989). We credit Cassel and Cobb for their seminal work on social support in 1976 (Cassel 1976; Cobb 1976). Social support has received substantial research attention since then (for reviews, see House, Umberson, and Landis 1988; Thoits 1995). By comparison, social capital as conceived of by Lin, particularly when measured through the position generator, uniquely captures structural positions possessed by individuals' network members. It is different from, but causally relevant to, the other network-based concepts. For example, social integration creates and maintains social ties and, furthermore, social capital; social cohesion may facilitate or constrain the accumulation of social capital; and social capital brings social support since we draw on network members' resources for various supportive purposes (Lin 2001a; Pearlin and Schooler 1978; Song and Lin 2009).

In addition, there are critics of specifying trust and norms of reciprocity as subjective components of social capital (Cook 2005; Foley and Edwards 1999; Lin 2001a). Social capital is neutral, objective, and rooted in social relationships, which contributes to its unique heuristic values. Trust and norms are inherently moral and psychological, and separated from network structures and social contexts. For example, studies on the associations of trust and norms with mental health are in particular questionable in terms of causal direction, considering the fact that researchers are trying to explain the relationship between psychological concepts. More theoretical efforts are needed for a coherent integration of social capital with the existing literature.

Does the network-based approach receive limited attention because of its limited implications for health? The answer is definitely no. Apart from its coherent integration with previous health literature as mentioned above, the network-based approach to social capital offers other important theoretical and methodological implications for future health research. First, this approach takes a conflict perspective, and contributes to linking health disparities with general stratification theories in sociology (Hawe and Shiell 2000; Song and Lin 2009). Second, this approach enhances the life-course perspective to health stratification (O'Rand 2001; Pevalin 2003). Bourdieu's argument on the production and reproduction process of stratification and Lin's argument on the reciprocal relationships between instrumental and expressive returns fit more into the cumulative advantage/disadvantage theory in the health literature. Also, this approach highlights social capital as an independent source of health disparities. Social capital as network members' resources exerts a health effect net of individuals' personal capital, in particular their own socioeconomic resources, the fundamental causes of disease and illness (Link and Phelan 1995). Its potential mechanisms include information, influence, social credential or symbolic profits, material profits, and reinforced identification.

Apart from its direct effect, social capital also interplays with other structural risk factors. Bourdieu argues for the convertibility between different forms of capital. Lin hypothesizes the reciprocal relationship between social capital and personal capital. Social capital could influence health by mediating the influence of prior personal capital, and indirectly by creating more personal capital. Medical sociologists are in a better position to explore multiple mechanisms linking social capital to health and the causal relationships between social capital, personal capital, and other structural risk factors such as gender and race in the production process of health inequality.

Next, the network-based approach strengthens the structural perspective in medical sociology, one unique sociological approach to health (Bird, Conrad, and Fremont 2000). Social capital can be another important approach to social structure and health because network members' structural positions reflect "structural arrangements in which individuals are embedded" (Pearlin 1989: 241). Furthermore, the network-based approach contributes to the social network tradition in medical sociology. It embeds social capital in networks beyond geographical location. One major research gap in the social network literature is whether the access to resources, in particular material resources, is one mechanism through which social networks shape health (Berkman et al. 2000). Occupation is one central indicator of hierarchical social locations in the stratification literature, and the position generator measures social capital as the occupational distribution of network members. Social capital measured through the position generator contributes to bridging that foregoing research gap in the social network and health literature (Webber and Huxley 2004).

What are the future research directions for the network-based approach? The theoretical adoption of Bourdieu's approach is still incomplete. Stephens (2008) concludes her research with the statement that "Bourdieu can help us only if we take account of his theory in its place." We would have to say that "Bourdieu can help us only if we take full rather than partial account of his theory." The lack of measurement in Bourdieu's work restricts its application to health and produces controversial theoretical and empirical applications. Instead of measuring social capital as in the normative approach or other established social factors such as social support (e.g., Carpiano 2006; Ziersch 2005), we suggest that Bourdieu's proposed elements of social capital (i.e., network size, network members' personal capital) are more consistent with Lin's notion and measurement. We reserve this for future discussion.

The empirical examination of Lin's theory and methodology relative to health is limited. For the purpose of generalizability and stronger causal inferences, longitudinal research designs containing appropriate network instruments, multiple health outcomes, and information for potential explanatory mechanisms are needed. Also, future research should examine not only the direct effect of social capital but also its mediating and moderating effect between health and other established structural risk factors, in particular personal capital over the life course. Furthermore, future research should measure network-based concepts including social capital independently and examine their causal relationships for a more systematic understanding of the role of social networks in the production of disease and illness. In addition, future studies should examine the mobilization process of social capital in the access to health resources. Available empirical studies only examine accessed social capital and its potential effects. Its limited explanatory power (Song and Lin 2009) may imply that social capital is expected to play a stronger role for individuals actually mobilizing social capital. For example, patients with more severe illness or people with insufficient personal capital are more motivated to resort to social capital for health resources. Besides, the dynamic paths between social capital and personal capital would encourage future research on the dynamics of disease and illness from onset to recovery (Pevalin 2003; Webber and Huxley 2004). Finally, Lin has only recently proposed his macro-level conceptualization of social capital. He specifies internal social capital at the collective level as the sum of members' resources. The established literature on the protective effect of community- and societal-level socioeconomic characteristics on various health outcomes implicitly demonstrates his conceptualization (for a review, see Robert and House 2000). Future theoretical clarification and methodological work is needed for a direct examination of his macro-level definition.

What are the major challenges and future directions for the normative approach? Collective efficacy theory proposed by Sampson and colleagues based on Coleman's work helps draw our attention to the neighborhood mechanisms of health inequality. Its limited empirical applications report mixed results. Different elements of collective efficacy exert varying effects. There is also evidence for an interaction of certain elements of collective efficacy with race and neighborhood deprivation. There is no doubt that Putnam's work contributes significantly to the health literature. Despite the fact that there is mixed evidence, multiple indicators and levels of social capital are associated with various health-related outcomes across populations and societies. Social capital not only exerts direct effects but also interplays with other factors such as gender, race, age, and neighborhood contexts. The mixed evidence for the normative approach to social capital provides a challenge for future theoretical and empirical research. Mixed results across societies suggest that future research should integrate institutional theory into the social capital literature. Mixed results across levels show that future research should elaborate the relationships between multiple levels of social capital. Mixed results across gender, race, and age groups imply that future studies should explore cultural and life-course explanations. Mixed results across health outcomes indicate that future research should theorize specific mechanisms for different outcomes. Mixed results across measurements of social capital point out that future studies should analyze each indicator and its mechanisms separately instead of combining indicators without theoretical justification. Also, most results are from cross-sectional data sets. For the purpose of stronger causal inferences, stricter research designs such as the collection of prospective data and twin data are needed.

The normative approach attracts not only more applications but also more theoretical critiques, such as their understatement of social conflict and social capital's negative consequences, the confusing stretching of social capital into the macrolevel, the mixed combination of established psychosocial factors, and tautological arguments of social capital as both a cause and an effect (Foley and Edwards 1999; Lin 2001a; Portes 1998). Future studies need to pay attention to the significance of social capital for health inequality. Also, more theoretical and methodological efforts are needed on the construct validity of multilevel measurements of social capital (Hawe and Shiell 2000; Lin 2001a; Muntaner and Lynch 2002; Portes 1998). To solve the tautological problem, we have to discriminate social capital from other relevant but distinct concepts. Such discrimination is not to deny the contribution of the normative approach to the revival of those concepts. To summarize, we suggest that future research should recognize the previous relevant research in medical sociology, and theorize and examine relevant concepts (e.g., social integration, social cohesion, informal social control, social support, and social networks) independently instead of subsuming them under the trendy umbrella of social capital. Otherwise, the picture is confusing. Our suggestion may disappoint some leading scholars in the area of public health, who are concerned that "at some future date, an international consensus conference of scholars might agree to reserve the use of the term 'social capital' only to network-based resources" (Kawachi, Subramanian, and Kim 2008b: 4).

Notes

1   The division of schools is controversial. For example, Adam and Rončević (2003) distinguish three schools: Bourdieu's approach, Lin's utilitarian network-based approach, and the normative approach of Coleman and Putnam. Moore et al. (2005) discern two schools: the network approach of Coleman and Bourdieu, and the communitarian approach of Putnam. Kawachi et al. (2008b) seem to classify two approaches: the social cohesion school of Coleman and Putnam, and the network school of Bourdieu and Lin.

2   For most recent systematic reviews of the empirical literature, see Kawachi, Subramanian, and Kim (2008a). This edited book devotes five chapters to summarizing empirical evidence.

References

Abrums, Mary. 2000. " 'Jesus Will Fix it After Awhile': Meanings and Health." *Social Science and Medicine* 50: 89–105.

Acock, Alan C. and Jeanne S. Hurlbert. 1993. "Social Networks, Marital Status, and Well-Being." *Social Networks* 15: 309–34.

Adam, Frane and Borut Rončević. 2003. "Social Capital: Recent Debates and Research Trends." *Social Science Information* 42: 155–83.

Almedom, Astier M. 2005. "Social Capital and Mental Health: An Interdisciplinary Review of Primary Evidence." *Social Science and Medicine* 61: 943–64.

Bain, K. and N. Hicks. 1998. "Building Social Capital and Reaching Out to Excluded Groups: The Challenge of Partnerships." Paper presented at CELAM meeting on the Struggle against Poverty towards the Turn of the Millennium, Washington DC.

Berkman, Lisa F., Thomas Glass, Ian Brissette, and Teresa E. Seeman. 2000. "From Social Integration to Health: Durkheim in the New Millennium." *Social Science and Medicine* 51: 843–57.

Bird, Chloe E., Peter Conrad, and Allen M. Fremont. 2000. "Medical Sociology at the Millennium." Pp. 1–32 in C. E. Bird, P. Conrad, and A. M. Fremont (eds.), *Handbook of Medical Sociology*. Upper Saddle River, NJ: Prentice-Hall.

Bourdieu, Pierre. 1984. *Distinction: A Social Critique of the Judgment of Taste*. London and New York: Routledge and Kegan Paul.

Bourdieu, Pierre. 1986 [1983]. "The Forms of Capital." Pp. 241–58 in J. G. Richardson (ed.), *Handbook of Theory and Research for the Sociology of Education*. Westport, CT: Greenwood Press.

Brissette, Ian, Sheldon Cohen, and Teresa E. Seeman. 2000. "Measuring Social Integration and Social Networks." Pp. 53–85 in Sheldon Cohen, Lynn G. Underwood, and Benjamin H. Gottlieb (eds.), *Social Support Measurement and Intervention*. New York: Oxford University Press.

Burt, Ronald S. 1984. "Network Items and the General Social Survey." *Social Networks* 6: 293–339.

Burt, Ronald S. 1992. *Structural Holes: The Social Structure of Competition*. Cambridge, MA: Harvard University Press.

Carpiano, Richard M. 2006. "Toward a Neighborhood Resource-Based Theory of Social Capital for Health: Can Bourdieu and Sociology Help?" *Social Science and Medicine* 62: 165–75.

Carpiano, Richard M. 2007. "Neighborhood Social Capital and Adult Health: An Empirical Test of a Bourdieu-Based Model." *Health and Place* 13(3): 639–55.

Carpiano, Richard M. 2008. "Actual or Potential Neighborhood Resources and Access to Them: Testing Hypotheses of Social Capital for the Health of Female Caregivers." *Social Science and Medicine* 67: 568–82.

Cassel, John. 1976. "The Contribution of the Social Environment to Host Resistance." *American Journal of Epidemiology* 104: 107–23.

Cobb, Sidney. 1976. "Social Support as a Moderator of Life Stress." *Psychosomatic Medicine* 38: 300–14.

Cockerham, William C. 2007. *Social Causes of Health and Disease*. Malden, MA: Polity Press.

Coleman, James S. 1988. "Social Capital in the Creation of Human Capital." *American Journal of Sociology* 94: 95–121.

Coleman, James S. 1990. *Foundations of Social Theory*. Cambridge: Belknap Press of Harvard University Press.

Cook, Karen Schweers. 2005. "Networks, Norms, and Trust: The Social Psychology of Social Capital." *Social Psychology Quarterly* 68: 4–14.

De Silva, Mary J. and Trudy Harpham. 2007. "Maternal Social Capital and Child Nutritional Status in Four Developing Countries." *Health and Place* 13: 341–55.

De Silva, Mary J., Sharon R. A. Huttly, Trudy Harpham, and Michael G. Kenward. 2007. "Social Capital and Mental Health: A Comparative Analysis of Four Low-Income Countries." *Social Science and Medicine* 64: 5–20.

De Silva, Mary J., Kwame McKenzie, Trudy Harpham, and Sharon R. A. Huttly. 2005. "Social Capital and Mental Illness: A Systematic Review." *Journal of Epidemiology and Community Health* 59: 619–27.

Drentea, Patricia and Jennifer L. Moren-Cross. 2005. "Social Capital and Social Support on the Web: The Case of an Internet Mother Site." *Sociology of Health and Illness* 27: 920–43.

Drukker, Marjan, Stephen L. Buka, Charles Kaplan, Kwame McKenzie, and Jim Van Os. 2005. "Social Capital and Young Adolescents' Perceived Health in Different Sociocultural Settings." *Social Science and Medicine* 61: 185–98.

Drukker, Marjan, Charles Kaplan, Frans Feron, and Jim Van Os. 2003. "Children's Health-Related Quality of Life, Neighborhood Socio-Economic Deprivation and Social Capital: A Contextual Analysis." *Social Science and Medicine* 57: 825–41.

Durkheim, Emile. 1951 [1897]. *Suicide: A Study in Sociology*, translated by John Spaulding and George Simpson. New York: Free Press.

Farr, James. 2004. "Social Capital: A Conceptual History." *Political Theory* 32: 6–33.

Foley, Michael W. and Bob Edwards. 1999. "Is It Time to Disinvest in Social Capital?" *Journal of Public Policy* 19: 141–73.

Fujiwara Takeo and Kawachi Ichiro. 2008a. "A Prospective Study of Individual-Level Social Capital and Major Depression in the United States." *Journal of Epidemiology and Community Health* 62: 627–33.

Fujiwara Takeo and Kawachi Ichiro. 2008b. "Social Capital and Health: A Study of Adult Twins in the US." *American Journal of Preventive Medicine* 35: 139–44.

Granovetter, Mark. 1973. "The Strength of Weak Ties." *American Journal of Sociology* 78: 1360–80.

Hanifan, Lyda Judson. 1916. "The Rural School Community Center." *Annals of the Academy of Political and Social Science* 67: 130–8.

Harpham, Trudy, Emma Grant, and Carlos Rodriguez. 2004. "Mental Health and Social Capital in Cali, Colombia." *Social Science and Medicine* 58: 2267–77.

Hawe, Penelope and Alan Shiell. 2000. "Social Capital and Health Promotion: A Review." *Social Science and Medicine* 51: 871–85.

House, James S., Karl R. Landis, and Debra Umberson. 1988. "Social Relationships and Health." *Science* 241: 540–5.

House, James S., Debra Umberson, and Karl R. Landis. 1988. "Structures of Processes of Social Support." *Annual Review of Sociology* 14: 293–318.

Islam, M. Kamrul, Juan Merlo, Kawachi Ichiro, Martin Lindstrom, and Ulf-G. Gerdtham. 2006. "Social Capital and Health: Does Egalitarianism Matter? A Literature Review." *International Journal for Equity in Health* 5: 3. Retrieved April 9, 2006 (www. equityhealthj.com/content/pdf/1475-9276-5-3.pdf).

Kawachi Ichiro. 1999. "Social Capital and Community Effects on Population and Individual Health." *Annals of the New York Academy of Sciences* 896: 120–30.

Kawachi Ichiro and Lisa F. Berkman. 2000. "Social Cohesion, Social Capital and Health." Pp. 174–90 in Lisa F. Berkman and Kawachi Ichiro (eds.), *Social Epidemiology*. New York: Oxford University Press.

Kawachi Ichiro, B. P. Kennedy, and R. Glass. 1999. "Social Capital and Self-Rated Health: A Contextual Analysis." *American Journal of Public Health* 89: 1187–93.

Kawachi Ichiro, B. P. Kennedy, K. Lochner, and D. Prothrow-Stith. 1997. "Social Capital, Income Inequality, and Mortality." *American Journal of Public Health* 87: 1491–8.

Kawachi Ichiro, B. P. Kennedy, and Richard Wilkinson (eds.). 1999. *Income Inequality and Health: A Reader*. New York: New Press.

Kawachi Ichiro, Daniel Kim, Adam Coutts, and S. V. Subramanian. 2004. "Commentary: Reconciling the Three Accounts of Social Capital." *International Journal of Epidemiology* 33: 682–90.

Kawachi Ichiro, S. V. Subramanian, and Daniel Kim (eds.). 2008a. *Social Capital and Health*. New York: Springer Science and Business Media.

Kawachi Ichiro, S. V. Subramanian, and Daniel Kim. 2008b. "Social Capital and Health: A Decade of Progress and Beyond." Pp. 1–26 in Kawachi Ichiro, S. V. Subramanian, and Daniel Kim (eds.), *Social Capital and Health*. New York: Springer Science and Business Media.

Kennelly, Brendan, Eamon O'Shea, and Eoghan Garvey. 2003. "Social Capital, Life Expectancy and Mortality: A Cross-National Examination." *Social Science and Medicine* 56: 2367–77.

Kim, Daniel and Kawachi Ichiro. 2007. "US State-Level Social Capital and Health-Related Quality of Life: Multilevel Evidence of Main, Mediating, and Modifying Effects." *Annals of Epidemiology* 17: 258–69.

Kim, Daniel, S. V. Subramanian, Steven L. Gortmaker, and Kawachi Ichiro. 2006. "US State- and County-Level Social Capital in Relation to Obesity and Physical Inactivity: A Multilevel, Multivariable Analysis." *Social Science and Medicine* 63: 1045–59.

Kim, Daniel, S. V. Subramanian, and Kawachi Ichiro. 2006. "Bonding versus Bridging Social Capital and Their Associations with Self-Rated Health: A Multilevel Analysis of 40 US Communities." *Journal of Epidemiology and Community Health* 60: 116–22.

Lakey, Brian and Sheldon Cohen. 2000. "Social Support Theory and Measurement." Pp. 29–52 in Sheldon Cohen, Lynn G. Underwood, and Benjamin H. Gottlieb (eds.), *Social Support Measurement and Intervention*. New York: Oxford University Press.

Lin, Nan. 1982. "Social Resources and Instrumental Action." Pp. 131–45 in P. V. Marsden and N. Lin (eds.), *Social Structure and Network Analysis*. Beverly Hills, CA: Sage.

Lin, Nan. 1999. "Social Networks and Status Attainment." *Annual Review of Sociology* 25: 467–88.

Lin, Nan. 2001a. *Social Capital: A Theory of Social Structure and Action*. Cambridge: Cambridge University Press.

Lin, Nan. 2001b. "Building a Network Theory of Social Capital." Pp. 3–29 in N. Lin, K. Cook, and R. S. Burt (eds.), *Social Capital: Theory and Research*. New York: Aldine de Gruyter.

Lin, Nan. 2008. "A Network Theory of Social Capital." Pp. 50–69 in D. Castiglione, J. van Deth, and G. Wolleb (eds.), *Handbook on Social Capital*. Oxford: Oxford University Press.

Lin, Nan, Paul Dayton, and Peter Greenwald. 1978. "Analyzing the Instrumental Use of Relations in the Context of Social Structure." *Sociological Methods and Research* 7: 149–66.

Lin, Nan and Mary Dumin. 1986. "Access to Occupations through Social Ties." *Social Networks* 8: 365–85.

Lin, Nan, Walter M. Ensel, and John C. Vaughn. 1981. "Social Resources and Strength of Ties: Structural Factors in Occupational Status Attainment." *American Sociological Review* 46: 393–405.

Lin, Nan, Yang-Chih Fu, and Ray-May Hsung. 2001. "The Position Generator: A Measurement Technique for Investigations of Social Capital." Pp. 57–81 in N. Lin, K. Cook, and R. S. Burt (eds.), *Social Capital: Theory and Research*. New York: Aldine de Gruyter.

Lin, Nan and M. Kristen Peek. 1999. "Social Networks and Mental Health." Pp. 241–58 in A. V. Horwitz and T. L. Scheid (eds.), *A Handbook for the Study of Mental Health: Social Contexts, Theories, and Systems*. Cambridge: Cambridge University Press.

Lindström, Christine and Martin Lindström. 2006. " 'Social Capital,' GNP per Capita, Relative Income, and Health: An Ecological Study of 23 Countries." *International Journal of Health Services* 36: 679–96.

Lindström, Martin. 2008. "Social Capital, Anticipated Ethnic Discrimination and Self-Reported Psychological Health: A Population-Based Study." *Social Science and Medicine* 66: 1–13.

Lindström, Martin, Bertil S. Hanson, and Per-Olof Östergren. 2001. "Socioeconomic Differences in Leisure-Time Physical Activity: The Role of Social Participation and Social Capital in Shaping Health-Related Behavior." *Social Science and Medicine* 52: 441–51.

Link, Bruce G. and Jo C. Phelan. 1995. "Social Conditions as Fundamental Causes of Disease." *Journal of Health and Social Behavior*, Extra Issue: 80–94.

Lochner, Kimberly A., Kawachi Ichiro, Robert T. Brennan, and Stephen L. Buka. 2003. "Social Capital and Neighborhood Mortality Rates in Chicago." *Social Science and Medicine* 56: 1797–1805.

Lundborg, Petter. 2005. "Social Capital and Substance Use among Swedish Adolescents: An Explorative Study." *Social Science and Medicine* 61: 1151–8.

Lynch, John W., Pernille Due, Carles Muntaner, and George Davey Smith. 2000a. "Social Capital: Is It a Good Investment Strategy for Public Health." *Journal of Epidemiology and Community Health* 54: 404–8.

Lynch, John W., George Davey Smith, George A. Kaplan, and James S. House. 2000b. "Income Inequality and Mortality: Importance to Health of Individual Income, Psychosocial Environment, or Material Conditions." *British Medical Journal* 320: 1200–4.

Macinko, James and Barbara Starfield. 2001. "The Utility of Social Capital in Research on Health Determinants." *Milbank Quarterly* 79: 387–427.

Macintyre, Sally and Anne Ellaway. 2000. "Ecological Approaches: Rediscovering the Role of the Physical and Social Environment." Pp. 332–48 in Lisa F. Berkman and Kawachi Ichiro (eds.), *Social Epidemiology*. Oxford: Oxford University Press.

Mansyur, Carol, Benjamin C. Amick, Ronald B. Harrist, and Luisa Franzini. 2008. "Social Capital, Income Inequality, and Self-Rated Health in 45 Countries." *Social Science and Medicine* 66: 43–56.

McCallister, Lynn and Claude S. Fischer. 1978. "A Procedure for Surveying Personal Networks." *Sociological Methods and Research* 7: 131–48.

McKenzie, Kwame and Trudy Harpham (eds.). 2006. *Social Capital and Mental Health*. London and Philadelphia: Jessica Kingsley.

Mellor, Jennifer M. and Jeffrey Milyo. 2005. "State Social Capital and Individual Health Status." *Journal of Health Politics, Policy and Law* 30: 1101–30.

Mitchell, J. C. 1969. "The Concept and Use of Social Networks." Pp. 1–50 in J. C. Mitchell (ed.), *Social Networks in Urban Situations*. Manchester: Manchester University Press.

Mitchell, J. C. 1974. "Social Networks." *Annual Review of Anthropology* 3: 279–99.

Moore, Spencer, Alan Shiell, Penelope Hawe, and Valerie A Haines. 2005. "The Privileging of Communitarian Ideas: Citation Practices and the Translation of Social Capital Into Public Health Research." *American Journal of Public Health* 95: 1330–7.

Morenoff, Jeffrey. 2003. "Neighborhood Mechanisms and the Spatial Dynamics of Birth Weight." *American Journal of Sociology* 108(5): 976–1017.

Muntaner, Carles and John Lynch. 1999. "Income Inequality, Social Cohesion, and Class Relations: A Critique of Wilkinson's Neo-Durkheimian Research Program." *International Journal of Health Services* 29: 59–81.

Muntaner, Carles and John Lynch. 2002. "Social Capital, Class, Race and Gender Conflict and Population Health." *International Journal of Epidemiology* 202(31): 261–7.

Muntaner, Carles, John Lynch, and George Davey Smith. 2001. "Social Capital, Disorganized Communities, and the Third Way: Understanding the Retreat from Structural Inequalities in Epidemiology and Public Health." *International Journal of Health Services* 31: 213–37.

Muntaner, Carles, John Lynch, Marianne Hillemeier, Ju Hee Lee, Richard David, Joan Benach, and Carme Borrell. 2002. "Economic Inequality, Working-Class Power, Social Capital, and Cause-Specific Mortality in Wealthy Countries." *International Journal of Health Services* 32: 629–56.

Nyqvist, Fredrica, Fjalar Finnäs, Gunborg Jakobsson, and Seppo Koskinen. 2008. "The Effect of Social Capital on Health: The Case of Two Language Groups in Finland." *Health and Place* 14: 347–60.

O'Rand, Angela M. 2001. "Stratification and the Life Course: The Forms of Life-Course Capital and Their Interrelationships." Pp. 197–213 in R. R. Binstrock and L. K. George (eds.), *Handbook of Aging and the Social Sciences*. San Diego: Academic Press.

Pearlin, Leonard I. 1989. "The Sociological Study of Stress." *Journal of Health and Social Behavior* 30: 241–56.

Pearlin, Leonard I. and Carmi Schooler. 1978. "The Structure of Coping." *Journal of Health and Social Behavior* 19: 2–21.

Pescosolido, Bernice A. 2007. "Sociology of Social Networks." Pp. 208–17 in Clifton D. Bryant and Dennis L. Peck (eds.), *21st Century Sociology: A Reference Book*. Thousand Oaks, CA: Sage.

Pescosolido, Bernice A. and Judith A. Levy. 2002. "The Role of Social Networks in Health, Illness, Disease and Healing: The Accepting Present, the Forgotten Past, and the Dangerous Potential for a Complacent Future." Pp. 3–25 in J. A. Levy and B. A. Pescosolido (eds.), *Social Networks and Health*. New York: Elsevier Science.

Petrou, Stavros, and Emil Kupek. 2008. "Social Capital and Its Relationship with Measures of Health Status: Evidence from the Health Survey for England 2003." *Health Economics* 17: 127–43.

Pevalin, David. 2003. "More to Social Capital than Putnam." *British Journal of Psychiatry* 182: 172–3.

Poortinga, Wouter. 2006. "Social Capital: An Individual or Collective Resource for Health?" *Social Science and Medicine* 62: 292–302.

Portes, Alejandro. 1998. "Social Capital: Its Origins and Applications in Modern Sociology." *Annual Review of Sociology* 24: 1–24.

Portes, Alejandro and Julia Sensenbrenner. 1993. "Embeddedness and Immigration: Notes on the Social Determinants of Economic Action." *American Journal of Sociology* 98: 1320–50.

Putnam, Robert D. 1993. *Making Democracy Work: Civic Traditions in Modern Italy*. Princeton, NJ: Princeton University Press.

Putnam, Robert D. 1995. "Bowling Alone: America's Declining Social Capital." *Journal of Democracy* 6: 65–78.

Putnam, Robert D. 2000. *Bowling Alone: The Collapse and Revival of American Community*. New York: Simon and Schuster.

Putnam, Robert D. 2004. "Commentary. 'Health by Association': Some Comments." *International Journal of Epidemiology* 33: 667–71.

Robert, Stephanie A. and James S. House. 2000. "Socioeconomic Inequalities in Health: Integrating Individual-, Community-, and Societal-Level Theory and Research." Pp. 115–35 in G. L. Albrecht, R. Fitzpatrick, and S. C. Scrimshaw (eds.), *Handbook of Social Studies in Health and Medicine*. Thousand Oaks, CA: Sage.

Sampson, Robert J., Jeffrey D. Morenoff, and Felton Earls. 1999. "Beyond Social Capital: Spatial Dynamics of Collective Efficacy for Children." *American Sociological Review* 64: 633–60.

Sampson, Robert J., Stephen W. Raudenbush, and Felton Earls. 1997. "Neighborhoods and Violent Crime: A Multilevel Study of Collective Efficacy." *Science* 277: 918–24.

Schultz, Jennifer, A. Maureen O'Brien, and Bedassa Tadesse. 2008. "Social Capital and Self-Rated Health: Results from the US 2006 Social Capital Survey of One Community." *Social Science and Medicine* 67: 606–17.

Semaan, Salaam, Maya Sternberg, Akbar Zaidi, and Sevgi O. Aral. 2007. "Social Capital and Rates of Gonorrhea and Syphilis in the United States: Spatial Regression Analyses of State-Level Associations." *Social Science and Medicine* 64: 2324–41.

Shortt, Samuel E. D. 2004. "Making Sense of Social Capital, Health and Policy." *Health Policy* 70: 11–22.

Smith, Kirsten P. and Nicholas A. Christakis. 2008. "Social Networks and Health." *Annual Review of Sociology* 34: 405–29.

Song, Lijun and Nan Lin. 2009. "Social Capital and Health Inequality: Evidence from Taiwan." *Journal of Health and Social Behavior* 50: 149–63.

Snijders, Tom A. B. 1999. "Prologue to the Measurement of Social Capital." *La Revue Tocqueville* 20: 27–44.

Stephens, Christine. 2008. "Social Capital in Its Place: Using Social Theory to Understand Social Capital and Inequalities in Health." *Social Science and Medicine* 66: 1174–84.

Szreter, Simon and Michael Woolcock. 2004. "Health By Association? Social Capital, Social Theory, and the Political Economy of Public Health." *International Journal of Epidemiology* 33: 650–67.

Thoits, Peggy A. 1995. "Stress, Coping, and Social Support Processes: Where Are We? What Next?" *Journal of Health and Social Behavior*, Extra Issue: 53–79.

Turner, Bryan. 2003. "Social Capital, Inequality and Health: The Durkheimian Revival." *Social Theory and Health* 1: 4–20.

Van der Gaag, Martin P. J. and Tom A. B. Snijders. 2005. "The Resource Generator: Social Capital Quantification with Concrete Items." *Social Networks* 27: 1–27.

Van der Gaag, Martin P. J., Tom A. B. Snijders, and Henk D. Flap. 2008. "Position Generator Measures and their Relationship to Other Social Capital Measures." Pp. 27–48 in N. Lin and B. Erickson (eds.), *Social Capital: Advances in Research*. New York: Oxford University Press.

Van der Linden, Jikke, Marjan Drukker, Nicole Gunther, Frans Feron, and Jim Van Os. 2003. "Children's Mental Health Service Use, Neighborhood Socioeconomic Deprivation, and Social Capital." *Social Psychiatry and Psychiatric Epidemiology* 38: 507–14.

Veenstra, Gerry. 2000. "Social Capital, SES and Health: An Individual-Level Analysis." *Social Science and Medicine* 50: 619–29.

Veenstra, Gerry, Isaac Luginaah, Sarah Wakefield, Stephen Birch, John Eyles, and Susan Elliott. 2005. "Who You Know, Where You Live: Social Capital, Neighborhood and Health in Hamilton, Canada." *Social Science and Medicine* 60: 2799–818.

Viswanath, Kasisomayajula, Whitney Randolph Steele, and John R Finnegan, Jr. 2006. "Social Capital and Health: Civic Engagement, Community Size, and Recall of Health Messages." *American Journal of Public Health* 96: 1456–61.

Weaver, Robert and Robert Rivello. 2006–7. "The Distribution of Mortality in the United States: The Effects of Income (Inequality), Social Capital, and Race." *OMEGA: Journal of Death and Dying* 54: 19–39.

Webber, Martin P. and Peter Huxley. 2004. "Mental Health and Social Capitals (letter)." *British Journal of Psychiatry* 184: 185–6.

Webber, Martin P. and Peter Huxley. 2007. "Measuring Access to Social Capital: The Validity and Reliability of the Resource Generator-UK and Its Association with Common Mental Disorder." *Social Science and Medicine* 65: 481–92.

Weitzman, Elissa R. and Ying-Yeh Chen. 2005. "Risk Modifying Effect of Social Capital on Measures Of Heavy Alcohol Consumption, Alcohol Abuse, Harms, and Secondhand Effects: National Survey Findings." *Journal of Epidemiology and Community Health* 59: 303–9.

Weitzman, Elissa R. and Kawachi Ichiro. 2000. "Giving Means Receiving: The Protective Effect of Social Capital on Binge Drinking on College Campuses." *American Journal of Public Health* 90: 1936–9.

Whitley, Rob and Kwame McKenzie. 2005. "Social Capital and Psychiatry: Review of the Literature." *Harvard Review of Psychiatry* 13: 71–84.

Wilkinson, Richard G. 1996. *Unhealthy Societies: The Afflictions of Inequality*. London and New York: Routledge.

Wilkinson, Richard G. 1999. "Income Inequality, Social Cohesion, and Health: Clarifying the Theory – A Reply to Muntaner and Lynch." *International Journal of Health Services* 29: 525–43.

Winstanley, Erin L., Donald M. Steinwachs, Margaret E. Ensminger, Carl A. Latkin, Maxine L. Stizer, and Yngvild Olsen. 2008. "The Association of Self-Reported Neighborhood Disorganization and Social Capital with Adolescent and Drug Use, Dependence, and Access to Treatment." *Drug and Alcohol Dependence* 92: 173–82.

Woolcock, Michael. 1998. "Social Capital and Economic Development: Toward a Theoretical Synthesis and Policy Framework." *Theory and Science* 27: 151–208.

Ziersch, Anna M. 2005. "Health Implications of Access to Social Capital: Findings from an Australian Study." *Social Science and Medicine* 61: 2119–31.

Ziersch, Anna M., Fran E. Baum, Colin MacDougall, and Christine Putland. 2005. "Health Implications of Access to Social Capital: Findings from an Australian Study." *Social Science and Medicine* 60: 71–86.

10

Medicalization, Social Control, and the Relief of Suffering

Joseph E. Davis

Through much of the short history of medical sociology, medicalization has been one of its most important and successful concepts. Medicalization is the name for the process by which medical definitions and practices are applied to behaviors, psychological phenomena, and somatic experiences not previously within the conceptual or therapeutic scope of medicine. Under various terminological rubrics, medicalization has been studied by many scholars, including sociologists, anthropologists, physicians, and historians, and is also regularly encountered in psychiatry, law, social work, and bioethics. Since the 1960s, scholars have produced a rich conceptual literature on medicalization and an extensive array of case studies and historiography. Not confined to academic journals, a concern with medicalization also figures prominently in the mass media and popular press, and has long provided analytical purchase for consumer movements in health.

If anything, the significance of medicalization is growing as its forms and expressions multiply and ever wider realms of behavior and feeling are brought within the ambit of medical explanation and management. The expansion of medical jurisdiction is a long-standing process. What is new is the pace and scope of the expansion. In a few short decades, a great many new diseases and disorders have been defined. Between 1968 and 1994, the *Diagnostic and Statistical Manual of Mental Disorders*, the US diagnostic system, grew from 180 categories of mental illness to over 350 (Healy 1997). The boundaries of disorders are also expanding, and new medical technologies and psychoactive medications, from Ritalin to Prozac, have proliferated and are utilized by millions worldwide. The synthesis of new pharmaceuticals, research in genetics and aging, and other developments promise to extend medicalization even further.

This chapter explores major conceptual issues and lines of research. This task is complicated by theoretical differences. There has never been a consensus on the meaning of medicalization. One difference arises over where to draw the line between medicine and other cultural discourses and institutional practices which employ the language of pathology but do so in non-medical conceptual models and/ or apart from medical interventions. Another difference concerns the question of medicalization as a transfer of conceptual and jurisdictional domains. This is how the concept was originally used but some no longer do so (sometimes signaled by the use of "biomedicalization," see, e.g., Clarke et al. 2003; Estes and Binney 1989). I will need, therefore, to offer an interpretation.

A further complicating factor is the sheer scope and diversity of the research literature. Previous assessments have distinguished two subtypes of medicalized phenomena: deviant behaviors, such as school misbehavior and child abuse, and "natural life processes," like childbirth and menopause. Over the past decade, as medical definitions and treatments spread to a wider range of experiences, the research grew more complex. I divide the new literature into two further subtypes. The first comprises studies investigating how problems of living and troubling experiences, from overeating to shyness, have been given medical definition. The second comprises studies examining biomedical enhancements – for example, new cosmetic procedures, human growth hormone for short stature – whose use is not to treat illness but to improve healthy people in one or another capacity. The conceptual shift constituted by medicalization is somewhat different in each of these four subtypes. There is also variation in terms of which features of the social environment are most salient, which groups are driving the process and which are affected, and what social consequences are theorized to follow. This variation requires sorting out. Generalizations one finds in the literature do not necessarily hold for every subtype.

The chapter, then, begins with definitional issues, tracing the evolution of the concept of medicalization over time, identifying key shifts in perspective, and providing some explanation for them. I next discuss the meaning of medicalization in the four subtypes and explore the variations. I conclude with a few thoughts on future directions.

THE EMERGENCE OF THE CONCEPT OF MEDICALIZATION

The concept of medicalization emerged from the intellectual and social ferment of the 1950s and 1960s as a critique of medicine and the expansion of its conceptual model to the analysis of social ills and attendant policy (Sutherland 1950; Szasz 1956, 1960; Wootton 1956, 1959). Most discussions characterize the concept's evolution as a single story (e.g., Ballard and Elston 2005; Lupton 1997; Nye 2003), creating something of a caricature in the process. I will argue that there were two distinct, if somewhat overlapping, lines of influence. The first tradition was a critique of medicine as authoritarian and imperialistic. The second was a critique of the expanding role of medicine in the social control of deviant behavior.

Medical imperialism

The first critique, reflecting the liberationist concerns of the 1960s and the deep sense of social crisis, directed a powerful challenge to the medical profession and its role in the capitalist/patriarchal social order. The pioneers of this perspective were the loosely assorted group in the United States and United Kingdom that came to be known as the anti-psychiatrists, including Thomas Szasz (1960), Erving Goffman (1961), David Cooper (1971), and R.D. Laing (1967; on anti-psychiatry see Crossley 2006: Ch. 5; Sedgwick 1982). Their views were diverse and reflected different theoretical orientations. In general, however, they shared a highly critical view of available therapies and psychiatric institutions, largely rejected the medical model of mental disorder, and regarded much mental illness as expectable responses to difficult circumstances. By the early 1970s, anti-psychiatric views were also being expressed by "radical therapists" with a Marxist critique of capitalism (Radical Therapist Collective 1971) and second-wave feminists with a stinging rebuke of patriarchy (e.g., Chesler 1972).

In the early 1970s, social scientists, feminists, and others widened the critique to mainstream medicine. A highly influential version of this left-libertarian argument was Ivan Illich's *Medical Nemesis*, which claimed that the "medical establishment" had become a "major threat to health" (1976: 3), both through the direct side effects of medical practices and through "social iatrogenesis." By the latter term, Illich (1976: 41) referred to the impact of medicine on the social environment – for example, increasing "disabling dependence," lowering "tolerance for discomfort," abolishing the "right to self-care" – and on the experience of suffering. Organized medicine, he argued, "has undermined the ability of individuals to face their reality, to express their own values, and to accept inevitable and often irremediable pain and impairment, decline, and death" (Illich 1976: 127–8). Other critiques of the political economy of health care at the time, Marxist and feminist, portrayed medicine as authoritarian, as continuously seeking to expand its professional empire (in service to the capitalist ruling class and/or the patriarchal order), as detracting from rather than improving people's health, and as depoliticizing social arrangements (e.g., Ehrenreich and English 1973; Frankfort 1972; Navarro 1976; Waitzkin and Waterman 1974).

Another influential contributor to this critical literature was the social philosopher Michel Foucault, whose early work on insanity and hospitals situated him among the anti-psychiatrists (Foucault 1965, 1973). In these writings, Foucault emphasized medical control and surveillance, the fabrication of scientific knowledge, the power of the profession to label and discipline, and the "docile body" of the patient caught in the "clinical gaze" exerted by medical practitioners. Over the course of the 1970s, however, Foucault published a series of essays dealing with medicalization that modified his earlier position (Nye 2003). He shifted away from an emphasis on medicalization as domination by doctors and the state and replaced it with a view of medical discourse and practice as moral/disciplinary guidelines by which patients are to understand and regulate their own lives. The power of medicine, he now argued, is exercised not primarily by direct coercion but rather, in the words of Deborah Lupton (1997: 99), "through persuading its subjects that certain ways of behaving and thinking are appropriate for them." In contrast with his earlier writings, Foucault characterized medical power as dispersed, emergent at sites outside of direct medical encounters, and involving the complicity and participation of ordinary people.

According to the historian Robert Nye, the shift in Foucault's thinking was "ultimately influential" in defeating what Philip Strong (1979), using the phrase common at the time, referred to as the "medical imperialism thesis." Beyond the influence of Foucault – an impact felt less in North American medical sociology than in other places and disciplines – the thesis was undone by empirical studies.

The evidence for it was always thin, as Strong (1979) argued, and subsequent research only complicated the picture further. Historical studies of medicalization in Western Europe and the United States, for instance, as Nye (2003: 121) documents, have not shown a direct relationship between "the process of medical professionalization and the growth of either a medical model of health or a medical regime allied to state power." Neither has the stream of sociological studies appearing over the past four decades.

Deviance and medical social control

The second tradition of medicalization critique, while influenced by the crises of the 1960s, the writings of Goffman and Szasz, and even the early work of Foucault, had different origins. Building on Talcott Parsons' (1951) functionalist analysis of medical practice, this critique grew out of new approaches to the study of deviant behavior and social control. For Parsons, illness is an inherently social and role-structured phenomenon. When people become sick, he argued, there is available a social role, the "sick role," which channels them to the doctor. If the doctor legitimates the sickness, the sick person is both relieved of responsibility for the illness and freed from some or all normal duties. Illness in this sense, like crime, is a form of deviance from normative role performances and is disruptive to society. Like crime, it is a problem of social control, and the doctor is a control agent who regulates entry to the sick role and "exposes the deviant to reintegrative forces" (Parsons 1951: 313). Reintegration, however, does not involve punishment but treatment. The sick role also imposes obligations: it requires the sick person to seek to "get well" and to comply with medical advice. In Parsons' view, individuals are often unconsciously motivated to seek illness (deviance) as a refuge from the strains and pressures of their normal roles and, in providing relief from such pressures, medical social control generally has positive effects for individuals and the social system.

While retaining the sick role analysis, sociologists in the 1960s rejected both Parsons' notion of deviance as motivated by personal needs and his optimistic view of medical social control. A key development was the emergence of the "labeling" or "societal reaction" perspective on deviance. In this counterintuitive approach, deviance is conceptualized as a property of social groups, a label which they apply to behavior rather than a quality intrinsic to the behavior itself (Becker 1963; Erikson 1966; Kitsuse 1962). Theoretical attention expands from the rule-breaker to the larger system of social control, both the socially defined norms or rules and the rewards and sanctions that enforce them. That system cannot be evaluated, as Parsons wanted, on the basis of universalistic, functional criteria because all of its elements are variable – relative to time, cultural context, and social group – and are shaped, in significant part, politically (Becker 1963: 7).

The labeling perspective, including applications in medical sociology such as Thomas Scheff's (1966) influential book on mental illness, fundamentally reoriented the study of deviance. Related theoretical developments, from phenomenological (Berger and Luckmann 1966) and conflict perspectives (e.g., Lofland 1969), further confirmed the importance of attending to the sociohistorical process by which deviance designations arise or change, and to the central role of social and political conflict in the process. By the late 1960s, sociologists were studying emerging categories of deviance, the competing interest groups driving the creation and application of deviance labels, and the evolution of social policy (Conrad and Schneider 1980). It was in this research context that new interest arose in the powerful social control aspects of medicine (Kittrie 1971; Pitts 1968) and in the application of "the belief system underlying medical science ... to more and more social problems" (Taber et al. 1969).

Medical sociologists called the extension of medical social control "medicalization" and widened the focus beyond psychiatry to the whole field of medicine (Freidson 1970; Pitts 1968; Zola 1972). They argued that medical jurisdiction over disapproved forms of behavior was expanding relative to the traditional institutions of religion, law, and the family, and was extending beyond medicine's original and, by implication, legitimate mandate into areas of life "far beyond concern with ordinary organic disease" (Zola 1972: 494) and any proven methods of treatment. They challenged the notion that medicine was a morally neutral enterprise, documented how physicians can act as moral entrepreneurs, and argued that shifting problems that were "not *ipso facto* medical problems" (Conrad 1975: 18) to the medical domain would concentrate inappropriate power in medical hands. They did not, however, identify medical imperialism as the primary stimulus for medicalization. It would be a mistake, Irving Zola (1972: 487) argued, to see medicalization as the "result of any professional 'imperialism'" on the part of physicians. Far larger cultural and institutional forces were at work, and studies showed that other interest groups were also drivers of the process.

Through the 1970s, medicalization research in this tradition focused on deviant behavior and medical social control. This work culminated in the influential text, *Deviance and Medicalization*, by Conrad and Schneider (1980, 1992). They described the medicalization of deviance as involving a shift from "badness to sickness." Behaviors, they argued, "that were once defined as immoral, sinful, or criminal have been given medical meanings" (Conrad and Schneider 1980: 1) and the medical profession mandated to provide treatments for them. The authors observed, however, that not all medicalization concerned deviant behavior or social problems. Other non-medical problems had been drawn into medical jurisdiction, including pregnancy, childbirth, and contraception (Conrad and Schneider 1980: 29; see Zola 1972). In subsequent years, as empirical studies accumulated, the early concern with deviant behavior was augmented by analyses of medicalization in many other areas. And as more phenomena were brought under the rubric of medicalization, the concept evolved.

THE EVOLVING MEANING OF MEDICALIZATION

As the concept of medicalization evolved, it shed some features of its original formulation and retained others. In order to better understand the specific types of medicalized phenomena and the differences between them, it will be helpful to first discuss these changes. Reappraisals of the lay role, the effects of medicalization for individuals, and the role of the medical profession all contributed to a far more nuanced and complex view of medicalization.

Active lay role

The imperialism thesis characterized patients as passive or victims and generally uncritical in the face of medicine's expansionist tendencies. By the 1990s, this picture had given way to a much more active conceptualization of the lay role in and contribution to the medicalization process. For those influenced by the later Foucault, the emphasis on medical surveillance came to include thinking about normalization and control in terms of "technologies of the self," Foucault's term for reflexive techniques people learn in order to manage their own emotions, inter-personal relationships, body, and so on (Foucault 1988). Writing in this vein, the historian Nye (2003: 117) argues that what replaced the imperialism thesis was a view of medicalization as "a process whereby medical and health precepts have been embodied in individuals who assume this responsibility for themselves." Though too narrow, this definition is consistent with Foucault's observation on the nature of discourse – it can be normative and coercive, yet also voluntary – and recognizes that contemporary medical practice requires active subjects not passive ones (Rose 2007: 110). Empirical cases of medicalization using the Foucauldian framework, therefore, often concentrate on the experiences and practices of everyday life, such as patient interactions with health care providers (e.g., Cowley, Mitcheson, and Houston 2004; Lupton 2003; Malacrida 2003; Williams and Calnan 1996), women's reactions to medical technologies (see, e.g., papers in Lock and Kaufert 1998), and so on. These studies demonstrate, *inter alia*, the complex and pragmatic ways in which people respond to medical authority and connect medical knowledge and practices to experiences of chaotic life events, healthcare needs, and self-definition.

Research in the deviance/social constructionist tradition also came to emphasize the active, collaborative role of the lay public in contributing to medicalization. Studies of specific cases demonstrated that medicine was not monolithic but fac-tionalized. Vested interests and subspecialties within the medical system differ in what they regard as legitimate diagnoses and exert differential pressure to medicalize problems (Strong 1979; Williams 2001). Studies showed that social movement, grassroots, and patient advocacy groups often worked aggressively to secure medical recognition for a favored condition or diagnosis, or, in the case of homosexuality, demedicalization, and were sometimes successful even in the face of medical resis-tance (e.g., Bayer 1981; Conrad and Schneider 1980; Scott 1990). Studies also began to explore the "lay perspective" and the ambivalent, calculated, and uncritical ways in which people respond to and struggle with medicalized definitions (e.g., Becker and Nachtigall 1992; Bransen 1992; Broom and Woodward 1996; Gabe and Calnan 1989; Treichler 1990).

Gains and losses

The recognition of an active lay role contributed to a less negative reading of the effects of medicalization. Early on, the contributors to the deviance literature rec-ognized that medicalization could have mixed effects (Conrad 1975; Pitts 1968). Though "skeptical of the social benefits of medical social control" and clearly emphasizing its "darker" consequences, Conrad and Schneider (1980) attributed a number of progressive aspects to the medicalization of deviance. Among others, these included the possibility of less punitive means of control; the extension of the sick role benefits, including institutional legitimation and removal of blame; and an optimistic prognosis (Conrad and Schneider 1980). In the following years, the literature increasingly noted particular clinical benefits and improvements in quality of life for individuals, as well as the symbolic, sick role advantages. Accordingly, definitions of medicalization took on a more neutral cast (e.g., Conrad 1992), permitting room for recognition of genuine medical advances and independent assessment of why people might seek medicalization and what might be socially or individually gained or lost when medicalization occurs.

Feminist critiques, which had often characterized women as victims of medicine and scientific medical knowledge as biased and sexist, were particularly affected. While claims of repressive medicalization remain, at least since Catherine Kohler Riessman's seminal article on "Women and Medicalization" (1983), and Emily Martin's *The Woman in the Body* (1987), feminists have also pointed to empowering possibilities in medicalization, the expansion of a discourse of rights and less stratified relations in the medical sphere, and possibilities for resistance and women's self-help activism. A less uniformly critical view and a lowered apprehension of the medical profession has come to prevail (e.g., Annandale and Clark 1996; Broom and Woodward 1996; Lock 2004; Oinas 1998; Riska 2003).

The medical complex

Along with a greater emphasis on the lay role, wider appraisals of the social transformations sweeping medicine, in the United States and elsewhere, brought attention to the growing institutional matrix in which medicine was embedded. Already in the 1970s, medical sociologists were observing how the changing organizational and economic infrastructure of medicine was undermining its professional strength. A rising consumer movement in health care – signaled by increasing litigation and other demands for accountability, "doctor-shopping" behavior, elaboration of lay referral systems, and patient advocacy – also indicated "a radical process of change" was underway in the doctor–patient relationship (Reeder 1972: 407; see Fox 1977; Haug 1976). Medicine was undergoing a "deprofessionalization" or "corporatization" in the view of some (e.g., McKinlay and Stoeckle 1988), while others argued medicine was being constrained by a growing number of "countervailing powers" including new government regulation, the rise of managed care, and consumer demand (Light 1991, 1993). These changes were widely read as an indication that medical authority was on the decline (e.g., Cockerham 1988; McKinlay and Stoeckle 1988; Starr 1982), that the so-called "golden age of doctoring" was over (McKinlay and Marceau 2002). New actors had entered and changed the social structure and practice of medical care and reduced the power and moral authority of physicians (Imber 2008; Rothman 1991).

In light of these realities, research on medicalization underwent a quiet but important change. Where the medicalization critique, writes Robert Dingwall (2006: 34), "had originally been focused on the disciplinary role of doctors as agents of social control ... it now became much more of a challenge to the extending influence of the medical-industrial complex as a whole." This complex included not only medical professionals and advocacy groups, but also consumers, managed care organizations, and commercial interests, particularly the pharmaceutical industry (Clarke et al. 2003; Conrad 2007; Gallagher and Sionean 2004). Together these forces had created a different, more dynamic world of medicine, enlarging the scope and generating new processes of medicalization. Research shifted in an effort to capture important changes in medical surveillance and self-monitoring, new discourses of risk and consumer choice, and the growing commercial promotion of medical technologies and medications.

Although in some instances the definition of medicalization got radically extended, losing sight of medicine (Davis 2006a), most research continued in practice to recognize the medical profession as the vital link in the medicalization process. It retains the power to define illness and control the technical procedures of intervention (Pescosolido 2006). At the same time, it has become clear that many additional actors influence, even co-constitute, the definition of disorder categories. These actors include social movements and advocacy groups (Conrad 2007: Ch. 3; Davis 2005; Moynihan and Cassels 2005), everyday clinical practices (Young 1995), new technologies – CT scans, ultrasounds, etc. – diagnostic techniques, and medications (Healy 2007; Rosenberg 2007), pharmaceutical marketing activities (Lane 2007; Singh 2007), and forms of popular medical communication from scientists, physicians, and journalists (Golden 2005; Watkins 2007a, 2007b). No doubt there are others. It has also become clear that other institutions play an important role in medical social control. These include, as always, the state (as I write the US government is considering linking food assistance for the poor to anti-obesity efforts [Black 2008]) and its agencies, as well as managed care organizations, insurance companies, pharmaceutical manufacturers, international NGOs, and more. And it has become clear that as Illich (1976) and research in the Foucauldian tradition have emphasized, discourses of health and illness have widely penetrated Western societies and become deeply embedded in individuals' subjectivity and interpretation of everyday experience (Turner 2004). As anthropologist Jean Comaroff (1982: 55) writes: "We look to medicine to provide us with key symbols for constructing a framework of meaning – a mythology of our state of being." People readily seek to be diagnosed, affecting not only the utilization of medical interventions but also the expansion of medical categories themselves (Conrad 2007; Tone 2008).

Medical social control

The more complex picture of how medicalization comes about greatly enriched but did not fundamentally change the definition of medicalization. *Medicalization is the extension of the conceptual and normative domain of medicine to problems, states, or processes not previously within the medical sphere, leading to medical management and treatment of them.* Medical jurisdiction remains crucial to the definition. As Thomas Szasz (2007: xiii) notes, "we ... do not speak of the medicalization of malaria or melanoma" as these are already and properly within the medical sphere (cross-cultural research is, of course, another matter). Medicalization also continues to signify an encroachment. The medicalization of a problem or process, however it comes about, involves medicine's norms and metaphors contravening and potentially driving out conceptual models or practices already used for that problem or process (Garry 2001). As noted above, the encroachment is not necessarily adjudged in negative or clear-cut terms. But the fact of an encroachment remains central to how the medicalization process is defined.

The encroachment, inconsistent and a matter of degree, is conceptual and normative. Some subtitles of recent books dealing with medicalization provide examples of the shift: *How Normal Behavior Became a Sickness* (Lane 2007); *How Psychiatry Transformed Normal Sorrow into Depressive Disorder* (Horwitz and Wakefield 2007); *On the Transformation of Human Conditions into Treatable Disorders* (Conrad 2007). With medicalization, a problem, state, or process nested within a pre-existing conceptual model, something "bad," or "normal," or "natural," is descriptively transformed into a disorder, illness, deficiency, or target of medical intervention. The transformation gives the problem a changed significance, individualizes it, and brings it within a new set of tacit assumptions. Once recast, the problem is now defined as a deviation from physiological or psychological ideals of proper functioning and is presumed to have a basis in some underlying process that necessitates or justifies technical intervention. The afflicted individual, separated from broader social context, is the "host" for these impersonal (asocial and amoral) processes and the symbols of healing marginalize or exclude his or her social relations (Comaroff 1982).

The normative meanings in the medicalized definition lie latent, as medicalization researchers have long stressed, in medicine's claims about nature and about value neutrality. In resetting and regulating the boundaries of acceptable behavior, bodily states, and subjectivity, medicalized approaches inescapably draw on cultural symbols and values. Ideals of proper functioning cannot but embody specific values and normative evaluations – of expectable self-control, the well-adjusted personality, the boundaries of individual responsibility, beauty, the tolerable level of discomfort, safe practices, proper social comportment, appropriate levels and expression of emotion, and so on – as well as images of selfhood. The unique power of medical knowledge and technique is that it "naturalizes" its underlying symbolic and normative frameworks (Lock 2004). That is, it gives them the status of empirically derived facts about the human organism. As such, naturalization disengages social and moral values and the answers these values propose to existential questions from the public languages of morality or social philosophy (Comaroff 1982; Zola 1975). Moral responsibility and feelings of guilt and abnormality, seemingly removed with the medical label, are often then reasserted by focusing, in Zola's words, on the "individual's role in his own demise, disability and even recovery" (Zola 1972: 491; see Becker and Nachtigall 1992). Because naturalized, medical morality denies value legitimacy to alternative possibilities and a patient's own good appears to mandate its careful observance. It is, as a result, very difficult to challenge.

As the conceptual and normative encroachment of the medical model remains primary, then, so too does the long-standing concern with the relationship of medicalization to the production, maintenance, and regulation of social order. Medicine is an institution of social control – in tandem, as noted above, with many other institutions – *and* it is concerned with the relief of suffering. Both aspects are now more clearly recognized. This recognition leads to a deeper understanding of the appeal of the individualizing and internalizing dynamic of the medical model, its implicit materialism, and its image of self-determining selfhood. And it permits a more subtle analysis of the role of medicine in promoting conformity to dominant

cultural values and definitions of the good life, depoliticizing social issues, reinforcing patterns of stratification, expanding the scope of pathology, and shrinking the
range of ordinary human variability. When wedded to the state, medical social
control can be directly coercive. More often than not, however, medicine functions
to create new expectations and secure adherence to social norms when responding
to individual needs and desires, when called upon by society to monitor and address
"at risk" and vulnerable populations, when employing the agency of people to regulate themselves, and when helping people return to their conventional social roles
or adjust to new ones. Social control is not so much the motivation of medicine as
it is its effect.

Finally, medicalization and medical social control involve medical supervision
and treatment. This dimension of medicalization has been analytically downplayed
in the literature, the definitional issue made primary. However, in reviewing the
literature, and once certain non-medical discourses are bracketed (see below), it is
clear that both a definition in terms of illness, or disorder, or deficiency, or relief
of suffering and a treatment modality are necessary for medicalization. Both dimensions are mutually constitutive and act back on one another in a complex feedback
loop. In many cases, clinical innovations – a new technology, diagnostic technique,
or medication – come first and create the possibility if not the impetus to consider
extending medical jurisdiction. In other cases, a medical conception is proffered
even in the absence of an effective treatment. However, medicine is an applied field,
and only that which it can in some way treat will it long define as medical, and that
which it treats it will legitimate as medically appropriate.

TYPES OF MEDICALIZED PHENOMENA

Without any attempt to be exhaustive, I want to consider the four subtypes or arenas
of medicalized phenomena (an overview is provided in Table 10.1). I distinguish
each subtype by the nature of the conceptual transfer involved, but the lines are not
rigid. Some cases can certainly be categorized in more than one way. There are also
several types of cases that I do not treat as instances of medicalization, and thus
exclude from this conceptualization. There is overlap in the medicalization literature
with cultural discourses and institutional practices at some remove from medicine
but which enlarge the sphere of human feeling and behavior deemed pathological.
These include discourses within feminism, such as "battered women's syndrome"
(Kurz 1987), and the broader "politics of victimhood" (Brown 1995), where "Identity can be legitimately claimed ... only to the extent that it can be represented as
denied, repressed, injured or excluded by others" (Rose 1999: 268). In articulating
a history of victimhood and survivorship, this politics draws on psychological
languages and models of suffering, but it does not involve a clinical medical model
or depoliticize problems, just the reverse.

Another discourse and set of institutionalized practices at some remove from
medicine is the "therapeutic" as a cultural ethic. In his pioneering study, *The
Triumph of the Therapeutic*, Philip Rieff (1966) observed that therapy, in the
narrow sense of treating psychic disorder, was becoming a wider cultural system of
meanings and symbols. Central to the therapeutic is a language for the management

Table 10.1 Subtypes of medicalized phenomena
Medicalization is the extension of the conceptual and normative domain of medicine to problems, states, or processes not previously within the medical sphere, leading to medical management and treatment of them.

	Deviant behavior	*Natural life processes*	*Everyday problems of living*	*Enhancements in healthy people*
Conceptual shift	From "badness to sickness"	From natural process or life event to medical–technical problem	From normal/ expectable behavior or feelings to medical pathology	From well to "better than well"
Social context	Liberal, humanitarian ideology; rationalistic approach to life	Advances in medicine and risk assessment; feminist efforts to gain control over biology	Expansion of mental illness categories; availability of SSRI drugs; consumer culture	Advances in neuroscience and genetics; competitive society; culture of self-fulfillment
Agents driving the process	Social movements; lay interest groups; the state	Medical specialties; consumers	Psychiatrists; pharmaceutical companies; patient advocacy groups; consumers	Medical specialties; pharmaceutical companies; consumers
Groups affected	Children; women; middle class	Women; the aged (including men)	Middle class and affluent	Middle class and affluent
Critique	Shift attention from environment to individual; eliminate alternative interventions	Medical surveillance and control; loss of autonomy and lay knowledge; narrow definitions of normal	Homogenization of life; blindness to environmental causes; less tolerance of minor problems; false promises	Reproduction of suspect norms; promotion of individual over social goods; undermine social solidarity

of subjectivity in which the self is characterized by its power to actualize itself and by its vulnerability to victimization from without and pathology from within (Furedi 2004; Nolan 1998; Rose 1999). Society is inherently repressive and unhappy childhoods, "toxic socialization," and personal dependencies lead to a wide variety of adult problems. These problems are often framed as "addictions" or "diseases" – for example, "co-dependency," "sex addiction" – and play a central role in identity narratives, which are utilized in self-help subcultures to explain why experience has fallen short of therapeutic ideals (Illouz 2008; Rice 1996, 2002). The conceptual model is not medical, but rather "therapeutic," though it is sometimes mistakenly characterized as medical in the medicalization literature.

Second, there is overlap in the medicalization literature with certain health discourses and attendant practices that enlarge the range of day-to-day experiences considered relevant to health and illness. Holistic health is an ideological movement and diverse collection of alternative therapies, which has traditionally operated from a non-medical conceptual framework (Gevitz 1988; Lowenberg and Davis 1994). Holistic health has been characterized both as representing further medicalization (e.g., Arney and Bergen 1984; Crawford 1980) and as a form of demedicalization (Berliner and Salmon 1980), but its techniques are principally directed to staving off problems already medically defined. The same is true of health promotion, a general designation for educational initiatives aimed to fix attention on behavioral risk factors and individual behavioral imperatives, such as physical fitness and general wellness activities. It is sometimes depicted as the medicalization of lifestyle, but it does not generally represent a conceptual transfer in the sense used here.

Deviant behavior

As already noted, the conceptual shift that distinguishes this arena is, in Conrad and Schneider's (1980) apt phrase, "from badness to sickness," where "badness" signifies socially problematic behaviors explicitly classified in moral terms, whether as immoral, sinful, criminal, or the like. Studies have explored a wide variety of cases, historical and contemporary: insanity (Scull 1975; Szasz 1970) and its relationship to social groups such as the poor and homeless (Snow et al. 1986; Weinberg 2005); many disapproved sexual practices, from homosexuality (Greenberg 1988) to pedophilia (Jenkins 1998; Sutherland 1950); some abusive behaviors, such as physical child abusing (Antler 1981; Pfohl 1977), and some forms of stigmatized victimhood, as in the cases of rape and sexual abuse (Davis 2005); many compulsive behaviors, including alcoholism (Appleton 1995; Conrad and Schneider 1980; Tournier 1985), opiate addiction (Conrad and Schneider 1980), excessive gambling (Rosecrance 1985; Rossol 2001), overeating (Salant and Santry 2006; Sobal 1995), and "uncontrolled" buying (Lee and Mysyk 2004); and many socially problematic behaviors of children, including disruptive and impulsive conduct at school (Conrad 1975; Malacrida 2003; Singh 2004), aggressive behavior, delinquency, and more (Harris 2005; Healy 2007).

Studies suggest that the medicalization of deviant behavior is much more likely for some groups than others. The group that stands out most sharply is children, perhaps especially middle-class boys. A great deal of attention has centered on the emergence and public controversy over the category of attention deficit/hyperactivity disorder (ADHD) for school misbehavior and inattention and, especially in the United States, Canada, and Australia but rising worldwide (Scheffler et al. 2007), its treatment with medication. A broader set of children's problems, from irritability and mood swings to verbal outbursts and "maladaptive aggression," is now also commonly diagnosed under new and emerging categories like *conduct disorder*, *pediatric bipolar disorder*, and *oppositional defiant disorder*, and treated with antidepressants, antipsychotics, anticonvulsants, and other medications (Findling, Steiner, and Weller 2005; Groopman 2007; Harris 2005; Martin 2007). Medical treatments, including medication, are being used alongside psychosocial interventions with children who have been maltreated – sexual, physical, and emotional abuse and neglect – or exposed to violence, and seen to be at risk for various mental illnesses and risky behaviors (Cohen et al. 2006).

Women's deviance, compared to men's, is more likely to be medicalized than to be criminalized. Women, for instance, represent a majority of those who physically abuse children. This category has been medicalized and is dealt with, at least in the United States, in the mental health system or through family support or reunification programs (Chaffin 2006; Newberger and Bourne 1978). Even in severe cases, it is rarely prosecuted (Chaffin 2006). Men, by contrast, represent a majority of those who sexually abuse children. This medicopsychiatric category is heavily criminalized (Jenkins 1998). Further, there is a clear social class dimension in this arena. The principle appears to be, in the words of Conrad and Schneider (1980: 275), that when "a particular kind of deviance becomes a middle-class rather than solely a lower-class 'problem,' the probability of medicalization increases" (see also Pitts 1968). They cite the medicalization of alcoholism, opiate addiction, hyperactivity, and abortion as examples. Rosecrance (1985) finds the same pattern with compulsive gambling.

Studies show the medicalization of deviant behavior is often very unevenly and insecurely institutionalized, with non-medical groups and the state often taking the lead in pressing for medicalization. Some cases are partly within medical jurisdiction and partly in other domains – the arenas of law, social services, therapeutic self-help, and so on. Some cases begin in the medical domain but then shift elsewhere. Physical child abuse, for example, was temporarily under medical jurisdiction as the "battered child syndrome" but eventually moved back to the jurisdiction of child protective services (Davis 2005). The overlap and instability is often related to pragmatic questions of effectiveness and disciplinary interest, as well as shifting social conditions, institutional demands, and political struggles (Weinberg 2005). Over the past few decades, for instance, a lack of psychiatric treatment success, combined with new and intense public concern, has shifted the management of sexual offenders in a far more stigmatized and criminalized direction (Jenkins 1998). It is also in this arena that the clearest case of demedicalization – homosexuality – can be found, which, predictably, followed a political fight (Bayer 1981; Spector 1977).

There is a strong tendency in this arena to label problems as "diseases" or "illnesses" for the sake of symbolic benefits, such as increasing tolerance, enhancing willingness to provide social services, and, perhaps most importantly, removing blame and stigma so as to motivate affected persons to adopt the sick role and seek help. Treating obesity itself as a disease is a clear example. Studies find that parents often welcome an ADHD diagnosis because it attributes their child's problems to an organic disorder rather than their own failings (Malacrida 2003). Alcoholism, to give another example, has been described as a disease by some within medicine and is included as a substance disorder in the official manuals. Except for treating the short-term effects of intoxication, however, medical professionals have little to offer by way of treatment. That role is typically played by lay therapeutic groups, like Alcoholics Anonymous, now a worldwide movement, which employ a disease concept but reject a medical model (Trice and Roman 1970). In the case of alcoholism, the meaning of "disease" may be primarily metaphoric (McHugh and

Slavney1998:182), aimed to secure normative benefits and treatment services but not traditional medical attention (Tournier 1985).

Research in the medicalization of deviant behavior has raised a number of concerns about its individual and social consequences. Medical answers to deviance and social problems deflect attention from the environment to the individual. The exclusion of social context obscures both the role of social structures and injustices in creating the conditions for problems to arise and the role structural change might play in ameliorating them. Individual, depoliticized answers are attractive in policy matters because adapting individuals to their social environment is far easier than the other way around. This is the path of least resistance, as Barbara Wootton (1959: 329) noted many years ago: "Always it is easier to put up a clinic than to pull down a slum." Medical answers can close off public deliberation of complex societal problems, deny value legitimacy to alternative social or political interpretations (see Lock 1991 on adolescent dissent in Japan), and eliminate other strategies of intervention. The medicalization of deviant behavior can, through the effects of labeling, create deviance and weaken a sense of agency. It can concentrate power in the hands of the medical profession and other elites for enforcing standards of normality, and, in some cases, lead to the violation of civil liberties. While there is recognition that medical means of social control may be humane, there is also concern – especially so in the case of children – that it is relentless and pervasive.

Natural life processes

Research on the medicalization of "natural life processes" followed closely on the heels of deviant behavior research and quickly outstripped it in sheer volume of work. The conceptual shift is a transformation in the meaning of everyday bodily processes and life-course events from natural human experiences to medical–technical problems. An immense body of research – historical, contemporary, cross-cultural – has been conducted in this arena. Studies have explored the medicalization of reproductive processes and events, including childbirth (Martin 1987; Treichler 1990; Wertz and Wertz 1989), birth control (Gordon 2002; Tone 2001), abortion (Riessman 1983), involuntary childlessness/infertility (Becker 2000; Becker and Nachtigall 1992), and menstruation (Bransen 1992; Chrisler and Caplan 2002; Oinas 1998), as well as medical interventions in life-cycle events and the aging process, as with menopause (Bell 1987; Lock 1993; Watkins 2007b), andropause (Conrad 2007; Watkins 2007a), impotence (Fishman 2007; Tiefer 1986, 1994), hair loss, and many other features of aging (Conrad 2007; Estes and Binney 1989; Rothman and Rothman 2003).

"Natural" in this context does not mean culturally unmanaged, nor does it imply that these processes and events are physically experienced in the same way. A study comparing Canadian and Japanese women, for instance, found that while the Canadians often used hot flashes to define themselves as menopausal, the Japanese used quite different types of physical markers (Lock 1993). Rather, "natural" is simply a way of identifying physiological experiences and events that are everywhere part of the human condition. In many cases of medicalization, medical definition is framed in terms of illness or disease. With natural life processes, however, that is far less clearly, or perhaps not at all, the case. There is some talk of disease in this arena. Studies of the medicalization of menopause, for instance, typically note the efforts of a small segment of medical experts in earlier eras to characterize menopause as a "deficiency disease" (Bell 1987; McCrea 1983). But the evidence in these studies suggests that in only a small minority of women did doctors see menopause as anything other than "a normal phase of the female life cycle" (Bell 1987: 538). There was concern for pathogenic processes related to menopause in this minority. There were also recommendations for widespread use of hormone replacement therapy (HRT) to give individual women relief from physical discomfort and restore their customary functioning. Additionally, HRT was recommended to address increased risk for some forms of cancer, and until recently, for risk of chronic conditions, such as osteoporosis and cardiovascular disease. But none of this indicates that doctors considered menopause itself a kind of sickness, or that women considering HRT do either (e.g., Griffiths 1999). When the word "disease" is used in this arena, it is used analogically or for a subset of people who experience severe distress (as, officially, with the clinical categories of premenstrual syndrome and premenstrual dysphoric disorder).

Rather than disease or illness, with natural life processes the common terms are words like "imbalance," "condition," or "dysfunction," which signify a departure from some biological standard which uses the youthful body or the absence of pain, suffering, or risk as the baseline. Setting the standard typically goes hand in hand with the development of new medical devices, diagnostic technologies, or medications that promise to more effectively, for example, relieve pain and resolve complications of the birthing process, smooth physiological and psychological changes related to menstruation, menopause, or andropause (male menopause), "solve the problem of childlessness" for couples (Becker and Nachtigall 1992: 460), control when pregnancy occurs, or address the "anguish" of declining sexual potency and the loss of hair and muscle mass. Studies show these standards not only shift with and replicate cultural norms, but are also in part constituted by the diagnostic technologies and treatments which, through the actions of doctors, marketers, medical popularizers, and others, redraw the boundaries of normal/abnormal, tolerable/intolerable, safe/unsafe, and lower the threshold for seeking medical attention (cf. Barsky and Boros 1995).

Further, because these interventions address bodily experiences that can be painful, distressing, dangerous, and disruptive, consumer demand has long played a very important role. As is obvious from the list above, women's natural life processes are much more likely to be medicalized than men's. Research, originating in the feminist version of the medical imperialism critique, has traditionally emphasized the role of the male-dominated medical profession, its ideology and economic interests, and the rise of new specialties, such as obstetrics and endocrinology, as agents of medicalization. However, studies over the past two decades have increasingly documented the demands of lay women, and now men, and social class differences in this arena. In many of these cases, from obstetric technologies to oral contraceptives, assisted reproduction to going on HRT (Lazarus 1997; Rothman and Rothman 2003; Tone 2001; Wertz and Wertz 1989), educated and "well-to-do women" have been at the forefront of efforts to "reduce the control that biology had over their lives" (Riessman 1983: 98). In general, this has led – very unevenly, to be sure – toward greater technological intervention, medication use, and medical supervision. Voluntary utilization rates of medical interventions in many natural life processes are high, and despite resistance, show little sign of slackening (though there are important cross-national differences, see DeVries 2005). Much the same class dynamic is at work among men in matters such as treating impotence and undergoing vasectomy (Conrad 2007: Ch. 2; Gordon 2002).

Research on the medicalization of natural life processes generally recognizes, at least implicitly, that sometimes medical interventions are necessary and life-saving. There has also been the trend among some feminists, noted above, to argue that women can and do find the use of medical technologies and medications an empowering experience (e.g., Annandale and Clark 1996; Beckett 2005). At the same time, the range of concerns and criticisms remains considerable. As with the medicalization of deviant behavior, there are concerns about the individualizing and depoliticizing dynamic of the medical model, the power of the medical profession, and its monopoly over the technologies of intervention. Studies have sought to highlight ideological components that shape medicalization in this arena, with criticisms centering on the reinforcement of gender roles and stereotypes, the devaluing of women's bodies, and the narrowing of the definition of "normal" with respect to the body and to specific processes, such as the length of labor or the intensity of menstruation. Studies have also emphasized the alienating nature of some medical procedures and hospital settings, the loss of patient autonomy, the extension of surveillance, the stripping away of lay knowledge of the body and practices, like midwifery, and the closing off of non-medical solutions, such as with infertility. Diagnostic technologies (such as fetal monitors) and physicians are criticized for overstating the risks of natural processes and understating the risks of medical technologies, increasing the danger of iatrogenesis, and generally fostering overutilization of high-tech and surgical procedures.

Everyday problems of living

The early work in this arena was centered on the medicalization of anxiety and tension and their treatment with minor tranquilizers, such as Valium and Librium (e.g., Cooperstock and Lennard 1979; Koumjian 1981; Lennard and Bernstein 1974). However, the medicalization of everyday life problems began to get sustained attention only in the 1990s. The conceptual shift is a transformation in the meaning of personal difficulties and responses to life events from normal and expectable behavior and feelings to medical disorders. The body of research is already extensive and has explored the medicalization of such emotional experiences as sadness, unhappiness, grief, loneliness, and alienation (Elliott 1998; Healy 1997; Horwitz and Wakefield 2007; Karp 2006: Ch. 7), anxiousness (Tone 2008), heightened mood (Martin 2007), shyness and fear of criticism (Lane 2007; Scott 2006), and outbursts of anger (Lane 2007) within new or expanded mental illness categories of major depressive disorder, generalized anxiety disorder, mania, social phobia/avoidant personality disorder, and intermittent explosive disorder. To these and other emotions and personality issues (premenstrual dysphoric disorder easily fits here; also see Chodoff 2002), studies have also explored the medicalization of problems of living such as perfectionism (Davis 2008), lack of libido (Hartley 2003; Hartley and Tiefer 2003), and work underperformance (Conrad 2007) under the categories of obsessive-compulsive personality disorder, female sexual dysfunction, and adult attention deficit/hyperactivity disorder. In virtually every case at least one of the treatments, and often the primary one, is pharmacologic.

Studies in this arena generally recognize or presuppose a boundary between normal and expectable experience and a chronic and debilitating condition. While this boundary is often difficult to draw with any precision, medicalization refers to its profound blurring, the shift in a very short period of time, for example, from regarding social phobia as "a rare and usually mild mental disorder" to one of "the most common" (Katzelnick and Greist 2001: 11). The literature identifies a number of key forces contributing to this conflation of normality and pathology. One major factor, widely documented, is the revolution in psychiatry occasioned by the 1980 and subsequent revisions of the *Diagnostic and Statistical Manual of Mental Disorders* (e.g., Horwitz 2002; Horwitz and Wakefield 2007; Kutchins and Kirk 1997; Lane 2007). Importantly, the *DSM* holds that mental disorders "must not be merely an expectable and culturally sanctioned response to a particular event, for example, the death of a loved one." Rather than circumstantially appropriate responses, they must be a "dysfunction in the individual" (quoted in Horwitz 2007: 214). The problem is, however, according to Allan Horwitz (2007: 214), "that many of the *DSM*'s criteria sets for particular disorders contradict its own definition." The formulaic and acontextual diagnostic criteria, he argues, fail to differentiate between expectable responses to life events and internal dysfunctions, a failure that has led to greatly inflated epidemiological estimates and a radical expansion of the scope of pathology.

Studies show that the *DSM* approach has benefited certain groups, who have played an active role in promoting the labeling of disagreeable emotions and experiences as symptoms of disorders and advocating the use of psychotropic drugs to resolve them. These groups include the psychiatric profession, patient advocacy groups, government agencies, and, perhaps most importantly, the pharmaceutical companies. Studies identify the minor tranquilizers in an earlier era (Smith 1991; Tone 2008) and especially the new antidepressants, like Prozac, launched in the late 1980s, as decisive developments for the redefinition of everyday problems in medical terms (e.g., Conrad 2007; Healy 1997; Horwitz and Wakefield 2007; Moynihan and Cassels 2005; Valenstein 1998). These medications (selective serotonin reuptake inhibitors) and others (stimulants, etc.) can treat a range of "symptoms" with relatively few side effects, have been approved by regulatory agencies for a large number of conditions, and are prescribed off-label for even more. They are often the favored form of treatment by managed care organizations and other payers (e.g., Frank, Conti, and Goldman 2005). Studies show they influence the definition of disorders and prescription rates in at least two ways. First, their clinical effect directly shapes what is regarded as clinically significant symptoms, shaping physician practice and psychiatric definitions (Healy 1997). Second, their marketing has brought pharmaceutical companies and the patient advocacy groups and physician experts they fund into the business of marketing not just medications but also the disorders they treat. This includes traditional and new forms of promotions to physicians (Greene 2004; Oldani 2002), as well as the marketing of medications to the public through "illness awareness" campaigns and commercials and, since the late 1990s, through direct-to-consumer advertising (only legal in the United States and New Zealand but seen over TV and the Internet elsewhere). These campaigns and ads work to undermine the boundary between normality and pathology and facilitate self-diagnosis by "showing how mental illness and everyday sufferings look and feel alike" (Davis 2006b: 77; see also, e.g., Grow, Park, and Han 2006).

Consumer demand, stimulated by pharmaceutical marketing, insurance coverage, and other practices, is yet another force contributing to the conflation. In exploring the popular appeal of medications and self-labeling, studies point to a number of factors beyond the relief of distress, particularly symbolic and sick role benefits. A diagnosis, for example, can provide a publicly recognized "account" that creates and organizes meaning for painful experience, gives it legitimacy, and may bring some relief from social obligations (Barker 2005; Broom and Woodward 1996; Davis 2000). Inferring the cause of problems from the effectiveness of the medications, doctors, pharmaceutical companies, and other medical popularizers have promoted the idea that for any given emotional or personality problem, "a chemical imbalance could be to blame." Emphasizing a physical cause operates to establish the problem as the sort of somatic difficulty that regular physicians treat, ruling out other explanations that might involve negative judgments of character or personality. This lifting of responsibility and blame, as Parsons argued long ago and media accounts confirm, comes as a relief (Valenstein 1998). Moreover, the chemical imbalance explanation comes with the sick role benefit of the promise of a positive prognosis – there is nothing psychologically enigmatic going on that the "safe and effective" medications can't correct (Davis 2006b).

There is no sure way to know if there are group differences in this arena. Studies report evidence suggesting that social class is a factor, noting that the use of psychotropic medications is far more prevalent among the middle classes and affluent. One of the concerns raised in the literature, then, has been with the overuse of scarce medical resources by those with minor problems and subsequent diversion of attention from the underserved population of those with serious mental illnesses. While there is criticism of psychiatry for the *DSM* and for close ties to the drug companies, there is also criticism, ironically, of physicians for yielding too readily to consumer self-diagnoses and dispensing prescriptions too freely. More generally, critiques emphasize that medicalizing everyday life problems misses the larger social and economic causes of individual distress and the role of change in those arrangements for influencing well-being. They argue that medicalization, through defining new norms and reproducing social judgments, has reset and narrowed the boundaries for what is acceptable and expected human variation. In echoes of Illich, Arthur Kleinman (2006: 9), for instance, argues that medicalizing "ordinary unhappiness and normal bereavement ... diminishes the person, thins out and homogenizes the deeply rich diversity of human experience," and undermines our moral life as a society. Among others, studies also raise concerns about medications – their long-term side effects and power to blunt emotions, decrease tolerance of minor discomfort, and reshape understandings of personhood – and the culture that produces the demand for them.

Enhancements in healthy people

Although medicine has long been involved in enhancing human traits, developments in gene therapy and new interventions, actual and potential, have made the medicalization of capacities and characteristics in healthy people a growing arena of research. The conceptual shift, to borrow a term from the psychiatrist Peter Kramer's *Listening to Prozac* (1993), is from "well" to "better than well." This arena is different from everyday life problems in that medicalization does not begin with a problem. The aim of enhancement "is not to cure a disease, to make a patient normal or remedy a deficit," but to improve or maximize human capacities or traits (Rothman and Rothman 2003: ix). However, in practice, it appears that medical treatments for healthy people are in fact legitimated not as simply "improvements" or in terms of "pursuing perfection" but as treatments for troubles (Davis in prep.; Elliott 2003, 2007; Haiken 1997). As the bioethicist Carl Elliott (2003: 120) writes, "Doctors treat 'patients,' not 'consumers,'" which means that generally enhancements must be transformed, however loosely, into treatments. Most human capacities and characteristics lie along a continuum, and those who find themselves on the end furthest from conventional expectations or feel they do not match up in some way may perceive disadvantage (President's Council on Bioethics 2003: 15). Being short has social drawbacks; blushing can be embarrassing; a creased brow can make one look perpetually angry. For many physicians, dispensing growth hormone or beta blockers or Botox is a way to help, even if no diagnosable pathology is present.

Research in this arena includes studies of specific cases, such as cosmetic surgery (Davis 1995; Haiken 1997; Sullivan 2001), hormone treatments for short stature (Conrad 2007; Rothman and Rothman 2003), new reproductive choices, such as sex selection or choosing a sperm or egg donor based on donor characteristics (Becker 2000; Sandel 2007), and the extensive off-label use of medications, such as the use of Viagra by young healthy males, the use of Ritalin to improve study habits, or the use of Prozac to "sculpt" a desired personality (Conrad 2007; Diller 1998: Ch. 13; Kramer 1993; Elliott 2003; Parens 1998; President's Council on Bioethics 2003; Sandel 2007). But these examples only scratch the surface, as advances in neuroscience and emerging neurotechnologies are rapidly opening up many new "quality of life" interventions with respect to mood and cognitive functioning (e.g., Chatterjee 2004; Wolpe 2002). Still mostly on the horizon but the subject of extensive commentary and popular press coverage are potential interventions based on discoveries in genomic research.

The possibility of enhancement uses of medical technologies and medications is created by the very development of those interventions. Synthetic growth hormone was developed to treat children with a growth hormone deficiency, and later given to those who were just short (Conrad 2007). Plastic surgery was developed to treat disfigured and severely burned soldiers beginning with the Crimean War and then later used to enhance the body (Davis 1995). A drug like Provigil was developed to treat narcolepsy and then later used to extend wakefulness and increase alertness (Williams et al. 2008; Wolpe 2002). And so it goes, the first use opening the possibility for the second. The medicalization of capacities and characteristics in healthy people is also facilitated by features of contemporary consumer culture. These features include a strong emphasis on expressing individuality, reinventing one's self, and revealing an identity that may be hidden by circumstance or accident of birth. In this environment, medical enhancements are appealing as a means by which people can express their true self, change their identity, or find happiness. Studies show that whether getting a facelift or undergoing a sex-change operation, people often speak in terms of achieving a more authentic and meaningful life (Elliott 2003). The relentless competitiveness and 24/7 demands of contemporary Western society have also been theorized to feed the desire for neurological aids to maintain or better one's position. Indeed, under these conditions, people may feel impelled: "To not take advantage of cosmetic neurology might mean being left behind" (Chatterjee 2004: 971). In this meritocratic world, mastery and control are among the most highly prized values.

The use of medical technologies for enhancement is generally paid for privately in both the United States and Europe (though see Davis 1995 on the Dutch experiment with covering cosmetic procedures). As a result, the middle class and affluent are the most likely to use them, and intense competition has emerged involving industry, scientists, and clinicians anxious to stake biotech claims and both foster and meet demand. Significant scientific innovations and transformations in the organization and practice of medicine are important driving forces. These include the public sponsorship of research and development by scientists and university research departments with subsequent privatization of the "commodifiable products and processes" that emerge (Clarke et al. 2003: 167). The publicly funded Human Genome Project is but a prime example. All the private and university patenting is in turn generating pressure to find any and every therapeutic use and to corner new markets. Pharmaceutical companies are increasingly funding research in academic medical centers, creating significant questions about how commercial sponsorship influences study results and subsequent claims about the safety and efficacy of tested drugs (Angell 2004). Pharmaceutical companies have also come to play a very large role in the continuing education of physicians, and, as noted above, aggressively market psychotropic medication and the disorders they treat as "everyday" drugs to both doctors and the general public (Mechanic 2006). Given the cultural emphasis on self-fulfillment and success, the producers of enhancement technologies, from drug companies to cosmetic surgeons, now market them as instruments of self-expression and liberation, promising just the right intervention to improve the quality of one's psychic experience, outer appearance, or social performance (Elliott 2003).

The medicalization of capacities and characteristics in healthy people touches on a wide array of issues, including concerns with distributive justice and social stratification, a trade-off between individual well-being and social goods, and the safety and side effects of clinical interventions. Critical observers argue that influential scientists and doctors, as well as the marketers, typically hype the benefits and downplay the dangers of enhancements, and that many physicians allow patient demand to drive their care. Studies express social and philosophical concerns that enhancements can create false hopes, weaken individual character, and threaten important features of what it means to be human. They can erode the "gifted character of human powers and achievements," ratcheting up individual responsibility for life outcomes, and diminishing "our sense of solidarity with those less fortunate than ourselves" (Sandel 2007: 86, 89). They can promote cultural norms that are "morally suspect" and "generate pressure to assimilate to an unjust paradigm," as with cosmetic procedures that involve unjust images of race and beauty (Little 1998: 166–7) or with the demand for "designer children." In this arena, as in all the others, the individualizing dynamic of medical conceptualization and treatment is joined to a concern with the insidious narrowing of norms and standards, the closing off of alternative ways to live, and the subtle but powerful pressures to conform.

TOWARD THE FUTURE

In conclusion, I want to briefly point to three areas for more focused research and emphasis. First, continuing work in each of the arenas could be usefully enlarged by attending not only to the social construction of medicalized categories but also to the etiology of the behavior or condition that is being medicalized. Studies exploring the dynamic interaction between cultural imperatives, cultural anxieties, and disease categories show that the experiences of suffering and feelings of inadequacy being medicalized are not simply being discovered, they are being generated by social change. A new tool for this type of work is the historicized form of conceptual analysis – "historical ontology" – developed by the philosopher Ian Hacking. In exploring transient mental illnesses, he employs the metaphor of an "ecological niche" and identifies four principal "vectors" which create it – the illness should fit into a taxonomy of illness; be socially observable "as suffering, as something to escape"; lie on a line between two elements of contemporary culture, one desired and the other feared; and, finally, the illness, "despite the pain it produces," should "provide some release that is not available elsewhere in the culture" (Hacking 1998: 1, 2). Historical ontology is one possible conceptual tool for moving beyond social constructionism (also see Horwitz 2002). We need others. The recent call for the development of a "sociology of disease" is a welcome development in this regard (Timmermans and Haas 2008).

Second, we need more research on resistance and constraints to medicalization. While undeniably a powerful process, medicalization is not monolithic or unidirectional but contingent. Research, however, has concentrated on the factors that push medicalization and has devoted far less attention to those that inhibit it. Our understanding is consequently skewed. After reading in this literature, one could easily come away with a picture of medicalization as an inexorable juggernaut. Over the years, various concepts have been introduced to capture the contingency analytically, including the concept of "demedicalization." There is no consensus on this concept and its use varies widely and confusingly. Conrad (1992: 224) argues that "Demedicalization does not occur until a problem is no longer defined in medical terms and medical treatments are no longer deemed to be appropriate solutions." This definition is clear enough, yet of doubtful utility since only a very few examples can be found. And given that medicalization is a response to pain, or problems, or some sense of being disadvantaged, it is unlikely that the number of examples will grow.

Yet constraints on medicalization are real. Resistance, passive or active, for instance, is widespread. Despite rising prescription rates in the US and elsewhere, there is considerable resistance to viewing certain behavioral problems of children as properly medical and pharmacologic treatments as appropriate (e.g., McLeod et al. 2004). Epidemiological studies always show a gap, often quite large, between diagnosed cases and estimated prevalence in many areas of psychiatry (e.g., Kessler et al. 2005) and well beyond. Not everyone is running to the doctor, and as noted above, patients often have their own perspective. Physicians can and do contest medicalized definitions and the extension of their role. There are new forms of backlash stirring, including the informal movement of medical journalists and academics criticizing the "disease mongering" of the pharmaceutical companies (Moynihan and Cassels 2005; Moynihan, Heath, and Henry 2002). And so on. Uneven, inconsistent, and contested: We need more research to balance our often one-sided picture of medicalization.

Finally, both medicine and society continue to change. Gathering steam for some time, a major, cross-national conversation has now erupted about the promises and perils of real and potential biomedical advances in neuroscience, genomics, assisted reproduction, and more. The issues, touched on only briefly above, are as fundamental as they are urgent: Who are we as human beings? What makes for a good life? What obligations do we have to one another? Can we establish normative limits on medical interventions, and if so, where? These and other such basic questions are being debated by politicians, philosophers, scientists of every stripe, bioethicists, theologians, activist groups, and others. The debates very often touch, directly and indirectly, on the question of medicalization. More clearly thematizing key features of medicalization research would bring the field more directly into this important conversation. Many studies of medicalization are windows not just on medicine but on culture and subjectivity. They illuminate how dominant social values and visions of the good life, standards of pathology and normality, and practices of social control are enacted and how they shift and change. And they shed light on the consequences, intended and unintended, for the conduct of life. These findings are relevant, and attending to and drawing them out would make them available to the larger debate about "life itself" (Rose 2007).

References

Angell, Marcia. 2004. *The Truth About the Drug Companies: How They Deceive Us and What to Do About It*. New York: Random House.

Annandale, Ellen and Judith Clark. 1996. "What is Gender? Feminist Theory and the Sociology of Human Reproduction." *Sociology of Health and Illness* 18: 17–44.

Antler, Stephen. 1981. "The Rediscovery of Child Abuse." Pp. 39–53 in L. H. Pelton (ed.), *The Social Context of Child Abuse and Neglect*. New York: Human Sciences Press.

Appleton, Lynn M. 1995. "Rethinking Medicalization: Alcoholism and Anomalies." Pp. 59–80 in J. Best (ed.), *Images of Issues: Typifying Contemporary Social Problems*, 2nd edition. New York: Aldine de Gruyter.

Arney, William Ray and Bernard J. Bergen. 1984. *Medicine and the Management of Living: Taming the Last Great Beast*. Chicago: University of Chicago Press.

Ballard, Karen and Mary Ann Elston. 2005. "Medicalisation: A Multi-dimensional Concept." *Social Theory and Health* 3: 228–41.

Barker, Kristin K. 2005. *The Fibromyalgia Story: Medical Authority and Women's Worlds of Pain*. Philadelphia: Temple University Press.

Barsky, Arthur J. and Jonathan F. Boros. 1995. "Somatization and Medicalization in the Era of Managed Care." *Journal of the American Medical Association* 274: 1931–4.

Bayer, Ronald. 1981. *Homosexuality and American Psychiatry: The Politics of Diagnosis.* New York: Basic Books.

Becker, Gay. 2000. *The Elusive Embryo: How Women and Men Approach New Reproductive Technologies.* Berkeley: University of California Press.

Becker, Gay and Robert D. Nachtigall. 1992. "Eager for Medicalisation: The Social Production of Infertility as a Disease." *Sociology of Health and Illness* 14: 456–71.

Becker, Howard S. 1963. *Outsiders: Studies in the Sociology of Deviance.* Glencoe, IL: Free Press.

Beckett, Katherine. 2005. "Choosing Cesarean: Feminism and the Politics of Childbirth in the United States." *Feminist Theory* 6: 251–75.

Bell, Susan. 1987. "Changing Ideas: The Medicalisation of Menopause." *Social Science and Medicine* 24: 535–42.

Berger, Peter L. and Thomas Luckmann. 1966. *The Social Construction of Reality.* New York: Anchor Books.

Berliner, Howard S. and J. Warren Salmon. 1980. "The Holistic Alternative to Scientific Medicine: History and Analysis." *International Journal of Health Services* 10: 133–47.

Black, Jane. 2008. "Targeting Obesity Alongside Hunger." *Washington Post*, December 24, p.A2.

Bransen, Els. 1992. "Has Menstruation been Medicalised? Or Will It Never Happen...?" *Sociology of Health and Illness* 14: 98–110.

Broom, Dorothy H. and Roslyn V. Woodward. 1996. "Medicalisation Reconsidered: Toward a Collaborative Approach to Care." *Sociology of Health and Illness* 18: 357–78.

Brown, Wendy. 1995. *States of Injury: Power and Freedom in Late Modernity.* Princeton, NJ: Princeton University Press.

Chaffin, Mark. 2006. "The Changing Focus of Child Maltreatment Research and Practice Within Psychology." *Journal of Social Issues* 62: 663–84.

Chatterjee, Anjan. 2004. "Cosmetic Neurology: The Controversy over Enhanced Movement, Mentation, and Mood." *Neurology* 63: 968–74.

Chesler, Phyllis. 1972. *Women and Madness.* Garden City, NY: Doubleday.

Chodoff, Paul. 2002. "The Medicalization of the Human Condition." *Psychiatric Services* 53: 627–8.

Chrisler, Joan C. and Paula Caplan. 2002. "The Strange Case of Dr. Jekyll and Ms. Hyde: How PMS Became a Cultural Phenomenon and a Psychiatric Disorder." *Annual Review of Sex Research* 13: 274–306.

Clarke, Adele E., Janet K. Shim, Laura Mamo, Jennifer Ruth Fosket, and Jennifer R. Fishman. 2003. "Biomedicalization: Technoscientific Transformations of Health, Illness, and US Biomedicine." *American Sociological Review* 68: 161–94.

Cockerham, William C. 1988. "Medical Sociology." Pp. 575–99 in N. J. Smelser (ed.), *Handbook of Sociology.* Newbury Park, CA: Sage.

Cohen, Judith A., Anthony P. Mannarino, Laura K. Murray, and Robyn Igelman. 2006. "Psychosocial Interventions for Maltreated and Violence-Exposed Children." *Journal of Social Issues* 62: 737–66.

Comaroff, Jean. 1982. "Medicine: Symbol and Ideology." Pp. 49–68 in P. Wright and A. Treacher (eds.), *The Problem of Medical Knowledge: Examining the Social Construction of Medicine.* Edinburgh: Edinburgh University Press.

Conrad, Peter. 1975. "The Discovery of Hyperkinesis: Notes on the Medicalization of Deviant Behavior." *Social Problems* 23: 12–21.

Conrad, Peter. 1992. "Medicalization and Social Control." *Annual Review of Sociology* 18: 209–32.

Conrad, Peter. 2007. *The Medicalization of Society: On the Transformation of Human Conditions into Treatable Disorders*. Baltimore: Johns Hopkins University Press.

Conrad, Peter and Joseph W. Schneider. 1980. *Deviance and Medicalization: From Badness to Sickness*. St. Louis, MO: C.V. Mosby.

Conrad, Peter and Joseph W. Schneider. 1992. *Deviance and Medicalization: From Badness to Sickness*, expanded edition. Philadelphia: Temple University Press.

Cooper, David. 1971. *Psychiatry and Anti-Psychiatry*. New York: Ballantine Books.

Cooperstock, Ruth and Henry L. Lennard. 1979. "Some Social Meanings of Tranquilizer Use." *Sociology of Health and Illness* 1: 331–47.

Cowley, Sarah, Jan Mitcheson, and Anna M. Houston. 2004. "Structuring Health Needs Assessments: The Medicalisation of Health Visiting." *Sociology of Health and Illness* 26: 503–26.

Crawford, Robert. 1980. "Healthism and the Medicalization of Everyday Life." *International Journal of Health Services* 10: 365–88.

Crossley, Nick. 2006. *Contesting Psychiatry: Social Movements in Mental Health*. London: Routledge.

Davis, Joseph E. 2000. "Accounts of False Memory Syndrome: Parents, 'Retractors,' and the Role of Institutions in Account Making." *Qualitative Sociology* 23: 29–56.

Davis, Joseph E. 2005. *Accounts of Innocence: Sexual Abuse, Trauma, and the Self*. Chicago: University of Chicago Press.

Davis, Joseph E. 2006a. "How Medicalization Lost its Way." *Society* 43(6): 51–6.

Davis, Joseph E. 2006b. "Suffering, Pharmaceutical Advertising, and the Face of Mental Illness." *The Hedgehog Review* 8(3): 62–77.

Davis, Joseph E. In prep. *After Psychology: Self and Suffering in the Age of Prozac*. Book manuscript.

Davis, Kathy. 1995. *Reshaping the Female Body: The Dilemma of Cosmetic Surgery*. New York: Routledge.

Davis, Lennard J. 2008. *Obsession: A History*. Chicago: University of Chicago Press.

DeVries, Raymond. 2005. *A Pleasing Birth: Midwives and Maternity Care in the Netherlands*. Philadelphia: Temple University Press.

Diller, Lawrence H. 1998. *Running on Ritalin: A Physician Reflects on Children, Society, and Performance in a Pill*. New York: Bantam Books.

Dingwall, Robert. 2006. "Imperialism or Encirclement?" *Society* 43(6): 30–6.

Ehrenreich, Barbara and Deirdre English. 1973. *Complaints and Disorders: The Sexual Politics of Sickness*. New York: Feminist Press.

Elliott, Carl. 1998. "The Tyranny of Happiness: Ethics and Cosmetic Psychopharmacology." Pp. 177–88 in E. Parens (ed.), *Enhancing Human Traits: Ethical and Social Implications*. Washington, DC: Georgetown University Press.

Elliott, Carl. 2003. *Better than Well: American Medicine Meets the American Dream*. New York: Norton.

Elliott, Carl. 2007. "The Mixed Promise of Genetic Medicine." *New England Journal of Medicine* 356: 2024–5.

Erikson, Kai T. 1966. *Wayward Puritans: A Study in the Sociology of Deviance*. New York: John Wiley.

Estes, Carroll L. and Elizabeth A. Binney. 1989. "The Biomedicalization of Ageing: Dangers and Dilemmas." *The Gerontologist* 29: 587–96.

Findling, Robert L., Hans Steiner, and Elizabeth B. Weller. 2005. "Use of Antipsychotics in Children and Adolescents." *Journal of Clinical Psychiatry* 66: 29–40.

Fishman, Jennifer R. 2007. "Making Viagra: From Impotence to Erectile Dysfunction." Pp. 229–52 in A. Tone and E. S. Watkins (eds.), *Medicating Modern America: Prescription Drugs in History.* New York: New York University Press.

Foucault, Michel. 1965. *Madness and Civilization: A History of Insanity in the Age of Reason.* New York: Pantheon Books.

Foucault, Michel. 1973. *The Birth of the Clinic: An Archaeology of Medical Perception.* New York: Pantheon Books.

Foucault, Michel. 1988. "Technologies of the Self." Pp. 16–49 in L. H. Martin, H. Gutman, and P. H. Hutton (eds.), *Technologies of the Self.* Amherst, MA: University of Massachusetts Press.

Fox, Renée C. 1977. "The Medicalization and Demedicalization of American Society." *Daedalus* 106(1): 9–22.

Frank, Richard G., Rena M. Conti, and Howard H. Goldman. 2005. "Mental Health Policy and Psychotropic Drugs." *The Milbank Quarterly* 83: 271–98.

Frankfort, Ellen. 1972. *Vaginal Politics.* New York: Quadrangle Books.

Freidson, Eliot. 1970. *Profession of Medicine: A Study of the Sociology of Applied Knowledge.* Chicago: University of Chicago Press.

Furedi, Frank. 2004. *Therapy Culture: Cultivating Vulnerability in an Uncertain Age.* London: Routledge.

Gabe, Jonathan and Michael Calnan. 1989. "The Limits of Medicine: Women's Perception of Medical Technology." *Social Science and Medicine* 28: 223–31.

Gallagher, Eugene B. and C. Kristina Sionean. 2004. "Where Medicalization Boulevard Meets Commercialization Alley." *Journal of Policy Studies* 16: 53–62.

Garry, Ann. 2001. "Medicine and Medicalization: A Response to Purdy." *Bioethics* 15: 262–9.

Gevitz, Norman. 1988. "Three Perspectives on Unorthodox Medicine." Pp. 1–28 in N. Gevitz (ed.), *Other Healers: Unorthodox Medicine in America.* Baltimore: Johns Hopkins University Press.

Goffman, Erving. 1961. *Asylums: Essays on the Social Situation of Mental Patients and Other Inmates.* Garden City, NY: Anchor Books.

Golden, Janet. 2005. *Message in a Bottle: The Making of Fetal Alcohol Syndrome.* Cambridge, MA: Harvard University Press.

Gordon, Linda. 2002. *The Moral Property of Women: A History of Birth Control Politics in America,* revised and updated edition. Urbana: University of Illinois Press.

Greenberg, David F. 1988. *The Construction of Homosexuality.* Chicago: University of Chicago Press.

Greene, Jeremy A. 2004. "Attention to 'Details': Etiquette and the Pharmaceutical Salesman in Postwar America." *Social Studies of Science* 34: 271–92.

Griffiths, Frances. 1999. "Women's Control and Choice Regarding HRT." *Social Science and Medicine* 49: 469–81.

Groopman, Jerome. 2007. "What's Normal? The Difficulty of Diagnosing Bipolar Disorder in Children." *The New Yorker,* April 9, pp. 28–34.

Grow, Jean M., Jin Seong Park, and Xiaoqi Han. 2006. " 'Your Life is Waiting!' Symbolic Meanings in Direct-to-Consumer Antidepressant Advertising." *Journal of Communication Inquiry* 30: 163–88.

Hacking, Ian. 1998. *Mad Travelers: Reflections on the Reality of Transient Mental Illnesses.* Charlottesville, VA: University Press of Virginia.

Haiken, Elizabeth. 1997. *Venus Envy: A History of Cosmetic Surgery.* Baltimore: Johns Hopkins University Press.

Harris, Jennifer. 2005. "The Increased Diagnosis of 'Juvenile Bipolar Disorder': What Are We Treating?" *Psychiatric Services* 56(5): 529–31.

Hartley, Heather. 2003. " 'Big Pharma' in Our Bedrooms: An Analysis of the Medicalization of Women's Sexual Problems." *Advances in Gender Research* 7: 89–129.

Hartley, Heather and Leonore Tiefer. 2003. "Taking a Biological Turn: The Push for a 'Female Viagra' and the Medicalization of Women's Sexual Problems." *Women's Studies Quarterly* 31(Spring/Summer): 42–54.

Haug, Marie R. 1976. "The Erosion of Professional Authority: A Cross-Cultural Inquiry in the Case of the Physician." *Milbank Memorial Fund Quarterly* 54: 83–106.

Healy, David. 1997. *The Antidepressant Era*. Cambridge, MA: Harvard University Press.

Healy, David. 2007. "Folie to Folly: The Modern Mania for Bipolar Disorders and Mood Stabilizers." Pp. 42–62 in A. Tone and E. Siegel Watkins (eds.), *Medicating Modern America: Prescription Drugs in History*. New York: New York University Press.

Horwitz, Allan V. 2002. *Creating Mental Illness*. Chicago: University of Chicago Press.

Horwitz, Allan V. 2007. "Transforming Normality into Pathology: The *DSM* and the Outcomes of Stressful Social Arrangements." *Journal of Health and Social Behavior* 48: 211–22.

Horwitz, Allan V. and Jerome Wakefield. 2007. *The Loss of Sadness: How Psychiatry Transformed Normal Sorrow into Depressive Disorder*. New York: Oxford University Press.

Illich, Ivan. 1976. *Medical Nemesis: The Expropriation of Health*. New York: Random House.

Illouz, Eva. 2008. *Saving the Modern Soul: Therapy, Emotions, and the Culture of Self-Help*. Berkeley: University of California Press.

Imber, Jonathan B. 2008. *Trusting Doctors: The Decline of Moral Authority in American Medicine*. Princeton, NJ: Princeton University Press.

Jenkins, Philip. 1998. *Moral Panic: Changing Concepts of the Child Molester in Modern America*. New Haven, CT: Yale University Press.

Karp, David A. 2006. *Is It Me or My Meds? Living with Antidepressants*. Cambridge, MA: Harvard University Press.

Katzelnick, David and John H. Greist. 2001. "Social Anxiety Disorder: An Unrecognized Problem in Primary Care." *Journal of Clinical Psychiatry* 62(Suppl.1): 11–15.

Kessler, Ronald C., Olga Demler, Richard G. Frank, Mark Olfson, Harold Alan Pincus, Ellen E. Walters, Philip Wang, Kenneth B. Wells, and Alan M. Zaslavsky. 2005. "Prevalence and Treatment of Mental Disorders 1990–2003." *New England Journal of Medicine* 352: 2515–23.

Kitsuse, John. 1962. "Societal Reaction to Deviance: Problems of Theory and Method." *Social Problems* 9: 247–56.

Kittrie, Nicholas N. 1971. *The Right to be Different: Deviance and Enforced Therapy*. Baltimore: Johns Hopkins University Press.

Kleinman, Arthur. 2006. *What Really Matters: Living a Moral Life Amidst Uncertainty and Danger*. New York: Oxford University Press.

Koumjian, Kevin. 1981. "The Use of Valium as a Form of Social Control." *Social Science and Medicine* 15E: 245–9.

Kramer, Peter D. 1993. *Listening to Prozac*. New York: Viking Penguin.

Kurz, Demie. 1987. "Emergency Department Responses to Battered Women: Resistance to Medicalization." *Social Problems* 34: 69–81.

Kutchins, Herb and Stuart A. Kirk. 1997. *Making Us Crazy: DSM: The Psychiatric Bible and the Creation of Mental Disorders*. New York: Free Press.

Laing, R.D. 1967. *The Politics of Experience and the Bird of Paradise*. New York: Ballantine Books.

Lane, Christopher. 2007. *Shyness: How Normal Behavior Became a Sickness*. New Haven, CT: Yale University Press.

Lazarus, Ellen. 1997. "What Do Women Want? Issues of Choice, Control, and Class in American Pregnancy and Childbirth." Pp. 132–158 in R. E. Davis-Floyd and C. F. Sargent (eds.), *Childbirth and Authoritative Knowledge: Cross-Cultural Perspectives*. Berkeley: University of California Press.

Lee, Shirley and Avis Mysyk. 2004. "The Medicalization of Compulsive Buying." *Social Science and Medicine* 58: 1709–18.

Lennard, Henry L. and Arnold Bernstein. 1974. "Perspectives on the New Psychoactive Drug Technology." Pp. 149–65 in R. Cooperstock (ed.), *Social Aspects of the Medical Use of Psychotropic Drugs*. Toronto: ARF Books.

Light, Donald W. 1991. "Professionalism as a Countervailing Power." *Journal of Health Politics, Policy and Law* 16: 499–506.

Light, Donald W. 1993. "Countervailing Power: The Changing Character of the Medical Profession in the United States." Pp. 69–80 in F. W. Hafferty and J. B. McKinley (eds.), *The Changing Medical Profession: An International Perspective*. New York: Oxford University Press.

Little, Margaret Olivia. 1998. "Cosmetic Surgery, Suspect Norms, and the Ethics of Complicity." Pp. 162–76 in E. Parens (ed.), *Enhancing Human Traits: Ethical and Social Implications*. Washington, DC: Georgetown University Press.

Lock, Margaret. 1991. "Flawed Jewels and National Dis/Order: Narratives on Adolescent Dissent in Japan." *Journal of Psychohistory* 18: 507–31.

Lock, Margaret. 1993. *Encounters with Aging: Mythologies of Menopause in Japan and North America*. Berkeley: University of California Press.

Lock, Margaret. 2004. "Medicalization and the Naturalization of Social Control." Pp. 116–25 in C. R. Ember and M. Ember (eds.), *Encyclopedia of Medical Anthropology*, vol. 1. New York: Kluwer Academic/Plenum.

Lock, Margaret and Patricia A. Kaufert (eds.). 1998. *Pragmatic Women and Body Politics*. Cambridge: Cambridge University Press.

Lofland, John. 1969. *Deviance and Identity*. Englewood Cliffs, NJ: Prentice-Hall.

Lowenberg, June S. and Fred Davis. 1994. "Beyond Medicalisation–Demedicalisation: The Case of Holistic Health." *Sociology of Health and Illness* 16: 579–99.

Lupton, Deborah. 1997. "Foucault and the Medicalisation Critique." Pp. 94–110 in A. Petersen and R. Bunton (eds.), *Foucault, Health and Medicine*. New York: Routledge.

Lupton, Deborah. 2003. *Medicine as Culture*, 2nd edition. London: Sage.

Malacrida, Claudia. 2003. *Cold Comfort: Mothers, Professionals, and Attention Deficit Disorder*. Toronto: University of Toronto Press.

Martin, Emily. 1987. *The Woman in the Body: A Cultural Analysis of Reproduction*. Boston: Beacon Press.

Martin, Emily. 2007. *Bipolar Expeditions: Mania and Depression in American Culture*. Princeton, NJ: Princeton University Press.

McCrea, Frances B. 1983. "The Politics of Menopause: The 'Discovery' of a Deficiency Disease." *Social Problems* 31: 111–23.

McHugh, Paul R. and Phillip R. Slavney. 1998. *The Perspectives of Psychiatry*, 2nd edition. Baltimore: Johns Hopkins University Press.

McKinlay, John B. and Lisa D. Marceau. 2002. "The End of the Golden Age of Doctoring." *International Journal of Health Services* 32: 379–416.

McKinlay, John. B. and John D. Stoeckle. 1988. "Corporatization and the Social Transformation of Doctoring." *International Journal of Health Services* 18: 191–205.

McLeod, Jane D., Bernice A. Pescosolido, David T. Takeuchi, and Terry Falkenberg White. 2004. "Public Attitudes toward the Use of Psychiatric Medications for Children." *Journal of Health and Social Behavior* 45: 53–67.

Mechanic, David. 2006. *The Truth About Health Care: Why Reform Is Not Working in America*. New Brunswick, NJ: Rutgers University Press.

Moynihan, Ray and Alan Cassels. 2005. *Selling Sickness*. New York: Nation Books.

Moynihan, Ray, Iona Heath, and David Henry. 2002. "Selling Sickness: The Pharmaceutical Industry and Disease Mongering." *British Medical Journal* 324: 886–91.

Navarro, Vicente. 1976. *Medicine Under Capitalism*. New York: Prodist.

Newberger, Eli H. and Richard Bourne. 1978. "The Medicalization and Legalization of Child Abuse." *American Journal of Orthopsychiatry* 48: 593–607.

Nolan, James L. 1998. *The Therapeutic State: Justifying Government at Century's End*. New York: New York University Press.

Nye, Robert A. 2003. "The Evolution of the Concept of Medicalization in the Late Twentieth Century." *Journal of the History of the Behavioral Sciences* 39: 115–29.

Oinas, Elina. 1998. "Medicalisation by Whom? Accounts of Menstruation Conveyed by Young Women and Medical Experts in Medical Advisory Columns." *Sociology of Health and Illness* 20: 52–70.

Oldani, Michael J. 2002. "Tales from the 'Script': An Insider/Outsider View of Pharmaceutical Sales Practices." *Kroeber Anthropological Society Papers* 87: 147–76.

Parens, Eric (ed.). 1998. *Enhancing Human Traits: Ethical and Social Implications*. Washington, DC: Georgetown University Press.

Parsons, Talcott. 1951. *The Social System*. Glencoe, IL: Free Press.

Pescosolido, Bernice A. 2006. "Professional Dominance and the Limits of Erosion." *Society* 43(6): 21–9.

Pfohl, Stephen J. 1977. "The 'Discovery' of Child Abuse." *Social Problems* 24: 310–23.

Pitts, Jesse R. 1968. "Social Control: The Concept." Pp. 381–96 in D. L. Sills (ed.), *International Encyclopedia of the Social Sciences*, vol. 14. New York: Macmillan and Free Press.

President's Council on Bioethics. 2003. *Beyond Therapy: Biotechnology and the Pursuit of Happiness*. Washington, DC: President's Council on Bioethics.

Radical Therapist Collective. 1971. *The Radical Therapist*, produced by J. Agel. New York: Ballantine Books.

Reeder, Leo G. 1972. "The Patient-Client as a Consumer: Some Observations on the Changing Professional–Client Relationship." *Journal of Health and Social Behavior* 13: 406–12.

Rice, John Steadman. 1996. *A Disease of One's Own: Psychotherapy, Addiction, and the Emergence of Co-Dependency*. New Brunswick, NJ: Transaction.

Rice, John Steadman. 2002. "'Getting Our Histories Straight': Culture, Narrative, and Identity in the Self-Help Movement." Pp. 79–99 in J. E. Davis (ed.), *Stories of Change: Narrative and Social Movements*. Albany, NY: State University of New York Press.

Rieff, Philip. 1966. *The Triumph of the Therapeutic: Uses of Faith After Freud*. New York: Harper and Row.

Riessman, Catherine Kohler. 1983. "Women and Medicalization: A New Perspective." *Social Policy* 14 (Summer): 3–18.

Riska, Elianne. 2003. "Gendering the Medicalization Thesis." *Advances in Gender Research* 7: 59–87.

Rose, Nikolas. 1999. *Governing the Soul: The Shaping of the Private Self*, 2nd edition. London: Free Association Books.

Rose, Nikolas. 2007. *The Politics of Life Itself: Biomedicine, Power, and Subjectivity in the Twenty-First Century*. Princeton, NJ: Princeton University Press.

Rosecrance, John. 1985. "Compulsive Gambling and the Medicalization of Deviance." *Social Problems* 32: 275–84.

Rosenberg, Charles E. 2007. *Our Present Complaint: American Medicine, Then and Now*. Baltimore: Johns Hopkins University Press.

Rossol, Josh. 2001. "The Medicalization of Deviance as an Interactive Achievement: The Construction of Compulsive Gambling." *Symbolic Interaction* 24: 315–41.

Rothman, David J. 1991. *Strangers at the Bedside: A History of How Law and Bioethics Transformed Medical Decision Making*. New York: Basic Books.

Rothman, Sheila M. and David J. Rothman. 2003. *The Pursuit of Perfection: The Promise and Perils of Medical Enhancement*. New York: Pantheon Books.

Salant, Talya and Heena P. Santry. 2006. "Internet Marketing of Bariatric Surgery: Contemporary Trends in the Medicalization of Obesity." *Social Science and Medicine* 62: 2445–57.

Sandel, Michael J. 2007. *The Case against Perfection: Ethics in the Age of Genetic Engineering*. Cambridge, MA: Harvard University Press.

Scheff, Thomas J. 1966. *Being Mentally Ill: A Sociological Theory*. Hawthorne, NY: Aldine.

Scheffler, Richard M., Stephen P. Hinshaw, Sepideh Modrek, and Peter Levine. 2007. "The Global Market for ADHD Medications." *Health Affairs* 26: 450–7.

Scott, Susie. 2006. "The Medicalisation of Shyness: From Social Misfits to Social Fitness." *Sociology of Health and Illness* 28: 133–53.

Scott, Wilbur J. 1990. "PTSD in *DSM-III*: A Case in the Politics of Diagnosis and Disease." *Social Problems* 37: 294–310.

Scull, Andrew T. 1975. "From Madness to Mental Illness: Medical Men as Moral Entrepreneurs." *Archives Européennes de Sociologie* 16: 218–61.

Sedgwick, Peter S. 1982. *Psycho Politics: Laing, Foucault, Goffman, Szasz and the Future of Mass Psychiatry*. New York: Harper and Row.

Singh, Ilina. 2004. "Doing Their Jobs: Mothering with Ritalin in a Culture of Mother-Blame." *Social Science and Medicine* 59: 1193–205.

Singh, Ilina. 2007. "Not Just Naughty: 50 Years of Stimulant Drug Advertising." Pp. 131–55 in A. Tone and E. S. Watkins (eds.), *Medicating Modern America: Prescription Drugs in History*. New York: New York University Press.

Smith, Mickey C. 1991. *A Social History of the Minor Tranquilizers: The Quest for Small Comfort in the Age of Anxiety*. New York: Pharmaceutical Products Press.

Snow, David A., Susan G. Baker, Leon Anderson, and Michael Martin. 1986. "The Myth of Pervasive Mental Illness among the Homeless." *Social Problems* 33: 407–23.

Sobal, Jeffery. 1995. "The Medicalization and Demedicalization of Obesity." Pp. 67–90 in D. Maurer and J. Sobal (eds.), *Eating Agendas: Food and Nutrition as Social Problems*. Hawthorne, NY: Aldine de Gruyter.

Spector, Malcolm. 1977. "Legitimizing Homosexuality." *Society* 14(5): 52–6.

Starr, Paul. 1982. *The Social Transformation of American Medicine*. New York: Basic Books.

Strong, P. M. 1979. "Sociological Imperialism and the Profession of Medicine: A Critical Examination of the Thesis of Medical Imperialism." *Social Science and Medicine* 13A: 199–215.

Sullivan, Deborah A. 2001. *Cosmetic Surgery: The Cutting Edge of Commercial Medicine in America*. New Brunswick, NJ: Rutgers University Press.

Sutherland, Edwin H. 1950. "The Diffusion of Sexual Psychopath Laws." *American Journal of Sociology* 56: 142–8.

Szasz, Thomas S. 1956. "Malingering: 'Diagnosis' or Social Condemnation?" *American Medical Association Archives of Neurology and Psychiatry* 76: 432–43.

Szasz, Thomas S. 1960. "The Myth of Mental Illness." *American Psychologist* 15: 113–18.

Szasz, Thomas S. 1970. *The Manufacture of Madness: A Comparative Study of the Inquisition and the Mental Health Movement*. New York: Harper and Row.

Szasz, Thomas S. 2007. *The Medicalization of Everyday Life: Selected Essays*. Syracuse, NY: Syracuse University Press.

Taber, Merlin, Herbert C. Quay, Harold Mark, and Vicki Nealey. 1969. "Disease Ideology and Mental Health Research." *Social Problems* 16: 349–57.

Tiefer, Leonore. 1986. "In Pursuit of the Perfect Penis: The Medicalization of Male Sexuality." *American Behavioral Scientist* 29: 579–99.

Tiefer, Leonore. 1994. "The Medicalization of Impotence: Normalizing Phallocentricism." *Gender and Society* 8: 363–77.

Timmermans, Stefan and Steven Haas. 2008. "Towards a Sociology of Disease." *Sociology of Health and Illness* 30: 659–76.

Tone, Andrea. 2001. *Devices and Desires: A History of Contraceptives in America*. New York: Hill and Wang.

Tone, Andrea. 2008. *The Age of Anxiety: A History of America's Turbulent Affair with Tranquilizers*. New York: Basic Books.

Tournier, Robert E. 1985. "The Medicalization of Alcoholism: Discontinuities in Ideologies of Deviance." *Journal of Drug Issues* 15(1): 39–49.

Treichler, Paula A. 1990. "Feminism, Medicine, and the Meaning of Childbirth." Pp. 113–38 in M. Jacobus, E. F. Keller, and S. Shuttleworth (eds.), *Body/Politics: Women and the Discourses of Science*. New York: Routledge.

Trice, Harrison M. and Paul Michael Roman. 1970. "Delabeling, Relabeling, and Alcoholics Anonymous." *Social Problems* 17: 538–46.

Turner, Bryan S. 2004. *The New Medical Sociology: Social Forms of Health and Illness*. New York: W.W. Norton.

Valenstein, Elliot S. 1998. *Blaming the Brain: The Truth about Drugs and Mental Health*. New York: Free Press.

Waitzkin, Howard and Barbara Waterman. 1974. *Exploitation of Illness in Capitalist Society*. Indianapolis: Bobbs-Merrill.

Watkins, Elizabeth Siegel. 2007a. "The Medicalisation of Male Menopause in America." *Social History of Medicine* 20: 369–88.

Watkins, Elizabeth Siegel. 2007b. *The Estrogen Elixir: A History of Hormone Replacement Therapy in America*. Baltimore: Johns Hopkins University Press.

Weinberg, Darin. 2005. *Of Others Inside: Insanity, Addiction, and Belonging in America*. Philadelphia: Temple University Press.

Wertz, Richard W. and Dorothy C. Wertz. 1989. *Lying-In: A History of Childbirth in America*, expanded edition. New Haven, CT: Yale University Press.

Williams, Simon J. 2001. "Sociological Imperialism and the Profession of Medicine Revisited: Where Are We Now?" *Sociology of Health and Illness* 23: 135–58.

Williams, Simon J. and Michael Calnan. 1996. "The 'Limits' of Medicalization? Modern Medicine and the Lay Populace in 'Late' Modernity." *Social Science and Medicine* 42: 1609–20.

Williams, Simon J., Clive Seale, Sharon Boden, and Pam Lowe. 2008. "Waking Up to Sleepiness: Modafinil, the Media and the Pharmaceuticalisation of Everyday/Night Life." *Sociology of Health and Illness* 30: 839–55.

Wolpe, Paul Root. 2002. "Treatment, Enhancement, and the Ethics of Neurotherapeutics." *Brain and Cognition* 50: 387–95.

Wootton, Barbara. 1956. "Sickness or Sin?" *The Twentieth Century* 159 (May): 433–42.

Wootton, Barbara. 1959. *Social Science and Social Pathology*. London: Allen and Unwin.

Young, Allan. 1995. *The Harmony of Illusions: Inventing Post-Traumatic Stress Disorder*. Princeton, NJ: Princeton University Press.

Zola, Irving Kenneth. 1972. "Medicine as an Institution of Social Control." *Sociological Review* 20: 487–504.

Zola, Irving Kenneth. 1975. "In the Name of Health and Illness: On Some Socio-Political Consequences of Medical Influence." *Social Science and Medicine* 9: 83–7.

11

Stress

William R. Avison and Stephanie S. Thomas

At some point, almost every person has felt overwhelmed by the demands of life. It is not uncommon for our family members, our friends, our co-workers, or other acquaintances to tell us that they are "stressed out." Indeed, stress has become part of the public lexicon concerning health and illness. Social scientists have played a significant role in identifying how various sources of stress manifest themselves as symptoms of mental or physical illness, disorder, or distress. Sociologists, in particular, have had a profound influence on the study of stress and illness.

In this chapter, we briefly review the historical antecedents of sociological research on stress and health and the emergence of a body of scientific knowledge about stress. We then review the evolution of the stress process paradigm, arguably the most influential model for understanding social differentials in health and illness. We next examine some of the most important developments in stress research and conclude by identifying promising new directions in the sociological study of stress. Our intent is not to present a comprehensive review of the literature, but rather to highlight research that is illustrative of the issues and ideas that we discuss.

Historical Background

The emergence of interest in life stress among social scientists is typically traced back to the early work of Hans Selye (1936) and W. B. Cannon (1932). In a series of experimental studies with laboratory animals, these scientists examined physiological responses to a controlled array of stressful circumstances. Selye's (1956) model of stress incorporated four components: (1) stressors in the form of electric shock or noise; (2) factors that altered or conditioned the impact of the stressor on the organism; (3) an adaptation process; and (4) responses to the stressor.

Behavioral scientists soon became interested in this research and began to develop measures of stress that were applicable to humans. Perhaps the best known example of this attempt to operationally define human stress is Holmes and Rahe's (1967) Schedule of Recent Experiences (SRE) and Social Readjustment Rating Scale (SRRS).

They asked a sample of respondents to rate the amount of life change that could be expected from the experience of 43 different life events. A life change score could then be computed for any individual who completed this inventory. So began the systematic study of stressful life events. In short order, psychologists, psychiatrists, epidemiologists, and sociologists produced a substantial body of research on the association between stressful life experience and a variety of health outcomes.

By the early 1980s, more than 16 different life events inventories had been developed (Zimmerman 1983) and over 15 reviews of the literature on measures of stressful life events had been published (Turner and Avison 1992). Despite differences in the contents of these inventories and in the mental health outcome assessed, there was consensus that life events were associated significantly with psychological disorder and distress. However, as Rabkin and Struening (1976) noted, the magnitude of this association was relatively modest. Explanations of this weak association tended to focus on problems of measuring life events, including problems of recall, content sampling, and intra- and inter-event variability (Thoits 1983).

Over time, there emerged two distinctive approaches to the measurement of stressful life events. One approach focused on inventories or life events checklists that were used in survey research in which respondents reported events that they had experienced over a specified period of time (typically, 12 months). Depending on the inventory, various probe questions allowed for the collection of additional information about each event (see Dohrenwend 2006; Turner and Wheaton 1995, for extensive reviews). Such checklist methods have been by far the more commonly used approaches in the study of stress and mental health, especially among North American researchers.

A second approach, developed by George Brown and his colleagues, focuses less on respondents' self-reports of stressful life events and more on the contextual meaning of life stress as assessed by the investigator. This approach is rooted in the Weberian concept of *Verstehen*, or understanding. The approach involves the generation of a consensus judgment among a team of researchers who consider the social context in which an event occurs and its likely meaning for the person who experienced that event (Brown 1989, 2002). Brown and Harris (1978, 1989) have described the use of this Life Events and Difficulties Schedule in a number of significant studies of physical and mental health. Variations on this approach have also been developed by Wethington, Brown, and Kessler (1997).

These two approaches to the study of stress set in motion a broad-ranging investigation of the impact of stressful life events on the psychological well-being of individuals. Sociologists, psychologists, epidemiologists, and psychiatrists all contributed importantly to the development of more sophisticated measures of stressful life experience and to a better understanding of the nature of the association between stress and health.

THE STRESS PROCESS

Although the study of stressful life events and their impact on health grew quickly in the 1970s and 1980s, it could be argued that, with a few notable exceptions, much of this work was relatively atheoretical. Bruce and Barbara Dohrenwend

(1981) provided a very useful conceptual model that advanced thinking about the effects of stressful life events on health. They proposed that life stress processes encompassed three components: recent life events, the ongoing situation, and personal dispositions. They argued that life events characterized by fateful loss (such as death of a loved one), those that are physically exhausting (such as illness or injury), and those that disrupt social support (such as divorce or job loss) constituted a "pathogenic triad" of particularly salient stressors.

During this same time period, other researchers developed conceptualizations of the ways in which stressful life experiences translated into symptoms of mental disorders. Brown and Harris (1978) emphasized the social context and ongoing difficulties that seemed to exacerbate the effects of stressful events on people's lives. Pearlin and Lieberman (1979) described role strains experienced by individuals as part of their everyday lives and how these contributed to psychological distress. In psychology, Lazarus (1966) focused on stress and coping mechanisms.

In the sociological study of stress, these ideas culminated in the stress process paradigm. Pearlin and colleagues' (1981) classic article on the stress process described a conceptual model that has continued to stimulate sociological research for over 25 years. The introductory paragraph of this article provides the essence of the stress process:

> The process of social stress can be seen as combining three major conceptual domains: the sources of stress, the mediators of stress, and the manifestations of stress. Each of these extended domains subsumes a variety of subparts that have been intensively studied in recent years. Thus, in the search for sources of stress, considerable interest has been directed to life events and to chronic life strains, especially the former; in work concerned with conditions capable of mediating the impact of stressful circumstances, coping and social supports have had a rather dramatic rise to prominence; and as for stress and its symptomatic manifestations, the expanding volume of research ranges from the microbiological substrates of stress to its overt emotional and behavioural expressions. (p. 337)

In a subsequent series of articles, Pearlin (1989, 1999) further elaborated the stress process to consider explicitly the social context in which the stress process occurs and to incorporate other features into the model. For Pearlin, the stress process is built upon three important assumptions. First, the process is a dense causal web that is dynamic in nature. Changes in one set of factors produce changes in others. Second, social stress is typical of ordinary life. The experience of stress is by no means unusual or abnormal. As Pearlin notes, this is a feature that is consistent with Durkheim's view of suicide as the result of the nature of social attachments or Merton's (1938) idea that anomie is a normative consequence of the disjunction between aspirations and access to opportunities. Third, it is assumed that the origins of stress are in the social world. This directs sociological stress researchers toward more proximal than distal sources of social stress and to a greater emphasis on social context than on history or biology.

With these assumptions in mind, Pearlin developed a model of the stress process containing four major components. *Sources of stress* include stressful life events as well as other dimensions of stressful experience including role-related strains, daily hassles, and life traumas. These sources of stress are potentially interactive in their effects on health outcomes. Indeed, many stress researchers (Brown and Harris 1978; Paykel 1978; Pearlin et al. 1981) argued that life events can intensify existing strains and vice versa. Moreover, stressful life experiences can create new role strains.

Manifestations of stress include an array of possible health outcomes. Sociologists have tended to focus on symptoms of mental illness or measures of psychological distress. These measures typically include symptoms of depressive illness; however, some sociologists have examined the effects of stressors on diagnosable disorders (Avison 2001; Brown and Harris 1978; Turner, Wheaton, and Lloyd 1995) and others have extended the study of stress to include alcohol consumption (Aneshensel, Rutter, and Lachenbruch 1991) and physical illness (Brown and Harris 1989).

The third component of the stress process model, *mediators of stress*, refers to a broad range of factors including social support, psychosocial resources such as mastery, self-esteem, mattering, interpersonal dependency, and coping strategies. These mediators are hypothesized to function as pathways that connect exposure to stress to its manifestations. So, for example, individuals exposed to stress experience the erosion of their sense of control over their lives. In turn, this decline in mastery manifests itself in symptoms of distress or depression. It has also been hypothesized that these factors sometimes buffer or moderate the effects of stressors on outcomes.

The interplay among sources of stress, mediators of stress, and outcomes all occurs in a social context that is defined by the social and economic statuses and roles that individuals occupy. A simplified version of the stress process is depicted in Figure 11.1. For Pearlin, the sociological study of stress is distinguished by the attention it places on the influences of statuses and roles in systems of social inequality. An individual's position in the structure of society affects his/her health indirectly through exposure to stressors and mediating resources.

Pearlin's emphasis on the social context in which the stress process operates rapidly became one of the dominant perspectives in the sociology of health and illness. It was apparent to researchers that this theoretical model had the potential to explain social patterns of health and illness. The stress process model stimulated a vast body of research literature on the impact of social and economic factors on physical and mental health problems. In general, these studies have demonstrated that individuals' social locations in society, in terms of their social statuses and social roles, have important implications for both the kinds and levels of stressors to which they are exposed. Indeed, one of the most important contributions of the sociology of mental health has been to demonstrate conclusively that stressors are not experienced randomly by individuals but, rather, that there is a social distribution of stressors.

MAJOR DEVELOPMENTS IN RESEARCH ON THE STRESS PROCESS

The stress process model provided a theoretical paradigm for the sociological study of stress. This motivated a number of sociologists to explore a wide range of issues

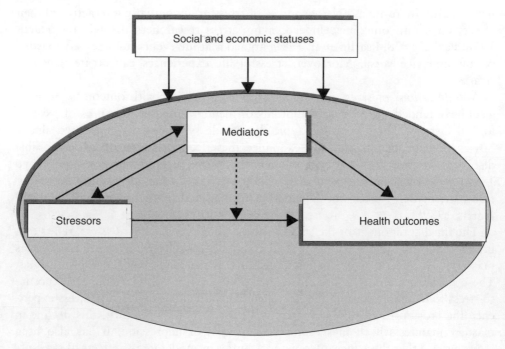

Figure 11.1 The stress process model.

concerning stress and health. These included both theoretical issues and method-ological problems.

The stress universe

Although much of the early work on stress and health focused on stressful life events, sociologists were always cognizant of the importance of more chronic kinds of stressors that were frequently experienced by individuals occupying various roles in society. For example, Pearlin (1983) provided a systematic description of the dimensions of role strain that might be incorporated into the sociological study of stress. He (Pearlin 1983: 5) argued that "as sociologists we are interested in ordinary people representative of major population groups rather than in exotic and extraor-dinary individuals, and to the extent that we are concerned with repeated and pat-terned behavior and experience rather than ephemeral, once-in-a-lifetime episodes, attention to social roles and the strains experienced within them serves us well."

Brown and Harris (1978) also recognized that some stressors are "ongoing dif-ficulties" and that such adversities had the potential to contribute to depression among individuals. They demonstrated that chronic strains such as a partner's drinking problem or prolonged stays in substandard housing had effects on mental health problems independent of life events.

Other researchers recognized that the contents of life events checklists might include ongoing, chronic stressors as well as eventful experiences. Avison and Turner (1988) showed that many items on life events checklists could be separated into discrete, eventful stressors and more chronic stressors.

In her review of stress research, Aneshensel (1992) drew attention to the distinction between random and systemic stressors. The former are stressors that occur with similar probabilities across different social groups; the latter are experiences that are integrally related to individuals' locations in the social structure. In Aneshensel's formulation, systemic stressors are directly relevant to understanding social differences in rates of mental disorder or levels of psychological distress. Random stressors contribute to the overall likelihood of disorder or distress but cannot account for group differentials.

Many of these considerations led Wheaton (1994) to argue for much more elaborate inventories of stressful experience. His concept of a *stress universe* specified the need to measure stressful experience in a more comprehensive manner than ever before. For Wheaton, the stress universe included not only stressful life events, chronic role strains, and ongoing difficulties, but also the experiences of sudden traumas, daily hassles, and ambient stressors in the social environment.

With measures derived from this conceptualization, Turner, Wheaton, and Lloyd (1995) established the utility of a more comprehensive strategy for measuring stressful experience. Their findings from a large community study reveal that younger people are more exposed to a variety of stressors than are older respondents. They also find this pattern among women compared to men, unmarried compared to married people, and individuals in lower compared to higher socioeconomic status positions in society. In their view, this clearly indicates that stressors are not experienced randomly in the population. Quite the contrary, they assert that their results reveal that a social distribution of stressors is characterized by greater exposure among members of disadvantaged social groups. Moreover, with this more comprehensive estimate of stressful experience, they draw attention to the importance of stress exposure for understanding social group differences in psychological distress and depressive disorder.

In a subsequent paper, Turner and Avison (2003) demonstrate the "value added" of including measures of chronic strain, traumatic stress, and discrimination as well as stressful life events when attempting to account for differences in psychological distress by race/ethnicity, social class, and gender. Their results reveal that the assessment of an array of measures that better represent the stress universe provides a more accurate estimate of exposure to stressors than does reliance solely on a life events checklist.

The growing awareness of the significance of multiple dimensions of stress for individuals' health has stimulated considerable research that seeks to expand our ability to measure the stress universe. The effects of adversities in childhood and adolescence on mental health problems in adulthood have attracted attention from a number of sociologists (Brown and Moran 1994; Davies, Avison, and McAlpine 1997; Harris, Brown, and Bifulco 1986; Kessler and Magee 1993; Turner and Lloyd 1995). This has generated a number of attempts to conceptualize and measure childhood adversities as a source of stress. For example, Turner and Lloyd (1995) use an inventory of traumatic experiences to test hypotheses about the significance of cumulative adversity. Brown and colleagues (2007) have examined childhood experiences of parental maltreatment and conclude that these early adversities are critical in the subsequent development of chronic depressive illness among women. They have developed a retrospective measure of childhood neglect and abuse to record these dimensions of stress.

Other sociologists have developed measures of perceived discrimination to add to inventories of stress. Kessler, Mickelson, and Williams (1999) have created measures of both lifetime discrimination and day-to-day perceived discrimination. These measures have effects on mental health that are comparable to other more commonly studied stressors.

Still other sociologists have drawn attention to more ambient stress that is characteristic of people's experiences in neighborhoods characterized by high rates of crime and social disorder. Aneshensel and Sucoff (1996) and Ross and Mirowsky (2001) independently document how the perception that one's neighborhood is dangerous is associated with higher levels of psychological distress. Other sociologists have shown how noxious occupational environments ("noisome occupations") contribute to mental illness (Link, Dohrenwend, and Skodol 1986).

With a steadily growing set of measures of stress, sociologists are now better able than ever to describe how exposure to stressors varies by individuals' location in the social structure. The mapping of these social distributions of stress is extremely important because it is now apparent that the association between stressful experience and mental health, when both are measured comprehensively, is more substantial than had been estimated previously.

The social distribution of stressors

With the emergence of the stress process model and the recognition of a multidimensional stress universe, sociologists have made substantial progress in documenting the ways in which social structure affects individuals' exposure to stressors. In thinking about the social distribution of stressors, social scientists have focused primarily on three major environmental determinants: social statuses, social roles, and the ambient environment. Most formulations of the stress process model take the view that individuals' locations in the structure of society place them at greater or lesser risk of encountering stressors. These locations are defined by the various statuses that individuals hold and by the social roles they occupy. Additionally, there are more ambient characteristics of the social environment that are not specific to statuses or roles but which may generate stressful experiences for individuals.

In the literature, individuals' positions in the structure of society are often defined by a number of status characteristics: age, gender, marital status, race/ethnicity, employment status, and socioeconomic status. Each of these social factors is associated with different levels of exposure to stressors.

There appears to be substantial agreement among researchers that exposure to stressful experiences declines with *age*. Whether the stressors in question are life events or chronic role strains, younger people report significantly more stress than do the elderly. Moreover, economic hardship tends to decline with age as does marital conflict among marriages that stay intact. Despite these findings, it is not yet clear whether the impact of age on exposure to stressors is a function of maturation processes, birth cohort or generational effects, or life-cycle processes (Mirowsky and Ross 1992).

Studies of *gender* differences in exposure to stressors have generated inconsistent findings. Some research concludes that women experience more stressful life events than men while other research finds no differences. Turner and Avison (2003) have conducted one of the more comprehensive studies of gender exposure to various dimensions of stress. Women report more stressful life events than men, but they experience fewer lifetime traumatic events and less discrimination stress. Women and men do not differ in their exposure to chronic stressors. When these various dimensions of stress are considered cumulatively, they find that men experience greater exposure compared to women, but this difference is relatively small. Turner and Avison (2003) conclude that these small gender variations in exposure to stressors are unlikely to account for gender differences in psychological distress, a view shared by Meyer, Schwartz, and Frost (2008).

Although other researchers report that women are more exposed than men to chronic strains due to financial hardship, workplace difficulties, and role overload associated with parenting and work, these differences are difficult to separate from the gendered roles that women and men play in the workplace and in the household division of labor. Indeed, one of the lessons of stress research in the sociology of mental health is that gender conditions the effects of a variety of roles and statuses on the exposure to stress.

One of the more robust findings in the study of social stress is the association between *marital status* and stress exposure. Married persons report considerably fewer stressors than either never married or formerly married individuals (Brown and Harris 1978; Turner et al. 1995). This pattern can be observed for chronic strains as well as for stressful life events. Unlike age and gender, however, the causal direction of the relationship between marital status and stressful experience is open to competing interpretations. A social selection interpretation suggests that people with high levels of stress in their lives are less likely to marry or, if they do so, they are more likely to separate and divorce. A social causation interpretation suggests that persons who have never married and those who have separated or divorced are more likely to experience an array of life events and chronic strains than are the married.

Some longitudinal research indicates that divorce leads to elevated levels of depression (Wade and Pevalin 2004) and that this change is accounted for by a decline in living standard, economic difficulties, and a reduction in social support (Kitson and Holmes 1992; McLanahan 1983). Even if the end of a marriage provides some escape from a stressful situation, divorce is accompanied by life stress that has depressive consequences. Other studies also report significant increases in psychological distress among divorced persons over and above their pre-divorce levels, but find virtually no evidence that changes in financial stressors, changes in role demands, or changes in geographic location mediate the relationship between marital disruption and distress. These are reflective of longitudinal studies on marital disruption and remarriage insofar as they generate few consistent findings other than the observations that marital disruption is associated with elevated psychological distress and that remarriage results in only a partial reduction in this elevation (Umberson and Williams 1999; Williams 2003).

Studies of *racial and ethnic* variations in exposure to stressors are relatively recent in the literature. There is general agreement that experiences of discrimination constitute an important set of stressors for African Americans, Hispanic Americans, and American Indians. In addition, stressors arising out of the social disadvantages of these groups have also been observed. Among Asian Americans, the experience of discrimination and the stress of migration have also been noted as important threats to their mental health.

Turner and Avison (2003) have systematically examined differences between African Americans and Whites in the United States in exposure to stressors. Across five different dimensions (recent life events, chronic stressors, total lifetime major events, lifetime major discrimination, and daily discrimination), African Americans experience significantly more stress than do Whites. It is interesting to note, however, that these elevated levels of stressors among racial and ethnic minority members do not necessarily translate into higher rates of distress or disorder for all groups. In their review of this issue, Williams and Harris-Reid (1999) conclude that African Americans have lower prevalence rates of psychiatric disorders than do Whites. The data are inconsistent when comparing Whites with Hispanic Americans or Asian Americans. What little data exist about the epidemiology of mental health among American Indians suggest that their rates of disorder, especially depression and alcohol abuse, are elevated.

It is difficult to interpret the meaning of these findings. Lower rates of disorder in the face of elevated levels of distress suggest that some racial and ethnic groups may be less vulnerable than others to these stressors or that countervailing effects of psychosocial resources may reduce the impact of stressors on their mental health. Turner and Avison (2003) have suggested that African Americans may exhibit a response tendency in which they underreport infrequent or mild experiences of distress, thus leading to an underestimation of their levels of distress. These researchers demonstrate that once this tendency is taken into account, there is clear evidence that African Americans' elevated exposure to stress manifests itself in significantly higher distress.

Research also leaves little doubt about the benefit of employment vis-à-vis stress exposure. Studies of individuals' job losses and their health problems have identified at least two major sources of environmental stressors that mediate this relationship (Kessler, House, and Turner 1987; Voydanoff 1990). Some researchers have shown that job loss and unemployment create financial strains that lead to mental health problems. Others have examined the mediating role of marital and family conflict. These studies report that unemployment leads to increasing conflicts between the unemployed worker and other family members. Avison (2001) has suggested that the elevated levels of distress observed among women whose husbands are experiencing job-related stress may be consistent with the "costs of caring" hypothesis (Kessler and McLeod 1984; Turner and Avison 1989).

Although there is general agreement that *socioeconomic status* (SES) and mental illness are inversely correlated and that exposure to stressors is a major determinant of mental health problems, there has been surprisingly little consensus among researchers about the SES–stress relationship. Whether SES is measured by some combination of education and income or by occupational prestige among those with jobs, contradictory results emerge. These inconsistent findings have led some researchers (McLeod and Nonnemaker 1999) to argue that it is not stress exposure that produces higher rates of mental illness among individuals from lower SES circumstances. Rather, they suggest that the impact of stressors on mental illness is more substantial among low SES than high SES individuals. In other words, they argue that lower-class individuals are differentially vulnerable to stressors. This issue of differences in exposure and vulnerability is addressed later; nevertheless, it seems clear that the debate over the influence of socioeconomic status has not been resolved. More recent studies suggest that when stressors are comprehensively measured, there is a significant social class gradient in exposure to stress.

Some of the most compelling evidence of the effects of economic hardship on marital relationships has been presented in studies of families during the Great Depression of the 1930s. This work clearly indicates that economic difficulties increase marital tensions in most families, and especially in those that were most vulnerable prior to the economic hardship (Elder and Liker 1982). Similar findings have been reported in studies of families whose lives have been affected by the farm crises of the 1980s in the Midwestern United States (Conger and Elder 1994).

A central focus of much research on the stress process has been on the ways in which the social roles that individuals occupy expose them to stressors. Pearlin (1983) has described these role strains in rich detail. For Pearlin, several types of stress may arise from role occupancy: (1) excessive demands of certain roles; (2) inequities in rewards; (3) the failure of reciprocity in roles; (4) role conflict; (5) role captivity; and (6) role restructuring. These various types of role strain are important sources of stress that may manifest themselves in symptoms of distress or disorder. Recent research on the family and mental health has focused on family structure in terms of the intersection of marital status and parenthood. In this context, there has been intense interest in the impact of single parenthood on symptoms of distress. Results consistently show higher levels of distress among single compared to married mothers (Avison, Ali, and Walters 2007). These studies of single parenthood clearly reveal that family structure and the roles imbedded in that structure are important determinants of women's mental health.

Research indicates that separation and divorce trigger chronic stressors such as income reduction and housing relocation (Ali and Avison 1997). In addition, the divorced experienced more life events than the married, particularly negative events involving loss. When children are involved, there may be additional strains associated with separation or divorce. The custodial parent, usually the mother, assumes many household, financial, and emotional responsibilities previously shared by two parents.

In addition to examining how differences in employment or work status influence exposure to stressors and subsequent mental health outcomes, social scientists have become aware of the importance of understanding how experiences in the work role are related to stress and health. Despite the observation that being employed generally has positive psychosocial consequences for individuals, not all employment circumstances are the same. Indeed, there are important variations in the stressors associated with any particular work situation. Work exposes individuals to various kinds of stressful experiences and provides different kinds of rewards for different people – financial rewards, self-esteem, a sense of control over one's life, and so on. It seems, then, that the net effect of paid employment for any individual will depend on the balance of these costs and benefits.

Recent contributions to the study of work and mental health have provided some useful models for this kind of research. In her comprehensive review of the literature on the interplay between work and family, Menaghan (1994) demonstrated clearly that work-related stressors are importantly associated with the mental health of family members. Other researchers have convincingly documented how role over-load and the sense of personal power have important implications for the effects of women's employment on their mental health (Lennon and Rosenfield 1992; Rosen-field 1989). Some investigations have shown how job characteristics such as full-time versus part-time work and substantive complexity have significant effects on mental health.

Research suggests a number of ways in which work and family roles interact in their effects upon women's psychological distress and depression. These studies highlight the importance of considering both family stressors to which women are exposed and work-related stress.

Relatively few studies have examined how single parenthood and paid employ-ment interact in their impact on mental health problems. Those studies that have investigated this issue conclude that differences between single-parent families and two-parent families in role obligations and opportunities may have significant effects on the balance between work and family responsibilities (Ali and Avison 1997). For married mothers, paid employment may be more easily integrated into daily family life. The presence of a spouse provides the opportunity to share some of the child care responsibilities. Alternatively, dual-income families have more funds for outside child care or paid assistance in the home.

Employment for single-parent mothers may represent more of a pressing respon-sibility than an opportunity for achievement and development. While income from employment may address a number of financial burdens of single-parent mothers, it nevertheless is the case that most single-parent families live in poverty or near poverty. In such circumstances, paid employment may alleviate some of the most pressing financial strains but other strains persist. Moreover, when single-parent mothers obtain employment, it is common for them to also bear continued sole responsibility for the care and nurturance of their children. Such dual demands may generate a cost to employment – role overload.

Under these circumstances, it seems probable that fewer psychosocial rewards associated with employment (greater self-esteem, self-efficacy, or social support) will accrue to single-parent mothers. This is all the more likely to be the case because single parents may be constrained to select jobs that are not their first choice but which are near their homes and have hours of work that fit with their children's schedules or with the availability of child care.

As we have noted, not all stressors are associated with statuses and roles. Ambient strains that are not attributable to a specific role but, rather, are diffuse in nature have a variety of sources. Some studies have demonstrated how ambient strains associated with the neighborhoods in which adolescents live magnify the impact of other stressors on their mental health (Ross and Mirowsky 2001). Others make the same point with respect to the ambient effect of economic environments.

For sociologists, there are at least two implications of documenting social pat-terns of exposure to stressors. First, these patterns remind us that stress arises from the experience of ordinary life. As Aneshensel (1992) states:

> Chance adversity intrudes on the lives of most persons, but stress also arises as a pre-
> dictable outcome of ordinary social organization. The psychiatric view of disorder as
> abnormal generates an implicit assumption that the social antecedents of disorder are

also abnormal. This orientation contrasts sharply with Merton's (1938) theoretical account of anomie and nonconforming behavior; social orders permitting normal emotional functioning also generate circumstances in which emotional disorder constitutes a normal or predictable response. The occurrence of social stress, therefore, can be seen as an inevitable consequence of social organization. (p. 33)

Second, this social distribution of stress and its consequences for health remind us of C. Wright Mills' (1959) well-known assertion that the appropriate study of private problems (such as mental health and illness) is the study of public problems (such as social inequality and disadvantage).

Differential exposure and differential vulnerability to stress

For sociologists who work within the parameters of the stress process model, a central goal has been to determine whether the social distribution of stress can assist in explaining the social pattern of psychological distress and mental illness. Substantial efforts have concentrated on the mechanisms or processes that link the social environment with differences in emotional or psychological distress. A major theme that emerged from these investigations concerns the importance of stressors as an explanation for these observed social differences in mental health outcomes.

Early work in this area argued that women (Gove 1978), the unmarried (Gove 1972; Gove and Tudor 1973), and the socioeconomically disadvantaged (Dohrenwend 1973; Dohrenwend and Dohrenwend 1969; Myers, Lindenthal, and Pepper 1975) were more exposed to socially induced stressors and, accordingly, were more likely to suffer from the distressful consequences of this differential exposure. However, initial attempts to test this differential exposure hypothesis largely failed to provide compelling empirical support. In reviewing the research contrary to this explanation, Kessler (1979a) argued that

Differential exposure to life stresses cannot, in itself, account for the commonly observed relationships between social status and psychological distress. We simply find too many psychologically healthy people who have suffered extreme life crises, and too many psychologically distressed people who have experienced only their normal share of life problems, to claim otherwise. (p. 101)

In the mid-1970s and early 1980s, attention shifted to explanations of social differences in mental health outcomes that emphasized the differential vulnerability of specific social groups to stressful experience. The first explicit statement of this differential vulnerability hypothesis appears to have been made by Kessler (1979a, 1979b), although he clearly acknowledges the earlier work of other researchers. Indeed, the idea that individuals occupying certain social statuses might be more likely to suffer from the experience of stress can be found in Bruce and Barbara Dohrenwend's (1974) and George Brown's (1974) discussions of substantial variations in mental health outcomes among individuals experiencing the same stressful event.

With this theoretical and empirical foundation, Kessler (1979a) specified a model for examining the distressful consequences of stressful experience and presented an

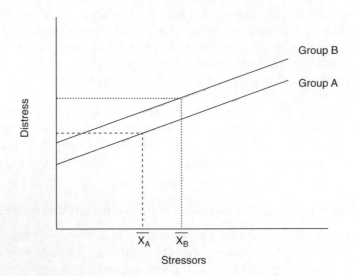

Figure 11.2 Differential exposure to stressors.

analytic strategy for estimating the relative impact of both exposure and vulnerability across social groups. In a subsequent article, he then presented preliminary evidence in support of the differential vulnerability hypothesis to account for variations in emotional distress by gender, marital status, and social class (Kessler 1979b).

Following the publication of these two articles, research on differential vulnerability to social stressors became a growth industry in the sociology of mental health (for reviews, cf. Aneshensel 1992; Aneshensel et al. 1991; Kessler, Price, and Wortman 1985). Given the substantial efforts that were expended in testing this hypothesis, it seems appropriate to examine critically the impact that this perspective has had on our understanding of social patterns of distress.

In his original formulation, Kessler (1979a) argued that mean differences in psychological distress could be decomposed into differences due to differential exposure to stress and differences due to differential vulnerability to stress. Figure 11.2 presents an example of a mean difference in distress that is solely due to differential exposure. As can be seen, the difference in mean distress scores for Group A and Group B is entirely a function of mean differences in exposure to stress. Small mean differences in stress exposure produce proportionately small mean differences in distress.

Kessler (1979a: 101) defined vulnerability as "the force with which a stress impacts on the distress of an individual." In other words, it is the rate at which stressors translate into distress. There appears to be consensus among stress researchers that vulnerability can be operationally defined as the slope of the regression of a measure of distress on a count of stressors. By extension, differential vulnerability refers to a difference in slopes between two contrast groups. The same mean difference between Group A and B in Figure 11.2 now translates into a much larger mean difference in mean distress because of the differences in slopes. This can be seen in Figure 11.3.

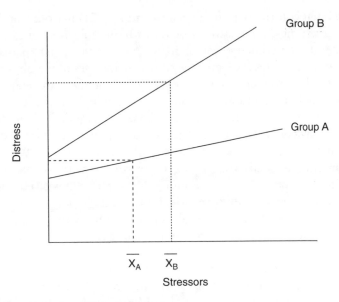

Figure 11.3 Differential vulnerability to stressors.

There are two important points to be emphasized in considering this operational definition. First, vulnerability is a relational construct (Turner and Avison 1989). Vulnerability in stress research is a construct defined by the association between stress and a mental health outcome. That is, any difference between contrast groups in the rates at which stressors translate into distress is specific to both the measures of stressful experience and the dimensions of distressful consequences that are examined. It follows, then, that any estimate of differential vulnerability involving a specific dimension of stress and a particular mental health outcome cannot be safely generalized to other domains of stress or to other outcomes.

The work of Pearlin (1989), Wheaton (1994), Aneshensel, Rutter, and Lachenbruch (1991), Turner, Wheaton, and Lloyd (1995), and others has made this idea a central principle of stress theory. We now recognize the need to measure the stress universe. We now understand that a more comprehensive evaluation of the impact of stressors may require that we consider a variety of outcomes. Among the lessons learned from this research is that unmeasured differences between social groups in exposure to stress may mistakenly be attributed to differential vulnerability.

Second, vulnerability is an inferred property of the contrasted groups rather than a measured characteristic of individuals comprising these groups. In the research that has employed Kessler's model of vulnerability, group differences in regression slopes provide the basis for inferring that individuals are more or less susceptible to stressors. This observation is descriptively useful insofar as it may draw our attention to the types of stressors that are most influential in contributing to distress among various social groups. It is, however, inaccurate to contend that differential vulnerability *explains* social group differences in distress. Rather, variations between social groups in the rate at which stressors translate into distress provide clues about the types of social experiences that are most distressful in their consequences. To Kessler's credit, he argued that vulnerability differentials might be due to (1) biological influences that contribute to fragile constitutions, (2) environmental factors such as subjective meanings, the relative absence of buffering resources, or socialization experiences, and (3) methodological artifacts. Nevertheless, an explanation of these differential effects requires theoretically informed analyses of the objective character of these particular stressors, the contexts in which they are experienced, their meaning for individuals, and the responses of individuals to them.

These challenges to the concept of group-based differential vulnerability limit the utility of the concept for understanding socially patterned differences in mental health. The usefulness of this construct is further challenged by Wheaton's (1990) research that demonstrated how the impact of role transitions commonly believed to be ubiquitously stressful were conditioned by social contexts. He shows how the distressful consequences of divorce, job loss, widowhood, and other significant transitions vary substantially by social context prior to the transition. Wheaton (1990: 220) concludes that "the stress potential of an event is neither an inherent characteristic of the event nor a result of 'coping' strategies, but instead is a product of the social environment prior to the occurrence of the transition."

These complex patterns of responses to stress that Wheaton uncovered seem to challenge the possibility that differential vulnerability to stressors is broadly patterned by gender, race, or class. Rather, it is the exposure to stressors that may be broadly patterned. It seems likely that the response to stressors by individuals is conditioned more by their microsocial and interactional contexts than by the broader influences of gender, race, class, or other social status or role. Moreover, there is now compelling evidence from several different studies (Avison et al. 2007; Turner and Avison 2003; Turner et al. 1995) that when the stress universe is comprehensively measured, differential exposure to stress is a much more powerful explanation of group differences in mental health than is differential vulnerability or responsiveness to stress.

Recognizing the inherent limitations of the idea of group-based differential vulnerability appears to have left a void in sociological thinking about the consequences of stress. Although sociologists have challenged the concept of group-based differential vulnerability on both theoretical and empirical grounds, they seem to have been unable either to jettison the construct or to develop an alternative conceptualization of vulnerability. After all, the idea that there is individual variation in people's responses to stressful experience is still intuitively appealing. Indeed, we often observe how two people encountering the same stressful experience respond in different ways. It may be that stress researchers have been searching for variations in vulnerability in the wrong social locations with the wrong method.

The use of the term *vulnerability* by sociologists of mental health to refer to group differences in the nature of the stress–distress relationship has introduced conceptual confusion to the interdisciplinary study of stressors and adversities. Researchers in psychology and psychiatry have for decades reserved the term to refer to experiences, interactions, or processes that exacerbate the impact of adversity on outcome. The sociological construct of vulnerability simply refers to observed group differences in the nature of the stress–distress relationship.

Sociologists have tried to document variations between groups (gender, class, race, etc.) in the impact of stressors because the sociological perspective emphasizes the search for socially patterned differences. It may be, however, that individual variations in the impact of stressors are greater within than between groups for the reasons that Wheaton has described: the complexity of social context trumps social structure.

Mediators and moderators of the stress–distress relationship

As we indicated earlier, a central postulate of the stress process is the existence of factors that alter in some manner the impact of stressors on the expression of symptoms of illness or dysfunction. These factors either mediate the relationship between stress and illness or they moderate or buffer the impact of stressors on distress and disorder. In this context, social resources or social supports, coping resources or psychosocial resources, and coping responses or behaviors are three critical groups of mediating factors.

Several important reviews of the literature on social support have been published (e.g., Cohen and Wills 1985; House, Umberson, and Landis 1988; Lin, Dean, and Ensel 1986; Turner and Turner 1999). These reviews attest to the important role played by social support in the stress process. They have also drawn attention to the multidimensional nature of the construct, including considerations of the structure of social networks, the functions of social support, and an awareness of the distinctions between perceived and actual support.

Individuals' psychosocial resources constitute a second important domain of mediators and moderators in stress process formulations. Research has shown that self-efficacy and self-esteem are especially important psychosocial resources that affect the ways in which stressors manifest themselves as distress or disorder. Studies have demonstrated that personal constructs such as locus of control, mastery, helplessness, and fatalism have significant effects on individuals' mental health (Mirowsky and Ross 1990; Ross and Sastry 1999; Turner and Roszell 1994). Similarly, there is substantial research documenting the benefits of self-esteem to mental health (Avison and McAlpine 1992; Rosenberg, Schooler, and Schoenbach 1989; Thoits 1999; Turner, Lloyd, and Roszell, 1999; Turner and Roszell 1994).

Third, variations in coping abilities and differences in the use of specific coping strategies are also central elements of stress process models. Early work on coping behaviors by Lazarus (1966) and Pearlin and Schooler (1978) stimulated interest among stress researchers. Subsequent research has provided significant insights into the ways in which situational contexts and cognitive appraisals influence the choice of coping responses by individuals who experience stressful circumstances (Eckenrode 1991; Menaghan 1983; Moos 1986). Sociologists seem to have abandoned the study of coping; however, Thoits (2006) recently called for a re-examination of the role of this construct in the stress process.

Despite the substantial body of theory and empirical research on the role of social support and personal resource variables in the stress process, there remains some conceptual vagueness about the mediating and moderating roles of constructs such as mastery, social support, or self-esteem. Part of this difficulty seems to emerge from the recognition that these resources may have multiple functions in the stress paradigm.

Wheaton (1985) has specified various models of stress buffering and stress mediation that reflect these multiple functions. He describes the potential roles that personal or coping resources such as mastery or social support might play in the stress process and specifies quantitative methods for testing these various effects. This provides a clear theoretical and methodological distinction between stress mediation and stress buffering.

Wheaton argues that there are two potential models of the stress-buffering functions of resources such as personal control. The first is perhaps the best known model in which the resource moderates the impact of stress on distress: the impact of stress on distress declines as levels of psychosocial resources increase. Empirically, this is equivalent to testing for the statistical interaction of the psychosocial resource and stress on distress. For most stress process researchers, this is the classic *interactive buffering effect*.

Another type of buffering effect occurs when a resource intervenes between stress and distress. Exposure to stressors results in an increase in the psychosocial resource that, in turn, results in a decline in distress. Presumably, stressful experiences mobilize resources that reduce distress. Conceptually, this *additive stress buffering* seems more likely to occur in the case of mobilizing social support or energizing one's coping efforts.

Wheaton also specifies three other models that depict personal resources either as mediators or as deterrent effects. The first model portrays these resources as a factor that intervenes between exposure to stressors and ensuing distress. In this instance, however, increased exposure to stressors is associated with an erosion of personal resources that manifests itself in increased psychological distress. This is the classic example of a personal resource operating as a *mediator variable*. A second model portrays personal resources as variables that reduce individuals' exposure to stressors. Resources affect distress only indirectly by reducing stressful experience. Wheaton refers to this as a *stress deterrence* model. Finally, psychosocial resources or social support and stress each have independent effects on distress. In this case, the impact of resources on distress is unrelated to the level of stress exposure. As Wheaton notes, the effect of these resources on distress may counteract the effect of stress on distress. He suggests that this is an example of a *distress deterrence* model in which mastery may operate as a "generalized health-maintenance resource."

There are several advantages to thinking about the role of social support and psychosocial resources in the stress process in terms of these models. They alert sociologists to the many ways in which support and resources may influence the stress process. Second, the existence of multiple models opens up the possibility that personal resources operate along multiple pathways or channels. Third, by attending to the distinctions among buffering, mediating, and deterrent models, we can better understand the influential roles that these resources play in affecting individuals' mental health. Moreover, Wheaton's formulation is consistent with a point more recently made by Pearlin (1999) in his reappraisal of the stress process:

> There is nothing inherent about coping, social support, or mastery that destines them to be treated as moderating resources. Casting them as moderators is a conceptual strategy, not an empirical imperative. Indeed, the three resources could as plausibly be regarded as mediating conditions, where the effects of the other components of the stress process on outcomes are channeled through resources. Their treatment as media-

tors assumes that resources are not immutable but can be diminished (or replenished) by the social and economic statuses surrounding the stress process and by the ensuing stressors. (pp. 405–6)

The volume of sociological research on the role of social support appears to have peaked in the late 1990s. Some recent work (Son, Lin, and George 2008) has focused on cross-cultural comparisons of the role of social support. Other work has examined the role of support as a vehicle that provides individuals with a sense of security (Ross and Mirowsky 2002). Some researchers have examined how social support in the workplace alleviates strain and contributes to job satisfaction (Chou and Robert 2008). Other investigations have focused on the mediating roles of social support in the context of the impact of functional disabilities on psychological distress (Yang 2006). Despite these contributions to the literature, contemporary sociological research on social support appears to have declined in recent years.

By contrast, sociological interest in the mediating and moderating effects of various psychosocial resources appears to have increased dramatically. Turner, Taylor, and Van Gundy (2004) have conducted a systematic assessment of the effects of a number of personal resources including mastery, self-esteem, assertion of autonomy, mattering, and emotional reliance. Thoits (2006) has raised several provocative ideas about the dynamics of personal agency in the context of social selection and social causation. These perspectives on the role of personal agency seem likely to generate continued research in this area of interest.

CONTEMPORARY DEVELOPMENTS IN RESEARCH ON THE STRESS PROCESS

The sociological study of stress continues to be a productive area of research. To some extent, the continuing interest in this area has been a function of at least three conceptual and methodological developments that have stimulated research. We briefly identify some of the most promising directions in which stress research appears to be headed.

Stress across the life course

Perhaps the most profound impact on the sociology of stress has been the synthesis of the life-course perspective with the stress process paradigm. Pearlin and Skaff (1996) argue that as people move through the life course, their lives are restructured so that their roles and statuses change, and, consequently, so too do the kinds of stressors to which they are exposed, and the levels and sources of social support to which they have access. This approach has been elaborated by George (1999, 2007), who argues that the persistent effects of early adversities such as childhood poverty, childhood abuse and neglect, and family violence impact subsequent mental health. She documents how the experience of mental illness early in one's life is associated with an array of negative social consequences that, in turn, generate recurrent episodes of illness. She also argues that an important characteristic of life-course research on mental health is its emphasis on linked lives, the notion that significant life experiences of one family member can have profound effects on other family members.

In their conceptual elaboration, Pearlin and colleagues (2005) identify a number of processes that have the potential to influence stress and health across the life course. These include the effects of economic strains and discriminatory experiences, stress proliferation, and the intersection of status attainment and stress exposure. These ideas will no doubt become the focus of future research in the sociology of stress.

One sign of the dramatic impact of taking a life-course perspective on the study of stress is the substantial increase in published research in this area. Indeed, Turner and Schieman's (2008a) edited collection of studies in this area reveals a wide range of topics, including stress and trajectories of mental health in adolescence, family and work transitions and mental health trajectories, as well as considerations of the life-course principle of linked lives and their effects on stress and mental health.

Contextual complexities

One of the continuing themes of stress research has been its appreciation of the social context in which stress is experienced. Wheaton (1990) has presented one of the most eloquent demonstrations of this in his studies of the ways in which social contexts condition the impact of various stressful life events on distress. He documents how the distressful consequences of events such as divorce depend upon whether this marked the end of a conflicted marriage or not. Similarly, he shows that the impact of job loss on distress is contingent on the perceived quality of the job.

Turner and colleagues (Reynolds and Turner 2008; Turner and Avison 1992) argue that the impact of life events and adversities is conditioned by the extent that individuals perceive these stressors to have been resolved. In this sense, the psycho social context of stress determines its impact.

Other researchers have pointed to the contextual significance of neighborhoods (Aneshensel and Sucoff 1996; Wheaton and Clarke 2003). These studies confirm that the ambient qualities of neighborhood life are important contexts for the experience of stress. Wheaton and Clarke further extend this by demonstrating that individuals' neighborhood experiences during their childhood have particularly enduring contextual effects.

Taken together, these various investigations confirm that the complexities of social experience need to be taken into account if sociologists are to understand the roles of stress in society. Social context exerts a profound effect on the stress process.

The continuing elaboration of the stress universe

Sociologists continue to think about aspects of everyday life that are experienced as stressful. We have already alluded to the work that has extended stress research into the study of chronic strains, adversities and traumas in childhood and adulthood, and perceived discrimination. It seems likely that there are other stressful experiences that can be incorporated into the stress paradigm that will enrich this perspective. For example, Evans-Campbell, Lincoln, and Takeuchi (2007) review the literature on the intergenerational transmission of trauma and its significance for mental health of the children of Holocaust survivors and the children of cultural genocide survivors. These "historical traumas" and their effects on mental health are as yet only partly understood.

In their study of people living with HIV, Wight and colleagues (2008) make a convincing case for treating future uncertainty as a stressor. They find that caregivers' uncertainty is not associated with their own depression but is correlated with depressive symptoms among the person living with HIV. This study demonstrates how life-course concepts (linked lives), social contexts, and the study of new types of stressors continue to make the stress process a fertile field of research.

Other sociologists have elaborated the stress universe by identifying different ways in which stressors are interrelated. Pearlin, Aneshensel, and LeBlanc (1997) describe the process of stress proliferation, the idea that a primary stressor creates or generates another, so-called secondary stressor. There are at least two contexts in which this occurs. From a life-course perspective, stress experienced by one individual may transfer or spill over to another. The second context is one in which one stressor sets in motion another stressor.

No doubt sociologists will continue to think about other sources of stress that are experienced in the social world. As the stress universe expands, future research will have to consider how these various stressors are connected to one another and how the stress process needs to be modified to take these new dimensions into account.

A CHALLENGE TO THE SOCIOLOGY OF STRESS

In 25 years, sociologists have discovered much about the stress process. The paradigm has been elaborated theoretically in a number of ways that has stimulated a rich body of research. This corpus of work draws attention to the possibility that different kinds of stressors have different kinds of consequences dependent upon individuals' locations in the social structure and their responses to stressful experience. While much has been accomplished in understanding individual responses to stress, the greater challenges are, first, to better map the complexities that condition the probabilities of exposure to various types of stressors and, second, to explore further how position in the social fabric of society affects individuals' experiences, perceptions, and evaluations of stressful experience and their consequences.

The challenge of mapping the complexities of stress exposure will require the continued elaboration of the stress model. What began as a parsimonious depiction of the effects of stress on individuals' well-being has grown into a sophisticated theoretical model with many conceptual additions. Nevertheless, the model remains clearly specified and, most important, capable of being tested empirically. Further specifications of the complexities of the stress process are likely to require creative research designs and state of the art methods. Turner and Schieman (2008b) describe some of these approaches.

The challenge of better understanding how the social fabric of society affects stress and its consequences seems deceptively simple. It seems to challenge sociologists to do what they already have done. It may be, however, that the influences of social statuses and roles and the contexts that these create are enormously complex. The sociology of stress will only meet this challenge if it incorporates ideas and methods that are available from other areas of the discipline.

It is fair to say that the sociology of stress has accomplished a great deal. Theoretically and empirically, much has been learned about stress and its manifestations. It is exciting to know that there is much more to be done.

References

Ali, Jennifer and William R. Avison. 1997. "Employment Transitions and Psychological Distress: The Contrasting Experiences of Single and Married Mothers." *Journal of Health and Social Behavior* 38: 345–62.

Aneshensel, Carol S. 1992. "Social Stress: Theory and Research." *Annual Review of Sociology* 18: 15–38.

Aneshensel, Carol S., Carolyn M. Rutter, and Peter A. Lachenbruch. 1991. "Competing Conceptual and Analytic Models: Social Structure, Stress, and Mental Health." *American Sociological Review* 56: 166–78.

Aneshensel, Carol S. and Clea A. Sucoff. 1996. "The Neighborhood Context of Adolescent Mental Health." *Journal of Health and Social Behavior* 37: 293–310.

Avison, William R. 2001. "Unemployment and Its Consequences for Mental Health." Pp. 177–200 in Victor W. Marshall, Walter Heinz, Helga Krueger, and Anil Verma (eds.), *Restructuring Work and the Life Course*. Toronto: University of Toronto Press.

Avison, William R., Jennifer Ali, and David Walters. 2007. "Family Structure, Stress, and Psychological Distress: A Demonstration of the Impact of Differential Exposure." *Journal of Health and Social Behavior* 48: 301–14.

Avison, William R. and Donna D. McAlpine. 1992. "Gender Differences in Symptoms and Depression among Adolescents." *Journal of Health and Social Behavior* 33: 77–96.

Avison, William R. and R. Jay Turner. 1988. "Stressful Life Events and Depressive Symptoms: Disaggregating the Effects of Acute Stressors and Chronic Strains." *Journal of Health and Social Behavior* 29: 253–64.

Brown, George W. 1974. "Meaning, Measurement, and Stress of Life Events." Pp. 217–44 in Barbara S. Dohrenwend and Bruce P. Dohrenwend (eds.), *Stressful Life Events: Their Nature and Effects*. New York: Wiley.

Brown, George W. 1989. "Life Events and Measurement." Pp. 3–48 in George W. Brown and Tirril O. Harris (eds.), *Life Events and Illness*. New York: Guilford Press.

Brown, George W. 2002. "Social Roles, Context and Evolution in the Origins of Depression." *Journal of Health and Social Behavior* 43: 255–76.

Brown, George W., Tom K. J. Craig, Tirril O. Harris, Rachel V. Handley, and Anita L. Harvey. 2007. "Development of a Retrospective Interview Measure of Parental Maltreatment Using the Childhood Experience of Care and Abuse (CECA) Instrument – A Life-Course Study of Adult Chronic Depression – 1." *Journal of Affective Disorders* 103: 205–15.

Brown, George W. and Tirrel O. Harris. 1978. *Social Origins of Depression*. New York: Free Press.

Brown, George W. and Tirrel O. Harris (eds.). 1989. *Life Events and Illness*. New York: Guilford Press.

Brown, George W. and Patricia M. Moran. 1994. "Clinical and Psychosocial Origins of Chronic Depressive Episodes. I: A Community Survey." *British Journal of Psychiatry* 165: 447–56.

Cannon, W. B. 1932. *The Wisdom of the Body*, 2nd edition. New York: Norton.

Chou, Rita Jing-Ann and Stephanie A. Robert. 2008. "Workplace Support, Role Overload, and Job Satisfaction of Direct Care Workers in Assisted Living." *Journal of Health and Social Behavior* 49: 208–22.

Cohen, Sheldon and Thomas A. Wills. 1985. "Stress, Social Support, and the Buffering Hypothesis." *Psychological Bulletin* 98: 310–57.

Conger, Rand D. and Glen H. Elder, Jr. 1994. *Families in Troubled Times*. Hawthorne, NY: Aldine de Gruyter.

Davies, Lorraine, William R. Avison, and Donna D. McAlpine. 1997. "Significant Life Experiences and Depression among Single and Married Mothers." *Journal of Marriage and the Family* 59: 294–308.

Dohrenwend, Barbara S. 1973. "Social Status and Stressful Life Events." *Journal of Personality and Social Psychology* 28: 225–35.

Dohrenwend, Bruce P. 2006. "Inventorying Stressful Life Events as Risk Factors for Psychopathology: Toward Resolution of the Problem of Intracategory Variability." *Psychological Bulletin* 132: 477–95.

Dohrenwend, Bruce P. and Barbara S. Dohrenwend. 1969. *Social Status and Psychological Disorder: A Causal Inquiry*. New York: Wiley.

Dohrenwend, Bruce P. and Barbara S. Dohrenwend. 1974. "Social and Cultural Influences on Psychopathology." *Annual Review of Psychology* 25: 417–52.

Dohrenwend, Bruce P. and Barbara S. Dohrenwend. 1981. "Socioenvironmental Factors, Stress, and Psychopathology. Part I: Quasi-Experimental Evidence on the Social Causation Social Selection Issue Posed by Class Differences." *American Journal of Community Psychology* 9: 129–46.

Eckenrode, John (ed.). 1991. *The Social Context of Coping*. New York: Plenum.

Elder, Glen H., Jr. and Jeffrey K. Liker. 1982. "Hard Times in Women's Lives: Historical Influences across Forty Years." *American Journal of Sociology* 88: 241–69.

Evans-Campbell, Teresa, Karen D. Lincoln, and David T. Takeuchi. 2007. "Race and Mental Health: Past Debates, New Opportunities." Pp. 169–89 in William R. Avison, Jane D. McLeod, and Bernice A. Pescosolido (eds.), *Mental Health, Social Mirror*. New York: Springer.

George, Linda K. 1999. "Life-Course Perspectives on Mental Health." Pp. 565–83 in Carol S. Aneshensel and Jo. C. Phelan (eds.), *Handbook of the Sociology of Mental Health*. New York: Kluwer Academic/Plenum.

George, Linda K. 2007. "Life Course Perspectives on Social Factors and Mental Illness." Pp. 191–218 in William R. Avison, Jane D. McLeod, and Bernice A. Pescosolido (eds.), *Mental Health, Social Mirror*. New York: Springer.

Gove, Walter R. 1972. "The Relationship Between Sex Roles, Marital Status, and Mental Illness." *Social Forces* 51: 33–44.

Gove, Walter R. 1978. "Sex Differences in Mental Illness among Adult Men and Women: Evaluation of Four Questions Raised Regarding Evidence on Higher Rates of Women." *Social Science and Medicine* 12: 187–98.

Gove, Walter R. and J. F. Tudor. 1973. "Adult Sex Roles and Mental Illness." *American Journal of Sociology* 78: 812–35.

Harris, Tirril O., George W. Brown, and Andrew Bifulco. 1986. "Loss of Parent in Childhood and Adult Psychiatric Disorder: Role of Lack of Adequate Parental Care." *Psychological Medicine* 16: 641–59.

Holmes, T. H. and R. H. Rahe. 1967. "The Social Readjustment Rating Scale." *Journal of Psychosomatic Research* 11: 213–18.

House, James S., Debra Umberson, and Karl R. Landis. 1988. "Structures and Processes of Social Support." *Annual Review of Sociology* 14: 293–318.

Kessler, Ronald C. 1979a. "A Strategy for Studying Differential Vulnerability to the Psychological Consequences of Stress." *Journal of Health and Social Behavior* 20: 100–8.

Kessler, Ronald C. 1979b. "Stress, Social Status, and Psychological Distress." *Journal of Health and Social Behavior* 20: 259–72.

Kessler, Ronald C., James S. House, and J. Blake Turner. 1987. "Unemployment and Health in a Community Sample." *Journal of Health and Social Behavior* 28: 51–9.

Kessler, Ronald C. and William J. Magee. 1993. "Childhood Adversities and Adult Depression: Basic Patterns of Association in a US National Survey." *Psychological Medicine* 23: 679–90.

Kessler, Ronald C. and Jane D. McLeod. 1984. "Sex Differences in Vulnerability to Undesirable Life Events." *American Sociological Review* 49: 620–31.

Kessler, Ronald C., Kristin D. Mickelson, and David R. Williams. 1999. "The Prevalence, Distribution, and Mental Health Correlates of Perceived Discrimination in the United States." *Journal of Health and Social Behavior* 40: 208–30.

Kessler, Ronald C., Richard H. Price, and Camille B. Wortman. 1985. "Social Factors in Psychopathology: Stress, Support, and Coping Processes." *Annual Review of Psychology* 36: 531–72.

Kitson, Gay C. and William M. Holmes. 1992. *Portrait of Divorce: Adjustment to Marital Breakdown*. New York: Guilford Press.

Lazarus, Richard S. 1966. *Psychological Stress and the Coping Process*. New York: McGraw-Hill.

Lennon, Mary Clare and Sarah Rosenfield. 1992. "Women and Mental Health: The Interaction of Work and Family Conditions." *Journal of Health and Social Behavior* 33: 316–27.

Lin, Nan, Alfred Dean, and Walter M. Ensel. 1986. *Social Support, Life Events, and Depression*. Orlando, FL: Academic Press.

Link, Bruce G., Bruce P. Dohrenwend, and Andrew E. Skodol. 1986. "Socio-Economic Status and Schizophrenia: Noisome Occupational Characteristics as a Risk Factor." *American Sociological Review* 51: 242–58.

McLanahan, Sara S. 1983. "Family Structure and Stress: A Longitudinal Comparison of Two-Parent and Female-Headed Families." *Journal of Marriage and the Family* 45: 347–57.

McLeod, Jane D. and James M. Nonnemaker. 1999. "Social Stratification and Inequality." Pp. 321–44 in Carol S. Aneshensel and Jo C. Phelan (eds.), *Handbook of the Sociology of Mental Health*. New York: Plenum.

Menaghan, Elizabeth G. 1983. "Individual Coping Efforts: Moderators of the Relationship between Life Stress and Mental Health Outcomes." Pp. 157–91 in Howard B. Kaplan (ed.), *Psychosocial Stress: Trends in Theory and Research*. New York: Academic Press.

Menaghan, Elizabeth G. 1994. "The Daily Grind: Work Stressors, Family Patterns, and Intergenerational Outcomes." Pp. 115–47 in William R. Avison and Ian H. Gotlib (eds.), *Stress and Mental Health: Contemporary Issues and Prospects for the Future*. New York: Plenum.

Merton, Robert K. 1938. "Social Structure and Anomie." *American Sociological Review* 3 (October): 672–82.

Meyer, Ilan H., Sharon Schwartz, and David M. Frost. 2008. "Social Patterning of Stress and Coping: Does Disadvantaged Social Status Confer More Stress and Fewer Coping Resources?" *Social Science and Medicine* 67: 368–79.

Mills, C. Wright. 1959. *The Sociological Imagination*. New York: Oxford University Press.

Mirowsky, John and Catherine E. Ross. 1990. "Control or Defense? Depression and the Sense of Control over Good and Bad Outcomes." *Journal of Health and Social Behavior* 31: 71–86.

Mirowsky, John and Catherine E. Ross. 1992. "Age and Depression." *Journal of Health and Social Behavior* 33: 187–205.

Moos, Richard H. 1986. *Coping with Life Crises*. New York: Plenum.

Myers, Jerome K., Jacob J. Lindenthal, and Max P. Pepper. 1975. "Life Events, Social Integration, and Psychiatric Symptomatology." *Journal of Health and Social Behavior* 16: 421–7.

Paykel, Eugene S. 1978. "Contribution of Life Events to Causation of Psychiatric Illness." *Psychological Medicine* 8: 245–53.

Pearlin, Leonard I. 1983. "Role Strains and Personal Stress." Pp. 3–32 in Howard B. Kaplan (ed.), *Psychosocial Stress: Trends in Theory and Research*. New York: Academic Press.

Pearlin, Leonard I. 1989. "The Sociological Study of Stress." *Journal of Health and Social Behavior* 30: 241–56.

Pearlin, Leonard I. 1999. "The Stress Concept Revisited: Reflections on Concepts and Their Interrelationships." Pp. 395–415 in Carol S. Aneshensel and Jo C. Phelan (eds.), *Handbook of the Sociology of Mental Health*. New York: Plenum.

Pearlin, Leonard I., Carol S. Aneshensel, and Allen J. LeBlanc. 1997. "The Forms and Mechanisms of Stress Proliferation: The Case of AIDS Caregivers." *Journal of Health and Social Behavior* 38: 223–36.

Pearlin, Leonard I. and Morton A. Lieberman. 1979. "Social Sources of Emotional Stress." Pp. 217–48 in Roberta Simmons (ed.), *Research in Community and Mental Health*, vol. 1. Greenwich, CT: JAI Press.

Pearlin, Leonard I., Morton A. Lieberman, Elizabeth G. Menaghan, and Joseph T. Mullan. 1981. "The Stress Process." *Journal of Health and Social Behavior* 22: 337–56.

Pearlin, Leonard I., Scott Schieman, Elena M. Fazio, and Stephen C. Meersman. 2005. "Stress, Health, and the Life Course: Some Conceptual Perspectives." *Journal of Health and Social Behavior* 46: 205–19.

Pearlin, Leonard I. and Carmi Schooler. 1978. "The Structure of Coping." *Journal of Health and Social Behavior* 19: 2–21.

Pearlin, Leonard I. and Marilyn McKean Skaff. 1996. "Stress and the Life Course: A Paradigmatic Alliance." *The Gerontologist* 36: 239–47.

Rabkin, Judith G. and Elmer L. Struening. 1976. "Life Events, Stress, and Illness." *Science* 194: 1013–20.

Reynolds, John R. and R. Jay Turner. 2008. "Major Life Events, Their Personal Meaning, Resolution, and Mental Health Significance." *Journal of Health and Social Behavior* 49: 223–37.

Rosenberg, Morris, Carmi Schooler, and Carrie Schoenbach. 1989. "Self-Esteem and Adolescent Problems: Modeling Reciprocal Effects." *American Sociological Review* 54: 1004–18.

Rosenfield, Sarah. 1989. "The Effect of Women's Employment: Personal Control and Sex Differences in Mental Health." *Journal of Health and Social Behavior* 30: 77–91.

Ross, Catherine E. and John Mirowsky. 2001. "Neighborhood Disadvantage, Disorder, and Health." *Journal of Health and Social Behavior* 42: 258–76.

Ross, Catherine E. and John Mirowsky. 2002. "Family Relationships, Social Support, and Subjective Life Expectancy." *Journal of Health and Social Behavior* 43: 469–89.

Ross, Catherine E. and Jay Sastry. 1999. "The Sense of Personal Control: Social-Structural Causes and Emotional Consequences." Pp. 360–94 in Carol S. Aneshensel and Jo C. Phelan (eds.), *Handbook of the Sociology of Mental Health*. New York: Plenum.

Selye, Hans. 1936. "A Syndrome Produced by Divers Nocuous Agents." *Nature* 138: 32.

Selye, Hans. 1956. *The Stress of Life*. New York: McGraw-Hill.

Son, Joonmo, Nan Lin, and Linda K. George. 2008. "Cross-National Comparison of Social Support Structures between Taiwan and the United States." *Journal of Health and Social Behavior* 49: 104–18.

Thoits, Peggy A. 1983. "Dimensions of Life Events That Influence Psychological Distress." Pp. 33–103 in Howard B. Kaplan (ed.), *Psychosocial Stress: Trends in Theory and Research*. New York: Academic Press.

Thoits, Peggy A. 1999. "Self, Identity, Stress, and Mental Health." Pp. 345–68 in Carol S. Aneshensel and Jo C. Phelan (eds.), *Handbook of the Sociology of Mental Health*. New York: Plenum.

Thoits, Peggy A. 2006. "Personal Agency in the Stress Process." *Journal of Health and Social Behavior* 47: 309–23.

Turner, Heather A. and Scott Schieman (eds.). 2008a. *Stress Processes across the Life Course*. New York: Elsevier.

Turner, Heather A. and Scott Schieman. 2008b. "Stress Processes across the Life Course: Introduction and Overview." Pp. 1–15 in Heather A. Turner and Scott Schieman (eds.), *Stress Processes across the Life Course*. New York: Elsevier.

Turner, R. Jay and William R. Avison. 1989. "Gender and Depression: Assessing Exposure and Vulnerability in a Chronically Strained Population." *Journal of Nervous and Mental Disease* 177: 433–55.

Turner, R. Jay and William R. Avison. 1992. "Innovations in the Measurement of Life Stress: Crisis Theory and the Significance of Event Resolution." *Journal of Health and Social Behavior* 33: 36–50.

Turner, R. Jay and William R. Avison. 2003. "Status Variations in Stress Exposure: Implications for the Interpretation of Research on Race, Socioeconomic Status, and Gender." *Journal of Health and Social Behavior* 44: 488–505.

Turner, R. Jay and Donald Lloyd. 1995. "Lifetime Traumas and Mental Health: The Significance of Cumulative Adversity." *Journal of Health and Social Behavior* 36: 360–76.

Turner, R. Jay, Donald A. Lloyd, and Patricia Roszell. 1999. "Personal Resources and the Social Distribution of Depression." *American Journal of Community Psychology* 27: 643–72.

Turner, R. Jay and Patricia Roszell. 1994. "Psychosocial Resources and the Stress Process." Pp. 179–210 in William R. Avison and Ian H. Gotlib (eds.), *Stress and Mental Health: Contemporary Issues and Prospects for the Future*. New York: Plenum.

Turner, R. Jay, John Taylor, and Karen Van Gundy. 2004. "Personal Resources and Depression in the Transition to Adulthood." *Journal of Health and Social Behavior* 45: 34–52.

Turner, R. Jay and J. Blake Turner. 1999. "Social Integration and Support." Pp. 301–19 in Carol S. Aneshensel and Jo. C. Phelan (eds.), *Handbook of the Sociology of Mental Health*. New York: Plenum.

Turner, R. Jay and Blair Wheaton. 1995. "Checklist Measures of Stressful Life Events." Pp. 29–58 in Lynn Gordon, Sheldon Cohen, and Ronald S. Kessler (eds.), *Measuring Stress: A Guide for Health and Social Scientists*. New York: Oxford University Press.

Turner, R. Jay, Blair Wheaton, and Donald A. Lloyd. 1995. "The Epidemiology of Social Stress." *American Sociological Review* 60: 104–25.

Umberson, Debra and Kristi Williams. 1999. "Family Status and Mental Health." Pp. 225–54 in Carol S. Aneshensel and Jo C. Phelan (eds.), *Handbook of the Sociology of Mental Health*. New York: Plenum.

Voydanoff, Patricia. 1990. "Economic Stress and Family Relations." *Journal of Marriage and the Family* 52: 1099–115.

Wade, Terrance J. and David J. Pevalin. 2004. "Marital Transitions and Health." *Journal of Health and Social Behavior* 45: 155–70.

Wethington, Elaine, George W. Brown, and Ronald C. Kessler. 1997. "Interview Measurement of Stressful Life Events." Pp. 59–79 in Sheldon Cohen et al. (eds.), *Measuring Stress: A Guide for Health and Social Scientists*. New York: Oxford University Press.

Wheaton, Blair. 1985. "Models for the Stress-Buffering Functions of Coping Resources." *Journal of Health and Social Behavior* 26: 352–65.

Wheaton, Blair. 1990. "Life Transitions, Role Histories, and Mental Health." *American Sociological Review* 55: 209–23.

Wheaton, Blair. 1994. "Sampling the Stress Universe." Pp. 77–114 in William R. Avison and Ian H. Gotlib (eds.), *Stress and Mental Health: Contemporary Issues and Prospects for the Future*. New York: Plenum.

Wheaton, Blair and Philippa Clarke. 2003. "Space Meets Time: Integrating Temporal and Contextual Influences on Mental Health in Early Adulthood." *American Sociological Review* 68: 680–706.

Wight, Richard G., Carol S. Aneshensel, Allen J. LeBlanc, and Kristin P. Beals. 2008. "Sharing an Uncertain Future: Improved Survival and Stress Proliferation among Persons with HIV and Their Caregivers." Pp. 369–97 in Heather A. Turner and Scott Schieman (eds.), *Stress Processes across the Life Course*. New York: Elsevier.

Williams, David R. and M. Harris-Reid. 1999. "Race and Mental Health: Emerging Patterns and Promising Approaches." Pp. 295–314 in Allan V. Horwitz and Teresa L. Scheid (eds.), *A Handbook for the Study of Mental Health: Social Contexts, Theories, and Systems*. Cambridge: Cambridge University Press.

Williams, Kristi. 2003. "Has the Future of Marriage Arrived? A Contemporary Examination of Gender, Marriage, and Psychological Well-Being." *Journal of Health and Social Behavior* 44: 470–87.

Yang, Yang. 2006. "How Does Functional Disability Affect Depressive Symptoms in Late Life? The Role of Perceived Social Support and Psychological Resources." *Journal of Health and Social Behavior* 47: 355–72.

Zimmerman, Mark. 1983. "Methodological Issues in the Assessment of Life Events: A Review of Issues and Research." *Clinical Psychology Review* 3: 339–70.

12

Stress in the Workplace

Johannes Siegrist

Medical sociology has traditionally been viewed as the scientific discipline that deals with two broad health-related areas. On the one hand, it is concerned with the sociological analysis of health care institutions, their professional groups and clients, as well as the larger socioeconomic and cultural frames of health care delivery. This field has been labeled "sociology of medicine." On the other hand, social determinants of health are the main focus of analysis where societal effects on the onset and course of diseases and on the promotion of health are explored ("sociology in medicine"; "sociology of health"). Although there are good reasons to criticize this taxonomy, it proves useful in supporting the development of cumulative knowledge within the broader field of sociological inquiry. This holds particularly true for scientific work on social determinants of health, where a growing body of theory-based internationally comparable knowledge has been produced in recent decades (Berkman and Kawachi 2000; Marmot and Wilkinson 2006). A significant part of this research is devoted to work and employment. In this chapter, using a sociological perspective, I provide an overview of currently available evidence on the health-related effects of work and employment. This overview is preceded by a discussion of the relevance of work in modern societies and its recent far-reaching changes due to technological and economic developments. In the final part of the chapter, future challenges for sociological research in this field and for policy measures based on available knowledge are addressed.

THE ROLE OF WORK IN SOCIETY: RECENT CHANGES

With the process of modernization of societies starting in Europe during the sixteenth and seventeenth centuries, the role of paid work in occupational or professional contexts became increasingly important (Weber 1958 [1904–5]). People's economic and social standing was largely based on their regular participation in the labor market, and individual work-related achievements were considered a crucial element in the formation of social identity and societal esteem. With the advent of the industrial and political revolutions in the late eighteenth and early nineteenth centuries, educational and occupational achievements became the main driving forces of social mobility. In fact, the "meritocratic triad" of education, occupation, and income was – and to some extent still is – a dominant feature of structuring social inequalities within modern societies. Waged work became a fundamental prerequisite for securing decent life chances that were independent of welfare support, and a prerequisite for developing people's options of individual autonomy and freedom. This development accompanied the industrialization of societies in the nineteenth and twentieth centuries, but was interrupted by brief periods of mass unemployment, in particular in the 1930s and in the early 1970s.

During the twentieth century, the nature of work underwent rather fundamental changes in economically advanced societies. Industrial mass production no longer dominates the labor market. This is due, in part, to technological progress, and in part to growth in the service sector. Many new jobs are confined to information processing, controlling, and coordination. Sedentary rather than physically strenuous work is becoming more and more dominant. Moreover, the traditional separation of the spheres of work and home is vanishing. Homework, telework, participation in virtual networks, and an unprecedented degree of flexibility in local and temporal work arrangements contribute to this process. Within organizations, flexible teams rather than fixed stable hierarchies are expanding, and traditional "life-long" occupational careers are increasingly being replaced by job change, requalification, fixed-term contracts, and contingent and temporary work. Self-employment, freelancing, and other types of non-standard work contracts challenge traditional notions of occupational position, status consistency, job career, and employment security.

With the advent of economic globalization, pressure toward an increase in return on investment has been growing over the past two decades. As a consequence, work pressure due to financial cuts increased considerably in private sectors, and is increasing in public sectors (Ostry and Spiegel 2004). Another consequence of economic globalization concerns the segmentation of the labor market and a related increase in income inequality. On one hand, there is a well-trained, skilled workforce with a high level of job satisfaction, fair promotion prospects, and adequate earnings. On the other hand, a large part of the workforce in advanced societies suffers from job insecurity, low wages and salaries, and a low level of safety at work. Less-qualified, less mobile, and older workers are more likely to belong to the latter segment. With the globalization of labor markets, competition among employees has been increasing, and a growing proportion have been exposed to the effects of mergers, downsizing, outsourcing, or redundancy (Landsbergis 2003).

In addition, demographic changes have had an impact on labor force participation and changing work conditions. Importantly, the workforce is getting older, and new challenges will be faced regarding premature retirement, the amount of work-related ill health, disability pensions among older workers, and other determinants of early exit from the labor market. As an increasing proportion of women enter the labor market, the second shift among women with children or, more generally, increases in dual-career families will be experienced, and related policies need to be developed.

Against this background, medical sociology is faced with two tasks. First, it has to tackle the problem of diversity and variability of workplaces and work conditions among different societies, and even within a single society. How is it possible to produce reliable and valid information on these aspects of the social world? Second, how does work affect human health and well-being? What is the evidence, and on what methodologies and study designs is such evidence based? The next section addresses these problems.

THEORETICAL MODELS AND THEIR MEASUREMENT

Why do we need a theory?

To address the first task of overcoming the difficulties of dealing with the diverse and variable social world of work and employment, a theoretical perspective needs to be developed. More specifically, we need theoretical models that can guide our analysis. A theoretical model is best understood as a heuristic device that selectively reduces the complex reality to meaningful components. These components are delineated at a level of generalization that allows for their application to a wide range of different occupations. A theory is commonly defined as a set of interrelated explanatory statements. Explanatory statements connect two or more single observations in a causal way by referring them to a general rule or principle. As such general principles are rarely available in the social sciences, so-called "middle-range theories" prevail in this field of inquiry where the range of conclusions is restricted with respect to time and place.

The design of a theory is at first a risky choice because its predictions have to deviate from expectations that are based on already existing knowledge. There is considerable probability that these predictions may fail as they can be contradicted by empirical observations. Thus, a successful theory is characterized by a set of far-reaching new predictions that are supported again and again by empirical observations (Popper 1959). There is always a trade-off between the limitations of a conceptual focus that is inherent in a theoretical model and the desire to understand the complexities of reality. Therefore, different middle-range theories do not exclude one another, but may be successfully combined to further advance our knowledge. Below, a few examples of such middle-range theories with regard to work and health are given. These theories are important, not only because they provide new explanations of phenomena that have been poorly understood so far, but also because they are instrumental in identifying targets of interventions and in guiding the development of intervention measures.

The second task of medical sociology consists of bridging two rather distinct phenomena: work and health. What is their relationship? What are the underlying mediating processes? Clearly, the relationship is bidirectional. Poor health reduces the opportunities of participating in the labor market. Conversely, stressful work may reduce working people's health. It is this latter argument that is central to our analysis. But then, the question arises of *how* work may affect human health. Traditionally, this question has been dealt with by occupational medicine or occupational health research. Occupational health research has long been concerned with the material dimensions of health-adverse work, such as heat, noise, and physical or chemical hazards at the workplace. While these hazards are still highly relevant in specific occupational groups, large proportions of the workforce in modern economies are exposed to mental and emotional demands and threats at work rather than material demands and hazards. As a result, psychological and social stressors (often termed psychosocial stressors) are increasingly frequent, and their contribution to health and well-being at work is likely to parallel or even outweigh the contribution of more traditional occupational stressors.

Yet, how can psychosocial stressors operating in working life be defined and how do they affect the mental and physical health of working people? In general terms, a stressor is defined as a challenge that taxes or threatens an exposed person due to her limited capability of successfully coping with it. In the context of work and employment, psychosocial stressors often become manifest as recurrent demands, threats or conflicts that cannot be disregarded or escaped, but require active coping efforts. Whether these demands or threats act as stressors depends on their quality and intensity, as well as on the coping ability and available resources of the person. Thus, the stress process is basically a transactional process involving characteristics of the work situation (organizational features) and characteristics of the working people (capabilities, resources).

A variety of theoretical models have been developed to identify psychosocial stressors at work and to explore their effects on working people (for reviews, see Antoniou and Cooper 2005; Cartwright and Cooper 2008; Perrewe and Ganster 2002). Among these theories, the following concepts, labeled as "person–environment fit" (Caplan et al. 1980), "job demand control" (Karasek and Theorell 1990), "effort–reward imbalance" (Siegrist 1996), "job resources" or "social support at work" (Hobfall and Shirom 2001; House 1981), and "organizational justice" (Greenberg and Cropanzano 2001), received special attention. Other models evolved from an action-theoretical approach to stressful work (Frese and Zapf 1994) or from a focus on coping (Lazarus and Folkman 1984; Ursin and Eriksen 2004; Warr 1996). Two criteria seem particularly helpful in making an informed choice about the usefulness of a theoretical model in the context of work and health: (1) the ability of a model to elaborate the psychobiological processes that link stressful work with human health and disease, and (2) the robustness of empirical evidence derived from tests of the model, in particular a model's ability to predict adverse health as an outcome of exposure to stressful work. A review of the models based on these two criteria follows.

Stress-theoretical bases: Control and reward

Earlier, stress was defined as a transactional process resulting from a misfit between organizational (structural) and personal (capabilities, resources) conditions. A general framework analyzing this misfit refers to basic human needs that are, or are not, fulfilled in people's working life. One such basic human need concerns security and continuity of income and related rewards, providing a sense of positive self-experience and *self-respect*. Conversely, people who are faced with job instability, job loss, and poverty due to a low wage or salary may suffer from a lack of positive self-experience and self-respect. Equally important is the need of *self-efficacy*, i.e., the experience of being able to meet challenging demands and to get favorable feedback, of developing skills, and of contributing to a significant product or service. Self-efficacy has been defined as the belief a person has in his or her ability to accomplish tasks. This belief is based on a favorable evaluation of one's competencies and of expected outcomes. Recurrent feelings of self-efficacy are essential for well-being, and workplaces often act as powerful drivers for experiencing self-efficacy. Yet, the reverse may also happen. In many instances, excessive demands or uncontrollable circumstances exceed the person's coping ability, inducing recurrent experiences of failure, inability, and defeat that weaken one's sense of self-efficacy.

Workplaces are instrumental for human health or ill health not only by providing or preventing self-respect and self-efficacy, but also by providing or preventing *self-esteem*, i.e., the continued positive experience of a person's self-worth. Self-esteem at work is strengthened if efforts spent (or challenges met) are compensated by adequate rewards. The norm of reciprocity, the justice or fairness of exchange between "give" and "take" in contractual transactions, such as the worker–employer transaction, is an essential prerequisite of human well-being. Frustration of justified reward expectancies and lack of appreciation in the case of successful performance elicit strong negative emotions and may threaten one's sense of favorable self-esteem.

As a result, work life plays a crucial role in securing or preventing basic human needs, in particular the needs for self-respect, self-efficacy, and self-esteem. By satisfying or frustrating these needs, workplaces and employment conditions can directly affect human health and well-being. In these instances, *control* and *reward* act as the two main psychobiological triggers.

Feelings and beliefs of control accompany positive self-experience, in particular self-efficacy and self-respect. The experience of personal control and the expectancy of a positive outcome from one's actions are the main triggers that activate or deactivate the stress mechanisms in the human brain. If personal control is threatened, the so-called "fight or flight reaction" is activated. This reaction induces intense arousal of the autonomic nervous system, the endocrine, and the immune system. By doing so, it prepares the organism for optimal use of its resources. While this type of active coping is beneficial in the short run, it may damage bodily systems in the long run due to excessive activation, adaptive dysfunction, and exhaustion (Henry and Stephens 1977; McEwen 1998). In the event of loss of control, feelings of helplessness are elicited that are paralleled by particular neuroendocrine and immune reactions of the so-called hypothalamic–pituitary–adrenocortical axis. Giving up and withdrawing from activity (passive coping) are behavioral manifestations of loss of control. Again, if experienced recurrently, this state may damage the organism by weakening the immune system and by disturbing hormonal and metabolic patterns that serve crucial functions in maintaining health (Weiner 1992). Thus, working conditions that threaten a person's sense of control or that induce a loss of control can directly affect the working person's health and well-being.

In a similar way, feelings and experiences of reward are paralleled by positive self-experience, in particular self-esteem. Conversely, threats to obtained rewards as well as frustrations of expected rewards act as powerful triggers of stress mechanisms in the brain, and specifically in the brain reward system, the so-called meso-limbic dopamine system. Intense feelings of anger, unfairness, and aggression may result in enhanced bodily stress reactions and elevated risks of stress-associated diseases, as well as in addiction and deviant social behavior (Blum et al. 1996; Rolls 2000). Again, working conditions that threaten obtained rewards or that induce reward frustration can directly affect the working person's health and well-being. The demand–control model focusing on the notion of control, and the effort–reward imbalance model focusing on the notion of reward, represent two theoretical approaches that hold promise in bridging the psychosocial work environment with the working person's health. These two models are described in more detail below.

The demand–control model and the effort–reward imbalance model

The *demand–control model* was introduced by sociologist Robert Karasek (1979) and further developed by Karasek and Theorell (1990). It posits that stressful experiences at work result from a distinct job task profile defined by two dimensions: the psychological demands put on the working person and the degree of control available to the person to perform the required tasks. Jobs defined by high demands and low control are stressful because they limit the individual's autonomy and sense of control while generating continued pressure (high job strain). Under these conditions, excessive arousal of the autonomic nervous system is expected to occur that is not compensated by a relaxation response following the experience of control and mastery.

Importantly, low levels of control or decision latitude manifest themselves in two ways; first as lack of decision authority over one's tasks, and second as low level of skill utilization, as evidenced by monotonous, repetitive work. While task profiles defined by low decision latitude in combination with low demands also may adversely affect health (although to a lesser extent than high-strain jobs), "active jobs" are expected to be health-protective. Such jobs are defined by challenging demands in combination with a high degree of autonomy. They offer opportunities for experiencing success and self-efficacy. It is obvious that some of the traditional high-strain jobs are highly prevalent in mass industry, especially in piecework and machine-paced assembly line work. Yet, several low-skilled jobs in administrations and in the service sector fit into this category as well. Overall, high-strain jobs seem to follow a social gradient. The higher one's level of professional training and skill, the less likely is one's probability of working in a "high demand–low control" job.

A third dimension, social support at work, was added to the original formulation where highest strain is expected to occur in jobs that are characterized by high demand, low control, and low social support at work or social isolation ("iso-strain jobs") (Johnson and Hall 1988). Thus, available social support at work may mitigate the amount of stress in people confined to high-strain jobs. In summary, this model is based on the stress concept of limited control in everyday job tasks. Unfortunately, it does not include characteristics of personal coping with demands and it focuses on job characteristics rather than the broader context of employment conditions; thus, this model would benefit from additional conceptualizations.

A complementary theory is provided by the *model of effort–reward imbalance*. This model is concerned with stressful features of the work contract rather than the profile of job tasks. Developed by this author and his group (Siegrist 1996), it builds on the notion of social reciprocity, a fundamental principle rooted in an "evolutionary-old" grammar of interpersonal exchange. Social reciprocity lies at the core of the employment (or work) contract, which defines distinct obligations or tasks to be performed in exchange for adequate rewards. These rewards include money, esteem, and career opportunities, including job security. Contractual reciprocity operates through norms of return expectancy where efforts spent by employees are reciprocated by equitable rewards from employers. The effort–reward imbalance model claims that lack of reciprocity occurs frequently under specific conditions and that failed reciprocity in terms of high cost and low gain elicits strong negative emotions with special propensity to sustained autonomic and neuroendocrine activation and their adverse long-term consequences for health. According to the theory, contractual non-reciprocity is observed if one or several of the following conditions are given: *dependency*, *strategic choice*, and *overcommitment* (Siegrist 1996; Siegrist and Theorell 2006).

Dependency reflects the structural constraints observed in certain types of employment contracts, especially in unskilled or semi-skilled workers, in elderly employees, in employees with restricted mobility or limited work ability, and in workers with short-term contracts. In all of these instances, incentives for paying non-equitable rewards are high for employers, while the risks of employees rejecting an unfair contractual transaction are low because they have no alternative choice. Dependency is relatively frequent in modern economies, which are characterized by a globalized labor market, mergers and organizational downsizing, rapid technological change, and a high level of job instability.

Strategic choice is a second condition of non-symmetrical exchange. Here, people accept high-cost/low-gain conditions of their employment for a certain time, often without being forced to do so, because they tend to improve their chances of career promotion and related rewards at a later stage. This pattern is frequently observed in early stages of professional careers and in jobs that are characterized by heavy competition. As anticipatory investments are made on the basis of insecure return expectancy, the risk of failed success after long-lasting efforts is considerable.

Third, there are psychological reasons for a recurrent mismatch between efforts and rewards at work. People characterized by a motivational pattern of excessive work-related *overcommitment* may strive toward continuously high achievement because of their underlying need for approval and esteem at work. Although these excessive efforts often are not met by adequate rewards, overcommitted people tend to maintain their level of involvement. Work-related overcommitment may also be triggered by informal social pressure at work, specifically in a highly competitive professional environment. Thus, it is elicited and reinforced by a variety of job environments, and is often experienced as self-rewarding over a period of years in occupational trajectories. However, in the long run, overcommitted people are susceptible to exhaustion and adaptive breakdown.

In summary, the model of effort–reward imbalance at work maintains that people experiencing dependency, strategic choice, and overcommitment, either separately or in combination, are often exposed to failed contractual reciprocity at work and its adverse health consequences. In stress-theoretical terms, this model is focused on the afflictions of self-esteem resulting from failed social reciprocity, i.e., the frustration of rewards following appropriate efforts spent. The model combines organizational features with personal coping characteristics.

These two models are usually measured by standardized, validated question-naires, although additional approaches are used as well (expert ratings, observa-tional methods, job exposure matrices based on occupational titles). The established instrument for measuring job tasks in the demand–control model is the *Job Content Questionnaire* (Karasek et al. 1998). The description of psychometric properties of the scales measuring demand, decision latitude, skill discretion, and social support at work is beyond the scope of this contribution, but these properties were generally found to be satisfactory in terms of reliability and validity, and several versions of the questionnaire have been applied in a multitude of studies in different countries, thus creating a bulk of new data on organizational determinants of health and well-being (Belkic et al. 2004; Karasek et al. 1998).

For the *effort–reward imbalance* model, a *standardized self-report questionnaire* contains three scales: effort (6 items), reward (11 items that represent the three dimensions of financial and career-related rewards, of esteem, and of job security in respective subscales), and overcommitment (6 items representing the personal or intrinsic model component) (Siegrist et al. 2004). Again, psychometric properties of this questionnaire were assessed to a substantial degree and were generally found to be satisfactory (De Jonge et al. 2008; Siegrist et al. 2004). More recently, a short version of the questionnaire was developed and tested, representing the full model on the basis of 16 Likert-scaled items (Siegrist et al. 2008).The questionnaires mea-suring the two models were translated into a number of languages and are widely used in international comparative research on work stress and health.

Several shortcomings of the above measurement approaches are obvious, notably the susceptibility of self-reported information to reporting bias, the limited compa-rability of the meaning of their content in cross-cultural research, or the imprecision of measurement of the theoretical notions. Moreover, there is no general consensus on how to best represent the theoretical notions by appropriate statistical modeling (e.g., test of interaction terms, use of general linear model). Therefore, it is of inter-est to know that supplementary methodological approaches were developed, such as the "momentary event assessment" approach using ambulatory diaries during the working day (Johnston, Beedie, and Jones 2006), or experimental designs that induce high demand and low control (e.g., Steptoe 2006), or reward frustration following task accomplishment (e.g., Siegrist et al. 2005). Nevertheless, based on the questionnaires measuring the two models, a rich amount of empirical evidence on health-adverse effects of stressful work was obtained in recent years from large-scale epidemiological investigations. This evidence is briefly summarized in the next section.

A SHORT REVIEW OF EMPIRICAL EVIDENCE

The prospective epidemiological observational study is considered a gold standard approach in this field because of its temporal sequence (exposure assessment pre-cedes disease onset), its sample size (based on statistical power calculation and allowing for adjustment for confounding variables in multivariate analysis), and the quantification of subsequent disease risk following exposure (odds ratio of disease in exposed vs. non-exposed individuals). Therefore, a short summary of the main findings based on prospective studies is given (for detailed reviews see Belkic et al. 2004; Kivimäki et al. 2006; Marmot, Siegrist, and Theorell 2006; Tsutsumi and Kawakami 2004; Van Vegchel et al. 2005).

The majority of prospective investigations studied work stress in relation to cardiovascular diseases and affective disorders. This choice is well justified in view of their contribution to the overall burden of disease (Murray and Lopez 1996). At present, at least 20 reports derived from prospective studies of associations between work stress and cardiovascular disease are available, and the findings of a majority of these studies are summarized in Table 12.1. Ten publications test the demand–control model and five publications test the effort–reward imbalance model, with two publications testing the two models simultaneously. Although measures were not fully comparable across these studies, the majority of findings support either the full theoretical models or their main components. Odds ratios or hazard ratios given in Table 12.1 are adjusted for relevant confounders (e.g., major biomedical and behavioral cardiovascular risk factors), and their statistical significance is estimated based on the respective 95 percent confidence intervals. These ratios vary considerably across the studies, but, overall, a twofold elevated risk is observed among individuals with high work stress in terms of job strain or effort–reward imbalance, compared to non-exposed individuals. Findings are more consistent in men than in women, and more consistent in middle-aged as compared to early old age populations. The observation period in these studies varies from 1 to 25 years, with a mean of 8 years.

A further summary can be drawn with regard to affective disorders, mainly depression. Findings from 12 reports on prospective epidemiological studies are summarized in Table 12.2. Overall, they indicate an 80 percent elevated relative risk of depression among men and women who were exposed to high demand and low control at work or who spent high efforts in combination with low rewards received in turn, compared to employed people who were free from these types of stressful work. Although the number of studies is still limited, the effects of effort–reward imbalance on depression seem to be stronger than those produced by job strain.

The results summarized in Tables 12.1 and 12.2 are based on a variety of occupational groups recruited from several modern Western countries in Europe and Northern America. Thus, it is likely that they can be generalized beyond the populations under study. Even if the reported odds ratios are not large, their effects in absolute terms are considerable, given the fact that between 10 and 25 percent of the samples were exposed to work stress in terms of these models. Thus, these findings justify the development and implementation of new policy measures to prevent major chronic diseases in working populations (see below).

Research on stress in the workplace and its effects on health is not restricted to these two major chronic diseases. Additional health outcomes include limited physical and mental functioning, alcohol dependence, metabolic syndrome, and diabetes, although the prospective evidence is less robust in some of these outcomes (Chandola, Brunner, and Marmot 2006; Head, Stansfeld, and Siegrist 2004; Kumari, Head, and Marmot 2004; Kuper et al. 2002; Stansfeld et al. 1998). Yet, taken together, the burden of disease produced by an adverse psychosocial work environment is considerable, and it strengthens the case of intervention efforts at work.

Table 12.1 Prospective studies on incidence of coronary heart disease (CHD) or cardiovascular diseases (CVD) risk respectively as a function of work stress (demand–control; effort–reward imbalance)

First author (year)	Sample (N) m = male, f = female (% f)	Outcome	Odds ratio; 95 % CI
Job demand–control model			
Alterman et al. (1994)	m N = 1,683	Non-fatal CHD	1.5 (0.8–2.8)
Bosma et al. (1998)	m, f N = 4,393 (33%)	CHD and/or angina pectoris	2.4 (1.3–4.3)[a]
De Bacquer et al. (2005)	m N = 14,337	CHD	1.3 (0.7–2.5)
Eaker et al. (2004)	m, f N = 3,039 (44%)	CHD	m 1.0 (0.8–1.2)[a] f 1.6 (1.1–2.4)[a]
Johnson, Hall, and Theorell (1989)	m N = 7,219	Fatal CVD	1.9 (1.1–3.2)
Kivimäki et al. (2002)	m, f N = 812 (33%)	Fatal CVD	2.2 (1.1–4.7)
Kuper et al. (2002)	m, f N = 10,308 (33%)	CHD	1.4 (1.1–1.7)
Lee et al. (2002)	f N = 35,038	CHD	0.7 (0.4–1.2)
Netterström, Kristensen, and Sjöl (2006)	m N = 659	CHD	2.4 (1.0–5.7)
Uchiyama et al. (2005)	f N = 1,615 (44%)	CVD	6.6 (0.9–47.7)
Effort–reward imbalance model			
Bosma et al. (1998)	m, f N = 10,308	CHD and/or angina pectoris	2.2 (1.1–4.0)
Kivimäki et al. (2002)	m, f N = 812 (33%)	Fatal CVD	2.4 (1.0–5.7)
Kuper et al. (2002)	m, f N = 10,308 (33%)	CHD	1.3 (1.0–1.5)
Lynch et al. (1997)	m N = 2,297	CHD	1.6 (0.8–3.2)[b]
Siegrist et al. (1990)	m N = 416	CHD	4.5 (1.4–14.3)

[a] low control; [b] high effort and low reward.
Source: Adapted from Siegrist and Dragano 2008.

Despite their methodological strengths, prospective epidemiological studies provide little insight into the mechanisms underlying the observed statistical associations. Two such mechanisms are generally considered: the mediation by health-adverse behaviors, such as smoking, poor diet, or lack of physical exercise (Siegrist

Table 12.2 Overview of results from prospective studies on associations of chronic psychosocial stress at work (demand–control; effort–reward imbalance) and depression

First author (year)	Sample (N, m and f)	Outcome	Odds ratio; 95% CI
Job demand–control model			
Ahola and Hakanen (2007)	2,555	Depressive symptoms	DC: 3.4 (2.0–5.7)
Marchand, Demers, and Durand (2005)	7,311	Physicians' diagnosis	D: 1.0 (0.9–1.1) C[3]: 1.1 (1.0–1.1)
Niedhammer et al. (1998)	11,552	Depressive symptoms	DC[1]: m 1.4 (1.2–1.6) f 1.4 (1.2–1.7)
Rugulies et al. (2006)	4,133	Depressive symptoms	D: m 0.5 (0.2–1.2) f 1.0 (0.5–1.7) C: m 0.6 (0.3–1.2) f 1.9 (1.1–3.4)
Shields (1999)	3,380	Major depressive episode	DC: m 3.3 (1.3–8.4) f 2.1 (1.1–4.0)
Stansfeld et al. (1999)	10,308	Depressive symptoms	DC: m 1.4 (1.2–1.6) f 1.2 (1.0–1.5)
Wang and Pattern (2004)	7,371	Physicians' diagnosis	D: 1.3 (1.1–1.6) C[2]: 1.2 (1.0–1.5)
Ylipaavalniemi et al. (2005)	4,815	Physicians' diagnosis	DC: 1.2 (0.9–1.6)
Effort–reward imbalance model			
Godin et al. (2005)	1,986	Depressive symptoms	ERI: m 2.8 (1.3–5.7) f 4.6 (2.3–9.0)
Kivimäki et al. (2007)	47,351	Physicians' diagnosis	ERI: 1.5 (1.2–1.8)
Kivimäki et al. (2007)	21,938	Physicians' diagnosis	ERI: 1.6 (0.9–2.7)
Stansfeld et al. (1999)	10,308	Depressive symptoms	ERI[4]: m 3.6 (2.8–4.8) f 1.9 (1.2–2.9)

[1] Demand–control ("Job strain"), [2] skill discretion only, [3] decision authority only, [4] ERI: combined measure of high effort and low reward.

Source: Adapted from Siegrist 2008.

and Rödel 2006), and the mediation by chronic stress reactions that contribute to the development of disease via psychobiological mechanisms, such as the ones discussed above.

Psychobiological processes are the pathways through which a health-adverse psychosocial work environment activates autonomic, neuroendocrine, immune, and inflammatory responses via the organism's stress axes. Recent experimental studies demonstrate associations of job strain or effort–reward imbalance with elevated heart rate and blood pressure, with reduced heart rate variability and with altered patterns of release of stress hormones into blood or saliva (Siegrist et al. 2005; Steptoe 2006; Vrijkotte, van Doornen, and de Geus 2000). Taken together, experimental studies supplement epidemiological evidence by demonstrating psychobiological processes that possibly mediate the observed associations of work stress with health.

A third approach toward estimating adverse consequences of stressful work deals with behavioral outcomes, such as (1) short-term sickness absence, (2) the intention to leave one's job, or (3) the probability of acting in an obstructive way. It is well known that a substantial part of sickness absence is due to lack of organizational commitment, and several investigations document a key role of psychosocial stress at work in this process (Marmot et al. 2006). In prospective studies, this was also demonstrated for the two work stress models discussed here (Ala-Mursula et al. 2005; Head et al. 2007).

Intention to leave one's job is considered a second indicator of behavioral outcomes. This outcome was studied in two large European surveys with regard to effort–reward imbalance at work. One such investigation, the NEXT study, examined the probability of quitting the job in the near future in relation to the degree of experienced non-reciprocity at work in some 21,729 registered nurses (Hasselhorn, Tackenberg, and Peter 2004). As demonstrated in Figure 12.1, a linear relationship was observed between the degree of imbalance, as measured by the effort/reward ratio, and the frequency of thoughts about leaving the profession. In view of a shortage of health care personnel, and particularly nurses, in many Western countries, this finding points to relevant policy implications.

The second study (SHARE) was performed in 10 European countries in 6,836 employed men and women aged 50 to 65, where determinants of intended early retirement were analyzed (Siegrist et al. 2007). Results showed that after adjustment for well-being the likelihood of intended early retirement was elevated by about 70 percent in the group of working men and women experiencing effort–reward imbalance at work and about 50 percent in the group experiencing low control at work, compared to those with adequate reward and control. This association was consistent across all countries under study despite variations in national retirement policies. These findings underline the need to improve the quality of work and organizational performance as a means of motivating elderly people to stay at work.

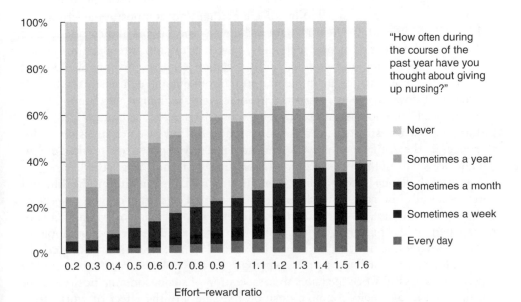

Figure 12.1 Work stress (effort–reward imbalance) and intention to leave the profession: The NEXT study (N = 21,729 registered nurses).
Source: Adapted from Hasselhorn et al. 2004.

Obstructive behavior may be a third behavioral response to frustrating and stressful working conditions. This topic has rarely been investigated in this context, but a recent report indicates that this assumption may be valid. In a survey of scientists' self-reported misbehaviors among 3,247 early- and mid-career researchers in the United States, it was found that a high effort–reward imbalance ratio was related to an increased probability of misbehavior in early-career, but not in mid-career scientists. Moreover, overcommitted researchers were more likely to report misbehavior, in particular if they additionally perceived a high degree of procedural injustice within their organization (Martinson et al. 2006).

This short review has dealt with three lines of scientific evidence: first, epidemiological investigations linking work stress with adverse health outcomes; second, experimental studies exploring possible psychobiological pathways underlying these associations; and third, studies of behavioral outcomes of stressful work, such as absenteeism, intention to leave one's job, and obstructive behavior. This evidence strengthens the case for improving organizational structure and functioning by appropriate measures.

FUTURE CHALLENGES

Despite recent scientific progress in medical sociology, as evidenced in research on social determinants of health in general, and of work stress in particular, future *challenges* remain to be met at the level of both science and policy.

At the level of scientific analysis, recent changes in work and employment mentioned earlier need to be incorporated into the theory and measurement of stressful work. A primary challenge consists in extending the frame of analysis into multilevel modeling where individual-level data on work stress are nested in contextual data and where the separate contribution of contextual and compositional effects on health can be estimated. Contextual data include macroeconomic indicators, such as level of unemployment or income inequality, as well as organizational features, such as downsizing, merging, outsourcing, or the speed of recent expansion (Siegrist and Theorell 2006). For instance, an influential study from Finland demonstrates that the experience of downsizing increased the prospective risk of mortality among those who "survived" the downsizing process by about 40 percent (Vahtera et al. 2004). And in a further investigation, it was shown that the effect of work stress on health is strongest in the group of employees who were recently exposed to a marked downsizing process within their organization (Dragano, Verde, and Siegrist 2005).

A second challenge concerns the explanation of social inequalities in health, and more specifically the role of work and employment. For instance, with respect to cardiovascular disease, it was shown that adverse health behavior explains a substantial part of the higher prevalence of coronary heart disease among people in lower socioeconomic positions (Kivimäki et al. 2008). Yet, stressful working conditions additionally contribute to this explanation in two ways. First, some studies suggest that stressful work mediates the association of socioeconomic position with health. Second, low socioeconomic position may amplify the effect of work stress on health, given an increased level of exposure to adversity and reduced capabilities of coping with adversity (Siegrist and Theorell 2006).

A further scientific challenge consists in testing the scope of generalization inherent in the propositions of the two work stress models discussed above. One could argue that the propositions of the two models should equally apply to types of social productivity or social exchange other than paid work. In fact, some first successful extensions have been developed. For instance, the demand–control model was modified to explain adverse health among housewives who had little control over their homework while being exposed to heavy demands (Chandola et al. 2004). The effort–reward imbalance model was applied to types of socially productive activities with non-monetary rewards, such as volunteering, informal help, and caring for a sick person. In a large comparative study of early old age populations it was observed that experienced non-reciprocity between efforts spent and rewards received (high cost/low gain) is associated with reduced well-being and an increased level of depressive symptoms in all three activities (Wahrendorf, Knesebeck, and Siegrist 2006). Likewise, experienced non-reciprocity in close social relationships, i.e., between partners, parents and children, or non-specified significant others, was consistently associated with reduced well-being (Chandola, Marmot, and Siegrist 2007; Knesebeck and Siegrist 2004). Thus, there are promising steps toward extending the scope of predictions derived from the two models.

At the level of *policy implications* of available scientific evidence, a major challenge consists in developing and implementing theory-based interventions and in demonstrating their beneficial effects on well-being. Improving the quality of work and employment is a target that can be tackled at several levels. International and national regulations and policies are far-reaching approaches. It is encouraging to see a growing interest among organizations such as the European Commission, the World Health Organization, and the International Labor Organization in dealing with measures to reduce work-related stress. National policies vary quite substantially in this regard, depending on the level of economic development, the type of welfare regime, and the prevailing political preferences (Mackenbach 2006). Single companies (especially medium- and large-scale organizations) are probably the most effective target of intervention approaches.

In this chapter, we have argued that two theoretical models hold particular promise in explaining work-related disease: the demand–control and effort–reward imbalance models. The conditions identified by these models provide a framework in which to understand and to modify the contribution of psychosocial factors at work to the development of disease. The conceptual differences between the models have direct implications for the design of intervention measures to improve health. Whereas the emphasis of the demand–control model is on change of the task structure (such as job enlargement, job enrichment, and increasing the amount of support within the job), the focus of the effort–reward imbalance model is on contractual fairness in terms of reciprocity between "cost" and "gain." This latter model offers measures at three levels, the individual level (e.g., reduction of overcommitment), the interpersonal level (e.g., improvement of leadership, of providing esteem reward), and the structural level (e.g., compensatory wage systems, models of gain sharing, and strengthening of non-monetary gratifications). Both models stress the need for better opportunities for job training, learning new skills, and increasing job security. In addition to general measures, more specific measures can be tailored for special risk groups at work, most importantly elderly workers.

A few intervention studies have already been conducted along these lines (e.g., Bond and Bunce 2001; Bourbonnais et al. 2006; Theorell et al. 2001), but much remains to be done to strengthen workers' health in a more pervasive way (Schnall et al. 2009). We cannot exclude the possibility that economic competition for cost saving and optimal performance may serve as an incentive for enterprises to get involved more readily in measures of organizational well-being. The same applies to the incentive of an improved return-on-investment once such measures are implemented (Pfeffer 1998). Clearly, joint efforts are needed from stakeholders, professionals, and national and international organizations to further improve quality of work and its beneficial effects on working people. In conclusion, medical sociology as applied to the study of stress in the workplace has made – and continues to make – a significant contribution to our understanding of how the social reality affects human health and well-being.

References

Ahola, Kirsi and Jari Hakanen. 2007. "Job Strain, Burnout, and Depressive Symptoms: A Prospective Study Among Dentists." *Journal of Affective Disorders* 104: 103–10.

Ala-Mursula, Leena, Jussi Vahtera, Anne Linna, Jaana Pentti, and Mika Kivimäki. 2005. "Employee Worktime Control Moderates the Effects of Job Strain and Effort–Reward Imbalance on Sickness Absence: The 10–Town Study." *Journal of Epidemiology and Community Health* 59: 851–7.

Alterman, Toni, Richard B. Shekelle, Sally W. Vernon, and Keith D. Burau. 1994. "Decision Latitude, Psychologic Demand, Job Strain, and Coronary Heart Disease in the Western Electric Study." *American Journal of Epidemiology* 139: 620–7.

Antoniou, Alexancer-Stamatios G. and Cary L. Cooper (eds.). 2005. *Research Companion to Organizational Health Psychology*. Cheltenham: Edward Elgar.

Belkic, Karen L., Paul A. Landsbergis, Peter L. Schnall, and Dean Baker. 2004. "Is Job Strain a Major Source of Cardiovascular Disease Risk?" *Scandinavian Journal of Work Environment and Health* 30: 85–128.

Berkman, Lisa F. and Kawachi Ichiro. 2000. *Social Epidemiology*. New York: Oxford University Press.

Blum, Kenneth, John G. Cull, Eric R. Braverman, and David E. Comings. 1996. "Reward Deficiency Syndrome: Addictive, Impulsive and Compulsive Disorders – Including Alcoholism, Attention Deficit Disorders, Drug Abuse and Food Bingeing – May Have a Common Genetic Basis." *American Scientist* 84: 132–45.

Bond, Frank W. and David Bunce. 2001. "Job Control Mediates Change in Work Organization Intervention for Stress Reduction." *Journal of Occupational Health Psychology* 6: 290–302.

Bosma, Hans, Richard Peter, Johannes Siegrist, and Michael Marmot. 1998. "Two Alternative Job Stress Models and the Risk of Coronary Heart Disease." *American Journal of Public Health* 88: 68–74.

Bourbonnais, R., C. Brisson, A. Vinet, M. Vezina, and A. Lower. 2006. "Development and Implementation of a Participative Intervention to Improve the Psychosocial Work Environment and Mental Health in an Acute Care Hospital." *Occupational and Environmental Medicine* 63: 326–34.

Caplan, R. D., S. Cobb, J. R. P. French, R. V. Harrison, and S. R. Pinneau. 1980. *Job Demand and Worker Health: Main Effects and Occupational Differences*. Ann Arbor, MI: Institute for Social Research.

Cartwright, Susan and Cary L. Cooper (eds.). 2008. *The Oxford Handbook of Organizational Well-Being*. Oxford: Oxford University Press.

Chandola, Tarani, Eric Brunner, and Michael Marmot. 2006. "Chronic Stress at Work and the Metabolic Syndrome: Prospective Study." *British Medical Journal* 332: 521–5.

Chandola, Tarani, Hannah Kuper, Archana Singh-Manoux, Mel Bartley, and Michael Marmot. 2004. "The Effect of Control at Home on CHD Events in the Whitehall II Study: Gender Differences in Psychosocial Domestic Pathways to Social Inequalities in CHD." *Social Science and Medicine* 58: 1501–9.

Chandola, Tarani, Michael Marmot, and Johannes Siegrist. 2007. "Failed Reciprocity in Close Social Relationships and Health: Findings From the Whitehall II Study." *Journal of Psychosomatic Research* 63: 403–11.

De Bacquer, Dirk, E. Pelfrene, E. Clays, R. Mak, M. Moreau, P. de Smet, M. Kornitzer, and G. De Backer. 2005. "Perceived Job Stress and Incidence of Coronary Events: 3-Year Follow-Up of the Belgian Job Stress Project Cohort." *American Journal of Epidemiology* 161: 434–41.

De Jonge, Jan, Sjaak van der Linden, Wilmar Schaufeli, Richard Peter, and Johannes Siegrist. 2008. "Factorial Invariance and Stability of the Effort–Reward Imbalance Scales: A Longitudinal Analysis of Two Samples with Different Time Lags." *International Journal of Behavioral Medicine* 15: 62–72.

Dragano, Nico, Pablo E. Verde, and Johannes Siegrist. 2005. "Organisational Downsizing and Work Stress: Testing Synergistic Health Effects in Employed Men and Women." *Journal of Epidemiology and Community Health* 59: 694–9.

Eaker, Elaine D., Lisa M. Sullivan, Margaret Kelly-Hayes, Ralph B. D'Agostino, Sr., and Emelia J. Benjamin. 2004. "Does Job Strain Increase the Risk for Coronary Heart Disease or Death in Men and Women? The Framingham Offspring Study." *American Journal of Epidemiology* 159: 950–8.

Frese, Michael and Dieter Zapf. 1994. "Action As the Core of Work Psychology: A German Approach." Pp. 271–340 in H. C. Triandis, M. D. Dunnette, and L. M. Hough (eds.), *Handbook of Industrial and Organizational Psychology*, vol. 4. Palo Alto, CA: Consulting Psychologists Press.

Godin, Isabelle, France Kittel, Yves Coppieters, and Johannes Siegrist. 2005. "A Prospective Study of Cumulative Job Stress in Relation to Mental Health." *BMC Public Health* 5: 67.

Greenberg, Jerald and Russell Cropanzano (eds.). 2001. *Advances in Organization Justice*. Stanford, CA: Stanford University Press.

Hasselhorn, Hans-Martin, Peter Tackenberg, and Richard Peter. 2004. "Effort–Reward Imbalance Among Nurses in Stable Countries and in Countries in Transition." *International Journal of Occupational and Environmental Health* 10: 401–8.

Head, Jenny, Mika Kivimäki, Johannes Siegrist, Jane E. Ferrie, Jussi Vahtera, Martin J. Shipley, and Michael G. Marmot. 2007. "Effort–Reward Imbalance and Relational Injustice at Work Predict Sickness Absence: The Whitehall II Study." *Journal of Psychosomatic Research* 63: 433–40.

Head, Jenny, Stephen A. Stansfeld, and Johannes Siegrist. 2004. "The Psychosocial Work Environment and Alcohol Dependence: A Prospective Study." *Occupational and Environmental Medicine* 61: 219–24.

Henry, James P. and Patricia M. Stephens. 1977. *Stress, Health, and the Social Environment*. New York: Springer.

Hobfall, Stephen E. and Arie Shirom. 2001. "Conservation of Resources Theory: Applications to Stress and Management in the Workplace." Pp. 57–80 in R. T. Golembiewski (ed.), *Handbook of Organizational Behavior*, 2nd edition. New York: Marcel Dekker.

House, James S. 1981. *Work, Stress and Social Support*. Reading, MA: Addison-Wesley.

Johnson, Jeffrey V. and Ellen M. Hall. 1988. "Job Strain, Workplace Social Support and Cardiovascular Disease: A Cross-Sectional Study of a Random Sample of the Swedish Working Population." *American Journal of Public Health* 78: 1336–42.

Johnson, Jeffrey V., Ellen M. Hall, and Töres Theorell. 1989. "Combined Effects of Job Strain and Social Isolation on Cardiovascular Disease Morbidity and Mortality in a Random Sample of Swedish Male Working Population." *Scandinavian Journal of Work and Environmental Health* 15: 271–9.

Johnston, Derek W., Alexis Beedie, and Martyn C. Jones. 2006. "Using Computerized Ambulatory Diaries for the Assessment of Job Characteristics and Work-Related Stress in Nurses." *Work and Stress* 20: 163–72.

Karasek, Robert A. 1979. "Job Demands, Job Decision Latitude, and Mental Strain: Implications for Job Redesign." *Administrative Science Quarterly* 24: 285–307.

Karasek, Robert A., Chantal Brisson, Norito Kawakami, Irene Houtman, Paulien Bongers, and Benjamin Amick. 1998. "The Job Content Questionnaire (JCQ): An Instrument for Internationally Comparative Assessment of Psychosocial Job Characteristics." *Journal of Occupational Health Psychology* 3: 322–55.

Karasek, Robert A. and Töres Theorell. 1990. *Healthy Work*. New York: Basic Books.

Kivimäki, Mika, Päivi Leino-Arjas, Ritva Luukkonen, Hilkka Riihimäki, Jussi Vahtera, and Juhani Kirjonen. 2002. "Work Stress and Risk of Cardiovascular Mortality: Prospective Cohort Study of Industrial Employees." *British Medical Journal* 325: 857–61.

Kivimäki, Mika, Martin J. Shipley, Jane E. Ferrie, Archana Singh-Manoux, G. David Batty, Tarani Chandola, Michael G Marmot, and George Davey Smith. 2008. "Best-Practice Interventions to Reduce Socioeconomic Inequalities of Coronary Heart Disease Mortality in UK: A Prospective Occupational Cohort Study." *The Lancet* 372: 1649–54.

Kivimäki, Mika, Jussi Vahtera, Marko Elovainio, Marianna Virtanen, and Johannes Siegrist. 2007. "Effort–Reward Imbalance, Procedural Injustice and Relational Injustice as Psychosocial Predictors of Health: Complementary or Redundant Models?" *Occupational and Environmental Medicine* 64: 659–65.

Kivimäki, Mika, Marianna Virtanen, Marko Elovainio, A. Kouvonen, A. Väänänen, and Jussi Vahtera. 2006. "Work Stress in the Etiology of Coronary Heart Disease: A Meta-Analysis." *Scandinavian Journal of Work, Environment and Health* 32: 431–42.

Knesebeck, Olaf von dem and Johannes Siegrist. 2004. "Reported Non-Reciprocity of Social Exchange and Depressive Symptoms: Extending the Model of Effort–Reward Imbalance Beyond Work." *Journal of Psychosomatic Research* 55: 209–14.

Kumari, Meena, Jenny Head, and Michael Marmot. 2004. "Prospective Study of Social and Other Risk Factors for Incidence of Type II Diabetes in Whitehall II Study." *Annals of Internal Medicine* 164: 1873–80.

Kuper, Hannah, Archana Singh-Manoux, Johannes Siegrist, and Michael Marmot. 2002. "When Reciprocity Fails: Effort–Reward Imbalance in Relation to Coronary Heart Disease and Health Functioning Within the Whitehall II Study." *Occupational and Environmental Medicine* 59: 777–84.

Landsbergis, Paul A. 2003. "The Changing Organization of Work and the Safety and Health of Working People: A Commentary." *Journal of Occupational and Environmental Medicine* 11: 61–71.

Lazarus, Richard S. and Susan Folkman. 1984. *Stress, Appraisal, and Coping*. New York: Springer.

Lee, Sunmin, Graham Colditz, Lisa Berkman, and Kawachi Ichiro. 2002. "A Prospective Study of Job Strain and Coronary Heart Disease in US Women." *International Journal of Epidemiology* 31: 1147–53.

Lynch, John, Niklas Krause, George A. Kaplan, Jaakko Tuomilehto, and Jukka T. Salonen. 1997. "Work Place Conditions, Socioeconomic Status, and the Risk of Mortality and Acute Myocardial Infarction: The Kuopio Ischemic Heart Disease Risk Factor Study." *American Journal of Public Health* 87: 617–22.

Mackenbach, Johan P. 2006. "Socio-Economic Inequalities in Health in Western Europe: From Description to Explanation to Intervention." Pp. 223–50 in Johannes Siegrist and Michael Marmot (eds.), *Social Inequalities in Health: New Evidence and Policy Implications*. Oxford: Oxford University Press.

Marchand, Alain, Andrée Demers, and Pierre Durand. 2005. "Does Work Really Cause Distress? The Contribution of Occupational Structure and Work Organization to the Experience of Psychological Distress." *Social Science and Medicine* 61: 1–14.

Marmot, Michael, Johannes Siegrist, and Töres Theorell. 2006. "Health and the Psychosocial Environment at Work." Pp. 97–130 in Michael Marmot and Richard G. Wilkinson (eds.), *Social Determinants of Health*. Oxford: Oxford University Press.

Marmot, Michael and Richard G. Wilkinson (eds.). 2006. *Social Determinants of Health*. Oxford: Oxford University Press.

Martinson, Brian C., Melissa S. Anderson, A. Lauren Crain, and Raymond De Vries. 2006. "Scientists' Perceptions of Organizational Justice and Self-Reported Misbehaviors." *Journal of Empirical Research on Human Research Ethics* 1: 51–66.

McEwen, Bruce S. 1998. "Protective and Damaging Effects of Stress Mediators." *New England Journal of Medicine* 338: S171–9.

Murray, Christopher and Alan D. Lopez. 1996. *The Global Burden of Disease*. Boston: Harvard University Press.

Netterström, Bo, Tage S. Kristensen, and Anette Sjöl. 2006. "Psychological Job Demands Increase the Risk of Ischaemic Heart Disease: A 14-Year Cohort Study of Employed Danish Men." *European Journal of Cardiovascular Prevention and Rehabilitation* 13: 414–20.

Niedhammer, Isabelle, Marcel Goldberg, Anette Leclerc, I. Bugel, and S. David. 1998. "Psychosocial Factors at Work and Subsequent Depressive Symptoms in the Gazel Cohort." *Scandinavian Journal of Work and Environmental Health* 24: 197–205.

Ostry, Aleck S. and Jerry M. Spiegel. 2004. "Labor Markets and Employment Insecurity: Impacts of Globalization on the Healthcare Workforce." *International Journal of Occupational and Environmental Health* 10: 368–74.

Perrewe, Pamela L. and Daniel C. Ganster (eds.). 2002. *Historical and Current Perspectives on Stress and Health*. Amsterdam: JAI Elsevier.

Pfeffer, Jeffrey. 1998. *Human Equation: Building Profit by Putting People First*. Boston: Harvard Business School Press.

Popper, Karl R. 1959. *The Logic of Scientific Discovery*. New York: Harper and Row.

Rolls, Edmund T. 2000. "The Orbitofrontal Cortex and Reward." *Cerebral Cortex* 10: 284–94.

Rugulies, Reiner, Ute Bültmann, Birgit Aust, and Hermann Burr. 2006. "Psychosocial Work Environment and Incidence of Severe Depressive Symptoms: Prospective Findings from a 5-Year Follow-Up of the Danish Work Environment Cohort Study." *American Journal of Epidemiology* 163: 877–87.

Schnall, Peter, Marnie Dobson, E. Ellen Rosskam, Dean Baker, and Paul Landsbergis (eds.). 2009. *Unhealthy Work: Causes, Consequences and Cures.* Amityville, NY: Baywood Press.

Shields, M. 1999. "Long Working Hours and Health." *Health Report* 11: 33–48.

Siegrist, Johannes. 1996. "Adverse Health Effects of High-Effort/Low-Reward Conditions." *Journal of Occupational Health Psychology* 1: 27–41.

Siegrist, Johannes. 2008. "Chronic Psychosocial Stress at Work and Risk of Depression: Evidence From Prospective Studies." *European Archives of Psychiatry and Clinical Neuroscience* 258: 115–19.

Siegrist, Johannes and Nico Dragano. 2008. "Psychosocial Stress and Disease Risks in Occupational Life: Results of International Studies on the Demand–Control and the Effort–Reward Imbalance Models." *Bundesgesundheitsblatt: Gesundheitsforschung Gesundheitsschutz* 51: 305–12.

Siegrist, Johannes, Ingo Menrath, Tony Stöcker, Martina Klein, Thilo Kellermann, N. Jon Shah, Karl Zilles, and Frank Schneider. 2005. "Differential Brain Activation According to Chronic Social Reward Frustration." *NeuroReport* 16: 1899–903.

Siegrist, Johannes, Richard Peter, Astrid Junge, Peter Cremer, and Dieter Seidel. 1990. "Low Status Control, High Effort at Work and Ischaemic Heart Disease: Prospective Evidence from Blue-Collar Men." *Social Science and Medicine* 31: 1127–34.

Siegrist, Johannes and Andreas Rödel. 2006. "Work Stress and Health Risk Behavior." *Scandinavian Journal of Work, Environment and Health* 32: 473–81.

Siegrist, Johannes, Dagmar Starke, Tarani Chandola, Isabelle Godin, Michael Marmot, Isabelle Niedhammer, and Richard Peter. 2004. "The Measurement of Effort–Reward Imbalance at Work: European Comparisons." *Social Science and Medicine* 58: 1483–99.

Siegrist, Johannes and Töres Theorell. 2006. "Socioeconomic Position and Health: The Role of Work and Employment." Pp. 73–100 in Johannes Siegrist and Michael Marmot (eds.), *Social Inequalities in Health: New Evidence and Policy Implications.* Oxford: Oxford University Press.

Siegrist, Johannes, Morten Wahrendorf, Olaf von dem Knesebeck, Hendrik Jürges, and Axel Börsch-Supan. 2007. "Quality of Work, Well-Being, and Intended Early Retirement of Older Employees: Baseline Results from the SHARE Study." *European Journal of Public Health* 17: 62–8.

Siegrist, Johannes, Natalia Wege, Frank Pühlhofer, and Morten Wahrendorf. 2008. "A Short Generic Measure of Work Stress in the Era of Globalization: Effort–Reward Imbalance." *International Archives of Occupational and Environmental Health* (published online).

Stansfeld, Stephen A., Hans Bosma, Harry Hemingway, and Michael Marmot. 1998. "Psychosocial Work Characteristics and Social Support as Predictors of SF-36 Functioning: The Whitehall II Study." *Psychosomatic Medicine* 60: 247–55.

Stansfeld, Stephen A., Rebecca Fuhrer, Martin J. Shipley, and Michael Marmot. 1999. "Work Characteristics Predict Psychiatric Disorder: Prospective Results from the Whitehall II Study." *Occupational and Environmental Medicine* 56: 302–7.

Steptoe, Andrew. 2006. "Psychobiological Processes Linking Socio-Economic Position With Health." Pp. 101–26 in Johannes Siegrist and Michael Marmot (eds.), *Social Inequalities in Health: New Evidence and Policy Implications.* Oxford: Oxford University Press.

Theorell, Töres, Reza Emdad, Bengt Arnetz, and Anna-Maria Weingarten. 2001. "Employee Effects of an Educational Program for Managers at an Insurance Company." *Psychosomatic Medicine* 63: 724–33.

Tsutsumi, Akizumi and Norito Kawakami. 2004. "A Review of Empirical Studies on the Model of Effort–Reward Imbalance at Work: Reducing Occupational Stress by Implementing a New Theory." *Social Science and Medicine* 59: 2335–59.

Uchiyama, Shuji, Takashi Kurasawa, Toshihiro Sekizawa, and Hiroshi Nakatsuka. 2005. "Job Strain and Risk of Cardiovascular Events in Treated Hypertensive Japanese Workers: Hypertension Follow-Up Group Study." *Journal of Occupational Health* 47: 102–11.

Ursin, Holger and Hege R. Eriksen. 2004. "The Cognitive Activation Theory of Stress." *Psychoneuroendocrinology* 29: 567–92.

Vahtera, Jussi, Mika Kivimäki, Jaana Pentti, Anne Linna, Marianna Virtanen, Pekka Virtanen, and Jane E. Ferrie. 2004. "Organisational Downsizing, Sickness Absence, and Mortality: 10-Town Prospective Cohort Study." *British Medical Journal* 328: 555.

Van Vegchel, Natasja, Jan de Jonge, Hans Bosma, and Wilmar Schaufeli. 2005. "Reviewing the Effort–Reward Imbalance Model: Drawing Up the Balance of 45 Empirical Studies." *Social Science and Medicine* 60: 1117–31.

Vrijkotte, Tanja, Lorenz van Doornen, and Eco de Geus. 2000. "Effect of Work Stress on Ambulatory Blood Pressure, Heart Rate, and Heart Rate Variability." *Hypertension* 35: 880–6.

Wahrendorf, Morten, Olaf von dem Knesebeck, and Johannes Siegrist. 2006. "Social Productivity and Well-Being of Older People: Baseline Results from the SHARE Study." *European Journal of Ageing* 3: 67–73.

Wang, Jian Li and S. B. Pattern. 2004. "Perceived Work Stress and Major Depressive Episodes in a Population of Employed Canadians Over 18 Years Old." *Journal of Nervous and Mental Disease* 192: 160–3.

Warr, Peter. 1996. "Employee Well-Being." In Peter Warr (ed.), *Psychology at Work*. London: Wiley.

Weber, Max. 1958 [1904–5]. *The Protestant Ethic and the Spirit of Capitalism*, translated by T. Parsons. New York: Scribner's.

Weiner, Herbert. 1992. *Perturbing the Organism. The Biology of Stressful Experience*. Chicago: Chicago University Press.

Ylipaavalniemi, Jaana, Mika Kivimäki, Marko Elovainio, Marianna Virtanen, Liisa Keltikangas-Järvinen, and Jussi Vahtera. 2005. "Psychosocial Work Characteristics and Incidence of Newly Diagnosed Depression: A Prospective Cohort Study of Three Different Models." *Social Science and Medicine* 61: 111–22.

Part IV
Health and Disease

13

Emerging Infectious Diseases, Urbanization, and Globalization in the Time of Global Warming

George J. Armelagos and Kristin N. Harper

Disease ecology in the modern world is often discussed as a consequence of three recent and independent developments – globalization, urbanization, and disease emergence. However, we argue that these processes are inextricably linked and that the foundations of the current disease-scape began millennia earlier than traditionally thought. Using an epidemiological model of disease transition as a means of understanding the changing pattern of disease ecology in human evolution, we will discuss the relationships between globalization, urbanization, and emerging disease. Situating them in an evolutionary and ecological context, we will also consider the effects of a process that will increasingly influence the type and prevalence of infectious diseases present in human populations: global warming.

To better understand changing ecological relationships between humans, pathogens, and other disease insults we will employ an epidemiological transition conceptual framework (Armelagos, Barnes, and Lin 1996; Barrett et al. 1998). Human populations have undergone three disease transitions (Armelagos and Barnes 1999; Armelagos and Harper 2005a; Barnes, Armelagos, and Morreale 1999; Barrett et al. 1998). The first epidemiological transition occurred around 10,000 years ago with a major shift in the subsistence economy from foraging to agriculture. This transition was marked by the emergence of novel infectious and nutritional diseases (Cohen and Armelagos 1984). The pattern of emerging diseases linked with nutritional disease continued with the urban transformation about 6,000 years ago and remains the dominant pattern to the present day in many parts of the world. About 200 years ago, however, some populations in developed nations underwent a second epidemiological transition in which improved nutrition, emerging public health measures, and medicine led to a decline in infectious disease and a rise in non-infectious, chronic, and degenerative diseases (Omran 1971, 1977, 1982, 2001). Humankind is now entering a third epidemiological transition (Barrett et al. 1998) in which there is a resurgence of infectious diseases previously thought to be under control. Many of these resurging pathogens are resistant to many antibiotics (Johnson et al. 2006; Upton, Lang, and Heffernan 2003; Webber and Piddock 2001;

Zager and McNerney 2008; Zhang and Young 1994) and some, such as the extremely drug-resistant tuberculosis strains that emerged recently in KwaZulu Natal, South Africa, are virtually untreatable (Raviglione 2006). Accompanying these resurgent diseases are a number of novel infections (Holmes and Rambaut 2004; Morse 1997; Satcher 1995). As recent experience with severe acute respiratory syndrome (SARS), West Nile Virus, and various drug-resistant strains of common pathogens has borne out, many emerging and resurging infectious diseases have the potential to be spread globally (Becker, Hu, and Biller-Andorno 2006; Jones et al. 2008; Woolhouse 2008). These spreading infections affect both populations that experienced the second disease transition and those that were never so fortunate.

An essential feature of modern disease ecology is the social and economic inequality that arose in post-Neolithic societies and has accelerated with advances in technology, urbanization, globalization, and global warming (Armelagos, Brown, and Turner 2005).

THE CONTEXT OF GLOBALIZATION

Paul Farmer (1996) has shown how global social inequities are at the center of many emerging diseases. According to Farmer (2004), those in power use structural violence to "erase history" by discouraging scrutiny of the political-economic factors that bring humans into contact with pathogens. Despite the high level of affluence in the United States at the national level, Americans are not immune to the impact of poverty. One famous study, for example, revealed that an adult man living in New York City's Harlem has a greater age-specific mortality than an adult man living in Bangladesh (McCord and Freeman 1990). The WHO *World Health Report* (World Health Organization 1995: 1) corroborated the importance of poverty in the health equation when it reported:

> The World's biggest killer and greatest cause of ill-health and suffering across the globe is listed almost at the end of the International Classification of Diseases. It is given in code Z59.5 – extreme poverty.

Urbanization and globalization are coupled in their impact upon social inequality and disease emergence (Armelagos and Harper 2005). Globalization is often mistakenly seen as a product of recent political-economic events. However, there is abundant evidence that the processes of globalization and urbanization began millennia ago. William McNeill (1976) describes the process in which urban centers coalesce and expand as they "digest" populations they encounter in their paths, easing their expansion into new habitats. The confluence of urban centers from 500 BCE until 1200 CE, according to McNeill, created the first major disease pools in Eurasia. The development of the Mongol Empire, from 1200 to 1500 CE, resulted in the second phase of globalization and emerging disease. Transoceanic exchange from 1500 to 1700 CE was the third phase in the historic process of globalization, resulting in one of the great periods of disease exchange (Crosby 1972, 1994, 2003, 2004).

Today, cities are the major feature of human habitation. Individual cities are growing to unprecedented size. Tokyo (33 million), New York City (24 million), Seoul (23 million), Delhi (21 million), and São Paulo (20 million) are the five largest cities in the world (Brinkhoff 2008), and many of the new megacities (defined as having populations greater than 10 million) can be found in low-income countries. In 1900, only 10 percent of the global populations were urban dwellers. This percentage now exceeds 50 percent and will increase even more in the next 50 years. More than 95 percent of this net increase will be in cities of the developing world, which will soon approach the 80 percent urbanization level of most industrialized nations (WorldResources1996–97 1996). Humankind's radical transformation from a rural to an urban animal has created what Stewart Brand (2006) described as a "city planet." In the modern era, the process of urbanization that gained momentum in the 1880s, in tandem with rapid transportation and the ecological impact of technological development, has driven social transformations that are marked by social inequalities. These forces shape the modern period of disease exchange.

MAJOR TRANSITIONS AND CHANGES IN DISEASE ECOLOGY

Having established the concept of disease transitions and discussing the context for globalization, we will now consider in more detail the changes in disease ecology that have occurred in human history.

Paleolithic baseline

Understanding the disease ecology of Paleolithic populations requires triangulation from a number of areas of investigation. Empirical evidence from paleopathology has shown that a shift from foraging to agriculture resulted in a pattern of emerging infectious disease, a finding that aids in establishing the Paleolithic as a baseline for studying the evolution of disease (Cohen and Armelagos 1984). A second line of evidence comes from the dwindling numbers of contemporary foragers who at one time lived in relative isolation. The disease ecology of contemporary gatherer-hunters provides a model for the diseases that would have afflicted Paleolithic foragers. Finally, the genomic analysis of humans, pathogens, and domesticated plants and animals provides information regarding both the origins of agriculture and disease emergence.

Ecological and social relationships that characterized the Paleolithic would have minimized the impact of infectious disease upon human populations. Paleolithic individuals would have retained many pathogens they shared with their primate ancestors (heirloom species) and would also have been exposed to zoonoses (souvenir species) that they acquired while foraging. However, sparse, mobile populations would have precluded the existence of many infectious diseases, such as measles, that can only persist in large populations. In addition to the reduced burden of infectious diseases suggested by small population size, well-balanced dietary patterns would have minimized susceptibility to infection. In fact, some have suggested the Paleolithic diet represents an ideal model modern humans can emulate (Eaton and Cordain 1997; Eaton and Eaton 2000; Eaton, Konner, and Shostak 1988a, 1988b).

While evidence suggests the Paleolithic was a relatively healthy time in human history, there is some controversy regarding the quality of living conditions and the demographic characteristics of this era. A perception of the Paleolithic as an idyllic setting where well-nourished populations lived in a disease-free environment has led some to suggest a "Paleolithic prescription" for better health in contemporary populations (Cordain et al. 2005; Cordain et al. 2000; Eaton and Eaton 2000). While Williams and Nesse (1991) believe that the human body reflects adaptation to the Stone Age, they attempt to move beyond this "Club Med" perception of the Paleolithic. They assert that populations were stable for much of the period because maximum fertility rates were balanced by very high mortality rates. They also argue that infectious disease burden increased during the Neolithic period. If this contention were true, however, it would have been difficult for the population to explode as it did following the Neolithic, since fertility rate would already be at a maximum while mortality rates would climb ever higher. An alternative scenario (Armelagos, Goodman, and Jacobs 1991) suggests fertility was not at its maximum during the Paleolithic. Thus, humans were later able to respond reproductively to the Neolithic economic demand for more children while experiencing increasing mortality from nutritional deficiencies and infectious disease (Cohen and Armelagos 1984).

The forensic application of genomic analysis (Cummings and Relman 2002) has stimulated the study of phylogenetic relationships between and among pathogens. The phylogenetic relationships of pathogens provide clues to their patterns of adaptation and their relationship to human hosts (Armelagos and Harper 2005b, 2005c). Such genomic analyses have forced a reanalysis of the theory that the majority of human infectious diseases emerged in the last 10,000 years. Using genetics, complemented by other sources of information, we are now able to fine tune our understanding of a pattern of emerging diseases dating thousands of years earlier than the advent of the Neolithic. The evidence suggests that as humans began the process of domestication, a process that in many areas began well before agriculture was adopted, they were exposed to the zoonotic diseases that these newly important animals carried.

Heirloom pathogens

Heirloom species that had long-standing relationships with our ape and hominid ancestors include most of the internal protozoa found in modern humans and also such bacteria as staphylococci (Cockburn 1967a, 1967b). *Bordetella pertussis*, the pathogen that causes whooping cough, was thought to be of very recent origin. Diavatopoulos and colleagues (2005: 0380) state:

> The whooping cough never appeared in Europe originally, but was transported thither from other parts of the world by means of merchandise, seamen, and animals. Its first appearance in Sweden cannot be determined with any certainty; but in France it began in the year 1414.

In contrast, sixteenth- and seventeenth-century descriptions of the disease and epidemics in Europe are frequently documented in the literature. This historical evidence suggested a recent introduction into European populations. New results, however, suggest that *B. pertussis* evolved from a lineage of *B. bronchiseptica*, a pathogen that infects and causes disease in a wide range of mammals (Diavatopoulos et al. 2005). This pathogen may already have had a preference for hominids up to 2.5 million years ago. Diavatopoulos and co-workers propose that the association of *B. pertussis* with humans is, in fact, ancient, but the introduction of *B. pertussis* into Europe may be more recent.

While the antiquity of some infections is well established, there is considerable controversy regarding others. For example, there is evidence that *Treponema pallidum* is an heirloom disease. A number of species of Old World primates, such as patas monkeys, baboons (Fribourg-Blanc and Mollaret 1969; Fribourg-Blanc, Mollaret, and Niel 1966), chimpanzees (Felsenfeld and Wolf 1971), and gorillas (Cousins 1972), contract a yaws-like infection. This suggests the pathogen may have been passed down from our last common ancestor (Froment 1994). In addition, Rothschild, Hershkovitz, and Rothschild (1995) describe possible yaws infection in Pleistocene remains, although the skeletal signs present are not pathognomonic for the infection. Finally, a phylogenetic examination of the *T. pallidum* family of bacteria indicates that the subspecies that causes yaws arose first in human history in either Africa or Asia, predating the subspecies that cause bejel and syphilis (Harper et al. 2008a; Harper et al. 2008b). This evidence for the antiquity of yaws, however, is puzzling in light of the absence of skeletal signs of yaws infection in many ancient populations (Baker and Armelagos 1988). Since yaws typically occurs in hot, humid environments, it is possible that preservation in affected areas is too poor to produce many cases. Additional genetic studies, with greater resolution, may help clarify the history of this pathogen.

The history of *Mycobacterium tuberculosis* is also still being explored; more evidence is suggesting this pathogen may have arisen very early in hominid evolution. One popular and widely cited theory has *M. tuberculosis* arising in the Neolithic when humans shared space with their newly domesticated animals (Stead 1997). This proximity would have exposed humans to the airborne pathogen *M. bovis*, carried by cattle, and mutants that could successfully exploit this new human niche would have been selected for in this environment. While this scenario is certainly plausible, it is not supported by genetic data. Analysis of single nucleotide polymorphisms (SNPs) at silent (synonymous) sites found in 26 different genes in bacteria sampled from all over the world indicates that *M. tuberculosis* did indeed emerge relatively recently in human history: from 15,000–20,000 years ago, a period roughly consistent with cattle domestication (Sreevatsan et al. 1997). Another, more recent, study of SNPs in antibiotic resistance genes also indicates that the population diversity in *M. tuberculosis* has accumulated relatively recently (Baker et al. 2004). However, a phylogeny based on deletions in the *M. tuberculosis* genome suggests the human pathogen diverged earlier than the form found in voles, seals, goats, and cows (Mostowy et al. 2002). This phylogeny is supported by another analysis of deletions which rules out the linear evolution of *M. tuberculosis* from *M. bovis* (Gordon et al. 1999). One study has even turned the original relationship on its head, suggesting that *M. bovis* evolved from the ancestor of today's *M. tuberculosis* strains, which may or may not have been a human pathogen (Brosch et al. 2001). While the relationship between *M. tuberculosis* and *M. bovis* is still unclear, it seems certain that *M. tuberculosis* was not likely to have arisen from *M. bovis* (Baker et al. 2004).

If tuberculosis did not arise in Neolithic European cattle domesticators, then where did it come from? A study of SNPs in antibiotic resistance genes found that no one subtype predominated in African-born patients, indicating that Africa is a sort of melting pot for genetic diversity in this pathogen (Baker et al. 2004). This suggests tuberculosis may have disseminated during ancient human migrations and along trade routes. This hypothesized African origin is supported by a recent study of East African strains which found human bacilli from this region represent extant bacteria of a much broader progenitor species from which the *M. tuberculosis* clonal group evolved (Gutierrez et al. 2005). Using the molecular clock, it was estimated that before the recent expansion of *M. tuberculosis*, this progenitor species may have existed for as long as 3 million years, possibly infecting early hominids. However, another SNP-based study has suggested that tuberculosis strains originated in India, only later spreading to East Africa (Filliol et al. 2006). It seems probable, based on newly available evidence, that *M. tuberculosis* became established in early hominid populations and did not emerge, as previously believed, in Neolithic Europe. However, additional genetic studies will help clarify the history of this pathogen in human populations.

Souvenir pathogens

In contrast to heirloom species, "souvenir" species are pathogens that are picked up as humans go about their daily activity. Insect bites, the preparation and consumption of contaminated flesh, bites of animals and contact with urine and feces of infected animals are sources of zoonotic disease. The pantheon of zoonotic diseases that most likely afflicted earlier gatherer-hunters includes: sleeping sickness (trypanosomiasis), relapsing fever caused by the spirochete *Borrelia*, trichinosis from the roundworm *Trichinella spiralis*, tetanus resulting from exposure to the toxin produced by *Clostridium tetani*, scrub typhus (*Orientia tsutsugamushi*), tularemia (*Francisella tularensis*), avian or ichthyic tuberculosis, leptospirosis (from the spirochete *Leptospira* spp), and schistosomiasis (Cockburn 1971).

The status of falciparum malaria as a souvenir disease in the Pleistocene is somewhat controversial. Recent reconstruction of the early hominid environment suggests they inhabited grassy woodlands that could have included the *Anopheles* mosquitoes. However, the threat of malaria in early hominids, while present, may not have been particularly large because the small population size of the foragers could not support endemic disease. Livingstone (1958, 1971, 1983) has shown the selection for the sickle cell allele, which protects against malaria in heterozygotes that also carry a normal copy of the gene, developed as slash-and-burn agriculture was introduced into West Africa during the last 3,000 years. Clearing land produced pools of clean water that are ideal for the breeding of the malaria vector *Anopheles gambiae* resulting in the spread of *Plasmodium falciparum*. Thus, slash-and-burn agriculture accompanying increases in human populations led to an explosion of the mosquito population.

Various genetic studies attempting to reconstruct the evolutionary history of this pathogen have arrived at different results. An early genetic study of *P. falciparum* indicated the pathogen originated 8 million years ago (Ayala, Escalante, and Rich 1999). These findings were challenged by a subsequent study suggesting malaria emerged between 9,500 and 23,000 years ago (Volkman et al. 2001). Most recently, results have been unveiled which help to reconcile these two scenarios (Joy et al. 2003). These data suggest that while *P. falciparum* originated 50,000 to 100,000 years ago, there was a "sudden increase in the African malaria parasite population about 10,000 years ago" that spread to other parts of the region. Thus, though malaria would have existed in Pleistocene humans, contraction of the disease was probably somewhat unusual.

The proposition that falciparum malaria did not become a significant human pathogen until after the Neolithic finds support in a study of the human genetic response to malaria. The genetic structure of variants of glucose-6-phosphate dehydrogenase confirms that malaria is a recent selective force in human populations (Tishkoff et al. 2001). The timing of the independent African "A" and Mediterranean "Med" mutations in GDP-6, dated to 3,840–11,760 and 1,600–6,640 years before present, respectively, suggest that *P. falciparum* infection began to exert a strong pressure upon human populations only in the last 10,000 years.

Pathogens that emerged and became established in the Pleistocene

Molecular analysis has provided some startling insights into the origins of the taenid tapeworms and their human host (Shipman 2002). The tapeworms that parasitize domesticated cattle (*T. saginata*) and pigs (*T. solium*) are prodigious egg producers that use their scolex to attach to the intestine of the definitive human host and can reach lengths of up to 30 feet. Each of the worm's 1,000 to 2,000 segments (proglottids) can carry 50,000 to 100,000 eggs. It had long been assumed that humans became infected by the taenid in the Neolithic period during the process of cattle and pig domestication. However, as a result of a phylogenetic and biogeographic analysis by Hoberg and his team (Hoberg et al. 2001; Hoberg et al. 2000), it now looks as if tapeworms originated as human parasites in the Paleolithic. Hoberg's molecular clock analysis suggests the human parasite sister species (*T. saginata* and *T. asiatica*) diverged from one another from 780,000 to 1.7 million years ago, long before humans migrated out of Africa. Hoberg and colleagues suggest hominids and carnivores preyed on similar animals. This supposes the humans transmitted tapeworms to domesticated cattle and swine. A regular pattern of scavenging and hunting appears to have originated on three separate occasions (Shipman 2002) and resulted in the transfer of taenids to humans from game animals. There has even been speculation that these processes were enhanced by the practice of cannibalism and the consumption of dogs (Hoberg et al. 2001).

Similarly, the two types of human lice appear to have emerged in the Pleistocene. Lice as ectoparasites have afflicted primate species such as Old World and New World monkeys since the Oligocene (Laird 1989). About 70,000 years ago, however, body lice (*Pediculus humanus humanus*) diverged from head lice (*Pediculus humanus capitas*) (Kittler, Kayser, and Stoneking 2003). This event may have occurred when clothing became a part of the human wardrobe, providing a habitat conducive to the evolution of a new, specialized pathogen.

In contrast to the two pathogens just discussed, *Salmonella typhi*, the causative agent of typhoid, was believed by some to be an heirloom pathogen until molecular data suggested it emerged in the Pleistocene. A phylogenetic study indicated the most recent common ancestor of all strains existed between 10,000 and 71,000 years ago (Roumagnac et al. 2006). The authors suggest the ancestral haplotype of *Salmonella typhus* arose after human migrations out of Africa but before the Neolithic period. The existence of an asymptomatic human carrier state could allow decades to pass between initial infection and new transmission. Thus, the human carrier state could have allowed the persistence of infection with *S. typhi* during periods of isolation and would have been essential for transmission between hunter-gatherer groups.

Although genetic studies have contributed significantly to our understanding of infectious disease in the past, it should be clear by now that genetic data are not always easy to interpret and should be considered in the light of other evidence. For example, *Shigella*, a pathogenic form of *E. coli* which has no carrier state or alternative host, was assumed to need a large population base to maintain it. Since Paleolithic groups would have been too small and too widely dispersed to support this bacterium, it was assumed to have arisen following the advent of major human civilizations. Recently, however, reports indicate that *Shigella* strains evolved 35,000 to 270,000 years ago (Pupo, Lan, and Reeves 2000). In addition, the *Shigella* strains suggest a complex origin in which convergent evolution has taken place (Pupo et al. 2000). Does this indicate that dysentery predated the agricultural transformation? If so, *Shigella* must either have a greater capacity to survive in small human bands than was previously thought, or human social organization was more complex in the Paleolithic than is currently believed. However, a more realistic explanation for the discrepancy between the expectation and the molecular data may be problems in calibrating the molecular clock, which appear to account for the frequent earlier-than-expected dates attributed to relatively recent evolutionary events (Ho and Larson 2006). Therefore, while molecular data can provide surprising insights into pathogen history, the results of molecular clock calculations must be considered in the light of other data.

The first epidemiological transition: Neolithic diseases

Agriculture or primary food production is usually dated to about 10,000 years ago in the Old World. In the Old World, the five major centers of domestication included areas of Mesopotamia, Sub-Saharan Africa, Southeast Asia, northern China, and southern China. In the New World, centers of maize domestication in Mesoamerica and potatoes in South America are the sixth and seventh independent centers of agriculture. Newly sedentary populations grew exponentially, and density increased as a consequence. The domestication of plants and animals transformed human ecology, disrupting the environment to which humans had adapted. Added to this was a rise in socioeconomic inequality associated with adoption of agriculture.

The transition from a nomadic to a sedentary lifestyle resulted in greater potential for parasitic infection. Suddenly, the living areas for both humans and domesticated animals, water sources, and the areas in which human waste were deposited could all be found in close proximity. This close relationship between humans and domesticated animals resulted in exposure to an array of zoonotic diseases. The milk, hair, and skin of domesticates, as well as the dust they raised, transmitted anthrax, Q fever, brucellosis, and bovine tuberculosis. Although tapeworm infection of humans may have arisen in the Pleistocene, infection by parasites associated with domesticated animals must have intensified during this time period. Peri-domesticates, such as rats, who lived near human permanent habitats must have also been a source of disease.

Independent of animal domestication, the actual practice of farming would have resulted in exposure to new diseases and higher incidence of known infections. During the course of their work, cultivators are susceptible to insect bites that transmit diseases such as scrub typhus (Audy 1961). As discussed earlier, slash-and-burn agriculture in West Africa exposed populations to the mosquito that is the vector for malaria (Livingstone 1958; Wiesenfeld 1968). In this way, falciparum malaria, present in the Paleolithic, became more common in the Neolithic. Other farming practices, such as the provision of artificial containers ideal for breeding the mosquito *Aedes aegypti*, also disturbed the existing ecology and increased human contact with arthropod vectors that carried yellow fever, dengue, trypanosomiasis, and filariasis. Finally, irrigation (Sattenspiel 2000; Watts et al. 1998), and the use of human feces as fertilizer, increased contact with non-vector parasites (Cockburn 1971). Emerging diseases in the Neolithic would have included many infections such as influenza, measles, mumps, and smallpox.

Surprisingly, primary food production resulted in dietary deficiencies that potentially exacerbated the infectious disease profile. Cohen and Armelagos (1984) provide numerous studies that show a decline in health following the Neolithic. In the past, agricultural subsistence invariably reduced the variety of foods available to farmers (Armelagos 1987). This is because agriculturalists frequently specialized in a single, central domesticate such as millet, rice, wheat, or maize. The narrowing of the dietary niche (Katz 1987) resulted in dietary deficiencies which can increase the impact of infectious disease (Hulsewe et al. 1999; Ulijaszek 2000). In addition, the necessity of food storage increased the potential for food poisoning (Brothwell 1972; Brothwell and Brothwell 1998). The combination of newly emerging complex societies, increasing division by class, epidemic disease, and dietary insufficiencies resulted in increased markers of biological stress levels in post-Agricultural populations (Goodman et al. 1984). For this reason, Diamond has declared that agriculture was humankind's greatest mistake (Diamond 1987), rather than its finest invention.

The second epidemiological transition

During the last century and a half, data from England, Wales, and Sweden showed a fundamental shift in disease patterns (Omran 1971: 162). Omran demonstrated a decrease in pathogen-induced infections and an increase in chronic, man-made diseases (Omran 1971: 163). He described a trend in which humans moved from an "age of pestilence and famine" to an "age of receding pandemics," ending in "the age of degenerative and man-made diseases." In Omran's model (1971, 1977, 1982, 1983), the elimination of infectious diseases allows a population to age, which results in increasing rates of chronic and degenerative diseases, or those of "man's"

making. While his use of the term "man-made" disease anticipated the roles pollution and other by-products of the industrial age play in the disease process (Caldwell
2001), it obscured the role of humans in creating the pattern of infectious disease.

It should be noted that this decline in infectious and rise in chronic disease
occurred only in certain high-income nations. Many countries have never experienced the second epidemiological transition, and others experience it in varied patterns (Barrett et al. 1998). In addition, in the last half century the rate of the decline
in infectious disease has decelerated in many countries (Gwatkin 1997), with some
not reaching the expectation for high-income nations (Gobalet 1989). Rapid urbanization, marked social inequalities, and a lack of public health infrastructure have
resulted in the urban underclasses' exposure to infectious diseases, while chronic
degenerative diseases have increased among the affluent and emerging middle classes
(Muktatkar 1995). In Mexico, Brazil, and other middle-income countries, socioeconomic status is inversely related to risk of chronic diseases such as obesity and
hypertension (Popkin 1994). This pattern is similar to the associations found in
affluent nations such as the United States and the United Kingdom (Kaplan and Keil
1993). This differential impact within and between nations reflects the role that
economic factors play in determining disease risk.

The factors responsible for the second epidemiological transition are controversial. It is often attributed to emergence of public health measures effective in com-
bating infectious diseases. However, Thomas McKeown (1976, 1983; McKeown
and Brown 1955) demonstrated a decline in infectious diseases long before most
pathogens were recognized, vaccinations developed, or effective medicines developed. McKeown and Brown (1955) claimed that improved nutrition was the major
factor in the decline of infectious disease. Frank and Mustard (1994) claim McKeown
did not fairly assess public health measures or behavioral features such as increased
birth spacing that led to a decline in infant mortality. In addition, some have claimed
(Szreter 2002) that McKeown failed to consider the historical importance of the
nineteenth-century redistributive social philosophy and the practical politics that
characterized the public health movement.

The third epidemiological transition

We are now witnessing the latest revision in the human–disease relationship, a
direct result of social, economic, and technological change on a global level.
There are six factors at the root of the re-emergence of infectious disease in the
third epidemiological transition: ecological change, human demographics and
behavior, international travel and commerce, technology and industry, microbial
adaptation and change, and the breakdown of public health measures (Institute
of Medicine 1992). We cannot overstate the importance of anthropogenic factors
in disease emergence. In this chapter, we highlight the role of globalization and
urbanization in the time of global warming, in this, the latest phase of the third
epidemiological transition.

Jones and colleagues (2008) have confirmed that emerging diseases are driven by
socioeconomic, environmental, and ecological factors. An examination of 335
instances of emerging disease from 1940 to 2004 demonstrated that, even after
considering reporting bias, there was a rise in emerging infectious disease that

peaked in the 1980s during the HIV pandemic. These emerging disease events were primarily contracted from zoonoses (60.3 percent), with most of them originating from wildlife (71.8 percent) (Jones et al. 2008: 990). Of these diseases, 54.3 percent were bacteria or rickettsia, many of which were antibiotic resistant.

This study also identified global clusters, or "hot spots" in which emerging diseases are likely to originate. For example, in the lower latitudes, in areas with substandard levels of reporting, there is a substantial risk of vector-borne and wildlife zoonotic disease. Unfortunately, as Jones and colleagues (2008) show, global scientific resources for surveillance are poorly located and most often found in countries where emerging diseases are least likely to appear. Given that emerging infectious diseases are a global economic and public health burden, this is not money well spent.

Urbanization

Within the last 125 years, the industrial transformation increased population size and density resulting in massive environmental change and the added stress of pollution, which now includes industrial waste. The mortality was so great that cities have been called the "graveyards of humanity." In the early 1800s, London and Beijing were the first cities to have over a million inhabitants. The pattern of social and economic disparity increases with squatters surrounding the cities. Disease epidemics with outbreaks of typhoid fever, typhus, smallpox, and yellow fever become a common part of the disease-scape. Industrial cities become a source of emerging disease to areas that had been free of epidemic disease until contact.

Urbanization is usually associated with a decline in birth and death rates following the pattern of the second epidemiological transition. Urbanites enjoy better health on average than rural inhabitants. However, there is an economic disparity, with the rich benefiting the most (Dye 2008). According to Christopher Dye (2008: 767), about 3.3 billion people representing over half of the world's population now live in an urban setting. He estimates that there are 50,000 settlements with 50,000 or more inhabitants. Within ten years, and continuing into the future, population growth will be in urban areas with 500 cities having between 1 and 10 million inhabitants, the majority of them in poorer, developing countries. Dye estimates that three-quarters of those who earn less than a dollar a day live in rural settings, while the number of the urban poor is rising. A billion people (a third of urban inhabitants) live in slums with a higher proportion in Sub-Saharan Africa and South Asia.

Anthony McMichael (2000) notes urban living is now the keystone of modern human ecology, with a crucial role in shaping emerging infectious disease. While there are many positive features of the urban revolution, there are health costs. McMichael (2000: 1117) calls urban centers the "incubators and gateways for infectious diseases." The positive aspects of urbanization are being slowed by the pressures and priorities of globalization. In addition to the risks of respiratory and diarrheal disease, according to McMichael, urban poor face the risk of vector-borne infections, lead and air pollution, traffic hazards, and urban heat load that is exacerbated by global warming.

The economic disparity in modern trends in urbanization is the primary issue in the pattern of urbanization and emerging diseases. In the last half century, the world population has increased from 2.5 billion to 6.1 billion. There are more than a billion people living as squatters in what Robert Neuwirth (2005) has called "shadow cities," and they do not reap the health benefits of the richer segments of their cities.

Globalization

The process of globalization and its impact on urbanization and emerging disease is well documented. However, what is less known is the impact of globalization on antibiotic use. The worldview of medicine in an era of antibiotics has always assumed that another antibiotic could be developed when a pathogen became resistant to a specific antibiotic. An understanding of evolutionary principles should have foretold that resistant antibiotics were inevitable. In fact, Alexander Fleming (1945: 93) in his Nobel Award acceptance speech forewarned of the inevitable crisis in antibiotic resistance:

> It is not difficult to make microbes resistant to penicillin in the laboratory by exposing them to concentrations not sufficient to kill them, and the same thing has occasionally happened in the body … Then there is the danger that the ignorant man may easily underdose himself and by exposing his microbes to non-lethal quantities of the drug make them resistant.

The indiscriminate use of antibiotics produces rapid selection in the pathogen. Over 40,000,000 pounds of antibiotics are manufactured yearly in the United States (Levy 1992), which represents an eightyfold increase from the 500,000 pounds produced in 1954. Antibiotic resistance in pathogens was inevitable given the intense selective pressures created by the massive amounts of antibiotic produced and used.

Just as infectious diseases have been subjected to globalization, antibiotic resistance has met the same fate (Schito 2002; Smith and Coast 2002; Zhang et al. 2006). Globalization increases the vulnerability of disease threats from other countries and the antibiotic-resistant pathogens they carry (Smith and Coast 2002). Johnston and co-workers (2006) showed that Mexican produce had *Enterococcus* isolates with a higher degree of resistance to antibiotics than domesticated products. Schito (2002) argues that there are global issues with antibiotic resistance. Schito showed there were profound geographic differences in the resistance profile of respiratory pathogens that could not be explained by local antibiotic use and that may result from the spread of resistant clones. The pattern of antibiotic resistance has been compared in China, Kuwait, and the United States (Zhang et al. 2006) with the purpose of understanding the global threat of the phenomenon. The "bug-drug" data from this study show China has the highest prevalence of antibiotic pathogens (41 percent) that are increasing at the greatest rate (22 percent growth from 1994 to 2003). Zhang and colleagues say that while there has not been an international convergence of antibiotic resistance, with the international travel that is part of globalization such a convergence is a possibility. Smith and Coast (2002) outline strategies and collective actions for containing resistance.

Global warming

Urbanization and globalization exist with the backdrop of global warming. It is now accepted that greenhouse gases have been the source of climate change (Haines et al. 2006). Githeko et al. (2000) estimate that in the next 100 years there will be an average rise of 1 to 3.5 degrees Celsius, increasing vector-borne disease in new areas.

One aspect of global warming is the spread of the Asian tiger mosquito (*Aedes albopictus*), a notorious daytime feeder (Enserink 2008). The Asian tiger mosquito was first discovered in Memphis, Tennessee, in 1983; by 2008, it had spread to 36 states and to Central and South America. The errant insect arrived in the United States inside the water found inside used tires that were brought to America to be recapped. The mosquito has an ability to survive desiccation and, hence, can deal with climatic variation (Enserink 2008: 865). The Asian tiger mosquito in nature breeds in tree holes and now has adapted to a variety of containers such as vases, buckets, and pots. The mosquito was also a stowaway on Lucky bamboo (*Dracaena sanderina*), a decorative plant imported from China. In addition to its nuisance as a daytime feeder, the Asian tiger mosquito is a carrier of a number of pathogens (Enserink 2008). The mosquito is a carrier of two debilitating diseases – dengue (*Flavirus*) and chikungunya (*Alphavirus*). The tiger mosquito is a non-discriminate feeder and may bite an infected human for one meal and then move to a lizard, breaking the chain of infection since the virus can only be transmitted to primates. Duane Gubler is more optimistic and has argued that *Aedes albopictus* can outcompete *Aedes aegypti* and may lead to less of a dengue disease threat (Enserink 2008). Morens and Fauci (2008) disagree and see *Ae. albopictus* becoming so ubiquitous that there will be widespread dengue in the United States.

Footnote: Bioterrorism

In containing the problem of emerging disease, we must confront the issue of bioterrorism, the purposeful transmission of infectious diseases for nefarious purposes (Khardori 2006; Meinhardt 2005; Moran, Talan, and Abrahamian 2008; Radosavljevic and Jakovljevic 2007). Rotz and colleagues (2002: 225) discuss a classification of bioterrorist threats based on their impact on the public health from illness and death, the mass delivery potential of a virulent agent and its ability to be transmitted person to person, the potential of civil disruption and the fear that the threat induces, and the special public preparedness that this threat requires. The greatest threats (Category A) include smallpox, anthrax, plague, botulism, tularemia, and viral hemorrhagic fevers (Filoviruses and Arenaviruses). Lesser threats include Q fever, brucellosis, glander, meliodosis, encephalitis, typhus fever, psittacosis, toxic syndrome (Ricin and Staphylococcus enterotoxin B), food (*Salmonella* and *E. coli* O157:H7) and water (Vibrio cholera and *Cryptosporidium parvum*) threats. Many of these diseases that emerged during the first epidemiological transition have become potential tools of bioterrorism.

CONCLUSION

Parasitic and infectious diseases have played a major role in the evolutionary journey of humankind. During the Paleolithic period, small nomadic populations would have been exposed to parasites and pathogens they shared with their anthropoid ancestors. With the shift to agriculture, there was the emergence of a number of zoonotic diseases that characterized human/pathogen interaction. The process of urbanization, beginning about 6,000 years ago, created a new disease environment that enhanced person-to-person contact.

About 150 years ago, humans experienced a second epidemiological transition with the decline of infectious disease and the rise of chronic and degenerative conditions. Improved nutrition, public health, and medical practice all contributed to this transition that occurred in developed nations. Many of the nations that underwent the second epidemiological transition are facing the burden of an onslaught of re-emerging and emerging infectious diseases. Human are now urban beings. More than half of the human population are living in cities and this number will increase significantly with time. The socioeconomic transition has created a "city planet" in which urbanization is increasing in the developing countries in lower latitudes, with many of their inhabitants living as squatters in "shadow cities." While the modern cities are healthy environments, many of the rising urban centers in developing nations challenge the health of their inhabitants.

A second challenge that has characterized the most recent phase of emerging disease has been the process of global warming. Models predict that in the next 60 years there will be a 3 to 5 degree increase in global temperature. While the cause has been debated, it now appears the earth is warming, the sea levels are rising, and snow cover is being depleted. These climatological changes are increasing the habitat of mosquitoes to the more temperate zones and increasing the range in mountain tropical regions where the insects can live at higher altitudes.

We are in the throes of a third epidemiological transition in which we have the re-emergence of diseases thought to be near extinction. Many of these diseases are resistant to at least one antibiotic; some are resistant to many antibiotics. Added to this dilemma, we have the emergence of a number of unique pathogens. These challenges are occurring in an era of globalization, unprecedented urbanization, and global warming as we are approaching the end of an antibiotic era. On December 4, 1967, William Stewart, Surgeon General of the United States, in a presentation to the Association of State and Territorial Health Officials (Novick 2008), stated: "It's time we close the book on infectious disease." Stewart was preparing the medical establishment to deal with chronic and degenerative diseases that were a problem for Americans. Unfortunately, we have to reopen the book on infectious disease. As we read chapters that deal with emerging infectious disease, we look wearily at an epilogue that adds chronic diseases to our disease burden. We now live in a world where we have to consider both infectious and chronic diseases. And it is a dilemma of our own making.

References

Armelagos, George J. 1987. "Biocultural Aspects of Food Choice." Pp. 579–94 in M. Harris and E. Ross (eds.), *Food and Evolution*. Philadelphia: Temple University Press.

Armelagos, George J. and Kathleen C. Barnes. 1999. "The Evolution of Human Disease and the Rise of Allergy: Epidemiological Transitions." *Medical Anthropology* 18: 187–213.

Armelagos, George J., Kathleen C. Barnes, and James Lin. 1996. "Disease in Human Evolution: The Re-Emergence of Infectious Disease in the Third Epidemiological Transition." *AnthroNotes* 18: 1–7.

Armelagos, George J., Peter J. Brown, and Bethany Turner. 2005. "Evolutionary, Historical and Political Economic Perspectives on Health and Disease." *Social Science and Medicine* 61: 755–65.

Armelagos, George J., Alan H. Goodman, and Kenneth H. Jacobs. 1991. "The Origins of Agriculture: Population Growth During a Period of Declining Health." *Population and Environment* 13: 9–22.

Armelagos, George J. and Kristin N. Harper. 2005a. "Disease Globalization in the Third Epidemiological Transition." Pp. 27–53 in G. Guest (ed.), *Globalization, Health, and the Environment: An Integrated Perspective*. Lanham, MD: Altamira Press. [was a and b]

Armelagos, George J. and Kristin N. Harper. 2005b. "Genomics at the Origins of Agriculture, Part One." *Evolutionary Anthropology: Issues, News, and Reviews* 14: 68–77. [was c]

Armelagos, George J. and Kristin N. Harper. 2005c. "Genomics at the Origins of Agriculture, Part Two." *Evolutionary Anthropology: Issues, News, and Reviews* 14: 109–21. [was d]

Audy, J. Ralph. 1961. "The Ecology of Scrub Typhus." Pp. 389–432 in J. M. May (ed.), *Studies in Disease Ecology*. New York: Hafner.

Ayala, Francisco J., Ananias A. Escalante, and Stephen M. Rich. 1999. "Evolution of Plasmodium and the Recent Origin of the World Populations of *Plasmodium falciparum*." *Parassitologia* 41: 55–68.

Baker, Brenda and George J. Armelagos. 1988. "Origin and Antiquity of Syphilis: A Dilemma in Paleopathological Diagnosis and Interpretation." *Current Anthropology* 29: 703–37.

Baker, Lucy, Tim Brown, Martin C. Maiden, and Francic Drobniewski. 2004. "Silent Nucleotide Polymorphisms and a Phylogeny for *Mycobacterium tuberculosis*." *Emerging Infectious Diseases* 10: 1568–77.

Barnes, Kathleen C., George J. Armelagos, and Steven C. Morreale. 1999. "Darwinian Medicine and the Emergence of Allergy." In W. Trevethan, J. McKenna, and E. O. Smith (eds.), *Evolutionary Medicine*. New York: Oxford University Press.

Barrett, Ronald, Christopher W. Kuzawa, Thomas McDade, and George J. Armelagos. 1998. "Emerging Infectious Disease and the Third Epidemiological Transition." Pp. 247–71 in W. Durham (ed.), *Annual Review of Anthropology*, vol. 27. Palo Alto, CA: Annual Reviews.

Becker, Katja, Ying Hu, and Nickola Biller-Andorno. 2006. "Infectious Diseases: A Global Challenge." *International Journal of Medical Microbiology* 296: 179–85.

Brand, Stewart. 2006. "City Planet." *Strategy + Business* 42: 1–4. Online (www.strategy-business.com/media/file/sb42_06109.pdf).

Brinkhoff, Thomas. 2008. "The Principal Agglomerations of the World." Online (www.citypopulation.de).

Brosch, Roland, Alexander S. Pym, Stephen V. Gordon, and Stewart T. Cole. 2001. "The Evolution of Mycobacterial Pathogenicity: Clues from Comparative Genomics." *Trends in Microbiology* 9: 452–8.

Brothwell, Don R. 1972. "The Question of Pollution in Earlier and Less Developed Societies." Pp. 15–27 in P. R. Cox and J. Peel (eds.), *Population and Pollution*. London: Academic Press.

Brothwell, Don R. and Patricia Brothwell. 1998. *Food in Antiquity: A Survey of the Diet of Early Peoples*. Baltimore: Johns Hopkins University Press.

Caldwell, John C. 2001. "Population Health in Transition." *Bulletin of the World Health Organization* 79: 159–60.

Cockburn, T. Aidan. 1967a. "The Evolution of Human Infectious Diseases." In T. A. Cockburn (ed.), *Infectious Diseases: Their Evolution and Eradication*. Springfield, IL: Charles C. Thomas.

Cockburn, T. Aidan. 1967b. "Infections of the Order Primates." In T. A. Cockburn (ed.), *Infectious Diseases: Their Evolution and Eradication*. Springfield, IL: Charles C. Thomas.

Cockburn, T. Aidan. 1971. "Infectious Disease in Ancient Populations." *Current Anthropology* 12: 45–62.

Cohen, Mark Nathan and George J. Armelagos. 1984. *Paleopathology at the Origins of Agriculture*. New York: Academic Press.

Cordain, Loren, S. Boyd Eaton, Anthony Sebastian, Neil Mann, Staffan Lindeberg, Bruce A. Watkins, James H. O'Keefe, and Janette Brand-Miller. 2005. "Origins and Evolution of the Western Diet: Health Implications for the 21st Century." *American Journal of Clinical Nutrition* 81: 341–54.

Cordain, Loren, Janette Brand Miller, S. Boyd Eaton, and Neil Mann. 2000. "Macronutrient Estimations in Hunter-Gatherer Diets." *American Journal of Clinical Nutrition* 72: 1589–90.

Cousins, Don. 1972. "Diseases and Injuries in Wild and Captive Gorillas: *Gorilla gorilla*." *International Zoo Yearbook* 12: 211–18.

Crosby, Alfred W. 1972. *The Columbian Exchange: Biological and Cultural Consequences of 1492*. Westport, CT: Greenwood Press.

Crosby, Alfred W. 1994. *Germs, Seeds and Animals: Studies in Ecological History*. Armonk, NY: M. E. Sharpe.

Crosby, Alfred W. 2003. *The Columbian Exchange: Biological and Cultural Consequences of 1492*, updated edition. Westport, CT: Praeger.

Crosby, Alfred W. 2004. *Ecological Imperialism: The Biological Expansion of Europe, 900–1900*. New York: Cambridge University Press.

Cummings, Craig A. and David A. Relman. 2002. "Microbial Forensics: Cross-Examining Pathogens." *Science* 296: 1976–9.

Diamond, Jared. 1987. "The Worst Mistake in the History of the Human Race." *Discover* 8: 64–6.

Diavatopoulos, Dimitri A., Craig A. Cummings, Leo M. Schouls, Mary M. Brinig, David A. Relman, and Frits R. Mooi. 2005. "*Bordetella pertussis*, the Causative Agent of Whooping Cough, Evolved from a Distinct, Human-Associated Lineage of *B. bronchiseptica*." *PLoS Pathogens* 1(4): e45.

Dye, Christopher. 2008. "Health and Urban Living." *Science* 319: 766–9.

Eaton, S. Boyd and Loren Cordain. 1997. "Evolutionary Aspects of Diet: Old Genes, New Fuels. Nutritional Changes Since Agriculture." *World Review of Nutrition and Dietetics* 81: 26–37.

Eaton, S. Boyd and S. B. Eaton, III. 2000. "Paleolithic vs. Modern Diets: Selected Pathophysiological Implications." *European Journal of Nutrition* 39: 67–70.

Eaton, S. Boyd, Melvin Konner, and Marjorie Shostak. 1988a. *The Paleolithic Prescription*. New York: Harper and Row.

Eaton, S. Boyd, Melvin Konner, and Marjorie Shostak. 1988b. "Stone Agers in the Fast Lane: Chronic Degenerative Diseases in Evolutionary Perspective." *American Journal of Medicine* 84: 739–49.

Enserink, Martin. 2008. "A Mosquito Goes Global." *Science* 320: 864–6.

Farmer, Paul. 1996. "Social Inequalities and Emerging Infectious Diseases." *Emerging Infectious Diseases* 2: 259–69.

Farmer, Paul. 2004. "An Anthropology of Structural Violence." *Current Anthropology* 45: 305–25.

Felsenfeld, Oscar and Robert H. Wolf. 1971. "Serological Reactions with Treponemal Antigens in Nonhuman Primates and the Natural History of Treponematosis in Man." *Folia Primat.* 16: 294–305.

Filliol, Ingrid, Alifiya S. Motiwala, Magali Cavatore, Weihong Qi, Manzour Hernando Hazbón, Miriam Bobadilla del Valle, Janet Fyfe, Lourdes García-García, Nalin Rastogi, Christophe Sola, Thierry Zozio, Marta Inírida Guerrero, Clara Inés León, Jonathan Crabtree, Sam Angiuoli, Kathleen D. Eisenach, Riza Durmaz, Moses L. Joloba, Adrian Rendón, José Sifuentes-Osornio, Alfredo Ponce de León, Donald Cave, Robert Fleischmann, Thomas S. Whittam, and David Alland. 2006. "Global Phylogeny of *Mycobacterium Tuberculosis* Based on Single Nucleotide Polymorphism (SNP) Analysis: Insights into Tuberculosis Evolution, Phylogenetic Accuracy of Other DNA Fingerprinting Systems, and Recommendations for a Minimal Standard SNP Set." *Journal of Bacteriology* 188: 759–72. (Erratum appears in *Journal of Bacteriology* 188 [April 2006]: 3162–3.)

Fleming, Alexander. 1945. "*Penicillin.*" Nobel Lecture, November 11. Online (nobelprize.org/nobel_prizes/medicine/laureates/1945/fleming-lecture.pdf).

Frank, John W. and J. Fraser Mustard. 1994 "The Determinants of Health from a Historical Perspective." *Daedalus* 123: 1–20.

Fribourg-Blanc, A. and H. H. Mollaret. 1969. "Natural Treponematosis of the African Primate." *Primates in Medicine* 3: 113–21.

Fribourg-Blanc, A., H. H. Mollaret, and G. Niel. 1966. "Serologic and Microscopic Confirmation of Treponematosis in Guinea Baboons." *Bulletin de la Société de Pathologie Exotique et de ses filiales* 59: 54–9.

Froment, Alain. 1994. "Epidemiology of African Endemic Treponematoses in Tropical Forest and Savanna." Pp. 41–7 in Olivier Dutour, György Pálfi, Jacques Bérato, and Jean-Pierre Brun (eds.), *The Origin of Syphilis in Europe: Before or After 1493?* Var: Centre Archéologique du Var.

Githeko, Andrew K., Steve W. Lindsay, Ulisses E. Confalonieri, and Jonathan A. Patz. 2000. "Climate Change and Vector-Borne Diseases: A Regional Analysis." *Bulletin of the World Health Organization* 78(9): 1136–47.

Gobalet, Jeanne C. 1989. *World Mortality Trends since 1870.* New York: Garland.

Goodman, Alan H., Debra Martin, George J. Armelagos, and George Clark. 1984. "Indications of Stress from Bones and Teeth." Pp. 13–49 in M. N. Cohen and G. J. Armelagos (eds.), *Paleopathology at the Origins of Agriculture.* Orlando, FL: Academic Press.

Gordon, Stephen V., Roland Brosch, Alain Billault, Thierry Garnier, Karin Eiglmeier, and
    Stewart T. Cole. 1999. "Identification of Variable Regions in the Genomes of Tubercle
    Bacilli Using Bacterial Artificial Chromosome Arrays." *Molecular Microbiology* 32:
    643–55.

Gutierrez, M. Cristina, Sylvain Brisse, Roland Brosch, Michel Fabre, Bahia Omaïs, Magali
    Marmiesse, Philip Supply, and Véronique Vincent. 2005. "Ancient Origin and Gene
    Mosaicism of the Progenitor of *Mycobacterium tuberculosis.*" *PLoS Pathogens* 1: e5.

Gwatkin, Davidson R. 1997. "Global Burden of Disease." Comment. *Lancet* 350: 141;
    author reply: 144–5.

Haines, A., R. S. Kovats, D. Campbell-Lendrum, and C. Corvalan. 2006. "Climate Change
    and Human Health: Impacts, Vulnerability and Public Health." *Public Health* 120:
    585–96.

Harper, Kristin N., Hsi Liu, Paolo S. Ocampo, Bret M. Steiner, Amy Martin, Keith Levert,
    Dongxia Wang, Madeline Sutton, and George J. Armelagos. 2008a. "The Sequence of
    the Acidic Repeat Protein (arp) Gene Differentiates Venereal from Nonvenereal *Trepo-
    nema pallidum* Subspecies, and the Gene has Evolved Under Strong Positive Selection in
    the Subspecies that Causes Syphilis." *FEMS Immunology and Medical Microbiology* 53:
    322–32.

Harper, Kristin N., Paolo S. Ocampo, Bret M. Steiner, Robert W. George, Michael S.
    Silverman, Shelly Bolotin, Allan Pillay, Nigel J. Saunders, and George J. Armelagos.
    2008b. "On the Origin of the Treponematoses: A Phylogenetic Approach." *PLoS
    Neglected Tropical Diseases* 1: e148.

Ho, Simon Y. W. and Greger Larson. 2006. "Molecular Clocks: When Times are A-
    Changin'." *Trends in Genetics* 22: 79–83.

Hoberg, Eric P., N. L. Alkire, A. de Queiroz, and A. Jones. 2001. "Out of Africa: Origins
    of the *Taenia* Tapeworms in Humans." *Proceedings of the Royal Society of London –
    Series B: Biological Sciences* 268: 781–7.

Hoberg, Eric P., Arlene Jones, Robert L. Rausch, Keeseon S. Eom, and S. L. Gardner. 2000.
    "A Phylogenetic Hypothesis for Species of the Genus *Taenia* (Eucestoda: Taeniidae)."
    Journal of Parasitology 86: 89–98.

Holmes, Edward C. and Andrew Rambaut. 2004. "Viral Evolution and the Emergence of
    SARS Coronavirus." *Philosophical Transactions of the Royal Society of London – Series
    B: Biological Sciences* 359: 1059–65.

Hulsewe, Karel W. E., Bernadette A. C. van Acker, Martin F. von Meyenfeldt, and Peter B.
    Soeters. 1999. "Nutritional Depletion and Dietary Manipulation: Effects on the Immune
    Response." *World Journal of Surgery* 23: 536–44.

Institute of Medicine (IOM). 1992. *Emerging Infections: Microbial Threats to Health in the
    United States*. Washington, DC: Institute of Medicine.

Johnson, Rabia, Elizabeth M. Streicher, Gail E. Louw, Robin M. Warren, Paul D. van
    Helden, and Thomas C. Victor. 2006. "Drug Resistance in *Mycobacterium tuberculo-
    sis.*" *Current Issues in Molecular Biology* 8: 97–111.

Johnston, Lynette M., Lee-Ann Jaykus, Deborah Moll, Juan Anciso, Brenda Mora, and
    Christine L. Moe. 2006. "A Field Study of the Microbiological Quality of Fresh Produce
    of Domestic and Mexican Origin." *International Journal of Food Microbiology* 112:
    83–95.

Jones, Kate E., Nikkita G. Patel, Marc A. Levy, Adam Storeygard, Deborah Balk, John L.
    Gittleman, and Peter Daszak. 2008. "Global Trends in Emerging Infectious Diseases."
    Nature 451: 990–3.

Joy, Deirdre A., Xiaorong Feng, Jianbing Mu, Tetsuya Furuya, Kesinee Chotivanich, Antoniana U. Krettli, May Ho, Alex Wang, Nicholas J. White, Edward Suh, Peter Beerli, and Xin-zhuan Su. 2003. "Early Origin and Recent Expansion of *Plasmodium falciparum*." *Science* 300: 318–21.

Kaplan, George A. and Julian E. Keil. 1993. "Socioeconomic Factors and Cardiovascular Disease: A Review of the Literature." *Circulation* 88: 1973–98.

Katz, Solomon H. 1987. "Food and Biocultural Evolution: A Model for the Investigation of Modern Nutritional Problems." Pp. 41–63 in F. E. Johnston (ed.), *Nutritional Anthropology*. New York: Alan R. Liss.

Khardori, Nancy. 2006. "Bioterrorism and Bioterrorism Preparedness: Historical Perspective and Overview." *Clinics of North America* 20: 179–211.

Kittler, Ralf, Manfred Kayser, and Mark Stoneking. 2003. "Molecular Evolution of *Pediculus humanus* and the Origin of Clothing." *Current Biology* 13: 1414–17.

Laird, Marshall. 1989. "Vector-Borne Disease Introduced into New Areas Due to Human Movements: A Historical Perspective." Pp. 17–33 in M. W. Service (ed.), *Demography and Vector-Borne Diseases*. Boca Raton, FL: CRC Press.

Levy, Stuart B. 1992. *The Antibiotic Paradox: How Miracle Drugs are Destroying the Miracle*. New York: Plenum.

Livingstone, Frank B. 1958. "Anthropological Implications of Sickle-Cell Distribution in West Africa." *American Anthropologist* 60: 533–62.

Livingstone, Frank B. 1971. "Malaria and Human Polymorphisms." *Annual Review of Genetics* 5: 33–64.

Livingstone, Frank B. 1983. "The Malaria Hypothesis." Pp. 15–44 in J. Bowman (ed.), *Distribution and Evolution of Hemoglobin and Globin Loci*, vol. 4. New York: Elsevier.

McCord, Colin and Harold P. Freeman. 1990. "Excess Mortality in Harlem." *New England Journal of Medicine* 322: 173–7.

McKeown, Thomas. 1976. *The Modern Rise of Population*. New York: Academic Press.

McKeown, Thomas. 1983. "Food, Infection and Population." *Journal of Interdisciplinary History* 14: 227–47.

McKeown, Thomas and R. G. Brown. 1955. "Medical Evidence Related to English Population Changes in the Eighteenth Century." *Population Studies* 9: 119–41.

McMichael, Anthony J. 2000. "The Urban Environment and Health in a World of Increasing Globalization: Issues for Developing Countries." *Bulletin of the World Health Organization* 78: 1117–26.

McNeill, William H. 1976. *Plagues and People*. Garden City, NY: Anchor/Doubleday.

Meinhardt, Patricia L. 2005. "Water and Bioterrorism: Preparing for the Potential Threat to US Water Supplies." *Annual Review of Public Health* 26: 213–37.

Moran, Gregory J., David A. Talan, and Fredrick M. Abrahamian. 2008. "Biological Terrorism." *Infectious Disease Clinics of North America* 22: 145–87.

Morens, David M. and Anthony S. Fauci. 2008. "Dengue and Hemorrhagic Fever: A Potential Threat to Public Health in the United States." *Journal of the American Medical Association* 299: 214–16.

Morse, Stephen S. 1997. "The Public Health Threat of Emerging Viral Disease." *Journal of Nutrition* 127: 951S–957S.

Mostowy, Serge, Debby Cousins, Jacqui Brinkman, Alicia Aranaz, and Marcel A. Behr. 2002. "Genomic Deletions Suggest a Phylogeny for the *Mycobacterium tuberculosis* Complex." *Journal of Infectious Diseases* 186: 74–80.

Muktatkar, R. 1995. "Public Health Problems of Urbanization." *Social Science and Medicine* 41: 977–81.

Neuwirth, Robert. 2005. *Shadow Cities: A Billion Squatters, a New Urban World*. New York: Routledge.

Novick, Lloyd F. 2008. "The Continuing First Revolution in Public Health: Infectious Disease." *Journal of Public Health Management Practice* 14: 418–19.

Omran, Abdel R. 1971. "The Epidemiologic Transition: A Theory of the Epidemiology of Population Change." *Millbank Memorial Fund Quarterly* 49: 509–38.

Omran, Abdel R. 1977. "A Century of Epidemiologic Transition in the United States." *Preventive Medicine* 6: 30–51.

Omran, Abdel R. 1982. "Epidemiological Transition." Pp. 172–83 in J. A. Ross (ed.), *International Encyclopedia of Population*. London: Free Press.

Omran, Abdel R. 1983. "The Epidemiologic Transition Theory: A Preliminary Update." *Journal of Tropical Pediatrics* 29: 305–16.

Omran, Abdel R. 2001. "The Epidemiologic Transition: A Theory of the Epidemiology of Population Change. 1971." *Bulletin of the World Health Organization* 79: 161–70.

Popkin, Barry M. 1994. "The Nutrition Transition in Low-Income Countries: An Emerging Crisis." *Nutrition Reviews* 52: 285–98.

Pupo, Gulietta M., Ruiting Lan, and Peter R. Reeves. 2000. "Multiple Independent Origins of Shigella Clones of *Escherichia coli* and Convergent Evolution of Many of their Characteristics." *Proceedings of the National Academy of Sciences* 97: 10567–72.

Radosavljevic, V. and B. Jakovljevic. 2007. "Bioterrorism: Types of Epidemics, New Epidemiological Paradigm and Levels of Prevention." *Public Health* 121: 549–57.

Raviglione, Mario. 2006. "XDR-TB: Entering the Post-Antibiotic Era?" *International Journal of Tuberculosis and Lung Disease* 10: 1185–7.

Rothschild, Bruce M., Israel Hershkovitz, and Christine Rothschild. 1995. "Origin of Yaws in Pleistocene East Africa: *Homo erectus* KNM-ER 1808." *Nature* 378: 343–4.

Rotz, Lisa D., Ali S. Khan, Scott R. Lillibridge, Stephen M. Ostroff, and James M. Hughes. 2002. "Public Health Assessment of Potential Biological Terrorism Agents." *Emerging Infectious Diseases* 8: 225–30.

Roumagnac, Philippe, Francois-Xavier Weill, Christiane Dolecek, Stephen Baker, Sylvain Brisse, Nguyen Tran Chinh, Thi Anh hong Le, Camilo J. Acosta, Jeremy Farrar, Gordon Dougan, and Mark Achtman. 2006. "Evolutionary History of *Salmonella typhi*." *Science* 314: 1301–4.

Satcher, David. 1995. "Emerging Infections: Getting Ahead of the Curve." *Emerging Infectious Diseases* 1.

Sattenspiel, Lisa. 2000. "Tropical Environments, Human Activities, and the Transmission of Infectious Diseases." *American Journal of Physical Anthropology*, Suppl. 31: 3–31.

Schito, Gian Carlo. 2002. "Is Antimicrobial Resistance Also Subject to Globalization?" *Clinical Microbiology and Infection* 8 Suppl. 3: 1–8; discussion 33–5.

Shipman, Pat. 2002. "A Worm's View of Human Evolution." *American Scientist* 90: 508–10.

Smith, Richard D. and Joanna Coast. 2002. "Antimicrobial Resistance: A Global Response." *Bulletin of the World Health Organization* 80: 126–33.

Sreevatsan, Srinand, Xi Pan, Kathryn E. Stockbauer, Nancy D. Connell, Barry N. Kreiswirth, Thomas S. Whittam, and James M. Musser. 1997. "Restricted Structural Gene Polymorphism in the *Mycobacterium tuberculosis* Complex Indicates Evolutionary Recent Global Dissemination." *Proceedings of the National Academy of Sciences* 94: 9869–74.

Stead, William W. 1997. "The Origin and Erratic Global Spread of Tuberculosis." *Clinical Chest Medicine* 18: 65–77.

Stewart, William H. 1967. "A Mandate for State Action." Presented at the Association of State and Territorial Health Officers, Washington, DC, December 4.

Szreter, Simon. 2002. "Rethinking McKeown: The Relationship between Public Health and Social Change." *American Journal of Public Health* 92: 722–35.

Tishkoff, Sarah A., Robert Varkonyi, Nelie Cahinhinan, Salem Abbes, George Argyropoulos, Giovanni Destro-Bisol, Anthi Drousiotou, Bruce Dangerfield, Gerard Lefranc, Jacques Loiselet, Anna Piro, Mark Stoneking, Antonio Tagarelli, Giuseppe Tagarelli, Elias H. Touma, Scott M. Williams, and Andrew G. Clark. 2001. "Haplotype Diversity and Linkage Disequilibrium at Human G6PD: Recent Origin of Alleles That Confer Malarial Resistance." *Science* 293: 455–62.

Ulijaszek, Stanley J. 2000. "Nutrition, Infection and Child Growth in Papua New Guinea." *Collegium Antropologicum* 24: 423–9.

Upton, A., S. Lang, and H. Heffernan. 2003. "Mupirocin and *Staphylococcus aureus*: A Recent Paradigm of Emerging Antibiotic Resistance." *Journal of Antimicrobial Chemotherapy* 51: 613–17.

Volkman, Sarah K., Alyssa E. Barry, Emily J. Lyons, Kaare M. Nielsen, Susan M. Thomas, Mehee Choi, Seema S. Thakore, Karen P. Day, Dyann F. Wirth, and Daniel L. Hartl. 2001. "Recent Origin of *Plasmodium falciparum* from a Single Progenitor." *Science* 293: 482–4.

Watts, S., K. Khallaayoune, R. Bensefia, H. Laamrani, and B. Gryseels. 1998. "The Study of Human Behavior and Schistosomiasis Transmission in an Irrigated Area in Morocco." *Social Science and Medicine* 46: 755–65.

Webber, Mark and Laura. J. V. Piddock. 2001. "Quinolone Resistance in *Escherichia coli*." *Veterinary Research* 32: 275–84.

Wiesenfeld, Stephen L. 1968. "African Agricultural Patterns and the Sickle Cell." *Science* 160: 1475.

Williams, George C. and Randolph M. Nesse. 1991. "The Dawn of Darwinian Medicine." *Quarterly Review of Biology* 66: 1–22.

Woolhouse, Mark E. 2008. "Epidemiology: Emerging Diseases Go Global." Comment. *Nature* 451: 898–9.

World Health Organization (WHO). 1995. *World Health Report 1995*. Geneva: WHO.

WorldResources1996–97. 1996. *A Guide to the Global Environment: The Urban Environment*. Washington, DC: WRI.

Zager, Ellen M. and Ruth McNerney. 2008. "Multidrug-Resistant Tuberculosis." *BMC Infectious Diseases* 8: 10.

Zhang, Ruifang, Karen Eggleston, Vincent Rotimi, and Richard Zeckhauser. 2006. "Antibiotic Resistance as a Global Threat: Evidence from China, Kuwait and the United States." *Globalization and Health* 2: 6.

Zhang, Ying and Douglas Young. 1994. "Molecular Genetics of Drug Resistance in *Mycobacterium tuberculosis*." Review. *Journal of Antimicrobial Chemotherapy* 34: 313–19.

14

Chronic Illness

KATHY CHARMAZ AND DANA ROSENFELD

Throughout the history of medical sociology, social scientific study of chronic conditions has taken two major directions: epidemiological studies of specific populations in relation to disease and analyses of the experience of illness, the primary focus of this chapter. In the sociological literature, disease and illness are neither interchangeable nor equivalent. Disease is the undesirable biological process or state affecting the individual, and illness is the person's experience of the disease, including its social and psychological impacts. Just as disease may be unrecognized and unfelt (see Conrad 1987: 2), deeply disturbing symptoms may arise without being diagnosed as a disease, even in the absence of perceivable organic causes. To study illness, then, is to study human experience without reference to organic causes, although it may include lay understandings of these causes and the experience of diagnosing them.

To an extent, these directions of inquiry reflect Robert Straus's (1957) distinction between a sociology *in* medicine and a sociology *of* medicine – a distinction that is not just heuristic but deeply political. According to Bryan Turner (1992), tensions between these two approaches are grounded in the core question of who the social-scientific study of health and illness serves: medicine itself (expanding and legitimating its existing powers) or the sociological understanding of human action. Sociology *in* medicine, Turner argues, is beholden to medicine's conceptual resources, concerns, and governing and funding bodies, working within these but remaining outside the ill person's experience (similarly, epidemiological studies use existing medical categories to directly serve health care professionals and policymakers). Sociologists *of* medicine, however, examine the nature and experience of health and illness, which medically derived categories cannot capture (see also Rosenfeld 2006a). At the same time, it remains free of the task of solving practical problems as established by medical agendas, and critically approaches the institution of medicine and its categories, assumptions, and agendas as social constructions and problematic areas of inquiry. William Cockerham (2010) has, however, critiqued the division between sociology in and sociology of medicine as overly simplistic[1] because the lines between them blur in policy research. Exploring the intriguing question of the extent to which his point applies to chronic illness goes beyond our focus here. This chapter also leaves aside the equally interesting sociological question of the social causes of the unequal distribution of chronic organic conditions; we emphasize the history and contributions of studies of the lived experience of chronic illness.[2]

Studies of the illness experience began with analyzing the realities of the lives of people with chronic conditions and focused on how they defined and managed their illnesses. The implications of this research ranged from practical contingencies to social relations and, finally, to self-image, identity, social relations, and imagined futures. Although the *temporary* incapacitation of acute illnesses inspired early medical sociologists (specifically, Parsons 1951) to consider the impact of illness on social structure, the *long-term* nature of chronic illness grounds sociological interest in how sufferers manage the personal experience of their disease's duration and uncertainty. The disease is not the focus; the illness is. Correspondingly, the emphasis in sociological studies of chronic illness is less on the actor's physical symptoms and more on (1) the meanings that actors impute to these symptoms (an emphasis criticized by some as overly cognitive – see below); (2) the consequences that these meanings have for daily living as they filter through such social concerns as stigma, social norms, expectations, and relations with self and other; and (3) how actors manage the impact of long-term, sometimes intermittent and unpredictable, physical incapacity on their respective selves and social worlds.

This chapter traces the rise of sociological research into chronic illness and reviews its core substantive foci and contributions. These studies illustrate the implications of chronic illness for self, identity, and social relations. Because these studies showed how people accomplished routine daily actions in the face of physical challenges to them, they drew on a wide range of sociological theories and approaches, primarily social constructionism, symbolic interactionism, and the sociology of the body. But their general focus on chronic illness in micro-social contexts (self and intimate others) has produced a literature that, while robust in its treatment of this arena, remains thin in its consideration of more meso- and macro- contexts and processes that shape chronic illness such as health care systems, community relations, medicalization, and the pharmaceutical industry. Although such studies exist, they tend to be seen as about these contexts and processes rather than about chronic illness itself. After reviewing the findings and contributions of sociological studies of chronic illness, we then discuss some works that take a more distal view of chronic illness and consider their possible linkages.

A BRIEF HISTORY OF CHRONIC ILLNESS SCHOLARSHIP

Chronic illness as an area of scholarly investigation was inspired by both an epidemiological shift and ethnographic challenges to the dominant sociological conception of illness. The epidemiological shift marked the emergence of chronic disease as the major cause of death, supplanting the acute illnesses that had prevailed in the era of infectious disease. This epidemiological transition (Omran 2005) occurred in tandem with three other key changes in the developed West: (1) the increase in life expectancy, (2) the drop in overall mortality and in infant and maternal mortality in particular, and (3) the surpassing of women's life expectancy over men's. The last century, then, produced a vastly different picture of Western health than had previous centuries. These changes spawned major concerns in medical sociology and the sociology of health about the relative distribution of health and illness (MacIntyre 1997) and the respective reasons for these distributions (Wilkinson 1996; Wilkinson and Marmot 2006). Most relevant to this chapter, the rise of chronic disease (specifically, cardiovascular disease, stroke, and cancer) as the most common cause of death led sociologists to recognize that Talcott Parsons' (1951) work on the "sick role," the seminal functionalist piece of work in medical sociology, was not only inapplicable to the chronic illness experience, but also problematic in its own right (see Charmaz 1999; Freidson 1961, 1970; Gallagher 1976; Parsons 1975; Twaddle 1969). This issue grounded a sociological concern with the experience and management of health and illness.

From sick role to biographical disruption

Parsons regarded illness as a form of deviance that the social system had to contain through institutionalized practices of social control over patients by medical agents and organizations. He began his analysis by looking at how the institution of medicine contributes to a functioning social system. For Parsons, illness was a safety valve that released pressures from the social system in general and the family system in particular, because being in the sick role temporarily removed a person from ordinary role obligations. Acute illness, in Parsons' view, necessitated that patients be temporarily exempted from their adult responsibilities but obligated them to seek help, to follow their physician's orders, and to concentrate on getting well. The sick role controlled and regulated the illness experience and held the ill person accountable to the larger social system.

Parsons uncovered the deeply social nature of illness by pointing to how illness could be problematic for the social system. Yet his theory suffered from major limitations. First, because it assumed acute illness, it posited a relatively straightforward curative pathway and an objective, authoritarian doctor–passive patient role relationship operating within a smoothly functioning institutionalized system. Yet these characteristics of the sick role do not fit people's experience of chronic illness or of disability. Rather than taking time out for illness, many people with chronic illnesses must learn to live with their conditions while keeping their jobs and maintaining their family obligations – managing a continuing and, often, deteriorating condition takes priority, and recovery cannot be assumed. Now, neither can physicians' authority, as national health services, insurance plans, and medical consumerism reshape their relations with patients (see also Bury and Taylor 2008). Moreover, because routine treatment and illness management occur at home rather than at the clinic, patients and families become active participants in treatment and care rather than the passive recipients of unilateral directives. Indeed, physicians must rely on patients and families to inform treatment planning and consult with them about treatment outcomes. Thus, the patient–physician role relationship shifts toward a partnership that relies on mutual efforts to manage the illness.

Second, Parsons' theoretical model remained limited because it adopted an outsider's rather than an insider's view. The concept of the sick role acknowledged physicians' expertise but not patients' experience, an important area of inquiry in its own right and an increasingly important feature of the doctor–patient interactional landscape. Within a decade of Parsons' publication of the sick role, medical sociologists recognized that understanding the actual experience of chronic illness, its consequences, and its management, as well as its definition and regulation, required an entirely new conceptual apparatus for investigating the social nature of chronic illness (see Gallagher 1976; Koos 1954; Levine and Kozloff 1978; Raynor 1981; Zola 1973).

The makings of an alternative conceptual model arose as ethnographers began to study patients' experience of illness and disability, which were linked in the early studies. Erving Goffman's (1961) *Asylums* pointed the way to looking at how the structure of care affected patients' lives. His 1963 book, *Stigma*, showed the effects of difference and disability on patients' social and personal identities. In early studies that followed, stigma and the sense of shame and loss of self attendant upon chronic illness were often central foci and have remained so (Charmaz 1983, 1991, 1994; Hopper 1981; Kelleher 1988; Locker 1983; MacDonald 1988; Mitteness 1987a, 1987b; Reif 1975; Schneider and Conrad 1980).

Elliott Freidson (1961, 1970) and Julius Roth (1963) both observed that patients attempted to negotiate with physicians, which challenged Parsons' view of medical authority and patient compliance. Fred Davis's (1963) study of children with poliomyelitis challenged notions of recovery because disability long outlasted the initial crisis. Davis (1972 [1956]) found that staff imposed their specialized – and limited – definitions of uncertainty and recovery on patients and their families. These definitions contradicted conventional notions and thus served to delay and control patients' and families' awareness of permanent disability. Patients' and families' hope for recovery kept them relatively compliant while their time projections stretched and the child's disability did not change. Both Roth and Davis brought the significance of time, interaction, and information control to the foreground in their respective studies and Glaser and Strauss (1965, 1968) advanced these concerns in their studies of dying.

Except for Goffman, the early studies of illness and disability addressed specific physical conditions. Anselm Strauss's (1975) *Chronic Illness and the Quality of Life* began to weave an analysis of problematic circumstances that cut across diverse chronic illnesses as Strauss and his colleagues explicitly made the experience of chronic illness their focus of inquiry and set the course for a new field in medical sociology. Like their predecessors, they offered an "insider's perspective" on the illness experience in explicit contrast to the sick role's "outsiders' perspective" (Lawton 2003: 23). In particular, Strauss and his colleagues emphasized the work that people with chronic illnesses and their families performed to manage their now problematic daily lives when illness created havoc with regimens, mobility, self-care, and routine interactions. By the second edition of *Chronic Illness and the Quality of Life*, Strauss and his colleagues (1984) initiated the idea that ill persons engaged in biographical work (reviewing, maintaining, and reconstructing accounts of their lives) to come to terms with waning health. Innovation and illness management are core themes of these studies. Thus, people with emphysema constructed routes for errands dotted with places where they could sit or lean, catch their breath, and go a little further (Fagerhaugh 1975) and people with colitis redesigned their lives to accommodate unpredictable episodes of diarrhea (Reif 1975).

As Janine Pierret (2003: 5) points out, earlier research shows "how illness upsets patients' interactions with persons close to them and leads to organizing family and occupational activities around it" (Charmaz 1983, 1991; Gerhardt and Brieskorn-Zinke 1986; Locker 1983; Schneider and Conrad 1983; Strauss 1975; Strauss et al. 1984; C. Williams 2000, 2002). Reciprocities and roles change as ill people and their kin learn what having a chronic illness means and as they work to strike a balance between independence and dependence (Brooks and Matson 1987; Kutner 1987; Strauss et al. 1984). Family strains increase when the illness results in sexual dysfunction, confusion, or uncontrolled anger such as may occur when kidney failure patients have blood pressure spikes (Kutner 1987) or people with diabetes have insulin reactions (Peyrot, McMurray, and Hedges 1987, 1988). Illness means adjusting to reduced activities, handling fatigue, learning to juggle and pace previously taken-for-granted daily tasks, and asking for help. All pose difficulties when relationships are strained or when expectations persist for the ill person to carry on as before. Brooks and Matson (1987) find that awareness of family obligations provided a powerful incentive to people with multiple sclerosis to keep going and to learn new ways of managing their lives. More recently, Susan Gregory (2005) showed that families attempted to normalize the unpredictability of illness and manage uncertainty and change.

In 1982, the focus on the experience of chronic illness was formalized in a special issue of *Social Science and Medicine* entitled "Social Factors in the Etiology of Chronic Disease" and invigorated by Michael Bury's seminal article "Chronic Illness as Biographical Disruption" in *Sociology of Health and Illness*. Bury (1982: 169) argued that chronic illness challenged how people understood the world and their position in it, disrupting both "the structures of everyday life and the forms of knowledge which underpin them." Sufferers were thus forced into a more reflexive, and uncertain, relationship with taken-for-granted forms of knowledge than they had enjoyed while physically well. His argument hinged on the following facts. First, chronic illness introduces a heightened and alien state of bodily awareness: determining the nature of initial symptoms requires "attention to bodily states not usually brought into consciousness and decisions about seeking help." Second, it challenges forms of knowledge, causing "a recognition of the worlds of pain and suffering, possibly even of death, which are normally only seen as distant possibilities or the plight of others," and disrupting "explanatory systems normally used by people, such that a fundamental re-thinking of the person's biography and self-concept is involved" (p. 169). Third, it has social repercussions, "bring[ing] individuals, their families, and wider social networks face to face with the character of their relationships in starker form, disrupting normal rules of reciprocity and mutual support" (p. 168), and calls for a responsive mobilization of resources. Finally, it forces the ill person to re-examine her "expectations and plans ... for the future" (p. 168).

Strengthened by the recognition of the increasing prevalence of chronic illness, Bury's framework spawned a wave of studies on the biographically disruptive nature of chronic illness (see Chamberlayne and King 1997; Ciambrone 2001), and, more recently, critiques of his implicit argument that chronic illnesses are universally and uniformly disruptive regardless of age and life-course location, life history, and socioeconomic context (see Carricaburu and Pierret 1995; Ciambrone 2001; Green, Todd, and Pevalin 2007; S. Williams 2000; Wilson 2007). While agreeing that chronic illness is essentially different from acute illness, these studies take the disruptiveness of the former as an empirical question rather than a basic assumption, asking under which conditions, to what extent, and when and how chronic illness is disruptive. Charmaz (1991) interviewed some chronically ill people who had modified and normalized their lives to accommodate symptoms before they knew that they had a chronic illness. They invoked other reasons such as stress or aging to account for their symptoms. Furthermore, the added troubles of chronic illness blend into the fabric of everyday life, when poverty and crises had long dominated people's lives (Charmaz 1991; Cornwall 1984).

Bury's concept of biographical disruption centers on adults and hence elides the complex relation that those who have come of age with a chronic illness might have with it (S. Williams 2003). Elderly people's experience may also differ as indicated by Sanders, Donovan, and Dieppe's (2002) comparisons of their elderly research participants' joint pain and disability with Bury's younger research participants who had rheumatoid arthritis. They argue that the gradual onset of osteoarthritis, its delimited locations of joint pain, and the perception of arthritis as normal in old age mitigate against biographical disruption. Here, then, chronic illness is a potential source of continuity rather than a later-life disruption. Two other studies uncovered chronic illness as biographically reinforcing. First, Carricaburu and Pierret (1995) found that for their HIV-positive informants, HIV infection reinforced components of their respective homosexual or hemophiliac identities that predated their HIV status. Second, Faircloth and colleagues (2004) outline discursive resources that their stroke-survivor informants used to construct a "biographical flow" that offset the stroke's disruptive effects.

Thus, while a chronic illness is undoubtedly disruptive in many ways, it does not always remain disruptive, or equally disruptive, over time, as actors bring biographical and narrative resources to bear. More recent work has uncovered other, perhaps more complex criticisms of Bury's biographical disruption. As Simon Williams (2003) notes, postmodern writers such as Nick Fox (1999) have critiqued the simplistic notion of the suffering self, wherein the self is depicted as distinct from her pain and distress, when the self is, in fact, constructed from the distress rather than an independent entity shaped by it; the suffering self also overshadows the potential secondary gains of chronic illness (e.g., the provision of support networks, and of a series of moral occasions through which the suffering actor can transform her situation, and her self, in positive ways – see Charmaz 1994, 1995, 2008; Hellström et al. 1999; Sandstrom 1990). Clare Williams (2002) also critiques Bury's "implied notion that bodies and selves are always taken for granted before the onset of disease" (Lawton 2003: 29) – a point that is becoming increasingly apposite as we become ever more aware of and attentive to our bodies in a postmodern, consumerist risk society.

These critiques signify the coming of age of much research into the chronic illness experience, as it takes stock of the need to expand the literature beyond the realm of managing illness to consider deep connections between self, biographical reconstruction, and bodily experience. This brings us to two other dimensions of chronic illness that remain underinvestigated: the body's *corporeal facticity* and *emotions*.

Bringing bodies and feelings in

Sociologists of the body argue that the chronic illness experience is no less social because it is also essentially physical, thus adding a much-needed corporeal dimension to a literature focused on (the cognitive process of) managing the effects of chronic illness on self, identity, and relationships. For example, Michael Kelly and David Field (1996: 250) argue that while bodily failures in chronic illness certainly have social consequences, the body has "a physical reality *sui generis*" unacknowledged by the literature. Although the meaning of physical pain and limitation remains key to the chronic illness experience, these authors argue that "physical restrictions and discomforts" are given short shrift in chronic illness studies, although "it is precisely these [restrictions] which have greatest weight in shaping interpretations and the attribution of meaning by sufferers" (Kelly and Field 1996: 243).

Research into emotions, health, and the body (see Freund 1990) similarly seeks to expand a chronic illness literature concerned with managing strategies. This literature notes that we become emotional not just *about* our bodies but *through* them as well, as emotion is intrinsically, if not exclusively, embodied (we feel shame, for example, on both a cognitive and a physical level – see Burkitt 1997). But, with the exception of Charmaz's 1991 book, in which emotions figure prominently, this research generally seeks to capture the physicality of emotions without reproducing the mind/body dualism that has grounded research into emotional life (see Newton 2003; Williams and Bendelow 1998), or explores the impact of emotions on physical health (see Freund 1998) or the emotion work conducted in the context of health care work (see Graham 2006; Meerabeau and Page 1998; Olesen and Bone 1998). In Charmaz's (1991: 56) words, "intrusive illness has spiraling effects that, in turn, further intrude upon life," and several researchers (see Blaxter 1983; Herzlich and Pierret 1987; Mitteness 1987a, 1987b; Nijhof 2002; Pinder 1988) have observed emotional responses, particularly embarrassment, sorrow, and shame, that intrusive illness causes. Other researchers have, however, treated such responses as a consequence of illness or treatment management failures rather than as either the focus for inquiry itself or a cause of further disruption (but see MacDonald 1988; Mitteness 1987a, 1987b).

We argue that people's emotional investment in particular bodies and relationships makes the experience of physical and social disruption emotionally disruptive in itself. The emotions this disruption occasions (i.e., shame and embarrassment over the loss of bodily control, fear and anxiety over the nature and implications of physical symptoms, guilt over upsetting or inconveniencing those called upon to respond or tend to the ill or injured person, and loneliness caused by the isolation of recovery) can further disrupt self, identity, relationships, and daily life (Rosenfeld 2006b). This point suggests that the illness experience is characterized by people's emotions elicited by physical and social disruption just as much as it is about physically compromised bodies and cognitive interpretation.

THE IMPACT OF UNCERTAIN CHRONIC DISEASE ON THE SELF

Despite the above gaps, recent research remains strong about the impact of chronic illness on everyday life, from the self and identity to relations in public centering on the management of stigmatized bodies and bodily behaviors caused by chronic disease. Although strategies for managing illness remain a strong theme in this literature, the research has also moved to address the implications of having an uncertain chronic condition on self and identity. Uncertainty pervades the course of illness – it undermines our "sense of constancy of the embodied self and the ability to plan and predict future actions" (Kelly and Field 1996: 244) – and thus imposes a central problem for people with intrusive chronic illnesses and for their families (Pitt 2006), although often in gender-specific ways. Men tend to have life-threatening chronic diseases in which uncertainty and risk of death loom large, whereas women tend to have more disabling conditions such as rheumatoid arthritis, multiple sclerosis, and fibromyalgia that may worsen suddenly but typically have a lengthy trajectory (Courtenay 2003; Verbrugge 1990).

Uncertainty becomes infused with "shoulds" and "oughts" because people view it as something to manage so as to reduce risk of further episodes or death. Meanings of uncertainty and risk figure in people's accounts of their health and illnesses. Consistent with Radley and Billig (1996), these accounts are ideological, showing that meanings of uncertainty elicit a moral discourse around legitimacy and credibility. For example, some chronic conditions such as epilepsy, heart disease, and AIDS bring uncertainty and risk into the foreground, but whether and how people attend to them elicit statements of moral evaluation and self and social scrutiny. Other chronic conditions such as chronic fatigue syndrome, environmental illness, and fibromyalgia are fraught with a more fundamental type of uncertainty: their legitimacy as real diseases. These conditions give rise to what Stockl (2007) calls "existential uncertainty" as sufferers struggle not only with symptoms but also with establishing the veracity of these symptoms and their own credibility as competent adults (Shriver and Waskul 2006; Travers and Lawler 2008; Ware 1992; Werner and Malterud 2003). Adamson (1997) and Broom and Woodward (1996), however, noted that "clinical uncertainty can provide grounds for hope, alleviating feelings of existential uncertainty associated with the contemplation of worst-case scenarios" (Adamson 1997: 136).

Crises underscore an uncertain course of illness. A life-threatening crisis or debilitating episode of illness suggests an uncertain future ahead – at least for a while. Strauss and his colleagues (1984), however, observe that the further away people are from experiencing a crisis, the less vigilant they become. Their attention to regimens and restrictions falters. In addition, ill people, their families, and health professionals may invoke conflicting definitions of uncertainty and risk that, in turn, affect what the person should do and who he or she can become. Speedling (1982) found that wives of men who had had heart attacks often viewed their husbands' health as uncertain and tried to restrict their activities while the men chafed to resume their earlier pursuits. Several of these men then focused on the tussle for control rather than on monitoring symptoms and following their regimens while their wives attempted to enlist physicians' concurrence of their definitions of uncertainty and what needed to be done about it.

People with chronic illnesses develop ways of handling uncertainty. They may give considerable efforts to reducing its potential deleterious effects. Certainly, people aim to reduce uncertainty by engaging in symptom control and following a regimen. Yet they may also try to protect themselves from uncertainties by testing the continuous applicability of a disease regimen to their own condition by, for example, withholding or manipulating their own medication use (Conrad 1985; Schneider and Conrad 1983: 194) and by reconceptualizing its meaning. Individuals may bracket uncertainty and treat it as though limited to crises (Charmaz 1999). They may also invoke idiosyncratic beliefs that they have already met a taken-for-granted measure of suffering and therefore should be exempt both from crises that make their lives uncertain and the day-to-day uncertainties of being able to live on their own terms. Under these conditions, they may be stunned by new concrete reminders that they still face uncertainty. In sum, meanings of uncertainty are imbedded in moral discourses about self, suffering, and action although, at first glance, uncertainty may seem like a characteristic of a disease process (see Werner et al. 2004).

SHAME AND STIGMA

Shame and stigma are interwoven in people's experience of chronic illness. Being stigmatized means that, however silently it occurs, other people mark the person as different and less than his or her peers. Those who stigmatize ill people separate and marginalize them, while simultaneously conferring and confirming their devalued identities. In turn, "identity spread" (Strauss et al. 1984) occurs as the stigmatized identity spreads over all other identities and redefines individuals in terms of the stigmatized attribute. Thus, a young mother with multiple sclerosis who uses a walker becomes a "disabled mother." Robert F. Murphy (1987), who used a wheelchair, states that the stigmatized identity leads to shame, guilt, and mortification, although the person realizes that he or she is undeserving of blame for the stigmatized disability. Quite possibly, such stigma increases when, like Murphy, people once applied the same stigmatizing definitions and marginalizing actions to others that they later experience themselves.

Whether stigmatizing definitions come from self in addition to others, the process of being stigmatized arises through interaction and relies on language and shared meanings. Stigma potential increases when the person: (1) has a condition such as AIDS and epilepsy that invoke other people's fear and dread, (2) has suffered disfigurement such as results from scleroderma, (3) behaves erratically or loses composure, (4) loses control of bodily functions (MacDonald 1988; Mitteness 1987a, 1987b), and (5) is viewed by other people as being culpable or morally suspect for having the condition (Nack 2008; Weitz 1991). A difference that might have once invoked sympathy and caring becomes the source of separation and marginalization. People who have unexplained illnesses (Kroll-Smith 1997; Nettleton et al. 2004) often find themselves blamed not only for their claims of being ill, but also for receiving stigmatized responses to these claims.

In re-examining how people with epilepsy experience stigma, Graham Scambler (1984) calls being stigmatized in the above ways the hidden distress model of epilepsy, which also applies to people with other chronic conditions, and argues that this model does not take into account structural conditions that make shame and its relationship to stigma more volatile. In the hidden distress model, people are viewed as or feel that they are "imperfect beings" (Scambler 1984: 31), possessing an "ontological deficit" because they cannot conform to cultural norms of identity. Scambler invokes his earlier distinction between enacted stigma (devaluation and/ or discrimination against those defined as different) and felt stigma, in which the person acknowledges and feels ashamed about this difference. Like other people whose symptoms and disabilities remain invisible, people with epilepsy live in a world in which they have become discreditable and live in fear of enacted stigma (Scambler and Hopkins 1986, 1988). Subsequently, they conceal their condition, which Scambler (1984) argues reduces chances of enacted stigma but makes felt stigma more disruptive.

Actors do not, however, passively accept stigma or simplistically experience shame. A crucial part of managing the consequences of chronic disease involves managing its stigmatizing nature, from personally engaging in information control (in the classical Goffmanian sense), in conversation and in the arrangement of the body's surface appearances and movements, to collectively agitating for the destigmatization of specific conditions. Much of this work is preventive in nature, as the chronically ill strive to avoid physical embarrassments that their compromised bodies might introduce. As Kelly and Field (1996: 247) note, "above all else coping with chronic illness involves coping with bodies." A strong line of research has documented the lengths to which the chronically ill go to conduct just this sort of management (see Fagerhaugh 1975; Reif 1975; Rosenfeld and Faircloth 2004; Sim and Madden 2008). Creative strategies to avoid embarrassing and stigmatizing moments are particularly invoked by people whose illnesses remain invisible on the body's surface but may unpredictably compromise that body's abilities to move or behave in appropriate ways (e.g., fibromyalgia, chronic fatigue syndrome, and epilepsy).

We (Charmaz and Rosenfeld 2006) explored the various meanings that the chronically ill body's public failures have for the public, and the subjective, self. Drawing on the work of symbolic interactionist theorists Cooley and Goffman, we write that "loss of bodily control – particularly public visibility of such loss – forces reflections about our physical status, threatens personal autonomy, and prompts feeling defeated by our body and viewing self as unacceptable" (Charmaz and Rosenfeld 2006: 41). That chronic illness may cause embodied "prop failures" (Goffman 1963) forces the chronically ill to plan and manage their bodily movements and positions in exceptionally reflexive ways, yet the very uncertainty of chronic illness, whose episodic failures are often unpredictable, "makes it difficult to plan movements, encounters, and interactions" (Charmaz and Rosenfeld 2006: 47). Nonetheless, the chronically ill work to manage the discrediting implications of failing bodies by preventing their public display and managing the shame and embarrassment that follow these displays when they occur. Thus, ill people and their caregivers learn to become attuned to subtle physical and emotional cues that signal changes. Mothers and wives particularly take the role of the alert assistant and smooth the way for their ill child or partner (Charmaz 1991: 91; C. Williams 2000, 2002).

Much of the research about the stigmatizing consequences of chronic illness and disability that documents this management, however, relied on interviews conducted in the 1980s and 1990s with people who lived in areas beyond the reach of emergent movements. Since then, Internet access has created possibilities for participating in the collectivization and politicization of illness and disability that has emerged long after the publication of Goffman's (1963) *Stigma*. Now people with illnesses and disabilities are not isolated actors navigating the world of the healthy, but are often members of support networks and political groups organized around specific conditions (e.g., HIV and cancer), and of a society that is increasingly aware of the needs of the chronically ill, if not always fully responsive to them. Although no evidence demonstrates that this politicization has encouraged a more public display of compromised embodiment, "health social movements," particularly "*embodied health movements* ... [which] address disease, disability or illness experience by challenging science on etiology, diagnosis, treatment and prevention" (Brown et al. 2004: 50), may supply the chronically ill with practical and emotional resources with which to negotiate the stigmatizing implications of chronic conditions. But despite the steadily growing body of work on health movements (see Allsop, Jones, and Baggott 2004; Scambler and Kelleher 2006; Williamson 2008), research has not yet adequately explored this potentially important dimension of the chronic illness experience (but see Barker 2002, 2008; Clarke 2000; Dumit 2006; Kelleher 1994).

A noteworthy exception is Klawiter's (2005) article on the impact of "culturally, spatially and historically specific regimes of practices" on the illness experience. Based on ethnographic research on breast cancer movements in San Francisco, Klawiter (2005: 845) highlights the "structural shaping of illness experience" through the term *disease regime*, and demonstrates that social movements can change the illness "sufferer or her relationship to the regime's practices." Here, then, is an example of the empirically grounded linking of social structure and illness experience of the sort Parsons launched half a century earlier, but that is explicitly concerned with chronic, as opposed to acute, illness. In the next, and final, section, we consider other areas of research that make these linkages and areas that provide the empirical and conceptual material to do so and to thus expand the sociology of the chronic illness experience's remit.

CHRONIC ILLNESS IN SOCIOSTRUCTURAL CONTEXT: MEDICALIZED ENVIRONMENTS, MEDICALIZED IDENTITIES, AND CHRONIC ILLNESS

As we argued at this chapter's outset, understanding the social impacts and experience of chronic illness requires considering how chronic illness plays out in wider social contexts and, indeed, social institutions, many of which have emerged specifically to handle chronic illnesses. Although we lack sufficient space to explore these wider contexts in full, we introduce a sociohistorical approach to medicine that has deep implications for the experience of chronic illness, and then briefly identify areas of research that merit more explicit inclusion in the quest to under-stand that experience.

Sociological analyses of what Klawiter (2005) termed *disease regimes* reside in two distinct approaches to the role of medicine in regulating social life: the Foucauldian approach, grounded in Foucault's (1975) *Birth of the Clinic* (see Armstrong 2002; Lupton 1995), and the medicalization thesis. A strong example of the first is Arney and Bergen's (1983) article tracing the emergence of the chronic patient not as a neutral reaction to epidemiological shifts but as a discursive and political construction emerging from changes in medical formulations. The authors note the shift from the nineteenth-century and earlier medical concern with making hidden bodily processes visible, which entails erasing the patient's personality and circumstances from the medical gaze and ceding compassionate responses to the patient's social needs to socio-moral agents, to a medicine that was, by the mid-twentieth century, equally concerned with the patient's organic and "socio-emotional developments." Arney and Bergen (1983: 10) cite medicine's postwar construction of alcoholism as a symptom of maladaptive responses to life that required "compassion *within* medicine." Thus "the search for non-maladaptive means of living a life became an explicit medical responsibility."

Arney and Bergen (1983: 12) argue that medicine's conscious adoption of new scientific reasoning practices sparked this construction and, by the 1940s, was replacing a Victorian mechanistic view (with the patient the victim of an internal breakage) with a dynamic understanding of the natural world in which the sick man is "an energy-system in which the balance of forces has been disturbed." Disease as a state of disequilibrium required a more totalizing program of disease manage-ment, hence new forms of health care delivery such as support teams and new connections between the clinic and the community were "deployed over a wide social space" (Arney and Bergen 1983: 13). The 1940s saw a massive growth in government-sponsored agencies in the United States designed to define, monitor, and manage chronic illness, framing these illnesses as economic as well as personal problems and seeking to find a productive place for the chronically ill. This trend fostered a more holistic medicine and medical regime that: (1) included prevention as well as management, (2) acknowledged the personal as well as the social, and (3) increasingly became organized around health promotion and prevention deployed through health care teams in a widening circle of contexts outside the clinic.

In the critical approach this article represents, proactive medical responses to chronic illness, while much sought after by patients and patient groups, can take on a less than positive or even benign form. Here, the management of chronic illness, and even more its prevention and screening, then becomes an insidious form of social control (to those adopting the medicalization thesis) or regulation in which patients themselves collude (to those holding to a Foucauldian approach). The medicalization thesis, initially offered by Illich (1975) and Zola (1975) and most widely known through Conrad's (1992, 2005) extensive work, tends to trace the medical framing of previously unproblematized (or problematized through religious or criminalizing frames) qualities and/or behaviors. Often using a social construc-tionist approach, medicalization theorizes this process of redefinition as originating in specific institutions' quest for professional power. While often engaged in the same process of tracing the emergence of medical categories, Foucauldian approaches view medicalization as one expression of more complex and diffuse power relations, and health promotion efforts as deeply enmeshed in the overall process of producing self-regulating actors (see Bunton, Nettleton, and Burrows 1995; Lupton 1993, 1997; Petersen 1996). Both approaches, however, highlight and deeply problematize the roles of agencies of social control in the construction of chronic illnesses, and call attention to the production of the "worried well" by newly dominant discourses of prevention and life/disease management (see Crawford 1980; Fitzpatrick 2001). They also, in their own ways, extend Parsons' recognition of the deeply social nature of illness, and of the sociopolitical and economic investment in healthy, self-regulating bodies that has increasingly insinuated itself into the fabric of social and moral life (see Turner 1992).

We do not depict the chronically ill as passive recipients of power. Just as sociological studies of chronic illness have demonstrated chronically ill persons' active engagement with their illness and its meanings and consequences, through which they craft a chronically ill self that is integrated into the social-moral order, so has sociology recognized and examined the social and political organizing in which the chronically ill have come to engage (see above). This organizing is not, it must be stressed, a simple rejection of medical diagnoses and forms of regulation: on the contrary, it often takes the form of demands for the development of medical diagnostic criteria, therapies, and identities. The chronically ill increasingly agitate for their own medicalization (Conrad 2005), a phenomenon perhaps most visible in the cases of post-traumatic stress disorder (Scott 1990), fibromyalgia (Barker 2006), chronic fatigue syndrome, and Gulf War Syndrome. To Foucauldians, this consumer quest for medicalization exemplifies the rise of new forms of self-governance rather than the beneficial growth of access to medical care. Here, then, the experience of chronic illness is not an exotic, exceptional domain but one deeply tied to the project of self-care, or "technologies of the self" (Foucault 1988), in which all social actors engage.

CONCLUSION

This chapter has (1) traced chronic illness research's exploration of the challenges that chronic disease poses to everyday life, social relations, and self and identity; (2) described how people with chronic illnesses manage those challenges; (3) noted the relatively new forms of collectivizing of and political organizing around the experience of chronic illness that have emerged over the past two decades; and (4) argued for the expansion of the scholastic project to capture the chronic illness experience beyond the micro-sociological domain. To conclude, we continue this argument by suggesting other new directions this scholarship might take.

Sociological studies of chronic illness are faced with the task of characterizing its experience in the face of continuous change; indeed, attempting to characterize chronic illness in stable and abiding terms is a virtual impossibility once one recognizes the sheer range of fast-changing factors that shape its experience. These include those shifts in scientific formulation and health care provision noted above, which, to critical sociologists, both ground and reflect tensions between medical and other agencies of social control and actors controlled and implicated by them.

But a raft of other meso- and macro-level changes and factors impact the chronic illness experience as well. Consider, for example, caregiving, which underwent major transformations given the need to provide long-term care for chronically ill and frail people rather than to provide curative care to the acutely ill and palliative care for the dying (Abel 1994). Here, too, the temporal dimension of chronic illness poses long-term challenges, not only for the recipients of care, but also for those providing it across a range of settings (home, community, and long-term care facilities). An impressive body of research into caregiving and the experience of receiving care has emerged over the last 30 years (see Abel 1991, 1994; Bury and Taylor 2008; Payne and Ellis-Hill 2001; Pearlin et al. 1990) which should, we argue, be recognized as being just as much about chronic illness as is the more local, individualized realm most often associated with the term (but see Corbin and Strauss 1984, 1985, 1988).

Relatedly, social, political, and financial institutions are also deeply affected by the demands of citizens of all ages suffering from chronic diseases. The political economy of care provision for the chronically ill merits inclusion in the sociological study of chronic illness because governmental and private insurance structures and policies shape the care and quality of life. Indeed, much of the political organizing by the chronically ill centers on agitating for more and/or different provision by these agencies. Medical care takes an increasingly significant place in discussions about citizenship, the rights of ill people, and the obligation of a nation's citizenry to remain healthy in the interest of the financial health of the polity. Much of the discourse about adherence to medical directives remains tied to issues of the financial viability of health care systems as well as to health outcomes: Vermeire and colleagues (2001: 331), for example, characterize non-adherence as "a major public health problem that imposes a considerable financial burden upon modern health care systems." Adherence became a pressing problem for the medical enterprise only when the long-term management of chronic illness became both possible and the central task of medical care. Finally, the role of the pharmaceutical industry in shaping the experience of chronic illness cannot be underestimated. In addition to strongly shaping medical care and provision, this industry provides medication that can vastly alter the severity, incidence, and even visibility of physical symptoms (though sometimes introducing painful, debilitating, and/or disfiguring side effects that may affect adherence to drug regimens), all of which offer new opportunities and challenges for the presentation of self. As a key claimsmaker in the medicalization process (Conrad 2005; Conrad and Schneider 1992), this industry also crafts and markets new categories of illness or redefines existing ones that may produce new categories of person or alter the membership of such categories (see Cohen, McCubbin, and Perodeau 2001; Hart, Grand, and Riley 2006; Marshall 2002). The effects of such macro-sociological factors on the micro-sociological dimensions of chronic illness must be explored to more fully appreciate the chronic disease experience.

Nonetheless, those dimensions of the chronic illness experience summarized above also merit further consideration. The situations that people with chronic illness face mirror and magnify less visible problems that others face throughout adult life. Living while under duress, experiencing biographical disruptions, facing uncertainty, constructing selves and identities, being viewed as acceptable, and relating to others all pose problems to many individuals in Western societies. Such topics raise numerous significant sociological questions that have not yet been fully explored. Thus, studying the experience of illness still offers rich opportunities for shaping sociological knowledge.

Notes

1 Cockerham (2007) points out that sociologists of medicine (who worked in sociology departments) held a stronger position to do research that met criteria of good sociology but sociologists in medicine had access to funding and the advantage of participating in the institution of medicine. In contrast to Turner's argument, Cockerham observes that the division between the two sociologies has blurred as sociologists in both areas have moved into health policy. In addition, medical sociologists may work in organizational settings that foster both directions of inquiry such as university departments of health and social care in the United Kingdom. Also, current enthusiasm about mixed methods encourages team projects that address questions reflecting both approaches.
2 We also limit our discussion to physical, rather than mental, chronic illnesses.

References

Abel, Emily K. 1991. *Who Cares for the Elderly? Public Policy and the Experiences of Adult Daughters*. Philadelphia: Temple University Press.

Abel, Emily K. 1994. "Historical Perspectives on Caregiving: Documenting Women's Experiences." Pp. 227–40 in Jaber F. Gubrium and Andrea Sankar (eds.), *Qualitative Methods in Aging Research*. Thousand Oaks, CA: Sage.

Adamson, Christopher. 1997. "Existential and Clinical Uncertainty in the Medical Encounter: An Idiographic Account of an Illness Trajectory Defined by Inflammatory Bowel Disease and Avascular Necrosis." *Sociology of Health and Illness* 19(2): 133–59.

Allsop, Judith, Kathryn Jones, and Rob Baggott. 2004. "Health Consumer Groups in the UK: A New Social Movement?" *Sociology of Health and Illness* 26(6): 737–56.

Armstrong, David. 2002. *A New History of Identity: A Sociology of Medical Knowledge*. London: Palgrave.

Arney, William R. and Bernard J. Bergen. 1983. "The Anomaly, the Chronic Patient and the Play of Medical Power." *Sociology of Health and Illness* 5(1): 1–24.

Barker, Kristin K. 2002. "Self-Help Literature and the Making of an Illness Identity: The Case of Fibromyalgia Syndrome (FMS)." *Social Problems* 49(3): 279–300.

Barker, Kristin K. 2006. *The Fibromyalgia Story: Medical Authority and Women's Worlds of Pain*. Philadelphia: Temple University Press.

Barker, Kristin K. 2008. "Electronic Support Groups, Patient-Consumers, and Medicalization: The Case of Contested Illness." *Journal of Health and Social Behavior* 49(1): 20–36.

Blaxter, Mildred. 1983. "The Cause of Disease: Women Talking." *Social Science and Medicine* 17: 59–69.

Brooks, Nancy A. and Ronald R. Matson. 1987. "Managing Multiple Sclerosis." Pp. 73–106 in J. A. Roth and P. Conrad (eds.), *Research in the Sociology of Health Care: The Experience and Management of Chronic Illness*, vol. 6. Greenwich, CT: JAI Press.

Broom, Dorothy H. and Roslyn V. Woodward. 1996. "Medicalisation Reconsidered: Toward a Collaborative Approach to Care." *Sociology of Health and Illness* 18: 357–78.

Brown, Phil, Stephen Zavestoski, Sabrina McCormick, Brian Mayer, Rachel Morello-Frosch, and Rebecca Gasior Altman. 2004. "Embodied Health Movements: New Approaches to Social Movements in Health." *Sociology of Health and Illness* 26(1): 50–8.

Bunton, Robin, Sarah Nettleton, and Roger Burrows (eds.). 1995. *The Sociology of Health Promotion: Critical Analyses of Consumption, Lifestyle, and Risk*. London: Routledge.

Burkitt, Ian. 1997. "Social Relationships and Emotions." *Sociology* 3: 37–55.

Bury, Michael. 1982. "Chronic Illness as Biographical Disruption." *Sociology of Health and Illness* 4: 167–82.

Bury, Michael and D. Taylor. 2008. "Toward a Theory of Care Transition: From Medical Dominance to Managed Consumerism." *Social Theory and Health* 6(3): 201–19.

Carricaburu, Danièle and Janine Pierret. 1995. "From Biographical Disruption to Biographical Reinforcement: The Case of HIV-Positive Men." *Sociology of Health and Illness* 17(1): 65–88.

Chamberlayne, Prue and Annette King. 1997. "The Biographical Challenge of Caring." *Sociology of Health and Illness* 19(5): 601–21.

Charmaz, Kathy. 1983. "Loss of Self: A Fundamental Form of Suffering in the Chronically Ill." *Sociology of Health and Illness* 5(2): 168–95.

Charmaz, Kathy. 1991. *Good Days, Bad Days: The Self in Chronic Illness and Time*. New Brunswick, NJ: Rutgers University Press.

Charmaz, Kathy. 1994. "Identity Dilemmas of Chronically Ill Men." *Sociological Quarterly* 35: 269–88.

Charmaz, Kathy. 1995. "The Body, Identity and Self." *Sociological Quarterly* 36: 657–80.

Charmaz, Kathy. 1999. "From the Sick Role to Stories of Self: Understanding the Self in Illness." Pp. 209–39 in R. Ashmore and R. Contrada (eds.), *Self and Identity. Vol. 2: Interdisciplinary Explorations in Physical Health*. New York: Oxford University Press.

Charmaz, Kathy. 2008. "Views from the Margins: Voices, Silences, and Suffering." *Qualitative Research in Psychology* 5(1): 7–18.

Charmaz, Kathy and Dana Rosenfeld. 2006. "Reflections of the Body, Images of Self: Visibility and Invisibility in Chronic Illness and Disability." Pp. 35–50 in D. D. Waskul and P. Vannini (eds.), *Body/Embodiment: Symbolic Interaction and the Sociology of the Body*. London: Ashgate.

Ciambrone, Desirée. 2001. "Illness and Other Assaults on Self: The Relative Impact of HIV/AIDS on Women's Lives." *Sociology of Health and Illness* 23(4): 517–40.

Clarke, Juanne N. 2000. "The Search for Legitimacy and the Expertization of the Lay Person: The Case of Chronic Fatigue Syndrome." *Social Work in Health Care* 30(3): 79–93.

Cockerham, William C. 2007. *Social Causes of Health and Disease*. Cambridge: Polity Press.

Cockerham, William. 2010. *Medical Sociology*, 11th edition. Upper Saddle River, NJ: Prentice-Hall.

Cohen, D., J. McCubbin, and G. Perodeau. 2001. "Medications as Social Phenomena." *Health* 5(4): 411–69.

Conrad, Peter. 1985. "The Meaning of Medications: Another Look at Compliance." *Social Science and Medicine* 20(1): 29–37.

Conrad, Peter. 1987. "The Experience of Illness: Recent and New Directions." Pp. 1–32 in J. A. Roth and P. Conrad (eds.), *Research in the Sociology of Health Care: The Experience and Management of Chronic Illness*, vol. 6. Greenwich, CT: JAI Press.

Conrad, Peter. 1992. "Medicalization and Social Control." *Annual Review of Sociology* 18: 209–32.

Conrad, Peter. 2005. "The Shifting Engines of Medicalization." *Journal of Health and Social Behavior* 46(1): 3–14.

Conrad, Peter and Joseph W. Schneider. 1992. *Deviance and Medicalization: From Badness to Sickness*, 3rd edition. Philadelphia: Temple University Press.

Corbin, Juliet M. and Anselm Strauss. 1984. "Collaboration: Couples Working Together to Manage Chronic Illness." *Image* 4: 109–15.

Corbin, Juliet M. and Anselm Strauss. 1985. "Managing Chronic Illness at Home: Three Lines of Work." *Qualitative Sociology* 8: 224–47.

Corbin, Juliet M. and Anselm Strauss. 1988. *Unending Work and Care: Managing Chronic Illness at Home*. San Francisco: Jossey-Bass.

Cornwall, Jocelyn. 1984. *Hard-Earned Lives: Accounts of Health and Illness from East London*. London: Tavistock.

Courtenay, Will H. 2003. "Key Determinants of the Health and the Well-Being of Men and Boys." *International Journal of Men's Health* 2(1): 1–27.

Crawford, Robert. 1980. "Healthism and the Medicalization of Everyday Life." *International Journal of Health Services* 10(3): 365–88.

Davis, Fred. 1963. *Passage Through Crisis: Polio Victims and Their Families*. Indianapolis: Bobbs-Merrill.

Davis, Fred. 1972 [1956]. "Definitions of Time and Recovery in Paralytic Polio Convalescence." Pp. 83–91 in F. Davis, *Illness, Interaction and the Self*. Belmont, CA: Wadsworth.

Dumit, Joseph. 2006. "Illnesses You Have to Fight to Get: Facts As Forces in Uncertain, Emergent Illnesses." *Social Science and Medicine* 62(3): 577–90.

Fagerhaugh, Shizuko. 1975. "Getting Around with Emphysema." Pp. 99–107 in A. L. Strauss (ed.), *Chronic Illness and the Quality of Life*. St. Louis, MO: Mosby.

Faircloth, Christopher A., Craig Boylstein, Maude Rittman, Mary Ellen Young, and Jaber Gubrium. 2004. "Sudden Illness and Biographical Flow in Narratives of Stroke Recovery." *Sociology of Health and Illness* 26(2): 242–61.

Fitzpatrick, Michael. 2001. *The Tyranny of Health: Doctors and the Regulation of Lifestyle*. London: Routledge.

Foucault, Michel. 1975. *The Birth of the Clinic: An Archaeology of Medical Perception*. New York: Vintage Books.

Foucault, Michel. 1988. "Technologies of the Self." Pp. 16–49 in L. H. Martin, H. Gutman, and P. H. Hutton (eds.), *Technologies of the Self*. Amherst: University of Massachusetts Press.

Fox, Nicholas J. 1999. *Beyond Health: Postmodernism and Embodiment*. London: Free Association Books.

Freidson, Eliot. 1961. *Patients' Views of Medical Practice: A Study of Subscribers to a Prepaid Medical Plan in the Bronx*. New York: Russell Sage Foundation.

Freidson, Eliot. 1970. *Profession of Medicine: A Study of the Sociology of Applied Knowledge*. New York: Harper and Row.

Freund, Peter E. S. 1990. "The Expressive Body: A Common Ground for the Sociology of Emotions and Health and Illness." *Sociology of Health and Illness* 12: 452–77.

Freund, Peter E. S. 1998. "Social Performances and Their Discontents: The Biopsychosocial Aspects of Dramaturgical Stress." Pp. 265–90 in S. J. Williams and G. Bendelow (eds.), *Emotions in Social Life: Critical Themes and Contemporary Issues*. London: Routledge.

Gallagher, Eugene B. 1976. "Lines of Reconstruction and Extension in the Parsonian Sociology of Illness." *Social Science and Medicine* 10: 207–18.

Gerhardt, Uta and Marianne Brieskorn-Zinke. 1986. "The Normalization of Hemodialysis at Home." Pp. 271–317 in J. A. Roth and S. B. Ruzek (eds.), *Research in the Sociology of Health Care: The Adoption and Social Consequences of Medical Technologies*, vol. 4. Greenwich, CT: JAI Press.

Glaser, Barney G. and Anselm L. Strauss. 1965. *Awareness of Dying*. Chicago: Aldine.

Glaser, Barney G. and Anselm L. Strauss. 1968. *Time for Dying*. Chicago: Aldine.

Goffman, Erving. 1961. *Asylums*. Garden City, NY: Doubleday.

Goffman, Erving. 1963. *Stigma: Notes on the Management of Spoiled Identity*. Englewood Cliffs, NJ: Prentice-Hall.

Graham, Ruth. 2006. "Lacking Compassion: Sociological Analyses of the Medical Profession." *Social Theory and Health* 4: 43–63.

Green, Gill, Jennifer Todd, and David Pevalin. 2007. "Biographical Disruption Associated with Multiple Sclerosis: Using Propensity Scoring to Assess the Impact." *Social Science and Medicine* 65: 524–35.

Gregory, Susan. 2005. "Living with Chronic Illness in the Family Setting." *Sociology of Health and Illness* 27(3): 372–92.

Hart, Nicky, Noah Grand, and Kevin Riley. 2006. "Making the Grade: The Gender Gap, ADHD, and the Medicalization of Boyhood." Pp. 132–64 in D. Rosenfeld and C. A. Faircloth (eds.), *Medicalized Masculinities*. Phialdelphia: Temple University Press.

Hellström, Olle, Jennifer Bullington, Gunnar Karlsson, Per Lindqvist, and Bengt Mattson. 1999. "A Phenomenological Study of Fibromyalgia: Patient Perspectives." *Scandinavian Journal of Primary Health Care* 17(1): 11–16.

Herzlich, Claudine and Janine Pierret. 1987. *Illness and Self in Society*. Baltimore: Johns Hopkins University Press.

Hopper, Susan. 1981. "Diabetes as a Stigmatized Condition." *Social Science and Medicine* 15B: 11–19.

Illich, Ivan. 1975. "The Medicalization of Life." Pp. 31–60 in I. Illich (ed.), *Medical Nemesis: The Expropriation of Health*. London: Caldon and Boyars.

Kelleher, David. 1988. *Diabetes*. London: Routledge.

Kelleher, David. 1994. "Self-Help Groups and Their Relationship to Modern Medicine." Pp. 104–17 in J. Gabe, D. Kelleher, and G. Williams (eds.), *Challenging Medicine*. London: Routledge.

Kelly, Michael O. and D. Field. 1996. "Medical Sociology, Chronic Illness and the Body." *Sociology of Health and Illness* 18(2): 241–57.

Klawiter, Maren. 2005. "Breast Cancer in Two Regimes: The Impact of Social Movements on Illness Experience." *Sociology of Health and Illness* 26(6): 845–74.

Koos, Earl L. 1954. *The Health of Regionville: What the People Thought and Did About It*. New York: Columbia University Press.

Kroll-Smith, J. Stephen. 1997. *Bodies in Protest: Environmental Illness and the Struggle Over Medical Knowledge*. New York: New York University Press.

Kutner, Nancy. 1987. "Social Worlds and Identity in End-Stage Renal Disease (ESRD)." Pp. 33–71 in J. A. Roth and P. Conrad (eds.), *Research in the Sociology of Health Care: The Experience and Management of Chronic Illness*, vol. 6. Greenwich, CT: JAI Press.

Lawton, Julia. 2003. "Lay Experiences of Health and Illness: Past Research and Future Agendas." *Sociology of Health and Illness* 25(3): 23–40.

Levine, Sol and Martin A. Kozloff. 1978. "The Sick Role: Assessment and Overview." *Annual Review of Sociology* 4: 317–43.

Locker, David. 1983. *Disability and Disadvantage: The Consequences of Chronic Illness*. London: Tavistock.

Lupton, Deborah. 1993. "Risk as Moral Danger: The Social and Political Functions of Risk Discourse in Public Health." *International Journal of Health Services* 23: 425–35.

Lupton, Deborah. 1995. *The Imperative of Health: Public Health and the Regulated Body*. London: Sage.

Lupton, Deborah. 1997. "Foucault and the Medicalization Critique." Pp. 94–110 in A. Petersen and R. Bunton (eds.), *Foucault, Health and Medicine*. New York: Routledge.

MacDonald, Lea. 1988. "The Experience of Stigma: Living with Rectal Cancer." Pp. 177–202 in R. Anderson and M. Bury (eds.), *Living with Chronic Illness*. London: Unwin Hyman.

MacIntyre, Sally. 1997. "The Black Report and Beyond: What Are the Issues?" *Social Science and Medicine* 44(6): 723–45.

Marshall, Barbara L. 2002. "Hard Science: Gendered Constructions of Sexual Dysfunction in the 'Viagra Age'." *Sexualities* 5(2): 131–58.

Meerabeau, Liz and Susie Page. 1998. "'Getting the Job Done': Emotion Management and Cardiopulmonary Resuscitation in Nursing." Pp. 291–308 in S. J. Williams and G. Bendelow (eds.), *Emotions in Social Life: Critical Themes and Contemporary Issues*. London: Routledge.

Mitteness, Linda S. 1987a. "The Management of Urinary Incontinence by Community-Living Elderly." *The Gerontologist* 27: 185–97.

Mitteness, Linda S. 1987b. "'So What Do You Expect When You're 85?': Urinary Incontinence in Late Life." Pp. 1–32 in J. A. Roth and P. Conrad (eds.), *Research in the Sociology of Health Care: The Experience and Management of Chronic Illness*, vol. 6. Greenwich, CT: JAI Press.

Murphy, Robert F. 1987. *The Body Silent*. New York: Henry Holt.

Nack, Adina. 2008. *Damaged Goods? Women Living With Incurable Sexually Transmitted Diseases*. Philadelphia: Temple University Press.

Nettleton, Sarah, Lisa O'Malley, Ian Watt, and Philip Duffey. 2004. "Enigmatic Illness: Narratives of Patients Who Live With Medically Unexplained Symptoms." *Social Theory and Health* 2: 47–66.

Newton, Tim. 2003. "Truly Embodied Sociology: Marrying the Social and the Biological?" *Sociological Review* 5: 20–42.

Nijhof, Gerhard. 2002. "Parkinson's Disease as a Problem of Shame in Public Appearance." Pp. 88–196 in S. Nettleton and U. Gustafsson (eds.), *The Sociology of Health and Illness Reader*. Cambridge: Polity Press.

Olesen, Virginia and Deborah Bone. 1998. "Emotions in Rationalizing Organizations: Conceptual Notes from Professional Nursing in the USA." Pp. 309–24 in S. J. Williams and G. Bendelow (eds.), *Emotions in Social Life: Critical Themes and Contemporary Issues*. London: Routledge.

Omran, Abdel R. 2005. "The Epidemiologic Transition: A Theory of the Epidemiology of Population Change." *Milbank Quarterly* 83(4): 731–57.

Parsons, Talcott. 1951. *The Social System*. Glencoe, IL: Free Press.

Parsons, Talcott. 1975. "The Sick Role and the Role of the Physician Reconsidered." *Milbank Memorial Fund Quarterly Health Society* 53(3): 257–78.

Payne, Sheila and Caroline Ellis-Hill. 2001. *Chronic and Terminal Illness: New Perspectives on Caring and Carers*. New York: Oxford University Press.

Pearlin, Leonard I., Joseph T. Mullan, Shirley J. Semple, and Marilyn M. Skaff. 1990. "Caregiving and the Stress Process: An Overview of Concepts and Their Measures." *The Gerontologist* 30(5): 583–94.

Petersen, Alan R. 1996. "Risk and the Regulated Self: The Discourse of Health Promotion as Politics of Uncertainty." *Journal of Sociology* 32(1): 44–57.

Peyrot, Mark, James F. McMurray, and Richard Hedges. 1987. "Living with Diabetes: The Role of Personal and Professional Knowledge in Symptom and Regimen Management." Pp. 107–46 in J. A. Roth and P. Conrad (eds.), *Research in the Sociology of Health Care: The Experience and Management of Chronic Illness*, vol. 6. Greenwich, CT: JAI Press.

Peyrot, Mark, James F. McMurray, and Richard Hedges. 1988. "Marital Adjustment to Adult Diabetes: Interpersonal Congruence and Spouse Satisfaction." *Journal of Marriage and the Family* 50: 363–76.

Pierret, Janine. 2003. "The Illness Experience: State of Knowledge and Perspectives for Research." *Sociology of Health and Illness* 25(3): 4–22.

Pinder, Ruth. 1988. "Striking Balances: Living with Parkinson's Disease." Pp. 67–88 in R. Anderson and M. Bury (eds.), *Living with Chronic Illness: The Experience of Patients and Their Families*. London: Unwin Hyman.

Pitt, Diane E. 2006. "*Hearts and Minds: Women, CHD and the Battle for Epistemic Authority in the Medical Consultation.*" Presented at the Humanity, Health, and Ethics Seminar Series in the Medical Humanities, University of Hull, UK.

Radley, Alan and Michael Billig. 1996. "Accounts of Health and Illness, Dilemmas and Representations." *Sociology of Health and Illness* 18(2): 220–40.

Raynor, Geof. 1981. "Medical Errors and the 'Sick Role': A Speculative Enquiry." *Sociology of Health and Illness* 3(3): 296–316.

Reif, Laura. 1975. "Ulcerative Colitis: Strategies for Managing Life." Pp. 81–8 in A. L. Strauss (ed.), *Chronic Illness and the Quality of Life*. St. Louis, MO: Mosby.

Rosenfeld, Dana. 2006a. "Similarities and Differences between Acute Illness and Injury Narratives and Their Implications for Medical Sociology." *Social Theory and Health* 4(1): 64–84.

Rosenfeld, Dana. 2006b. "Transcending the Acute/Chronic Illness Divide: The Physical and Social Experience of Acute Illness and Injury." Presented at the Section on Medical Sociology Refereed Roundtables. 101st Annual Meeting of the American Sociological Association, Montreal, Canada.

Rosenfeld, Dana and Christopher Faircloth. 2004. "Embodied Fluidity and the Commitment to Movement: Constructing the Moral Self through Arthritis Narratives." *Symbolic Interaction* 27(4): 507–29.

Roth, Julius A. 1963. *Timetables: Structuring the Passage of Time in Hospital Treatment and Other Careers*. Indianapolis: Bobbs-Merrill.

Sanders, Caroline, Jenny Donovan, and Paul Dieppe. 2002. "The Significance and Consequences of Having Painful and Disabled Joints in Older Age: Co-Existing Accounts of Normal and Disrupted Biographies." *Sociology of Health and Illness* 24(2): 227–53.

Sandstrom, Kent L. 1990. "Confronting Deadly Disease: The Drama of Identity Construction Among Gay Men with AIDS." *Journal of Contemporary Ethnography* 19: 271–94.

Scambler, Graham. 1984. "Perceiving and Coping with Stigmatizing Illness." Pp. 203–26 in R. Fitzpatrick, J. Hinton, S. Newman, G. Scambler, and J. Thompson (eds.), *The Experience of Illness*. London: Tavistock.

Scambler, Graham. 2004. "Reframing Stigma: Felt and Enacted Stigma and Challenges to the Sociology of Chronic and Disabling Conditions." *Social Theory and Health* 2(1): 29–46.

Scambler, Graham and Anthony Hopkins. 1986. "Being Epileptic: Coming to Terms with Stigma." *Sociology of Health and Illness* 8(1): 26–43.

Scambler, Graham and Anthony Hopkins. 1988. "Accommodating Epilepsy in Families." Pp. 156–76 in R. Anderson and M. Bury (eds.), *Living with Chronic Illness: The Experience of Patients and Their Families*. London: Unwin Hyman.

Scambler, Graham and David Kelleher. 2006. "New Social and Health Movements: Issues of Representation and Change." *Critical Public Health* 16(3): 219–31.

Schneider, Joseph W. and Peter Conrad. 1980. "In the Closet with Illness: Epilepsy, Stigma Potential and Information Control." *Social Problems* 28(1): 32–44.

Schneider, Joseph W. and Peter Conrad. 1983. *Having Epilepsy: The Experience and Control of Illness*. Philadelphia: Temple University Press.

Scott, Wilbur J. 1990. "PTSD in *DSM-III*: A Case Study in the Politics of Diagnosis and Disease." *Social Problems* 37(3): 294–310.

Shriver, Thomas E. and Dennis D. Waskul. 2006. "Managing the Uncertainties of Gulf War Illness: The Challenges of Living with Contested Illness." *Symbolic Interaction* 29(4): 465–86.

Sim, Julius and Sue Madden. 2008. "Illness Experience in Fibromyalgia Syndrome: A Meta-synthesis of Qualitative Studies." *Social Science and Medicine* 67: 57–67.

Speedling, Edward. 1982. *Heart Attack: The Family Response at Home and in the Hospital*. New York: Tavistock.

Stockl, Andrea. 2007. "Complex Syndromes, Ambivalent Diagnosis, and Existential Uncertainty: The Case of Systemic Lupus Erythematosus (SLE)." *Social Science and Medicine* 65(7): 1549–59.

Straus, Robert. 1957. "The Nature and Status of Medical Sociology." *American Sociological Review* 22(2): 200–4.

Strauss, Anselm L. (ed.). 1975. *Chronic Illness and the Quality of Life*. St. Louis, MO: Mosby.

Strauss, Anselm L., Juliet M. Corbin, Shizuko Fagerhaugh, Barney G. Glaser, David Maines, Barbara Suczek, and Carolyn L. Wiener. 1984. *Chronic Illness and the Quality of Life*, 2nd edition. St. Louis, MO: Mosby.

Travers, Michele Kerry and Jocalyn Lawler. 2008. "Self within a Climate of Contention: Experiences of Chronic Fatigue Syndrome." *Social Science and Medicine* 66(2): 315–26.

Turner, Bryan. 1992. *Regulating Bodies: Essays in Medical Sociology*. London: Routledge.

Twaddle, Albert C. 1969. "Health Decisions and Sick Role Variations: An Exploration." *Journal of Health and Social Behavior* 10(2): 105–15.

Verbrugge, Lois M. 1990. "Pathways to Health and Death." Pp. 41–79 in R. D. Apple (ed.), *Women, Health, and Medicine in America*. New York: Garland.

Vermeire, E., H. Hearnshaw, P. Van Royen, and J. Denekens. 2001. "Patient Adherence to Treatment: Three Decades of Research. A Comprehensive Review." *Journal of Clinical Pharmacy and Therapeutics* 26(5): 331–42.

Ware, Norma C. 1992. "Suffering and the Social Construction of Illness: The Delegitimation of Illness Experience in Chronic Fatigue Syndrome." *Medical Anthropology Quarterly* 6(4): 347–61.

Weitz, Rose. 1991. *Life with AIDS*. New Brunswick, NJ: Rutgers University Press.

Werner, Anne, L. W. Isaksen, Lise Widding, and Kirsti Malterud. 2004. " 'I Am Not the Kind of Woman Who Complains of Everything': Illness Stories on Self and Shame in Women with Chronic Pain." *Social Science and Medicine* 59(5): 1035–45.

Werner, Anne and Kirsti Malterud. 2003. "It Is Hard Work Behaving as a Credible Patient: Encounters between Women with Chronic Pain and Their Doctors." *Social Science and Medicine* 57(8): 1409–19.

Wilkinson, Richard. 1996. *Unhealthy Societies: The Afflictions of Inequality*. London: Routledge.

Wilkinson, Richard and Michael Marmot (eds.). 2006. *Social Determinants of Health*. Oxford: Oxford University Press.

Williams, Clare. 2000. "Alert Assistants in Managing Chronic Illness: The Case of Mothers and Teenage Sons." *Sociology of Health and Illness* 22: 254–72.

Williams, Clare. 2002. *Mothers, Young People and Chronic Illness*. Aldershot: Ashgate.

Williams, Simon J. 2000. "Chronic Illness as Biographical Disruption or Biographical Disruption as Chronic Illness? Reflections on a Core Concept." *Sociology of Health and Illness* 22(1): 40–67.

Williams, Simon J. 2003. *Medicine and the Body*. London: Sage.

Williams, Simon J. and Gillian A. Bendelow. 1998. "The Emotionally Expressive Body." Pp. 131–54 in S. Williams and G. Bendelow (eds.), *The Lived Body: Sociological Themes, Embodied Issues*. London: Routledge.

Williamson, Charlotte. 2008. "The Patient Movement as an Emancipation Movement." *Health Expectations* 11(2): 102–12.

Wilson, Sarah. 2007. "'When You Have Children, You're Obliged to Live': Motherhood, Chronic Illness and Biographical Disruption." *Sociology of Health and Illness* 29(4): 610–26.

Zola, Irving K. 1973. "Pathways to the Doctor: From Person to Patient." *Social Science and Medicine* 7(9): 677–89.

Zola, Irving K. 1975. "In the Name of Health and Illness: On Some Socio-Political Consequences of Medical Influence." *Social Science and Medicine* 9: 83–7.

Part V
Health Care Delivery

15

Health Professions and Occupations

ELIANNE RISKA

Over the past 30 years, sociologists have debated the state and future of the health professions. While the theoretical discussion in the 1960s was characterized by a belief in the future of powerful professions, the debate in the field since the mid-1980s has predicted the demise of such groups. It has been suggested that most professions are losing their special skills and autonomy because of organizational and knowledge-based changes and are becoming ordinary occupations. Still others have argued that the distinction between professions and occupations is an artifact of the vocabulary of sociologists on different continents. Sciulli (2005: 915) has asserted that "not a single continental language either before or after the Second World War developed indigenously a term synonymous with or generally equivalent to the English term 'profession'" and that "professions play no role whatsoever in European sociology" (Sciulli 2005: 916). While this observation is certainly based on the fact that theorizing about professions emerged in American sociology, it does not mean that theorizing and research about health professions and occupations have been totally absent from European sociology. The debated issues have been different because of the organizational settings for knowledge-based groups in Europe (Evetts 2006). As Evetts and her colleagues suggest, the Anglo-American market-oriented society created free professions and an intellectual endeavor – a sociology of professions – to understand the power of these groups. In Europe, by contrast, the close cooperation between government bureaucracies, public universities, and the professions turned the focus of sociological attention to class and organizations because there were few free professions (Evetts et al. 2009: 140).

This chapter will try to bridge the theoretical models of professions with the contextual issues that have emerged in the study of professions in different countries. The chapter is organized into four parts. The first part will look at the early theorizing about professions and the use of the medical profession as a prototype of knowledge-based professional groups that emerged with the modernization and rationalization of society. It presents the major theoretical perspectives on the power of the medical profession. The second part presents another type of theoretical discussion that has used the concepts of medicalization and biopower as analytical tools to examine the power of the medical profession. The third part will look at the gendered aspects of health professions. The fourth and concluding section will present a summary of the major issues presented in the chapter but also indicate the current challenges in the sociology of professions.

PHYSICIAN-CENTERED THEORIES: HEALTH CARE AS THE WORK OF AND TRUST IN THE MEDICAL PROFESSION

Since the 1960s, there has been a clearly identifiable scholarly debate on health professions. In fact, few other fields in sociology are represented by such a linear development of the theoretical discussion as in the sociology of the professions. This section and the following ones will present the major theoretical perspectives on the power and social position of the medical profession that have emerged during the past five decades. Eight theoretical perspectives on the power and structure of health professions and occupations will be reviewed: the functionalist, the interactionist, the neo-Weberian, the neo-Marxist, neo-system theories, the social constructionist, the poststructuralist, and the feminist perspectives. A summary of the characteristics of these theoretical frameworks is presented in Table 15.1. The table lists each perspective by the assumptions about the structure underlying the power of health professions, the focus of the analysis, and the characteristics of the internal structure of the medical profession.

The functionalist theory of professions derives from the structural views on status, roles, and normative aspects of social behavior that appeared in the writings of Emile Durkheim and Max Weber. For Durkheim, the role of intermediary organizations and the organic solidarity growing out of the modern division of labor signaled the rise of the functions that occupations and professions would come to serve in the modern world. Influenced by the works of Durkheim and Weber, Talcott Parsons presented a theoretical framework – a theory of social action – for the understanding of modern society. Parsons saw in the profession of law, and especially in the medical profession, the prototype of occupations based on expertise (Parsons 1949, 1951). The status and authority of the professions were based on possession of knowledge, and on a service and collective orientation that provided the kind of expertise and trust that clients required. For Parsons, the professions harbored a particular relationship of trust vis-à-vis the client, in contrast to the businessmen whose behavior was guided by a profit motive. Hence, Parsons distinguished the "professional man" from the "business man." He depicted the former as an altruistic servant of his clients, and the latter as mainly pursuing his own self-interest in the transaction (Parsons 1949: 186–7). The difference in behavior, Parsons argued, was not motivational but resided in different institutional patterns and structures governing the two fields of action.

Parsons' view on professions can be characterized as a normative theory. The norms of the professions, expressed as professionalism in behavior and thought, were the criteria by which sociologists could set these groups apart from regular occupational groups. For Parsons' students, the task was to map how new recruits to the professions were socialized to the norms that guided professional thinking

Table 15.1 Theoretical perspectives on the power of the medical profession

Perspective	Underlying structure	Focus of analysis	Structure of the profession
Functionalist:			
Parsons	Normative consensus	Professional role of physicians	United body
Interactionist:			
Hughes	Social drama of work	Occupational culture	Contractual and relational power
Goffman	Team work	Tinkering service	Management of impressions
Freidson	Professional knowledge	Professional autonomy	Professional dominance/ professionalism of physicians
Neo-Weberian	Modern society and rationalization	Professional projects	United profession due to professional closure
Neo-Marxist	Capitalist economy	Corporate and bureaucratic structure of health care	Corporate control of health care and power of physicians
Neo-system theories	Marketization of medicine	Jurisdictions and allies	Pluralist notion of power
Social constructionist:			
Conrad	Cultural power of medicine	Medicalization	United profession but new groups get definitional power
Poststructuralist:			
Foucault	Medical knowledge	Medical discourse and biopolitics	Fragmented character of power
Feminist	Patriarchy/gendered structures	Gendered organization of health care	Gender segregation of work

and behavior. A classic in this genre of studies was *The Student-Physician*, which was headed by one of Parsons' students, Robert Merton (Merton, Reader, and Kendall 1957). Known as the Columbia University study, it examined how students at three US medical schools learned the behavior and attitudes of the medical profession. The medical school is said "to shape the novice into the effective practitioner of medicine, to give him the best available knowledge and skills, and to provide him with a professional identity so that he comes to think, act and feel like a physician," and the final product, the physician, is called "a medical man" (Merton 1957: 7). This theme of the unmarked character of the gender of the professions in the early literature on professions will be examined later in this chapter.

A consensual perspective of society and a view of professions' work as based on mutual trust between the client and the professional has been attributed to Parsons' work. However, Parsons was not unaware of the special market position of the American medical profession in the 1950s. He identified the contemporary

American industrial economy as characterized by giant corporations and mass commodity production, and he drew attention to the fact that the medical profession was acting outside of this economy. Parsons noted that organized medicine defended the profession's entrepreneurial and autonomous position by appealing not to scientific expertise but to the profession's particularistic relation to the family and the local community (Parsons 1963: 26).

The functionalist theory of professions was the dominant perspective for studying the medical profession in the 1950s and 1960s. Yet it is important to remember that in American sociology there were from the start different approaches to understanding the character of occupations and professions. Everett Hughes' (1958) collection of essays, *Men and Their Work*, offered an alternative interpretation of work, occupations, and professions. For Hughes (1958: 53), a study of any kind of occupations entailed an analysis of the "social drama of work." In his view, most occupations bring together people in definable roles and it is in the interaction that the content of work and status are defined. An occupation is not, by means of its expertise and knowledge, a profession *a priori* but a social status that is socially constructed (Hughes 1958: 44–5). According to Hughes (1958: 48), the aim of the study of the work of occupations and professions should therefore be "to *penetrate more deeply* into the personal and social drama of work, to understand the social and social-psychological arrangements and devices by which men make their work tolerable, or even glorious to themselves and others." More recently, this approach has been called the "negotiation perspective" and been used to explain the intraprofessional dynamics and developments of American surgery and obstetrics and gynecology (Zetka 2003, 2008a, 2008b).

The interactionist and dramaturgical approach to work was also represented by Erving Goffman (1961). He viewed an occupation as a service relation between the server and the served. Like Hughes, Goffman (1961: 325–6) viewed professions not as intrinsically distinct from occupations but as a particular type of personal-service occupation based on expertise. An expert provided a special type of "tinkering service." Goffman (1961: 330) characterized the expert-servicing as a practice in which "the server has a complex physical system to repair, construct, or tinker with – the system here being the client's personal object or possession." Tinkering services can be broken down into a series of distinct phases that constitute the "repair cycle" (Goffman 1961: 330). But medical tinkering confronts a major problem – the body. It is a possession of the served that cannot be left under the care of the server while the client goes about his or her other business. Therefore, a large part of the medical encounter involves, according to Goffman (1961: 341), "non-person treatment" or ways of handling the patient/the body as "a possession someone has left behind." Furthermore, the verbal part of the server's exchange has three components: a technical part that contains the relevant repair information, a contractual part that specifies the terms of the repair task, and the sociable part that involves courtesies, civilities, and signs of deference (Goffman 1961: 328–9). During the past decades, the problem of the presence of the body in medical encounters and the physician's preference for focusing on the technical part while being oblivious to the social part of the verbal exchange have been in focus in a whole new genre of research. Based on an interactionist framework, several studies have examined the interaction between clients and health care experts. A special method – conversational analysis (CA) – has been one of the upshots of this research (Arminen 2005; Silverman 1987).

While Goffman continued to inspire sociologists interested in the dynamics of the micro-level aspects of the patient–physician relationship, Hughes' work seems to have been less referred to in the 1970s and 1980s. During those decades, the mainstream functionalist perspective in the sociology of professions was challenged. The major challenge came from Eliot Freidson (1970a), who in his book *The Profession of Medicine* analyzed the normative basis of the Parsonian model of the physician's behavior. According to Freidson, Parsons' theoretical framework for understanding the normative basis of professions – the pattern variables – did not fit the doctor's behavior. In Freidson's view, medical practice is characterized by pragmatism, subjectivism, and indeterminacy, a feature he called the "clinical mentality." As Freidson (1970a: 170–1) put it, "The practitioner is particularistic, not universalistic" and "manifests a strain toward functional diffuseness, again contrary to Parsons' expectation." The special power of the medical profession was, he suggested, based on its knowledge monopoly and dominance over other health professions (Freidson 1970b). This perspective on the medical profession's power and status has been known as the professional dominance or monopolization thesis.

A decade later, Freidson (1984, 1985) presented another version of his thesis. In his addendum – the so-called restratification thesis – he proposed that, despite changes, the American medical profession would be able to maintain its dominance because it had adapted by differentiating into three segments, each with its specific task: an administrative segment, a knowledge elite, and practitioners. This internal differentiation would guarantee the status quo for the profession's traditional power position. Although such an internal differentiation has indeed taken place, critics have argued that the managerial positions are no longer filled by physicians and that the knowledge elite itself is internally differentiated into small expert circles, with their own associations and with little affinity for advancing the interests of the profession as a whole (e.g., Hafferty and Light 1995).

A third phase of Freidson's work would emerge yet another decade later, when Freidson re-evaluated the American scene in his last book, *Professionalism: The Third Logic* (Freidson 2001). The title refers to the three logics of service provision: the market, bureaucratic organizations, and professions. Here Freidson is returning to the concept of professionalism introduced in his first book. He suggests that the professions have occupied an autonomous position between the market and big organizations and this autonomy guarantees the special service and trust that professions can offer their clientele. Commentators on Freidson's final perspective on professions see a return here to the Parsonian normative view on professions (see Evetts 2006; Evetts et al. 2009: 142). But as yet another scholar comments, "*Third Logic* is not, then, an exercise in nostalgia. It tries to come to terms with a world that has changed in ways that were not acknowledged in the original intellectual project" (Dingwall 2006: 97).

The Profession of Medicine by Freidson (1970a) had offered a fresh look at an old theme and showed a way forward from the theoretical and hegemonic status of the functionalist approach to professions that had characterized the field for two decades. Freidson's perspective sparked a debate on health professions. The positive aspect of this debate in the 1970s and 1980s was the ensuing alternative interpretations of the power of the medical profession and numerous reports of the development and power of that profession in various countries in the 1990s and 2000s (e.g., Hafferty and McKinlay 1993; Hellberg, Saks, and Benoit 1999; Johnson, Larkin, and Saks 1995; Jones 1991; Kuhlmann 2006). The drawback has been that it kept the focus on only one health profession – that of physicians – and so postponed the exploration of the character, clientele, and function of other health professions and alternative health occupations.

In retrospect, the intense phase of research on the American medical profession between 1975 and the end of the 1980s was related to the dramatic change of the American health care system that began during those years and that witnessed the rise of corporate medicine and managed care (Starr 1982). There were two main directions in this research. One direction, represented by the neo-Weberian and the neo-Marxist perspectives, focused on the extraordinary power that the medical profession had acquired in the American health care system. The other direction projected the demise of this power as a sign of a structural change of American health care characterized by a bureaucratic and consumer-challenging structure.

The neo-Weberian perspective became the major theoretical framework for those who tried to explain the united power of the medical profession and the challenges or professional projects pursued by other health professions and occupations. Larson's (1977) work was influential in starting this genre of research, and the concepts of professional projects and social closure were used to describe the jurisdictions, mandates, licensure, and power of professions vis-à-vis occupation (see Table 15.1). The neo-Weberian framework of market closure was used to map the history of the current medical profession and how it succeeded in becoming a united professional body among competing medical sects in various national contexts. It was applied in studies on how certain types of physicians managed to achieve a specialty status, and on the professionalization of a variety of health occupations and the steps they had to take to achieve a professional status. This framework has been used by American and European scholars to explain the power of the medical profession and the division of labor within their health care systems (e.g., Hafferty and McKinlay 1993; Johnson et al. 1995; Jones 1991; Kuhlmann and Saks 2008; Witz 1992).

In addition to the neo-Weberian perspective, there emerged a neo-Marxist perspective that offered its interpretation of the power of the medical profession. This perspective was introduced by Vicente Navarro (1976) and later elaborated by Howard Waitzkin (Jasso-Aguilar, Waitzkin, and Landwehr 2004; Waitzkin 2000 [1983]), who pointed to the ties of the American profession to corporate capitalism and biomedical industries. The connections of the biomedical corporations and pharmaceutical industries to the medical profession and the issue of medicine as a system of social control have been central themes explored in later social constructionist and poststructuralist perspectives on the professions.

The second direction in American research on the medical profession that began in the mid-1980s pointed to the decline of the power of the American profession (see also Haug 1975). A challenge to the view of the American medical profession as gaining its power from corporate medicine came from McKinlay and his colleagues (McKinlay and Arches 1985; McKinlay and Marceau 2002), who foresaw the gradual decline of the professional dominance of the American medical profession due to the growing corporate and bureaucratic structure of American medicine. American physicians, they argued, were increasingly becoming salaried, and the power was no longer in the hands of the profession but in those of large health care corporations that composed the expanding medical industrial complex.

Recently, McKinlay and Marceau (2008) have presented a refurbished version of their argument and pointed to the declining role of the government in US health care and the increasing impact of private interests. They do not envision a demise of the medical profession as a group under these new conditions, but instead see the disappearance of primary care physicians in the US because "what used to be termed 'primary care' will be conducted digitally, or be delivered by non-physician providers, or specialists" (McKinlay and Marceau 2008: 1489). A major force in this process, they argue, is the support by state authorities of other subordinate health professions that take over the tasks previously done by primary care physicians. This process has also been observed in the Canadian health care system, which has witnessed an expanded professional domain for female-dominated health professions propelled by neoliberal cost-saving health policy initiatives (Bourgeault 2005). In the UK context it has been predicted that the growing importance of the Internet as a source of production of medical knowledge will "alter the degree of trust in medical practice" and "the relationship between patients and professionals," a process dubbed the rise of "e-scaped medicine" (Nettleton and Burrows 2003: 180).

A new effort to introduce a general theory of professions was presented by Andrew Abbott (1988) in *The System of Professions*. Abbott examines professional work and the professions' claims to their jurisdictions. According to Abbott (1988: 33), the power of a profession lies in the achieved right to its jurisdiction, and the profession is linked to other professions through a system of professions, where jurisdictional boundaries are constantly negotiated. This approach is exemplified by three case studies: a presentation of the historical roots of the jurisdiction of information professions, law, and experts on personal problems. In his more recent work, Abbott (2005) has tended to move even further into a neofunctionalist framework by viewing the system of professions as an "ecology," with fluid boundaries between interacting groups and audiences.

Abbott's system model seems to have been applied more to studies of service occupations than to studies of health professions or occupations that have tended to be well organized and strive for professional recognition and status. As MacDonald (1995: 14–17) suggests, Abbott's concept of system is a theoretical hybrid, suggesting partly an interdependence (systems theory) and partly a market model of actors (Weberian theory) and a Chicago School approach to the empirical study of work. A similar hybrid is Light's (1995) concept of "countervailing powers," which suggests a pluralist perception of power in the area of health care. In this respect, both Abbott and Light fall into the category of neo-system theories listed in Table 15.1.

THE POWER OF THE MEDICAL PROFESSION:
MEDICALIZATION AND BIOPOWER

The social constructionist perspective on medical work is not primarily focused on the work of the medical profession but rather on how medicine acts as an institution of social control and the role of the profession as a chief agent in applying and constructing categories of illnesses (Table 15.1). The medicalization argument is based on the notion of the power of the medical profession to define and even expand its jurisdiction to include phenomena that are social rather than biological. When the term *medicalization* was introduced in the early 1970s, Irving Zola (1972) suggested that medical culture would increasingly influence the way that social problems are identified and solved. This cultural trend – "medicalizing of society" (Zola 1972: 496) – relied on physicians as experts in providing medical solutions to a variety of non-medical conditions in a society that increasingly depended on experts and technology. During the past 30 years, Peter Conrad has empirically explored the usefulness of the concept as an analytical tool in understanding emerging new categories of disease. Over the years, Conrad's (1992, 2005, 2007) own theoretical approach has shifted from theory of deviance to a social constructionist position. The analytical focus has continued to be on the definition of the problem: how and by whom new medical categories are constructed, with a subsequent expansion of medical jurisdiction for the medical profession (Conrad 2007: 13). Conrad argues that the agents behind medicalization have shifted over the past 30 years. It is no longer the medical profession that solely defines the criteria of new diseases (for example, as in the case of the expanded jurisdiction of psychosocial pediatrics [Halpern 1990]) – specific interest groups do, too. And more recently, consumers and pharmaceutical companies have become agents in the definitional process.

Over the past decade, poststructuralist theorizing has supplemented the previous dominant social constructionist approach in the literature on medicalization. For example, Adele Clarke and her colleagues (2003) use this approach in their analysis of the increased importance of the role of sciences, technologies, and experts in biomedicine *per se* and in enhancement of the body. They argue that the term "biomedicalization" more aptly describes the current phase of medicalization. Medical interventions in the form of "technologies of the body" enable an enhancement of a certain type of revered notion of the self, for example, by means of cosmetic surgery or lifestyle drugs such as Viagra. They suggest that in the creation of "technoscientific identities," the boundaries between the material body and social identity have come to be blurred (Clarke et al. 2003: 182). Their arguments rest on the French philosopher Michel Foucault's view on the disciplinary power of medicine.

Foucault (1975, 1988) presents medical knowledge as a discourse, a way of seeing and reading the body. He points to the role of science and experts in the construction of new regimens of social control. The argument here is that medical science and medical and biotechnologies serve as hidden instruments of social control so that a self-disciplining governance permeates society at various levels. The term biopolitics refers to knowledge, practices, and norms that have developed to regulate the quality of life of individuals and populations. It extends the use of new technologies in the government of the self, new forms of self-regulation, and self-disciplinary measures that are internalized so that society seems to be self-regulated and self-corrective.

This argument is also presented by the British scholar Nikolas Rose (2001, 2007), who has expanded the Foucauldian perspective on biopolitics and offers three phases of biopolitics to understand new forms of medical culture and social control. *Risk politics* characterizes the first half of the twentieth century, when the focus was on prevention of major public health problems. Two new types of biopolitics followed during the second half of the century. *Molecular politics* is a reorganization of the medical gaze at the molecular level. This politics is represented by, for example, biological psychiatry, a discipline that looks at the neurotransmitters of the brain to identify chemical imbalances that are seen as the causes of mental pathologies. Current biopolitics has taken the character of *ethopolitics*: it demands an optimization of one's corporeality to embrace an enlarged will to health and concerns itself with "the self-techniques by which human beings should judge themselves and act upon themselves to make themselves better than they are" (Rose 2001: 18; 2007: 27). It is argued that this new regimen blurs the boundaries between expert knowledge and the individual's will to self-regulation. In this kind of society, individuals are still dependent on experts who provide the technologies for rational management of the self.

Tied to ethopolitics is a notion of biological citizenship that rests on the conviction that individuals have a right to a good life and that biology is no longer a biological constraint but a matter of choice and enhancement. Individuals can turn to *professionals of vitality* – physicians, genetic counselors, drug companies – to achieve the revered goals (Rose 2001: 22). In his latest work, Rose identifies the emergence of ethopolitics experts, a group called the *new pastorate* (Rose 2007: 73). These experts have "new pastoral powers" that are no longer concerned merely with the population as a whole. Instead, the new biopolitics is pursued by an array of experts involved in risk assessment for special groups and individuals. These endeavors entail the subjects' involvement not only in the form of informed consent, but also in the form of self-examination and self-mastery (Rose 2007: 74–6).

As Table 15.1 suggests, medical discourse offers the medical profession a tool for practice, and at the macro-level the disciplinary regimen of medicine takes the form of a certain kind of biopolitics. Although the medical profession enjoys power, the Foucauldian notion of power is not monolithic but fragmented (Lupton 1998).

GENDER AND THE PROFESSIONS

The theories on professions tend to present health professions in gender-neutral terms. This derives from the early functionalist perspective on professions that delegated the notion of gender to the particularistic character of the family and considered the world of professional work to be guided by other (gender-neutral) norms. The two early studies on professional socialization – *The Student-Physician* and *Boys in White* – solidified this tradition by depicting the professional education of doctors as mainly an enterprise of training (white) men and thereby made gender, race, and ethnicity invisible (Lorber 1975: 85). For example, Merton's study *The Student-Physician* (Merton et al. 1957) presents medical students in gender-neutral or in masculine terms and does not mention women as medical students, nor even whether they were included in the study. And the authors of *Boys in White* confessed that women were not included in that study because of the overwhelmingly male composition of the medical profession. They concluded, therefore, that "we shall talk mainly of boys becoming medical men" (Becker et al. 1961: 3).

The feminist perspective on health professions has therefore pointed out that the major theoretical perspectives on professions have, since their inception, been unmarked by gender even though the very behavior depicted as professional is not gender-neutral but male-gendered (Beagan 2000; Davies 1996). The early efforts that pointed to the gendered character of the attitudes and behavior of doctors tied it to the power structure of men – patriarchy. In the US, such an interpretation was advanced in the works of Ehrenreich and English (1973, 1978), which paved the way for later feminist and structural perspectives on the medical profession, such as Judith Lorber's (1984) pioneering study, *Women Physicians*. In the UK, Anne Witz's (1992) *Professions and Patriarchy* combined a feminist and neo-Weberian perspective on professions and included an analysis of health professions such as medicine and midwifery. These works documented and theorized how different structural mechanisms (Lorber) and discursive strategies and social closures (Witz) had prevented women from entering into or advancing in the medical profession on equal terms with men and how other subordinate health professions – nursing, midwifery – had become women's work. While nursing still continues to be sparsely researched by sociologists (Allen 2001), sociological research on midwifery has proliferated during the past decade (DeVries et al. 2001; Rothman, Simonds, and Norman 2007).

When women began to enter medicine in increasing numbers, some saw the development in an optimistic light while others were more pessimistic in their con-clusions. The optimists have interpreted this upward trend as a sign that values in medicine are going to shift toward more humanistic and holistic concerns and that women are going to advance to all levels and ranks of medicine in numbers cor-responding to their proportion in the profession. Figures from different countries – for example, Sweden, Finland, and the US – show that women currently constitute at least half of the students entering medical school. These figures have been inter-preted as an indicator that women will eventually take over positions in all sectors and ranks of medicine.

On the other hand, the critics have shown that, despite women's numerical and proportional increase in the profession, gender segregation of medical prac-tice has continued. In fact, gender segregation is a persistent feature in different types of health care systems: in market-driven health care systems like that of the US, in welfare states with a public gender-equality policy like Scandinavia, and in post-Soviet societies like Russia and Lithuania, where for the past five decades a majority of the doctors have been women (Riska 2001). To illustrate this point, the pattern of gender segregation in selected medical specialties in Finland, Sweden, Lithuania, and the US could be used as an example. Early research looking at the gender segregation of medical specialties interpreted the pattern as following the gender-stereotyping of work in general (e.g., Lorber

1984). Women physicians tend to practice in specialties that fit their assumed, traditional female-gender qualities: They tend to work in primary care areas that are high-interaction fields and other fields that cater to children and elderly, such as pediatrics, child psychiatry, and geriatrics. By contrast, low-interaction fields and fields associated with "heroic" medicine like surgery, sports medicine, and internal medicine tend to be male dominated.

The gender-essentialist argument for the division of tasks by gender in the medical profession is partially supported in women's high proportion in certain specialties. For example, although women constitute a majority (70 percent) of the physicians in Lithuania, they are sparsely represented in surgery (11 percent) while pediatrics is overwhelmingly female dominated (93 percent) (Riska and Novelskaite 2008). A similar pattern is found in Scandinavia. The proportion of women in surgery is rather low in Finland (20 percent) and Sweden (18 percent), although in 2008 women constituted almost half or more of all doctors (Finnish Medical Association 2008; Swedish Medical Association 2008). By contrast, the proportion of women in pediatrics is relatively high in Finland (63 percent). The same trends are confirmed in the US, where in 2006 a much lower proportion of women practiced in surgery (12 percent) than in pediatrics (54 percent) (American Medical Association 2008; Association of American Medical Colleges 2006: 7).

These trends point to underlying value structures in medicine. The question pondered by researchers is whether the gender segregation reflects the traditional preferences in the career choices of men and women or the persistence of gendered structures (Acker 1990). A challenge to the explanations that point to women's subordinate position in the profession is the remarkable change that has taken place in women physicians' position in obstetrics and gynecology where women are in a majority – for example, in Sweden (62 percent), Finland (70 percent), and Lithuania (76 percent). A high rate (44 percent) is also documented in the US. The entrants into obstetrics and gynecology in the UK and the US indicate that the profile is approaching that in the preceding countries. Women constituted 15 percent of the residents in obstetrics and gynecology in US medical schools in 1975, but they constituted 70 percent in 2000. Furthermore, women are expected to amount to 60 percent of the obstetrics and gynecology practitioners in the US in 2020 (Emmons et al. 2004: 331).

In short, two types of explanation have been given for the gender-segregated character of medical work, one structural and one voluntaristic. The structural explanation points to barriers that keep women from advancing in medicine, such as a lack of mentors and a persistence of gendered structures in medicine (Acker 1990; Lorber 1984). More recently, the term *inequality regimes* (Acker 2006) has been introduced as a way of understanding the production of gender, race, and class in organizations and of shedding light on why so many organized equality projects have failed or have had only minor impact.

The voluntaristic interpretation covers a broad range of frameworks, including the socialization/sex-role theory and gender-essentialist explanations. According to the former, women are socialized to follow stereotypic gender expectations and hence tend to make occupational choices that fit these expectations. According to the latter, women are essentially different from men – more empathic, less interested in the heroic aspects of medicine than men – and tend therefore to choose specialties that give them opportunities to practice the kind of medicine that they prefer and in areas where they can use their gender-specific skills.

Besides examining explanations for the gender segregation of medical practice, researchers have also asked what impact women doctors will have on medicine. The increasing number of women in the profession has not automatically entailed a dramatic change in medical practice. The reviews of the literature on gender and practice styles point to how hard it is to provide a clear-cut answer to the question of women doctors' impact on medicine (e.g., Heru 2005; Kilminster et al. 2007; Lorber 2000; Roter and Hall 2004). The processes are complex and contain both structural and selection aspects – for example, the self-selection of both physicians and patients to certain practice settings that are already gender segregated.

Health care systems and biomedicine are changing rapidly, but some of the structural changes have been mainly linked to women's entry, as if male doctors had nothing to do with these changes. The term *feminization* has been used both to indicate a female majority in medicine and as a term that signals the gradual decline of the status and autonomy of medical work when women enter medicine (Boulis and Jacobs 2008; Riska 2008). The welcome aspect of this discussion in the public media and in the research literature is that it has pointed to the existence of different styles of doctoring. The task is to degender them to meet the demands for new skills in medicine.

CONCLUSIONS

This chapter has reviewed eight theoretical perspectives on the power and structure of health professions and occupations: the functionalist, the interactionist, the neo-Weberian, the neo-Marxist, neo-system theories, the social constructionist, the poststructuralist, and the feminist perspectives. A summary of the characteristics of these theoretical frameworks (Table 15.1) lists each perspective according to the assumptions about the structure underlying the power of various health professions, the focus of analysis, and the characteristics of the internal structure of the medical profession.

The sociology of professions emerged along with the functionalist framework, which saw the institutionalization and authority of the medical profession as based on trust in the profession. The issues of the benevolence of and the trust in the medical profession continue to characterize the debate and to be challenged by alternative theoretical frameworks. Research on the health professions has been heavily focused on the medical profession and its characteristics. In order to revitalize the sociological professionalization literature, scholars have called for more research "in which the results do not lead to an either-or position on professional power but elaborate and revise dominant theoretical assumptions in the medical sociological literature" (Timmermans and Kolker 2004: 188).

Another way of exploring the power of the medical profession instead of looking at its attributes has been to examine the culture of medicine. The concept of "medicalization" was introduced early as an analytical tool to describe the unique power of the medical profession not only in its own domain, but also in its efforts to integrate many aspects of life and behavior under its jurisdiction, as with, for example, birth, adolescence, aging, alcoholism, and premenstrual syndrome (PMS). Feminist researchers have shown that these expansionist endeavors have primarily been directed at women's bodies and therefore perceive medicalization as evidence that medicine is a patriarchal institution (Riska 2003). Empowerment of women as patients, and care by other health professionals – midwives and nurses – and practitioners of alternative medicine became central themes in the non-physician-oriented research.

British research on health professions and occupations has been less physician-centered than American research and has presented a broad view of the division of labor between various health professions and even included lay carers as health workers. Furthermore, European, Canadian, and Latin American research has given the state a central role in shaping the conditions of health professions (DeVries et al. 2001; Jones 1991; Kuhlmann and Saks 2008) and for obvious reasons: Health care systems with publicly financed and run medical care, with a large fraction of physicians being salaried employees, and public health nurses and general practitioners working at local health centers, constitute a different arena for the relationships between various health professions than the market-oriented American health care context.

There are, however, several topics that have been but sparsely covered in current research on health professions and occupations. There are, for example, few sociological studies of work pursued in the hospital setting. A number of sociological classics on the hospital as a social organization – studies on work done in the wards and on the external ties of hospitals to the community – were done in the 1960s, but at present this institutional setting of medical work seems mostly to be a research field of health services researchers. While clinics and office-based practice have been in the focus of sociologists using an ethnographic and symbolic interactionist approach, the hospital setting has had less attention.

Another area related to hospital medicine is the vast array of health professionals who do work that does not entail any caring. Laboratory medicine, medical research, and health care managers include a variety of occupational groups with diverse educational backgrounds and occupational loyalties (Leicht and Fennell 2001). These groups have so far been largely ignored in the sociology of health professions and occupations. Furthermore, efforts to control and regulate the therapy traditions of physicians by means of evidence-based data sources constitute a new feature of public health policy. In many countries, evidence-based medicine and its emphasis on clinical guidelines and rules for "good practice" represent a professional reform movement composed of a coalition of various health professionals (Timmermans and Berg 2003). Timmermans has noted that clinical practice guidelines are influenced by experts in the area and that the system is therefore not a serious external challenge to the clinical power of the medical profession. A major change is that the scientific basis for medical knowledge in evidence-based medicine tends to shift toward epidemiology and public health-based knowledge (Timmermans 2008; Timmermans and Kolker 2004: 188).

Obviously, more studies on the occupational culture of specialist physicians and other health professions will provide a greater understanding of how health workers construct the content of their work, and how they accommodate or overturn the effects of the large structural changes that are currently taking place in most health care systems (e.g., Kuhlmann 2006). Here the work by Hughes, Goffman, and Foucault provides useful theoretical frameworks for understanding the workplace, the larger institutional context, the impact of new technologies, and the cultural arrangements and practices embedded in health care work.

The interactionist and phenomenological accounts of the work conducted in health care settings provide a much needed understanding of what Hughes and Goffman called the social drama of work. But in these days of the revival of the micro-level analysis of health care work, it is important to continue the examination of two powerful macro-level systems – the market-driven economic system and the gender system. Both systems shape the broader structural framework within which the members of health professions and occupations do their everyday work.

References

Abbott, Andrew. 1988. *The System of Professions*. Chicago: University of Chicago Press.

Abbott, Andrew. 2005. "Linked Ecologies: States and Universities as Environments for Professions." *Sociological Theory* 23: 245–74.

Acker, Joan. 1990. "Hierarchies, Jobs, Bodies: A Theory of Gendered Organizations." *Gender and Society* 4: 139–58.

Acker, Joan. 2006. "Inequality Regimes: Gender, Class, and Race in Organizations." *Gender and Society* 20: 441–64.

Allen, Davina. 2001. *The Changing Shape of Nursing Practice: The Role of Nurses in the Hospital Division of Labour*. London: Routledge.

American Medical Association (AMA). 2008. *Physician Characteristics in the US, 2008* edition. Chicago: AMA.

Arminen, Ilkka. 2005. *Institutional Interaction Studies of Talk at Work*. Aldershot: Ashgate.

Association of American Medical Colleges (AAMC). 2006. *Physician Specialty Data: A Chart Book*. Center for Workforce Studies, AAMC.

Beagan, Brenda L. 2000. "Neutralizing Differences: Producing Neutral Doctors for (almost) Neutral Patients." *Social Science and Medicine* 51: 1253–65.

Becker, Howard S., Blanche Geer, Everett C. Hughes, and Anselm L. Strauss. 1961. *Boys in White: Student Culture in Medical School*. Chicago: University of Chicago Press.

Boulis, Ann K. and Jerry A. Jacobs. 2008. *The Changing Face of Medicine: Women Doctors and the Evolution of Health Care in America*. Ithaca, NY: Cornell University Press.

Bourgeault, Ivy Lynn. 2005. "Rationalization of Health Care and Female Professional Projects: Reconceptualizing the Role of Medicine, the State and Health Care Institutions from a Gendered Perspective." *Knowledge, Work and Society* 3: 25–52.

Clarke, Adele E., Janet K. Shim, Laura Mamo, Jennifer Ruth Fosket, and Jennifer R. Fishman. 2003. "Biomedicalization: Technoscientific Transformations of Health, Illness, and US Biomedicine." *American Sociological Review* 68: 161–94.

Conrad, Peter. 1992. "Medicalization and Social Control." *Annual Review of Sociology* 18: 209–32.

Conrad, Peter. 2005. "The Shifting Engines of Medicalization." *Journal of Health and Social Behavior* 46: 3–14.

Conrad, Peter. 2007. *The Medicalization of Society: On the Transformation of Human Conditions into Treatable Disorders*. Baltimore: Johns Hopkins University Press.

Davies, Celia. 1996. "The Sociology of Professions and the Profession of Gender." *Sociology* 30: 661–78.

DeVries, Raymond, Cecilia Benoit, Edwin R. van Teijlingen, and Sirpa Wrede (eds.). 2001. *Birth By Design: Pregnancy, Maternity Care, and Midwifery in North America and Europe*. New York: Routledge.

Dingwall, Robert. 2006. "The Enduring Relevance of the Professional Dominance." *Knowledge, Work and Society* 4: 77–98.

Ehrenreich, Barbara and Deirdre English. 1973. *Witches, Midwives and Nurses: A History of Women Healers*. Old Westbury: Feminist Press.

Ehrenreich, Barbara and Deirdre English. 1978. *For Her Own Good: 150 Years of Experts' Advice to Women*. New York: Anchor Press.

Emmons, Sandra L., Karen E. Adams, Mark Nichols, and Joanna Cain. 2004. "The Impact of Perceived Gender Bias on Obstetrics and Gynecology Skills Acquisition by Third-Year Medical Students." *Academic Medicine* 79: 326–32.

Evetts, Julia. 2006. "The Sociology of Professional Groups: New Directions." *Current Sociology* 54: 133–43.

Evetts, Julia, Charles Gadea, Mariano Sanchez, and Juan Saez. 2009. "Sociological Theories of Professions: Conflict, Competitions and Cooperation." Pp. 140–54 in A. Denis and D. Kalekin-Fishman (eds.), *The ISA Handbook in Contemporary Sociology: Conflict, Competition, Cooperation*. London: Sage.

Finnish Medical Association (FMA). 2008. "Statistics on Physicians 2008." *Retrieved February* 18, 2009 (www.laakariliitto.fi/tilastot/laakaritilastot/erikoislaakarit.html).

Foucault, Michel. 1975. *The Birth of the Clinic: An Archaeology of Medical Perception*. New York: Vintage Books.

Foucault, Michel. 1988. "Technologies of the Self." Pp. 16–49 in L. M. H. Martin, H. Gutman, and P. H. Hutton (eds.), *Technologies of the Self*. Amherst: University of Massachusetts Press.

Freidson, Eliot. 1970a. *The Profession of Medicine*. New York: Mead and Company.

Freidson, Eliot. 1970b. *Professional Dominance: The Social Structure of Medical Care*. New York: Atherton.

Freidson, Eliot. 1984. "The Changing Nature of Professional Control." *Annual Review of Sociology* 10: 1–20.

Freidson, Eliot. 1985. "The Reorganization of the Medical Profession." *Medical Care Review* 42: 11–35.

Freidson, Eliot. 2001. *Professionalism: The Third Logic*. Chicago: University of Chicago Press.

Goffman, Erving. 1961. "The Medical Model and Mental Hospitalization: Some Notes on the Vicissitudes of the Tinkering Trades." Pp. 321–86 in *Erving Goffman, Asylums*. Garden City: Anchor Books.

Hafferty, Frederic W. and Donald Light. 1995. "Professional Dynamics and the Changing Nature of Medical Work." *Journal of Health and Social Behavior* (Extra issue): 132–53.

Hafferty, Frederic W. and John B. McKinlay (eds.). 1993. *The Changing Medical Profession: An International Perspective*. New York: Oxford University Press.

Halpern, Sydney A. 1990. "Medicalization as Professional Process: Postwar Trends in Pediatrics." *Journal of Health and Social Behavior* 31: 28–42.

Haug, Marie. 1975. "The Deprofessionalization of Everyone?" *Sociological Focus* 3: 197–213.

Hellberg, Inga, Mike Saks, and Cecilia Benoit (eds.) 1999. *Professional Identities in Transition: Cross-Cultural Dimensions*. Södertälje: Almqvist and Wiksell International.

Heru, Alison M. 2005. "Pink-Collar Medicine: Women and the Future of Medicine." *Gender Issues* 22: 20–34.

Hughes, Everett C. 1958. *Men and Their Work*. Glencoe, IL: Free Press.

Jasso-Aguilar, Rebeca, Howard Waitzkin, and Angela Landwehr. 2004. "Multinational Corporations and Health Care in the United States and Latin America." *Journal of Health and Social Behavior* 45 (Extra issue): 136–57.

Johnson, Terence, Gerry Larkin, and Mike Saks (eds.). 1995. *Health Professions and the State in Europe*. London: Routledge.

Jones, Anthony (ed.). 1991. *Professions and the State: Expertise and Autonomy in the Soviet Union and Eastern Europe*. Philadelphia: Temple University Press.

Kilminster, Sue, Julia Downes, Brendan Gough, Deborah Murdoch-Eaton, and Trudie Roberts. 2007. "Women in Medicine – Is there a Problem? A Literature Review of the Changing Gender Composition, Structures and Occupational Cultures in Medicine." *Medical Education* 41: 39–49.

Kuhlmann, Ellen. 2006. *Modernising Health Care: Reinventing Professions, the State and the Public*. Boston: Policy Press.

Kuhlmann, Ellen and Mike Saks (eds.). 2008. *Rethinking Professional Governance: International Directions in Healthcare*. Bristol: Policy Press.

Larson, Magali Sarfatti. 1977. *The Rise of Professionalism*. Berkeley: University of California Press.

Leicht, Kevin T. and Mary L. Fennell. 2001. *Professional Work: A Sociological Approach*. Malden, MA: Blackwell.

Light, Donald. 1995. "Countervailing Powers: A Framework for Professions in Transition." Pp. 25–41 in T. Johnson, G. Larkin, and M. Saks (eds.), *Health Professions and the State in Europe*. London: Routledge.

Lorber, Judith. 1975. "Women and Medical Sociology: Invisible Professionals and Ubiquitous Patients." Pp. 75–105 in M. Millman and R. Moss Kanter (eds.), *Another Voice: Feminist Perspective on Social Life and Social Science*. New York: Anchor Press/Doubleday.

Lorber, Judith. 1984. *Women Physicians*. London: Tavistock.

Lorber, Judith. 2000. "What Impact Have Women Physicians Had on Women's Health?" *Journal of the American Medical Women's Association* 55(1): 13–15.

Lupton, Deborah. 1998. "Foucault and the Medicalization Critique." Pp. 94–110 in A. Petersen and R. Bunton (eds.), *Foucault: Health and Medicine*. London: Routledge.

MacDonald, Keith. 1995. *The Sociology of the Professions*. London: Sage.

McKinlay, John B. and Joan Arches. 1985. "Towards the Proletarianization of Physicians." *International Journal of Health Services* 15: 161–95.

McKinlay, John B. and Lisa D. Marceau. 2002. "The End of the Golden Age of Doctoring." *International Journal of Health Services* 33: 379–416.

McKinlay, John B. and Lisa D. Marceau. 2008. "When There is No Doctor: Reasons for the Disappearance of Primary Care Physicians in the US during the early 21st Century." *Social Science and Medicine* 67: 1481–91.

Merton, Robert K. 1957. "Some Preliminaries to a Sociology of Medical Education." Pp. 3–79 in R. K. Merton, G. G. Reader, and P. L. Kendall (eds.), *The Student-Physician: Introductory Studies in the Sociology of Medical Education*. Cambridge, MA: Harvard University Press.

Merton, Robert K., George G. Reader, and Patricia L. Kendall (eds.). 1957. *The Student-Physician: Introductory Studies in the Sociology of Medical Education*. Cambridge, MA: Harvard University Press.

Navarro, Vicente. 1976. *Medicine under Capitalism*. New York: Prodist.

Nettleton, Sarah and Roger Burrows. 2003. "E-Scaped Medicine? Information, Reflexivity and Health." *Critical Social Policy* 23: 165–85.

Parsons, Talcott. 1949. "Professions and Social Structure." Pp. 185–99 in *T. Parsons, Essays in Sociological Theory: Pure and Applied*. Glencoe, IL: Free Press.

Parsons, Talcott. 1951. *The Social System*. New York: Free Press.

Parsons, Talcott. 1963. "Social Change and Medical Organization in the United States: A Sociological Perspective." *Annals of the American Academy of Political and Social Sciences* 346: 21–33.

Riska, Elianne. 2001. *Medical Careers and Feminist Agendas: American, Scandinavian, and Russian Women Physicians*. New York: Aldine de Gruyter.

Riska, Elianne. 2003. "Gendering the Medicalization Thesis." *Advances in Gender Research: Gender Perspectives on Health and Medicine* 7: 59–87.

Riska, Elianne. 2008. "The Feminization Thesis: Discourses on Gender and Medicine." *NORA: Nordic Journal of Feminist and Gender Research* 16: 3–18.

Riska, Elianne and Aurelija Novelskaite. 2008. "Gendered Careers in Post-Soviet Society: Views on Professional Qualifications in Surgery and Pediatrics." *Gender Issues* 25(4): 229–45.

Rose, Nikolas. 2001. "The Politics of Life Itself." *Theory, Culture and Society* 18(6): 1–30.

Rose, Nikolas. 2007. *The Politics of Life Itself: Biomedicine, Power, and Subjectivity in the Twenty-First Century*. Princeton, NJ: Princeton University Press.

Roter, Debra L. and Judith A. Hall. 2004. "Physician Gender and Patient-Centered Communication: A Critical Review of Empirical Research." *Annual Review of Public Health* 25: 497–519.

Rothman, Barbara Katz, Wendy Simonds, and Bari Meltzer Norman. 2007. *Laboring On: Birth in Transition in the United States*. New York: Routledge.

Sciulli, David. 2005. "Continental Sociology of Professions Today: Conceptual Contributions." *Current Sociology* 53: 915–42.

Silverman, David. 1987. *Communication and Medical Practice: Social Relations in the Clinic*. London: Sage.

Starr, Paul. 1982. *The Social Transformation of American Medicine*. New York: Basic Books.

Swedish Medical Association (SMA). 2008. *Statistics on Physicians 2008* (Läkarfakta 2007). Online (www.lakarforbundet.se).

Timmermans, Stefan. 2008. "Oh Look, There is a Doctor After All: About the Resilience of Professional Medicine." *Social Science and Medicine* 67: 1492–6.

Timmermans, Stefan and Marc Berg. 2003. *The Gold Standard: The Challenge of Evidence-Based Medicine and Standardization in Health Care*. Philadelphia: Temple University Press.

Timmermans, Stefan and Emily Kolker. 2004. "Evidence-Based Medicine and the Reconfiguration of Medical Knowledge." *Journal of Health and Social Behavior* 45 (Extra issue): 177–93.

Waitzkin, Howard. 2000 [1983]. *The Second Sickness: Contradictions of Capitalist Health Care*, revised edition. Lanham, MD: Rowman and Littlefield.

Witz, Anne. 1992. *Professions and Patriarchy*. London: Routledge.

Zetka, James R. 2003. *Surgeons and the Scope*. Ithaca, NY: Cornell University Press.

Zetka, James R. 2008a. "Radical Logics and their Carriers in Medicine: The Case of Psychopathology and American Obstetricians and Gynecologists." *Social Problems* 55(1): 95–116.

Zetka, James R. 2008b. "The Making of the 'Women's Physician' in American Obstetrics and Gynecology: Re-forging an Occupational Identity and a Division of Labor." *Journal of Health and Social Behavior* 49(3): 335–51.

Zola, Irving K. 1972. "Medicine as an Institution of Social Control." *Sociological Review* 20: 487–504.

16

Challenges to the Doctor–Patient Relationship in the Twenty-First Century

JENNIFER VANDERMINDEN AND SHARYN J. POTTER

The doctor–patient relationship is the primary foundation of all modern health care. It is where we start and ultimately where we finish. From its beginnings to the present day, health care has involved interaction between two kinds of people – one who seeks help and a consultant who is believed capable of helping. (Freidson 1989: 3)

The steady rise of the medical profession during the first half of the twentieth century and the control it ultimately exerted over all aspects (Goode 1960; Starr 1982) has fascinated sociologists and medical professionals. Of particular interest are the relationships physicians develop with their patients. A quick search on doctor–patient relationship in Medline finds that 1,733 articles have been published on the subject between 1965 and 2008, making it one of the most studied types of professional relationships. The large literature on the doctor–patient relationship includes theories that offer insight into this complex relationship (e.g., Bloom 1963; Freidson 1989; Parsons 1951). Additionally, there is research on different aspects of this relationship, including how the knowledge differential between a physician and patient impacts their interactions (Arrow 1963), how the medical socialization process impacts physicians' perceptions of patients (Gawande 2003; Konner 1987; Liederman and Grisso 1985; Williams 1985), and how physicians use language to deal with uncertainty (Anspach 1988).

The increasing authority of the physician that occurred during the first half of the twentieth century, coupled with the breakthroughs in medical technology, gave physicians a role unlike other professionals (e.g., teachers, bankers) in that "they serve as intermediaries between science and private experience, interpreting personal trouble in the abstract language of scientific knowledge" (Starr 1982: 4). Physicians' professional ascent and ability to help patients negotiate life and death situations provided them with even greater occupational prestige. Furthermore, the idealized American view of the doctor–patient relationship (Emanuel and Dubler 1995), based on nineteenth- and twentieth-century conceptualizations, stressed patient trust and physician availability (Bellin 1986; Potter and McKinlay 2005). Yet recently, some have argued that these traditional relationships have weakened or have even become nonexistent (Potter and McKinlay 2005).

THE USE OF THE WORD "RELATIONSHIP"

Recently, social scientists have debated whether the term "relationship" appropriately describes the interaction between a physician and a patient. The concept of "relationship" has been criticized as being an "inappropriate description of the experience" (Potter and McKinlay 2005) and a "simplification, and in some cases an obfuscation of reality, or even an outright fiction" (Wilde 2007: 16 printed version). Some have proposed terms like "encounter" (Potter and McKinlay 2005), "interaction," or "clinical interaction" (Wilde 2007). Further, the term "doctor–patient relationship" implies that the relationship is limited to two people, while in reality the crowding of this relationship by family, friends, alternative healers, and nurses has been documented as far back as the 1890s (Wilde 2007). Finally, the multidimensional context in which the doctor–patient interaction occurs is sometimes ignored when using the term "relationship" (May 2007). For the purposes of this chapter, we use the term "association" to describe what occurs between physicians and patients. The term "association" allows specification of the strength of the interaction as well as multidimensional contexts in which this dynamic interchange takes place.

Doctoring in the twenty-first century

In thinking about associations between doctors and their patients in the twenty-first century, it is important to discuss the wider context of the relationship. It could be argued that the association between a physician and patient has been weakened through introduction of other players who now also influence the doctor–patient association. The once strong association between a doctor and patient, characterized by intimacy and trust, now includes others who focus not only on patient care, but also on financial gains and losses. In addition to changing the way physicians practice medicine, the ways in which patients view their doctor and the health care system have also changed. Since the late twentieth century, many patients view themselves as consumers and see the medical consultation as a transaction for which they seek a better price or shorter wait time (McKinlay and Marceau 2002; Potter and McKinlay 2005).

In this chapter, we examine how corporate, regulatory, and technological changes from the late twentieth century and into the twenty-first have affected the doctor–patient relationships within the disease patterns that characterize this time frame.

THE INCREASING CORPORATIZATION OF HEALTH CARE

In recent years, health care entities have been viewed as growth opportunities for investors. In 1960, national (US) health care expenditures were a mere $27.5 billion

(National Center for Health Statistics 2008). Today, it is estimated that health care in the United States is a $1.8 trillion industry (Becker, Walsh, and Werling 2007). Investors in the manufacturing industry assume that an infusion of capital will increase the production of widgets, thereby increasing investor returns. Yet, an infusion of capital in the health care industry may result in arrangements that are not in the best interests of physicians and patients. When health care becomes a commodity, providers are forced to speed up their care by increasing the number of patients seen or procedures performed per day. Pressures on physician productivity increase the risk of patients becoming objectified. Patients are no longer seen as a human, but rather become a case of a migraine, a bunion, or a kidney.

The objectification resulting from pressure to speed up can result in patient care without physician feeling, what some call *assembly-line medicine* (McKinlay and Marceau 2002). Speeding up is also occurring in other industries, like the banking industry where human interactions have become increasingly rare. Like banking, the health care industry is dealing with strict guidelines, pre-authorization, centralization, and financial awards for increased output. "Leaders of economic entities increasingly make decisions that once were considered to be in the jurisdiction of the physician," leading to physicians' loss of autonomy and consequently dissatisfaction (Marceau et al. 2005: 4).

The insurance industry has contributed to the increased corporatization of health care in different ways. Below we discuss how increased corporatization has affected associations between doctors and patients.

The insurance industry

By the end of the twentieth century, traditional fee-for-service arrangements between physician and patient were fairly uncommon, with the exception of patients seeking elective procedures. Fee-for-service arrangements have waned as insurance companies now administer payments to physicians and health care organizations (Budrys 2005). Health insurance companies have changed the ways individuals pay for health care services. They have consolidated their control over the dynamics between doctors and patients by guiding and limiting the physicians from whom patients may seek care (McKinlay and Marceau 2002). Insurance companies control physicians' medical decision-making processes by requiring physicians to obtain approval before prescribing tests, procedures, and even medication (McKinlay and Marceau 2002).

The introduction of managed care promised to streamline the provision of health care, reduce inefficiencies, and ultimately reduce costs. These promises remain unfulfilled while the portion of the gross domestic product spent on health care continues to increase annually (DoBias, Lubell, and Becker 2007; Keehan et al. 2008). Furthermore, managed care has weakened the association between doctors and patients. Researchers argue that under managed care, patients are acting more like consumers than patients, viewing the medical field as a market (Kronenfeld 2001) and dismissing the trusting doctor–patient association as a thing of the past.

On the whole, managed care has experienced a great deal of negative press for its restrictions on both physician and patient. Mechanic argues that managed care is viewed negatively because it brings to light the notion that health care is something to be "rationed." Even when physician and patient agree that a treatment or procedure is necessary, it can be denied by managed care, thus taking a portion of control out of the hands of both the physician and the patient (Mechanic 2001).

While corporatization of health care increases the association between physicians and patients, physician accountability has increased, taking on forms that were once limited to corporate employees.

Accountability

With increased patient dissatisfaction with the health care system, with distancing of relations between physician and patient, and with greater corporatization, there is a stronger call for physician accountability. Health outcomes, time spent with patients, and many other performance criteria are evaluated to ensure that physicians are working efficiently and effectively. Physicians are held accountable for both providing health care to patients and meeting the performance standards laid out by the employing organization.

Performance evaluations. With the increased relational distance between physicians and patients, some scholars argue that there is also a breakdown of trust and that this trust is being replaced with accountability (Budrys 2005; McKinlay and Marceau 2002). Current changes in accountability of the health care professions include supervision from both private and public sectors, regulation, heightened standards, and guidelines (Lanier et al. 2004). The actions of physicians are routinely scrutinized, and any actions outside conformity with overall practice norms are corrected through the physician's employer (McKinlay and Marceau 2002). Performance evaluations can serve to better a physician's care, but they may also place time and resource constraints on the physician, weakening the association between physician and patient.

Medical errors. In the United States alone it is estimated that medical errors cause between 44,000 and 98,000 deaths per year (Ball and Lillis 2001). Some researchers argue that litigation against physicians as a result of medical errors is a result of the weakening association between physicians and patients (Budrys 2005). In recent years, researchers have analyzed the occurrence of medical errors in hospital settings. Findings indicate diagnostic and prevention errors are less common than errors in the performance of a procedure or surgery. However, 75 percent of diagnostic errors and 60 percent of prevention errors were classified as negligent, compared to only 35 percent of the errors resulting from a procedure or surgery (Brennan et al. 1991; Leape et al. 1991).

Although these studies demonstrate the need for research focused on diagnostic errors and prevention recommendations, researchers have not yet extensively examined the occurrence of medical errors resulting from the prescription of preventive tests and treatments in general practice offices. Currently, the physician is responsible for disclosing a medical error, minor or major, to the patient affected (Kaidjian et al. 2007). Communication between the physician and patient is crucial for disclosure of medical errors (Mazor et al. 2004). The weakening of bonds between doctors and patients makes the discussion of errors increasingly strained. In cases where there is a strong association between a physician and patient, increased accountability and increased recognition of the potential for medical errors can strengthen the association by building trust.

REGULATORY CHANGE

Until the late 1960s, physicians enjoyed control over all aspects of their profession. Autonomy and control were granted by both federal and state governments (Haug 1988; Wilensky 1964) and enabled the physicians to influence and monitor the scope of their responsibilities and those of the associated medical professions. The physician was able to retain control over most medical practices, and state laws required that licensed physicians supervise all non-clinician physicians (McKinlay and Marceau 2002). The 1965 passage of the Medicare and Medicaid federal insurance programs continued the fee-for-service arrangement, protecting the financial well-being of the physician profession. In the 1970s, the states' allegiance shifted from protecting physicians to protection of corporate health care (McKinlay and Marceau 2002). As corporate revenue became a focus of the states, professional privileges once limited for physicians became legal responsibilities of other medical professions as well (e.g., nurse practitioners who were given permission to write prescriptions). In addition, states invested more money in training other medical professionals, increasing their numbers (McKinlay and Marceau 2002; Potter and McKinlay 2005).

In the next section, we describe how increasing diversity in health care providers impacts the doctor–patient relationship, how the rise of complementary and alternative medicine affects a patient's relationship with his or her physician, and the rise of medical tourism. Finally, we examine how changes in laws governing pharmaceutical advertising have impacted interactions between doctors and patients.

Increasing number and variety of health care providers

The health care domain has recently seen greater specialization and consequently more varied occupations within the field. Some attribute the increased complexity to the advent of managed care (Hoff, Whitcomb, and Nelson 2000). Today, nursing has expanded beyond "nurse" to include nurse practitioners, nurse anesthetists, registered nurses, licensed practical nurses, and medical assistants. Within the field, there are now X-ray technicians, phlebotomists, and a myriad assortment of other positions. Specializations and even sub-specializations among physicians have grown enormously. Today, there are specialists for every part of the body, and even physicians who specialize in hospital care (hospitalists).

The settings in which patients see physicians have been transformed also. Patients can be seen in outpatient clinics, hospitals, or private practice facilities. In 2006, according to the National Health Interview Survey, 80 percent considered a physician's office to be their primary source of health care, 17 percent a clinic or health center, and 3 percent considered an emergency room or hospital to be their primary source of health care (Pleis and Lethbridge-Çejku 2007). Along with the expansion of specialties within mainstream medicine, other options are becoming available for patients, such as complementary and alternative medicine (which is increasingly being incorporated into hospitals) and medical tourism.

Complementary and alternative medicine

Complementary and alternative medicine (CAM) has been used as an umbrella term for therapies outside mainstream medicine, for example, acupuncture, chiropractic care, and massage therapy. A widely held notion about complementary and alternative medicine is that its popularity is a testament to increasing dissatisfaction with modern Western medicine. Many studies have argued that people seek CAM because of the rejection of paternalism (Jonas 1998), calling into question the locus of control (Bishop, Yardley, and Lewith 2007).

Little research exists on the doctor–patient association for CAM or on how patients' interaction with CAM providers affects interactions with primary physicians. However, there is research on the interactions, communication, duration of visit, and satisfaction of relationship (Matter-Walstra et al. 2008; Pappas and Perlman 2002). Ernst (2000) discusses patient motivations for trying CAM, including the dimensions of ample time, equality, empathy, emotional connectedness, and an overall closer relationship between provider and client (Ernst 2000).

It is possible the primary physician's status could be weakened with the increasing integration of CAM into hospitals. Complementary and alternative medicine presents additional options to conventional mainstream medicine, calling into question the position of the physician as the one in power. Complementary and alternative medicine is said to conform to the needs of the patient in ways that conventional practice rarely does (Frank and Stollberg 2004). Potential awkwardness can arise between a patient and conventional medical doctor regarding disclosure of using CAM. At the same time, discussion of CAM may facilitate a more whole (holistic) experience of medical care and allow for the traditional physician to recommend alternative providers who may meet the needs of many patients.

Although not a direct offshoot of regulatory change, medical tourism has also increased medical care options for patients, further complicating the associations between physicians and patients.

Medical tourism

Medical tourism, sometimes called vacation medicine, is a trend in the United States and other Western nations to travel abroad for health care procedures. Examples range from elective cosmetic surgeries (Connell 2006), heart surgery, fertility treatment (Burkett 2007), and assisted suicide (Gray and Poland 2008). Medical tourism has become increasingly popular for two main reasons. First, the cost of health care is high in the United States and elsewhere. Second, where there is universal health care, as in the United Kingdom and Canada, the waiting time for procedures is lengthy. It is estimated that between 50,000 and 500,000 Americans travel abroad for medical treatment (York 2008). These estimates are imprecise because many patients often do no report seeking treatment abroad.

What, then, does this trend mean for the doctor–patient relationship? There is surprisingly little research on how this new trend will affect the doctor–patient association and continuity of care, both before and after the patient goes abroad. The lack of research may reflect the impersonal nature of the doctor–patient association as it is today. Because the doctor–patient association is now complex, often disjointed, and distant, the effects of medical tourism may not be highly relevant. The association between physician and patient has become more like a transaction, where the patient, as a consumer, is shopping for a better price or a shorter wait. Outsourcing surgeries and procedures reflect a growing distance in the doctor–patient association.

The increased prevalence of individuals who cannot afford health care in the United States, but instead travel abroad for treatments, may create a perception of empowerment for the patients. Reasons to seek health care abroad include: unaffordable procedures at home (United States); long waits for procedures (United Kingdom, Scandinavian countries, and Canada); or the procedures are illegal or unavailable in the native country (abortion, stem cell, novel cancer therapies). It appears that patients are empowered by having more options to any of the preceding reasons. New options for care abroad also come with risks that are sometimes overlooked. Countries offering medical tourism destinations are countries that may be less developed and where health care is, therefore, more affordable. However, affordability can come at the expense of safety or quality.

What are the impacts on the association between the primary physician at home and the patient who travels abroad for medical treatment? What little that has been written suggests that there is a broker who is the go-between for the patient and foreign doctor (Burkett 2007). Once the procedure abroad is completed the association between that doctor and patient is over. The doctor in the patient's native country is not involved unless there are necessary follow-up appointments or complications (Connell 2006). Some researchers examining medical tourism argue the future of the doctor–patient association, and medical care in general, is headed toward increased outsourcing (Milstein and Smith 2007) and greater distance between the physician and the patient: "the adage that 'all health care is local' will recede" (Milstein and Smith 2007: 141).

Pharmaceutical advertising

During the first three-quarters of the twentieth century, the American Medical Association (AMA) and the Food and Drug Administration (FDA) banned pharmaceutical companies from advertising directly to consumers (Starr 1982). During the last quarter of the twentieth century, federal regulations reversed the ban, bringing an explosion of prescription drug advertising directly to consumers (DTC). Patients are now inundated with information about medical conditions and treatments, in their periodicals and on television (Hollen 1999). In 2004, pharmaceutical companies spent approximately $4 billion to advertise prescription drugs directly to consumers (Gagnon and Lexchin 2008).

Pharmaceutical companies, with approval of the FDA, spend billions of advertising dollars *educating* patients about existing and potential problems, thereby reducing the role of the physician from expert/educator to a prescription writer. Patients are encouraged to seek relief for medical problems by asking their physician for specific remedies advertised in the media. While advertisements can make it easier for patients to discuss conditions with their doctors, physicians need to make sure that patients are not taking appointment times from those in need of medical help (Murray et al. 2004). Research indicates consumers are likely to inquire about a treatment seen advertised in the press or on television when they had previously lived with or ignored the condition (Freudenheim 1998). Patients today often visit physicians armed with information from advertisements seen in periodicals or on television and the Internet (Stolberg 2000). Interactions between a doctor and a patient may turn antagonistic when patients demand the medications they see advertised. Doctors may feel their diagnostic skills are being questioned, and patients may be angry when they can't obtain a prescription for the advertised medication.

Pharmaceutical companies have found the most successful prescription drug advertisements describe conditions that are easy for the consumer to identify (Stolberg 2000). These problems include allergies, stomach problems, erectile dysfunction, postmenopausal problems, and depression. Medication advertisements for conditions that are not easily identifiable, such as high blood pressure, have not been as successful. Economists find that pharmaceutical advertising results in consumers paying higher prices for prescription drugs (Rizzo 1999).

TECHNOLOGICAL CHANGE

The accelerated pace of technological innovation has caused spiraling expectations that medical care will be delivered at a certain speed and be characterized by the latest technology. Akerkar and Bichile (2004) call the result of this pressure the creation of the *impatient patient*. The modern medical consumer pressures the physician to deliver quality care at a rapid rate, much like the speed demanded by ATMs, cell phones, and high-speed Internet (Akerkar and Bichile 2004). Technology has enabled physicians to access global resources such as medical record keeping, altering communication between physicians and patients, and revolutionizing diagnostics. Below are some examples of the transformative effects of technology.

Medical records

Patient medical records are now being transferred to and stored on computers. Many functions can easily be performed electronically, for example, recording of clinical notes, patient demographics, diagnosis, allergies, scheduling, patient education materials, and weight-based dosing calculations (Menachemi et al. 2006). The transition to digital has the potential to save time and money by eliminating paper and time needed to sift through paper records and prescriptions (Ball and Lillis 2001). The use of electronic charts is also thought to reduce medical errors and improve health outcomes (Ball and Lillis 2001; Krizner 2002). Some researchers go so far as to argue that electronic health records "hold significant promise for improving the quality and safety of health care" (Menachemi et al. 2006: 5 of printed version).

A major concern with the trend toward electronic medical records focuses on safeguarding patient privacy and confidentiality. Other concerns include financial, productivity, and technical barriers (Menachemi et al. 2006). Online medical records can ease the transition from one physician to another at the patient's discretion. Electronic medical records are just the beginning of the potential for technology to transform the medical field, including the doctor–patient association.

The Internet and the doctor–patient relationship

The Internet is a technological innovation that has and continues to change the face of medicine and the physician–patient relationship. The Internet has inevitably affected the interaction between doctor and patient. In a typical office today, it is common for a physician to use a computer during the consultation to access information on the Internet for the patient (Srinivasan, Keenan, and Yager 2006), for a patient to present his or her own Internet findings to the doctor (Murray et al. 2003), or for a physician to send diagnostic tests overseas to be read. Over the past two decades, the Internet also has changed how patients access physician support and served to empower patients facing medical problems with access to information.

The Internet and physician access. Currently, increasing numbers of individuals are accessing the Internet for medical information and to communicate with or seek out a physician (Cotten and Gupta 2004; Jadad and Gagliardi 1998). Researchers estimate that 90 percent of patients would welcome the opportunity to email their physician (Car and Sheikh 2004). At present, software has been developed for secure doctor–patient communication. The creation of software specifically for physicians is intended to address fears that online communication could breach confidentiality, and to allow physicians to follow up with patients, to monitor disease management (Ball and Lillis 2001), and/or to act as a "visit extender" for issues not resolved during the office visit (Baur 2000).

While the Internet can provide more immediate access to information, it also enables patients to communicate with their physician without involving office staff such as a triage nurse. Allowing patient access to a physician over the Internet enables patients to ask questions they might have forgotten or felt uncomfortable asking at the office or hospital. This could potentially free up time for the physician, allowing her to answer emails at her convenience, rather than via a randomly timed phone call or a scheduled office visit (Ball and Lillis 2001). Accessing a physician online has two opposing implications: a positive sign that patients are getting answers to questions they didn't have time or felt uncomfortable asking at their last visit; and alternatively, displacing face-to-face visits or hands-on care, resulting in lower-quality care (Baur 2000).

The introduction of the Internet to the field of medicine has potential to challenge the authority and status of the physician. Researchers argue physicians will have to learn the latest technology in addition to keeping current with other medical knowledge to "remain leaders in the delivery of medical care" (Srinivasan et al. 2006: 480). Technology has allowed some functions previously performed only by physicians to be relocated overseas; for example, diagnostic test reading and medical information and consultation (telemedicine). The internationalization of medicine has created yet an additional demand for physicians to keep up with technology (Srinivasan et al. 2006). The Internet has facilitated the practice of medical outsourcing. Medical outsourcing increasingly is relocating medical procedures like X-ray interpretation abroad where costs are less, or, where it's daytime there and nighttime here, outsourcing to "nighthawk radiology." While challenging the physician status in some ways, outsourcing also allows physicians to concentrate their energies on other aspects of their work.

The Internet has provided empowerment for those who are educated and computer literate, including convenience, control, and choice (Ball and Lillis 2001). These options allow consumers/patients to avoid long waits and time away from work, giving them a greater role in their own health care through information as well as choices for health care services (Ball and Lillis 2001). In addition, the patient has the option of emailing questions or concerns to the physician after their consultation, which are often rushed.

The Internet as a source of patient information. The Internet has given patients immediate access to materials once reserved for medical professionals. Patients' ability to access medical information independently has the potential to strengthen the doctor–patient association through trust building (Andreassen et al. 2006). Akerkar and Bichile (2004) found that "blind trust" is being replaced by "informed trust." Patients are now able to better understand their medications and treatments through access to information independent of their physician. A more educated patient can ideally contribute to a closer relationship through informed mutual trust. When the physician is a good communicator in an established relationship, the effect of the Internet on the doctor–patient association can be very positive (Murray et al. 2003). Conversely, access to medical information can be potentially harmful if a patient uses the information inappropriately or decides not to see a doctor and be his or her own "expert." This is especially dangerous because much of the medical information found on the Internet is unreliable and not necessarily accepted or endorsed by any formal medical authority.

Studies estimate the number of people of using the Internet for health care information is on the rise. Research finds that 55 percent of respondents used the Internet for medical information at least once or twice in the last year (Cotten and Gupta 2004). Socioeconomic status, age (the younger are more likely to use), and better education were all predictors of use of Internet (Cotten and Gupta 2004). Many patients look for information on the Internet right after a diagnosis, even before starting prescribed treatment (Eysenbach 2008). The US National Library of Medicine and the National Institutes of Health sponsor www.pubmed.gov, a website on which the public can access health information. Another website that allows individuals to look up symptoms, diagnoses, treatments, drugs, and more is www. WebMD.com. The symptom checker on WebMD allows "the patient" to click on the part of the body experiencing symptoms. Next, "the patient" is prompted with questions (like an online triage). Ultimately, the user is given a list of conditions associated with the symptoms. It is common for physicians to refer to the Internet during consultation, even giving patients printouts to bring home and read for a better understanding of their condition or further topics to research on the Internet (Srinivasan et al. 2006).

Does access to health care information by the public take power away from physicians (Broom 2005)? The Internet does permit a narrowing of the gap between lay person and expert on medical issues (Cotten and Gupta 2004). Prior to the information revolution, physicians were the primary source of health care information, "thus they have held almost exclusive access to this information or expert knowledge" (Cotten and Gupta 2004: 1796). Physicians can no longer control "how much a patient can know – or hope" (Prevost 1999).

Several researchers have reported that access to information on the Internet is empowering for the patient (Akerkar and Bichile 2004), "transforming the patient into a reflexive consumer who makes active decisions" (Ayme, Kole, and Groft 2008: 2048).The Internet allows wider access to information (Akerkar and Bichile 2004; Broom 2005; Murray et al. 2003), particularly for embarrassing or sensitive issues (Cotten and Gupta 2004). Like a "cloak of confidentiality," it allows patients to access information that they might not feel comfortable asking a physician (Cotten and Gupta 2004: 1797).

The Internet can relieve the physician of being the sole supplier of information and allow greater concentration on treatment (Akerkar and Bichile 2004), which can potentially strengthen the doctor–patient relationship. The "locus of power in health care is shifting" instead of the doctor acting as "sole manager of patient care" (Akerkar and Bichile 2004: 121). Scholars like Murray et al. (2003) question whether the Internet is acting as an equalizer in the doctor–patient relationship. Overall, their data show that when the doctor communicated well, the Internet improved the doctor–patient association, and often the patient relied on the doctor to help interpret the Internet findings (Murray et al. 2003).

Medical support through the Internet. In the past communities were physical gatherings. Those with stigmatized illnesses might not find an accepting and supportive community. Individuals with such illnesses might not tell their closest friends or family because of bleak prognoses and stigmatization. The Internet has allowed individuals with rare or stigmatizing illness to communicate with one another while maintaining complete privacy. Individuals can research on the Internet and connect with others in a similar situation across the world. The Internet has become a source of support for patients seeking to understand their diagnosis and to share their experiences with others. The Internet community is particularly important for those with stigmatized illnesses because of social aspects of their diseases (Berger, Wagner, and Baker 2005; Franck, Noble, and McEvoy 2008).

Patients participating in online support groups have positive results, such as satisfaction, confidence, and more information (Akerkar and Bichile 2004). Online support groups and communities are said to have important benefits in terms of outcomes for patients, particularly in cancer cases (Eysenbach 2008). The association between doctor and patient can be improved when an Internet community supports the patient in ways the physician is likely to be too busy to perform. There is also potential for online groups to communicate anxieties and even misinformation, which the physician ultimately has to handle.

Corporatization, regulation, and technology have all impinged upon the association between physician and patient, weakening it and often reallocating the power that once existed between the two actors and displacing it elsewhere. The change in disease patterns in the twenty-first century begs for a stronger association than currently exists. Ironically, as the larger context of these relationships continues to change, changes in patient disease patterns require a partnership between doctors and their patients.

CHANGE IN DISEASE PATTERNS

"Improvements in health care, medical technology, food production, sanitation, and working conditions have increased life expectancy for the average American from 47 years in 1900 to 77 years in 2000" (Centers for Disease Control and Prevention 2003). Acute illness diagnoses that were fatal in earlier centuries are now curable and often preventable (McKinlay and McKinlay 1977). Even diseases that were characterized by a shortened lifespan, including HIV/AIDS, cardiovascular disease, and diabetes, have seen enormous advances in treatment and prevention. Ironically, the immunizations, medications, and other breakthroughs in technology that helped physicians ascend to the apex of occupational prestige by the mid-twentieth century have also brought challenges to the twenty-first-century doctor–patient association. People are now living longer, inevitability long enough to be diagnosed with a chronic illness. Unlike acute illness, chronic illnesses require more than a diagnosis and a prescription. As the population ages, patients need more advice on lifestyle changes and long-term disease management.

In addition to a higher prevalence of chronic diseases, patients now seek treatment for a range of problems that were historically not part of the medial purview. The medicalization of conditions that were previously considered non-medical problems has widened the spectrum of medical conditions (Conrad 2005). Many medical problems treated as such today were not considered medical problems in the past, for example insomnia, restless leg syndrome, attention deficit disorder, post-traumatic stress disorder (PTSD), fibromyalgia, and social anxiety disorder to name a few, not to mention the cosmetic surgery industry, which has enjoyed tremendous growth. The medicalization of more problems and conditions requires physicians to broaden their medical knowledge.

Despite the improvement in the overall health status of Americans as evidenced by increasing longevity, declining infant mortality, and other societal health markers (National Center for Health Statistics 2009), Americans have become less satisfied with their health (Barsky 1988). Progress in health care has led many to believe that there is a cure for everything – that all of our discomforts, infirmities, and impairments are curable, and we are frustrated when we find things to be incurable (Barsky 1988). These findings are corroborated by a cross-cultural study that highlights the American notion that the body is analogous to a machine and that broken parts are fixable (Payer 1988).

"The number of people over the age of 65 years has more than doubled since the 1930s" (Carroll 2004). This leads to a need for experts on geriatric care and care for the disabled. These needs are paralleled by the weakening of the association between patients and their primary care physicians. Many older Americans now require ongoing medical care and/or assistance with activities of daily living as a consequence of their increased lifespan.[1] Concurrent with the medical discoveries and innovations that have extended average life expectancy, demographic changes have resulted in a fractured system of elderly care. The majority of elderly care was provided by family members until the late twentieth century, when unprecedented numbers of women entered the paid labor force, increasing the demand for paid caregivers (Potter, Churilla, and Smith 2006).

The change in disease patterns and classifications would ideally require a strong association between patients and medical providers. Ironically, though, the changing context of the relationship has made the association tenuous when it needs to be strong. In sum, while there are more people in need of a physician, and arguably a closer relationship with that physician, the changing context has made the development of these associations increasingly difficult.

CONCLUSION

Throughout this chapter we have shown how the association once characterized as a paternalistic, close relationship is now a crowded association between physician and patient. Corporate, regulatory, and technological changes have altered the status of the once powerful profession. These factors, coupled with the change in disease patterns and medicalization, complicate, and in many cases weaken, the association between a physician and patient.

What of this association, then? Is medicine intrinsically different than banking? Is medicine different because it deals with human adversity? Marx makes the argument that schoolchildren are no different than sausages and what is important is how many are educated or produced. But human beings and their health care are intrinsically different from sausages or widgets. Taking care of people's health, therefore, is a job that is different and of higher status than that of factory workers and bankers. While we are not advancing a romantic notion of the physician–patient relationship, we are advocating that things need to be done to protect interactions between patients and doctors from events occurring in the larger environment. We are not advocating against drive-by flu shots and technology inventions that enable patients to take a greater role in their care. We do, however, feel that there are instances where a close association between doctor and patient is imperative, such as the case of a chronic disease or a high-risk pregnancy.

What can be done to insulate the doctor–patient relationship? Globalization has increased the diversity and complexity of options within health care systems. It has allowed physicians and patients to access resources around the world, but also requires that physicians are diverse in their cultural understanding of medicine and language. Physicians face challenges today that were unimaginable when sociologists were first fascinated by the interactions between doctors and their patients. Disease patterns have changed from acute to chronic, leaving patients with conditions that require a partnership between patients and doctors rather than a five-minute interaction. Physicians no longer serve as the gatekeepers for health care information and delivery. As information available to patients' increases, the weakening association between doctor and patient permits less time for physicians to help patients filter this information. Corporatization and regulatory and technological changes have taken control of access, price, quality, and distribution of health care. Perhaps it is time for regulatory change that would provide incentives for doctors and patients to develop stronger associations. Trusting relationships between doctors and patients can motivate patients to follow the protocols for maintaining chronic diseases. Further, patients might feel more comfortable seeking medical care at the onset of medical problems rather than after the problems worsen. This would ultimately help reduce health care costs.

Doctors and patients alike would suffer from a drive-through-like association. While remembering the history of the doctor–patient association, we need to look forward to see how an association can be maintained in a modern society. There remains potential for these modern changes to enable physicians and patients to better access one another and for medical technologies to improve the quality of care the physician provides and the patient receives. Future research will need to look in greater depth at how these challenges of the twenty-first century impact the association between doctor and patient.

Acknowledgments

We would like to thank Dr. Michael Bell for generously sharing his expertise with us.

Note

1   The Paraprofessional Healthcare Institute (2001) estimates that 6 million people aged 65 and over "require assistance to manage the everyday activities of caring for themselves" resulting from "cognitive or physical disabilities associated with aging."

References

Akerkar, Shashank M. and L. S. Bichile. 2004. "Doctor–Patient Relationship: Changing Dynamics in the Information Age." *Journal Postgrad Medicine* 50: 120–2.

Andreassen, Hege K., Marianne Trondsen, Per Egil Kummervold, Deede Gammon, and Per Hjortdahl. 2006. "Patients Who Use E-Mediated Communication with Their Doctor: New Constructions of Trust in the Patient–Doctor Relationship." *Qualitative Health Research* 16: 238–48.

Anspach, Renee R. 1988. "Notes on the Sociology of Medical Discourse: The Language of Case Presentation." *Journal of Health and Social Behavior* 29: 357–75.

Arrow, Kenneth J. 1963. "*Uncertainty and the Welfare Economics of Medical Care.*" *American Economic Review* 53: 941–73.

Ayme, Segolene, Anna Kole, and Stephen Groft. 2008. "Empowerment of Patients: Lessons from the Rare Diseases Community." *Lancet* 371: 2048–51.

Ball, Marion J. and Jennifer Lillis. 2001. "E-Health: Transforming the Physician/Patient Relationship." *International Journal of Medical Informatics* 61: 1–10.

Barsky, Arthur J. 1988. "The Paradox of Health." *New England Journal of Medicine* 318: 414.

Baur, Cynthia. 2000. "Limiting Factors on the Transformative Powers of E-Mail in the Patient–Physician Relationships: A Critical Analysis." *Health Communication* 12: 239–59.

Becker, Scott, Amber Walsh, and Krist Werling. 2007. "Investing in Health Care: A Story of Political Clout, Successful Niches, and Recurring Cycles." *Journal of Health Care Finance* 34: 8–18.

Bellin, Lowell Eliezer 1986. "Shrinking Autonomy of the Practicing Physician and its Impact on Quality." *Journal of Community Health* 11: 155–64.

Berger, Magdalena, Todd H. Wagner, and Laurence C. Baker. 2005. "Internet Use and Stigmatized Illness." *Social Science and Medicine* 61: 1821–7.

Bishop, Felicity L., Lucy Yardley, and George T. Lewith. 2007. "A Systematic Review of Beliefs Involved in the Use of Complementary and Alternative Medicine." *Journal of Health Psychology* 12: 851–67.

Bloom, Samuel W. 1963. *The Doctor and His Patient*. New York: Free Press.

Brennan, T. A., L. L. Leape, N. M. Laird, L. Hebert, A. R. Localio, A. G. Lawthers, J. P. Newhouse, P. C. Weiler, and H. H. Hiatt. 1991. "Incidence of Adverse Events and Negligence in Hospitalized Patients: Results of the Harvard Medical Practice Study I." *New England Journal of Medicine* 324: 370–6.

Broom, Alex. 2005. "Medical Specialists' Accounts of the Impact of the Internet on the Doctor/Patient Relationship." *Health* 9: 319–38.

Budrys, Grace. 2005. *Our Unsystematic Health Care System*, 2nd edition. Lanham, MD: Rowman and Littlefield.

Burkett, Levi. 2007. "Medical Tourism." *Journal of Legal Medicine* 28: 223–45.

Car, Josip and Aziz Sheikh. 2004. "Email Consultations in Health Care 2: Acceptability and Safe Application." *British Medical Journal* 329.

Carroll, Carmen. 2004. "What Does Leadership Mean for Geriatricians?" *CME Geriatric Medicine* 6: 124–9.

Centers for Disease Control and Prevention. 2003. "HHS Study Finds Life Expectancy in the US Rose to 77.2 Years in 2001." Retrieved December 14, 2005 (www.cdc.gov/nchs/releases/03news/lifeex.htm).

Connell, John. 2006. "Medical Tourism: Sea, Sun, Sand and … Surgery." *Tourism Management* 27: 1093–100.

Conrad, Peter. 2005. "The Shifting Engines of Medicalization." *Journal of Health and Social Behavior* 46: 3–14.

Cotten, Sheila R. and Sipi S. Gupta. 2004. "Characteristics of Online and Offline Health Information Seekers and Factors that Discriminate Between Them." *Social Science and Medicine* 59: 1795–806.

DoBias, Matthew, Jennifer Lubell, and C. Becker. 2007. "CMS: Spending Growth Slows. However, Experts Say GDP Projections Alarming." *Modern Healthcare* 26.

Emanuel, Ezekiel J. and Nancy N. Dubler. 1995. "Preserving the Physician–Patient Relationship in the Era of Managed Care." *Journal of the American Medical Association* 275: 1693–7.

Ernst, Edzard. 2000. "The Role of Complementary and Alternative Medicine." *British Medical Journal* 321.

Eysenbach, Gunther. 2008. "The Impact of the Internet on Cancer Outcomes." *CA Cander Journal for Clinicians* 53: 356–71.

Franck, Linda, Genevieve Noble, and Marcella McEvoy. 2008. "Enquiring Minds Want to Know: Topics Requested by Users of a Children's Health Information Website." *Patient Education and Counseling* 72: 168–71.

Frank, Robert and Gunnar Stollberg. 2004. "Medical Acupuncture in Germany: Patterns of Consumerism among Physicians and Patients." *Sociology of Health and Illness* 26.

Freidson, Eliot. 1989. *Medical Work in America: Essays on Health Care*. New Haven, CT: Yale University Press.

Freudenheim, Milt. 1998. "Influencing Doctors' Orders: Ads Help Sales of Prescription Drugs, but at What Cost?" *New York Times*, November 17.

Gagnon, Marc-André and Joel Lexchin. 2008. "The Cost of Pushing Pills: A New Estimate of Pharmaceutical Promotion Expenditures in the United States." *PLoS Medicine* 5: e1.

Gawande, Atul. 2003. *Complications*. New York: Picador.

Goode, William J. 1960. "Encroachment, Charlatanism, and the Emerging Profession: Psychology, Sociology, and Medicine." *American Sociological Review* 25: 902–14.

Gray, Harriet Hutson and Susan Cartier Poland. 2008. "Medical Tourism: Crossing Borders to Access Health Care." *Kennedy Institute of Ethics Journal* 18: 193–201.

Haug, Marie R. 1988. "A Re-Examination of the Hypothesis of Physician Deprofessionalization." *Milbank Quarterly* 60: 48–56.

Hoff, Timothy, Winthrop F. Whitcomb, and John R. Nelson. 2000. "Thriving and Surviving in a New Medical Career: The Case of Hospitalist Physicians." *Journal of Health and Social Behavior* 43: 72–91.

Hollen, Matthew F. 1999. "Direct-to-Consumer Marketing of Prescription Drugs." *Journal of the American Medical Association* 281.

Jadad, Alejandro R. and Anna Gagliardi. 1998. "Rating Health Information on the Internet: Navigating to Knowledge or Babel?" *Journal of the American Medical Association* 279: 611–14.

Jonas, Wayne B. 1998. "Alternative Medicine: Learning from the Past, Examining the Present, Advancing to the Future." *Journal of the American Medical Association* 289.

Kaidjian, Lauris C., Elizabeth W. Jones, Barry J. Wu, Valerie L. Forman-Hoffman, Benjamin H. Levi, and Gary E. Rosenthal. 2007. "Disclosing Medical Errors to Patients: Attitudes and Practices of Physicians and Trainees." *JGIM: Journal of General Internal Medicine* 22: 988–96.

Keehan, Sean, Andrea Sisko, Christopher Truffer, Sheila Smith, Cathy Cowan, John Poisal, and M. Kent Clemens. 2008. "Health Spending Projections through 2017: The Baby-Boom Generation is Coming to Medicare." *Health Affairs (Project Hope)* 27: 145–55.

Konner, Melvin. 1987. *Becoming a Doctor: A Journey of Initiation in Medical School*. New York: Viking.

Krizner, Ken. 2002. "Technology is the Right Prescription for Minimizing Medical Errors." *Managed Healthcare Executive* 12: 44.

Kronenfeld, Jennie Jacobs. 2001. "New Trends in the Doctor–Patient Relationship: Impacts of Managed Care on the Growth of the Consumer Protections Model." *Sociological Spectrum* 21: 293–317.

Lanier, David C., Martin Roland, Helen Burstin, and J. André Knottnerus. 2004. "Doctor Performance and Public Accountability." *Lancet* 363: 171–2.

Leape, L. L., T. A. Brennan, N. Laird, A. G. Lawthers, A. R. Localio, B. A. Barnes, L. Hebert, J. P. Newhouse, P. C. Weiler, and H. Hiatt. 1991. "The Nature of Adverse Events in Hospitalized Patients: Results of the Harvard Medical Practice Study II." *New England Journal of Medicine* 324: 377–84.

Liederman, Deborah B. and Jean-Anne Grisso. 1985. "The Gomer Phenomenon." *Journal of Health and Social Behavior* 26: 222–32.

Marceau, Lisa D., Sharyn J. Potter, Carol L. Link, John B. McKinlay, and Amy B. O'Donnell. 2005. "Does Level of Autonomy Affect Physician Satisfaction? Results of the USUK Clinical Decision Making Study." Unpublished manuscript. Watertown, MA: New England Research Institute.

Matter-Walstra, Klazien, Franziska Schoeni-Affolter, Marcel Widmer, and Andre Busato. 2008. "Patient-Based Evaluations of Primary Care for Cardiovascular Diseases: A Comparison between Conventional and Complementary Medicine." *Journal of Evaluation in Clinical Practice* 14: 75–82.

May, Carl. 2007. "The Clinical Encounter and the Problem of Context." *Sociology* 41: 29–45.

Mazor, Kathleen M., Steven R. Simon, Jerry H. Gurwitz, Robert A. Yood, Brian C. Martinson, Margaret J. Gunter, and George W. Reed. 2004. "Health Plan Members' Views about Disclosure of Medical Errors." *Annals of Internal Medicine* 140: 409–23.

McKinlay, John B. and Lisa D. Marceau. 2002. "The End of the Golden Age of Doctoring." *International Journal of Health Services* 33: 379–416.

McKinlay, John B. and Sonja M. McKinlay. 1977. "The Questionable Contribution of Medical Measures to the Decline of Mortality in the United States in the Twentieth Century." *Milbank Memorial Fund Quarterly* (Summer): 405–28.

Mechanic, David. 2001. "The Managed Care Backlash: Perceptions and Rhetoric in Health Care Policy and the Potential for Health Care Reform." *Milbank Quarterly* 79: 35.

Menachemi, Nir, Donna L. Ettel, Robert G. Brooks, and Lisa Simpson. 2006. "Charting the Use of Electronic Health Records and Other Information Technologies among Child Health Providers." *BMC Pediatrics* 6.

Milstein, Arnold and Mark Smith. 2007. "Will the Surgical World Become Flat?" *Health Affairs* 26: 137–41.

Murray, Elizabeth, Bernard Lo, Lance Pollack, Karen Donelan, Joe Catania, Ken Lee, Kinga Zapert, and Rachel Turner. 2003. "The Impact of Health Information on the Internet on Health Care and the Physician–Patient Relationship: National US Survey among 1,050 US Physicians." *Journal of Medical Internet Research* 5: e17.

Murray, Elizabeth, Bernard Lo, Lance Pollack, Karen Donelan, and Ken Lee. 2004. "Direct-to-Consumer Advertising: Public Perceptions of its Effects on Health Behaviors, Health Care, and the Doctor–Patient Relationship." *Journal of the American Board of Family Practice* 17.

National Center for Health Statistics. 2008. "National Health Expenditures, Average Annual Percent Change, and Percent Distribution, by Type of Expenditure: United States, Selected Years 1960–2006 (Table 127)." Retrieved December 2008 (www.cdc.gov/nchs/).

National Center for Health Statistics. 2009. *National Vital Statistics Report*, vol. 57 (www.cdc.gov/nchs/products/nvsr.htm#vol57).

Pappas, Sam and Adam Perlman. 2002. "Complementary and Alternative Medicine: The Importance of Doctor–Patient Communication." *Medical Clinics of North America* 86: 1–10.

Paraprofessional Healthcare Institute. 2001. *Direct-Care Health Workers: The Unnecessary Crisis in Long-Term Care*. Washington, DC: Aspen Institute.

Parsons, Talcott. 1951. *The Social System*. Glencoe, IL: Free Press.

Payer, Lynn. 1988. *Varieties of Treatment in the United States, England, West Germany, and France*. New York: Henry Holt.

Pleis, John R. and Margaret Lethbridge-Çejku. 2007. "Summary Health Statistics for US Adults: National Health Interview Survey, 2006." *National Center for Health Statistics Vital Health Statistics* 10.

Potter, Sharyn J., Allison Churilla, and Kristen Smith. 2006. "Meeting Elderly Needs in the United States: An Examination of Full-Time Employment in the Direct-Care Workforce." *Journal of Applied Gerontology* 25: 356–74.

Potter, Sharyn J. and John B. McKinlay. 2005. "From a Relationship to Encounter: An Examination of Longitudinal and Lateral Dimensions in the Doctor–Patient Relationship." *Social Science and Medicine* 61: 465–79.

Prevost, Lisa. 1999. "healme.com." *Civilization* 6: 100–6.

Rizzo, John A. 1999. "Advertising and Competition in the Ethical Pharmaceutical Industry: The Case of Antihypertensive Drugs." *Journal of Law and Economics* 42: 89–116.

Srinivasan, Malathi, Craig R. Keenan, and Joel Yager. 2006. "Visualizing the Future: Technology Competency Development in Clinical Medicine, and Implications for Medical Education." *Academic Psychiatry* 30: 480–90.

Starr, Paul. 1982. *The Social Transformation of American Medicine.* New York: Basic Books.

Stolberg, Sheryl Gay. 2000. "Want a New Drug? Plenty to Choose From on TV." *New York Times,* January 23.

Wilde, Sally. 2007. "The Elephants in the Doctor–Patient Relationship: Patients' Clinical Encounters and the Changing Surgical Landscape of the 1890s." *Health and History* 9(1). Online.

Wilensky, Harold L. 1964. "The Professionalization of Everyone?" *American Journal of Sociology* 70: 137–58.

Williams, William Carlos. 1985. *The Doctor Stories.* New York: W. W. Norton.

York, Diane. 2008. "Medical Tourism: The Trend toward Outsourcing Medical Procedures to Foreign Countries." *Journal of Continuing Education in the Health Professions* 28: 99–102.

17

Complementary and Alternative Medicine

Processes of Legimation, Professionalization, and Cooption

Hans A. Baer

Historically, medical sociologists have focused on various aspects of biomedicine, including medical dominance and professionalism, while tending to ignore alternative medical systems. Exceptions include the work of Walter Wardwell (1992), Lesley Biggs (1991), David Coburn (1991), Ian Coulter (1991), and Evan Willis (1989) on chiropractors in the United States, Canada, and Australia. Conversely, medical anthropologists have conducted studies of shamanism and other indigenous and folk medical systems as well as the phenomenon of medical pluralism in complex societies. In modern industrial or postindustrial societies, in addition to biomedicine – the dominant medical subsystem – one finds other medical subsystems, such as homeopathy, osteopathy, chiropractic, naturopathy, religious healing systems, and popular and folk medical systems. Patterns of medical pluralism tend to reflect hierarchical relations in the larger society, including ones based upon class, caste, and racial, ethnic, regional, religious, and gender divisions. The medical system of a complex society consists of the totality of medical subsystems coexisting in a generally competitive, but sometimes collaborative or even cooptative, relationship with one another.

Although only a few sociologists, such as Cant and Sharma (1999), have employed the concept of medical pluralism, growing interest on the part of particularly upper- and upper-middle-class people in alternative medicine in Western societies appears to have prompted a growing number of medical sociologists and medical anthropologists to examine issues such as the sociopolitical relationship between biomedicine and alternative therapies, the holistic health movement, and patient utilization of alternative therapies.

What has come to be termed *complementary and alternative medicine* (CAM) is an amorphous category encompassing many medical systems and therapies in various national contexts but particularly Anglophone countries, such as the United

States, Canada, United Kingdom, Australia, and New Zealand. A panel convened by the US Office of Alternative Medicine in 1995 defined it as follows:

> Complementary and alternative medicine (CAM) is a broad domain of healing resources that encompasses all health systems, modalities, and practices and their accompanying theories and beliefs, other than those intrinsic to the politically dominant health system of a particular society or culture in a given historical period. CAM includes all such practices and ideas self-defined by their users as preventing or treating illness or promoting well-being. Boundaries within CAM and between the CAM domain and the domain of the dominant system are not always sharp or fixed. (Office of Alternative Medicine 1997: 50)

Whereas alternative practitioners and lay people have tended to speak of holistic health, CAM and integrative medicine are in large part biomedical constructions.

What started out as the popular holistic health movement in the early 1970s has largely evolved into the professionalized entity generally referred to as CAM or *integrative medicine*. Alternative medicine generally refers to all medical systems or therapies lying outside of the purview of biomedicine that are used instead of it. Complementary medicine refers to medical systems or therapies that are used alongside or as adjuncts to biomedicine. Finally, integrative medicine refers to the effort on the part of conventional physicians to blend biomedical and CAM therapies or the collaborative efforts between biomedical practitioners and CAM practitioners in addressing health care needs of specific patients.

TYPOLOGIES OF COMPLEMENTARY AND ALTERNATIVE MEDICINE (CAM)

Scholars have proposed various typologies of CAM therapies. Fulder (1996: 107) delineates five "therapeutic modalities of complementary medicine": (1) ethnic medical systems, such as acupuncture, Chinese medicine, and Ayurveda; (2) manual medical systems, such as osteopathy, chiropractic, massage, Alexander technique, and reflexology; (3) "mind–body" therapies, such as hypnotherapy, psychic healing, radionics, and anthrosophical medicine; (4) nature-cure therapies, such as naturopathy and hygienic methods; and (5) nonallopathic medicinal systems, such as homeopathy and herbalism. This typology and most other typologies of CAM tend to privilege Western and Asian therapies over indigenous, folk, and religious therapies (see also Kaptchuk and Eisenberg 2001; Tataryn 2002). In contrast to most schemes that exclude biomedicine, Nienstedt (1998) presents a "model of complementary medicine and practice" that includes it. Her typology delineates four categories or quadrants: (1) biomedicine, which includes MDs, osteopathic physicians, dentists, optometrists, podiatrists, psychologists, pharmacists, nurses, physician assistants, medical technologists, physical therapists, and so on; (2) body-healing alternatives (e.g., chiropractors, homeopaths, medical herbalists, naturopaths, massage therapists, reflexologists); (3) mind/spirit alternatives (e.g., Christian Scientists, faith healers, psychic healers, transcendental meditation); and (4) cross-cultural alternatives (e.g., shamanism, folk medicine, Ayurveda, Chinese medicine,

Reiki therapists). Although Nienstedt's scheme includes biomedicine, it does not make any reference to the power difference that exists between it and other therapeutic systems.

Bearing this thought in mind, in my own work on medical pluralism I have proposed the notion of dominative medical system attempts to recognize the fact that both biomedicine and a wide array of CAM systems coexist within a hierarchical social arrangement (Baer 2001, 2004; Singer and Baer 2007). Medical pluralism in the modern world is characterized by a pattern in which biomedicine exerts dominance over alternative medical systems, whether they are professionalized or not. With European expansion, allopathic medicine, or what eventually became biomedicine, came to supersede in prestige and influence both professionalized indigenous medical systems, such as Ayurveda and Unani in India and Chinese medicine, and a wide array of folk medical systems. The US dominative medical system consists of several levels that tend to reflect class, racial, ethnic, and gender relations in the larger society (Baer 2001). In rank order of prestige, these include (1) biomedicine; (2) osteopathic medicine as a parallel medical system focusing on primary care and incorporating spinal manipulation as an adjunct; (3) professionalized heterodox medical systems (namely, chiropractic, naturopathy, and acupuncture); (4) partially professionalized or lay heterodox medical systems (e.g., homeopathy, herbalism, bodywork, and midwifery); (5) Anglo-American religious healing systems (e.g., Spiritualism, Christian Science, Pentecostalism, and Scientology); and (6) folk medical systems (e.g., Southern Appalachian herbal medicine, African American folk medicine, *curanderismo* among Mexican Americans, and Native American healing systems). With some modification, the model of the dominative medical system can be applied to other modern societies. For the most part, the therapeutic systems that fall under the rubric of CAM tend to be situated under the categories of professionalized, partially professionalized, and lay heterodox medical systems. Within this framework, although it is changing, MDs tend to be white, upper- and upper-middle-class males, while folk healers tend to be working-class women of color. Alternative medical systems often exhibit counterhegemonic elements that resist, often in subtle forms, the elitist, hierarchical, and bureaucratic patterns of biomedicine. Conversely, corporate and governmental elites around the world have come to express growing interest in CAM therapies as cost-cutting measures in an era of rising health care costs.

THE SHIFT FROM HOLISTIC HEALTH TO COMPLEMENTARY AND ALTERNATIVE MEDICINE AND INTEGRATIVE MEDICINE

New medical systems or synthetic ensembles of therapies, such as the hygiene movement in the nineteenth century or the holistic health movement in the late twentieth century, emerge as popular health movements. They often undergo a process of professionalization and may in time even be absorbed by biomedicine. The holistic health movement began to emerge on the US West Coast, especially the San Francisco Bay Area, by the early 1970s if not earlier. It quickly spread to other parts of the United States and also other countries, especially Anglophone ones but also Western European countries, such as Germany, the Netherlands, and Denmark. It began as a popular movement or medical revitalization movement that in various ways challenged the bureaucratic, high-tech, and iatrogenic aspects of biomedicine. The holistic health movement was by no means a monolithic phenomenon and varied considerably from society to society where it had emerged. It encompassed numerous alternative medical systems (such as homeopathy, herbalism, naturopathy, and bodywork) with divergent philosophical premises. Although it appeared to have its strongest expression in Western societies, it also drew heavily on various Eastern healing systems such as Chinese medicine and Ayurveda. To a large extent, the holistic health movement overlapped with the New Age movement, which also became very popular in particularly Western societies. Like the holistic health movement, the New Age movement focuses upon a balance in the interaction of mind, body, and spirit in its attempts to achieve experiential health and well-being. New Age also incorporates many therapeutic techniques and practices, including meditation, guided visualization, channeling, psychic healing, and neo-shamanism.

THE PREMISES OF HOLISTIC HEALTH

While proponents of the holistic health movement vary in terms of what they regard to be the basic premises of the movement, Lowenberg (1989: 15–50) presents a comprehensive overview of the core beliefs, meanings, and values exhibited by holistic health practitioners and patients. She delineates seven elements of the holistic health model: (1) holism, which entails the recognition of the uniqueness of each individual and the notion that this humanness entails the "interrelation of the physical, mental, emotional, spiritual, and social dimensions" (Lowenberg 1989: 19); (2) an emphasis on health promotion; (3) the recognition that illness represents a state of imbalance or "dis-ease" in a person's life and provides an opportunity to alter one's lifestyle; (4) the belief that the patient's health ultimately is the patient's responsibility; (5) the notion that the health practitioner should mobilize the patient's innate healing capacity and act as an educator, consultant, and facilitator in an egalitarian and mutual relationship with the patient; (6) an openness to a variety of healing traditions and practices from many cultures, including Eastern and indigenous ones; and (7) a new consciousness that includes a present-time orientation as well as subjective and intuitive approaches to life. These elements of holistic medicine are ideals, some of which are not fully adhered to in practice. For example, the holistic health movement often subscribes to the assertion that an individual is part of a larger internal system that consists of body, mind, and spirit and that this internal system is embedded in a larger sociocultural and natural environment. However, in most cases holistic practitioners give priority to mind–body–spirit connections over mind–body–spirit–society connections, thus engaging a limited holism.

Two ethnographic overviews of the holistic health subculture

The holistic health/New Age movement established a number of centers around the United States, including in small cities such as Santa Cruz (California), Santa Fe (New Mexico), Sedona (Arizona), Boulder (Colorado), and Ashville (North Carolina). However, the only detailed ethnography of such a place was conducted by

English-Lueck (1990), who studied Paraiso (pseudonym for a California town). Paraiso was made up largely of white upper-middle- and upper-class residents but also had small enclaves of Chicanos (10 percent), Asians (2 percent), and Native Americans (nearly 1 percent). Despite this relative ethnic homogeneity, Paraiso's residents followed a variety of lifestyles: there were millionaires who tended to live in the city's higher elevations, university students, street people, resident vagabonds, and members of religious groups such as the Unitarian-Universalist Church, the Unity School of Christianity, and the Church of Religious Science. Paraiso had exercise centers, numerous self-help groups, and 36 schools offering workshops and lectures on holistic health. Workshops on alternative therapies were offered at the local community college, a university extension program, the YMCA, herbal stores, a Taoist sanctuary, and Yogic Institute/ashram. English-Lueck (1990: 27) presents the following characterization of holistic healers in Paraiso:

> Holistic health practitioners are not a monolithic block. Besides diverse personalities and practices, there is a variety of functional roles. A few visiting and local practitioners are renowned catalysts, founders of well-known therapies. Most holistic healers who are visible to the public are practitioners who are also teachers. Some rarely or never teach and prefer just to practice. Among this category are those who choose to work in informal, confidential networks. They may, or may not, choose to practice with the blessing of the law. Novice practitioners, not yet through their rites of passage, may also have informal networks of clients.

More recently, Schneirov and Geczik (2003) conducted an ethnography of two holistic health networks in Pittsburgh, namely the Holistic Living Quest and the Committee for Freedom of Choice. The former constitutes an informal coalition of well-educated, progressive people who disseminate information on CAM practices, grassroots activism, and New Age spirituality; the latter tends to be made up of conservative Christian, rural, working-class people who seek to acquaint their audience with a range of CAM therapies for cancer and other diseases. Schneirov and Geczik (2003) view "alternative health" as a new social movement or site in which diverse communities and discourses challenge what Jürgen Habermas terms the "colonization of the lifeworld" by a health care system dominated by high technology, invasive medical procedures, and profit-driven bureaucratic institutions. They maintain that alternative health encompasses both offensive new social movements that seek to create new social structures and ecologically sustainable lifestyles and defensive new social movements that seek to preserve traditional values and lifestyles. Ironically, both progressives and conservatives in alternative health tend to engage in an "incomplete holism that fails to appreciate the social and class dimensions of illness" (Schneirov and Geczik 2003: 23).

BIOMEDICAL PHYSICIANS AND NURSES DISCOVER HOLISTIC HEALTH

By the late 1970s, an increasing number of biomedical and osteopathic physicians as well as nurses, particularly in the United States and Great Britain, began to recognize the limitations of their conventional approach to illness and that they were losing many of their more affluent patients to alternative or heterodox practitioners. A group of MDs and osteopathic physicians (DOs) established the American Holistic Medical Association in 1978. Nurses in particular, given their person-orientation, expressed interest in holistic health, forming the American Holistic Nurses' Association in 1981.

In the case of the United Kingdom, Adams and Tovey (2004: 158) portray the growing interest of nurses in holistic health or CAM as follows:

> [M]embership figures for the Complementary Therapies Forum of the Royal College of Nursing (RCN) give some indication of the extent of interest within the profession, and of the growth of interest during the late 1990s. In 1997, membership (which is simply a reflection of interest and not of active practice) stood at 1,600; by 2000 this had risen to 11,400.

Ironically, holistic health as a popular movement has by and large been tamed, evolving into a professionalized entity referred to as *complementary and alternative* medicine or even *integrative medicine*. The shift from a discussion of holistic health, holistic medicine, or simply alternative medicine to CAM over the past decade or so is perhaps most apparent in the titles of various books and periodicals. During this time, numerous biomedical physicians and nurses have written overviews of CAM (Bratman 1997; Diamond 2001; Jonas and Levin 1999; Micozzi 2007; Novey 2000; Rosenfeld 1996; Snyder and Lindquist 2006; Yuan, Bieber, and Bauer 2006). The shift from holistic health to CAM is also exemplified by an article titled "The Evolution of Complementary and Alternative Medicine in the United States: The Push and Pull of Holistic Health Care into the Medical Mainstream" (Caplan, Harrison, and Galantiono 2003).

Cassidy (2002: 894) correctly argues that biomedical hegemony pervades the notion of CAM:

> This issue of the dominant practice versus "all others" lies behind the whole concept of CAM, which is surely a misperception that we should be just about ready to give up. For, if we are agreed that there are many medicines and they can be sorted in terms of their philosophical underpinnings, then we must come to see that *all* are alternatives, and *all* can complement others. In short, biomedicine ought not to be treated as the standard against which all others are compared (which remains all too common) but as one among many, itself a complementary and alternative practice.

Indeed, Wolpe (2002: 165) argues that CAM is "what sociologists refer to as a residual category" in that it is "defined not by its internal coherence but by its exclusion from other categories of medicine."

In some circles, the term *integrative medicine* has come to supplant *complementary and alternative medicine*. According to Cohen (1998: 2), integrative medicine or integrative health care refers to a "system of medicine that integrates conventional care with CAM." Diamond (2001: 14) argues that the terms *alternative* and *complementary* are divisive and should be discarded by integrative or integrated medicine. In many cases, however, the terms *CAM* and *integrative medicine* are used interchangeably (see Milton and Benjamin 1999). In *Integrative Health Care: Complementary and Alternative Therapies for the Whole Person*, Sierpina (2001: 3) delineates eight aspects of integrative health care: (1) patient-centered care; (2) encouragement of personal responsibility for health; (3) recognition of interaction of mind, body, and spirit in health and healing; (4) an emphasis on wellness; (5) "collaborative partnerships involving interdisciplinary teams of health-care providers and the patient"; (6) openness to CA therapies "that they have a record of safety and efficacy but are outside of the conventional biomedical model"; (7) reliance on evidence-based scientific thinking when integrating biomedical and CAM therapies; and (8) recognition of the fact that health and healing are individualistic processes. Other than an emphasis on evidence-based science and reliance on safety and efficacy studies, Sierpina's model of integrative health care is virtually identical with the old holistic health model, suggesting that integrative medicine is nothing more than "new wine in old wineskins."

As noted previously, while alternative practitioners and lay people have tended to speak of holistic health, CAM and integrative medicine are in large part biomedical constructions. While CAM or integrative medicine often continues to adhere to some notion of holism, in reality it appears to function as a style of health care in which biomedicine treats alternative therapists as subordinates and alternative therapies as adjuncts. Although some MDs subscribe to the philosophical underpinnings of various alternative therapies, including their vitalist perspectives, others adopt these techniques without wholeheartedly subscribing to their ideologies or reinterpreting them in terms of biomedical concepts or evidence-based medicine.

SOCIAL PROFILES OF PATIENTS UTILIZING CAM AND THEIR REASONS FOR DOING SO

Numerous studies examining patient utilization of CAM, too many to review in detail here, have been published over the past 20 years or so. David Eisenberg and his colleagues have been involved in a couple of renowned and frequently cited national surveys of patient utilization of CAM therapies (Eisenberg et al. 1993, 1998). The first study, which entailed a 1990 telephone survey of 1,539 English-speaking adults, estimated that one-third of the US population used some type of CAM therapy. Respondents most often noted the use of exercise and prayer, but approximately one-third said that in the last year, they had used at least one CAM therapy, such as relaxation techniques, self-help groups, biofeedback, hypnosis, chiropractic, massage, imagery, spiritual healing, lifestyle diets, herbal medicine, energy healing, homeopathy, acupuncture, and folk remedies. Almost two-thirds of CAM users did not consult a provider but treated themselves. The remainder consulted a provider, making an average of 19 visits each over the two-month period. Forty-four percent of CAM users had attended college, 39 percent were middle-class adults with incomes exceeding $35,000, and 44 percent resided in western states. Virtually all respondents (96 percent) utilizing CAM consulted a conventional physician (MD or DO). None of the respondents saw a CAM practitioner for treatment of serious medical complications such as cancer, diabetes, lung ailments, hypertension, urinary tract problems, and dental problems. Based on their findings, Eisenberg and colleagues projected that 61 million Americans used at least one of 16 CAM therapies and that 22 million Americans consulted a CAM practitioner in 1990.

The follow-up study conducted in 1997 found that the use of CAM had increased to 42.1 percent. Eisenberg and his colleagues (1998: 1571) report that in 1997:

> Use was more common among women (48.9%) than men (37.8%) (p = .001) and less common among African Americans (33.1%) than members of other racial groups (44.5%) (p = .004). People aged 35 to 49 years reported higher rates of use (50.6%) than people either older (39.1%) (p = .001) or younger (p = .003). Use was higher among those who had some college education (50.6%) than those with no college education (36.4%) (p = .001) and more common among people with annual incomes above $50,000 (48.1%) than with lower incomes (42.6%) (p = .03). Use was more common in the West (50.1%) than elsewhere in the United States (42.1%) (p = .004).

The percentage of users paying out of pocket for CAM services had decreased somewhat from 64.0 percent in 1990 to 58.3 percent in 1997. Total expenditures for CAM therapies came to an estimated $27.0 billion, $12.2 billion of which was paid out of pocket.

Whereas most CAM utilization studies focus on the social characteristics of patients who actually seek out CAM therapies, Jain and Astin (2001) conducted a survey in which they focused on barriers to CAM utilization among respondents derived from a randomly selected sample of 1,680 Stanford University alumni. They found that those less inclined to use CAM are men, people in good health, and those who believe that CAM is generally ineffective or inferior to conventional medicine, or who think they do not know enough about CAM therapies.

While most studies examining patient utilization of CAM therapies tend to focus on those provided by professionalized or partially professionalized heterodox practitioners, some studies have examined utilization of various folk medical systems in the United States, particularly among ethnic minorities. Bailey (1991) found that among a sample of African Americans in Detroit, 24 percent of the women and 10 percent of the men reported using folk or "personal" care treatments for hypertension. Rivera (1988) reported 32 percent of the Mexican Americans in urban barrios in Colorado sought treatment from curanderas or curanderos. In a survey of 2,103 people born in Mexico but residing or working in San Diego, Chavez (1984: 34) found that only 27 (1.3 percent) reported that they had actually used a curandera or curandero, but 429 (23.3 percent) were willing to do so.

More than a decade ago, Sharma (1995) reported that one quarter of the British population were utilizing CAM. Utilization studies of patients accessing CAM also demonstrate its popularity in Canada and Western Europe (Fisher and Ward 1994; Kelner and Wellman 1997). Complementary medicine appears to be even more popular down under than in the United States, Canada, and the United Kingdom as a whole, although the Australian pattern seems to resemble the US West Coast pattern. The Australian government estimates more than 60 percent of Australians utilize complementary medicine and spend some $2 billion (Australian) on complementary medicine, with two-thirds of this expenditure going to complementary practitioners (Eastwood 2002: 223). Based upon interview and focus group research in Oceanport (pseudonym), a suburb of a New South Wales city, she found 27 (24 percent) of her 111 subjects indicated they or another household member had engaged in a pattern of *mixed therapy regimens* – a scenario in which "people may be using multiple types of therapists and therapies simultaneously, or shift from one type of therapy or practitioner to another in seeking to solve their health problems." A review of studies on patient utilization of complementary medicine in Australia indicates that, as in other Western societies, users tend to be female, relatively young, employed, highly educated, and often, but not necessarily, involved in alternative lifestyles (MacLennan, Wilson, and Taylor 1996). Conversely, complementary medicine has found some reception among working-class Australians, including those living in country towns (Wilkinson and Simpson 2001).

THE DRIVE FOR PROFESSIONALIZATION AND LEGITIMATION ON THE PART OF CAM THERAPISTS

In their drive for professionalization and legitimation, CAM practitioners often emulate biomedicine by pursuing some form of state-mandated recognition and/or accreditation, even one internal to the occupational group. CAM practitioners around the world have a long history of conducting intense campaigns to obtain state sponsorship and have found support among sympathetic politicians and other patrons. In struggles among rival medical systems, the state, which holds to power to confer legislative recognition, has tended to side with biomedicine while making concessions to CAM groups. According to Willis (1994: 70), in theory the state may engage in several forms of patronage with respect to complementary health occupations: (1) subsidization of training programs in either private or public institutions of higher learning; (2) licensing or statutory registration of practitioners; (3) the granting of research funds; and (4) the incorporation of CAM practitioners into the national health insurance system. To avoid dramatic changes in the larger health care system, the legitimation granted to CAM systems by the state is generally only partial. CAM practitioners are forced to comply with structures, standards, and processes that are dominated by biomedicine. Cohen (2000: 17) argues that while regulatory legislation purportedly serves to protect the public from charlatans and incompetent practitioners, it often fails to achieve this and essentially creates social closure or barriers to entry into a public health occupation.

Cant and Sharma (1999: 77) maintain that CAM systems function as "cottage" industries in their early stages in which their practitioners often learn their skills through apprenticeships or even from visits to therapists in other countries. In time, CAM practitioners see that it is politically expedient to establish "professional associations, pan organizations and training colleges – what might be seen as the rationalization of complementary medicine" (Cant and Sharma 1999: 77). Such efforts, however, are often awkward and frequently result in numerous competing professional bodies and colleges, often spearheaded by strong-willed and charismatic individuals who reflect both the *laissez-faire* mentality of CAM and its difficulty in presenting a unified front to the larger society, particularly the state. For example, naturopathy, which has yet to achieve statutory registration in any Australian state or territory, is represented by several organizations, including the National Herbalists Association of Australia, the Australian Natural Therapies

Association, the Australian Naturopathic Practitioners, the Australian Traditional-Medicine Society, and the Federation of Natural and Traditional Therapists (Baer 2006a: 1777). To complicate matters further, some of these bodies represent not only naturopaths but also other complementary practitioners, such as Chinese medicine practitioners, Western herbalists, and homeopaths.

While CAM practitioners – particularly osteopaths, chiropractors, Chinese medicine physicians, and naturopaths – have indeed made gains within the context of various dominative medical systems, including those in the United States, Canada, United Kingdom, Australia, and New Zealand, this development has not seriously eroded biomedical dominance. As Willis (1988: 176) observes, "[p]ractitioners of complementary care modalities have been so far unsuccessful in gaining access to the hospital system [with some recent notable exceptions], either in public or private." However, biomedical dominance is eroding somewhat as national and state or provincial governments – as well as corporations – have come to play a more important role in the creation of health policy, which in turn has begun to adopt a greater tolerance of CAM systems.

Saks (2003) compares and contrasts the routes by which biomedicine and allied health occupations and various CAM systems embarked on professionalization in Britain and the United States since the sixteenth century. He defines professionalization in neo-Weberian terms as a process "based upon the establishment of patterns of legally underwritten exclusionary social closure, gained by some occupation in the politics of work" (Saks 2003: 4). Whereas in the sixteenth and seventeenth centuries health care in both national settings was extremely pluralistic, by the mid-twentieth century biomedicine had achieved clear-cut, but incomplete, domination over CAM systems. British CAM practitioners theoretically have had a freer hand to function under common law in contrast to CAM practitioners, such as chiropractors and naturopaths, who were forced to abide by state licensing regulations and basic science examinations. Conversely, a large underground of unlicensed CAM practitioners, including those who term themselves "traditional naturopaths," has emerged in the United States since at least the early 1970s, many of whom have obtained training in profit-making distance-learning programs (Baer 2004: 59–64). Osteopaths and chiropractors managed to achieve social closure under the guise of statutory registration in the UK in the early 1990s and achieved the same in Australia between the 1980s and 1990s, as have Chinese medicine practitioners in the state of Victoria in 2000 (Baer 2006a, 2006b, 2007).

CAM AND INTEGRATIVE MEDICINE IN BIOMEDICAL AND NURSING SCHOOLS, WORKSHOPS, JOURNALS, CLINICS, AND HOSPITALS

CAM, often within the larger rubric of integrative medicine, has become part and parcel of biomedical and nursing education, workshops, journals, clinics, and hospitals in many settings around the world. A growing number of biomedical and nursing students in developed countries have come to express interest in CAM or integrative medicine. In response to this interest, more and more biomedical schools began to offer courses on alternative medicine – a process that is still occurring – as it became apparent that the bread-and-butter patients of biomedicine, those with disposable incomes, could afford to pay for alternative therapies out of their pockets. The first teaching program in alternative medicine at a US biomedical institution was established in the 1970s at Montefiore Medical Center in the Bronx (Abrams 1994: 99). In 2002, at least 81 out of 125 biomedical schools offered instruction in CAM, either in required courses, electives, or both (Courses on Complementary Medicine 2002). The Consortium of Academic Health Centers has been seeking to introduce programs of integrative medicine in US medical schools (Rees 2001). Andrew Weil directs the Program in Integrative Medicine at the University of Arizona, which provides continuing medical education (including quarterly mini-conferences) and a two-year fellowship for MDs and DOs who have completed residencies in primary care specialties (Goldstein 1999: 120). Training in CAM is also increasingly available in UK and European biomedical schools.

Nursing schools have embraced holistic health or CAM even more enthusiastically than have biomedical schools. The New York University Advanced Practice Holistic Practice Nursing Graduate Program (est. 1998) offers a master's degree as holistic nurse practitioner and teaches meditation, therapeutic touch, and homeopathy (Dean 2001). The University of Minnesota School of Nursing has incorporated CAM into its curriculum and offers instruction in storytelling, journaling, aromatherapy, energy healing, tai chi, yoga, massage, and prayers (Halcon et al. 2001). Nursing schools in many parts of the world also train their students in various CAM therapies.

In addition to CAM training at biomedical and nursing schools, many MDs, nurses, and other health professionals are receiving training in CAM at a wide assortment of conferences and workshops. Acupuncture in particular has captured relatively wide appeal among US conventional physicians. UCLA, for example, enrolls some 5,000 to 6,000 MDs a year in a 300-hour acupuncture training program (Brunk 2000). Conventional physicians and other health professionals, both biomedical and CAM, may acquaint themselves with CAM or integrative medicine by consulting a growing number of research journals, such as *Alternative Medicine*, the *Journal of Alternative and Complementary Medicine*, *Advances in Mind–Body Medicine*, *Alternative and Complementary Therapies*, *Alternative Therapies*, *Alternative Healthcare Management*, and *Focus on Alternative and Complementary Therapies: An Evidence-Based Approach*.

A growing number of biomedical schools and university hospitals have created centers of integrative medicine or CAM where they treat patients. The Stress Reduction Center at the University of Massachusetts–Worcester Medical School teaches Buddhist meditation and yoga to its patients. The UCLA Center for East–West Medicine was created in 1993 to merge principles of Chinese medicine and biomedicine (Hui et al. 2002). Thomas Jefferson University Hospital in Philadephia and George Washington University Medical Center are among the various medical schools operating centers of integrative medicine (Baer 2004). Most of the growing number of integrative medical centers, whether affiliated with medical schools or independent of them, tend to be directed by one or more conventional physicians and staffed by an array of CAM practioners.

GOVERNMENTAL AND CORPORATE INVOLVEMENT IN CAM AND INTEGRATIVE MEDICINE

Health services have become matters of public concern, particularly to third-party payers such as government, industry, business, insurance companies, and labor. Salmon (1985) argues that a "class-conscious corporate directorship" has come to wield considerable power over health policy decision-making. According to Berliner and Salmon (1989: 538):

> Because holistic health is generally provided on an ambulatory basis and stresses prevention and health maintenance, alternative modalities tend to be less expensive than scientific medicine interventions; thus, they may gain an advantage in policy discussions if their efficacy can be assured.

As a result of a Congressional mandate, the National Institutes of Health (NIH) established the Office of Alternative Medicine (OAM) in 1992. The office reportedly was created "under pressure from Congress alarmed by the soaring costs of high-tech healing and the frustrating fact that so many ailments – AIDS, cancer, arthritis, back pain – have yet to yield to standard medicine" (Toufexis 1993: 43). OAM received a mandate to explore the efficacy of various heterodox therapies. The funding for OAM and its successor body, the National Center for Complementary and Alternative Medicine (NCCAM), has increased from $2 million in fiscal year 1992 to $121.4 million in fiscal year 2007.

On March 7, 2000, President Bill Clinton created the White House Commission on Complementary and Alternative Medicine Policy in response to heavy political lobbying. The Final Report of the White House Commission on Complementary and Alternative Medicine (2002) made 22 recommendations on topics such as increased funding for CAM training and research, guidelines for scientific research on CAM, the need for dialogue and collaboration between biomedical and CAM practitioners, the incorporation of CAM into the biomedical curriculum, the provision of training in biomedical principles and practices to CAM practitioners, and the dissemination of information on CAM to the general public.

Health insurance companies, health maintenance organizations (HMOs), and hospitals have become increasingly interested in CAM therapies as a way of satisfying patient demands and curtailing costs. Most large HMOs in California now offer chiropractic and acupuncture care (Rees 2001: 4). HMOs in other parts of the United States now reimburse CAM treatment. Indeed, Washington State requires health insurers to cover naturopathic medicine, acupuncture, massage therapy, and other types of licensed CAM care. Various health care corporations and numerous practices also offer CAM or integrative treatment.

Collyer (2004) discusses the corporatization and commercialization of CAM, particularly in Australia but also elsewhere, noting it has evolved from a cottage industry into a corporate endeavor. She observes complementary medicines have increasingly come to be manufactured by pharmaceutical companies that produce biomedical drugs, and CAM practitioners increasingly are working in corporate-owned integrative medical centers. Collyer (2004: 95) argues that the mainstreaming of CAM will ultimately increase costs for consumers, governments, and third-party payers, and that CAM ultimately has come to have "little relation to the enhancement of well-being, patient safety, altruism or the curing of disease."

IS BIOMEDICINE COOPTING CAM?

Various medical social scientists have warned that holistic health or CAM faces the danger of being coopted by biomedicine. Biomedicine historically has often incorporated alternative therapies rather than losing patients en masse to heterodox practitioners. Alster (1989: 163) maintains that biomedical calls for CAM or integrative medicine may in reality "serve the purpose of preserving the hegemony of medicine by co-opting the most attractive components of holism." In a similar vein, Wolpe (2002: 169) states: "The conventionalization of CAM into the academic medical centers is part of a long history of medicine gaining control over modalities by co-opting them." In the process, he maintains, the CAM that conventional physicians adopt is stripped of the "very ritual and therapeutic philosophy that made it attractive to many patients in the first place" (Wolpe 2002: 171). Cross-cultural research has repeatedly indicated the integration of biomedicine and CAM tends to preserve rather than eradicate biomedical hegemony (Cant and Sharma 1999: 183; Yoshida 2002; Baer 2008). Indeed, Rakel and Weil (2003: 7), both biomedical physicians and staunch proponents of integrative medicine, observe that biomedicine often views CAM as "tools that are simply added to the current model, one that attempts to understand healing by studying the tools in the tool box."

The dominance of biomedicine often becomes apparent in CAM or integrative medical centers. Goldner (2000: 228) found this to be the case in her ethnographic observations in an integrative clinic in the San Francisco Bay area:

> At the integrative clinic, one practitioner mentioned that the "physician here likes to be the physician and wave her title. So I have to be respectful, but not necessarily back down" … On several occasions, members thanked physicians for attending workshops, especially since they were "putting themselves out there" when "they don't have to [do this]." The alternative practitioners seemed so appreciative that physicians were giving them any level of credibility, that they did not seem to mind differences in power.

Fadlon (2005) conducted an ethnographic study of what she terms a non-conventional medicine (NCM) clinic loosely affiliated with an Israeli hospital. In this setting, despite the fact that NCM practitioners tended to have more extensive training in specific NCM systems, such as homeopathy, MDs who performed the same modality with less training in it exerted more authority. Most patients also felt more assured if they knew they were being administered NCM by an MD rather than by an NCM practitioner. In her conclusion, Fadlon (2005: 117) asserts that in the case of Israel:

> While NCM may embody countercultural ideologies that lead to differentiation, in practice its major and most successful thrust has been through selective integration and

ultimately domestication. ... Through the mechanisms of dissemination, institutionalization, and consumption, NCM has been incorporated, appropriated, and tamed.

At a more institutional setting, a recent report drafted by the Committee on the
Use of Complementary and Alternative Medicine by the American Public indirectly
indicates the degree to which biomedicine has been coopting CAM, at least in the
United States (Institute of Medicine 2005). The composition of this committee is,
in large part, a who's who of many of the major policy makers relating to CAM
and integrative medicine – and it draws heavily upon some of the most prestigious
biomedical institutions in the country.

While biomedicine has not gone nearly as far in its efforts to coopt CAM in
Australia as in the United States, biomedicine continues to exert dominance over
complementary medicine down under as well. Indeed, Australian biomedical physicians are increasingly redefining complementary therapeutic systems as modalities
within biomedicine or closely related to biomedicine. For example, some general
practitioners have come to term chiropractic and osteopathy as physical medicine
or manual medicine (Eastwood 1997: 14). Dietetics and nutritional advice as
treatment modalities integral to naturopathy, homeopathy, and Western herbal
medicine have been incorporated by biomedical physicians under the designation
of nutritional and environmental medicine. According to Eastwood (1997: 14),
"Acupuncture, in the context of general practice, has been redefined as medical
acupuncture."

CONCLUSION

This chapter provides a partial overview of the issues that have become part and
parcel of the social scientific study of CAM. While some scholars posit the existence of a new holistic health or CAM social movement with counterhegemonic
elements, others point to the growing biomedical cooption of CAM under the
guise of integrative medicine, the commercialization of CAM therapies, and the
emergence of a lucrative CAM industry. Furthermore, some sociologists have been
examining the implications of the application of evidence-based medicine to CAM
(Heller 2005; Heller, Hills, and Weatherly-Jones 2005). Willis and White (2004)
argue that as CAM therapies have become more acceptable to biomedicine, the
issue of subjecting them to the rigors of randomized, double-blind, controlled
testing has moved to the forefront, as a means to validate or discredit them.
Randomized controlled testing methodology functions most easily when treatment
is fairly straightforward, but becomes much more difficult to administer in the
case of many CAM treatments that entail a combination of treatments for individual patients.

While sociological and anthropological studies of a wide array of alternative
medical systems in modern societies have been elucidating much about CAM, most
of this research has relied upon archival sources and survey research, although there
a growing number of notable exceptions. What is desperately needed are in-depth
studies of CAM practitioners, their educational institutions, associations, conferences, and clinical practices, and the vitalist subcultures within which they and their

patients or clients function as well as the increasing number of settings in which biomedical and CAM practitioners interact with one another.

References

Abrams, Maxine. 1994. "Alternative Medicine: Quackery or Miracle?" *Good Housekeeping*, March: 99–119.

Adams, Jon and Philip Tovey. 2004. "CAM and Nursing: From Advocacy to Critical Sociology." Pp. 158–74 in Philip Tovey, Gary Easthope, and Jon Adams (eds.), *The Mainstreaming of Complementary and Alternative Medicine*. London: Routledge.

Alster, K. B. 1989. *The Holistic Health Movement*. Tuscaloosa: University of Alabama Press.

Baer, Hans A. 2001. *Biomedicine and Alternative Healing Systems in America: Issues of Class, Race, Ethnicity, and Gender*. Madison: University of Wisconsin Press.

Baer, Hans A. 2004. *Towards an Integrative Medicine: From Holistic Health to Complementary and Alternative Medicine*. Walnut Creek, CA: Altamira Press.

Baer, Hans A. 2006a. "The Drive for Legitimation in Australian Naturopathy: Successes and Dilemmas." *Social Science and Medicine* 63: 1771–83.

Baer, Hans A. 2006b. "The Drive for Legitimation by Osteopathy and Chiropractic in Australia: Between Heterodoxy and Orthodoxy." *Complementary Health Practice Review* 11: 77–94.

Baer, Hans A. 2007. "The Drive for Legimition in Chinese Medicine and Acupuncture in Australia: Successes and Dilemmas." *Complementary Health Practice Review* 12: 87–98.

Baer, Hans A. 2008. "The Emergence of Integrative Medicine in Australia: The Growing Interest of Biomedicine and Nursing in a Southern Developed Society." *Medical Anthropology Quarterly* 22: 52–66.

Bailey, Eric J. 1991. "Hypertension: An Analysis of Detroit African American Health Care Treatment Patterns." *Human Organization* 50: 287–96.

Berliner, Howard and J. Warren Salmon. 1989. "The Holistic Alternative to Scientific Medicine: History and Analysis." *International Journal of Health Services* 10: 133–47.

Biggs, Lesley. 1991. "Chiropractic Education: A Struggle for Survival." *Journal of Manipulative and Physiological Therapeutics* 14: 22–8.

Bratman, Steven. 1997. *The Alternative Medicine Sourcebook: A Realistic Evaluation of Alternative Healing Methods*. Los Angeles: Lowell House.

Brunk, Doug. 2000. "Marketplace Demands Physicians Offer More CAM." *Family Practice News*, May 1, p. 1.

Cant, Sarah and Ursula Sharma. 1999. *A New Medical Pluralism? Alternative Medicine, Doctors, Patients, and the State*. London: Taylor and Francis.

Caplan, R., K. Harrison, and M. L. Galantiono. 2003. "The Evolution of Complementary and Alternative Medicine in the United States: The Push and Pull of Holistic Health Care into the Medical Mainstream." Pp. 9–22 in Jodie L. Carson (ed.), *Complementary Therapies and Wellness Practice Essentials for Holistic Health Care*. Upper Saddle River, NJ: Prentice-Hall.

Cassidy, Claire M. 2002. "Commentary on Terminology and Therapeutic Principles: Challenges in Classifying Complementary and Alternative Medicine Practices." *Journal of Alternative and Complementary Medicine* 8: 893–6.

Chavez, Leo R. 1984. "Doctors, *Curanderos*, and *Brujas*: Health Care Delivery and Mexican Immigrants in San Diego." *Medical Anthropology Quarterly* 15(2): 31–7.

Coburn, David. 1991. "Legitimacy at the Expense of Narrowing of Scope of Practice: Chiropractic in Canada." *Journal of Manipulative and Physiological Therapeutics* 14: 14–21.

Cohen, Michael H. 1998. *Complementary and Alternative Medicine: Legal Boundaries and Regulatory Perspectives*. Baltimore: Johns Hopkins University Press.

Cohen, Michael H. 2000. *Beyond Complementary Medicine: Legal and Ethical Perspectives on Health Care and Human Evolution*. Ann Arbor: University of Michigan Press.

Collyer, Fran. 2004. "The Corporatisation and Commercialisation of CAM." Pp. 81–9 Philip Tovey, Gary Easthope, and Jon Adams (eds.), *The Mainstreaming of Complementary and Alternative Medicine*. London: Routledge.

Coulter, Ian D. 1991. "Sociological Studies of the Role of the Chiropractors: An Exercise in Ideological Hegemony?" *Journal of Manipulative and Physiological Therapeutics* 14: 51–8.

Courses on Complementary Medicine and Alternative Therapies (CAM) Taught at Conventional US Medical Schools. 2002. Retrieved August 4, 2004 (www.healthwweb.com/courses.html).

Dean, Karen L. 2001. "NYU's Holistic Nursing Program: Expanding the Conventional Boundaries of Nursing." *Alternative and Complementary Therapies* 7(3): 183–7.

Diamond, W. J. 2001. *The Clinical Practice of Complementary, Alternative, and Western Medicine*. Boca Raton, FL: CRC.

Eastwood, Heather. 1997. "*General Medical Practice, Alternative Medicine, and the Globalization of Health*." PhD thesis, Department of Sociology and Anthropology, University of Queensland.

Eastwood, Heather. 2002. "Globalisation, Complementary Medicine, and Australian Health Policy: The Role of Consumerism." Pp. 222–45 in H. Gardner and S. Barraclough (eds.), *Health Policy in Australia*. Melbourne: Oxford University Press.

Eisenberg, David M., Roger Davis, Susan L. Ettner, Scott Appel, Sonja Wilkey, Maria Van Rompay, and Ronald C. Kessler. 1993. "Unconventional Medicine in the United States: Prevalence, Costs, and Patterns of Use." *New England Journal of Medicine* 328: 246–52.

Eisenberg, David M., Roger Davis, Susan L. Ettner, Scott Appel, Sonja Wilkey, Maria Van Rompay, and Ronald C. Kessler. 1998. "Trends in Alternative Medicine Use in the United States, 1990–1997." *Journal of the American Medical Association* 280: 1569–75.

English-Lueck, Jan A. 1990. *Health in the New Age: A Study in California Holistic Practices*. Englewood Cliffs, NJ: Prentice-Hall.

Fadlon, Judith. 2005. *Negotiating the Holistic Turn: The Domestication of Alternative Medicine*. Albany: State University of New York Press.

Fisher, Peter and Adama Ward. 1994. "Complementary Medicine in Europe." *British Medical Journal* 309: 107–10.

Fulder, Stephen. 1996. *The Handbook of Complementary and Alternative Medicine*, 3rd edition. Oxford: Oxford University Press.

Goldner, Melinda. 2000. "Integrative Medicine: Issues to Consider in the Emerging Form of Health Care." *Research in the Sociology of Health Care* 16: 55–74.

Goldstein, Michael S. 1999. *Alternative Health Care*. Philadelphia: Temple University Press.

Halcon, L. et al. 2001. "Incorporating Alternative and Complementary Health Practices Within University-Based Nursing Education." *Complementary Health Practice Review* 6(2): 127–35.

Heller, Tom. 2005. "Researching CAM Interventions." Pp. 195–228 in Geraldine Lee-Treweek, Tom Heller, Hilary McQueen, Julie Stone, and Sue Spurr (eds.), *Complementary and Alternative Medicine: Structures and Safeguards*. London: Routledge.

Heller, T., D. Hills, and E. Weatherly-Jones. 2005. "Evaluating Practice in Complementary and Alternative Medicine." Pp. 229–55 in Geraldine Lee-Treweek, Tom Heller, Hilary McQueen, Julie Stone, and Sue Spurr (eds.), *Complementary and Alternative Medicine: Structures and Safeguards*. London: Routledge.

Hui, Ka-Kit, Lidia Zylowska, Edward K. Hui, Jun Liang Yu, and Jie Jia Li. 2002. "Introducing East–West Medicine to Medical Students and Residents." *Journal of Alternative and Complementary Medicine* 8: 507–15.

Institute of Medicine (IOM). 2005. *Complementary and Alternative Medicine in the United States*. Washington, DC: National Academies Press.

Jain, N. and J. A. Astin. 2001. "Barriers to Acceptance: An Exploratory Study of Complementary/Alternative Medicine Disuse." *Journal of Alternative and Complementary Medicine* 7: 689–96.

Jonas, Wayne and Jeffrey S. Levin (eds.). 1999. *Essentials of Alternative and Complementary Medicine*. Philadelphia: Lippincott, Williams, and Williams.

Kaptchuk, Ted and David Eisenberg. 2001. "Varieties of Healing, 2: A Taxonomy of Unconventional Healing Practices." *Annals of Internal Medicine* 135(3): 196–204.

Kelner, Merrijoy and Beverly Wellman. 1997. "Health Care and Consumer Choice: Medical and Alternative Therapies." *Social Science and Medicine* 45: 202–12.

Lowenberg, Judith S. 1989. *Caring and Responsibility: The Crossroads Between Holistic Health Practice and Traditional Medicine*. Philadelphia. University of Pennsylvania Press.

MacLennan, A. H., D. H. Wilson, and A. W. Taylor. 1996. "Prevalence and Cost of Alternative Medicine in Australia." *Lancet* 347: 569–73.

Micozzi, Marc. S. (ed.). 2007. *Fundamentals of Complementary and Alternative Medicine*, 3rd edition. New York: Churchill Livingstone.

Milton, D. and S. Benjamin. 1999. *Complementary and Alternative Therapies: An Implementation Guide*. Chicago: AHA.

Nienstedt, Barbara Cable. 1998. "The Federal Approach to Alternative Medicine: Co-opting, Quackbusting, or Complementing?" Pp. 27–43 in Rena J. Gordon and Barbara Cable Nienstedt (eds.), *Alternative Therapies: Expanding Options in Health Care*. New York: Springer.

Novey, Donald W. (ed.). 2000. *Clinician's Complete Reference to Complementary/Alternative Medicine*. St. Louis, MO: Mosby.

Office of Alternative Medicine Committee on Definition and Description. 1997. " 'Defining and Describing Complementary and Alternative Medicine'." *Alternative Medicines in Health and Medicine* 3(2): 49–57.

Rakel, David and Andrew Weil. 2003. "Philosophy of Integrative Medicine." Pp. 3–9 in David Rakel (ed.), *Integrative Medicine*. Philadelphia: Saunders.

Rees, Alan M. (ed.). 2001. *The Complementary and Alternative Information Source Book*. Westport, CT: Oryx.

Rivera, G., Jr. 1988. "Hispanic Folk Medicine Utilization in Urban Colorado." *Social Science Review* 72: 237–41.

Rosenfeld, Isadore. 1996. *Dr. Rosenfeld's Guide to Alternative Medicine: What Works, What Doesn't*. New York: Random House.

Saks, Michael. 2003. *Orthodox and Alternative Medicine*. New York: Continuum.

Salmon, J. Warren. 1985. "Profit and Health Care: Trends in Corporatization and Proprietization." *International Journal of Health Services* 15: 395–418.

Schneirov, Matthew and Jonathan D. Geczik. 2003. *A Diagnosis for Our Times: Alternative Health from Lifeworld to Politics*. Albany: State University of New York Press.

Sharma, Ursula. 1995. *Complementary Medicine Today: Patients and Practitioners*. London: Routledge.

Sierpina, Victor S. 2001. *Integrative Health Care: Complementary and Alternative Therapies for the Whole Person*. Philadelphia: Davis.

Singer, Merrill and Hans A. Baer. 2007. *Introducing Medical Anthropology: A Discipline in Action*. Walnut Creek: CA: Altamira Press.

Snyder, Mariah and Ruth Lindquist (eds.) 2006. *Complementary/Alternative Therapies in Nursing*, 5th edition. New York: Springer.

Tataryn, Douglas J. 2002. "Paradigms of Health and Disease: A Framework for Classifying and Understanding Complementary and Alternative Medicine." *Journal of Alternative and Complementary Medicine* 8(6): 877–92.

Toufexis, A. 1993. "Dr. Jacob's Alternative Mission." *Time*, March 1, pp. 43–4.

Wardwell, Walter I. 1992. *Chiropractic: History and Evolution of a New Practice*. St. Louis, MO: Mosby Year Book.

White House Commission on Complementary and Alternative Medicine Policy. 2002. *White House Commission on Complementary and Alternative Medicine Policy: Final Report*. Washington, DC: US Government Printing Office.

Wilkinson, J. M. and M. D. Simpson. 2001. "High Use of Complementary Therapies in a NSW Rural Community." *Australian Journal of Rural Health* 9: 166–71.

Willis, Evan. 1988. "Doctoring in Australia: A View at the Bicentenary." *Milbank Quarterly* 66: 167–81.

Willis, Evan. 1989. *Medical Dominance*, revised edition. St. Leonards, New South Wales, Australia: Allen and Unwin.

Willis, Evan. 1994. *Illness and Social Relations: Issues in the Sociology of Health Care*. Sydney: Allen and Unwin.

Willis, Evan and Kevin White. 2004. "Evidence-Based Medicine and CAM." Pp. 49–63 in Philip Tovey, Gary Easthope, and Jon Adams (eds.), *Mainstreaming Complementary and Alternative Medicine: Studies in Social Context*. London: Routledge.

Wolpe, Paul R. 2002. "Medical Culture and CAM Culture: Science and Ritual in the Academic Medical Center." Pp. 163–71 in Daniel Callahan (ed.), *The Role of Complementary and Alternative Medicine: Accommodating Pluralism*. Washington, DC: Georgetown University Press.

Yoshida, M. 2002. "A Theoretical Model of Biomedical Professional's Legitimization of Alternative Therapies." *Complementary Health Practice Review* 7: 187–208.

Yuan, Chun-Su, Eric J. Bieber, and Brent A. Bauer (eds.). 2006. *Textbook of Complementary and Alternative Medicine*, 2nd edition. Abindgon, Oxon, England: Informa Health.

18

The American Health Care System

Beginning the Twenty-First Century with High Risk, Major Challenges, and Great Opportunities

BERNICE A. PESCOSOLIDO AND CAROL A. BOYER

At the end of the nineteenth century the medical profession stood in the midst of great change in America. The coming of the industrial revolution coupled with new scientific theories for the practice and training of physicians resulted in the modern profession of medicine. With that great social transformation of American medicine (Starr 1982), there was little doubt in the minds of the leaders of the new scientific profession that the American health care system would be substantially different from the one at the beginning of the nineteenth century or even at mid-century. As it evolved during the twentieth century, the modern health care system in the United States took a very different form from many of its European counterparts, building a mixed private and public system of care with powerful physician direction.

What was less anticipated but equally remarkable was the contrast between the health care system at the beginning of the twenty-first century and its predecessor in the early 1990s. Escalating costs, the increasing burden of chronic and degenerative diseases, the growing number of Americans not covered by any form of health insurance, and a weak relationship between health care spending and some important markers of success (e.g., the infant mortality rate) compared to other countries led to major efforts to restructure the American health care system. The failure of the Clinton health care plan in the early 1990s led to employers and state governments launching managed care strategies to transform the structure and financing of health services. A backlash against managed care began in the mid-1990s and resulted in the weakening of many of its strategies that limited choice of physicians, access to specialists, and other forms of explicit and strict rationing of health care services to what has been described as "managed care lite" (Mechanic 2004). Without the constraints on utilization under managed care, health care costs began to escalate at the same time that the number of uninsured continued to increase. Health care services continued to remain fragmented and uncoordinated. Currently, the richest country in the world with almost 300 million people is undergoing social experiments in reconfiguring federal–state partnerships and the use of individual and employer mandates to cover more of the uninsured, increase access, and improve the quality of health services. The recent presidential election also signaled potential change emanating from the federal level, although the difference between campaign proposals and enacted policy is often substantial.

The purpose of this chapter is to provide an overview of the different eras in providing health care in the United States, concentrating on the challenges and opportunities in the current context of a health care system under stress. We begin with a review of the evolution of the American health care system, focusing on the authority of its major practitioners, physicians, and the limits on their autonomy in determining recent arrangements under which health care is provided. Several challenges are described that now figure prominently in the changes taking place in American health care as continuing efforts attempt to assure access to more of the population and to improve quality of care in a cost-effective manner.

THE RISE OF A HEALTH CARE SYSTEM IN THE UNITED STATES

Historians and sociologists alike have argued that the discovery of a bacillus that caused anthrax, the routine use of antiseptics, and the introduction of anesthesia combined to produce the great break between medicine of the past and the modern form of science-based practice. While different societies embraced the new science in different ways in shaping their health care systems, the industrializing countries of the United States and Europe used political, social, and economic mechanisms to place scientific physicians at the center of modern health care systems. Figure 18.1 provides a simple heuristic device charting the relative authority of physicians in the American health care system over time. As Figure 18.1 indicates, the authority and reach of modern physicians grew dramatically from 1860 to 1910. The Flexner Report, instrumental in establishing physician authority, gave rise to the scientific model of medical education in the United States, with the recommendation

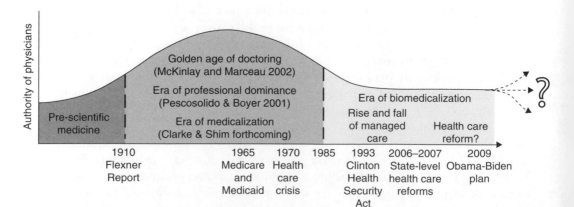

Figure 18.1 Eras in the American health care system.

that only medical schools following the German model of biomedical training and stronger clinical practice receive financial assistance and public support. Suppressed were the itinerant medicine men delivering elixirs laced with opium or alcohol and practices that purged disease by cleansing the body through vomiting or elimination. Gone also was the standard practice of "regular" physicians (i.e., the precursors of the scientific physician such as Benjamin Rush) who bled the ill person to remove tainted blood. Other alternative providers such as "Granny" midwives who delivered babies at home and female and minority physicians who learned medicine through apprenticeships were also eliminated through the establishment of licensing laws.

Licensing laws required all those wishing to practice medicine to take state examinations that were written by physicians at the newly established, scientific-based medical schools such as The Johns Hopkins University in Baltimore. Both aspiring and practicing medical providers not trained at these modern medical schools failed the examinations and were prohibited from practicing medicine in the United States (Brown 1979). Even the well-established chiropractors and homeo-paths, who were the preferred providers of the upper classes in the United States, found themselves without substantial support, even though they were not barred from practice. The scientific medical profession became a successful, if not total, monopoly (Berlant 1975; Collins 1979; Starr 1982).

The medical profession's role in establishing the American health care system looms large and substantial (Quadagno 2006). Formed in 1847, the American Medical Association became extremely powerful and helped direct the use of resources generated by wealthy industrialists in the United States. Corporate inter-ests, while backing the large infusion of wealth into the emerging system of modern medicine, contributed indirectly through their newly established philanthropic foun-dations. The government, whether federal or state, played a minimal early role in the design of the American health care system. The role of the American government differed substantially from the European experience. For example, in Germany, the federal government played an early and active role in directing general and employer taxes to cover the services of scientific medical practice (Berlant 1975; Rosen 1963).

Health care in the United States could only loosely be referred to as a system of health care financed by private and public sources. It was, and still is at best, a patchwork of providers in the private/nonprofit sector including solo-practitioners, incorporated groups of physicians, voluntary, community hospitals, private hospi-tals, and some early health maintenance organizations such as Kaiser Permanente in California, which arose from the lack of physicians to serve the workers in important railroad and mining industries that developed beyond urban centers. The private sector was supplemented by a weak public sector that included city and county hospitals, long-term care facilities (e.g., mental hospitals, TB sanitariums), a Veterans Administration System established at the end of the Civil War in the 1860s, public health nursing, and specialized community clinics (e.g., the Commu-nity Mental Health Centers or CMHCs, which were established with the decision to deinstitutionalize the treatment of persons with mental illness). Only in the 1960s did the federal government introduce programs to provide health insurance coverage for the elderly, the disabled, and eventually those with end-stage renal disease (Medicare) and partner with the states to offer coverage for the poor and medically needy (Medicaid).

The period from 1910 through 1970 represented an era of significant growth, success, and authority of the medical profession. After World War II with the large federal government infusion of support for research and development and hospital construction, American physicians became the most prominent medical professional group in the world. This era has been described by McKinlay and Marceau (2002) as the "Golden Age of Doctoring," by Clarke and her colleagues as the "Medicalization Era" (Clarke and Shim forthcoming), and by us, using Eliot Freidson's (1970) terms, as "The Era of Professional Dominance" (see Figure 18.1). Working in a primarily private health care system, physicians determined both the nature of medical care and the arrangements under which it was provided (Freidson 1970). Physicians set their fees, worked in predominantly solo-practices, and joined the American Medical Association. The New Deal, which introduced several major economic and social programs including Social Security in response to the Great Depression of the 1930s, was not extended to the public provision of health care characteristic of health insurance systems of Europe. Beginning in the 1940s, for the most part, patients could choose the physician of their choice for treatment and purchase private health insurance.

THE END OF UNQUESTIONED DOMINANCE

In 1970 President Richard Nixon announced the existence of a health care crisis in the United States (see Figure 18.1). The number of uninsured Americans and those underinsured who had limited access to medical care was growing. Although the Medicare and Medicaid programs offered insurance coverage to several significant groups, these programs left millions without health care insurance. At the same time, these programs, notably Medicare, resulted in escalating costs and profit-taking at a time of rapid inflation in the economy. A "two-tiered" or "two-class" system of health care in the United States had also become more prominent as inequalities in care rose to the forefront of policy debates. The limits of medical care were especially evident with chronic illnesses such as cancer, heart disease, and other degenerative illnesses that could not be understood and treated under the germ theory or an acute care model, a central tenet of modern, scientific medicine. While medicine offered increasingly more sophisticated, technological solutions to diagnosis and treatment, Americans who were better educated than before and with higher expectations questioned established practices such as routine resort to surgery for problems (e.g., prostate surgery and back pain) and the extension of life through artificial means (e.g., life support in end-stage cases). As Figure 18.1 indicates, 1985 marks the beginning of the "Biomedicalization Era," according to Clarke and colleagues (Clarke and Shim forthcoming), which brought dramatic and largely technoscientific changes to both the practice and the organization of American medicine.

Simultaneously, there was a growing interest in both older and newer forms of complementary and alternative medicine, including midwifery, acupuncture, chiropractic, and homeopathy. Scholars began to write about the second social contract between modern medicine and society with scientific medicine's deprofessionalization; patients' rights and a growing consumer movement; anti-trust regulation for professions; and the use of alternative and holistic approaches to health care (Pescosolido and Kronenfeld 1995; Pescosolido, McLeod, and Alegría 2000). As health care insurance began to cover alternative medicines, albeit on a very limited basis (e.g., chiropractic), and greater numbers of physicians declined to join the American Medical Association and joined specialty groups instead, professional dominance was unraveling. Sociologists shifted their discussion from issues of professional dominance to corporatization, proletarianization, and countervailing powers; anthropologists talked about alternative medical systems being complementary rather than competing and discussed the potential for integration among different systems of medical care (Light 1995; Light and Levine 1988; Unschuld 1976). A well-known critique of American medical schools has described them as "vassals of the marketplace," reflecting their retreat from a public mission (Ludmerer 1999).

This disillusionment was not exclusive to modern medicine and, perhaps, reflected larger changes in modern society (Pescosolido and Rubin 2000). Rubin (1996) has argued that the social and economic bases of modern society tarnished in the early 1970s and marked a turning point. The postwar growth that had fueled prosperity in all sectors, including medicine, diminished. A long decline in expansion resulted in the downsizing of corporations and displacement of large numbers of workers. While new jobs continued to be created, some were also increasingly part-time, temporary, low wage, and without important benefits including health insurance (Kronick and Gilmer 1999). The costs of medical care in the United States continued to rise at rates higher than inflation in other sectors at the same time that individuals experienced greater barriers to access and faced substantial medical problems. Old problems, thought to have been solved, returned (e.g., the resurgence of tuberculosis), new ones that perplexed medical researchers and strained the limits of scientific medicine arose (e.g., HIV/AIDS, antibiotic-resistant bacterial infection), and persistent failures plagued the country that continued to spend the most on health care in the world, but without consistently good outcomes (e.g., the relatively higher infant mortality rate in the United States compared with countries with lower national spending for health care, such as Japan, Poland, Italy, and Sweden).

HEALTH CARE REFORM OF THE 1990S AND ITS BACKLASH

For the first time in a century, health care became a central political issue in national debates in the 1990s (see Figure 18.1). In the presidential election of 1990, Democratic candidates Bob Kerry and, later, Bill Clinton focused on the crisis in health care as a central issue. To the surprise of many, this issue became a lightning rod among the American people. After his election, President Clinton sought major reform in the health care system and appointed his wife, Hillary Clinton, to chair a Task Force that between 1992 and 1994 deliberated and crafted the Clinton Health Security Act. Based on the triad of managed competition, global budget, and universal coverage, the plan sought to achieve improved access to health care through privately provided health insurance and to control costs simultaneously (see Zelman 1996).

The original ideas about managed competition focused on the creation of health alliances, a group of individuals who would enroll in a health insurance plan together and purchase insurance from a private group (see Enthoven 1978). The system would be employer-based and would allow the invisible hand of the market to set competition in motion among plans to provide the best and widest range of coverage at the lowest prices. A public agency would be established to certify these managed care plans, monitor quality, and guarantee yearly enrollment. The global budget provision was to move the United States to a single payer system where the federal government would cap the overall health care budget and reduce the high costs of administration. With the goal of universal coverage, health alliances would be created for all citizens. Through various provisions (e.g., Medicaid would no longer exist; Medicare would be folded into a health alliance), the Clinton Plan proposed for the first time that health care in America was a right and not a privilege based on ability to pay. The Clinton Plan also preserved the private nature of health care in the United States while ensuring it as a public good.

While scholars, politicians, and policy makers debated the merits of the approach (e.g., Relman 1993), the Clinton Health Reform Act was gutted and eventually abandoned in 1994 after lengthy report recommendations were issued and due to strong public opposition (see Domhoff 1996; Quadagno 2006; Skocpol 1997). In its demise, the private health insurance market was transformed with the introduction of managed care and the private centralization of large health plans. Facing total health benefit costs increasing more than 20 percent each year (Higgins 1991), fiscal constraints resulting from a mounting federal budget deficit, and more skepticism about the value of health care given its costs under mostly a fee-for-service system, private employers and eventually state governments sought and achieved substantial changes in the allocation of care and services under managed care.

The last decade of the twentieth century represented an historic turn in the American health care system with the expansion of managed care, but with an extraordinary popular backlash against managed care that followed in the mid- to late 1990s. Initially a number of diverse insurance options and organizations integrated the financing and delivery of care into what has been defined as managed care (Gold 1998). Key features included: (1) the use of a fixed prepayment, capitated, or negotiated fee for a defined set of services for a specified population of enrollees; (2) the assumption of insurance risk shared by a managed care organization (MCO) and/or providers to provide necessary services; (3) selective contracting where enrollees are limited to a panel of providers; (4) the use of primary care gatekeepers to coordinate care and control the use of services; (5) utilization review to assess the appropriateness of care and provider decisions before services are provided, including pre-certification, concurrent review, and high-cost case management; (6) the managing of quality of care through the use of clinical practice standards or guidelines; and (7) the tracking of patient and organizational outcomes, referred to as performance monitoring and used to identify poor-quality plans, care, and providers.

Managed care also presented a challenge to the autonomy and clinical decision-making authority of physicians as they faced control of their practices through utilization management, profiling, and capitated payments and financial incentives that fit uneasily with medical professional ethics (Mechanic 2004). Sociologists (e.g., Hafferty and Castellani forthcoming) have argued that this challenge prompted a professionalism movement that reasserted the primacy of physicians' altruistic and community-oriented duties. Hostility to managed care by physicians was also equaled by an outcry against the restrictions in access and services by the general public, special interest groups, politicians, and the media. A substantial literature has been devoted to analyzing the managed care backlash and the reasons for the backlash, which were seen to arise from several sources including American cultural values of independence, autonomy, choice, barriers to access, threatened stakeholders, frustrated providers, the rejection of explicit rationing by the public, administrative complexity, and media portrayals of the denial of allegedly lifesaving services and care (*Journal of Health Politics, Policy and Law*, entire issue 1999; Mechanic 2004; Robinson 2001).

While only a small portion of the insurance market retains the traditional indemnity plan, where the insurer pays for the costs of services included in the benefit package after they are delivered without any pre-negotiation of fees or oversight, the strategies of managed care have been substantially weakened as a result of the widespread backlash. Although managed care contained health care cost increases under its most stringent practices, both costs and premiums have risen substantially since the withdrawal of some of its strategies (Center for Studying Health System Change 2002; Draper et al. 2002; Strunk, Ginsburg, and Gabel 2001). Increasing health care costs are also attributed to the widespread use of new medical technologies, increasing rates of obesity, direct-to-consumer pharmaceutical advertising, and higher public expectations about treatment and services, with population aging playing only a minor role (Ginsburg 2008).

COMPLEXITY IN THE CURRENT HEALTH CARE SYSTEM

The arrangements in the American health care system among consumers, employers, health care providers, and health insurers were fundamentally reconfigured under managed care and continue to evolve. The current system is considerably more complex than in the past, with changed and complicated relationships among diverse actors and stakeholders. Under managed care, insurers and managed care organizations (MCOs) made treatment decisions that previously had been controlled by providers and their patients. Now MCOs have been introduced as additional actors into models of utilization (Mechanic, Schlesinger, and McAlpine 1995). Health plans not only pay for services, but also, although less restrictive in some cases, still define how and which services are delivered.

Employers have been and continue to be major players in the American health care system. Employers responded to rising health care costs when the government failed to enact legislation under the Clinton Administration. Within big business groups, many self-insure and hire insurance companies to process the paperwork of claims and payments. Business communities also have varying and different agendas for insuring their employees. Over time, employers have become more attentive to health insurance options for their employees and have been more engaged in selecting how health benefit packages will be managed. As premiums increase, employers have employees pay higher co-pays and deductibles.

Managed care also placed greater responsibility for providing care after a hospital discharge on individuals themselves and on their families (Pescosolido and

Kronenfeld 1995). Families may be the recipients of services, and they have also been required to provide greater levels of care and treatment as allowable days of hospitalization decreased and outpatient surgeries expanded.

The greater complexity of arrangements in the health care system means that the multiple perspectives of many key stakeholders, beyond the provider–patient relationship, must be taken into account in health outcomes, professional norms, and behaviors. Their interdependence also makes significant change in the health care system more difficult. The interests of these multiple actors may be compatible at times, but they are more likely to result in increased tensions and conflicts in the provision of medical care and in efforts to seek reform. Physicians, patients, and the courts are struggling with denied requests for treatment and the grievance procedures following from them (Rodwin 1995). There are also continuing concerns about offering financial incentives to physicians that may result in conflicts of interest and the compromising of care.

While the most restrictive strategies of managed care, especially limited choices of providers, the use of gatekeepers, and utilization reviews, have been diluted, functional forms of managed care remain in place. For some treatment decisions, more discretion has been returned to physicians (Freudenheim 1999). Managed behavioral health care has expanded and now dominates how mental health services are organized and financed (Mechanic 2008). Newer managed care models offer more choice in providers and more flexibility (e.g., co-payments for the use of specialists). However, there is also evidence that as health care costs have escalated and with the recent slowdown in the economy, health plans and employers are reintroducing stronger cost containment and care management approaches that were relaxed during the height of the managed care backlash (Mays, Claxton, and White 2004).

Surveys showed that under managed care the public had concerns about quality of health care, denial of services when sick, difficulty in getting referrals to specialists, and that health plans valued cost control over the best medical care. The public also seemed to regard possibly rare events, such as the denial of cancer treatment for a child, as a common occurrence among managed care plans (Blendon et al. 1998). Still, most Americans, although not always certain if they were in a managed care plan (Nelson et al. 2000), remained relatively satisfied with their own health insurance plan, whether it was managed or not (Blendon et al. 1998). This contradictory finding of individuals being satisfied with their own managed care plan, yet skeptical of managed care generally, fit with a long tradition of research that similarly showed Americans as being satisfied with their own physician but critical of the larger system of health care.

In the end, managed care was primarily an economic success in *initially* constraining health care cost increases (Robinson 2001). Managed care did not fundamentally alter the patchwork system of care in the United States, nor has it resolved the great disparities in health and health care access for disadvantaged and racial/ethnic minority groups. The expectation that managed care would lead to better integrated systems and promote continuity of care has yet to be demonstrated. The coordination of care, especially for those with chronic illnesses, is especially fragmented, and both overutilization of treatments that have no established value and underutilization of less expensive but evidenced-based services exist. Broadly speaking, most research shows mixed results and few significant differences in how patients fare in managed care compared to the more traditional fee-for-service arrangements (Miller and Luft 1994, 1997, 2002). There are some studies showing that the poor, elderly, and others with chronic illnesses receive less appropriate treatments under managed care (Miller and Luft 1994; Ware et al. 1996). For children and adolescents, there is some indication that managed care may compromise quality of care, but insufficient data exist to be fully certain about its impact (Wickizer, Lessler and Boyd-Wickizer 1999). Enrollees in HMOs and other managed care plans are more likely to receive preventive services (e.g., mammograms), but the long-term benefits of these services across populations with different risks is unknown. Few studies are available that compare various forms and arrangements of managed care to fee-for-service plans, so little is known about which financing strategies work most effectively to ensure quality of care.

The devolution of responsibility in health care reform to the states has added additional complexity to the American health care system. With policy differences across the states, states have made efforts to improve access for Medicaid beneficiaries and expand coverage to the uninsured, especially focused on children through the State Children's Health Insurance Programs (SCHIP). Reforms to the Medicaid program have also been underway while attempting to control costs (Gold 1997). In the absence of federal action, "expectations for state leadership promoting health reform have reached an all-time high" (Weil 2008). Yet, as Weil (2008) argues, without a strong state–federal partnership, strong experimentation in health reform at the state level, sufficient diffusion of knowledge about successes and failures, and adequate federal resources, significant reform across states may not be achieved.

CHALLENGES FACING THE AMERICAN HEALTH CARE SYSTEM

Although frequently characterized as one of the best in the world, improving the performance of the American health care system in areas of access to quality care, cost control, and good outcomes are major challenges the country faces. Fortunately, recent electoral politics in 2008 returned health care reform to the center of policy debates.

While pundits and citizens debated whether the downturn in the global economy or the war in Iraq trumped health care concerns, there was little doubt that both presidential candidates agreed on the need for health care reform. While platform commonalities included investment in information technology, particularly electronic medical records, and disease management, they revealed expected ideological party differences on the relative roles of the competitive marketplace and the government. The Obama plan that will serve as a starting point for reform discussions targets expanding insurance coverage; a variety of individual and small business subsidies; expanded eligibility for public, means-tested programs; and increased federal regulation of private insurance (Antos, Wilensky, and Kuttner 2008; Pauly 2008). Ultimately the success of ongoing efforts at reform and anticipation of reform under the new federal administration will be measured by addressing the increasingly visible and persistent problem of the uninsured while at the same time achieving some measure of cost control, a factor notably underplayed in the Obama plan (Oberlander 2008).

Two other challenges deserve attention as policy makers and other stakeholders try to create a workable framework to improve access for the uninsured and cost efficiency. Major providers in the health care system, especially doctors and nurses, have significant responsibilities not only in improving quality of care through evi-denced-based practices, but also in taking on expanded professional roles in serving the public in their relationships with patients and more broadly in enhancing popu-lation health (Mechanic 2000; Mechanic and Reinhard 2002; Stevens 2001). Another challenge focuses clearly on a twenty-first-century issue. Global economies and the interdependence among the world's population have resulted in a rise in pandemics, the spread of new and old infectious diseases, and rising rates of chronic illnesses with grave warning signs of the increasing global burden of disease. Those in our health care system have a moral imperative as well as a self-interest in contributing to reducing the spread of disease that threatens all populations (Benatar 2001). The challenges that face the United States in reforming its health care system involve not only internal issues, but increasingly also those of an interdependent world of nations. Below, we describe the five major challenges that policy makers and other stakeholders face in their efforts to reform the American health care system.

Challenge 1
Controlling costs: Health care spending in a comparative perspective

For a very short period of time in the mid-1990s, a slowing in the growth of health care expenditures occurred between 1993 and 1996 as health care's share of the GDP fluctuated between 13.5 and 13.7 percent, an unexpected plateau given the previous trend and predictions at the start of the decade (Smith et al. 1999). The decline in health expenditure growth as a share of GDP was also accompanied by increases in the GDP. In this time period the average annual growth in health spending was 3.3 percent for the private sector and 7.1 percent for public spending. Tighter constraints on Medicare payment rates associated with the Balanced Budget Act of 1997 also resulted in declines in the rate of growth of spending in the Medi-care program (Smith et al. 1999). The control of health care costs that might have resulted from the more stringent practices under managed care was short-lived. Typically, cost reductions resulted from imposing lower rates of reimbursement for physicians, hospitals, other providers, and services. Utilization reviews limited use of technology and access to some services. Once restrictive managed care practices were eliminated, health care costs increased. A steep rise in health care costs occurred during the 1996 to 2001 period (Strunk and Ginsburg 2003). The experi-ence with managed care and the later retreat from some of its restrictive strategies did not produce a long-term mechanism for containing the rising costs of health care in the United States (Reinhardt, Hussey, and Anderson 2004).

All industrialized countries have encountered escalating health care costs, and various forms of rationing, however openly discussed, have helped slow growth in health expenditures cross-nationally (Mechanic 1999). Yet, the latest figures for 2006 show the United States still continuing to spend a substantially greater share of its GDP (15.3 percent) on health than the median (8.9 percent) for the OECD countries (OECD 2008). Furthermore, in comparison with these countries, per capita health spending continued to diverge substantially between the United States ($6,714) and the OECD countries ($2,824) for the same time period (OECD 2008; White 2007). Multiple factors are associated with the rising costs of health care in the United States. Recent reviews of the causes show that the adoption and diffusion of medical technology contributed most importantly to spending increases over time with other factors such as the aging of the population playing a less important role (Congressional Budget Office 2007; Ginsburg 2008). Effectiveness is not always demonstrated in the use of technology, and it is questionable whether and when benefits accrue in the broad use of technology. Other factors that have been associated with rising health care costs include administrative costs across a complex system of payers, defensive medicine by practitioners, increasing expectations by consumers for more treatments, overuse of treatments and inappropriate care, increasing rates of obesity, and medicalization of more problems (Congressional Budget Office 2007; Ginsburg 2008; Mechanic 2006).

A host of troubling issues arises with escalating health care costs. There are higher premiums for workers, workers are less likely to buy into insurance coverage, employers decide to restrict benefit designs or not to offer coverage, and higher out-of-pocket costs prompt individuals to use health care services only when ill. As health care premiums increase, the uninsured population also rises (Oberlander 2008).

The question at the center of the current controversy in the United States is how to provide greater access for the uninsured population and assure quality of care within the context of what the federal and state governments, employers, and consumers are willing to pay. A growing federal deficit, constrained state budgets, and rising unemployment place the health care system in the United States under great stress. A political will among various stakeholder groups is needed to undertake the reforms needed to address cost control in the context of one of the most pressing concerns in the health care system, the rising number of uninsured individuals (Mechanic 2006).

Challenge 2
The rising uninsured population

The most recent estimate from the Census Bureau's 2007 Current Population Survey was that 47 million people or 15.8 percent of the population had no health insurance in 2006, an increase of about 3.7 million people since 1997 (United States Department of Commerce 2007). Employer-sponsored health insurance remains the largest source of health insurance coverage and covers 59.7 percent of the population, a decline from 60.2 percent in 2005. As fewer employees are covered by their employer-sponsored health insurance, the number of uninsured is increasing. Approximately 27 percent of the population were covered by government-sponsored insurance in 2006.

Several specific population groups characterize the uninsured population. The highest uninsured rate (29.3 percent) of any age group is disproportionately aged 18 to 24 years old and has a family income below $25,000. But 38 percent of the uninsured also have family incomes above $50,000. Although the number of uninsured children has been declining since 1998, the percentage of uninsured children under 18 years of age rose from 10.9 percent in 2005 to 11.7 percent in 2006 (United States Department of Commerce 2007). Those of Hispanic origin have the highest rate of being uninsured (34 percent) within racial and ethnic groups. Among the Black population, 20 percent lacked health insurance for a full year. In general, not having insurance declined as educational level increased, but among the poor, no differences in uninsurance rates exist across educational levels. Further, among the poor, workers were less likely to be insured than non-workers, creating a growing pool of uninsured workers (i.e., approximately one-half or 47.5 percent of poor, full-time workers in 1998). Workers employed by smaller firms (with fewer than 25 employees) were least likely to be insured (Cooper and Schone 1997; Ginsburg, Gabel, and Hunt 1998; Kronick and Gilmer 1999).

The decline in the number of Americans with health insurance appears to be linked to increases in health care spending relative to real family income (Custer 1999; Kronick and Gilmer 1999). As personal health care costs consumed a larger portion of personal and family budgets, health insurance premiums and the proportion of premiums paid by employees became less affordable. Nine million people lost employer-sponsored health insurance during the economic downturn of 2001 to 2003, but declines continued between 2003 and 2004 when the economy began to grow, suggesting the influence of both premium costs and labor market tightness (Reschovsky, Strunk, and Ginsburg 2006).

One of the major legislative efforts to address the growing number of uninsured is directed to children through the State Children's Health Insurance Program (SCHIP), enacted as part of the Balanced Budget Act of 1997. The program has been a federal–state government partnership that gives considerable discretion to the states in implementing the program. SCHIP provides three options for increasing affordable insurance coverage to low-income, uninsured children in working families who earn too much to be insured through the Medicaid program but whose income is insufficient to afford private coverage. The options include designing a new children's health insurance program, expanding the current state Medicaid programs, or introducing a combination of both strategies.

Unlike the rising rates of the uninsured among adults, the numbers of uninsured children have decreased substantially as a result of SCHIP legislation. Ambiguities in the legislation and conflicting state policy agendas hampered initial enrollment and implementation (Halfon et al. 1999; Rosenbaum 1998), but over a ten-year period the number of uninsured low-income children in the United States has declined by approximately one-third (Kenney and Yee 2007). Over the past few years, however, uninsured rates among children have reached a plateau in some states as outreach and enrollment efforts declined with states facing budget shortfalls. The erosion in employer-sponsored health insurance may have also resulted in a growing number of uninsured children.

Outcome studies have shown that access to health care for children has improved, although the impact of SCHIP on discrete measures of health such as immunization rates, asthmatic attacks, and quality of life measures have been mixed. The SCHIP program also faces some major hurdles in the near future. Currently, SCHIP is operating under an extension that expires in March 2009, and the Bush administration resisted expanding income eligibility for the program above 250 percent of the federal poverty level. The new administration is likely to extend SCHIP authorization and possibly overturn restrictions on income eligibility. An individual mandate for children also has some likelihood. If the states are given opportunities to expand the SCHIP program, the major uncertainty is whether they will have the revenue and resources to implement far-reaching or even modest changes.

Among at least 39 states and the District of Columbia enacting laws since 2006 to improve access, quality, and costs (McDonough, Miller, and Barber 2008) has been the highly visible Massachusetts health reform law to provide basic health coverage for the state's uninsured residents. Passed in 2006, this legislation involved a "shared responsibility" among the stakeholders including the uninsured, businesses, and government that resulted in both an individual mandate and employer ("pay or play approach") requirements (Altman and Doonan 2006). Several major strategies have been used to reduce the number of uninsured residents and make insurance more affordable, including expanding eligibility in the state's Medicaid program, publicly paid coverage for all residents with incomes below 100 percent of the poverty level, government subsidies to help individuals with incomes between 100 percent to 300 percent of the poverty level to buy insurance, and establishing a quasi-public independent authority, the Commonwealth Health Insurance Connector, to connect people and small businesses with certified private health insurance plans. Businesses employing more than ten people and not providing health insurance are also assessed fees for subsidizing their care.

Early results show success in reducing the estimated 650,000 uninsured by 50 percent and an increase in the number of individuals with employer-based coverage (Kaiser Commission on Medicaid and the Uninsured 2008). The problems with the Massachusetts health reform have been higher than expected cost increases that are likely to result in employers dropping coverage because of premium increases and unsustainable costs to state government through the expansion in Medicaid and subsidies for the near poor. Diminishing tax revenues will also result from rising unemployment (Woolhandler and Himmelstein 2006).

Beyond the serious financing concerns for state health reforms is how the federal government will participate and partner with the states in sustaining the reforms (McDonough et al. 2008). Without federal leadership and a coherent national strategy the problems of access, quality, and costs facing the American health care system are not likely to be addressed successfully. National standards that create uniformity across the states are also needed in areas of program administration and regulation for well-functioning health care systems (Weil 2008).

Challenge 3
The call for a "new professionalism" for physicians and its reception among entering cohorts

As the organization and financing of health care have changed in the United States, so has the practice of medicine been transformed in significant ways. Starr (1982) predicted that the coming of corporate medicine and the financial behavior of large corporations in the 1980s would threaten the autonomy and power of the medical profession. As Figure 18.1 indicates, the relative authority of physicians declined in the era of managed care, but unknown is whether, how, and if this loss of authority will plateau, be reversed, or continue downward (see dotted lines). While the various strategies of managed care are no longer in place, physicians still encounter many of its controls. Representatives in organizations beyond physicians dictate the process of referrals, certify admission and discharge decisions, profile the services that physicians use, and recommend services. Managed care organizations establish the networks in which physicians operate and from which clients seek care. Treatment guidelines have been established in an effort to standardize care and reduce variations in practice that can limit the independent decision-making of physicians. Physicians may be dropped from networks and health plans if they are not performing to standards set by the MCO. Some treatments that were previously provided by physicians are now also assumed by other health professionals. All of these changes remove power over medical care from the physician and transfer it to others.

The significant change has not been the sole introduction of financial considerations in client–provider relationships. Financial incentives have always existed for physicians in their medical work beyond even the early forms of pre-paid practices where physicians were paid a salary or a capitated fee to provide necessary medical services. The medical profession has portrayed itself as having erected a wall between money and medicine. Although the professional ideology has been that "doctors' decisions and recommendations were dictated by the best interests of the patient and by science and distinctly not by the pecuniary interests of the doctor" (Stone 1997), the reality has always been much more complicated from this idealized conception of professional practice (Pescosolido and Martin 2004).

With frustration and dissatisfaction among physicians over their loss of authority in clinical decision-making and in the ethical dilemmas they face in balancing financial incentives with the best interests of patients (Grumbach et al. 1998; Hadley et al. 1999), physicians still have much credibility with their patients (Pescosolido et al. 2001). Yet, with the erosion of autonomy, fairness issues in remuneration, public criticism of the profession, and troubling issues of disparities within the health care system, discussions about a reassertion of medical professionalism have arisen. "Responsive medical professionalism" (Frankford and Konrad 1998) has brought attention to the potential of physicians, especially given the loyalty of their patients, to recapture levels of leadership, albeit in different ways than under the era of professional dominance. Mechanic (2000) calls for a "new professional ethic" in the education and socialization of physicians. The most important elements of this new professionalism include responsible and just patient advocacy, collaboration with public health practitioners in assuming more responsibility for population health, forging new partnerships and collaborations with patients as they take on a greater role in treatment decisions, and increased participation in an evidenced-based culture. Significant impediments exist to realizing these changes for organized medicine and, as Hafferty and Castellani (forthcoming) among others have noted, the current cohort of medical students appears less than enthusiastic about engaging in a new professionalism.

Achieving medical excellence in the quality and effectiveness of care requires accepting an expanded role for patients in decision-making, sensitivity to their preferences, and physician knowledge and use of evidenced-based practices. A shared balance of power would exist under the new medical professionalism with a collaboration of physicians, other health care professionals in public–private partnerships, consumers, and MCOs.

Challenge 4
Crafting health care reform in cultural context

As Ruggie (forthcoming) points out, the United States has much to learn from the experiences of other countries. But, wisely, she points to the limits of a naïve view that extols the virtues of other systems and advocates for wholesale adoption of their programs, policies, and reforms. Although similar pressures exist for health care systems from rising costs, aging populations, and the increased burden of diseases, providers and policy makers across countries confront different local pressures. The implicit social contract between the state, physicians, other providers, employers, insurers, and consumers places critical limits on policy decisions. Public support for health care system change reflects current economic and demographic challenges. However, they tend to cluster more directly around the history and tradition of the countries' health care arrangements (Kikuzawa, Olafsdottir, and Pescosolido 2008). That is, in countries where the nation-state directly provides health care, whether the government exerts a little (the National Health Service Model; e.g., Norway, Italy, Spain) or a great deal of control (the Centralized Model of Health Care Delivery; e.g., Latvia, Russia, Slovenia), citizens are more supportive of government intervention in health care compared to countries where the state's role is limited to maintaining the health care system (the Insurance Model, e.g., Japan, Germany, US). This historical legacy must also confront current levels of spending and health outcomes. In those countries where most is spent and where the outcomes are relatively poorer, citizens are relatively less supportive of the government's role. However, the impact of these two factors pales in comparison to the historical trajectory that shapes the political climate in which reform is undertaken.

Despite similar pressures on health care systems around the world, public pressure within countries places limits on acceptable change. Stakeholder expectations will likely result in different paths to reform, producing policies shaped by the interplay of the sociohistorical institutional arrangements, the nature of pressures on the health care system, and the profile of individuals' needs and expectations.

Challenge 5
Facing threats to global health

In an increasingly interdependent world, the transmission of both infectious and chronic illnesses threatens the population health of all countries. With the growth of foreign travel and markets for international food and other products and services, diseases can spread rapidly throughout the world, resulting in high morbidity and mortality rates. A global influenza pandemic is a grave and inevitable infectious disease threat, and even a mild pandemic is expected to result in the loss of millions of lives (Osterholm 2005). Newer and emerging diseases that pose significant threats of global proportions include the recent "swine flu" strain (H1N1), severe acute respiratory syndrome (SARS), the avian influenza virus strain (H5N1), and the Marburg virus, while malaria, tuberculosis, and HIV/AIDS continue to afflict populations in many regions of the world.

There is substantial evidence that the research and technology for preparing for a pandemic (e.g., limited production capacity for vaccines) as well as the multinational commitment and planning to addressing the global health challenge fall far short of what is required (Osterholm 2005; Sandman and Lanard 2005). Beyond these severe limitations in production and management are two relevant issues for sociologists. First, while the growing economies of the world have generated considerable wealth enhancing the lives of many people, at the same time the income gap between the rich and poor has widened throughout the world. Incredible poverty and malnutrition are associated with many of the old as well as new diseases that disproportionately affect the poor. The relationship between socioeconomic status and health and mortality is well established (Benatar 2001; Mechanic 2002; Wilkinson 1996). Second, the social values and distribution of wealth and power that have shaped health care systems throughout the world and the profession of medicine have not been mobilized to respond effectively to the growing burden of disease (Benatar 2001). Scientific progress and advances in technology have not been matched by sufficient improvements in health care access to preventive and life-saving treatments.

The interdependence of the world creates conditions for widening the spread of old and new infectious diseases into pandemics and ill health and reduced functioning from chronic diseases. The gravity of these global problems has been documented for several years, but the priorities in health care spending, research, and treatment and services have not matched the threats (Benatar 2001).

Conclusion: Where to Now?

Health care reform is once again near the top of the political agenda in the United States. Organizational and financial changes continue to be made, especially at the state level, with over 75 percent of states and the District of Columbia recently enacting laws in one or more areas of access, quality, and costs and with 15 of these states enacting comprehensive reform or starting the process (McDonough et al. 2008). Whether broad changes at the federal level will be made under the new administration that took office in January 2009 is uncertain given federal and state budgetary constraints and the role of interest group politics.

From a comparative perspective, the United States, as well as other countries with very different health care systems, continue to search for strategies to contain costs, provide access to high-quality and effective care, manage care for chronic illnesses and disabilities and the treatment of old and new infectious diseases, and reconfigure new professional roles and responsibilities. Although the various health care systems of the world operate under different organizing principles and evolve from unique political and social cultures, economic climates, and the roles of professional groups, many fundamental problems and challenges exist cross-nationally. The stakeholders in the American health care system, including medical leaders, can benefit greatly from sharing strategies and learning from what is happening beyond its borders. Giving a higher priority to global health issues in partnership with other nations will also benefit the United States as well as other countries.

References

Altman, Stuart H. and Michael Doonan. 2006. "Can Massachusetts Lead the Way in Health Care Reform?" *New England Journal of Medicine* 354: 2093–5.

Antos, Joseph, Gail Wilensky, and Hanns Kuttner. 2008. "The Obama Plan: More Regulation, Unsustainable Spending." *Health Affairs* 27(6): w462–w471.

Benatar, Solomon R. 2001. "The Coming Catastrophe in International Health." *International Journal* 61: 611–31.

Berlant, Jeffrey. 1975. *Profession and Monopoly: A Study of Medicine in the United States and Great Britain*. Berkeley: University of California Press.

Blendon, Robert J., Mollyann Brodie, John M. Benson, Drew E. Altman, Larry Levitt, Tina Hoff, and Larry Hugick. 1998. "Understanding the Managed Care Backlash." *Health Affairs* 17: 80–94.

Brown, E. Richard. 1979. *Rockefeller Medicine Men: Medicine and Capitalism in America*. Berkeley: University of California Press.

Center for Studying Health System Change. 2002. *Navigating a Changing Health System, 2001 Annual Report*. Washington, DC: Health System Change. Retrieved December 8, 2004 (www.hschange.com/CONTENT/452).

Clarke, Adele and Janet Shim. Forthcoming. "Medicalization and Biomedicalization Revisited: Technoscience and Transformations of Health and Illness." In Bernice A. Pescosolido, Jack K. Martin, Jane D. McLeod, and Anne Rogers (eds.), *The Handbook of the Sociology of Health, Illness, and Healing*. New York: Springer.

Collins, Randall. 1979. *The Credential Society*. New York: Academic Press.

Congressional Budget Office. 2007. *The Long-Term Outlook for Health Care Spending*. Washington, DC: Congressional Budget Office.

Cooper, Philip F. and Barbara S. Schone. 1997. "More Offers, Fewer Takers for Employment-Based Health Insurance: 1987 and 1996." *Health Affairs* 16: 103–10.

Custer, William S. 1999. "Health Insurance Coverage and the Uninsured." *A Report to the Health Insurance Association of America*. Washington, DC: Health Insurance Association of America.

Domhoff, G. William. 1996. *State Autonomy or Class Dominance? Case Studies on Policy Making in America*. New York: Aldine.

Draper, Debra A., Robert E. Hurley, Cara S. Lesser, and Bradley C. Strunk. 2002. "The Changing Face of Managed Care." *Health Affairs* 21: 11–23.

Enthoven, Alain C. 1978. "Consumer-Choice Health Plan: Inflation and Inequity in Health Care Today: Alternatives for Cost Control and an Analysis of Proposals for National Health Insurance." *New England Journal of Medicine* 298: 650–85.

Frankford, David M. and Thomas R. Konrad. 1998. "Responsive Medical Professionalism: Integrating Education, Practice and Community in a Market-Driven Era." *Academic Medicine* 73: 138–45.

Freidson, Eliot. 1970. *Professional Dominance*. New York: Atherton Press.

Freudenheim, Milt. 1999. "Big HMO to Give Decisions on Care Back to Doctors." *New York Times*, November 9, pp. A1, C8.

Ginsburg, Paul B. 2008. *High and Rising Health Care Costs: Demystifying US Health Care Spending*. Princeton, NJ: Robert Wood Johnson Foundation.

Ginsburg, Paul B., Jon R. Gabel, and Kelly A. Hunt. 1998. "Tracking Small-Firm Coverage, 1989–1996." *Health Affairs* 17: 167–71.

Gold, Marsha R. 1997. "Markets and Public Programs: Insights from Oregon and Tennessee." *Journal of Health Politics, Policy, and Law* 22: 633–6.

Gold, Marsha R. 1998. "Understanding the Roots: Health Maintenance Organizations in Historical Context." Pp. 7–16 in Marsha R. Gold (ed.), *Contemporary Managed Care: Readings in Structure, Operations, and Public Policy*. Chicago: Health Administration Press.

Grumbach, Kevin, Dennis Osmond, Karen Vranizan, Deborah Jaffe, and Andrew B. Bindman. 1998. "Primary Care Physicians' Experience of Financial Incentives in Managed-Care Systems." *New England Journal of Medicine* 339: 1516–21.

Hadley, Jack, Jean M. Mitchell, Daniel P. Sulmasy, and M. Gregg Bloche. 1999. "Perceived Financial Incentives, HMO Market Penetration, and Physicians' Practice Styles and Satisfaction." *Health Services Research* 34: 307–19.

Hafferty, Frederick W. and Brian Castellani. Forthcoming. "Two Cultures – Two Ships: The Rise of a Professionalism Movement within Modern Medicine and Medical Sociology's Disappearance from the Professionalism Debate." In Bernice A. Pescosolido, Jack K. Martin, Jane D. McLeod, and Anne Rogers (eds.), *The Handbook of the Sociology of Health, Illness, and Healing*. New York: Springer.

Halfon, Neil, Moira Inkelas, Helen DuPlessis, and Paul W. Newacheck. 1999. "Challenges in Securing Access to Care for Children." *Health Affairs* 18: 48–63.

Higgins, A. Foster. 1991. *Health Care Benefits Survey*, vol. 1. New Jersey: Health Care Benefits Survey. *Journal of Health Politics, Policy and Law*. 1999. Special Issue. "The Managed Care Backlash." 24: 873–1218.

Kaiser Commission on Medicaid and the Uninsured. 2008. *Massachusetts Health Care Reform: Two Years Later*. Washington, DC: The Henry J. Kaiser Family Foundation.

Kenney, Genevieve and Justin Yee. 2007. "SCHIP at a Crossroads: Experiences to Date and Challenges Ahead." *Health Affairs* 26: 356–69.

Kikuzawa, Saeko, Sigrun Olafsdottir, and Bernice A. Pescosolido. 2008. "Similar Pressures, Different Contexts: Public Attitudes toward Government Intervention for Health Care in 21 Nations." *Journal of Health and Social Behavior* 49: 385–99.

Kronick, Richard and Todd Gilmer. 1999. "Explaining the Decline in Health Insurance Coverage, 1979–1995." *Health Affairs* 18: 30–47.

Light, Donald. 1995. "Countervailing Powers: A Framework for Professions in Transition." Pp. 25–41 in Terry Johnson, Gerald Larking, and Mike Saks (eds.), *Health Professions and the State in Europe*. London: Routledge.

Light, Donald and Sol Levine. 1988. "The Changing Character of the Medical Profession: A Theoretical Overview." *Milbank Quarterly* 66 (Supplement): 10–32.

Ludmerer, Kenneth M. 1999. *Time to Heal: American Medical Education from the Turn of the Century to the Era of Managed Care*. New York: Oxford University Press.

Mays, Glen P., Gary Claxton, and Justin White. 2004. "MarketWatch: Managed Care Rebound? Recent Changes in Health Plans' Cost Containment Strategies." *Health Affairs*, Web Exclusive. Retrieved August 11, 2004 (content.healthaffairs.org).

McDonough, John E., Michael Miller, and Christine Barber. 2008. "A Progress Report on State Health Access Reform." *Health Affairs*, Web Exclusive. Retrieved January 29, 2008 (content.healthaffairs.org).

McKinlay, John B. and Lisa D. Marceau. 2002. "The End of the Golden Age of Doctoring." *International Journal of Health Services* 32(2): 379–417.

Mechanic, David. 1999. "Lessons from Abroad: A Comparative Perspective." Pp. 25–34 in Francis Powell and Albert Wesson (eds.), *Health Care Systems in Transition: An International Perspective*. Newbury Park, CA: Sage.

Mechanic, David. 2000. "Managed Care and the Imperative for A New Professional Ethic." *Health Affairs* 19: 100–11.

Mechanic, David. 2002. "Disadvantage, Inequality, and Social Policy. *Health Affairs* 21: 48–59.

Mechanic, David. 2004. "The Rise and Fall of Managed Care." *Journal of Health and Social Behavior* 45: 76–86.

Mechanic, David. 2006. *The Truth About Health Care: Why Reform Is Not Working in America.* New Brunswick, NJ: Rutgers University Press.

Mechanic, David. 2008. *Mental Health and Social Policy: Beyond Managed Care,* 5th edition. Boston: Allyn and Bacon.

Mechanic, David and Susan C. Reinhard. 2002. "Contributions of Nurses to Health Policy: Challenges and Opportunities." *Nursing and Health Policy Review* 1: 7–15.

Mechanic, David and Mark Schlesinger. 1996. "The Impact of Managed Care on Patients' Trust in Medical Care and Their Physicians." *Journal of the American Medical Association* 275: 1693–7.

Mechanic, David, Mark Schlesinger, and Donna D. McAlpine. 1995. "Management of Mental Health and Substance Abuse Services: State of the Art and Early Results." *Milbank Quarterly* 73: 19–55.

Miller, Robert H. and Harold S. Luft. 1994. "Managed Care Plan Performance Since 1980: A Literature Analysis." *Journal of the American Medical Association* 271: 1512–19.

Miller, Robert H. and Harold S. Luft. 1997. "Does Managed Care Lead to Better or Worse Quality of Care?" *Health Affairs* 16: 7–25.

Miller, Robert H. and Harold S. Luft. 2002. "HMO Plan Performance Update: An Analysis of the Literature, 1997–2001." *Health Affairs* 21: 63–86.

Nelson, David E., Betsy L. Thompson, Nancy J. Davenport, and Linda J. Penaloza. 2000. "What People Really Know about Their Health Insurance: A Comparison of Information Obtained from Individuals and their Insurers." *American Journal of Public Health* 90: 924–8.

Oberlander, Jonathan. 2008. "The Politics of Paying for Health Reform: Zombies, Payroll Taxes, and the Holy Grail." *Health Affairs* 27(6): w544–w555.

Organization for Economic Cooperation and Development (OECD). 2008. *OECD Health Data 2008: Statistics and Indicators for 30 Countries.* Paris: Organization for Economic Cooperation and Development.

Osterholm, Michael T. 2005. "Preparing for the Next Pandemic." *New England Journal of Medicine* 352: 1839–42.

Pauly, Mark V. 2008. "Blending Better Ingredients for Health Reform." *Health Affairs* 27(6): w482–w491.

Pescosolido, Bernice A. and Carol A. Boyer. 2001. "The American Health Care System: Entering the 21st Century with High Risk, Major Challenges and Great Opportunities." Pp. 180–98 in W. C. Cockerham (ed.), *The Blackwell Companion to Medical Sociology.* Oxford: Blackwell.

Pescosolido, Bernice A. and Jennie J. Kronenfeld. 1995. "Sociological Understandings of Health, Illness, and Healing: The Challenge from and for Medical Sociology."*Journal of Health and Social Behavior* (Extra Issue): 5–33.

Pescosolido, Bernice A. and Jack K. Martin. 2004. "Cultural Authority and the Sovereignty of American Medicine: The Role of Networks, Class, and Community." *Journal of Health Politics, Policy, and Law* 29(4–5): 735–56.

Pescosolido, Bernice A., Jane D. McLeod, and Margarita Alegría. 2000. "Confronting the Second Social Contract: The Place of Medical Sociology in Research and Policy for the

21st Century." Pp. 411–26 in Chloe Bird, Peter Conrad, and Allen Fremont (eds.), *The Handbook of Medical Sociology*, 5th edition. Upper Saddle River, NJ: Prentice-Hall.

Pescosolido, Bernice A. and Beth A. Rubin. 2000. "The Web of Group Affiliations Revisited: Social Life, Postmodernism and Sociology." *American Sociological Review* 65: 52–76.

Pescosolido, Bernice A., Stephen A. Tuch, and Jack K. Martin. 2001. "The Profession of Medicine and the Public: Examining Americans' Changing Confidence in Physician Authority from the Beginning of the 'Health Care Crisis' to the Era of Health Care Reform." *Journal of Health and Social Behavior* 42 (March): 1–16.

Quadagno, Jill. 2006. *One Nation, Uninsured: Why the US Has No National Health Insurance*. New York: Oxford University Press.

Reinhardt, Uwe E., Peter S. Hussey, and Gerard F. Anderson. 2004. "US Health Care Spending in An International Context." *Health Affairs* 23: 10–25.

Relman, Arnold S. 1993. "Controlling Costs by 'Managed Competition' – Would It Work?" *New England Journal of Medicine* 328: 133–5.

Reschovsky, James D., Bradley C. Strunk, and Paul Ginsburg. 2006. "Why Employer-Sponsored Insurance Coverage Changed, 1997–2003." *Health Affairs* 25: 774–82.

Robinson, James C. 2001. "The End of Managed Care." *Journal of the American Medical Association* 285: 2622–8.

Rodwin, Marc A. 1995. "Conflicts in Managed Care." *New England Journal of Medicine* 332: 604–7.

Rosen, George. 1963. "The Hospital." Pp. 1–36 in Eliot Freidson (ed.), *The Hospital in Modern Society*. New York: Free Press.

Rosenbaum, Sara. 1998. "The Children's Hour: The State Children's Health Insurance Program." *Health Affairs* 17: 75–89.

Rubin, Beth A. 1996. *Shifts in the Social Contract*. Thousand Oaks, CA: Pine Forge Press.

Ruggie, Mary. Forthcoming. "Learning from Other Countries: Comparing Experiences and Drawing Lessons for the United States." In Bernice A. Pescosolido, Jack K. Martin, Jane D. McLeod, and Anne Rogers (eds.), *The Handbook of the Sociology of Health, Illness, and Healing*. New York: Springer.

Sandman Peter M. and Jody Lanard. 2005. "Pandemic Influenza Risk Communication: The Teachable Moment." Retrieved from www.psandman.com/col/pandemic.htm.

Skocpol, Theda. 1997. *Boomerang: Health Care Reform and the Turn Against Government*. New York: North.

Smith, Sheila, Stephen Heffler, Mark Freeland, and the National Health Expenditures Projection Team. 1999. "The Next Decade of Health Spending: A New Outlook." *Health Affairs* 18: 86–95.

Starr, Paul. 1982. *The Social Transformation of American Medicine*. New York: Basic Books.

Stevens, Rosemary A. 2001. "Public Roles for the Medical Profession in the United States: Beyond Theories of Decline and Fall." *Milbank Quarterly* 79: 327–53.

Stone, Deborah A. 1997. "The Doctor as Businessman: The Changing Politics of a Cultural Icon." *Journal of Health Politics, Policy and Law* 22: 533–56.

Strunk, Bradley C. and Paul B. Ginsburg. 2003. "Tracking Health Care Costs: Trends Stabilize But Remain High in 2002." *Health Affairs*, Web Exclusive. Retrieved June 11, 2003 (content.healthaffairs.org).

Strunk, Bradley C., Paul B. Ginsburg, and Jon Gabel. 2001. "Tracking Health Care Costs." *Health Affairs*, Web Exclusive. Retrieved September 26, 2001 (content.healthaffairs.org).

United States Department of Commerce, Bureau of the Census. 2007. *Income, Poverty, and Health Insurance Coverage in the United States: 2006*. Washington, DC: Department of Commerce.

Unschuld, Paul. 1976. "Western Medicine and Traditional Healing Systems: Competition, Cooperation, or Integration?" *Ethics in Science and Medicine* 3: 1–20.

Ware, John E., Martha S. Bayliss, William H. Rogers, Mark Kosinski, and Alvin R. Tarlov. 1996. "Differences in 4-Year Health Outcomes for Elderly and Poor Chronically Ill Patients Treated in HMO and Fee-for-Service Systems." *Journal of the American Medical Association* 276: 1039–47.

Weil, Alan. 2008. "How Far Can States Take Health Reform?" *Health Affairs* 27: 736–47.

White, Chapin. 2007. "Health Care Spending Growth: How Different is the United States from the Rest of the OECD?" *Health Affairs* 26: 154–61.

Wickizer, Thomas M., Daniel Lessler, and Jodie Boyd-Wickizer. 1999. "Readmissions among Children and Adolescents." *American Journal of Public Health* 89: 1353–8.

Wilkinson Richard G. 1996. *Unhealthy Societies: The Afflictions of Inequality*. London: Routledge.

Woolhandler, Steffie and David U. Himmelstein. 2006. "The New Massachusetts Health Reform: Half a Step Forward and Three Steps Back." *Hastings Center Report* 36: 19–21.

Zelman, Walter A. 1996. *The Changing Health Care Marketplace*. San Francisco: Jossey-Bass.

19

The British Health Care System*

Michael Bury

Two terms in the title of this chapter require an introductory comment. The first concerns the reference to the *British* health care system. Under conditions of devolved government, the constituent parts of the United Kingdom (England, Northern Ireland, Scotland, and Wales) have separate health care systems, albeit as parts of an overall National Health Service (NHS). The term *Britain* is often used in everyday language as a synonym for the United Kingdom. Most of the discussion in this chapter will refer to developments and policies in England and the English Department of Health (DoH), though similar arrangements or initiatives will sometimes be found in other parts of the system. The other issue lies in the term *health care system*. In most developed European countries, health care systems are socialized in character; that is, they rely on social insurance schemes in order to provide coverage for all citizens. The British system is different to the extent that it is a "universal" system, providing access for every citizen as a right, paid for out of taxation. Health care in Britain is free at the point of delivery, and nearly all of the hospitals and facilities of the NHS are owned by the state, with only a small private sector. As we shall see, however, this is a simplified picture of a rather complex and evolving pattern.

Health services in Britain, as in other developed countries, are going through a period of rapid change. The NHS constitutes one of the largest organizations to be found in any country. In 2007, it spent some £100 billion and employed over a million people, about 375,000 of whom were nurses (Buchan 2004). By contrast, the largest private company in Britain, in terms of people employed, Tesco, came a distant second: it had a turnover in 2007 of £46.6 billion and employed about 200,000 people. It is therefore unsurprising that attempts to develop and run a huge enterprise such as the NHS have been fraught with difficulty. Many different structures and interest groups are at work, and the "product" of the organization – health care – comes in many shapes and sizes. Attempts to fashion new working practices,

*This is a revised version of a chapter that appeared in David Wainwright (ed.), *A Sociology of Health* (Sage, 2008).

new funding arrangements, and introduce new relationships within the organization, often by a government operating with short-term political goals, raise, to say the least, complex issues.

In order to provide a workable focus for the chapter, two dimensions of the British health care system will be examined: the changing role of the medical profession and medical practice, and the role of patients and the public. Through examining these two dimensions, a number of features of the British system should become visible, including changes in the power of the medical profession, the growth of a more plural form of health care delivery, and the growth of managed consumerism in health care. What will also become clear is that the organization of the health care system in Britain has, to a degree, departed from a centrally organized NHS that is both state funded and state provided. While state funding remains important, local control of finances (through, for example, Foundation Trusts, which run hospitals and other services) and a more plural system of providers, including those from the private sector, have moved center stage. Paradoxically, many of the changes being promulgated by the British government that are aimed at loosening central control require strong political direction from the center.

THE CHANGING NATURE OF THE MEDICAL PROFESSION AND PRACTICE

At the time of the 2005 general election in the UK, the King's Fund (a London-based health policy think tank) was commissioned by the *Sunday Times* newspaper to draw up an NHS audit. This provided an overview of a range of changes in the NHS and attempted to assess whether their goals had been met. With some provisos, the answer was, largely yes. The audit noted that since the turn of the century, the Labour government had committed itself to raising the level of health care expenditure year by year, in order to reach 9 percent of GDP (around the European average) by 2008. In this the government has been on target, as has been the case with organizational issues such as reducing waiting times for services and increasing the numbers of doctors and nurses working in the system. Ten thousand more doctors, 20,000 more nurses, and 6,500 more therapists were apparently recruited into the service (King's Fund 2005). The audit also found that patient satisfaction with the NHS remained high overall, despite negative media stories. Regular large-scale surveys, by the Picker Institute, also report year-by-year improvements in patient satisfaction, with most if not all aspects of the system such as inpatient care (Picker Institute 2008).

Professional power and managerialism

Useful though such data are in keeping a sense of perspective of developments in the health services, they cannot tell us much about the changing relationships that are accompanying the British government's attempts to fashion what it often refers to as health care "reform." For example, though targets such as shorter waiting times can bring about real benefits to some patients, they may be at the expense of others, whose need may be greater but who do not yet pose a threat to the achievement of the target. Much public discussion and comment has focused on such contradictions and unintended consequences of health care "modernization." In particular, tensions between NHS managers, whose task it is to meet targets, and health care providers, who may have other priorities, are built into the system. Critics of the new NHS, such as Pollock, point to the conflicts that arise under these conditions. In the past, she argues, a professional medical ethos underpinned health care organization and management, but now a more entrepreneurial and "distinctly 'macho' management style" has come to the fore (Pollock 2004). For Pollock the shift from medical authority and expertise to management systems based on political decisions and top-down initiatives marks a break with planning to meet need. She argues that this is part of an attempt essentially to privatize the service, an issue to which the chapter returns below.

For the present purposes, it is the nature of social relations within the health care system that is of concern here, and especially the central position of the medical profession. In this respect, changes introduced under the Labour government's modernization agenda have continued those set in motion during the Thatcher years. Labour's modernizing intentions were set out soon after the 1997 election in a document entitled *The New NHS: Modern, Dependable* (DoH 1997). A raft of initiatives followed this initial statement. Over the years, the changes involved have sought progressively to give more power to managers and reduce the influence of senior doctors in decision-making and funding. Thus, treasury-driven policies may bypass resistance from the medical profession and be implemented directly by NHS managers. For example, managers have come under intense pressure to reduce costs and stay within their budgets, despite predictions of substantial deficits across the system (Mooney 2005). The failure to meet such goals on the part of managers could lead to the termination of their contracts, a matter far more difficult to achieve if senior hospital consultants were still in charge of hospital finances.

Having said this, the long-term decline in the influence and power of the medical profession in the health services (and the rise of managerialism) has been much debated. In the 1970s, medical sociology was strongly influenced by Eliot Freidson's thesis on the medical profession. This held that, in the US and other advanced health care systems such as that in Britain, the medical profession held sway. According to Freidson's approach to the professions, it was the degree of autonomy over work practices that provided the basis of medical power. This independence from scrutiny or regulation was then used and extended beyond the borders of medical practice. Insofar as the medical profession made *claims* to have jurisdiction over wide areas of life (labeling particular conditions as illness, for example) and over the forms and delivery of medical treatment, they were acting, according to Freidson, essentially on a moral terrain. That is, health, illness, and health care were seen as issues being decided by the medical profession alone, divorced from lay perspectives (Freidson 1988 [1970]). But for Freidson, the medical profession had no more right to decide on health-related issues than any other group in society. Medical knowledge and technical expertise should not, in this view, be used to underpin medical dominance over all matters to do with health and society. The special claims of the professional to have privileged status over health and health care were seen to be illegitimate and in need of challenge by the wider society.

In an afterword to the second edition of *Profession of Medicine*, Freidson noted changes in health care organization that had occurred since his first edition, which, he said, covered the "Golden Age" of medicine between 1945 and 1965. In particular, the rise of Medicare and Medicaid in the US, which provided state involvement in "paying the bills of the elderly and the poor," and of "large corporate employers" paying for medical insurance moved the center of gravity away from the medical profession. Even so, Freidson (1988 [1970]: 385) maintained that "the loss of extensive political influence and economic independence does not represent the loss of professionalism as I have described it." Whilst the loss of clinical freedom was "virtually complete," Freidson could see that all kinds of informal moves by the profession to evade constraints and maintain a high degree of control were always possible. One thinks today of doctors in the British context, despite the growth in the power of managers, working their way around waiting time targets and trying to assert clinical judgment against political interference. To the extent that such actions are successful, the loss of power by the medical profession may be more apparent than real. Freidson saw such power as being diffused throughout the profession and exercised in everyday practices, not simply being held or lost by a national unitary body.

Corporatization and globalization in health care

There are other factors that point to a more radical shift in the role of the medical profession in health care systems. Partly in debate with Freidson, McKinlay and Marceau (2002), for example, have argued that the external context of medical practice (in the US context, though much of what they say is applicable increasingly to Britain) marks a major break with the past. Most notably, they argue that "medical dominance" has now given way to "corporate dominance." Where once fee-for-service held sway in the US system, "increasingly concentrated and globalized financial and industrial interests" dominate (McKinlay and Marceau 2002: 381). These interests influence not only the financing of health care but also the way health care organizations are run and medicine practiced. Such practice takes on an increasingly assembly-line character, with the timing, type, and tempo of practice being monitored and regulated. Achieving targets and standardizing and costing treatments in the new NHS are in many respects similar matters of volume and throughput of activity characterized by such specifications.

McKinlay and Marceau make two other points that are relevant to the discussion here. One of these concerns an additional feature of the external environment: the increasingly globalized character of health care. In the US and in Britain the movement of medical personnel across national boundaries is becoming increasingly common. The European Union, for example, is providing greater opportunities for mobility of doctors between countries, subject to local licensing and training requirements. Press reports have been appearing of GPs flying into Britain from different parts of Europe to provide weekend cover. There are now several hundred registered doctors in Britain from France, Germany, and Italy alone. Clearly, such movements will tend to undermine the position of national professional bodies such as the British Medical Association, as individual doctors operate outside of their influence or control.

Additionally, globalization also means that health care corporations can operate on an increasingly international basis. Pollock makes the point that private health care companies are looking to increase their penetration into socialized health care systems such as exist in Europe. Pollock argues that a series of meetings of the World Trade Organization and the General Agreement on Trade in Services in the 1990s paved the way for expanding the range of services being put forward for private investment and competition (Pollock 2004: 61). Health care is one such service. Debates about the role of US companies such as the United Health Care group and its attempts to offer packages of care for the chronically ill to the NHS through a scheme called "Evercare" are only one example of a growing international trend in health care organization that can be seen to bypass medical jurisdiction (Mayor 2005; Smith 2003).

The second point made by McKinlay and Marceau concerns the increasing competition among health care workers. The rise of what in the US is often called "non-physician clinicians" (NPCs) – ranging from nurses through chiropractors and herbalists to optometrists and podiatrists – constitutes a major challenge to medical dominance. Even though the "overall pie" of health care, as these authors put it, is likely to increase, so too is the competition between doctors and NPCs. Cooper and Stoflet (2004) make the point that the rapid increase in NPCs raises critical issues concerning the quality of care. Of importance here, however, is their observation that the best results from NPC care tend to be at the less complex end of health care and when such workers are under the direction of a medical physician. In other words, although NPCs are on the rise (nurses' sphere of practice in particular is expanding rapidly), they may be operating in such a way as to offer limited challenges to medical dominance. Although a much more pluralistic health care system is likely to develop in countries such as Britain, as it has in the US, whether this constitutes a major plank in the reduction in the power of medicine, as McKinlay and Marceau seem to think, is open to debate.

From the foregoing discussion it is possible to see important processes at work in the new forms of health care organization appearing in countries such as Britain and the US. Most importantly, perhaps, the role of the medical profession is being transformed by the increase in bureaucratic and corporate pressures. Whilst the US system has adopted more "managed" forms of care, the British NHS has developed greater pluralism, in which private health care delivery will be increasingly evident (though still within the overall national system). It is important, however, not to see a simple process of convergence happening here. Despite changes in medical practice in the US, writers such as Wholey and Burns (2000) argue that these do not constitute moves toward the socialization of health care as a whole, if only because such managed care is not offered to uninsured populations. Similarly, though changes in health care organization in Britain (more aggressive management, stricter financial control, and target setting) offer major challenges to the former dominant position of the medical profession, the NHS remains a centrally funded system of care, with doctors still occupying a key role in the delivery of that care, in what Salter (2004) refers to as the "disposal of resources": deciding on tests, treatment options, discharge of patients, and the like. Nonetheless, changes in both systems are marked by a significant change in direction for the medical profession toward less clinical freedom and a reduction in power.

Before the chapter turns to related and perhaps contrasting changes occurring in the patient's role, there are two other aspects of the context of medical organization and practice that need briefly to be considered. Both are arguably central to understanding the pattern of health care organization in the current period.

Litigation and health care

The first of these is the change in the legal context of medical practice. It is clear that the protected status of medical practice, enjoyed within national systems such as the British NHS, has in the past reinforced the autonomy and authority of the medical profession. Whilst mistakes and errors may well have occurred, these were seen largely as internal matters. The public either accepted the situation or, more cynically, saw medicine as a "closed shop" in which the members – doctors – would protect one another. Unlike the US, litigation was rare in Britain, and the courts, let alone the police, were not likely to spend much time on medical matters.

During the 1980s and 1990s, claims for medical negligence began to spiral. A report from 2001 stated that in one English region alone, "clinical negligence claims increased by 72 percent between 1990 and 1998" (National Audit Office 2001). The report went on to say that, nationally, claims had doubled from £1.3 billion in 1996–7 to £2.6 billion in 1999–2000. These trends are a sign, the report stated, of an "increased litigiousness on the part of patients." Individual claims for conditions such as cerebral palsy, as the result of mistakes occurring at birth or shortly afterwards, can now amount to millions of pounds. The risk of having to pay such sums from health service budgets has to be anticipated in financial planning within local health care organizations.

More important, perhaps, from a sociological viewpoint is what this tells us about the changing nature of health care, and especially the position of doctors within the system. Having enjoyed special privileges, the profession is now exposed to potential criticism and censure on a regular basis. There is an added level of complexity as a result: the implications for medical care are not always those anticipated by the litigant. In 2005, for example, a leading pediatrician in Britain, Sir Roy Meadow, was struck off the medical register by the General Medical Council (GMC), which regulates medical practice in the UK. This followed the case of Sally Clark, who had been convicted of the murder of her two sons. Mrs. Clark's conviction was overturned in 2003 after a second appeal. The GMC ruled that Meadow's evidence in Mrs. Clark's trial (including statistical estimates of the probability that both children had suffered natural deaths) amounted to serious professional misconduct. The chairwoman of the GMC hearing told Meadow that his conduct had "undermined public confidence in doctors who play a pivotal role in the criminal justice system" (Dyer 2005). Whilst Mrs. Clark welcomed the verdict, Alan Craft, president of the Royal College of Paediatrics, argued that "there will be a huge knock-on effect on expert witnesses, both in child protection ... and right across the whole field of medicine" (Dyer 2005). A reduction in the privileged position of the medical profession may make them more accountable. But it may also have the unintended consequence of damaging positive aspects of the wider role that medical practitioners have carried out in the past, with widespread withdrawal from high-risk specialties (*Lancet* 2005). Meadow went on to win an appeal against the GMC's ruling in February 2006.

Regulation and accountability in the NHS

The second aspect of the organization and practice in health care that needs to be noted here concerns increasing regulation and monitoring, alongside accountability through litigation. The influence of scandal on health services is not confined to expert opinion offered in criminal trials. Britain has witnessed a stream of events in the last ten years or more that have led to increasing regulation. Two very different cases stand out. The first is the events surrounding a pediatric unit at Bristol Royal Infirmary in the 1980s where 29 deaths among children undergoing heart surgery were investigated. As a result, two doctors were struck off the medical register in 1998. An inquiry lasting three years, costing a reported £14 million and involving 577 witnesses and over 900,000 documents, made a host of recommendations and criticisms (DoH 2001). Secrecy and arrogance among doctors were particularly highlighted. The chairman of the inquiry, Sir Ian Kennedy, went on to set up and then chair the Healthcare Commission, whose role it is to "assess the performance of healthcare organisations, [and] award annual performance ratings" on behalf of the DoH (Healthcare Commission N.d.).

The other case that received enormous professional, policy, and public attention concerns the conduct of Dr. Harold Shipman, a general practitioner in Manchester, who was found guilty in July 2000 of murdering 15 of his elderly patients but who had probably killed over 200. After his conviction, inquiries were held into the circumstances surrounding his actions and recommendations were made for future medical practice (Shipman committed suicide in prison in January 2004). In response to this case and other inquiries into medical practice at the time, the Chief Medical Officer, Sir Liam Donaldson, received a report from the GMC in 2005 on new procedures for "clinical performance and medical regulation" (GMC 2005). Among a range of measures aimed at increasing public confidence in medical practice, the GMC stated that one of its main challenges was to "ensure the maintenance of national standards and principles of good practice at local level through effective appraisal and clinical governance mechanisms." Here, again, the autonomy of medical practitioners was being circumscribed by new organizational forms which aimed explicitly at limiting the ability of doctors to practice without formal oversight or accountability.

Linked to this process is the last aspect of the changing role of medical practice to be discussed here, namely, the advent of "evidence-based health care." Part of the "clinical governance" process is the setting of standards and the use of research evidence in the delivery of care in the NHS. Both of these processes mark a departure from the idea that the individual practitioner should be allowed, indeed encouraged, to use clinical judgment based on initial training and accumulated experience. Now, National Service Frameworks specify the content and form of care for a given area (cancer, older people, mental health) that aim to increase the quality of care and reduce variation. These frameworks are drawn up by "external reference groups" comprising professionals, patients, managers, and others. Under the auspices of the DoH, these reference groups then manage the process of implementation. The DoH sees such developments as a key feature of its modernization agenda, set in motion in the NHS Plan (DoH 2000).

From the more academic direction, evidence-based health care (EBHC) seeks to bring research evidence to bear on treatment decisions. Advocates of this approach, such as Sackett and colleagues (1996: 71), have argued that variations in treatment and the need to keep abreast of recent advances in research mean that doctors who employ "selective, efficient patient-driven searching, appraisal, and incorporation of the best available evidence can practice evidence-based medicine." In this way, these authors hope that EBHC will not be seen simply as an "ivory tower" initiative. Armstrong (2002) has pointed out that, in fact, EBHC can be seen not so much as an ivory tower activity than as a move by professional elites to demonstrate to governments their willingness to undertake internal regulation of their activities and embrace clinical governance more fully: that is, embracing a form of "scientific-bureaucratic" medicine (Harrison 2002). In this way, as with the GMC's recommendations, more severe regulation of practice and managerial control imposed from above may be minimized. In addition, as Rogers, Bury, and Kennedy (2009) point out, such processes reinforce the standardization and thus the costing of treatment modules.

Of course, as argued earlier, changes in the organization of care and medical practice do not mean that the position of doctors has lost all continuity with the past. As Hunter (2005) has pointed out, doctors retain a high degree of social standing. In seeking help for pain and distress, it is understandable that, despite a loss in public confidence in the medical profession, the authority of individual doctors remains high. It also has to be noted that despite much discussion of the loss of faith in the "grand narrative" of science, medical knowledge and technology retain a legitimacy that outweighs intermittent crises. If this were not the case, patients would not be presenting themselves for medical treatment in record numbers. The demand for medical care shows no sign of abatement. Thus, organizational change and political agendas may have profound effects on health care systems, but continuity as well as discontinuity needs to be recognized.

THE CHANGING POSITION OF THE PATIENT IN HEALTH CARE ORGANIZATION

The chapter now alters its angle of perception in order to examine contemporary health care organization from the patient vantage point. Against the background of what has been said so far, a number of key issues immediately come into view. These include: ideas currently being developed to base health care organization around the "needs of the patient"; the role of the patient *as* a patient and as a consumer in a system that increasingly emphasizes choice; the nature of "partnership" in health care and specifically in decision-making about treatment; initiatives to support self-care and especially the "Expert Patients Programme," in which responsibility for improvements in care shifts from professional providers to patients themselves. Each of these topics will be looked at in turn.

A patient-led NHS?

In a paper published in the *British Medical Journal* in 1998, Rogers, Entwistle, and Pencheon (1998: 1816) argue that "the model of health care in which knowledge-able and skilful doctors make decisions on behalf of patients is being increasingly criticised, and more patient centred models of care in which patients play an impor-tant role in decisions about their treatment are becoming the norm." Such new models of health care, these authors argue, should be based on the actions already being taken by lay people in the community. Self-care, the processing of appropri-ate and culturally sensitive information, and decisions about seeking professional help should all, they argue, be the bedrock of the health care system. In this way, "encouraging demand" for some forms of professional health care can be balanced with "promoting self-care for other problems" (Rogers et al. 1998: 1816). The overall effect would be to deal with growing demand in the NHS with a form of "graduated access," where alternative sources of help (self-help groups, helplines, and so on) would link informal systems with more formal ones. This graduated approach would restructure health care organization in ways "that are sensitive to people's needs and acknowledge that people's use of services is shaped over time" (Rogers et al. 1998: 1819).

In the years that followed, a range of ideas concerning the role of the patient in the health care system in the UK emerged. By 2005, Sir Nigel Crisp (DoH 2005), the then Chief Executive of the NHS, was able to argue that having built up the capacity of the NHS, together with improved access and clinical gover-nance to improve quality, a more profound change was appearing on the agenda. Now, Crisp stated, it was necessary "to change the whole system so that there is more choice, more personalised care, real empowerment of people to improve their health – a fundamental change in our relationships with patients and the public. In other words, to move from a service that does things *to* and *for* its patients to one which is patient led, where the service works *with* patients to support them with their health needs" (DoH 2005: 3). Quoting developments such as the NHS Live programme (local initiatives aimed at involving patients and public in improving services) and the *NHS Improvement Plan* (DoH 2004), which sets out the terms of change in an NHS being "patient led," Crisp argued that, despite some difficulties, the path forward is clear. All organizations will need to develop new service models, building on "current experience and innova-tion," in which patients are given more choice and control wherever possible. This would result in offering high-quality, integrated emergency and specialist care and ensuring that all services contribute to "health promotion, protection, and improvement" (DoH 2005: 13).

This somewhat heady vision is now part and parcel of the British government's modernization agenda. In 2008, the Darzi Report (DoH 2008) (after Lord Darzi, its author) reinforced the need for a personalized NHS "tailored to the needs and wants of each individual." However rhetorical some aspects of this vision may appear, it clearly marks a departure from earlier forms of official thinking. This is evident in bodies such as the Healthcare Commission, mentioned above, where the performance ratings of health care organizations in the future will be based on patients' experiences as well as on objective criteria of quality. In a new system being planned, called the Annual Health Check, the Commission will for the first time offer patients and public representatives a formal role in judging the quality of services. In conjunction with the Commission for Patient and Public Involvement in Health, the Healthcare Commission is aiming to involve the wider community in judging the quality of health care.

The idea of a patient-led NHS has an attractive and populist ring to it. In many respects, putting patients' needs in the driver's seat and building services around the patient seems logical. Who else's interests should be dominant? The old approach in which "doctor knows best" and health care is organized for the convenience of the professional is now consigned to history, at least in official health policy circles. As Coulter (1999) has argued, "patients have grown up and there is no going back." Paternalistic health care gives way to a patient-based system, at least as long as patients do not make demands for forms of health care that go completely against accepted medical opinion.

As I have pointed out elsewhere (Bury 2005: 104), a patient-oriented system of health care does not, of course, guarantee a reduction in problems between providers and consumers. It may have quite the opposite effect. The stress on the patient's view and, where necessary, on patients being encouraged to complain and hold doctors to account may exacerbate forms of "contestable culture" to be found in late modern societies. Conflict rather than cooperation may result. There have been several examples of this in recent years in the NHS. Mention has already been made of the difficulties surrounding child protection and the role of pediatricians as expert witnesses in court cases. In such circumstances, the open criticism of medical expertise may have consequences that go far beyond the immediate cases in hand. Whilst the lay people involved are likely to feel vindicated, the medical profession may feel confused and betrayed by its own professional bodies. Far from producing a new form of cooperation between patients and doctors, resentment and low morale may become widespread.

Added to this are cases in which conflict arises as to the most appropriate form of treatment. If patients are to be given more choice and control "wherever possible," who is to decide when this point is reached? Can the wants of patients referred to by Lord Darzi really be met? In the well-documented case of the combined vaccine for measles, mumps, and rubella – MMR – medical researchers in Britain first raised the possibility of serious side effects in the form of gastrointestinal disease and even autism, and then the medical profession entered into public dispute as parents began to demand separate vaccination for the three diseases. The Chief Medical Officer, a strong advocate of a patient-led NHS, then found himself marshaling all the forces he could to overcome the demand for separate vaccines. In this case, medical opinion saw the patient's view as mistaken. As Richard Smith, editor of the *British Medical Journal* at the time, stated, although the DoH and government had been stressing choice and the patient view, this could not encompass patients making wrong or foolish decisions, even if telling parents this in the clinic would be difficult (Smith 2002). Although the British government may envisage a health care system in which patients are in the driver's seat, the much-vaunted "direction of travel" has many humps and traffic jams to deal with.

Consumerism and choice in health care

This brings us to the related question of consumerism and choice, again two central mantras in today's British health care system. There is, of course, always a political dimension to health policies and thus to health care organization. The emphasis on choice to be found in documents such as Sir Nigel Crisp's *Creating a Patient-Led NHS* (DoH 2005) is bound up with attempts to decentralize the NHS and create a market-type approach. NHS Trusts (hospitals, community services) from this viewpoint will become providers competing with one another for health care business. Foundation Trusts "will become 'public benefit corporations' to be run as non-profit but nonetheless commercial concerns" (Pollock 2004: 71). Independent of central government control, they will then be free to borrow money on the open market, determine their own priorities, and enter into contracts with the private health care sector. Primary Care Trusts will cease almost entirely to provide care directly and will instead commission (that is, purchase) services from both public and private sectors. Although Pollock (2004: 72) argues that patient need will give way to health care based on economic considerations of effectiveness and efficiency, the aim is to create an atmosphere in which patient preferences and demands act as market forces in shaping provision. Though Pollock may be right that wider planning becomes more difficult under such circumstances, she may underestimate the level of activity that could be generated around "unglamorous, complex, costly kinds of care." This chapter has already mentioned schemes such as Evercare, which aim to sell care packages for those with long-term conditions to the NHS. The marketization of health care within the NHS (where no fees for treatment to patients will be charged) can extend across the whole range of health care provision.

The changing role of the patient can be seen to help underpin and deliver these new forms of health care. The idea of the informed consumer in health care chimes in with ideas of the patient view and a patient-led service. In fact, as Calnan and Gabe (2001) have shown, a market approach to health care in which the patient is seen as a consumer dates from the period in the late 1980s when, under a Conservative government, the idea of hospitals and community units becoming Trusts was first mooted. At that time, too, general practitioners in primary care were turned into "fundholders" and began commissioning services. As these authors (Calnan and Gabe 2001: 120) state, this altered "the culture of the NHS from one determined by the preferences and decisions of professionals to one shaped by the views and wishes of its users." In such circumstances, the GP would act as a proxy for patients, channeling their choices upwards through the system, advocating but not controlling.

Calnan and Gabe (2001: 121) go on to note that those general practices that opted to become fundholders delivered shorter waiting times, quicker test results, and a more responsive service than those that did not become fundholders. At the same time, Calnan and Gabe (2001) argue that the setting up of Trusts could also reduce choice if this meant that provision in a given area ceased as the result of a loss of a contract through competition. In any event, changes throughout the 1990s, including the *Patient's Charter* (DoH 1991), led to a rise in patient complaints. Paradoxically, policies aimed to give patients more of a say in health care can lead to a decline in satisfaction rather than an increase. Whether this is the result of improvements in care is difficult to say. Calnan and Gabe argue that it may be the case that these forms of consumerism in health care actually strengthen the position of managers and politicians in the NHS as they increasingly act "on behalf of the patient" – just as doctors have claimed in the past.

The current choice agenda constitutes a strong political plank of health policy. It marks a shift from a Fordist emphasis on the production and regulation of health care to a post-Fordist emphasis on consumption (Harrison 2002; Pickstone 2000). In a series of papers and policy pronouncements since the turn of the century, choice has become the keyword in health care thinking. For example, in December 2003, a strategy paper, *Building on the Best: Choice, Responsiveness and Equity in the NHS*, set out a series of proposals concerning choice that played to a strongly populist agenda. Choice, the document argued, was not simply a province of the affluent middle classes but something that all of us want. From 2004, the document stated, patients would be able "to begin recording their own information securely on the internet in their own Health Space. In time this will link to their electronic medical record so they can make their preferences known to the clinical team" (DoH 2003: 8). Moreover, a wider range of primary care services, easier repeat prescriptions, a choice of hospitals especially if waiting time for surgery extends beyond six months, and greater choice in maternity care and in care at the end of life are all offered. The right information to inform these choices will be "kitemarked" so that patients will know what they can rely on.

Further papers on "guiding choice at six months" and information for service providers followed this strategy announcement. *The NHS Improvement Plan* (DoH 2004), mentioned above, set out clearly the implications of choice and consumerism for health care organization in the future. In an introduction, the then Prime Minister, Tony Blair, stated that "Our aim is to reshape the NHS, building on the *NHS Plan* so it is not just a national health service but also a personal health service for every patient. We want to provide more choice for every patient, irrespective of the money in their pocket." *The NHS Improvement Plan* went on to state that by the year 2007–8, spending would rise to £90 billion per year, and a raft of measures would be put in place to improve patient choice. These reiterated many of those from previous documents, such as *Building on the Best*, and added others concerning long-term care. Patients, the *Plan* (p. 6) stated, will be able to choose between a range of providers, and will "be able to be treated at any facility that meets NHS standards, within the maximum price that the NHS pays for the treatment they need." In this way, choice is linked directly to the development of private as well as public provision within the NHS. It is clear that whatever the limits of consumerism in health care (unlike a CD player or motor car, one cannot take a surgical operation "back to the shop"), the idea of state provision and professional control over health care has been abandoned in favor of a mixed economy of care (though still within a tax-based national health service) in which patients will increasingly be expected to be active consumers. The most recent development – "choose and book" – where patients can choose between four hospitals when referred for treatment, only serves to underline the point. In March 2008, the Secretary for Health, Alan Johnson, pronounced that a "one size fits all NHS is over" (BBC, March 2).

From consumerism to partnership?

Another element is running parallel to the developments discussed above. This concerns the idea of "partnership." As many governments have found, an overemphasis on patients' rights and preferences carries the risk of alienating professionals and overstating how far patients are in a position to choose their health care. In both situations, serious limitations arise. For example, if a patient is offered the choice of hospitals by a GP, unless that patient is particularly well informed and has a great deal of information about their respective performance, it is very likely that the question will bounce back – "what hospital would you choose, doctor?" Indeed, patients may express the preference for good-quality local services rather than choice as envisaged in government rhetoric. When it comes to decisions about treatment once a service is accessed, again, patients may wish to be involved but find it difficult to balance the risks and benefits of treatment options. In such circumstances, paternalistic medical advice may be valued.

In dealing with the reactions of professionals to the emphasis on a patient-led NHS and the ambiguities of transferring responsibility for choice to the patient, ideas such as partnership have come to the fore. This appears to be less threatening to professionals and somewhat less unrealistic to patients. A 2005 *Lancet* editorial expressed the professional stance when it stated that the government view is that "the NHS should be patient-led, patients need to complain more, people should have choice and control over the care they get. And doctors are obstacles to this patient-friendly agenda." Rather, the editorial opined, there is a "need to strengthen the patient–doctor partnership" (*Lancet* 2005: 277). Note the ordering of words here. In previous decades, it is likely that sentiments such as this would have been expressed in terms of the "doctor–patient relationship," a phrase regularly used by the medical profession to explain its position on one or another health care issue. In this way, actions could be justified in terms of the patient interest rather than the self-interest of the medical profession. By embracing partnership (and by reversing "doctor–patient" to "patient–doctor"), the profession signals its intention to try to meet the government half way. Indeed, the term partnership is one much favored by contemporary governments. It seeks to legitimize a range of activities, from collaboration between private and public sectors in the financing and construction of public services (including building hospitals, schools, and prisons) to various initiatives at the community level, including tackling crime and antisocial behavior. In these areas of public policy, the emphasis is on "shared information, shared evaluations and shared responsibility" (Calnan and Gabe 2001: 127).

In the health care sector, partnership has come to take on several meanings. As Coulter (2002) has pointed out, the idea of partnership in health goes beyond public representatives serving on health policy committees, or even serving as lay members on health care bodies such as Trusts. In such circumstances, patient involvement may amount to little more than non-representative individuals serving on bodies where other stakeholders and political priorities (such as meeting government targets) hold sway. For Coulter, the idea of partnership goes much further, to the heart of the "one-to-one clinical encounter." This means that partnership should cover "shared decision-making, including patients' information needs, the evaluation and use of patient decision aids, and strategies for training health professionals to elicit patients' values and preferences and engage them in decisions about their care" (Coulter 2002: 186). Citing a wide body of research and a special issue of the *British Medical Journal* (1999) given over to the topic, Coulter (2002: 719) asked: "is shared decision-making doomed to remain the obsession of a few academic pointy heads?" and "what can be done to move it into the mainstream?"

Three years later, in a further discussion of the topic, Coulter (2005) sounded even less sure that shared decision-making would prove to be the hallmark of partnership in health care in the future. New studies, Coulter argued, showed that a full picture of partnership displays many different features. As with choice, it seems clear that patients' views may not always coincide with the dominant ideas of policy makers, or, indeed, those of "pointy head" academics. Although some of the latter argue that professionals should always seek to help "patients to make informed medical decisions for themselves," Coulter noted that research also indicates that "some patients prefer to remain uninformed and to delegate shared decision-making responsibility to the doctor." Coulter (2005: 95) went on to outline a series of debating points about partnership and shared decision-making, including findings that indicated that patients wish to know doctors' opinions as well as wanting "objective information."

Whatever the difficulties facing the implementation of shared decision-making as part of a partnership approach to health care organization, it is clear that it will remain a key feature of government policy. Gabe, Olumide, and Bury (2004) argue that shared decision-making and the exchange of information between patients and doctors may take different forms as an illness trajectory unfolds – as Charles and her colleagues have shown (Charles, Gafni, and Whelan 1997, 1999). Thus in the early stages, when diagnosis and tests need to be undertaken, a range of expert opinion may come into play and be the dominant voice. During a period of reflection and decision-making about treatment options, a more shared approach may be feasible, though time and other constraints play a part here. Following treatment, and hopefully during recovery, the emphasis may shift once again toward the patient, with the professional supporting self-care and rehabilitation.

One of the difficulties in fashioning partnership and shared decision-making strategies is that health care covers a very wide range of health-related experiences, with patients and health care professionals bringing many different factors into a given encounter. In health care, one size cannot fit all. Gabe and colleagues (2004) raise a crucial factor in this context, namely, age. In the case of pediatric care, for example, the question of the legal and social status of the child (or young person) in the health care system introduces a particular dynamic into proceedings. In these circumstances, it is rarely the case that "the patient" appears alone in the clinical encounter, and equally rare that decisions about treatment will be made by the young person without the influence of a parent. Indeed, for infants and very young children, such parental involvement may be the only way to make relevant decisions. Whilst there is emphasis today on "children's rights" in health care (as in other areas of life), Gabe and colleagues (2004: 1073) argue that this complicates as much as clarifies the situation. National and international policies concerning children in health care stress the need *both* for professionals to act to protect the child *and* for the "child's voice to be heard." These two strictures may cut across each other in given situations, for example in undertaking invasive life-saving treatment, or judging that the child's preferences will lead to a "failure to protect."

Children are not alone in posing a major challenge to the development of patient partnership. Older patients, especially those whose cognitive abilities are impaired or who are being cared for by a close relative or friend, may not be (or wish to be) the sole decision-maker interacting with the professional. Indeed, many if not most patients are likely to be embedded in a network of more or less supportive relationships. In some cultural settings, it may be quite unrealistic to think of patients as individual actors, equivalent, on the other side of the table, to the autonomous professional. The clinical encounter, in this sense at least, is not a meeting of equals. For patients, encounters with doctors are surrounded by a range of emotional and social factors all bearing on the agenda they bring to the partnership process. For doctors, bureaucratic, legal, and professional factors provide guidelines for approaching each "case" in turn. Whilst some aspects of the encounter can therefore be regarded as open to the development of partnership and perhaps shared decision-making, this is unlikely ever to characterize the encounter as a whole. Patients' and doctors' respective roles and "assumptive worlds" are too distinct.

One other aspect of partnership is worth noting at this point. A great deal of medical activity in health care organizations deals with the prescribing of drugs. Here, too, the government has proposed changes in the patient's role and thus in the organization of health care. In 2003, as part of the government's £30 million "Pharmacy in the Future" programme, a new body entitled "Medicines Partnership" set out a series of new steps to modernize public health pharmacy and outline new roles for both professionals (including nurses and community pharmacists) and patients alike. In this new vision, the earlier emphasis on encouraging patient compliance, in which patients were expected to follow "doctor's orders," is supplanted by the notion of concordance. This new approach emphasizes the idea that prescriber and consumer should enter into a shared decision-making process and arrive at a mutually agreed approach to the prescribing and taking of medicines. The resulting "concordance" between patient and prescriber should overcome, it is hoped, the faults of compliance where patients' views remained unexamined in the prescribing process. Non-compliance, and the waste of drugs never taken, should both be addressed by this route. The Medicines Partnership states that: "The initiative is aimed at helping patients to get the most out of medication by involving them as partners in prescribing decisions and supporting them in medicine taking" (National Prescribing Centre N.d.).

As elsewhere on this new health care terrain, questions have been quick to emerge. Britten (2004), for example, has argued that where research has been carefully conducted, it indicates that the expression of patient preferences may lead to the issuing of prescriptions that are not clinically needed. In one study, when asked why they had done so, doctors stated that it had occurred "in order to maintain relationships with patients" (Britten 2004: 416). This suggests that some patients may be pressurizing their doctors to take decisions against their clinical judgment. It appears that patients' priorities may be very different from prescribers' priorities, or indeed from the priorities that the prescribers presume their patients to have (Britten 2003: 840). The agendas, again, of both "partners" may simply be too different for "concordance" to be arrived at with any ease. Patients may be more concerned with the demands of their social situation and "moral concerns" (that is, with not taking drugs unnecessarily and appearing not to be seen as dependent on medication; Horne, Weinman, and Hankins 1999) than worrying too much about the fine detail of medicine taking itself. Britten states that "clinicians who are trying to give their patients the best evidence about treatment options and to present balanced information about risks and benefits may find it difficult to take this on board" (Britten 2003: 840). As with shared decision-making more generally, pursuing concordance may alter some aspects of health care delivery, but the jury must be out as to how meaningful this may become as a part of new organizational structure.

Self-care and the expert patient

This brings us to the final aspect of changes in the role of the patient in the new NHS – that of self-care and the "expert patient." *The NHS Improvement Plan* contains a central chapter that deals with "Supporting people with long-term conditions to live healthy lives." The chapter states that "about 60% of adults report some form of long-term or chronic health problem" (DoH 2004: 34). As a result, the use of health care increases with the number of problems reported ("the 15% of people with three or more problems account for almost 30% of inpatient days"; DoH 2004: 34). Although it is not clear how the 60 percent figure has been arrived at and what range of problems it is referring to, the *Improvement Plan* goes on to describe a set of arrangements that will meet the challenge of chronic illness in the community. At the more severe end of the spectrum, those with highly complex conditions will be offered case management. This will involve the advent of over 3,000 "community matrons" by 2008, who will "co-ordinate the contribution of all the different professionals who can help, anticipate and deal with problems before they lead to worsening health or hospitalisation" (DoH 2004: 38). Since the publication of the *Plan*, two reports have cast doubt on the effectiveness of this approach (Hutt, Rosen, and McCauley 2004; Roland et al. 2005), but it is still being pursued.

At the intermediate level, higher-risk patients with serious chronic disease that is not complex in character (such as asthma, diabetes, or depression) will receive disease management, largely within the primary care setting. In heart disease, for example, measures such as checking blood pressure or cholesterol levels and ensuring that support is given for stopping smoking will be offered. The development of National Service Frameworks, together with guidance from the National Institute of Health and Clinical Excellence, will help to underpin this kind of approach. "Strong financial incentives" under the new GP contract, it is hoped, will help doctors "seek out patients who can benefit from this kind of support and demonstrate that they are making a real difference to their health" (DoH 2004: 37).

However, it is at the third level, affecting 70–80 percent of patients, that self-management is seen as the cornerstone of the *Improvement Plan*. This combines the idea of self-care in "population-wide prevention" and self-management with respect to the bulk of existing chronic conditions. In the case of prevention, self-care shades across into the well-worn paths of stressing individuals' responsibility for maintaining their health. But it is in the area of chronic illness that newer and more innovative forms of health care are proposed. Central to this, and drawing on "international experience," the *Plan* states, is the Expert Patients Programme (EPP). In this programme, "using trained non-medical leaders as educators, people with arthritis and other long-term conditions have been equipped with the skills to manage their own conditions." "By 2008," the *Plan* states, "it will have been rolled out throughout the NHS, enabling thousands more patients to take greater control of their own health and their own lives" (DoH 2004: 38).

The international experience alluded to in the *Plan* comes from one particular source, Stanford University in the United States. There, a "chronic disease self-management programme" (CDSMP) pioneered and led by Kate Lorig (Lorig et al. 2001; Lorig et al. 1999) has trained "lay tutors" in key self-management skills. These tutors then run courses for other chronically ill patients, without the oversight of medical practitioners. The EPP in Britain has been essentially the CDSMP, with minor changes. The course in question comprises six two-hour weekly sessions, teaching the participants not about their disease (in the British version anyone suffering from a long-term condition can sign up to go on the EPP) but skills in areas such as exercise, fatigue management, communication with professionals, and diet. The underlying theory of the programme, based on the work of the American psychologist Albert Bandura, is that an increase in the level of self-efficacy will help people feel more in control of their condition and of their lives.

The EPP runs an active website for patients and health care practitioners, and is now focusing on people at work (EPP CIC N.d.). Those interested can sign up to a regular "e-update" on the EPP and find out how to participate, or even become a lay tutor. It is clear from the website, as well as recent media coverage, that many patients who have volunteered to go to the course and who have completed at least most of the six modules claim to have benefited from the experience. On the EPP website, under a "views from patients and professionals" heading, "Cathy," for example, states that as a result of being on the programme she has been able "to take some positive steps for the future." In a poem written by a "Sue Jump," Sue states that "So now, I am a tutor helping others to find the pearl." And despite misgivings, especially the notion of patients as "experts" among some sections of the medical profession (Shaw and Baker 2004), even some doctors have welcomed the programme. On the EPP website, GP Anita Campbell states that the programme "transforms people's lives, especially those without higher education and who may have poor self esteem. It is good to see our patients taking control of their medical condition and their interactions with clinicians."

The problem arises, however, when a wider evaluation of the programme is attempted. To date there has been limited systematic study of the programme in the UK, though an evaluation of its implementation and a randomised controlled trial have been carried out by the National Primary Care Research and Development Centre at Manchester. Their two reviews of the programme's progress paint a mixed picture, both of the practical problems encountered in setting up the course and recruiting patients and tutors, and embedding the programme fully in the NHS (EPP Evaluation Team 2005; Kennedy, Gately, and Rogers 2004). Recently published results of a randomized controlled trial of the EPP show small to moderate levels of effectiveness (Kennedy et al. 2007).

Most of the studies of self-management in chronic illness (whether using the kind of approach advocated by Lorig in the US and the EPP in Britain or not) are of "condition-specific" programmes, for disorders such as arthritis or asthma. A recent review of this literature, covering three conditions, showed some benefits in the short term, in some studies, but little if any long-term effectiveness (Bury, Newbould, and Taylor 2005; Newman, Steed, and Mulligan 2004). Lorig's own research on the CDSMP showed some positive outcomes in the short term at six months (though not on all measures, including psychological well-being), but much less in an uncontrolled follow up at 2 years (Lorig et al. 2001; Lorig et al. 1999). Such findings are, perhaps, understandable. If the attraction of being involved in the programme helps overcome participants' previous sense of isolation, short-term benefits may be evident. It is quite a different matter to sustain positive changes over a longer time span – essential in the case of chronic conditions. It is highly likely that social factors and the progression of the condition may reassert themselves with the passage of time.

Conclusion

Initiatives such as the EPP hold out the promise of new forms of health care organization that will be radically different from the past. This chapter has explored changes in the role of both the doctor and the patient that seem to be emblematic of these proposed changes. What ties them together, perhaps, is the emphasis on the patient's viewpoint, whether we consider reductions in professional power, the growth of regulation, or the rise of a patient-led NHS. Taylor and Bury have called this process "care transition" (Bury and Taylor 2008; Taylor and Bury 2007), suggesting a major break with the past. There is much to commend such a refocusing of health care systems and service delivery to meet new demands. Enough has been said to indicate that a number of agendas are at work here. Health care and health services are at base political issues, and new forms of heath care organization as described above clearly chime in with New Labour's approach to the public sector more generally. Here, private financing, private provision, and an emphasis of consumerism are brought to bear on "monolithic" public services such as the British NHS.

The underlying contradiction in such an approach lies in the fact that the emphasis on the patient view or on patient self-care has not emerged directly from patients themselves, but from a centralized "top-down" set of initiatives and reorganization coming from government. This is why, when careful research is undertaken, patients do not often or regularly confirm the assumptions held. It is unlikely that they could. The idea of the patient viewpoint is fundamentally problematic, if only because patients are many and various. In addition, there are many areas of health care in which high-quality medical expertise is essential to good outcomes. Shifting the balance of power (to use the title of yet another and earlier government document) toward the patient may be important in offsetting the dysfunctional aspects of a paternalistic form of medicine and too much professional control in shaping health care organization. But however useful the rhetoric of the patient's viewpoint may be in this process, it is unlikely to alter the experience of the vast majority of practitioners and patients in the health care system as a whole. Whether a more realistic approach to health care organization can be developed in Britain, in which clinical expertise and patients' varying needs can be reconciled more appropriately, only time will tell.

References

Armstrong, David. 2002. "Clinical Autonomy, Individual and Collective: The Problem of Changing Doctors' Behaviour." *Social Science and Medicine* 55: 1771–7.

British Medical Journal. 1999. 319 Special Theme Issue: Embracing Patient Partnership (September 18).

Britten, Nicky. 2003. "Does a Prescribed Treatment Match a Patient's Priorities?" *British Medical Journal* 327: 840.

Britten, Nicky. 2004. "Patients' Expectations of Consultations." *British Medical Journal* 328: 416–17.

Buchan, James. 2004. "International Rescue? The Dynamics and Policy Implications of the International Recruitment of Nurses to the UK." *Health Services Research and Policy* 9 (Supplement 1): 10–15.

Bury, Michael. 2005. *Health and Illness.* Cambridge: Polity Press.

Bury, Michael, Jenny Newbould, and David Taylor. 2005. *A Rapid Review of Knowledge Regarding Lay-Led Self-Management of Chronic Illness.* London: National Institute for Health and Clinical Excellence.

Bury, Michael and David Taylor. 2008. "Towards a Theory of Care Transition: From Medical Dominance to Managed Consumerism." *Social Theory and Health* 6: 210–19.

Calnan, Michael and Jonathan Gabe. 2001. "From Consumerism to Partnership? Britain's National Health Service at the Turn of the Century." *International Journal of Health Services* 31(1): 119–31.

Charles, Cathy, Amiram Gafni, and Tim Whelan. 1997. "Shared Decision-Making in the Medical Encounter: What Does it Mean? (Or It Takes at Least Two to Tango)." *Social Science and Medicine* 44(5): 681–92.

Charles, Cathy, Amiram Gafni, and Tim Whelan. 1999. "Decision-Making in the Physician–Patient Encounter: Revisiting the Shared Treatment Decision-Making Model." *Social Science and Medicine* 49: 651–61.

Cooper, Richard and Sandra Stoflet. 2004. "Diversity and Consistency: The Challenge of Maintaining Quality in a Multidisciplinary Workforce." *Journal of Health Services Research and Policy* 9 (Supplement 1): 39–47.

Coulter, Angela. 1999. "Paternalism or Partnership? Patients Have Grown Up – And There's No Going Back." *British Medical Journal* 319: 719–20.

Coulter, Angela. 2002. "Whatever Happened to Shared Decision Making?" *Health Expectations* 5: 185–6.

Coulter, Angela. 2005. "Shared Decision-Making: The Debate Continues." *Health Expectations* 8: 95–6.

Department of Health (DoH). 1991. *The Patient's Charter.* London: Department of Health.

Department of Health (DoH). 1997. *The New NHS: Modern, Dependable.* Cmnd 3807. London: Department of Health.

Department of Health (DoH). 2000. *The NHS Plan: A Plan for Investment and a Plan for Reform*. Cmnd 4818–1. London: The Stationery Office.

Department of Health (DoH). 2001. *Report of the Public Inquiry Into Children's Heart Surgery at the Bristol Royal Infirmary 1984–1985*. Cmnd 5207. London: The Stationery Office.

Department of Health (DoH). 2003. *Building on the Best: Choice, Responsiveness and Equity in the NHS*. London: Department of Health.

Department of Health (DoH). 2004. *The NHS Improvement Plan: Putting People at the Heart of Public Services*. Cmnd 6268. London: The Stationery Office.

Department of Health (DoH). 2005. *Creating a Patient-Led NHS: Delivering the NHS Improvement Plan*. London: Department of Health.

Department of Health (DoH). 2007. *The New NHS: Modern, Dependable*. Cmnd 3807. London: Department of Health.

Department of Health (DoH). 2008. *High Quality Care for All: NHS Stage Review Final Report – Summary*. London: Department of Health.

Dyer, Clare. 2005. "Professor Roy Meadow Struck Off." *British Medical Journal* 331: 177.

EPP Evaluation Team. 2005. *Process Evaluation of the EPP – Report II*. Manchester: National Primary Care Research and Development Centre, University of Manchester.

Expert Patients Programme Community Interest Company (EPP CIC). N.d. Retrieved December 15, 2008 (www.expertpatients.nhs.uk).

Freidson, Eliot. 1988 [1970]. *Profession of Medicine: A Study of the Sociology of Applied Knowledge*, 2nd edition. Chicago: University of Chicago Press.

Gabe, Jon, Gillian Olumide, and Michael Bury. 2004. "'It Takes Three to Tango': A Framework for Understanding Patient Partnership in Paediatric Clinics." *Social Science and Medicine* 59: 1071–9.

General Medical Council (GMC). 2005. *Developing Medical Regulation: A Vision for the Future*. London: General Medical Council.

Harrison, Stephen. 2002. "New Labour, Modernisation and the Medical Labour Process." *Journal of Social Policy* 31(3): 465–85.

Healthcare Commission. N.d. Retrieved December 15, 2008 (www.healthcarecommission.org.uk).

Horne, Robert, John Weinman, and Maittew Hankins. 1999. "The Beliefs About Medicines Questionnaire: The Development and Evaluation of a New Method for Assessing the Cognitive Representation of Medication." *Psychology and Health* 14(1): 1–24.

Hunter, David. 2005. "From Tribalism to Corporatism: The Managerial Challenge to Medical Dominance." Pp. 1–23 in J. Gabe, D. Kelleher, and G. Williams (eds.), *Challenging Medicine*, 2nd edition. London: Routledge.

Hutt, Ruth, Rebecca Rosen, and Janet McCauley. 2004. *Case Managing Long-Term Conditions: What Impact Does It Have in the Treatment of Older People?* London: King's Fund.

Kennedy, Anne, Clare Gately, and Anne Rogers. 2004. *Assessing the Process of Embedding EPP in the NHS: Preliminary Study of PCT Pilot Sites*. Manchester: National Primary Care Research and Development Centre.

Kennedy, Anne, David Reeves, Peter Bower, Victoria Lee, Elizabeth Middleton, Gerry Richardson, Caroline Gardner, Clare Gately, and Anne Rogers. 2007. "The Effectiveness and Cost Effectiveness of a National Lay-Led Self-Care Support Programme for Patients with Long-Term Conditions: A Pragmatic Randomised Controlled Trial." *Journal of Epidemiology and Community Health* 61: 254–61.

King's Fund. 2005. *An Independent Audit of the NHS Under Labour*. London: King's Fund.

Lancet. 2005. "A Dismal and Dangerous Verdict Against Roy Meadow." *Lancet* 366: 277.

Lorig, Kate, Philip Ritter, Anita Stewart, David Sobel, Byron Brown, Albert Bandura, Virginia Gonzalez, Dian Laurent, and Halsted Holman. 2001. "Chronic Disease Self-Management Program, 2-Year Health Status and Health Care Utilization Outcomes." *Medical Care* 39(11): 1217–23.

Lorig, Kate, David Sobel, Anita Stewart, Byron Brown, Albert Bandura, Philip Ritter, Virginia Gonzalez, Dian Laurent, and Halsted Holman. 1999. "Evidence Suggesting that a Chronic Disease Self-Management Program Can Improve Health Status While Reducing Hospitalization, a Randomized Trial." *Medical Care* 37(1): 5–14.

McKinlay, John and Lisa Marceau. 2002. "The End of the Golden Age of Doctoring." *International Journal of Health Services* 32(2): 379–416.

Mayor, Susan. 2005. "Case Management to Be Used for People With Chronic Conditions." *British Medical Journal* 330: 112.

Mooney, Helen. 2005. "Mass Redundancies Expected as SHAs Tackle £750 Shortfall." *Health Services Journal*, July 13.

National Audit Office. 2001. *Handling Clinical Negligence Claims in England*. London: National Audit Office.

National Prescribing Centre. N.d. "Medicines Partnership." Retrieved December 15, 2008 (www.npc.co.uk/med_partnership/index.htm).

Newman, Stanton, Liz Steed, and Kathleen Mulligan. 2004. "Self-Management Interventions for Chronic Illness." *Lancet* 364: 1523–37.

Picker Institute. 2008. *The Key Findings Report for the 2007 Inpatient Survey*. Oxford: Picker Institute Europe.

Pickstone, John. 2000. "Production, Community and Consumption: The Political Economy of Twentieth-Century Medicine." Pp 1–19 in R. Cooter and J. E. Pickstone (eds.), *Medicine in the Twentieth Century*. London: Harwood.

Pollock, Allyson. 2004. *NHS PLC: The Privatisation of Our Health Care*. London: Verso.

Rogers, Anne, Michael Bury, and Anne Kennedy. 2009. "Rationality, Rhetoric and Religiosity in Health Care: The Case of the Expert Patients Programme." *International Journal of Health Services*, in press.

Rogers, Anne, Vicky Entwistle, and David Pencheon. 1998. "Managing Demand: A Patient-Led NHS: Managing Demand at the Interface Between Lay and Primary Care." *British Medical Journal* 316: 1816–19.

Roland, Martin, Mark Dusheiko, Hugh Gravelle, and Stuart Parker. 2005. "Follow-Up of People Aged 65 and Over with a History of Emergency Admissions: Analysis of Routine Admission Data." *British Medical Journal* 330: 289–92.

Sackett, David, William Rosenberg, Muir Gray, Brian Haynes, and W. Scott Richardson. 1996. "Evidence-Based Medicine: What It Is and What It Isn't." *British Medical Journal* 312: 71–2.

Salter, Brian. 2004. *The New Politics of Medicine*. Basingstoke: Palgrave Macmillan.

Shaw, Joanne and Mary Baker. 2004. "'Expert Patient' – Dream or Nightmare?" *British Medical Journal* 328: 723–4.

Smith, Richard. 2002. "The Discomfort of Patient Power." *British Medical Journal* 324: 497–8.

Smith, Richard. 2003. "Improving the Management of Chronic Disease." *British Medical Journal* 327: 12.

Taylor, David and Michael Bury. 2007. "Chronic Illness, Expert Patients and Care Transition." *Sociology of Health and Illness* 29(1): 27–45.

Wholey, Douglas and Lawton Burns. 2000. "Tides of Change: The Evolution of Managed Care in the United States." Pp. 217–37 in C. E. Bird, P. Conrad, and A. M. Fremont (eds.), *Handbook of Medical Sociology*, 5th edition. Upper Saddle River, NJ: Prentice-Hall.

20

The Convergence and Divergence of Modern Health Care Systems

Fred Stevens

Do countries at about the same stage of industrial development adopt the same approach to the organization and management of their health care system? Or are cultural heritages distinctive enough that each society fashions its own political and administrative structure? And to what extent do national and international policies affect and determine the organizational structures located in and emerging from the institution of health care?

A widespread view in reflections on modern health care systems is that they are becoming increasingly similar. This view is based on the fact that modern societies are faced with analogue problems impinging on their health care organization. Most important are an aging population, technological developments, and rising costs of health care. The percentage of very old people will continue to rise. With this, we see a shift in disease patterns from acute to chronic illnesses. As people age, the chance that they will maintain good health decreases. Combined with advances in science and medical technology, these factors influence public expectations and demands for health care, and consequently result in higher expenditures on health care.

The scope of this chapter is to review developments in health care organization of modern societies in the context of current debates on health care reform, with a specific focus on the structural and cultural context of health services. We argue that the organization of health care in modern societies reflects a wide range of convergences and divergences. This is illuminated by a discussion of international trends in health care and of basic health care organization models used in Europe, the Americas, Africa, and Asia.

INTERNATIONAL TRENDS IN HEALTH CARE ORGANIZATION

During the last decades industrialized nations have felt an increasing need to reform health care. This need is due to a general dissatisfaction with overall performance, evidence of inefficiencies in the use of resources, and a lack of responsiveness of services to users. The latter is particularly reflected in attempts to increase patient choice and in demands for more public accountability and participation in the organization and management of services. More and more nations are seeking ways to decrease inequalities and to increase the choices of patients in selecting their general practitioner, specialists, and hospital.

Dissatisfaction is further manifested in attempts to change the balance between public health, prevention, and primary health care on the one side, and secondary care on the other. It has been recognized that, in the past, too much priority has been given to hospital care at the expense of the development of primary care, community care, and public health. By means of budgetary incentives, health care services are refashioned, for example, with regard to the relation between primary and secondary care provision and with regard to measures to improve continuity of care. New professions come into existence at the interface of nurse and physician, while the content of nursing practice is changing. Particularly in primary health care the role of nursing is expanding.

Another general trend is that the future role of the hospital in health care is increasingly being questioned (Ginzberg 1996; McKee and Healy 2002). Epidemiological and demographic transitions, as well as new technological developments in the field of diagnosis and treatment, have a tremendous impact on the delivery of services. Many services that, until recently, were only delivered in hospitals have found their way into the homes of patients. Typical examples are renal dialysis and diabetes care, where patients and their relatives are taught to deal with low- and high-tech medical equipment (Gallagher 1999). The number of acute beds in hospitals and the average length of stay have dropped substantially in all industrialized countries (OECD 2007). This is a direct result of changes in treatment procedures, new diagnostic techniques, the changing role of primary health care, early discharge procedures, and overall cost-containment measures.

With the changing role of hospitals in health care we see that the responsibilities of health professionals in health services are also changing. The roles of doctors regarding professional accountability and cost containment have widened. This has resulted in a shift of focus from professional norms exclusively targeted at the quality of professional care to one also focusing on issues of cost containment, management, and service reduction (General Medical Council 2003; Leicht and Fennell 1997). A variety of initiatives have been launched, such as the purchaser–provider split in the UK, where groups of general practitioners are held responsible for purchasing hospital services. Groups of primary care physicians receive the allocation for their patients' health care to purchase all services, including hospital care. In other countries, for example in the Netherlands, doctors will have a greater responsibility in the efficient use of services. In the US, shifts in decision-making have taken place as a result of contract relationships and reimbursement policies. For example, physicians are forming associations to negotiate managed care contracts. But also, as was predicted several decades ago, medical work is coming more and more under bureaucratic control (Mechanic 1975; Starr 1982). The overall impact of these developments on professional autonomy is not clear. Indeed, professionals will lose some of their professional control. But then again, professionals are moving into organizational positions that create new opportunities for control and satisfaction (Stevens, Diederiks, and Philipsen 1992; Warren, Weitz, and Kulis 1998; Zeitz 1984).

The thread through all these developments is a continuing debate on the financing of health care. Dependent on the country under consideration, these debates focus on overall expenditures (e.g., in the US), on the role of the government in cost containment (e.g., in Sweden and Canada), on policies regarding health care coverage restrictions (e.g., in Germany and the Netherlands), or on improving solidarity and equity (e.g., in South Africa and Colombia). In most countries, an increasing interest has been shown in the introduction of competition between providers. This is considered as a reform strategy to tackle inefficiencies and to enlarge the responsiveness of providers to users. Policy makers everywhere are trying to find a position in the middle between competition on the one hand and managed care on the other. Countries where competition lies at the heart of service provision, as is the case in the US, are moving toward more regulated and managed care. In countries with a long tradition of governmental planning and regulation, as, for example, in Sweden, the Netherlands, or the UK, we see a movement in the opposite direction toward more competition on the basis of market mechanisms. Not surprisingly, the overall trend in health care reform is managed competition, being a mixture of competition on the one side and management on the other. But as Saltman and Figueras (1998: 87–8) noted in an early overview of health care reforms in Europe: "There is no single concept of a market that can be adopted for use within a health care system. Rather, market-style mechanisms include a number of different specific instruments such as consumer sovereignty (patient choice), negotiated contracts and open bidding, which can be introduced on the funding, allocation, or production subsectors of the system."

Because of these congruent cross-national patterns and policies seeking an optimal mix of public and individual responsibility, there is a growing interest in the comparison of health care systems. Countries in the process of health care reform seek to adopt suitable financial and organizational solutions, but also try to learn from each other's mistakes. The necessity of making health care available and accessible for whole populations within certain budget restrictions gives rise to dilemmas in priority setting and rationing. Making choices about the allocation of resources has traditionally been considered an almost exclusive part of the jurisdiction of the medical profession. What we see now, however, is that priority setting and rationing are becoming part of the public debate.

Priority setting and rationing are not purely technical operations. The course and direction of these activities are influenced by the dominant belief system of a nation. Many countries try to find ways to combine the values of equity, efficiency, and autonomy. Equity implies that health care should be accessible for everyone who is in need of it. It reflects a *collectivist* approach with regard to the equal distribution of health care resources among all strata of the population. The contrasting value of individual autonomy reflects the ability of self-determination and independence in health care. It signifies that people should have a free choice, and preferably would have the means to decide for themselves what they would need from health care, irrespective of the distribution of resources. Efficiency indicates that resources for health care should be spent as economically as possible. In their priority setting, all modern nations try to combine these three values in one way or another. Some nations, however, put more emphasis on the collectivist approach (equity), others on individual autonomy. But for all modern nations, efficiency has become the more dominant orientation in the light of the increasing costs of health care.

A major dilemma is whether values of efficiency and self-determination can be sustained without losing principles of equity and solidarity. But as priority setting and rationing in health care have become important policy issues in many countries, the outcomes of the political debate are not spectacular. As Mossialos and King (1999: 131) note: "Greater relative awareness of rationing and priority setting issues in countries such as the Netherlands, Sweden and the UK is accompanied by some ambivalence about the actual need for rationing or priority setting." Indeed, in Scandinavian countries and in countries like Israel and the Netherlands, with their long tradition of equity and solidarity principles, governments have always been rather reluctant to introduce measures to restrict payment for services, a situation that is changing now (Saltman and Figueras 1997).

HEALTH CARE AS A SOCIETAL SECTOR

While the comparison of health care systems has grown in popularity during recent years, some may have wondered at the quasi-absence of studies relating health care and health care organization to the broader societal and institutional environment. The literature on the comparison of health care systems has strongly been influenced by (neoclassical) economic, managerial, and policy perspectives. These focus on issues of macro- and micro-efficiency, on organizational arrangements conducive to effectiveness, on quality of services, and on measures to improve the continuity and accessibility of care. Many studies try to answer the question how, in the context of changing circumstances, goals and priorities in health care can be reached within the limits of political and legislative boundaries, and using resources economically. In essence, this question regards the *effectiveness* of health care.

For their survival and continuity, however, health care systems also must be assessed on their *legitimacy*. Societies have to solve the problem of how health care goals and priorities can be set and achieved in such a way that the actions of health care actors and the effects of these actions, intentionally or unintentionally, will be judged as socially acceptable. To evaluate the effectiveness of health care, but in particular its legitimacy, it is important to envisage health care as a societal sector, and to take its societal and institutional environment into consideration.

Societal sectors are defined as collections of actors who are functionally inter-connected, who operate in the same domain (e.g., health, education, economics, or welfare), and who have a set of similar or interrelated functions (Powell and DiMaggio 1991; Scott and Meyer 1991). Defining health care as a societal sector would imply a focus on the collectivity of actors working within the context of that specific institution. In other words, it comprises focal organizations, services, and functions delivering specific products, but also includes all other organizations, providers, facilities, and services that directly or indirectly influence the core actors. These include facilities such as hospitals, medical practices, nursing homes, and the health professions (medical and non-medical), their clients, client organizations, funding sources on a national, federal, and regional level, local governmental bodies, suppliers of facilities such as the pharmaceutical industry, and so on.

Societal sectors have their primary orientation on one societal core function, in this case, health and illness (Lammers 1993: 321–39). They further have a (social) structure, and a specific pattern of relationships between actors in super/subordinate or egalitarian positions. Societal sectors also have their specific institutional culture. This includes a dominant belief system, a specific system of routines, norms, and values, and specific notions of their "bond." In some sectors, for example in economy, these bindings will be primarily competitive. In health care, they are more cooperative. Analyzing health care systems as societal sectors would also imply the recognition of their distinctive history over time, their specific values and value patterns that go beyond technological requirements, and their commitment to a set of normative standards (Parsons 1951; Selznick 1957). In the comparison of health care systems across nations it may seem that goals do not vary much, but that, over time, variations are primarily found in the implementation of technologies used to reach these goals. Where health care systems vary is in their emphasis on goals and priorities; this is mainly due to long-term cultural and structural developments. Consequently, it can be argued that every health care system is typified by its structure of relations of actors and organizations. Every health care system is further typified by its unique pattern of underlying norms, values, and value orientations.

The Structure of Health Care Systems

To conceptualize health care systems as societal sectors indicates a high degree of specialization and vertical integration of system elements (Scott and Meyer 1991). Vertical integration denotes that in a production chain activities are controlled at both ends. The health economist Robert Evans, however, argues that, because of their distinctive structure, health care systems are characterized by incomplete vertical integration (Evans 1981). As relatively independent subsections are involved, such as hospitals, medical services, drugs prescribers, and so forth, vertical integration is difficult to achieve.

Vertical integration is further complicated by the fact that regulatory authority is for the major part delegated by the government to the suppliers. Also, the provision of health insurance is directly linked to one or more of the other transactors in health care (Evans 1981). Consumers permit providers to act as their agents. But professional organizations enjoy, to a substantial degree, independence from other actors, which indicates that the integration between first-line providers and consumers is far from complete. This incompleteness also regards the physician–hospital relations. In general, physicians do not own or manage hospitals, although in some countries, as in Japan, this is different.

Also, the role of the government in health care can vary considerably. In some countries, the state has only very limited control of the insurance activities, as is the case in the US. In other countries, for example in Canada and in the UK, the state is in control of insurance by means of taxation.

Health care systems vary in structural relationships and in formal interactions between system elements. A traditional market structure presupposes bilateral relations between buyers and suppliers. The health care sector differs essentially from the market sector, because interactions between the actors are not organized in bidirectional relations of pairs of producers and consumers. In contrast to these typical market structures, the exchange relations between the actors in health care are much more complex (Evans 1981). Multilateral transactions involve many participants who have limited independence and jurisdictions. The organization of health care, therefore, consists of multidirectional relations within an interacting system of five principle actors. These are the consumers, first-line providers (general practitioners), second-line providers (hospitals), governments, and insurers (Evans 1981). How these five actors are connected reflects the basic structure of a system.

HEALTH CARE MODELS OF EUROPEAN HEALTH CARE SYSTEMS

Although health care systems diverge in their methods of financing, organization, and regulation, certain organizational configurations dominate, dependent on the role and position of the respective (trans)actors. From the relations between these transactors, typical health care systems can be modeled: the social insurance system, the centralized system of (former) communist countries, and the UK national health care system (Evans 1981; Hurst 1992; Marrée and Groenewegen 1997). These are found in Eastern and Western Europe, as well as in the Americas and Asia.

The social insurance model. The first model is the social insurance or "Bismarck" model, named after its founder. Typical for the social insurance system or Bismarck model, patients pay an insurance premium to the sick fund, which has a contract with first-line and second-line providers. The role of the state is limited and is confined to setting the overall conditions of the contracts between patients, providers, and insurers. The social insurance system is funded by premiums paid and controlled by employers and labor unions. These, however, have little influence on the provision of services. This is left to the professions, specifically the medical profession, and to charity organizations (e.g., home nursing, home help). For people with lower- and middle-class salaried incomes, collective and enforced arrangements are available. This social security model was founded in Germany at the end of the nineteenth century, and then almost immediately adopted by Czechoslovakia during Austrian–Hungarian rule, and by Austria, Hungary, and Poland. During World War II, it was enforced on the Netherlands (1941), and later also adopted by Belgium and France. The social insurance system survived two world wars and national socialism, and essentially still exists, although in a modified fashion, in Germany, the Netherlands, Belgium, France, Austria, Switzerland, Luxembourg, and Japan.

The socialized model. Founded in 1918, the second major European health care model is the centralized communist model or, after its founding father, the "Semashko" model. This model is characterized by a strong position of the state, which guarantees free access to health care for everyone. This is realized by state ownership of health care facilities, by funding from the state budget, and by geographical distribution of services throughout the country. The state-dominated socialized model is funded by taxation. Health services are provided by state employees, planned by hierarchical provision, and organized as a hierarchy of hospitals, with outpatient clinics (polyclinics) as the lowest levels of entrance. Among the nations that, until recently, had a health care system based on the Semashko model are Russia, Belarus, the Central Asian republics of the former USSR, and some countries in Central and Eastern Europe. Many former Soviet republics have undergone a process of transition toward a social insurance-based system. But even today, the health care infrastructure remains in disrepair across much of the former Soviet region.

Outside Europe, the socialized Cuban health care system also underwent shortages following the collapse of the Soviet Union. But while Cuban secondary and tertiary care suffered from the crisis, the well-functioning universal and equitable health care system from before the crisis remained largely intact, due to the government's support and grassroots organizations-based networks of solidarity (Nayeri and Lopez-Pardo 2005). The country further remained faithful to the premises of an integrated national health system with the improvement of first-line health care as one of its priorities (De Vos, De Ceukelaire, and Van der Stuyft 2006).

The national health service model. The third European model is the UK National Health Service (NHS) or "Beveridge" model. The basic model is virtually similar to the socialized model. It is also centralized, funded by means of taxation, and the state is responsible for the provision of institution-based care (hospitals). The major difference between the NHS model and the socialized model, however, is that in the former model the medical profession has a more independent position. Further, self-employed general practitioners have an important role as the gatekeepers in primary health care. This implies that before visiting the hospital or a medical specialist, it is obligatory to have a referral from a general practitioner. Another difference is that the NHS model has less government regulation and leaves more room for private medicine.

Through processes of diffusion and adaptation, the Beveridge model was first adopted in Sweden, and then by the other Nordic countries: Denmark, Norway, and Finland. At present, the NHS model applies to the United Kingdom, Ireland, Denmark, Norway, Sweden, Finland, and Iceland, and outside Europe to Australia and New Zealand. Four Southern European countries adopted the tax-based model more recently: Italy, in 1978; Portugal, 1979; Greece, 1983; and Spain, 1986.

NORTH AMERICAN HEALTH CARE SYSTEMS: CANADA AND THE UNITED STATES

It has been argued that a crucial element of ways in which health care systems are structured, in essence, depends on the relationship between three principal actors: the medical profession, the state, and the insurers (Johnson, Larkin, and Saks 1995; Tuohy 1999). There is a mix of mechanisms of social control systemizing and legitimizing relationships between these actors. The first is by the market, characterized by voluntary exchange relationships. The second is through a hierarchy, based on a chain of command and on obedience to rules. The third is characterized by collegiality, based on common norms and values and on a common knowledge base. While the National Health Service in the UK is a typical example of the hierarchy model (strong position of the state; rules), the US and Canada reflect the market and the collegiality models (Tuohy 1999). In the United States, the logic of the market and entrepreneurialism dominate. Canada relies more on collegial mechanisms.

While during past decades many health care systems underwent major structural reforms, the Canadian health care system remained remarkably stable. There has been continuing public and political support for maintaining a system that provides universal access to medical services for those in need regardless of economic position. In the late 1960s, Canada adopted universal hospital and medical care insurance, based on tax financing, while the provision of professional services remained in private hands. Most physicians (about two-thirds) are in private, self-employed, fee-for-service practice. Provincial governments were the exclusive payers for most services, and the allocation of services was negotiated with the medical profession. Prior to the introduction of universal public programs, the financing of hospital and medical care occurred in a mixture of funding modalities. State-provider negotiations promoted enormous discretion for the profession, which explains, in part, why the Canadian health care system ranked among the high spenders of publicly financed systems. Physicians' fees tended to rise faster than the general income level. In the early 1970s, Canada broke with this previous trend.

As Evans (1985) notes, the Canadian health care system is quite clearly not "socialized medicine," despite the rhetoric. Only the insurance can be typified as socialized, because it is exclusive, without competition, and superimposed by the government upon a delivery system that is virtually private. For a long period, using this model, Canada succeeded in complying with the effectiveness and legitimacy criterion in health care, in providing all citizens with access to all the medically necessary hospital and medical services, without financial barriers, and at a reasonable and acceptable price in terms of share of the national income.

As elsewhere in the world, however, Canadian physicians favor the use of state power to ensure their professional monopoly without being publicly accountable. Consequently, continuing profession–government tensions and public concerns on rising costs and limited access resulted in several modifications of the Canadian health care system. According to recent figures (2008), the Canadians spend 10 percent of their gross domestic product (GDP) on health care, which is again quite high. It places Canada in the eighth position of high spenders among 31 OECD countries. One of the questions in Canada is whether market competition should be introduced by permitting private entrepreneurs to provide for-profit services, next to the well-established Canadian Medicare model. On this issue, the Canadian medical profession is divided between whether to continue to accommodate with the state or to press for more entrepreneurial freedom. On a provincial level, the accommodation of the state with the medical profession, serving purposes on both sides for more than two decades, has become more and more of an uneasy relationship since the 1990s (Tuohy 1999).

While Medicare and Medicaid provide services to the poor and to the elderly, the basic model of the United States health care system is a voluntary reimbursement model, with four actors playing a key role (Hurst 1992). First-level (general practitioners) and second-level providers (hospitals) deliver services to patients who are reimbursed for their medical bill, in part or in full. Patients pay a voluntary risk-related premium to voluntary insurers, who reimburse them for medical expenses.

In principle, there is no or minimal interaction between insurer and provider. Only the patient interacts with both parties.

This private reimbursement model has two major drawbacks (Hurst 1992). One is that it does not have built-in incentives to restrict demand and, therefore, is often accompanied by cost sharing. Another drawback is that it does not have built-in mechanisms to prevent inequities. For reasons of profit maximization, private insurers have an incentive to select against poor risks. Moreover, access to voluntary insurance is only open to those who are willing or can afford to pay. This has enormous consequences for health care insurance coverage in the US. While most OECD countries achieved universal coverage, US figures showed that, in 2005, 15 percent of the population (nearly 46 million people) were without health insurance, varying between 8 percent for the population of Minnesota and 24 percent in Texas (US Bureau of the Census 2007). This problem has been put on the political agenda again and again, but still has not seen any substantial improvements (Mechanic 2006). Reforming health care, however, is becoming a domestic priority. United States per capita health spending, currently above 15 percent of GDP, continues to exceed per capita health spending in the other OECD countries by huge margins. In the period between 1991 and 2001, the US average annual growth in health spending was 3.1, compared to 2.1 in Canada and 3.0 for the OECD median. Despite managed care initiatives and government attempts at regulation, costs keep increasing in the United States. Lack of (hospital) budget control, fragmented and complex payment systems that weaken the demand side, and excessive administrative overhead may account for the high health care spending (Anderson 1997; Anderson and Poullier 1999; OECD 2007; Reinhardt, Hussey, and Anderson 2004). Failure to overcome the current health system's dysfunction seems not to be a matter of organizational capacity but of will, commitment, and cultural constraints (Mechanic 2006). Most Americans, getting their health insurance through their employers, hardly have an idea of what anything costs. While Americans love fancy technology, the doctor gets paid for anything he or she does or prescribes, which is an incentive to perform costly procedures. Costs are passed on to insurers who, in turn, pass them on to employers in the form of higher premiums, and then to employees, resulting in lower salaries. The rising costs of coverage squeeze ordinary Americans' wages and/or result in dropping health care coverage overall.

Just like in other industrial societies, health care reforms in the US are essentially focused on cost containment. Managed care initiatives, for example health maintenance organizations (HMOs), were developed to increase competition, to change methods of payment for medical services, and to curb the power of the medical profession. The fundamental model of the health maintenance organization is to be typified as a voluntary contract model (Hurst 1992). It involves contractual relationships between insurers and independent providers, which give these providers an exclusive right to supply complete services, mainly free of charge. Patients pay a voluntary, risk-related premium to voluntary insurers who have contracts with providers. The difference with the voluntary reimbursement model is that insurers now have contractual relationships with providers. Variations on this voluntary contract model are the Individual Practice Organizations, where insurers are controlled by providers. These managed care models are all aimed at controlling the costs of health care by monitoring the work of doctors and hospitals, and by limiting the visit to second-level hospital care. In practice, this is often done by means of a "case manager," who, on behalf of the insurer, is authorized to decide whether the care to be rendered is effective and efficient. Another feature is that patients are only allowed to see a specialist after they have visited a general practitioner. This gatekeeper role of the primary care physician to the use of specialist care is similar to the role of GPs in European countries like Denmark, Norway, Italy, the Netherlands, Portugal, Spain, and the UK (Kroneman, Maarse, and Van der Zee 2006).

At the end of the 1990s, almost 90 percent of practicing physicians in the US participated in at least one or more managed care organizations (Tuohy 1999). Their share in patient enrollment rose from 12 percent in 1981 to 53 percent in 2006. Therefore, managed care is the most significant development in the US health care arena. But the "competition revolution" in US health care in the 1990s was driven more by the increasing activism of purchasers than by the supply side (Tuohy 1999). As a result of government efforts to introduce tighter payment schemes under Medicare, hospital providers sought to shift some of their costs from public to private payers. Within the context of changing economic circumstances, this alarmed purchasers and provoked them to play a more substantial role in the organization and management of the use of services. For the medical profession, the increasing importance of bargaining relationships and contracting with entrepreneurs ultimately led to a dramatic decline of their influence in the private-market-oriented US health care arena.

HEALTH CARE SYSTEMS IN ASIA: THE CASE OF JAPAN AND CHINA

Conceptually, the Japanese health care system can be typified as a social insurance model with mixed public and private providers (Abell-Smith 1996). Japan adopted the Bismarckian health care model of Germany in 1927. It has achieved universal health insurance coverage since 1961, with one insurance program for employees and their dependents (paid by employers and employees), and one national program for all others (paid by taxes). Japan has one of the most equitable health care systems in the world (Ikegami 1991; Ikegami and Campbell 1999). An insured person is free to go to any hospital or clinic, with no difference in costs. Despite this nationwide insurance scheme, the delivery of services is highly privatized, with an overwhelming amount of physicians in solo practices working on a fee-for-service basis (Nakahara 1997). These physicians are essentially general practitioners, similar to European GPs, but prefer to see themselves as more specialized (Nakahara 1997).

The Japanese health care system would benefit from greater differentiation and vertical integration. Private practitioners are not allowed to practice medicine in the hospital, just as is the case in several European countries (Garland 1995). But, unlike the situation in other countries, there is no referral relation between first-level services of these office-based physicians and second-level services provided in hospitals. As a consequence of the fee structure, office-based physicians compete with hospitals for patients and try to keep them in their own practice as much as possible. Hospitals do the same, because they are in the main owned by physicians, who also serve as prescribers and dispensers of medications (Ikegami and Campbell 1999).

Also, long-term care for the elderly is burdened by the absence of a differentiated and vertically integrated health care system. While the rate of institutionalized elderly does not deviate from figures in other industrialized societies, care is provided in hospitals rather than in nursing homes. A consequence of this is the high average hospital length of stay, the highest among OECD countries (OECD 2007). Incomplete vertical integration of Japanese health care services is due significantly to the high degree of autonomy of the medical profession in medical practice and in capital expenditures. This is evident in the availability of medical equipment. Japan has the highest rate of CT scanners and MRI equipment in the world, because not only hospitals but also private clinics are allowed to purchase expensive equipment (OECD 2007).

While having adopted a basic European health care model, Japan kept many of its typical cultural peculiarities. Traditional medicine continues to be widely practiced in Japan (Anderson, Oscarson, and Yu 1995; Garland 1995). As Anderson and colleagues (1995) have noted, since Western medicine was introduced in Japan it has been shaped and molded to fit into the cultural context of East Asian medicine. Despite the long average intramural length of stay, Japan has the lowest rate of hospital admissions in the world (OECD 2007). One reason is the cultural antipathy for invasive procedures and a preference for more conservative treatments. Another is that invasive procedures are discouraged by low fees for physicians to conduct surgery (Ikegami and Campbell 1999).

In recent years, the Japanese health care system has been faced with rising costs, an aging population, and growing consumer consciousness. This has led the government to initiate proposals to reform the system, similar to those in other industrialized countries. However, the necessity of health care reform in Japan should be considered in the circumstance that its health spending is still among the lowest in industrialized societies. There may be greater reasons to reform because of organizational problems than financial ones (Ikegami and Campbell 1999).

The Chinese health care system, created in 1949, was also a typical example of the now largely extinct twentieth-century communist model. By the early 1980s, the Chinese government virtually dismantled it (Blumenthal and Hsiao 2005). Its way of financing was dramatically changed by reducing government investments, the imposition of price regulation, and the decentralization and underfinancing of its public health system. China now has a private health care system, with its typical failures: a large part of the population not covered by health insurance (about 70 percent), unaffordable services for many, high national spending, and overuse of (profitable) pharmaceuticals and high-tech care (Blumenthal and Hsiao 2005). Currently, the government is trying to repair the damage done, which ultimately may result in a mixed public–private system (McIntyre et al. 2007). The outline is already clear: the role of the government will be stronger, more money will come from a central budget, and there is a move toward universal health insurance. Many problems still exist. The medical insurance scheme introduced in the countryside in 2003 is only a slight relief for the poor. But many urban residents also fare badly. The reforms reversed the market-driven policies of the past decades. China proves negatively that government involvement in health care is essential to keep the health care system intact, to protect patients, and to provide affordable access to services.

LATIN AMERICA: COLOMBIA AS THE MODEL TO FOLLOW?

Just as in some European health care systems, the model of managed competition gained ground throughout Latin American countries, most notably in Colombia, Argentina, and Chile (Cavagnero 2008). These Latin American health systems, traditionally characterized by the coexistence of a private, social, and public sector, were drastically overhauled by reforms that started in the early 1990s. The general framework, pushed by the International Monetary Fund (IMF) and the World Bank, was that they shift the role of the government from the operator of public health services to one of regulating a mixed public and private system. Whereas the government used to be the purchaser and provider of health services, these tasks were separated by means of an insurance system. Decentralized units and private organizations implemented the reforms (Bossert et al. 1998). A typical example of such reform is the Colombian health care system, which has often been suggested to other countries as the model to follow (Homedes and Ugalde 2005).

In the mid-1990s, the Colombian health care system underwent a very ambitious and complex reform in order to achieve universality, equity, solidarity, and efficiency. Up until that time, the health care system was considered highly inefficient and badly targeted, in particular to health care for the poor. The system was composed of three different subsystems: a national health system aimed at the poor and financed from a national budget; a social security system aimed at public and private employees, financed from a national budget and run by insurance companies; and a private sector mainly for the rich (and poor) without NHS (out-of-pocket delivery). In 1993, Colombia introduced one system for all with two different funding mechanisms, a contributory and a subsidized one. The essence of the model was universal access to a relatively large package of services and the participation of the private sector in collecting premiums and delivering health services. Employers and employees contribute a percentage (12 percent) of income to a solidarity fund. Insurance agencies (*Entidad Promotora de Salud*) act on behalf of individuals in purchasing services, after which services are provided as health services packages (*Plan Obligatorio de Salud*). For lower-income groups (between 55 and 60 percent of the population), there is a subsidized regimen, funded through the contributions of the government. Equity in financing is realized through cross-subsidizing, resulting in higher access to health care to the poor. While in 1993, 23 percent of the population had access to health care insurance, this percentage had increased to 62 percent ten years later. Among the poor, insurance coverage increased from 9 to 48 percent in the same period. Not surprisingly, the poor are the greatest supporters of the new system (Tono 2008).

Changing the system to the current one has required a technically and politically demanding effort. The Colombian subsidized health system managed to provide insurance coverage to approximately half of the poor population. Notwithstanding important achievements, in particular in the first years, there is a continuing debate on the realization of universality, equity, and solidarity, on resources wasted, modest insurance coverage, and bad management (Castano and Zambrano 2006; De Vos et al. 2006; Homedes and Ugalde 2005; Plaza, Barona, and Hearst 2001). Colombia is still far from offering universal coverage and the equitable provision of health services (Rosa and Alberto 2004). There is also the question of financial sustainability, considering the current economic crisis, corruption, and inaccurate financial forecasting. The health care reform led to a significant increase in total expenditures (Tono 2008). Therefore, difficulties in financing health care for the poor will continue. Reduced revenues were caused by the recession at the end of the 1990s. Public hospitals (two-thirds of the total), traditionally on historically decided budgets, had great difficulties when they were required to bill and to reduce their increasing expenditures – mainly caused by the increase in personnel expenditures – to match their revenues. Also, some health professionals, in particular high-earning hospital physicians, were unhappy when their high-bracket earnings were reduced (Tono 2008).

HEALTH CARE IN SOUTH AFRICA:
THE FAILING PUBLIC–PRIVATE MIX

Health systems in many low- and middle-income countries are failing not only the poor but also other income groups, who are faced with wide-ranging barriers to accessing the health care they need (McIntyre et al. 2007). South Africa is, in terms of income distribution, one of the most unequal countries in the world. This situation has worsened since the end of apartheid in 1994, which means that economic growth has mostly benefited a small elite. Forty percent of the richest South Africans account for 86 percent of income. The South African health care system is far removed from what Colombia has realized up until now. South Africa has an underperforming health sector despite the fact that it spends a greater proportion of its GDP on health than any other African country (McIntyre 2008). But it ranks very poorly (3.5 percent) compared to some other low- and middle-income countries (Colombia, 6.7 percent; Cuba, 5.5 percent; Brazil, 4.8 percent), while its infant mortality rate per 1,000 living births is 55, compared to 6 in Cuba, 17 in Colombia, and 31 in Brazil.

South Africa's health system is a mixed public–private system and consists of a large public sector and a smaller but fast-growing private sector. Health care varies from the most basic primary health care, offered free by the state, to highly specialized hi-tech health services available in the private sector for those who can afford it. Inequity and inefficiency in relation to the segmentation between the public and private sector are among the main contributing factors to the poor performance of the health care system. Compared to the public sector, the private sector spends approximately seven times more per capita on only less than 20 percent of the population. The public sector mainly serves the uninsured and poor, approximately 84 percent of the population. Its spending is approximately 40 percent of the total health funding (Health Systems Trust 2005). While the public sector is overused and underresourced, the private sector employs most of South African health professionals and serves the middle- and high-income groups. In the private sector, there is one medical specialist for every 500 patients; in the public sector, there are 11,000 patients per specialist. The private curative sector continues to grow, which is typical of supply increasing the demand: the building of new private hospitals attracts specialists, who increase the utilization, income, and profits. Private sector growth is further stimulated by the public sector shifting its emphasis from hospital care to primary care. With the public sector's shift in emphasis from acute to primary health care in recent years, private hospitals have begun to take over many tertiary and specialist health services.

The current situation is that the public system is systematically underresourced and barely keeps pace with inflation and population growth. There is a declining number of staff taking care of the increasing health care needs due to HIV/AIDS, tuberculosis epidemics, and the growing burden of non-communicable (chronic) diseases. There is an urgent need to strengthen public health services that have been systematically neglected over the past few decades while also regulating the worst excesses of the private health sector.

One way to address the disparities between the public and the private sector is by introducing a national health insurance system, in line with the NHS model or the social insurance model. Such intervention to fundamentally change the health system is essential to break the vicious cycle of poverty, ill health, and (further) impoverishment. Cross-subsidization, from wealthy to poor and from healthy to ill, which could be achieved by increasing allocation from general tax revenues and by pooling of funds for everyone's benefit (McIntyre et al. 2007). Additionally needed measures include restoring public hospitals, human resources development and retention strategies, and the upgrade of primary care facilities to a gatekeeper's service.

CULTURE AND VALUE ORIENTATIONS IN HEALTH CARE

Anthropologists have argued that differences between health care systems are imbedded in the values and social structure of the societies involved (Helman 1996). Based on specific histories, traditions, customs, and so on, differences in health care organization reflect the way in which societies define and deal with issues of health and illness. For example, in some societies, health care is considered a collective good for the benefit of all citizens. In others, health care is treated as a "commodity" that can be bought or sold on a free market. As Gallagher (1988: 65) notes, "The concept of health care as a calculable resource is an essential feature in its role as a carrier of modernity." The notion of health care as a commodity, however, has not been rooted everywhere. It appears that it has been more established in the essentially market-oriented organization of health care in the US than elswhere. Nowhere in Europe has it become part of health policy objectives, notwithstanding a wide range of health care reforms in recent years introducing market-oriented approaches with incentives to introduce greater competition between providers and to use resources more economically (Saltman and Figueras 1997).

Cultures or nations can vary in value orientations to a considerable degree. For example, values of equity, solidarity, and autonomy may have different significance across cultures (Hofstede 1984). As will be discussed, emphasis on hospital care versus home care or care for the elderly, on individual responsibilities or on solidarity between people, reflects general value orientations that have priority in a society (Hofstede 1984; Philipsen 1980; Stevens and Diederiks 1995). The cultural embeddedness of health care in industrialized societies, however, is an often discussed but rather underresearched topic (Saltman and Figueras 1997; Stevens and Diederiks 1995). There is little research on core values underlying the organization of health care systems in modern societies.

One notable exception is Lynn Payer's (1990) *Medicine and Culture*. She compared medical culture and health practices in Germany, Great Britain, France, and the United States on the basis of her own observations, literature study, and interviews with key persons. Not unexpectedly, she found the largest differences between the US and the European systems. For example, the dominant attitude of doctors in the US is described by her as "aggressive" and "action oriented," in accordance with a kind of "frontier mentality." American doctors appear to favor surgery above drug therapy. But when drug therapy is used, they do it more aggressively than in Europe. European doctors were found to prefer less radical approaches, although the differences between Germany, France, and Great Britain were also substantial, in particular with regard to procedures in diagnosis and treatment (Payer 1990).

Another study is Hofstede's research on international differences in value orientations. For his *Culture's Consequences: International Differences in Work-Related Values*, Hofstede (1984) surveyed employees of IBM plants in 40 different nations. He found that national cultures could be classified along four different value orientations: (1) individualism versus collectivism, (2) large versus small power distance, (3) strong versus weak uncertainty avoidance, and (4) masculinity versus femininity.

Individualism/collectivism refers to whether, in a particular society, the individual opinion and the individual interest is considered as more important than collective opinions and collective interest, or vice versa. It indicates the weight of our own interests versus the weight of the public good. The second dimension, *power distance*, indicates the extent to which the less powerful members in a society expect and accept that power is unequally distributed. Power distance, therefore, points to the degree of inequality in a society. The third dimension, *uncertainty avoidance*, reflects the extent to which members of a society feel threatened by uncertain or unknown situations, and whether people can cope with this. It also indicates whether people are willing to take certain risks in life. Finally, *masculinity/femininity* refers to the division of social roles between the sexes and indicates whether achievement and competitiveness (masculine behavior) prevails above "tender" relations and care for others (feminine behavior).

Hofstede's study was not designed to analyze health care systems. But his work goes beyond the settings that were subject to his research, and indeed applies to the organization of health care services (Hofstede 1991). For example, in health care, the masculinity/femininity dimension would indicate the importance of rationality, efficiency, justice, and so forth on the one side (masculinity), and solidarity, continuity, importance of care and caring relationships, on the other (femininity). Uncertainty avoidance has been related to the nurse–physician ratio in a country (Hofstede 1984, 1991). When people in a society have difficulty in dealing with uncertain situations, they are more likely to consult the doctor (the "expert") rather than a nurse. Consequently, the work of physicians is considered as more important than that of nurses. Comparing doctor–nurse ratios in different European countries gives some support for Hofstede's hypothesis. The group of *Northern* European countries, consisting of Sweden, Norway, Finland, Denmark, and the Netherlands, share high scores on femininity and low scores on uncertainty avoidance. These countries are characterized by their long-standing tradition of social democratic policies and their well-developed systems of social security and health insurance coverage. All have a well-established system of "care" provision with regard to the delivery of home care, mental health care services, and care for the elderly. All these countries also have many more nurses than physicians (Saltman and Figueras 1997: 240; World Health Organization 1998). Alternatively, in the *Southern* European countries with high scores on masculinity and on uncertainty avoidance, specifically in Italy and Greece, there are more physicians than nurses.

But there is another inference to be made from these data that regards the development of professional home care nursing. Because doctors and nurses have different work, it is likely that in countries where the medical profession dominates health care, professional home care provided by the nursing profession is less in existence. Philipsen (1988) hypothesizes that in societies typified by a high degree of *uncertainty avoidance* and a *masculinity* orientation, it is more likely that: (1) "cure" (medical intervention) instead of "care" will prevail; (2) the physician has a dominant position in the health care system; (3) social positions are ascribed according to traditional sex roles.

Philipsen's hypothesis is also consistent with a north–south division in Europe, whereby in southern regions priority would be given to the cure and treatment of health care problems, while care activities would be dealt with more in family relations than by professional nursing (Giarchi 1996; Philipsen 1980). This is supported in an OECD study of the early 1990s, showing that the lowest percentages of institutionalized care (nursing home care) were found in Southern Europe (Greece, Italy, Portugal, Spain, Turkey). Most institutional care for the elderly was found in Northern Europe (the Netherlands, Finland, Norway, Luxembourg) and in Canada.

However, the absence of institutional care for the elderly is not compensated for by professional home care everywhere. For example, this is the case in the US, Canada, Austria, Germany, Ireland, and Japan. All these countries are considered as masculine societies, but divide on the uncertainty avoidance dimension. High levels of institutional and professional home care were found in Denmark, Finland, and Norway, while low levels of both types of care were found in Southern Europe (Italy, Spain, Portugal). Other countries were somewhat in the middle (Belgium, France, Sweden, UK, the Netherlands). From these data it appears that there is indeed evidence of a north–south division in Europe, whereby institutional care for the elderly in the north is not paralleled by professional home care in the south, but more by family care (Mossialos and Le Grand 1999: 56). This latter conclusion also applies to Japan, which has the highest masculinity score among countries that were under consideration (Hofstede 1984). Also, even though Canada and the US are considered masculine societies, they are low on uncertainty avoidance in contrast to Japan.

CONCLUSIONS: THE CONVERGENCE AND DIVERGENCE OF HEALTH CARE SYSTEMS

In this chapter, models of health care organization have been presented within the context of their cultural environment. While these models are the major ones that can be found in industrialized countries in Europe, America, and Asia, and in several middle-income countries, since the 1990s there is no system that fully complies to any one of these (Stevens and Van der Zee 2008). Because of financing problems necessitating cost containment, and through processes of adaptation and diffusion, national health care systems vary. Bismarckian health care systems and the entrepreneurial system of the US were confronted with problems of rising costs in the 1960s and 1970s. The NHS systems and socialized-like systems of Eastern Europe had problems of neglect, underfunding, and extensive bureaucracy. In some countries this led to more state regulation to curb the costs of health care. In other countries it resulted in less state intervention and in the introduction of experiments with different forms of managed competition. For example, in Eastern Europe after the fall of the Berlin Wall, we see the demise of state funding and state provision because of economic deficits. In the countries that have adopted the Bismarck model, we see more state and market regulation in order to introduce more planning and to curb the rising costs of health care. One of the results has been a stronger position for hospitals. In the United Kingdom, we have seen a movement toward greater decentralization, which was realized by the earlier noted split between purchasers and providers (Saltman and Figueras 1997; Tuohy 1999).

Health care organization, however, is also influenced by cultural circumstances. For example, nations with a strong collective orientation have more state intervention, a small private sector, have a preference for tax rather than insurance funding, and prefer comprehensive coverage with universal entitlement based on the notion of rights. In contrast, societies steeped in individualism prefer private enterprise and insurance funding with selective coverage and high responsiveness to consumer demand (Mechanic 2006). In societies that have equity as an important root, we see explicit attempts to avoid discrimination and to facilitate public participation.

We started this chapter with the question of whether countries at the same stage of industrial development have the same approach to the organization and management of health care services. Indeed, institutional patterns are converging. There is ample evidence that contingencies like increasing health care costs, an aging population, changing disease patterns, technological developments, growing public demand, and so forth impose a common logic in terms of institutional performance and in the structuring of modern health care systems. In the literature, a wide range of convergences in health policy and health care organization have been listed (Field 1989; Mechanic and Rochefort 1996; Raffel 1997; Saltman and Figueras 1997). These include (1) the concern of governments to control health care costs while at the same time improving the effectiveness and efficiency of the system; (2) the increasing attention for health promotion and healthy lifestyles such as abstinence from substance use (alcohol, smoking, drugs) and the promotion of healthy behavior; (3) reduction of health care inequalities and differences in access; (4) the stimulation of primary health care at the expense of cutting back further medical specialization; (5) the promotion of patient participation and improving patient satisfaction; and (6) the reduction of fragmentation of services and the promotion of continuity of care.

The convergence of modern health care systems, however, is not undisputed. Even if societies are faced with similar contingencies, their societal structures have to be consonant with culturally derived expectations (Lammers and Hickson 1979). Consequently, while there is substantial evidence that modern societies are evolving in the same direction, with efficiency, equity, and utilitarian individualism as core value orientations, differences exist in degree and similarity of these developments. Modern societies still vary considerably in the way they deal with issues of health and illness (Anderson et al. 1995). Moreover, while nations may have similar goals, alternative options are available to reach these. National health systems are the outcome of a dialectical tension between universal aspects of technology and medicine on the one hand, and particularistic cultural characteristics of each nation on the other (Field 1989). These particularistic cultural characteristics refer to the historical foundations of health care systems, to the societal and national context, and to specific values and value orientations of societies and health care systems under consideration. According to Pomey and Poullier (1997), health care institutions are still largely country-specific. Such country-specific elements would include the social, economic, institutional, and ideological structures, the dominant belief system, the role of the state versus the market, patterns of health care coverage, and centralization or decentralization of political authority (Saltman and Figueras 1997, 1998). As Saltman and Figueras (1998: 105) note, "Given unbridgeable conceptual differences and divergence in organizational principles, suggestions of convergence among the health care systems of industrialized countries seem to be misplaced." Whether health care systems and not only policy objectives will converge remains to be seen.

References

Abell-Smith, Brian. 1996. *The Reform of Health Care Systems: A Review of Seventeen OECD Countries*. Paris: Organization for Economic Cooperation and Development.

Anderson, Gerard F. 1997. "In Search of Value: An International Comparison of Cost, Access, and Outcomes." *Health Affairs* 16: 163–71.

Anderson, Gerard F. and Jean-Pierre Poullier. 1999. "Health Spending, Access, and Outcomes: Trends in Industrialized Countries." *Health Affairs* 18: 178–92.

Anderson, James G., Renee Oscarson, and Yan Yu. 1995. "Japan's Health Care System: Western and East Asian Influences." Pp. 32–44 in E. Gallagher and J. Subedi (eds.), *Global Perspectives on Health Care*. Englewood Cliffs, NJ: Prentice-Hall.

Blumenthal, D. and W. Hsiao, 2005. "Privatization and its Discontents: The Evolving Chinese Health Care System." *New England Journal of Medicine* 353: 1165–70.

Bossert, Thomas, William Hsiao, Mariela Barrera, Lida Alarcon, Maria Leo, and Carolana Cacares. 1998. "Transformation of Ministries of Health in an Era of Health Reform: The Case of Colombia." *Health Policy and Planning* 13: 59–77.

Castano, Ramon and Andres Zambrano. 2006. "Biased Selection within the Social Health Insurance Market in Colombia." *Health Policy* 79: 313–24.

Cavagnero, Eleonora. 2008. "Health Sector Reforms in Argentina and the Performance of the Health Financing System." *Health Policy* 88: 88–99.

De Vos, Pol, Wim De Ceukelaire, and Patrick Van der Stuyft. 2006. "Colombia and Cuba, Contrasting Models in Latin America's Health Sector Reform." *Tropical Medinine and International Health* 11: 1604–12.

Evans, Robert G. 1981. "Incomplete Vertical Integration: The Distinctive Structure of the Health-Care Industry." Pp. 329–54 in J. Van der Gaag and M. Perlman (eds.), *Health, Economics, and Health Economics. Proceedings of the World Congress on Health Economics, Leiden, The Netherlands, September 1980*. Amsterdam: North-Holland.

Evans, Robert G. 1985. "The Grass on Our Side is Actually Quite Green ... Health Care Funding in Canada." *Gezondheid and Samenleving* 6: 245–55.

Field, Mark. 1989. "The Comparative Evolution of Health Systems: Convergence, Diversity and Cross-Cutting Issues." Pp. 15–30 in G. Lüschen, W. Cockerham, and G. Kunz (eds.), *Health and Illness in America and Germany*. Munich: Oldenbourg.

Gallagher, Eugene. 1988. "Modernization and Medical Care." *Sociological Perspectives* 31: 59–87.

Gallagher, Eugene. 1999. "'Hi-Tech' Home Treatment for Patients with Serious Chronic Illness: Sociological Questions." Paper presented to the International Conference on Socio-Cultural and Policy Dimensions of Health Care, Singapore.

Garland, Neal T. 1995. "Major Orientations in Japanese Health Care." Pp. 255–67 in E. Gallagher and J. Subedi (eds.), *Global Perspectives on Health Care*. Englewood Cliffs, NJ: Prentice-Hall.

General Medical Council (GMC). 2003. *Tomorrow's Doctors*. London: General Medical Council.

Giarchi, George Giacinto. 1996. *Caring for Older Europeans: Comparative Studies in Twenty-Nine Countries*. Aldershot: Arena.

Ginzberg, Eli. 1996. *Tomorrow's Hospital: A Look to the Twenty-First Century*. New Haven, CT: Yale University Press.

Health Systems Trust (HST). 2005. *South African Health Review 2005*. Johannesburg: Health Systems Trust.

Helman, Cecil G. 1996. *Culture, Health and Illness*. London: Wright.

Hofstede, Geert. 1984. *Culture's Consequences: International Differences in Work-Related Values*. London: Sage.

Hofstede, Geert. 1991. *Cultures and Organizations: Software of the Mind*. London: McGraw-Hill.

Homedes, Núria and Antonio Ugalde. 2005. "Why Neoliberal Health Reforms have Failed in Latin America." *Health Policy* 71: 83–96.

Hurst, Jeremy. 1992. *The Reform of Health Care: A Comparative Analysis of Seven OECD Countries*. Paris: Organization for Economic Cooperation and Development.

Ikegami, Naoki. 1991. "Japanese Health Care: Low Cost Through Regulated Fees." *Health Affairs* 10: 87–109.

Ikegami, Naoki and John Creighton Campbell. 1999. "Health Care Reform in Japan: The Virtues of Muddling Through." *Health Affairs* 18: 56–75.

Johnson, Terry, Gerry Larkin, and Mike Saks. 1995. *Health Professions and the State in Europe*. London and New York: Routledge.

Kroneman, Madelon W., Hans Maarse, and Jouke Van der Zee. 2006. "Direct Access to Primary Care and Patient Satisfaction: A European Study." *Health Policy* 76: 72–9.

Lammers, Cornelius J. 1993. *Organiseren van Bovenaf en Onderop* [Organizations in Comparison]. Utrecht: Het Spectrum.

Lammers, Cornelius J. and David J. Hickson. 1979. *Organizations Alike and Unlike: International and Inter-Institutional Studies in the Sociology of Organizations*. London: Routledge and Kegan Paul.

Leicht, Kevin T. and Mary Fennell. 1997. "The Changing Organizational Context of Professional Work." *Annual Review of Sociology* 23: 215–31.

Marrée, Jorgen and Peter P. Groenewegen. 1997. *Back to Bismarck: Eastern European Health Care in Transition.* Aldershot: Avebury.

McIntyre, Diane. 2008. Unpublished Inaugural Lecture, University of Cape Town, South Africa.

McIntyre, Diane, Margaret Whitehead, Lucy Gilson, Göran Dahlgren, and Shenglan Tang. 2007. "Equity Impacts of Neoliberal Reforms: What Should the Policy Responses Be?" *International Journal of Health Services* 37: 693–709.

McKee, Martin and Judith Healy. 2002. *Hospitals in a Changing Europe.* Buckingham: Open University Press.

Mechanic, David. 1975. *The Growth of Bureaucratic Medicine.* New York: Wiley.

Mechanic, David. 2006. *The Truth About Health Care: Why Reform Is Not Working in America.* New Brunswick, NJ: Rutgers University Press.

Mechanic, David and David A. Rochefort. 1996. "Comparative Medical Systems." *Annual Review of Sociology* 22: 239–70.

Mossialos, Elias and Derek King. 1999. "Citizens and Rationing: Analysis of a European Survey." *Health Policy* 49: 75–135.

Mossialos, Elias and Julian Le Grand. 1999. *Health Care and Cost Containment in the European Union.* Aldershot: Ashgate.

Nakahara, Toshitaka. 1997. "The Health System of Japan." In M. Raffel (ed.), *Health Care and Reform in Industrialized Countries.* University Park, PA: Pennsylvania State University Press.

Nayeri, K. and C. M. Lopez-Pardo, 2005. "Economic Crisis and Access to Care: Cuba's Health Care System Since the Collapse of the Soviet Union." *International Journal of Health Services* 35: 797–816.

Organization for Economic Cooperation and Development (OECD). 2007. *Health at a Glance: OECD Indicators 2007.* Paris: Organization for Economic Cooperation and Development.

Parsons, Talcott. 1951. *The Social System.* New York: Free Press.

Payer, Lynn. 1990. *Medicine and Culture: Notions of Health and Sickness in Britain, the US, France and West Germany.* London: Gollancz.

Philipsen, H. 1980. "Internationale vergelijking van welvaart, gezondheidszorg en levensduur: het probleem van Galton" ["International Comparisons of Prosperity, Health Care, and Life Expectancy: Galton's Problem"]. *Gezondheid en Samenleving* 1: 5–17.

Philipsen, H. 1988. *Gezondheidszorg als project en bejegening. Waarden ten aanzien van ziekte, gezondheid en samenleving [Health Care as a Project and Attitude: Values in Illness, Health, and Society].* Maastricht: Rijksuniversiteit Limburg.

Plaza, Beatriz, Ana B. Barona, and Norman Hearst. 2001. "Managed Competition for the Poor or Poorly Managed Competition? Lessons from the Colombian Health Reform Experience." *Health Policy and Planning* 16 (Supplement): 44–51.

Pomey, Marie-Pascal and Jean-Pierre Poullier. 1997. "France." In M. Raffel (ed.), *Health Care and Reform in Industrialized Countries.* University Park, PA: Pennsylvania State University Press.

Powell, Walter W. and Paul J. DiMaggio. 1991. *The New Institutionalism in Organizational Analysis.* Chicago: University of Chicago Press.

Raffel, Marshall W. 1997. "Dominant Issues: Convergence, Decentralization, Competition, Health Services." Pp. 291–303 in M. Raffel (ed.), *Health Care and Reform in Industrialized Countries.* University Park, PA: Pennsylvania State University Press.

Reinhardt, Uwe E., Peter S. Hussey, and Gerard F. Anderson. 2004. "Cross-National Comparisons of Health Systems Using OECD Data, 1999." *Health Affairs* 21: 169–81.

Rosa, Rodríguez-Monguió and Infante Campos Alberto. 2004. "Universal Health Care for Colombians 10 Years after Law 100: Challenges and Opportunities." *Health Policy* 68: 129–42.

Saltman, Richard B. and Josep Figueras. 1997. "European Health Care Reform." In *WHO Regional Publications, European series*. Copenhagen: World Health Organization, Regional Office for Europe.

Saltman, Richard B. and Josep Figueras. 1998. "Analyzing the Evidence on European Health Care Reforms." *Health Affairs* 17: 85–105.

Scott, W. Richard and John W. Meyer. 1991. "The Organization of Societal Sectors: Propositions and Early Evidence." Pp. 108–40 in W. Powell and P. DiMaggio (eds.), *The New Institutionalism in Organizational Analysis*. Chicago: University of Chicago Press.

Selznick, Philip. 1957. *Leadership in Administration*. New York: Harper and Row.

Starr, Paul. 1982. *The Social Transformation of American Medicine*. New York: Basic Books.

Stevens, Fred C. J. and Joseph P. M. Diederiks. 1995. "Health Culture: An Exploration of National and Social Differences in Health-Related Values." Pp. 137–44 in G. Lüschen, W. Cockerham, and J. Van der Zee (eds.), *Health Systems in the European Union: Diversity, Convergence, and Integration*. Munich: Oldenbourg.

Stevens, Fred C. J., Joseph P. M. Diederiks, and Hans Philipsen. 1992. "Physician Satisfaction, Professional Characteristics, and Behavior Formalization in Hospitals." *Social Science and Medicine* 35: 295–303.

Stevens, Fred C. J. and J. Van der Zee. 2008. "Health System Organization Models (Including Targets and Goals for Health Systems)." Pp. 247–56 in Kris Heggenhougen and Stella Quah (eds.), *International Encyclopedia of Public Health*, vol. 3. San Diego: Academic Press.

Tono, Teresa M. 2008. "*Thirteen Years of Healthcare Reform in Colombia*." Lecture presented at the Network Annual Conference, *Towards Unity for Health*, Bogotá, Colombia, September.

Tuohy, Carolyn Hughes. 1999. "Dynamics of a Changing Health Sphere: The United States, Britain, and Canada." *Health Affairs* 18: 114–31.

US Bureau of the Census. 2007. *Current Population Reports*. Washington, DC: Department of Commerce.

Warren, Mary Guptill, Rose Weitz, and Stephen Kulis. 1998. "Physician Satisfaction in a Changing Health Care Environment: The Impact of Challenges to Professional Autonomy, Authority, and Dominance." *Journal of Health and Social Behavior* 39: 356–67.

World Health Organization (WHO). 1998. *Health for All Database*. Copenhagen: Regional Office for Europe.

Zeitz, Gerald. 1984. "Bureaucratic Role Characteristics and Member Affective Response in Organizations." *Sociological Quarterly* 25: 301–18.

21

Social Policies and Health Inequalities

AMÉLIE QUESNEL-VALLÉE AND TANIA JENKINS

The relationship between low social status and poor health and mortality is undoubt-edly one of the most persistent empirical findings of contemporary research on population health, as demographers, sociologists, epidemiologists, and, more recently, economists have devoted enormous attention to the study of socioeco-nomic inequities in health. In the United States as in other developed countries, individuals with higher socioeconomic status have better health and lower mortal-ity than individuals below them in the social structure (Antonovsky 1967; Williams 1990). Moreover, this holds true – whether socioeconomic status is measured as education, income, or occupation – for different populations, through varied time periods, and using diverse analytic methods (Robert and House 2000).

In contrast with inequalities in health that stem from biological differences brought about by age or genetics, *social* inequalities in health are mutable and avoidable, as they are affected by public policies. In addition, they are also inher-ently unfair, as the preamble of the constitution of the World Health Organization (1948: 1) states: "The enjoyment of the highest attainable standard of health is one of the fundamental rights of every human being without distinction of race, religion, political belief, economic or social condition."

In this chapter we focus on ways in which health inequalities are linked to social policies. We will begin with an overview of the field of social inequalities in health, followed by a brief summary of the social determinants of health and the life-course theoretical perspectives, both of which inform our approach. Next, we will turn to a discussion of some of the most important macro-determinants of health to high-light how they may lead to social inequalities in health, drawing out policy implica-tions for each. Following a life-course perspective, we will treat in turn early life, housing, education, employment, health insurance, income, and social exclusion. Finally, we will end the chapter with a discussion of future challenges in the field, touching upon issues of international comparisons, the importance of life-course research that properly accounts for the dynamic relations of these factors over time, the difficulties inherent with binding research with a life-course perspective to policy making, and finally, the importance of this research for developing countries.

SOCIAL INEQUALITIES IN HEALTH

Whereas the notion of social inequalities in health has all but become common sense nowadays (Popay et al. 2003), this was not always so. In fact, increases in standards of living, medical advances, and the deployment of systems of universal health insurance coverage led many to think in the 1960s and 1970s that inequalities in health would fade away. Yet, in the early 1980s, two seminal pieces of evidence, namely the Black Report (Townsend, Davison, and Whitehead 1982) and the White-hall studies (Marmot, Shipley and Rose 1984), shattered these assumptions and heralded the onset of this prolific research enterprise.

The Black Report (Townsend et al. 1982) was in fact the end result of a British government-mandated Research Working Group on Inequalities in Health chaired by Sir Douglas Black. The impetus for this working group came from the realization that despite 30 years of strong welfare state policies, and especially the implementation of the National Health Service (NHS), Great Britain was lagging behind some other countries in terms of population health improvements (mainly measured in terms of mortality).

Mortality rates by social class over the previous century and in different countries were examined in what was arguably the first government-initiated attempt to explain trends in socioeconomic inequities in life expectancy and relate them to policy interventions. Briefly put, this report showed that a socioeconomic gradient in life expectancy existed in the early 1900s and has persisted ever since in Great Britain. Moreover, while the diseases associated with these inequities evolved over time, the gradient itself remained mainly impervious to change and was observed in several other developed nations. In addition, the development of a universal health care (or at least coverage) system in many countries did not appear to lessen this gradient. Finally, individuals' lifestyles could explain part of but not the total effects of socioeconomic status on mortality.

This report generated substantial political controversy in Great Britain as it challenged several assumptions that guided policy interventions up until then (MacIntyre 1997; Townsend et al. 1982). In particular, this report dealt a strong blow to the premise that a universal health care system was a sufficient condition for the eradication of social inequities in life expectancy. In addition, it also provided the first evidence of a social gradient in mortality, whereby life expectancy increases linearly with each additional step in occupational class structure. These findings disputed the notion that inequalities in health concerned only the most deprived segments of society, and that successful interventions could be directed solely at these populations.

But it was through the Whitehall studies that the gradient in health really struck the imagination of researchers. In these studies, Sir Marmot and his colleagues followed more than 10,000 British civil servants for close to two decades. An important feature of this sample lies in its status groupings, as British civil servants are clearly and unambiguously ordered hierarchically according to both their income and their rank. Marmot found that, among males aged 40 to 64, age-standardized mortality in the lowest grades (clerical and manual) was three times as high as in the highest grade (administrative). Moreover, these findings also uncovered a gradient in mortality from the top to the bottom of this social hierarchy. Indeed, the less "fortunate" were characterized by poorer health, and this, even in the presence of the universal access to the British medical system.

Furthermore, none of the respondents could be considered deprived materially in terms of absolute poverty. In fact, these findings went beyond the Black Report in contradicting the common view that surmised that socioeconomic differences in health were found because the poor suffered from the deprivation associated with their material circumstances. On the contrary, Marmot's findings tellingly indicated that socioeconomic differences in health were not limited to a few individuals at the very bottom of society, but rather that they were widespread in all of society, and presumably operated at all levels of the social ladder. Moreover, this gradient was again apparent for a number of illnesses, as well as for morbidity (not just mortality). The existence of this socioeconomic gradient for various illnesses suggests that it is caused by a common factor anterior to the illnesses themselves.

These studies' main findings were replicated in the United States (Pappas et al. 1993), Canada (Evans, Barer, and Marmor 1994), and in other countries as well (Marmot, Kogevinas, and Elston 1987). The accumulation of these results has led governments in most developed countries to designate the reduction of socioeconomic inequities in health as a primary health goal; in the United States, for instance, the eradication of these inequities is a stated goal of the United States Department of Health and Human Services' (2000) *Healthy People 2010*.

Overall, these findings establish the importance of the social environment as a health determinant, shifting the focus away from the medical, individualistic, and problem-oriented approach to a population-level view of health. At such a level of analysis, individual differences in health do not appear to be random, but rather to be patterned by socioeconomic status. Many terms have been used to describe these associations, such as health disparities (mainly in the US), health inequities (to denote a value judgment on the unfairness of those inequalities), and social inequalities in health (a descriptive statement useful to distinguish inequalities stemming from social and other factors). We have used the latter term up until now, but for parsimony, we will refer to these inequalities in the remainder of the text as simply "health inequalities."

SOCIAL DETERMINANTS OF HEALTH

While the environment was never completely absent from models of disease causation, the recognition that exposure to deleterious environmental conditions is socially patterned did not receive widespread acceptance until quite recently, after mounting evidence and anomalous findings became too weighty to ignore. In fact, according to Krieger (2001), Cassel's (1976) paper titled "The Contribution of the Social Environment to Host Resistance" marked a defining moment for the recognition of the salience of the social environment for health.

Following a period of rapid, almost geometric, growth of this field of research in the 1970s and 1980s, the 1990s saw the crystallization of knowledge in a plethora of reference documents and governmental initiatives. Calls for a change of paradigm in the study of the health of populations were made in response to the growing realization that while more and more funds were injected in universal health care systems, socioeconomic inequalities in health nevertheless persisted (Evans et al. 1994).

According to an authoritative eponymous book edited by Marmot and Wilkinson (1999), the social determinants of health encompass individuals' material and psychosocial circumstances, and range from the more micro-level of health behaviors and social support to the more macro-level of unemployment rates and policies regarding food and transportation.

These determinants are very aptly graphically represented in Figure 21.1, which was presented in the report of the British Independent Inquiry into Inequalities in Health chaired by Sir Donald Acheson (1998),[1] upon which the following discussion will draw. To explain this figure briefly, note that human populations appear at the center and are conceptualized as being endowed with age, sex, biological, and genetic characteristics. As such, this model is not mutually exclusive of the biomedical model, but rather incorporates it and broadens its scope. Yet, while these factors undoubtedly influence health, they are, however, considered as fixed and not amenable to intervention insofar as public health policies are concerned.

In contrast, the layers surrounding individuals are considered to be alterable by policy interventions. The innermost layer includes individuals' personal behaviors and lifestyles, which would include, for instance, smoking and eating habits and physical activity. These behaviors have the potential to promote or damage health.

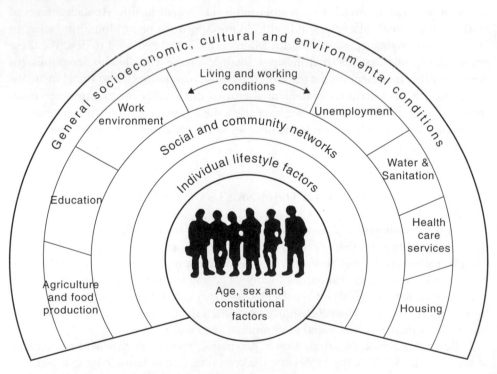

Figure 21.1 The main determinants of health.
Source: Acheson (1998).

The next layer highlights that individuals do not exist in a social vacuum. Their interactions with relatives, friends, and their immediate community expose them to influences that can impact their health directly through stress and social support, or indirectly, by molding their behaviors. For instance, the direct influence of the family of origin on health can be found at this level, as well as on the levels it circumscribes.

The third layer presents the wider social conditions that may influence individuals' ability to maintain their health, which include living and working conditions, as well as the provisions of the welfare state (or lack thereof) through education and health care, for instance. Finally, the outermost layer represents the overall economic, cultural, and environmental conditions prevalent in society as a whole at a given point in time.

We have limited the scope of this chapter to the third layer, as it is the one that is most pertinent to the study of social policies, which we define as "[s]tate and government interventions that contribute to the well-being of individuals and communities and foster full citizenship" (Vaillancourt et al. 2004: 313).[2] Within the realm of determinants that constitute this third layer, we restricted our analysis further to those that have received the most attention in the field of social inequalities in health, namely, education, employment (which subsumes the work environment and unemployment), health care services (or health insurance in this case), and housing.

We have also added to this list two determinants that have horizontal policy implications which cannot be confined in traditional governmental "silos." In other words, these are social determinants that do not fit within a given ministry or department, but demand policies that cut across departments. Thus, we added the topic of social exclusion, since it has more recently become the focus of much attention in many initiatives pertaining to the policy implications of social determinants of health (Commission on Social Determinants of Health 2008; Wilkinson and Marmot 2003), as well as early life, in recognition of the life-course perspective that also informs our approach.

HEALTH AND SOCIOECONOMIC STATUS OVER THE LIFE COURSE

While the life-course perspective has oriented a substantial amount of research in sociology over the past 30 years (George 2003), it has only recently become a unifying framework in the study of disease etiology (Ben-Shlomo and Kuh 2002) and socioeconomic inequities in health (Hertzman 1999). As O'Rand (2003: 693) puts it succinctly,

> [the] life course – when defined as interdependent sequences of age-related social roles across life domains (family, education, work, health, leisure) – is a product of the linkages among state (welfare), market and familial (gender) institutions and demographic behaviors across the life span.

Thus, the life-course perspective in sociology focuses on the intersection of individual biographies, social change, and social structure. More specifically, this perspective also pays particular attention to both the impact of early experiences on development and the timing and sequencing of roles throughout life. Naturally, similar themes can be found in conceptual models of life-course epidemiology. This section will expose the three main ways in which socioeconomic status over the life course has been postulated to affect health, namely, the latent, pathway, and cumulative effects.

Latent effects

According to this hypothesis, adverse socioeconomic conditions *in utero* and during infancy and childhood act as critical determinants of poor health in adulthood, irrespective of intervening social circumstances (Barker 2003; Barker et al. 2002; Hertzman 1999). Thus, this hypothesis encompasses both the eponymous "Barker hypothesis" and Hertzman's "biological embedding" model. Essentially, these authors argue that socioeconomic status may be associated with specific biological disadvantage at developmentally critical moments in the life course. In turn, this biological impairment may have an impact on health and well-being that emerges only much later in life, without having affected or having been affected by intervening socioeconomic circumstances.

Empirically, research on the impact of early-life experiences on adult health has intensified in the past decade with findings convincing enough to warrant the establishment of social policies and interventions to ensure the optimal psychological and physical development of infants and children (Gouvernement du Québec 2002; Health Canada 2001). Studies have indeed found that adverse socioeconomic conditions during childhood were associated with greater risk of health outcomes such as poor self-reported health, cardiovascular disease, and higher mortality independent of adult social circumstances (Gliksman et al. 1995; Goya-Wannamethee et al. 1996; Kaplan and Salonen 1990; Lynch et al. 1994; Nystrom-Peck 1994; Vågerö and Leon 1994).

Cumulative effects

This hypothesis suggests that socioeconomic status (SES) over the life course has cumulative effects on health, regardless of when adversity is experienced in the life course (Power, Manor, and Matthews 1999). For instance, taking the medical analogy of a dose–response mechanism, every additional dollar increase in lifetime income or additional year of education will have a positive effect on adult health. Perhaps the most compelling evidence for this hypothesis is found in studies that show that the relationship between income and mortality becomes stronger when earnings are measured over several years (Benzeval and Judge 2001; McDonough et al. 1997). More generally, exposure to cumulative socioeconomic disadvantage[3] across the life course was associated with higher mortality from multiple causes, worse mental health, poorer self-rated health, and impaired cognitive function (Beebe-Dimmer et al. 2004; Frank et al. 2003; Hayward and Gorman 2004; Mustard, Vermeulen, and Lavis 2003; Pensola and Martikainen 2003, 2004).

Pathway effects

Of the three mechanisms, pathway effects hypothesize the most complex interaction between individual and environment, whereby early life environments may shape the life trajectories of individuals. For instance, a typical pathway effect would occur when low SES in childhood restricts educational opportunities, which in turn impairs entry into the labor force in early adulthood, with dire consequences for accumulated SES and, finally, health in adulthood (Graham 2002).

Pathway effects do not postulate deterministic mechanisms, but they do represent probabilities whereby positive outcomes at one stage increase the likelihood of positive outcomes at the next in a process of cumulative advantage – or, conversely, of cumulative disadvantage (Evans 2002; O'Rand 1996, 2002). Moreover, while the latent effects hypothesis is essentially biological at its roots, the pathway hypothesis has a more sociologically salient interpretation that can be linked to the impact of structural constraints on transitions in a life-course perspective.

The evidence regarding pathways is at this point more suggestive than definitive, as they are less often hypothesized (and adequately tested) than the other two mechanisms. A good example of a pathway effect is provided by Hayward and Gorman's (2004) "long arm of childhood" US study (also see Pensola and Martikainen 2004 for a comparable study – and findings – with a Finnish population). Hayward and Gorman's (2004) study cogently suggests that the pathways through which SES influences mortality, and presumably health, over the life course are multiple and not interchangeable. Moreover, this study highlights the fact that pathway effects can potentially coexist with – or perhaps subsume – both cumulative and latent effects.

The life-course perspective underlies much of the results we present in this chapter, as many of the relationships we will discuss can be taken to have cumulative or pathway effects. In addition, we treat specifically latent (and potential pathway) effects in the "Early Life" section.

SOCIAL POLICIES AND HEALTH INEQUALITIES

One of the most prolific – and hotly debated – areas of research on social inequities in health postulates the existence of an independent effect of the extent of inequality in a society on individuals' health and longevity. However, seldom have studies considered how institutional factors that antecede these macro-level inequities could change the relationship between individual SES and health (Coburn 2004; Lynch et al. 2000). In this section, we review the evidence on some of the most prominent social determinants of health and highlight the policy implications that this research suggests.

Early life

Promoting healthy, happy childhoods can be considered a wise social investment for the future (Ridge 2008). Early childhood development that occurs in the first eight years of life (including physical, social, emotional, and cognitive development) is crucial for health outcomes later in life, since it sets the stage for future health afflictions, employment potential, and social relationships (Commission on Social Determinants of Health 2008). It is therefore little wonder that childhood health has been found to be an important predictor of both adult health and socioeconomic status (Wadsworth 1999). For example, the experience of socioeconomic deprivation in early life can increase the chances of poor physical development and low educational attainment in childhood, which can then lead to lower SES in adulthood (Ben-Shlomo and Kuh 2002; Case, Fertig, and Paxson 2005; Case and Paxson 2006). Given the importance of early life, then, what are the specific social factors which pose an increased risk to health in early childhood?

Social inequalities can first emerge from deleterious exposures *in utero*, particularly those related to the mother's nutrition and health behaviors such as smoking, alcohol or drug consumption, and exercise (Wadsworth 1999). For instance, Barker (2003) has argued that the link between low birth weight and the development of cardiovascular disease more than half a century later provides evidence of long-lasting effects of poor growth *in utero*. Support for this hypothesis has also come from cohort studies of individuals having suffered through "natural experiments" of starvation, such as studies of the Dutch Famine Birth. During World War II, a period of five or six months of extreme food shortage occurred in the Netherlands, then occupied by the German Army. Official food rations were below 1,000 calories per person per day from January through April 1945, or half the current recommended minimal caloric intake for an average height and weight pregnant woman (Institute of Medicine 2002). These studies found individuals who were severely undernourished in early gestation to be at higher risk of obesity, coronary heart disease, and lower self-reported health, which suggests they may also exhibit higher mortality in the future (Roseboom et al. 2001).

Following birth, social variations in breastfeeding can also have long-lasting effects throughout the life course. Exclusive breastfeeding is recommended for the first six months of an infant's life, as it has been linked with decreased risk of gastrointestinal tract infection and atopic eczema in the first year of life, and improved cognitive development at age 6, among other benefits (Kramer et al. 2008; Kramer et al. 2001; World Health Organization 2008b). Even so, breastfeeding rates are notoriously lower amongst socioeconomically deprived groups in developed countries; purchasing formula puts additional pressure on already strained finances and can increase the risk of a number of nutritional and developmental deficiencies for their children (Amir and Donath 2008).

Other studies have also found adverse socioeconomic conditions during childhood were associated with greater risk of health outcomes such as poor self-reported health, cardiovascular disease, and higher mortality independent of adult social circumstances (Gliksman et al. 1995; Goya-Wannamethee et al. 1996; Kaplan and Salonen 1990; Lynch et al. 1994; Nystrom-Peck 1994; Vågerö and Leon 1994). The first of these factors is family poverty. Poverty in childhood has been linked to inadequate nutrition, stunted growth, increased incidence of infection, higher risk of smoking in the household, poorer parental self-esteem, and comparatively poorer access to medical care (Mayer 1998; Wadsworth 1999). All of these effects can lead to increased incidence of premature morbidity and mortality later in life.

Early childhood exposures also involve intergenerational processes of deprivation. For instance, parental unemployment has been known to have deleterious effects on their children's health and well-being. Indeed, it has been associated with poor mental health in adults, increased social isolation, and reduced self-esteem, all of which are known to impact childrearing (Downey and Coyne 1990; Salsali and Silverstone 2003; Wadsworth 1999). Parental social inclusion, health, and well-being, therefore, can be just as important to the well-being of a child as his or her own health.

Policy implications

The research summarized above highlights the importance of investing now to create healthy social circumstances for children, as this can be used as "money in the bank" for future generations and to prevent the onset of processes of cumulative disadvantage (O'Rand 1996; Ridge 2008). While most women in developed countries receive adequate prenatal care, socioeconomic differences in perinatal outcomes (premature births and small-for-gestational-age babies) are still evident (Committee to Study Outreach for Prenatal Care: Division of Health Promotion and Disease Prevention 1988). Nutritional differences may be at play here, and programs such as OLO (oeuf, lait, orange), which provides one egg, one pint of milk, and one orange a day to pregnant women in need, have been found to be relatively inexpensive ways to improve perinatal outcomes among those populations (Fondation OLO 2007). Breastfeeding can also be promoted by ensuring optimal conditions for mother–newborn bonding in birthing centers and maternity wards, such as allowing the newborn to nurse at the breast within an hour of birth and using formula, bottles, and pacifiers only in last recourse. The WHO developed a certification process to recognize birthing units that follow those policy recommendations and are therefore deemed "baby-friendly" (World Health Organization 2008a).

Policies aimed at stopping the circle of intergenerational disadvantage involve strengthening and improving early childhood development programs and making them universally accessible so that all children begin school on an equal footing, regardless of their social background. Other initiatives have revolved around providing adequate child care options to parents and improved diet and nutrition for children (Commission on Social Determinants of Health 2008; Ridge 2008; Wadsworth 1999). Ultimately, the most efficient policies will ensure coherence across different departments such that a comprehensive approach to child health may be implemented (Commission on Social Determinants of Health 2008). An example of such a concerted effort is the "Every Child Matters" agenda in Britain, which promotes children's health, safety, academic achievement, civic involvement and responsibility, and economic well-being (Ridge 2008).

Housing

Adequate housing is not only important for individuals facing poor living conditions, it is also crucial for population health in general. Increasing levels of urbanization bring about new health risks such as increased air pollution as well as violence and accidents, while overcrowdedness facilitates the spread of infectious diseases (Commission on Social Determinants of Health 2008). In addition, studies show that the most common occupants of poor-quality housing include families with children (and particularly lone-parent households), the elderly, the sick, and the disabled (Murie 2008). This situation has been aggravated over the past three decades by diminishing governmental funding for affordable and subsidized housing in many developed countries, including Canada, the United States, and the United Kingdom (McLean 2008; Murie 2008; Shapcott 2008).

Lo and O'Connell (2005) argue that inadequate housing has been associated with a number of negative health outcomes, including asthma, poisoning, and injuries. More specifically, individuals living in poor-quality housing tend to be exposed to different hazards, including lead poisoning (particularly harmful to children and pregnant women), pesticides, allergens from cockroaches and dust mites, mold, nitrogen dioxide from poor ventilation, and higher risk of injuries from structural hazards. Overcrowding is also harmful, as it can lead to the proliferation of infectious diseases such as tuberculosis and increased stress levels. Lo and O'Connell point out that low-income individuals are more likely to live in these types of conditions given the limited housing options available to them.

Another consequence of the welfare state retrenchment in affordable and subsidized housing (often coupled with health care reforms centered around deinstitutionalization of mentally ill individuals) has been a secular rise in homelessness in many of the same countries (Baumohl 2004). In a meta-analysis of the relationship between homelessness and health, Hwang (2001) found that homeless individuals have higher mortality rates than the general population (though this is less true in Canada than in the US, due in part to universal health care). The homeless are also prone to more severe diseases due to delays in seeking treatment, extreme poverty, non-compliance with medical instructions, and cognitive or mental impairment. Particularly prevalent are poorly controlled chronic diseases, infectious diseases (tuberculosis and various sexually transmitted infections, including most prominently HIV/AIDS), and injuries and accidents. Finally, mental illness and substance abuse are rampant, as schizophrenia and alcoholism are disproportionately represented in the homeless (male) population.

Policy implications

It is therefore evident that healthy living spaces are essential to reduce social inequalities in health (Commission on Social Determinants of Health 2008). As the recommendations of the WHO's report on the social determinants of health note, there is a need for a greater availability of affordable housing (Commission on Social Determinants of Health 2008; Murie 2008). This may include government-subsidized residential projects or programs to encourage home ownership (Murie 2008). A harm-reduction approach should be applied to urban slums by providing basic services such as water, garbage disposal, paved roads and utilities to all, regardless of ability to pay. In addition, improved urban planning must include adequate public transport services and regulated retail planning so as to improve the availability and affordability of healthy foods (and limit the availability of less healthy options, like unwholesome foods and alcohol). Finally, these initiatives should also take into account the fact that homelessness, landlessness, poverty, and displaced individuals also exist in rural areas and these problems are not just the purview of urban areas.

Education

The relationship between education and income has long been documented. In 1973, Kitagawa and Hauser produced one of the first studies in the field demonstrating that higher levels of education are associated with lower mortality levels. Since then, the evidence has accrued on the positive effects of education on both physical and mental health (Grossman and Kaestner 1997; Lleras-Muney 2005; Mirowsky and Ross 2003; Mirowsky, Ross, and Reynolds 2000; Ross and Wu 1995). Better-educated people tend to be healthier, as evidenced by higher self-rated health and lower levels of morbidity, mortality, and disability, both cross-sectionally and over time (Goesling 2007; Ross and Wu 1995).

So what is it about education that makes individuals healthier? Most experts tend to agree that the relationship between education and health is largely indirect, in that it is mediated by other factors. Broadly speaking, those other factors include employability, income, psychosocial resources, and health behaviors. Individuals with more education are more likely to be employed full time, occupying safer, more autonomous, and more fulfilling positions than their less educated counterparts (Mirowsky and Ross 2003; Ross and Wu 1995; West 2008). The educated also tend to be more likely to have control over their work and engage in relatively rewarding activities, whereas the less educated are often faced with repetitive, routine, or non-stimulating jobs that increase their likelihood of poor physical and mental health (Mirowsky et al. 2000; Ross and Willigen 1997; Ross and Wu 1995; Vosko 2006). Low education also increases one's likelihood of working under dangerous conditions (Mirowsky et al. 2000; Vosko 2006).

The beneficial effect of education on one's health may also largely be mediated by income (Mirowsky and Ross 2003). Individuals with poor education often occupy jobs of lower quality, which often offer lower benefits and do not pay well (Kalleberg, Reskin, and Hudson 2000). Conversely, findings show that education does pay off since individuals with more education earn more than their less educated counterparts (Cheeseman Day and Newburger 2002). But even when controlling for income, better-educated people have been found to suffer less from economic hardship, in part because of an improved ability to cope with stress (Ross and Wu 1995).

Similarly, educated individuals are less likely to experience powerlessness (Mirowsky and Ross 2003; Mirowsky et al. 2000; Ross and Wu 1995). The feeling that one cannot do anything to change one's current circumstances can be devastating for mental health, as well as physical health, in particular since it can lead to poor health-related behaviors (like increased alcohol consumption) and suppressed immune systems (Mirowsky et al. 2000; Ross and Wu 1995). Conversely, the more educated tend to feel as though they have more personal control over their lives, which promotes self-confidence and staves off depression (Kim 2003). Education is also associated with increased self-discipline and motivation, as well as effective communication, problem-solving, and critical thinking skills, all of which give individuals an impression that they have the power to change their circumstances.

Individuals with lower education levels have also been found to have lower social support levels, which brings increased risks for depression and mortality (Kim 2003; Ross and Wu 1995). In addition, propinquity (or the homophily bias) implies that more educated individuals will tend to congregate with peers who resemble them and are, therefore, on average more likely to have socially well-positioned individuals in their social networks, thus increasing access to valued resources like health care (Alter, Basinski, and Naylor 1998; Shortt 1999).

The better educated tend to adopt healthier lifestyle habits, including being less likely to smoke, drink, or eat excessively (Grossman and Kaestner 1997; Mirowsky and Ross 2003; Mirowsky et al. 2000; Regidor et al. 2003; Ross and Wu 1995). They are also more likely to seek routine medical care not only because of their knowledge of the importance of those behaviors (Link and Phelan 1995), but also because they have the financial resources – or insurance and social networks – required to do so. In developing countries, a community's education level has also been found to be positively associated with increased use of prenatal care, child health prevention, and more adequate nutrition (Kravdal 2004).

Education's effect on health can be summed up by Mirowsky and Ross's concept of learned effectiveness. In this process of cumulative advantage, education cultivates a sense of self-direction which ultimately leads to healthier outcomes (Mirowsky and Ross 2003, 2005). Conversely, the negative effects of poor education can also be felt across the life course. Some authors have found that health disparities have increased over time in all age groups between adults with and without college education, while others find that this trend only holds true amongst older cohorts (aged 70 and older) (Goesling 2007; Lynch 2003).

Policy implications

Given the evidence outlined above, it seems hardly surprising that one of the most effective ways to reduce health inequalities could be to invest in universal education for all (Commission on Social Determinants of Health 2008; Lleras-Muney 2005; Mirowsky and Ross 2003). In Canada, research shows that such social investments in education have indeed succeeded in improving socioeconomic position for most Canadians who undergo compulsory education (Oreopoulos 2005). In addition, as highlighted in the early childhood section, education initiatives should begin as early as possible to foster cognitive and social development at an early age, thus improving chances of succeeding at K12 schooling (Low et al. 2005). Low and colleagues (2005) have proposed an "Education Starts at Birth" policy scheme, which would involve combining comprehensive child care, parental education, and childhood education initiatives into a single policy goal in order to improve educational outcomes and, ultimately, reduce health disparities. Similarly, the World Health Organization's Commission on the Social Determinants of Health (2008) recently recommended "equity from the start," which includes universal child care, education, and early childhood programs for all, regardless of ability to pay.

Employment

Gainful employment is one of the most significant social activities in which we partake, both in terms of the time we devote to it (or prepare for it through formal training) over the life course, and because of its importance in providing social standing and facilitating social participation (Canadian Mental Health Association 1995; Canadian Public Health Association 1996; Deacon 2000). It should come as no surprise that not having a job can in fact have significant consequences on our health and well-being.

Unemployment

Consistently and over time, studies have shown that there is a strong and statistically robust association between unemployment and higher morbidity and mortality, especially with regard to cardiovascular disease and suicide (Bartley, Ferrie, and Montgomery 1999; Beland, Birch, and Stoddart 2001; Canadian Public Health Association 1996; Jin, Shah, and Svoboda 1995; Lewis and Sloggett 1998). Poor mental health is also dynamically associated with unemployment (independent of previous mental health), as it can improve once employment is regained (Canadian Public Health Association 1996; Montgomery et al. 1999). The result, of course, is that the unemployed are also more likely to use medical services, which makes the social costs related to unemployment even more significant than the underutilization of human resources (Canadian Public Health Association 1996; Jin et al. 1995).

Despite these unambiguous associations, the pathways through which unemployment affects health remain unclear. Some have posited that the relationship between employment and health may be due to a selection effect, whereby poor health leads to higher risk of unemployment. Overall, however, the main explanatory mechanisms are thought to run causally from employment to health (Bartley et al. 1999). A first pathway involves poverty: most agree that gainful employment is more highly valued than other types of work (like volunteering or childrearing) because of the income it generates (Canadian Public Health Association 1996). As such, unemployment inevitably jeopardizes income stability, which can lead to lower standards of living and the need to borrow money and/or sell property, all of which has been associated with higher rates of depression (Bartley et al. 1999).

Another pathway could involve the psychosocial stressors inherent to unemployment. In addition to earnings, a secure job provides a daily routine and socialization opportunities which are lost when unemployment occurs (Jahoda 1942). As such, decreased self-esteem – and increased alienation and isolation – are associated with unemployment (Deacon 2000; Salsali and Silverstone 2003). The impact of these stressors could also manifest itself through poor health behaviors (smoking, drinking, drug use, and overeating), which have been found to occur more frequently among the unemployed (Khlat, Sermet, and Le Pape 2004; Laitinen et al. 2002; Montgomery et al. 1998).

Work conditions

The effects of employment on health are not limited to those who are out of work. Jobs where people are unhappy, insecure, or unsafe can also have just as negative effects on health as unemployment (Bartley et al. 1999; Marmot et al. 1991). In particular, precarious or contingent employment which involves "a cumulative combination of atypical employment contracts, limited social benefits, poor statutory entitlements, job insecurity, short tenure and low wages" (Lewchuk et al. 2003:

23) has indeed been associated with poorer health outcomes. Precarious jobs thus feature a combination of decreased job security, fewer benefits, lower wages, and increased likelihood of hazardous work conditions, all of which can have negative effects on health (Vosko 2006).

Explanations of these relationships have come notably from job demand–control theories. These contend that control over the amount and type of work you engage in can mitigate the negative effects of high psychological and physical demands (Lewchuk et al. 2003). Thus, jobs characterized by high demands and low control (high-strain jobs) have been associated with poor mental health, including depression and exhaustion, and poor physical health over time, particularly cardiovascular disease (Karasek and Theorell 1990). Individuals in precarious employment tend to experience less control over their jobs, and thus experience higher levels of ill health associated with their work (Lewchuk et al. 2003).

Policy implications

High rates of employment (also referred to as labor market activation) are good for any government, since the population tends to be happier (and healthier), and there is more tax revenue and fewer expenditures on social benefits such as unemployment insurance (Deacon 2000). However, policies need to go beyond approaches to reduce unemployment, taking into account the complex needs of unemployed individuals (who may in fact be experiencing other social problems concurrently) and not just providing them with a temporary monthly wage. According to Bartley and colleagues (1999), governments should provide spring boards, not simply safety nets, for the unemployed. For example, Britain's "Welfare-to-Work" policy implemented in 1998 aims at increasing the number of jobs available to welfare recipients, while also improving their eligibility for such positions by encouraging motivation and skill development through training programs with generous participation incentives (Deacon 2000). It has also been suggested that these benefits be provided as soon as possible to recently unemployed individuals in order to mitigate the impact such a shock may have on their mental and physical health (Montgomery et al. 1999).

Health insurance

While one of the goals of mandatory health care coverage was to reduce inequities in access to the medical institution and, through this, health inequalities (Robert and House 2000), the case of the UK's NHS unambiguously proves that universal health insurance is not a sufficient condition to eliminate socioeconomic inequities in mortality (Townsend et al. 1982). However, recent evidence indicates that universal health insurance coverage may mitigate health inequalities (Quesnel-Vallée 2004).

Indeed, in countries like the United States that still do not guarantee health insurance coverage to all their citizens, social inequalities in health are often amplified, with dire consequences for health across the life course. As such, compared with public insurance, risk-rated private insurance may contribute to social differentials in health by amplifying the positive effects of socioeconomic position on health. In contrast, coverage through public means should mitigate socioeconomic differentials in health as it can remove – and even reverse through progressive taxation – one pathway whereby advantaged socioeconomic positions may contribute to better health. Conceptually, public insurance should therefore reduce the total effect of social position on health.

In the most comprehensive observational study to date, the Black Report revealed that, far from having diminished, social inequalities in health and mortality had increased since the implementation of the NHS in the United Kingdom (Townsend et al. 1982). However, because part of this growing gap was due to improvements in mortality among the wealthier classes, and not caused by declines among the lower socioeconomic groups, these results suggested that the upper classes were making greater (or somehow "better") use of the improved access to medical resources.

In contrast, Canadian studies using income as a marker of social position (rather than class as in the United Kingdom) found that access to care for the poor increased substantially after the introduction of national health insurance (Enterline et al. 1973; McDonald et al. 1974). Moreover, this increase in access also translated into improved health outcomes, as Hanratty (1996) found that the introduction of Medicare was associated with a 4 percent decline in infant mortality, along with a decrease in the incidence of low birth weight that was particularly notable among single parents. Infant mortality is well known to be more sensitive than general population mortality to social inequalities in health (Gwatkin 2001a), suggesting that the introduction of a national health insurance system disproportionately benefited the most destitute in Canada. Similarly, international research examining access to care outcomes found that while access to general practitioners was equitably distributed in OECD countries, access to specialists exhibited such a pro-rich gradient that overall access to physicians appeared to favor the wealthiest segments of the population (Van Doorslaer et al. 2006). Moreover, this relationship was exacerbated in countries with private health insurance. Yet, this research only speaks to access to care, and thus future studies should examine whether these inequities in access also translate into morbidity and mortality differentials.

Policy implications

Over the past decade, health spending in developed countries has grown faster than gross domestic product, leading governments to search for alternative financing structures (OECD 2007). In Canada, for instance, this has resulted in close to a 100 percent increase from 1988 to 2004 in the proportion of total health expenditures accounted for by private health insurance spending, from 7.4 to 13 percent. Few studies exist on the health consequences of this growth, but the RAND Health Insurance Experiment (HIE), a randomized trial of cost sharing conducted in the United States in the 1970s, can shed some light on issues that are pertinent to this debate. Consistent with economic theory, the authors found that higher cost sharing led to reductions in service use. However, while cost sharing had no effect on the health of the general population, the poorest and sickest of the group had better health outcomes (hypertension, vision, dental, and fewer serious symptoms) under the free care plan (P. Newhouse and Insurance Experiment Group 1993). This suggests that cost sharing might help achieve cost containment, but that the poor and chronically ill should benefit from free access to care.

In addition, while the evidence on the public–private mix of insurance and its impact on social inequalities in health has global policy implications for equity, the United States faces a particular challenge posed by its lack of mandatory coverage. Indeed, the young (18–24) and racial and ethnic minorities are overrepresented among the uninsured (Mills and Bhandari 2003). In a recent article, Keppel (2007) identified the ten largest health disparities in the US, and found that the bulk of those were related to social inequalities and lack of access to monitoring or testing. As the second goal of *Healthy People 2010* is the elimination of health disparities, it appears that insuring the uninsured is a pressing necessity, and it will be most interesting in coming years to see if state initiatives to achieve this, like that of Massachusetts, will be successful.

Income

It is widely accepted that individuals with lower income tend to experience poorer health, as measured through both morbidity and mortality (Direction de la santé publique 2002; Marmot et al. 1991; Mirowsky et al. 2000; Shaw, Dorling, and Smith 1999). Many have found that this relationship follows a linear income gradient, whereby each additional dollar of income brings health benefits (Adler et al. 1993; Marmot et al. 1991). However, yet others have found that income has a non-linear (logarithmic) relationship with morbidity and mortality such that the positive effects of income on health mainly or only occur at lower income levels (Backlund, Sorlie, and Johnson 1996; House et al. 1994; McDonough et al. 1997).

Poverty, and the material deprivation that it brings, has also long been recognized as a strong determinant of poor health (McDonough, Sacker, and Wiggins 2005). The poor have been found to be more likely to experience higher accident mortality rates, higher degrees of activity restriction, and poorer self-rated health (Direction de la santé publique 2002). They are also more likely to engage in unhealthy behaviors, such as smoking or drinking (Lynch, Kaplan, and Salonen 1997; Shaw et al. 1999).

Low income can also have significant effects on self-esteem (Salsali and Silverstone 2003) and is thus sometimes associated with high rates of suicide and depression (Leo 2006; Patel 2006). In addition, women and children tend to be disproportionately affected by low income (Mirowsky et al. 2000). For instance, low income has been associated with higher infant mortality rates, higher hospital admission rates, and increased risk of injuries, illness, and developmental problems among children (Bloch et al. 2008; Seguin et al. 2003). Despite this, people with lower income have been found to have poorer access to physicians than their richer counterparts, even when controlling for health need (Dunlop, Coyte, and McIsaac 2000; Wilson and Rosenberg 2004).

Income inequality

A large body of research has examined the ways in which income inequality at the aggregate level of a given geographical unit can have an impact on individual and population health and mortality (Wilkinson 1992). Discounting the possibility that this association is simply the aggregation of individual-level relationships between income and mortality, Lynch et al. (2000) argue that two main explanations can account for this effect of the social context: the psychosocial explanation and the neo-material framework.

According to the psychosocial environment interpretation, which is often associated with Wilkinson's (1997) and Marmot's (2004) research, health is affected through perceptions of social standing related to income. This perception of relative disadvantage can lead to emotional and physiological stress, which can act as a catalyst for a cascade of deleterious health consequences. Lynch et al. (2000) argue, however, that although the effects of relative deprivation are important, they must be understood within the context of structural inequality. Indeed, the individualistic perspective of the psychosocial model impedes its capacity to distinguish between the structural, societal *causes* of inequality and the psychosocial, individual *consequences* of those causes. As a result, this perspective offers limited potential for policy making.

While it concedes that psychosocial factors may exist, the neo-materialist approach argues that we first need to recognize that income inequality is associated with structural conditions, and that it may be these structural constraints that have an impact on health. As such, the effect of income inequality on health may be spurious as it "reflects a combination of negative exposures and lack of resources held by individuals, along with systematic underinvestment across a wide range of human, physical, health, and social infrastructure" (Lynch et al. 2000: 1202). Societies that exhibit the highest levels of income inequality may also be those that provide the lowest levels of public support for individual well-being (such as occupational structures, legal systems, and insurance schemes), and it is from this low level of support that individuals are suffering.

Policy implications

With poverty rates and inequality on the rise across Europe and Canada, redistributive income policies should be a priority for policy makers (Canadian Public Health Association 2004; Shaw et al. 1999). As the Public Health Association of Canada (2004) notes, "[n]o amount of money or reform within the healthcare system will effectively reduce inequalities in health status until geographically-based income and social disparities are addressed." There is also a need for providing adequate employment, education, training, housing, and child care opportunities for low-income families in order to mitigate the effects of their social circumstances on their health (Canadian Public Health Association 2004; McKay and Rowlingson 2008). Finally, physicians should be encouraged to look beyond personal risk factors for disease, broadening their scope to social factors, such as income, which may be affecting their patients' health (Bloch et al. 2008).

Social exclusion

Social exclusion is a relatively recent concept in the field of social determinants of health, which finds its conceptual roots in Europe and the UK, in a broadening of the concept of poverty. According to Shaw and colleagues (1999: 222):

"Poverty" emphasizes lack of economic resources, and the term "relative deprivation" stresses the conditions of living. "Social exclusion" refers not only to the economic hardship or relative economic poverty, but also incorporates the notion of the *process* of marginalization – how individuals come, through their lives, to be excluded and marginalized from various aspects of social and community life.

Thus, while poverty increases the risk of social exclusion, not all socially excluded individuals are necessarily poor. In addition, as mentioned earlier, social exclusion is a prime example of a social determinant that cuts across many policy areas due to its multidimensionality. It therefore encompasses cultural dimensions as well as economic ones and emphasizes the many aspects of discrimination, stigmatization, and marginalization.

More specifically, White (1998) recognizes that social exclusion emerges from four basic processes: (1) legal constraints or regulation that limit participation in civil society (e.g., when citizenship is denied for certain groups of migrants and their dependants, even if they are born in the country, as is the case in Germany, for instance); (2) lack of certain goods or social services that limit full participation in society (e.g., adapted facilities for the disabled); (3) exclusion from social production (e.g., labeling of certain groups as undesirable); (4) economic exclusion from average consumption (e.g., through relative or absolute poverty). As such, the specific groups affected are likely to vary from society to society, but as reviewed by Shaw and colleagues (1999), some are often more vulnerable than others: those living in poverty, the unemployed, refugees, migrants, ethnic and racial minorities, and the homeless. We have in this chapter already discussed some of these groups: the homeless in the housing section, the unemployed in the employment section, and the poor in the income section. Other chapters in this volume treat of racial and ethnic variations in health that also bear elements of social exclusion.

Policy implications

Given its multifactorial nature, policies addressing social exclusion cannot be confined to one specific ministry or department. Indeed, this social problem must be addressed by intersectorial policies and involves a concerted effort from many actors in government. This section will draw mainly from Wilkinson and Marmot (2003) to summarize some of the most pressing policy issues with regard to social exclusion. Of course, the elimination of absolute poverty (especially among children) at both the individual and neighborhood level should constitute a priority. But the amount of relative inequality should also be controlled with policies affecting the distribution of income, such as minimum income guarantees, unemployment benefits set at a higher proportion of wages, and minimum wage laws. Access to a minimum of universal coverage of social and health services should be ensured, including affordable housing. Anti-discrimination and universal access (for the disabled) legislation ensures optimal participation for all to education and work. Finally, at the broadest level, welfare policies should be directed at reducing stratification through increased access to education and to the labor market, and the protection of families.

FUTURE CHALLENGES FOR SOCIAL POLICY AND HEALTH INEQUALITIES

The promise of comparative research

Students of the association between social policy and health inequalities are often faced with issues of lack of variation in exposure (when these policies are universal in a given country) or the absence of individual-level measurements of the receipt of certain benefits (when these are available only to certain subgroups of the population). Yet, these very limitations point the way toward promising areas of inquiry in research contrasting units over time (historically) or space (across legal jurisdictions). This type of research can take advantage of policy changes over time or between units to construct "natural policy experiments" to approximate with observational studies, an experimental context that facilitates the adjudication of causality. However, the power of this research hinges on the availability of comparable data across time periods or geographical units. This challenge is compounded when one adopts a life-course perspective that requires data with multiple measurements across time for the same individuals.

Fortunately, a number of initiatives have been launched recently to remedy this situation, such as the cross-national equivalent file (CNEF), which has harmonized household panel data sets from Australia, Canada, Germany, the US, the UK, and Switzerland (CNEF 2009). However, most of these initiatives focus on developed countries, because data on health inequalities are still scarce in many developing countries and emerging economies (Gwatkin 2001b).

With regard to policy, the most promising ongoing initiatives are attempting to synthesize the evidence on strategies that reduce disparities in health using statistical methods (meta-analyses mostly) drawing from evidence-based medicine (e.g. DETERMINE; Cochrane Health Equity field; CAMPBELL collaboration).

But qualitative research is also of great importance in the development of this field of research, particularly through documentary analysis of policy texts. By documenting the timeline and nature of policy changes, these longitudinal harmonized data sets can then be supplemented with policy measurements, thus allowing direct and more precise quantitative assessments of the effects of policy changes on population health.

Life-course perspective

We have shown above that much attention has been directed recently at the ways through which socioeconomic status over the life course has an impact on adult health. Yet, substantial questions remain, particularly in the United States. First, much of this research has been conducted with European populations, not because of lack of interest from US researchers, but rather because of lack of data, as the most compelling findings in this field of research have come from studies of British or Scandinavian birth cohorts.

Another related consequence of the European preeminence in this field of research is that much of the evidence pertains to the effects of social class[4] on health and mortality, while income has received much less attention. In addition, while a handful of studies have substantiated a cumulative impact of income on mortality in the United States (Frank et al. 2003; Hayward and Gorman 2004; Lynch et al. 1997; McDonough et al. 1997), none have examined the effects of timing or mobility in income, and all bear on respondents 40 years and older. Thus, it is unclear how these patterns play out in early and mid-adulthood or with other measures of health. More broadly, it is obvious that the cumulative, latent, and pathway explanations offered above are only conceptually mutually exclusive. Indeed, whereas scant studies have explicitly tested this possibility, it is likely that all three processes coexist throughout individuals' lives.

Finally, it was also evident that few of these studies have relied on theoretical models of the evolution of socioeconomic status itself over the life course, despite the fact that social stratification research has made significant strides in understanding these mechanisms. In addition, according to Robert and House (2000), a first step toward a greater understanding of the pathways linking adult SES and health would be the acknowledgment that the study of socioeconomic inequalities in health is truly a problem of social stratification.

Challenges of enacting healthy public policy

While this area of research has thrived since the 1970s, it is only in the past decade that governments have begun enacting policies that explicitly tackle health inequalities and the unequal distribution of their social determinants (Graham and Power 2004). Thus, public health policy in many countries now has broadened its mandate from a concern with population health to the protection of health equity. This is true mainly in Europe, but can also be found in the United States with its *Healthy People 2010* program, or in Canada with its definition of population health as "an approach to health that aims to improve the health of the entire population and to reduce health disparities among population groups" (Health Canada 2008).

Yet, Graham and Power (2004) contend that these initiatives conflate the (social) determinants of health and the social processes that create an unequal distribution of those determinants in society. This confusion has led to policy perspectives that wrongly assume that addressing health determinants will also *de facto* reduce inequalities. Thus, while recent decades have seen improvements in determinants of health (e.g., rising living standards, higher average education, lower smoking rates), with concomitant benefits in population health, health inequalities have persisted or even increased. In line with Link and Phelan's (1995) fundamental cause perspective, many have therefore come to recommend that, to truly address health inequalities, policy agendas will have to tackle not only the social determinants of health, but also the determinants of social inequality that shape the myriad ways in which social advantage cumulates over the life course and across generations (Coburn 2004; Graham and Power 2004).

Exworthy (2008) identifies seven challenges inherent to the social determinants of health approach that compound the conceptual difficulties highlighted by Graham and Power (2004). Among those, we have noted above the demanding task of enacting policies in the face of multifactorial exposures and complex causal chains that summon concerted initiatives across many governmental departments and beg better data collection. In addition, the life-course perspective that underlies much of this research poses the additional problem that the policy cycle is ill-equipped to deal with such long-term processes (since most electoral processes follow timelines measured in years, not decades). While issues relating to the need to rethink policy in the face of new risks across the life course have recently been addressed by policy makers at the request of the OECD (2007), Exworthy (2008) argues that part of the solution to these challenges may come from researchers, through the development of conceptual models and appropriate methodologies that better conform to the subtleties of the social determinants of health approach in a policy setting. It is therefore at this interdisciplinary frontier between health and social sciences and quantitative and qualitative methodologies that the future of this area of research lies, and from where the next improvements for those who need it the most may come.

Notes

1 This figure was based on a working document by Dahlgren and Whitehead (1991), retrieved from www.framtidsstudier.se/filebank/files/20080109$110739$fil$mZ8UVQv2 wQFShMRF6cuT.pdf.
2 See Chapter 8 for a discussion of individual lifestyle factors.
3 With measures of SES including education, occupation, work conditions, income, financial hardship, and occupational class (generally the Erikson–Goldthorpe [EGP] class schema, but also the manual/non-manual dichotomy).
4 The British Office for National Statistics adopted a variant of the EGP class schema in most of its studies, thus providing a rich source of socioeconomic information on this population, which can be linked to morbidity and mortality data.

References

Acheson, Donald. 1998. *Independent Inquiry into Inequalities in Health*. London: Her Majesty's Stationery Office.

Adler, Nancy E., W. Thomas Boyce, Margaret A. Chesney, Susan Folkman, and S. Leonard Syme. 1993. "Socioeconomic Inequalities in Health: No Easy Solution." *Journal of the American Medical Association* 269: 3140–5.

Alter, David A., Antoni S. H. Basinski, and C. David Naylor. 1998. "A Survey of Provider Experiences and Perceptions of Preferential Access to Cardiovascular Care in Ontario, Canada." *Annals of Internal Medicine* 129: 567–72.

Amir, Lisa H. and Susan M. Donath. 2008. "Socioeconomic Status and Rates of Breastfeeding in Australia: Evidence from Three Recent National Health Surveys." *Medical Journal of Australia* 189: 254–6.

Antonovsky, Aaron. 1967. "Social Class, Life Expectancy, and Overall Mortality." *Milbank Memorial Fund Quarterly* 45: 31–73.

Backlund, Eric, Paul D. Sorlie, and Norman J. Johnson. 1996. "The Shape of the Relationship between Income and Mortality in the United States: Evidence from the National Longitudinal Mortality Study." *Annals of Epidemiology* 6: 12–20.

Barker, David J. P. 2003. "Coronary Heart Disease: A Disorder of Growth." *Hormone Research* 59: 35–41.

Barker, D. J. P., J. G. Eriksson, T. Forsen, and C. Osmond. 2002. "Fetal Origins of Adult Disease: Strength of Effects and Biological Basis." *International Journal of Epidemiology* 31: 1235–9.

Bartley, Mel, Jane Ferrie, and Scott M. Montgomery. 1999. "Living in a High-Unemployment Economy: Understanding the Health Consequences." Pp. 81–104 in M. Marmot and R. G. Wilkinson (eds.), *Social Determinants of Health*. Oxford: Oxford University Press.

Baumohl, Jim. 2004. "Deinstitutionalization." Pp. 110–13 in D. Levinson (ed.), *Encyclopedia of Homelessness*. Thousand Oaks, CA: Sage.

Beebe-Dimmer, Jennifer, John W. Lynch, Gavin Turrell, Stephanie Lustgarten, Trivellore Raghunathan, and George A. Kaplan. 2004. "Childhood and Adult Socioeconomic Conditions and 31-Year Mortality Risk in Women." *American Journal of Epidemiology* 159: 481–90.

Beland, François, Stephen Birch, and Greg Stoddart. 2001. "Unemployment and Health: Contextual-Level Influences on the Production of Health in Populations." *Social and Economic Dimensions of an Aging Population Research Papers* 54.

Ben-Shlomo, Yoav and Diana Kuh. 2002. "A Life Course Approach to Chronic Disease Epidemiology: Conceptual Models, Empirical Challenges and Interdisciplinary Perspectives." *International Journal of Epidemiology* 31: 285–93.

Benzeval, Michaela and Ken Judge. 2001. "Income and Health: The Time Dimension." *Social Science and Medicine* 52: 1371–90.

Bloch, Gary, Vera Etches, Charles Gardner, Rosana Pellizzari, Michael Rachlis, Fran Scott, and Itamar Tamari. 2008. "Why Poverty Makes Us Sick: Physician Backgrounder." *Ontario Medical Review* 75: 32–7.

Canadian Mental Health Association. 1995. "Mental Health and Unemployment." Retrieved 8 October, 2008 (www.cmha.ca/bins/content_page.asp?cid=5-33-165).

Canadian Public Health Association. 1996. "Discussion Paper on the Health Impact of Unemployment." Retrieved October 17, 2008 (www.cpha.ca/uploads/resolutions/1996-dp1_e.pdf).

Canadian Public Health Association. 2004. "The Social Determinants of Health: Income Inequality as a Determinant of Health." Retrieved October 15, 2008 (www.phac-aspc.gc.ca/ph-sp/oi-ar/02_income-eng.php).

Case, Anne, Angela Fertig, and Christina Paxson. 2005. "The Lasting Impact of Childhood Health and Circumstance." *Journal of Health Economics* 24: 365–89.

Case, Anne and Christina Paxson. 2006. "Children's Health and Social Mobility." *The Future of Children* 16: 151–73.

Cassel, John. 1976. "The Contribution of the Social Environment to Host Resistance." *American Journal of Epidemiology* 104: 107–23.

Cheeseman Day, Jennifer and Eric C. Newburger. 2002. "The Big Payoff: Educational Attainment and Synthetic Estimates of Work-Life Earnings." Washington, DC: US Census Bureau.

CNEF. 2009. "CNEF." Ithaca, NY: Cornell University. Retrieved February 13, 2009 (www.human.cornell.edu/che/PAM/Research/Centers-Programs/German-Panel/cnef.cfm).

Coburn, David. 2004. "Beyond the Income Inequality Hypothesis: Class, Neo-Liberalism, and Health Inequalities." *Social Science and Medicine* 58: 41–56.

Commission on Social Determinants of Health. 2008. "Closing the Gap in a Generation: Health Equity through Action on the Social Determinants of Health." Geneva: World Health Organization.

Committee to Study Outreach for Prenatal Care: Division of Health Promotion and Disease Prevention. 1988. "Prenatal Care Outreach: An International Perspective." Pp. 210–28 in S. Brown (ed.), *Prenatal Care: Reaching Mothers, Reaching Infants*. Washington, DC: National Academy Press.

Deacon, Alan. 2000. "Employment." Pp. 311–17 in P. Alcock, M. May, and K. Rowlingson (eds.), *The Student's Companion to Social Policy*. Oxford: Blackwell.

Direction de la santé publique. 2002. *"Urban Health: A Vital Factor in Montreal's Development."* Montreal: Régie régionale de la santé et des services sociaux de Montréal-Centre.

Downey, Geraldine and James C. Coyne. 1990. "Children of Depressed Parents: An Integrative Review." *Psychological Bulletin* 108: 50–76.

Dunlop, Sheryl, Peter C. Coyte, and Warren McIsaac. 2000. "Socio-Economic Status and the Utilisation of Physicians' Services: Results from the Canadian National Population Health Survey." *Social Science and Medicine* 51: 123–33.

Enterline, Philip E., Vera Salter, Alison D. McDonald, and J. Corbett McDonald. 1973. "The Distribution of Medical Services before and after "Free" Medical Care: The Quebec Experience." *New England Journal of Medicine* 289: 1174–8.

Evans, Robert. 2002. *Interpreting and Addressing Inequalities in Health: From Black to Acheson to Blair to … ?* London: Office of Health Economics.

Evans, Robert G., M. L. Barer, and Theodore R. Marmor. 1994. *Why Are Some People Healthy and Others Not? The Social Determinants of Health of Populations*. New York: Aldine de Gruyter.

Exworthy, Mark. 2008. "Policy to Tackle the Social Determinants of Health: Using Conceptual Models to Understand the Policy Process." *Health Policy and Planning* 23: 318–27.

Fondation OLO. 2007. "Fondation OLO pour naître en santé." Retrieved November 10, 2008 (www.olo.ca/).

Frank, John W., Richard Cohen, Irene Yen, Jennifer Balfour, and Margot Smith. 2003. "Socioeconomic Gradients in Health Status over 29 Years of Follow-Up after Midlife: The Alameda County Study." *Social Science and Medicine* 57: 2305–23.

George, Linda K. 2003. "Life Course Research: Achievements and Potential." Pp. 671–80 in Jeylan T. Mortimer and Michael J. Shanahan (eds.), *Handbook of the Life Course*. New York: Kluwer Academic/Plenum.

Gliksman, M. D., Kawachi Ichiro, D. Hunter, G. A. Colditz, J. E. Manson, M. J. Stampfer, F. E. Speizer, W. C. Willett, and C. H. Hennekens. 1995. "Childhood Socioeconomic Status and the Risk of Cardiovascular Disease in Middle-Aged US Women: A Prospective Study." *Journal of Epidemiology and Community Health* 49: 10–15.

Goesling, Brian. 2007. "The Rising Significance of Education for Health?" *Social Forces* 85: 1621–44.

Gouvernement du Québec. 2002. *Rapport Annuel de Gestion 2001–2002. Ministère de la Famille et de l'Enfance*. Sainte-Foy, QC: Les Publications du Québec.

Goya-Wannamethee, S., Peter H. Whincup, Gerald Shaper, and Mary Walker. 1996. "Influence of Father's Social Class on Cardiovascular Disease in Middle-Aged Men." *Lancet* 348: 1259–63.

Graham, Hilary. 2002. "Building an Inter-Disciplinary Science of Health Inequalities: The Example of Lifecourse Research." *Social Science and Medicine* 55: 2005–16.

Graham, Hilary and C. Power. 2004. "Childhood Disadvantage and Health Inequalities: A Framework for Policy Based on Lifecourse Research." *Child Care Health and Development* 30: 671–8.

Grossman, Michael and Robert Kaestner. 1997. "Effects of Education on Health." Pp. 69–124 in J. R. Berhman and N. Stacey (eds.), *The Social Benefits of Education*. Ann Arbor: University of Michigan Press.

Gwatkin, Davidson R. 2001a. "The Need for Equity-Oriented Health Sector Reforms." *International Journal of Epidemiology* 30: 720–3.

Gwatkin, Davidson R. 2001b. "Poverty and Inequalities in Health Within Developing Countries." Pp. 217–46 in D. Leon and G. Walt (eds.), *Poverty, Inequality, and Health in International Perspective: A Divided World?* Oxford: Oxford University Press.

Hanratty, Maria J. 1996. "Canadian National Health Insurance and Infant Health." *American Economic Review* 86: 276–84.

Hayward, Mark D. and Bridget K. Gorman. 2004. "The Long Arm of Childhood: The Influence of Early-Life Social Conditions on Men's Mortality." *Demography* 41: 87–107.

Health Canada. 2001. "Federal/Provincial/Territorial Early Childhood Development Agreement. Report on Canada Activities and Expenditures 2000–2001." Ottawa.

Health Canada. 2008. "Population Health." Retrieved November 1, 2008 (www.hc-sc.gc.ca/ahc-asc/activit/strateg/population-eng.php).

Hertzman, Clyde. 1999. "The Biological Embedding of Early Experience and Its Effects On Health in Adulthood." *Socioeconomic Status and Health in Industrial Nations* 896: 85–95.

House, James S., James M. Lepkowski, Anne M. Kinney, Richard P. Mero, Ronald C. Kessler, and A. Regula Herzog. 1994. "The Social Stratification of Aging and Health." *Journal of Health and Social Behavior* 35: 213–34.

Hwang, Stephen W. 2001. "Homelessness and Health." *Canadian Medical Association Journal* 164: 229–33.

Institute of Medicine. 2002. *Dietary Reference Intakes for Energy, Carbohydrate, Fiber, Fat, Fatty Acids, Cholesterol, Protein, and Amino Acids (Macronutrients).* Washington, DC: National Academies Press.

Jahoda, Marie. 1942. "Incentives to Work: A Study of Unemployed Adults in a Special Situation." *Occupational Psychology* 16: 20–30.

Jin, R. L., C. P. Shah, and T. J. Svoboda. 1995. "The Impact of Unemployment on Health: A Review of the Evidence." *Canadian Medical Association Journal* 153: 529–40.

Kalleberg, Arne L., Barbara F. Reskin, and Kenneth Hudson. 2000. "Bad Jobs in America: Standard and Nonstandard Employment Relations and Job Quality in the United States." *American Sociological Review* 65: 256–78.

Kaplan, George A. and Jukka T. Salonen. 1990. "Socioeconomic Conditions in Childhood and Ischaemic Heart Disease During Middle Age." *British Medical Journal* 301: 1121–3.

Karasek, Robert and T. Theorell. 1990. *Work, Stress, Productivity and the Reconstruction of Working Life.* New York: Basic Books.

Keppel, Kenneth G. 2007. "Ten Largest Racial and Ethnic Health Disparities in the United States Based on Healthy People 2010 Objectives." *American Journal of Epidemiology* 166: 97–103.

Khlat, Myriam, Catherine Sermet, and Annick Le Pape. 2004. "Increased Prevalence of Depression, Smoking, Heavy Drinking and Use of Psycho-Active Drugs among Unemployed Men in France." *European Journal of Epidemiology* 19: 445–51.

Kim, Jinyoung. 2003. "Education, Work, Personal Control, and Depression." Paper presented at the annual meeting of the American Sociological Association, Atlanta, GA.

Kramer, Michael S., Frances Aboud, Elena Mironova, Irina Vanilovich, Robert W. Platt, Lidia Matush, Sergei Igumnov, Eric Fombonne, Natalia Bogdanovich, Thierry Ducruet, Jean-Paul Collet, Beverley Chalmers, Ellen Hodnett, Sergei Davidovsky, Oleg Skugarevsky, Oleg Trofimovich, Ludmila Kozlova, Stanley Shapiro, and Group for the Promotion of Breastfeeding Intervention Trial Study. 2008. "Breastfeeding and Child Cognitive Development: New Evidence from a Large Randomized Trial." *Archives of General Psychiatry* 65: 578–84.

Kramer, Michael S., Beverley Chalmers, Ellen D. Hodnett, Zinaida Sevkovskaya, Irina Dzikovich, Stanley Shapiro, Jean-Paul Collet, Irina Vanilovich, Irina Mezen, Thierry Ducruet, George Shishko, Vyacheslav Zubovich, Dimitri Mknuik, Elena Gluchanina, Viktor Dombrovskiy, Anatoly Ustinovitch, Tamara Kot, Natalia Bogdanovich, Lydia Ovchinikova, Elisabet Helsing, and Probit Study Group. 2001. "Promotion of Breast-feeding Intervention Trial (PROBIT): A Randomized Trial in the Republic of Belarus." *Journal of the American Medical Association* 285: 413–20.

Kravdal, Øystein. 2004. "Child Mortality in India: The Community-Level Effect of Education." *Population Studies* 58: 177–92.

Krieger, Nancy. 2001. "Theories for Social Epidemiology in the 21st Century: An Ecosocial Perspective." *International Journal of Epidemiology* 30: 668–77.

Laitinen, Jaana, C. Power, E. Ek, Ulla Sovio, and Marjo-Riitta Järvelin. 2002. "Unemployment and Obesity among Young Adults in a Northern Finland 1966 Birth Cohort." *International Journal of Obesity* 26: 1329–38.

Leo, Sher. 2006. "Per Capita Income is Related to Suicide Rates in Men But Not in Women." *Journal of Men's Health* 3: 39–42.

Lewchuk, Wayne, Alice de Wolff, Andy King, and Michael Polanyi. 2003. "From Job Strain to Employment Strain: Health Effects of Precarious Employment." *Just Labour* 3: 23–35.

Lewis, Glyn and Andy Sloggett. 1998. "Suicide, Deprivation, and Unemployment: Record Linkage Study." *British Medical Journal* 317: 1283–6.

Link, Bruce G. and Jo C. Phelan. 1995. "Social Conditions as Fundamental Causes of Diseases." *Journal of Health and Social Behavior* 35 (Extra issue): 80–94.

Lleras-Muney, Adriana. 2005. "The Relationship Between Education and Adult Mortality in the United States." *Review of Economic Studies* 72: 189–221.

Lo, B. and M. E. O'Connell (eds.). 2005. *Ethical Considerations for Research on Housing-Related Health Hazards Involving Children*. Washington, DC: National Academies Press.

Low, M. David, Barbara J. Low, Elizabeth R. Baumler, and Phuong T. Huynh. 2005. "Can Education Policy Be Health Policy? Implications of Research on the Social Determinants of Health." *Journal of Health Politics Policy and Law* 30: 1131–62.

Lynch, John W., George Davey Smith, S. A. M. Harper, Marianne Hillemeier, Nancy Ross, George A. Kaplan, and Michael Wolfson. 2004. "Is Income Inequality a Determinant of Population Health? Part 1. A Systematic Review." *Milbank Quarterly* 82: 5–99.

Lynch, John W., George Davey Smith, George A. Kaplan, and James S. House. 2000. "Income Inequality and Mortality: Importance to Health of Individual Income, Psychosocial Environment, or Material Conditions." *British Medical Journal* 320: 1200–4.

Lynch, John W., George A. Kaplan, Richard D. Cohen, and Thomas W. Wilson. 1994. "Childhood and Adult Socioeconomic Status as Predictors of Mortality in Finland." *Lancet* 343: 524.

Lynch, John W., George A. Kaplan, and Jukka T. Salonen. 1997. "Why Do Poor People Behave Poorly? Variation in Adult Health Behaviours and Psychosocial Characteristics by Stages of the Socioeconomic Lifecourse." *Social Science and Medicine* 44: 809–19.

Lynch, Scott M. 2003. "Cohort and Life-Course Patterns in the Relationship Between Education and Health: A Hierarchical Approach." *Demography* 40: 309–31.

MacIntyre, Sally. 1997. "The Black Report and Beyond: What Are the Issues?" *Social Science and Medicine* 44: 723–45.

Marmot, Michael. 2004. *The Status Syndrome: How Social Standing Affects Our Health and Longevity*. New York: Times Books.

Marmot, Michael G., Manolis Kogevinas, and Mary Anne Elston. 1987. "Social-Economic Status and Disease." *Annual Review of Public Health* 8: 111–35.

Marmot, Michael G., Martin J. Shipley, and Geoffrey Rose. 1984. "Inequalities in Death: Specific Explanations of a General Pattern." *Lancet* 1: 1003–6.

Marmot, Michel G., George Davey Smith, Stephen Stansfeld, C. Patel, F. North, J. Head, I. White, E. Brunner, and A. Feeney. 1991. "Health Inequalities among British Civil Servants: The Whitehall II Study." *Lancet* 337: 1387–93.

Marmot, Michael G. and Richard Wilkinson. 1999. *The Social Determinants of Health*. Oxford: Oxford University Press.

Mayer, Susan E. 1998. *What Money Can't Buy: Family Income and Children's Life Chances*. Cambridge, MA: Harvard University Press.

McDonald, Alison D., J. Corbett McDonald, Vera Salter, and Philip E. Enterline. 1974. "Effects of Quebec Medicare on Physician Consultation for Selected Symptoms." *New England Journal of Medicine* 291: 649–52.

McDonough, Peggy, Greg J. Duncan, David R. Williams, and Jim S. House. 1997. "Income Dynamics and Adult Mortality in the United States, 1972 through 1989." *American Journal of Public Health* 87: 1476–83.

McDonough, Peggy, Amanda Sacker, and Richard D. Wiggins. 2005. "Time On My Side? Life Course Trajectories of Poverty and Health." *Social Science and Medicine* 61: 1795–1808.

McKay, Stephen and Karen Rowlingson. 2008. "Income Maintenance and Social Security." Pp. 303–10 in P. Alcock, M. May, and K. Rowlingson (eds.), *The Student's Companion to Social Policy*. Oxford: Blackwell.

McLean, Mike. 2008. "Affordable Housing Gap Widens." *Spokane Journal of Business*. Retrieved November 9, 2008 (www.spokanejournal.com/spokane_id=article&sub=3732).

Mills, Robert J. and Shailesh Bhandari. 2003. *Health Insurance Coverage in the United States: 2002*, edited by US Census Bureau. Washington, DC: US Government Printing Office.

Mirowsky, John and Catherine E. Ross. 2003. *Education, Social Status, and Health*. Hawthorne, NY: Aldine de Gruyter.

Mirowsky, John and Catherine E. Ross. 2005. "Education, Learned Effectiveness and Health." *London Review of Education* 3: 205–20.

Mirowsky, John, Catherine E. Ross, and John Reynolds. 2000. "Links Between Social Status and Health Status." Pp. 47–67 in C. E. Bird, P. Conrad, and A. M. Fremont (eds.), *Handbook of Medical Sociology*. Upper Saddle River, NJ: Prentice-Hall.

Montgomery, Scott M., Derek G. Cook, Mel J. Bartley, and Michael E. J. Wadsworth. 1998. "Unemployment, Cigarette Smoking, Alcohol Consumption and Body Weight in Young British Men." *European Journal of Public Health* 8: 21–7.

Montgomery, Scott M., Derek G. Cook, Mel J. Bartley, and Michael E. J. Wadsworth. 1999. "Unemployment Pre-Dates Symptoms of Depression and Anxiety Resulting in Medical Consultation in Young Men." *International Journal of Epidemiology* 28: 95–100.

Murie, Alan. 2008. "Housing." Pp. 343–50 in P. Alcock, M. May, and K. Rowlingson (eds.), *The Student's Companion to Social Policy*. Oxford: Blackwell.

Mustard, Cameron A., Marian Vermeulen, and John N. Lavis. 2003. "Is Position in the Occupational Hierarchy a Determinant of Decline in Perceived Health Status?" *Social Science and Medicine* 57: 2291–303.

National Research Council and Institute of Medicine. 2005. "Housing and Health." In B. Lo and M. E. O'Connell (eds.), *Ethical Considerations for Research on Housing-Related Health Hazards Involving Children*. Washington, DC: National Academies Press.

Newhouse, Joseph P. and The Insurance Experiment Group. 1993. *Free for All? Lessons from the RAND Health Experiment*. Cambridge, MA: Harvard University Press.

Nystrom-Peck, Maria. 1994. "The Importance of Childhood Socioeconomic Group for Adult Health." *Social Science and Medicine* 39: 553–62.

O'Rand, Angela M. 1996. "The Precious and the Precocious: Understanding Cumulative Disadvantage and Cumulative Advantage Over the Life Course." *The Gerontologist* 36: 230–8.

O'Rand, Angela M. 2002. "Cumulative Advantage Theory in Life Course Research." Pp. 14–30 in Stephen Crystal, Dennis Shea, and K. Warner Schaie (eds.), *Annual Review of Gerontology and Geriatrics*. New York: Springer.

O'Rand, Angela M. 2003. "The Future of the Life Course: Late Modernity and Life Course Risks." Pp. 693–702 in Jeylan T. Mortimer and Michael J. Shanahan (eds.), *Handbook of the Life Course*. New York: Kluwer Academic/Plenum.

Oreopoulos, Phil. 2005. "Canadian Compulsory School Laws and Their Impact on Educational Attainment and Future Earnings." *Statistics Canada Analytical Studies Branch Research Paper Series*.

Organization for Economic Cooperation and Development (OECD). 2007. *Modernising Social Policy for the New Life Course*. Paris: OECD.

Pappas, Gregory, Susan Queen, Wilbur C. Hadden, and Gail F. Fisher. 1993. "The Increasing Disparity in Mortality Between Socioeconomic Groups in the United States, 1960 and 1986." *New England Journal of Medicine* 329: 103–9.

Patel, Vikram. 2006. "Is Depression a Disease of Poverty?" *Regional Health Forum WHO South-East Asia Region* 5(1).

Pensola, Tiina H. and Pekka Martikainen. 2003. "Cumulative Social Class and Mortality from Various Causes of Adult Men." *Journal of Epidemiology and Community Health* 57: 745–51.

Pensola, Tiina and Pekka Martikainen. 2004. "Life-Course Experiences and Mortality by Adult Social Class Among Young Men." *Social Science and Medicine* 58: 2149–70.

Popay, Jennie, Sharon Bennett, Carol Thomas, Gareth Williams, Anthony Gatrell, and Lisa Bostock. 2003. "Beyond 'Beer, Fags, Egg and Chips'? Exploring Lay Understandings of Social Inequalities in Health." *Sociology of Health and Illness* 25: 1–23.

Power, Chris, Orly Manor, and Sharon Matthews. 1999. "The Duration and Timing of Exposure: Effects of Socioeconomic Environment on Adult Health." *American Journal of Public Health* 89: 1059–65.

Quesnel-Vallée, Amélie. 2004. "Is it Really Worse to Have Public Health Insurance than to Have No Insurance at All? Health Insurance and Adult Health in the United States." *Journal of Health and Social Behavior* 45: 376–92.

Regidor, Enrique, Luis de la Fuente, M. Elisa Calle, Pedro Navarro, and Vicente Dominguez. 2003. "Unusually Strong Association between Education and Mortality in Young Adults in a Community with a High Rate of Injection-Drug Users." *European Journal of Public Health* 13: 334–9.

Ridge, Tess. 2008. "Children." Pp. 378–85 in P. Alcock, M. May, and K. Rowlingson (eds.), *The Student's Companion to Social Policy*. Oxford: Blackwell.

Robert, Stephanie A. and James S. House. 2000. "Socioeconomic Inequalities in Health: An Enduring Sociological Problem." Pp. 79–97 in C. E. Bird, P. Conrad, and A. M. Fremont (eds.), *Handbook of Medical Sociology*, vol. 5. Upper Saddle River, NJ: Prentice-Hall.

Roseboom, Tessa J., Jan H. P. van der Meulen, Clive Osmond, David J. Barker, Anita C. J. Ravelli, and Otto P. Bleker. 2001. "Adult Survival after Prenatal Exposure to the Dutch Famine 1944–45." *Paediatric Perinatal Epidemiology* 15: 220–5.

Ross, Catherine E. and Marieke Van Willigen. 1997. "Education and the Subjective Quality of Life." *Journal of Health and Social Behavior* 38: 275–97.

Ross, Catherine E. and Chia-Ling Wu. 1995. "The Links Between Education and Health." *American Sociological Review* 60: 719–45.

Salsali, Mahnaz and Peter Silverstone. 2003. "Low Self-Esteem and Psychiatric Patients: Part II – The Relationship between Self-Esteem and Demographic Factors and Psychosocial Stressors in Psychiatric Patients." *Annals of General Hospital Psychiatry* 2: 3.

Seguin, Louise, Qian Xu, Louise Potvin, Maria-Victoria Zunzunegui, and Katherine L. Frohlich. 2003. "Effects of Low Income on Infant Health." *Canadian Medical Association Journal* 168: 1533–8.

Shapcott, Michael. 2008. "Wellesley Institute National Housing Report Card 2008." Toronto: Wellesley Institute.

Shaw, Mary, Danny Dorling, and George Davey Smith. 1999. "Poverty, Social Exclusion and Minorities." Pp. 211–39 in M. Marmot and R. G. Wilkinson (eds.), *Social Determinants of Health*. Oxford: Oxford University Press.

Shortt, Samuel E. D. 1999. "Waiting for Medical Care: Is it Who you Know that Counts?" *Canadian Medical Association Journal* 161: 823–4.

Townsend, Peter, Nick Davison, and Margaret Whitehead. 1982. *Inequalities in Health: The Black Report*. London: Pelican Books.

United States Department of Health and Human Services. 2000. *Healthy People 2010: Understanding and Improving Health*, 2nd edition. Washington, DC: US Government Printing Office.

Vågerö, Denny and D. Leon. 1994. "Effect of Social Class in Childhood and Adulthood on Adult Mortality." *Lancet* 343: 1224–5.

Vaillancourt, Yves, Francois Aubry, Muriel Kearny, Luc Theriault, and Louise Tremblay. 2004. "The Contribution of the Social Economy towards Healthy Social Policy Reforms in Canada: A Quebec Viewpoint." In D. Raphael (ed.), *Social Determinants of Health: Canadian Perspectives*. Toronto: Canadian Scholars' Press.

Van Doorslaer, Eddy, Cristina Masseria, Xander Koolman, and OECD Health Equity Research Group. 2006. "Inequalities in Access to Medical Care by Income in Developed Countries." *Canadian Medical Association Journal* 174: 177–83.

Vosko, Leah F. 2006. *Precarious Employment: Understanding Labour Market Insecurity in Canada*. Montreal: McGill-Queens University Press.

Wadsworth, Michael. 1999. "Early Life." Pp. 44–63 in M. Marmot and R. G. Wilkinson (eds.), *Social Determinants of Health*. Oxford: Oxford University Press.

West, Anne. 2008. "Education in Schools." Pp. 326–34 in by P. Alcock, M. May, and K. Rowlingson (eds.), *The Student's Companion to Social Policy*, 3rd edition. Oxford: Blackwell.

White, Paul E. 1998. "Urban Life and Social Stress." In D. Pinder (ed.), *The New Europe: Economy, Society and Environment*. Chichester: Wiley.

Wilkinson, Richard. 1992. "Income Distribution and Life Expectancy." *British Medical Journal* 304: 165–8.

Wilkinson, Richard. 1997. "Socioeconomic Determinants of Health: Health Inequalities: Relative or Absolute Material Standards?" *British Medical Journal* 314: 591.

Wilkinson, Richard and Michael Marmot. 2003. *Social Determinants of Health: The Solid Facts*, 2nd edition. Copenhagen: World Health Organization (www.euro.who.int/DOCUMENT/E81384.PDF).

Williams, David R. 1990. "Socioeconomic Differentials in Health: A Review and Redirection." *Social Psychology Quarterly* 53: 81–99.

Wilson, Kathi and Mark W. Rosenberg. 2004. "Accessibility and the Canadian Health Care System: Squaring Perceptions and Realities." *Health Policy* 67: 137–48.

World Health Organization. 1948. "Preamble to the Constitution of the World Health Organization as adopted by the International Health Conference, New York, 19–22 June, 1946; signed on 22 July 1946 by the representatives of 61 States (Official Records of the World Health Organization, no. 2, p. 100) and entered into force on 7 April 1948" (www.who.int/about/definition/en/print.html).

World Health Organization. 2008a. "Baby-Friendly Hospital Initiative." Retrieved November 10, 2008 (www.who.int/nutrition/topics/bfhi/en/index.html).

World Health Organization. 2008b. "Breastfeeding." Retrieved October 1, 2008 (www.who.int/topics/breastfeeding/en/).

Part VI
New Developments

22

A Sociological Gaze on Bioethics

Kristina Orfali and Raymond G. DeVries

In America the purely practical part of science is admirably understood, and careful attention is paid to the theoretical portion which is immediately requisite to application. On this head the Americans always display a clear, free, original, and inventive power of mind.

Alexis de Tocqueville, "Why the Americans are more addicted to
Practical than to Theoretical Science," in *Democracy in America*,
Vol. II, 1840, p. 139

INTRODUCTION

Textbooks in bioethics sometimes start as early as Hippocrates, making today's bioethics a generic term that includes medical ethics, medical humanities, deontology, and even medical etiquette. True, medical ethics is not a new field, and there has long been a concern with moral questions occasioned by medicine and medical research. But the field was not known as bioethics, nor did it have – as it does now – the institutional support of centers for bioethics, professional journals, government commissions, or graduate programs and professorships. By the beginning of the twenty-first century, however, bioethics has become an important part of medicine and life sciences, "an industry," as quoted by *The Economist*, not only in the US but worldwide. Yet few can clearly define the field, often viewed as "in transition, if not confusion" (Faden 2004: 276).

Bioethics emerged as a movement concerned with the moral dimensions of life sciences and health care in the 1960s in the United States, from where it spread all over the world. In historical accounts, bioethics is often described as starting in the aftermath of World War II, but emerging as a distinct discipline and discourse in the 1960s and becoming increasingly institutionalized and professionalized in the late 1960s to early 1970s. How did this development take place? Why did the moral questions within research and then medical practice itself become ethical dilemmas? Why did a distinctive field concerned with advances in biology and medicine emerge beyond medicine and academia, in legislatures and courts of the land and in society overall, to become such an important social-cultural phenomenon? How did medicine evolve from the authoritarian paternalism of yesterday to today's obsession with patient autonomy, accepting "strangers at the bedside" who called themselves bioethicists? How was this field institutionalized and organized into a professionalized expertise, yet not a profession?

There are multiple narratives around the birth of bioethics, attesting to the difficulties of defining a unified field or a clear object of classical sociological study (unlike, for example, education or religion). Moreover, the sociology of bioethics is an emerging field of study. This is somewhat surprising given the fact that sociology was defined by Durkheim as the "science of moral facts." While he did conceive sociology as the science of morality, medicine hardly caught his attention as a "moral fact" – it being a "technique" and an activity which, contrary to morality, "didn't regulate the ends."[1]

Although bioethics was coming into its own in the late 1960s and early 1970s, sociological analysis of the field – as a distinct area of intellectual inquiry, as a social movement, as a service in clinical and research settings, and as a profession – did not begin until the mid-1980s. This tardiness, which we explore more fully below, is the result of several features of both sociology and bioethics, including sociological unease with matters ethical and bioethical displeasure with sociological descriptions of the field.

This chapter begins by emphasizing the necessary distinction between the two (sometimes overlapping) components of the bioethics movement: research ethics focused on human experimentation on the one hand, and health care and bedside ethics on the other. Research ethics appears first in the narrative of bioethical beginnings, leading to new regulations, lay oversight, and accountability in the US. The second dimension within the bioethics movement appears when requirements of informed consent of the research subject are extended to the ordinary patient within clinical care, leading to one of the most drastic reforms of the practice of medicine. We focus on the articulation between research ethics and health care ethics, exploring the different factors that contributed, in the US and elsewhere, to this unique extension of the debates regarding human experimentation and the rights for human subjects to an ethical critique of how medicine treated patients.

Secondly, we discuss the uneasy relationship between sociology and bioethics. Interestingly, when medical sociology was starting to establish itself as a specific field, calling attention to the deprofessionalization of medicine, emphasizing a lay perspective on medical knowledge, and fostering a more patient-centered approach, it did not include the study of the bioethics movement in such transformations. Yet both were advocating for almost the same changes. We analyze sociology's tardiness in addressing these issues, from an uneasy relationship to an emerging field linked to the uncertainty around the object of inquiry, its blurred boundaries and inherent multidisciplinarity. We explore the social organization of bioethics as a new area of professionalized expertise.

The Birth of Bioethics in the US

The emergence of the bioethical enterprise

While the bioethics movement developed in a context of intense debates in moral philosophy (Jonas 1966; Toulmin 1982), theology, and even medicine around questions raised by science, medicine, and progress, most chronological accounts focus first on the birth of research ethics and the problem of informed consent by human subjects. In fact, modern bioethics, starting with the doctrine of informed consent and the codes for human experimentation and protection for research subjects so prevalent in modern bioethics, is often said to be rooted in the Nuremberg trials of the Nazi doctors (Annas 2004; Annas and Grodin 1992; Jonsen 1998). The Nuremberg code, promulgated in 1947, is viewed generally as the first authoritative statement of consent requirements in biomedical ethics or more precisely in research ethics, and is presented as one of the founding texts in any classical teaching of a bioethical course.[2]

However, other authors note that, *de facto*, the Nuremberg code had little, if any, impact on American medical practice. After all, the horrific events of World War II and the monstrosity of Nazi experiments had nothing to do with the medical research that was being carried out in the US or even elsewhere.[3] Rothman (1991), an American historian, argues that Nuremberg had little effect on the American world of medical research. Between 1945 and 1966, the National Institutes of Health (NIH) funded more than 2,000 research projects and none of them used informed consent. In fact, until the late 1950s to early 1960s, accounts of human experimentation in the media were surprisingly laudatory (Halpern 2001). Then, a dramatic shift took place in public narratives related to human experimentation. According to Rothman (1991: 15), bioethics emerged as a response to questionable practices in human experimentation in the US context; American bioethics "began with a whistleblower and a scandal." The whistleblower in question was Dr. Henry Beecher, a scientist who created a scandal in the field of medical research in 1966 when the *New England Journal of Medicine* published an exposé of the abuse of human subjects taking place during research procedures. This article identified 22 cases where the life and health of subjects were placed in jeopardy and where the subjects were not informed that they were being used in an experiment. Beecher's exposé, together with additional revelations in the media about other instances of mistreatment of research subjects – the most infamous of which were the abuse of poor black men in the Tuskegee syphilis study[4] and the Willowbrook study involving injecting retarded children with hepatitis B in order to test a vaccine – led to the creation of administrative structures for the regulation of research. In the 1960s and 1970s, human experimentation became an identified public problem.

The National Commission for the Protection of Human Subjects of Biomedical and Behavioral Research was finally established in 1973, after strong resistance against any outside public or governmental scrutiny for researchers (Rothman 1991). The Commission was in charge of identifying the basic ethical principles that should govern medical research involving people and then recommending steps to improve the regulations for the protection of human subjects. After four years of work, in 1979 the Commission issued the Belmont Report, which made the informed consent process the essential component for the protection of human research subjects.

As a consequence, in medical research, Institutional Review Boards (IRBs) were created to ensure that medical experiments were carried out with the patients' explicit informed consent and that research protocols followed ethical standards. Federal regulation 45 CFR 46, known as the "common rule," stipulates that all federally funded research involving human subjects be reviewed by a local IRB. IRBs are today interdisciplinary committees involving the scrutiny of volunteer members recruited from the research institution and from the local community over medical research.

In fact, the guidelines provided by the common rule are rather loose, reflecting an effort to appease several parties. While nearly everyone agrees that there must be a system to protect research subjects, scientists and research institutions have resisted mandates from Washington bureaucrats that would slow scientific progress. The result of this political dance is a highly decentralized system that allows great variation in IRB membership, principles, and operating procedures. This decentralized system is flexible and sensitive to local culture, but does it work? Research on IRBs shows that human subjects are minimally protected, that researchers are upset about what they see as unnecessary roadblocks to their work, and that IRB members and administrators feel overburdened by the large volume of research for which they have responsibility (Keith-Spiegel and Koocher 2005). Still, it gave lay people a unique possibility of oversight as they were invited to review research protocols and ensure that the vulnerable research subjects would be sufficiently protected. Interestingly, this regulation – a distinctive American feature – was extended to all academic or industrial research taking place in the US, even if non-medical.[5] Following the American model, many countries have implemented new ethical regulations for human experiments within scientific and medical research but rarely beyond these fields.

From informed consent in research to informed consent in the clinic

The previous narrative describes how, despite much resistance, what is now known as the American model of bioethics prevailed, shaping scientific and medical research worldwide. Equally remarkable was the process that led to the extension of the scope of the new requirements introduced by bioethics, from research practice to the situation of ordinary patient in the clinic. The principal characteristic of the American bioethics sociocultural movement is perhaps a radical transformation of modes of accountability and oversight that took place, not only within the context of research, but also in the more private world of care, and that medical practice itself deeply changed, switching from professional and self-regulated peer accountability to accountability to the patient and to lay people. Strikingly, this evolution was mostly an American specificity: while, as mentioned above, the emergence of research ethics became a global phenomenon, it did not generate outside the US such a drastic transformation within the care setting, unveiling a world of secrets, taboos, power relationships, benevolent lies and pretense which, until then, pervaded so strongly the paternalistic context of health care and which has been largely studied by medical sociology.[6]

Which are the main factors that contributed to this radical transformation within medicine? What brought bioethics into the political and public policy arena in Washington? Several factors have contributed to the emergence of the so-called bioethics movement: the role of "moral entrepreneurs," the context of the anti-authoritarian movements of the 1960s, the impact of new medical technologies leading to unprecedented ethical dilemmas in transplantation, end of life, assisted reproduction, or other domains, the transformation of medicine with the increasing erosion of trust, and the influence of the legal system. We now briefly review some of these factors.

The "open agenda"

A first factor has certainly been the specific situation of America in the 1960s. In a context of waning authority of science and general questioning of the consequences and the legitimacy of progress, it was no longer acceptable, at least in the US, that significant social policy decisions should not be on an "open public agenda."[7] The informed consent process, for so long an implicit, tenuous, private assent between a physician and her patient, had to become an explicit contract between the two parties. Halpern (2001) describes how the bioethics movement of the 1960s benefited from the sponsorship of the legislative and executive branches of the government which, when the human experiment problem became highly controversial as a matter of public debate, selected members of the emerging movement to testify at Congressional hearings, at staff commissions, and at committees on ethical issues in human research. Thus, the movement got direct access to crucial arenas of public policy and discourse. The bioethics movement was the opposite of a grassroots movement: it was a cultural movement of critique, both within and outside the medical world, which became strongly institutionalized over a short period.

Elite academic physicians, as well as external forces, mostly within academia, played the role of "moral entrepreneurs," but they would not have gained so much success if earlier patient rights activists, focusing for example on such psychiatric issues as civil commitment and the right to refuse treatment, had not prepared the cultural and media terrain. Both modern bioethics and the modern patient rights movement can be seen as reactions to medical paternalism – but, in America at least, the patient rights movement has been considerably more powerful (Fox and Swazey 2008). In a way, bioethics, a top-down enterprise with a more powerful voice (as belonging to the elite and having access to the public, the political, and the institutional channels), met the concerns of those living with these issues and advocating for more participation in health matters; but the bioethical rhetoric has tended to make these claims their own.

Anti-authoritarian movements in the 1960s

Most narratives emphasize the specific context of the 1960s, with the civil unrest and popular rebellion linked to anti-authoritarian movements (Vietnam War, civil rights movements) to explain a crisis of legitimacy in the US. In fact, there was arguably a more general political movement and legitimacy crisis worldwide (end of decolonization; France, Germany, Prague Spring, and so on). The bioethics movement emerged in a wider context, which perceived the side effects and iatrogenic consequences of progress, and particularly of scientific and technological advances, as increasingly threatening. At the same time, traditional institutions were under heavy critique; books like Illich's *Deschooling Society* (1971) or *Medical Nemesis* (1975) had an influential role among the public. The idea of "progress," constitutive of modernity, was being challenged, for example, with the publication in 1972 by the Club of Rome, a global think tank that dealt with a variety of international political issues, of a report called "The Limits to Growth." Nisbet (1986) describes how, in the 1970s, all the debates were about the limits of knowledge and the end of scientific inquiry, the unreliability of claims to objective truth.

The changing structure of medicine

Among many other factors, the changing structure of American medicine (Pescosolido and Boyer 2005; Rothman 1991; see also Chapter 18 in this volume) and the erosion of trust are often mentioned as having played a central role in the success of the bioethics rhetoric advocating for patients' rights, both in research and in care. It is true that the proportion of Americans expressing trust in medicine declined sharply between the mid-1960s and the 1980s.[8] The dual role of the physician as researcher in an academic institution and as caregiver was revealed as a conflict of interest, unveiling the contradiction between pursuing the "common good" while simultaneously defending one's own patient's best interest. The traditional paradigm of research, which had long emphasized the sacrifice of the individual for the common good, shifted to putting the rights of the individual first and above all. At the same time, it allowed the scientific and medical research agenda in the US to advance and prosper with a new moral imprimatur. After all, many of the scandals and abuses that had been revealed concerned government-sponsored research. In a country prone historically to suspicion toward any control by the state, federal regulations in research brought a long-needed public oversight and transparency. But surprisingly, other areas in bioethics remained immune to federal regulations: the field of reproductive technologies, for instance, remains mostly unregulated.

In the absence of a universal health care system, the integrity of doctor–patient relationships was and still is increasingly viewed as compromised by the intervention of the insurer and the other bureaucrats who populate the health care industrial complex known as managed care, translating the patient "into an abstraction," according to Jennings (2008), who adds: "and some doctors seemed to regard me as a rare pelt, a fascinating wrinkle in their volume business in prostates."

The fact that doctors in the US operate under the influence of considerable external forces and often hidden incentives has probably played a crucial role in the accelerated shift of informed consent and patients' rights from research to health care. In the absence of a government playing a central role in providing health care, there is a more acute need than anywhere else to regulate the rights of individuals who will have to bear the costs of choices made by others. Not surprisingly, the paternalistic medical context cannot prevail in a world with increasing means to withdraw or prolong life, resuscitate at the threshold of viability or manufacture disability. The values and choices of physicians can less be justified in the patient's best interests as uncertainty increases around what such interests are and how to define quality-of-life issues with long-term consequences. The medical profession becomes more vulnerable to the moral specter raised by the image of an increasingly unscrupulous physician who has not (or cannot have) the patient's best interest solely at heart (Stone 1997).

During the same period, the landscape of illness also changed expectations within the health care system, with the shift from acute care to chronic illness and advocacy for a more symmetrical partnership (Bury 1982; Charmaz 1991; Strauss and Glaser 1975) increasing the presence of a more powerful lay voice in medicine. The medical sociological literature emphasized patients' experience and narratives long before narratives of ethics (Charon and Montello 2002) came into being. Bioethics translated these narratives more formally into the patient's final authority through the recognition of her absolute autonomy to make decisions regarding her own health.

Medical technology, new ethical issues

Among the constellation of issues that triggered debates in the 1960s, from fertility control to human experimentation and from abortion to death and dying, most were linked to technological advances in medicine – such as dialysis, organ transplant, and respirators. Rothman (1991) even argued that bioethics was established to find a way to live with new technology and to find answers to questions that were unimaginable a few decades ago: When is someone "dead enough" to allow the harvesting of organs? What conditions justify creating a human clone? Should there be an upper age limit for *in vitro* fertilization? Bioethics, from the very beginning, was concerned with the "*future*" of humanity and the impact of science, technology, and medicine on the human being, echoing concerns worldwide around the idea of progress. For Potter – a research oncologist who coined the word "bioethics' in 1971 – biology guided by ethics would bring humanity to a better life. The search for public oversight and experts' accountability to society and humanity as a whole became a key component of the early bioethics movement, moving from the world of scholarly debates in philosophy and theology to the more mundane matters of bedside ethics. In that sense, the evolution of bioethics can be seen as both a continuity and a rupture.

The way in which issues around end of life evolved in the US is particularly salient to our point. It is true that scientific innovations and technological advances have made possible situations no one could have foretold, leading to novel and agonizing ethical dilemmas. Renal dialysis technology in the 1960s created the issue of determining which patients should receive the benefit of a scarce life-saving resource (Fox and Swazey 1974). The first heart transplant in 1967 made necessary a new definition of death that seemed as unprecedented as the heart transplant itself. In the late 1960s the quest for criteria to define death, as well as standards for withdrawing care from the living, led to the creation of numerous committees and symposiums in several countries. Transplant possibilities led to the definition of death as a medical (and later legal) category, leading to the notion of "brain death" introduced by the Harvard Committee in 1968; even today, debates around organ donation after a cardiac arrest by someone not brain dead continue to pose challenging ethical problems.

It is interesting to note that, despite media coverage and public attention, the brain death criteria was at first less a product of any lay debate or bioethical discussion than an issue of medical technicality. As such, it was viewed as a purely medical prerogative by most of the Harvard committee members, such as H. Beecher, while at the same time a mode to reassure the public against reminiscences of nineteenth-century body-snatching by strictly regulating death. Interestingly, until 1977, the American Medical Association (AMA) rejected all proposed standards of brain death as "violating the professional discretion of the individual physician" (Pernick 1999: 17) – against Beecher's view demanding united action by physicians to defend the profession's collective authority over death.

The definition of death thus became a matter of bioethical debate only when it shifted from the sphere of (medical and philosophical) expert debates (Jonsen 1998) into the public arena. When concerns around the medicalization of dying became publicly discussed with the publication from 1971 to 1974 of at least 36 articles in the *New York Times* on such issues, it became a "bioethical issue." The uncertainties around the human functions that define human life and how their presence or absence could be recognized, which were not clear from the Harvard report, spurred debates that were, according to historical accounts, produced by the intellectual entrepreneurs of the emerging bioethics movement (Jonsen 1998). These debates extended analyses regarding end-of-life matters into issues of personhood, identity, and spiritual meaning. The shift to remove brain death from the needs of transplantation to the needs of patients to die with dignity was endorsed by the President's Commission in 1981, showing how bioethics evolved from an intellectual academic discipline to not only a more clinical one, but also a larger sociocultural phenomenon. From defining death (a matter of clinical, philosophical, theological, and legal expertise), the issue became linked to the more practical clinical problem of discontinuing life support and who should make that decision.

In 1973, Duff and Campbell's article in the *New England Journal of Medicine* on withdrawal of life support for severely compromised neonates and a plea for an increased parental involvement drew considerable attention, revealing from within the clinic the ethical dilemmas of medical work and the secrecy surrounding them. Yet the paper didn't support the complete shift of decision-making in life and death choices to parents such as defended in the current autonomy model. It did, however, call for the courts' help to decide in cases of disagreement "when death may be chosen, not (now) that generally death cannot be chosen" (Duff and Campbell 1973: 893). The question of who should draw the line of what is ethically acceptable became not only an issue between physicians, as it used to be, or even between solely the doctors and the parents, but a matter of public debate and a wider social issue.

The role of law

The law (Annas 1993) has played an influential role in the shaping of bioethics and in the promotion of "a right to decide rather than in terms of the right thing to do." In a way, it emphasized the American bioethics shift from questions of substantive content of right and wrong to focus more strongly on who should decide, or as Evans (2002) expresses it, from "thick" rationality (debates over ends) to "thin" rationality (formal), thus promoting the autonomy paradigm more clearly than ever even in cases in which the patient could not decide. In 1976, the father of a young girl in a coma petitioned the court to be her guardian and to be allowed to disconnect her from the respirator that kept her alive for years. The *Quinlan* case (1976), and later the *Cruzan* case (1990), and finally the Patient Self-Determination Act can be viewed as the legal milestones of the bioethical enterprise enacting the right to refuse life-sustaining treatments even when one lacks competency. It created an arsenal of diverse means, from the durable power of attorney to living wills, to ensure that the patient's autonomy as a decision-maker could be respected even when that patient no longer was competent. The law – in the *Quinlan* case – by turning to a hospital ethics committee to find "clear and convincing evidence" (Capron 1999: 307) of what Karen Quinlan would have wanted had she been aware, gave bioethics the legitimation it lacked until then. In a way, the law validated bioethical expertise (Capron 1999) more than medical expertise and triggered the extensive institutionalization of the field with the adoption by the Joint Commission of Accreditation of Healthcare Organizations (JCAHO) of the requirement of clinical ethics committees for hospital accreditation. A jurisprudence of medical dying was taking place, giving bioethicists a greater role than ever not only in philosophical debates or in research ethics, but also within the private world of the clinic. While life-and-death issues are not the sole topics of bioethics, they are the ones that are the most relevant for lay people; they are the ones (as much as matters around birth or abortion) that are viewed as the most private issues yet the ones that are matters of public concern. In the US, the law played a role as an instrument of accountability in health care unparalleled in other societies (Morreim 2001).

THE INSTITUTIONALIZATION OF BIOETHICS

When the Hastings Center was created in the 1970s, gathering scholars from different disciplines, it avoided any affiliation with academic institutions, thus providing an independent forum to discuss and disseminate analysis around bioethical issues such as death, genetic counseling transplantation, and other topics. The Kennedy Institute fostered a more academic path to bioethics. Both organizations stimulated debates and ideas to federal activities in bioethics.

As mentioned by Bosk (2007), today in the US, there are more than 50 medical schools that have established centers in bioethics. Philosophy has become very much the core discipline of bioethics, although theology was first to appear on the scene. The most spectacular growth of bioethics is certainly within the health care world. From IRBs to clinical ethics committees, bioethicists have found new employment opportunities. In 1980, 7,000 hospitals reported the implementation of some kind of ethics committee (Randall 1983). The mandates of the JCAHO in the mid-1990s, requiring that institutions seeking its approval should have a mechanism for resolving problems in clinical ethics, boosted the development of clinical ethics committees all over the country, bringing more formally "strangers at the bedside" and allowing for an external authority over medicine. Non-clinicians became advice givers to clinicians and "moral experts" before even any specific qualification beyond theology, philosophy, or humanities was required. The role of an ethics consultant was seen as being the patient advocate, the guardian of her autonomy.

The pragmatic triumph of autonomy

Principlism is viewed as the prevailing approach of bioethics, and autonomy has emerged as the most powerful principle in American bioethics (Wolpe 1998). In fact the triumph of the "thin" instrumental reasoning (Evans) or "proceduralism" instead of normative conclusions can be viewed through the prism of the triumph of this autonomy principle – despite Beauchamp and Childress's (1979) willingness to give equal moral weight to four core principles (autonomy, beneficence, non-maleficence, and justice) in a world unified by a "common morality." The efficiency of such formal principles, as reflected in the extract from Tocqueville in the introduction, maybe more than his entrenched allusion to American individualism, explains the success of the autonomy paradigm over all other principles in American bioethics. In a way, autonomy has become the *ideology* of bioethics. Wolpe (1998) gives an account of how autonomy became the central and most powerful principle in medical decision-making, showing its practical value in decision-making particularly in a society with no universal health coverage. Callahan (1999) emphasizes how much autonomy is linked to a right-centered society, while other authors (Annas and Miller 1994) point to the fact that the dominant US version of informed consent is grounded on principles of patient/consumer autonomy and seems to enhance market choice. Not surprisingly, "personal autonomy [...] enjoy[s] its most zealous protection under US jurisprudence" (Annas and Miller 1994: 358).

Autonomy has its detractors. Some lament the overwhelming "mandatory" autonomy imposed upon vulnerable patients (Schneider 1998); others denounce the triumph of autonomy over all other principles as an "ethnocentric phenomenon" (Fox and Swazey 2005), a negative individualism, and an instrumental autonomy which finally serves the patient or the family less than the needs of a health care team or a society that eschews its responsibilities and duties. Another concern is that ideologies identifying with one single principle tend to become political and ideological instruments for justifying a ruling elite, be it economical, political, civil, or cultural (Touraine 1995). Autonomy can be viewed as an endogenous principle, a quick fix to get rid of responsibility (leading to "defense medicine"). It can also be viewed as a way to resolve the apparently insurmountable contradiction between the reign of a universal reason and the resistance of particular cultures. Autonomy is the minimal principle that can hold together a multicultural and pluralistic society by promoting, even minimally, a stable "rational" reference.

Bioethics as an American product

Among the factors leading to the success of the bioethics movement, which we briefly reviewed above, many are not specific to the American context. After all, the anti-authoritarian movements of the 1960s, and the debates about the ends of science, were not unique to American culture; questions surrounding moral progress haunted the majority of scholarly publications and the media in most Western countries, and medical technology was changing the field of medicine abroad just as in the US (indeed, the first heart transplant took place in South Africa!). Yet, contrary to many historical accounts (Rothman, Fox, and Rieser 1974), these same factors did not result, outside the US, in a bioethics movement comparable to the US model. The rights language of the 1960s and 1970s, which has been so strongly legally implemented in the US, did convert very late and in a looser way into patients' rights elsewhere. In fact, outside the US, matters of research and clinical ethics remain mostly separate; the general landscape is often one of a state-regulated field of research ethics coexisting with a still silent world of clinical ethics in which medical discretion largely prevails. The accountability of the researcher and the physician to the human research subject has not so easily expanded to the ordinary patient in other countries. From a sociological perspective, the articulation between research and bedside ethics remains the specific attribute and contribution of the American bioethics movement. In many countries, despite recent legal changes to promote patients' rights, medical authority remains strong in the clinical context.

Among many of the factors which played a role in the coming of bioethics, the most salient to the American context is probably the importance of the law in formally promoting a lay voice into medical matters. Several authors (Annas 2004; Capron 1999: 296) emphasize the crucial and "disproportionate influence" of American law in "shaping the content and methodology of the field." In American society there is an implicit reliance on courts, a commitment to due process and formal legal equality which translates "into an unwillingness to defer to expert authority" (Capron 1999: 296). California courts have been the most influential in shaping the doctrine of informed consent (*Cobbs v. Grant*, 502 P. 2d 1 (Cal 1972)). Law played a crucial role in end-of-life issues, in the recognition of advance directives, the right to refuse treatment, and so on. Law and medical ethics have constructed as a "co-production" (Wolf 2004) the field of American bioethics. Another feature is the public visibility given by the different cases that have shaped issues that were normally kept in the private world of the doctor–patient relationship, hospitals, and families. Cases – a recent example being Florida's *Schiavo* case – trigger media uproar and debates which, in turn, help define stakes and allow for mediation and a practical solution, thus vitalizing the bioethical debate in the public.

In a sense, the autonomy paradigm is indeed an ethnocentric product; other cultural references may be more suitable to different health care systems, especially if these claim to be more oriented toward the "common good" than individual welfare. Not surprisingly, a stronger focus on vulnerability, dignity, and solidarity has developed in the bioethics discourse outside the English-speaking world, particularly in cultures with a socialized health care system.

SOCIOLOGY AND BIOETHICS

Sociology, except for the work of a few sociologists such as Bernard Barber and colleagues (1973) reporting in his study about the lack of social control in most medical experimentation, has been conspicuously absent from the world of bioethics – although, interestingly, bioethics developed historically at the very same time medical sociology was taking root in the American landscape. Very much like medical sociology in the twentieth century (Cockerham 2005), it was concerned with the same topics and was intended to help solve a clinical problem or a policy issue, often being funded by agencies less interested in theoretical work than in practical utility. Their parallel development and their mutual unawareness of each other have been little explored. As much as medical sociology moved away from medicine, setting its own research agenda as "defining a medical practice and policy as an *object* of study" (Cockerham 2005: 4), the sociology of bioethics has increasingly become a distinctive field of inquiry since the late 1990s.

Yet while the field of bioethics is about 40 years old, its emergence and growth have only recently become an object of study for social scientists (Bosk 2007; DeVries et al. 2007). The body of work in the very recent sociology of bioethics can be classified into three main strands. The first line of work is a recurrent critique of the bioethical project and is strongly embedded in a contentious relationship which, nevertheless, has forced bioethics to define more clearly the very task of bioethics (Callahan 1999). The second body of work develops in relation to more classical approaches and topics in medical sociology around ethical dilemmas, information control, medical decision-making, and patient autonomy. The third approach focuses on both the bioethical work in specific new areas generated by the bioethics movement, such as ethics consultation or research ethics, IRB reviews, and on the professionalization of bioethics.

The relationship between sociology and bioethics has been an uneasy one. Although sociology had (and has) much to offer to the work of bioethics in the way of theoretical insights and well-tested strategies for data collection, bioethics remained a lonely outpost for a few sociologists until the twenty-first century. Why this lack of interest in bioethics on the part of sociology? For a number of reasons, sociologists have been reluctant to get mixed up in bioethics. From its beginning, bioethics was seen as a task for philosophers, physicians, and lawyers, not for sociologists. Sociologists and bioethicists have, after all, different approaches to the study of medicine: sociologists attempt to study the medical world as it is, bioethicists write about medicine as it ought to be. Sociology tends to be a descriptive discipline that eschews explicit moral judgments. Conversely, bioethics is a prescriptive discipline, its basic work is moral evaluation. Bioethics take social science into the uncertain area of "values," a place that social scientists are taught to avoid. Speaking of his graduate school years, Bosk (2004: 2) notes: "In graduate school nothing so much attracted my teachers' attention, ire, and red pen as any sentence containing the grammatical structure *ought*, *should*, or *must* plus a verb form. I learned first to give up this grammatical structure, then, like some subject trapped in some elaborately bizarre socio-psycho-linguistic experiment, I stopped thinking in these terms altogether. It was as if I had developed an allergy to normative arguments." Although sociological work is, of course, rife with values, sociologists have steered clear of *studying* values.

Second, bioethicists are not easy to study. Sociologists find it easier to "study down" rather than to "study up." Sociologists are quick to study prostitutes, drug users, and "street corner men," and less likely to study CEOs. Although some high-status members of society are flattered by the attention of researchers, bioethicists are counted among those who do not necessarily enjoy the sociological spotlight. Bioethicists welcome the methods of sociology when those methods are used to study already bioethically defined "problems," but they are less eager to have those methods turned to the analysis of bioethics itself. For example, bioethicists were not pleased when a sociologist pointed out that they are training far too many students: using data collected by the American Society for Bioethics and the Humanities (ASBH), Bosk (2002: 21–2) concluded that in ten years' time, "close to 2,500 bioethicists will be chasing 600 jobs." Thinking sociologically about this fact, Bosk notes that "a buyer's market does not encourage fledgling bioethicists to take positions that go against the grain, to do work that ruffles feathers, or to take positions that challenge the conventional wisdom." Bioethicists, who view themselves as advocates for patients and research subjects facing the power of medicine and the medical-industrial complex, are made uneasy by this type of sociological analysis. Although we sociologists find this kind of analysis both interesting and useful – after all, effective bioethics must understand how the health system can deflect its goals – critical commentary has not eased the entrée of sociologists into the worlds of bioethics.

The sociology of bioethics has thus mostly been a critique of bioethics. Several authors, among them Evans (2002), emphasize how government agencies recruited bioethicists to "translate" thick reasoning into a formally rational discourse, transforming the "watchdogs" protecting the public against the scientific elite into "lapdogs" of the research establishment. Others (Stevens 2000) contend that the bioethics movement fostered the illusion of lay ethical oversight but, in fact, served the needs of physicians and biomedical researchers in an area of newly emerging biomedical technologies. Many sociological narratives of the bioethics movement tend to denounce a hidden agenda, a manipulation, a flawed conceptual framework, a blindness to issues of social justice and resource allocation, a cultural myopia. Fox and Swazey (2005, 2008) show the lacks and weakness of the bioethical enterprise – a moral enterprise – that despite its incredible growth went awry, unable to live up to its initial expectations.

As Callahan (1999: 275), one of the co-founders of the Hastings Center, expresses it, bioethics, despite its strong institutionalization, is in a "lingering uncertainty about its purpose and value." Like other interdisciplines, bioethics continues to struggle with the well-known institutional impediments to interdisciplinarity – including problems related to funding, tenure, and promotion – and with the challenge of bringing together different disciplinary "languages," cultures, and methods of research.

But détente among the disciplines of bioethics is also hampered by *peculiar* features of the field. Included here are: the identity problem of bioethics, an unusual share of disciplino-centrism, the "quandary of critical distance," and varied "moralities of method." While some of these peculiarities stand in the way of progress in bioethics, others are important sources of bioethical insight. If all in bioethics "gets along," the generative tensions of the field are lost.

The identity problem – "Are you fish or fowl?" – exists for all interdisciplinarians, but it is especially acute in bioethics. Unlike other interdisciplines, several important scholars in bioethics actively disavow the identity of bioethicist. While there are some descriptive social scientists who proudly call themselves bioethicists, there are many prescriptive bioethicists who eschew the moniker, describing themselves as "philosophers (or theologians, or lawyers) who study bioethical issues."

This identity problem presents a structural challenge to bioethics: if bioethicists cannot agree on who is, and is not, a member of the interdiscipline, it will be well nigh impossible to secure a distinct place for themselves. An unusual share of disciplino-centrism contributes to this problem of identity. Scholars tend to be reductionistic, to see the world through the lenses of the disciplines to which they have devoted their lives. This tendency is aggravated in bioethics where members of different disciplines vie for the last word on what is *morally* right and wrong.

Another tension among the disciplines of bioethics is found in their varied "moralities of method." One of the strengths of interdisciplines is their ability to bring many methods of inquiry to bear on a research question, for example, on life-and-death decisions (Botti, Orfali, and Iyengar 2009). Scholars in science and technology studies, for example, use historical research methods, surveys, qualitative methods (including focus groups, in-depth interviews, and ethnographies), and philosophical reflection to explore the emergence, adoption, and consequences of new biotechnologies. Bioethicists also rely on multiple methods, but the nature of their work demands reflection on the moralities embedded in these different methods. We do not refer here to whether the research is done ethically (i.e., no cheating, no harm to subjects), but rather to the moral standpoint assumed by the method. What is the moral vision that drives the sociological imagination? How is that similar to, and different from, the moral vision of the philosophical imagination?

Another hindrance to the peaceful coexistence of the disciplines within bioethics is the quandary of critical distance. Bioethics was born as a critique of harmful research and clinical practices: when bioethicists reflect on their history they see themselves as speaking truth to (medical) power, as advocates of vulnerable patients and research subjects. What happens when the critics are welcomed into the system they criticize? Yes, being admitted to the institutions of medicine and medical research allows one to work for change from the inside out, but it also weakens the critical distance that generated the original wisdom of bioethics. Bioethics gains both power and insight to the extent that there is a conversation between those who work in the system and those who remain outside. Bosk and Frader (1998), in their paper on clinical ethics committees, speculated about sociology's unexpected lack of interest in studying the social construction of ethical authority. According to these authors, it might be that sociologists tend to view ethicists' role as "nothing more than an attempt to preserve professional power by internalizing a critique and thereby disarming it" (Bosk and Frader 1998: 113).

While the so-called "sociology of bioethics" is a very recent denomination, one can say that the study of ethical problems in medicine existed much earlier. Many sociological studies focused on the moral issues of medicine (Bosk 1979; Fox 1959; Fox and Swazey 1974; Gray 1975) long before the emergence of a specific field called bioethics. Thus, the sociology of bioethics can be viewed as a subfield within medical sociology long ignored by bioethicists preoccupied by the very same topic, namely, the patient or, more generally, the promotion of a lay voice within medicine. Just as sociologists were seen as "imperialist rivals" to medical professionals (Strong 1979), they have become rivals to the bioethicists as the field of bioethics itself grew more and more medicalized.

Around the 1990s a sociological perspective on bioethics began to develop more clearly, with empirical studies of ways in which right and wrong were interpreted and justified and emerged out of the complex social situations of patients, families, and teams in the clinical setting (Clark, Potter, and McKinlay 1991; Muller 1991). Zussman (1994) examined how medical decision-making in intensive care units was negotiated while Guillemin and Holmstrom (1986), Anspach (1993), and Heimer and Staffen (1998) looked similarly at neonatal intensive care units. From studies of life-and-death decisions to genetic counselors doing mop-up work (Bosk 1992) or the construction of medical responsibility in geriatrics (Kauffman 1995), sociology has begun to give accounts on those values that underlie decisions and on how values became articulated in context. The study of local worlds and individual decision-making processes informs, at a macro-level, on the values of a given profession or society, and on the powers and interests at stake. Other areas (Elliott 2002), such as the ethics of medical research, have been studied by Dresser (2001) and Halpern (2001) and expand on the "morality of risk" in medical experiments.

Yet most sociological work has been a "deconstruction" of the reality of the prevailing model of autonomy offered by bioethics. Studies of informed consent emphasize the way it "manufactures assent" (Anspach 1993; see also Corrigan 2003), turns moral issues into professional and technical ones (Zussman 1994), or uses uncertainty to maintain medical authority (Orfali 2004). While medical ethics, a longtime stronghold of medical authority, has supposedly been challenged, most sociological works suggest that medicine was more or less successful in turning to its own purposes the attempts of others (including medical ethicists) to regulate it.

Another venue of sociological approaches concerns the new areas directly generated by the bioethics movement, for example, the studies of bioethical work such as clinical ethics committees or within research and in IRBs. An oft-made criticism of bioethicists is that they are full of good ideas and policy suggestions, but that they never stop to consider how these ideas and suggestions are actually working. Do end-of-life directives actually succeed in directing end-of-life care? Do ethics consultants steer corporations toward better behavior? Do elaborate rules for controlling conflicts of interest on the part of medical researchers work? Do IRBs really protect subjects of research? This kind of work, most often conducted by social scientists, allows bioethicists to see if their contributions to the biosciences are making a difference, if bioethics – measured on its own terms – is a success. This is best thought of as the evaluation research wing of bioethics.

CLINICAL ETHICS

The hospital context has been the privileged location for many studies, although work on clinical ethicists or on the inner workings of ethics consultations still remains scarce (Marshall 2001). Regarding bioethicists' work in the clinic, some in the field speak pejoratively of "beeper ethics" – the image here is of a bioethicist who responds to a page, rushing into a patient's room to render an ethical judgment. The work of clinical ethicists is to help caregivers, patients, and members of patients' families make decisions in circumstances that are ethically murky.

Social scientists have taken a cynical view of the role played by clinical ethicists, describing them variously as: doers of the "dirty work" of medicine (Bosk 1992) and deflectors of criticism of hospitals (Chambliss 1996). For their part, clinical ethicists do not always agree on the value of their services. Their efforts at self-assessment are hampered by the lack of a clear definition of what counts as success in bioethics consultation. Is it level of satisfaction? If so, whose satisfaction? Clients? Families? Caregivers? Judged by this criterion, clinical ethicists seem to have little effect – the SUPPORT study (1995) showed that even well-planned ethics interventions at the end of life did little to improve the satisfaction of any of the participants. Yet, more recent interdisciplinary studies by Schneiderman and colleagues (2003) show that ethics consultation significantly reduced the use of life-sustaining treatments *and* was regarded as helpful by a majority of nurses, patients, surrogates, and physicians.

The role of a clinical bioethicist resembles that of a public defender in the American legal system. The formal role of each is to represent the interests of a client in a large and confusing organization, but both must also maintain good relationships with other members of that organization, many of whom are working against their clients. Given this situation, both are inclined to represent the interests of professionals and institutions over those who are merely passing through – patients and families (Feeley 1979). Their work is often associated with messy emotional, relationship, or spiritual/religious issues: Bosk (1992), for example, describes genetic counselors as a "mop-up service" – a way for physicians to delegate the awkward task of dealing with distraught parents.

Finally, clinical bioethicists in the US seem to be doing a form of social work or dispute resolution: listening to patients (or staff), suggesting options, and finding ways to reconcile individual and institutional agendas. Picking up some of the "dirty work" (Hughes 1958) of medicine might well hinder bioethicists' desire to acquire professional status: it might finally become another subordinate profession in the medically dominated division of labor as shown by these approaches.

RESEARCH ETHICS

Many studies look at IRBs, examining both their characteristics and their decision-making processes. After their survey of a stratified sample of IRB administrators, DeVries and Forsberg (2002) concluded:

> A close look at the composition and workload of IRBs shows that not all voices are represented in board deliberations, that the existing structure of IRBs inclines researchers and research institutions to put their interests before the interests of the subjects of research, and that there are too few staff to monitor the many protocols IRBs are required to manage.

The most popular method of examining IRB decisions has been to look at how several different IRBs respond to the same protocol. In the 1980s, these studies were done with "mock" protocols or with "mock IRBs" (Goldman and Katz 1982). In the 1990s, with the rise of multi-center trials, there was less need to create mock protocols – researchers were gaining first-hand experience with different IRB reactions to the same protocols, and a few of these researchers began to analyze and write about the variations they saw (Silverman, Hull, and Sugarman 2001). Studies of informed consent and recruitment include analysis of the readability of consent forms (Goldstein et al. 1996) and in-depth studies of subjects' understanding of what their consent involved (Corrigan 2003). For the most part, researchers interested in questions about conflicts of interest have studied administrative rules and procedures. In 2000, Cho and her colleagues studied policies on faculty conflicts of interest at 89 universities in the United States. They discovered wide variation in the management of these conflicts and concluded that this variation "may cause unnecessary confusion among potential industrial partners or competition among universities for corporate sponsorship that could erode academic standards" (Cho et al. 2000: 2203). Ethnographic studies on scientists conducting research with human embryonic stem cells by Wainwright, Williams, and their colleagues (2007) are another example of social science's growing interest in research ethics.

THE PROFESSIONALIZATION OF BIOETHICAL EXPERTISE

The question of what moral expertise is and what legitimizes someone to speak as a "bioethicist" remains an ongoing issue within bioethics and has gained increased attention from a sociological perspective (DeVries, Dingwall, and Orfali 2009). While bioethics has been widely institutionalized in the US, it still remains very much a profession in transition. Bioethicists' struggle to find a collectively acceptable way of organizing themselves has been more challenging than the creation of an intellectual framework. Despite establishing training programs, occupational associations, graduate programs, journals, and the like all over the country, there has been an ongoing debate about what credentials should be required for those working in hospital ethics committees and Institutional Review Boards that review and approve research involving human subjects. Hospital accreditation in the US requires institutions to have an ethics committee, normally made up of various health and social work professionals, local clergy, community members, and administrators. What qualifies one to participate in ethical decision-making? In the late 1990s, the credentials of ethics committee members were debated on the "biomed-l listserv" (biomed-l@listserv.nodak.edu). This debate reflected the ambivalence about professionalization among bioethicists at that time. It began with a simple question: does any member of the hospital ethics committee need to be licensed/certified? The responses varied. At one end were those suspicious of licensing; others found licensure to be a useful tool. Still others reflected on the problem of credentialing in bioethics because, given the different backgrounds of participants, there could be no unified basis for judging the competency of any candidate.

In the case of this "profession in transition," the task of separating sheep from goats was complicated by the fact that the best-known bioethicists have not had professional training in bioethics. The founders of bioethics come from a variety of backgrounds, with degrees in philosophy, medicine, theology, and law. Many of these "original bioethicists" insisted that the proper way to become a bioethicist was to first get an advanced degree in one of these fields and then to come into bioethics. They justified this position by explaining that bioethics was a rich, interdisciplinary field that drew some of its best insights from the conversation between disciplines. To narrow the focus of training to bioethics would diminish the field.

By 1997, these attitudes were changing. The demand for a professional identity has led many bioethicists to rethink their stance on professional education and to establish university-based masters and PhD programs in bioethics.

This debate started nearly 20 years ago, but bioethicists continue to argue about the value of, and need for, certification. In 1998, the ASBH adopted and published the report of the Task Force on Standards for Bioethics Consultation, a report that takes a strong stand *against* certification. The Task Force rejected certification for a number of reasons, including: (1) fear that certification would increase the risk of displacing providers and patients as the primary moral decision-makers, and (2) concern that certification could undermine the disciplinary diversity of bioethics (see American Society for Bioethics and Humanities 1998; Aulisio, Arnold, and Youngner 2000; Churchill 1999).

At the same time, there also is a trend that favors certification of bioethical decision-makers. In its report, *Ethical and Policy Issues in Research Involving Human Participants*, the National Bioethics Advisory Council (2001) recommended that "all investigators, IRB members, and IRB staff should be certified prior to conducting or reviewing research involving human participants." The professionalization of bioethics will probably lead to a clarification of its boundaries, changing further the very nature of bioethical expertise and authority in American health care.

Conclusion

Medical sociology and bioethics came into being at the same time, in the same place – namely, the US – with a very similar focus on patient rights, yet with mutual inattention to each other. When sociologists started to pay more attention to the growing distinctive field emerging as bioethics, they structured their approaches "against" bioethics, pointing to the lacks and limits of "a monistic conception of ethical universalism which is coupled with a tendency to disregard context" (Fox and Swazey 2008: 13). The recurrent social science critique of the bioethical enterprise has probably hampered a more theoretical and richer empirical approach on the emergence and development of bioethics. At the same time, it has helped construct and identify bioethics as a new territory, a distinctive object to study (Callahan 1999). One of the early books collecting essays on the relationship between bioethics and social science (DeVries and Subedi 1998) was a strongly critical appraisal of the bioethical enterprise and a call for more convergence between the two. In 2001 (Hoffmaster 2001), essays using qualitative research methods exposed the multiple contexts within which the problems of bioethics arose and were debated. Ethnography appeared as the privileged approach. A recent version on bioethics as an object of study for social scientists (DeVries et al. 2007) moves toward a clearer identification of a sociological body of knowledge exploring research ethics, the way moral boundaries are negotiated in biomedicine, issues of ethics policies in different cultural contexts, and other topics. We are now past the point where that argument must be made: for better or for worse, the social sciences are now part of the bioethical enterprise. In that sense, Bosk's (2008) recent book looks at the emergent social organization of the everyday ethical dilemmas of clinical care and research as a distinctive field organized by experts in bioethics and at the same time examines ethnography through the lens of ethics.

Of course (as sociologists would predict), the place of social science in bioethics varies by cultural and social context. In the Netherlands and Belgium, the creation of "empirical bioethics" has given social science an established voice in the bioethical conversation (Borry, Schotsmans, and Dierickx 2005; Van der Scheer and Widdershoven 2004). In North America and the UK, social science methods are widely used in bioethics, but social scientists remain, to a certain extent, strangers to the field (De Vries 2004; Hedgecoe 2004). There are advantages to both insider and outsider statuses. We North Americans who stand at a distance from bioethics can take comfort in Simmel's (1950) observation that the stranger "is freer practically and theoretically ... he surveys conditions with less prejudice [and] is not tied down in his action by habit, piety, and precedent." Simmel pointed out that those who do not "own the soil" are in a unique position, one that combines nearness and distance, indifference and involvement, a social location that allows them to become the recipients of a "most surprising openness" from group members. On the other hand, there are undeniable benefits that come with "owning the soil" of bioethics. The collaborative work that gets done under the rubric of empirical bioethics moves the important ideas of philosophical bioethics into the real world of medicine and medical research where human beings live and work, and help and harm each other (Borry, Schotsmans, and Dierickx 2004; Molewijk et al. 2003). This tension between the "voice in the wilderness" (that no one hears) and "going native" (thereby losing the distinctive, critical perspective offered by sociology) can be used productively: distance allows challenges to the common sense of bioethics and closeness allows the analyses of social scientists to be incorporated into the work of bioethicists (De Vries et al. 2007).

Finally, bioethics can be viewed as an unsettled field, the very project of modernity itself, a constant tense relationship between *reason* and *subject*. Our Western culture evolved not from irrationality to rationality but from an integrated view of the universe, which was considered (in the Enlightenment model) both as rational and created by God, to a growing separation between the objective and subjective universes (Touraine 1995). The bioethical enterprise can be viewed as the reformulation of modernity, no more a quest for a unified world or principle, be it rationalization, cultural identity, or any other principle, but as a necessary but tense relationship between rationalization and individualism or subjectivism. If one component wins over the other, rationalization becomes an instrument of power and individualism a negative cultural identity (fundamentalism, nationalism, and so on). So in a sense, the sociological critics of bioethics are right and wrong at the same time: bioethics is the critique of modernity and can only retain its vitality and be renewed by remaining unsettled, evolving in disagreement and temporary consensus.

Notes

1   E. Durkheim, "Introduction à la morale," *Revue Philosophique* 89 (1920).
2   The *Declaration of Helsinki,* which followed in 1964 (and was revised in 2004) sets out stricter requirements for consent, but it is less quoted in medical textbooks. It is interest-

ing to note that the Nuremberg code was drafted by Americans, making it a more native contribution to American bioethics.

3   The fact that eugenics in the twentieth century preceded the Nazi experiments and was developed by physicians from Germany, the US, and other countries has been largely ignored (Caplan 1992; Katz 1995: 227).

4   For 40 years, the US Public Health Service had conducted a study on 600 black men, mostly poor and uneducated, to study the natural history of syphilis in the untreated patient even after a therapy became available.

5   The IRB requirements tend today to extend to any international research involving US academics.

6   See Glaser and Strauss 1965; Quint 1972 and others. Even in medical literature a fair amount of articles around truth-telling in cancer wards, for example, emerged at the same time.

7   Dr. Kenneth Ryan, chairman of the National Commission for the Protection of Human Subjects of Biomedical and Behavioral Research (1974–8), 1986.

8   Decline of two-thirds to just one-half: General Social Survey (National Opinion Research Center, University of Chicago, 1990).

References

American Society for Bioethics and Humanities. 1998. *Core Competencies for Health Care Ethics Consultation*. Glenview, IL: American Society for Bioethics and Humanities.

Annas, Georges J. 1993. *Standard of Care: The Law of American Bioethics*. New York: Oxford University Press.

Annas, Georges J. 2004. "'Culture of Life': Politics at the Bedside – The Case of Terri Schiavo." *New England Journal of Medicine* 352: 1710–15.

Annas, Georges J. and Michael A. Grodin (eds.). 1992. *The Nazi Doctors and the Nuremberg Code*. New York: Oxford University Press.

Annas, Georges J. and Frances H. Miller. 1994. "The Empire of Death: How Culture and Economics Affect Informed Consent in the US, the UK, and in Japan." *American Journal of Law and Medicine* 20(4): 357–94.

Anspach, Renée. 1993. *Deciding Who Lives: Fateful Choices in the Intensive Care Nursery*. Chicago: University of Chicago Press.

Aulisio, Mark, Robert Arnold, and Stuart Youngner. 2000. "Health Care Ethics Consultation: A Position Paper from the Society for Health and Human Values–Society for Bioethics Consultation Task Force on Standards for Bioethics Consultation." *Annals of Internal Medicine* 133: 59–69.

Barber, Bernard, John Lally, Julia Laughlin Makarushka, and Daniel Sullivan. 1973. *Problems and Processes of Social Control in Bio-Medical Experimentation*. New York: Russell Sage Foundation.

Beauchamp, Tom and James Childress. 1979. *Principles of Biomedical Ethics*. New York: Oxford University Press.

Beecher, Henry K. 1966. "Ethics and Clinical Research." *New England Journal of Medicine* 274: 1354–60.

Borry, Pascal, Paul Schotsmans, and Kris Dierickx. 2004. "What Is the Role of Empirical Research in Bioethical Reflection and Decision-Making? An Ethical Analysis." *Medicine, Health Care and Philosophy* 7: 41–53.

Borry, Pascal, Paul Schotsmans, and Kris Dierickx. 2005. "The Birth of the Empirical Turn in Bioethics." *Bioethics* 19(1): 49–71.

Bosk, Charles. 1979. *Forgive and Remember: Managing Medical Failure.* Chicago: University of Chicago Press.

Bosk, Charles. 1992. *All God's Mistakes: Genetic Counseling in a Pediatric Hospital.* Chicago: University of Chicago Press.

Bosk, Charles. 2002. "Now That We Have the Data, What Was the Question?" *American Journal of Bioethics* 2: 21–3.

Bosk, Charles. 2004. "Professional Expertise and Moral Cowardice: 'Counterfeit Courage' and the 'Non-Combatant'." Presented at the School of Social Science, Institute for Advanced Study, Princeton, NJ, October.

Bosk, Charles. 2007. "The Sociological Imagination." Pp. 398–410 in C. E. Bird, P. Conrad, and A. M. Fremont (eds.), *The Handbook of Medical Sociology.* New York: Macmillan.

Bosk, Charles. 2008. *What Would You Do? The Collision of Ethics and Ethnography.* Chicago: University of Chicago Press.

Bosk, Charles and Joel Frader. 1998. "Institutional Ethics Committees: Sociological Oxymoron, Empirical Black Box." Pp. 94–116 in R. De Vries and J. Subedi (eds.), *Bioethics and Society: Constructing the Ethical Enterprise.* Upper Saddle River, NJ: Prentice Hall.

Botti, Simona, Kristina Orfali, and Sheena S. Iyengar. 2009. "Tragic Choices: Autonomy and Emotional Responses to Medical Decisions." *Journal of Consumer Research*: published online (www.journals.uchicago.edu/doi/abs/10.1086/598969).

Bury, Michael R. 1982. "Chronic Illness as Biographical Disruption." *Sociology of Health and Illness* 4: 167–82.

Callahan, Daniel. 1999. "The Social Sciences and the Task of Bioethics." *Daedalus, Journal of the American Academy of Arts and Sciences* 128: 275–94.

Caplan, Arthur (ed.). 1992. *When Medicine Went Mad: Bioethics and the Holocaust.* Totowa, NJ: Humanities Press.

Capron, Alexander M. 1999. "What Contributions Have Social Science and the Law Made to the Development of Policy on Bioethics?" *Daedalus, Journal of the American Academy of Arts and Sciences* 128: 295–325.

Chambliss, Daniel. 1996. *Beyond Caring: Hospitals, Nurses, and the Social Organization of Ethics.* Chicago: University of Chicago Press.

Charmaz, Kathy. 1991. *Good Days, Bad Days: The Self in Chronic Illness and Time.* New Brunswick, NJ: Rutgers University Press.

Charon, Rita and Martha Montello. 2002. *Stories Matter: The Role of Narrative in Medical Ethics.* London: Routledge.

Cho, M., R. Shohara, A. Schissel, and R. Drummond. 2000. "Policies on Faculty Conflicts of Interest at US Universities." *Journal of the American Medical Association* 284: 2203–8.

Churchill, Larry R. 1999. "Are We Professionals? A Critical Look at the Social Role of Bioethicists." *Daedalus, Journal of the American Academy of Arts and Sciences* 128: 253–74.

Clark, Jack, Deborah A. Potter, and John B. McKinlay. 1991. "Bringing Social Structure Back into Clinical Decision Making." *Social Science and Medicine* 32: 853–66.

Cobbs v. Grant, 502 P. 2d 1 (Cal 1972).

Cockerham, William. 2005. "Medical Sociology and Sociological Theory." Pp. 3–22 in W. Cockerham (ed.), *The Blackwell Companion to Medical Sociology.* Oxford: Blackwell.

Corrigan, Oonagh. 2003. "Empty Ethics: The Problem with Informed Consent." *Sociology of Health and Illness* 25: 768–92.

Cruzan v. Missouri Department of Health, 497 U.S. 261 (1990).

DeVries, Raymond. 2004. "How Can We Help? From 'Sociology In' Bioethics to 'Sociology of' Bioethics." *Journal of Law, Medicine and Ethics* 32: 279–92.

DeVries, Raymond, Robert Dingwall, and Kristina Orfali. 2009. "The Moral Organization of the Professions: Bioethics in the United States and France." *Current Sociology* 57: 555–79.

DeVries, Raymond and C. Forsberg. 2002. "What Do IRBs Look Like, What Kind of Support Do They Receive?" *Accountability in Research* 9: 199–216.

DeVries, Raymond and Janardan Subedi (eds.). 1998. *Bioethics and Society: Constructing the Ethical Enterprise*. Upper Saddle River, NJ: Prentice-Hall.

DeVries Raymond, Leigh Turner, Kristina Orfali, and Charles Bosk (eds.). 2007. *The View from Here: Bioethics and the Social Sciences*. Oxford: Blackwell.

Dresser, Rebecca. 2001. *When Science Offers Salvation: Patient Advocacy and Research Ethics*. Oxford: Oxford University Press.

Duff, Raymond S. and A. G. M. Campbell. 1973. "Moral and Ethical Dilemmas in the Special Care Nursery." *New England Journal of Medicine* 289: 890–4.

Elliott, Carl. 2002. "Diary: The Ethics of Bioethics." *London Review of Books* 24: 40.

Evans, J. H. 2002. *Playing God? Human Genetic Engineering and the Rationalization of Public Bioethical Debate*. Chicago: University of Chicago Press.

Faden, Ruth R. 2004. "Bioethics: A Field in Transition." *Journal of Law, Medicine and Ethics* 32: 276–8.

Feeley, Malcolm M. 1979. *The Process Is the Punishment: Handling Cases in a Lower Criminal Court*. New York: Russell Sage Foundation.

Fox, Renée C. 1959. *Experiment Perilous: Physicians and Patients Facing the Unknown*. Glencoe, IL: Free Press.

Fox, Renée C. and Judith Swazey. 1974. *The Courage to Fail: A Social View of Organ Transplant and Dialysis*. Chicago: Chicago University Press.

Fox, Renée C. and Judith Swazey. 2005. "Examining American Bioethics: Its Problems and Prospects. Quo Vadis? Mapping the Future of Bioethics, Special Section." *Cambridge Quarterly of Health Care Ethics* 14: 361–73.

Fox, Renée C. and Judith Swazey. 2008. *Observing Bioethics*. Oxford: Oxford University Press.

Glaser, Barney G. and Anselm Strauss. 1965. *Awareness of Dying*. Chicago: Aldine.

Goldman, J. and M. Katz. 1982. "Inconsistency and Institutional Review Boards." *Journal of the American Medical Association* 248: 197–202.

Goldstein, A., P. Frasier, A. Curtis et al. 1996. "Consent Form Readability in University-Sponsored Research." *Journal of Family Practice* 42: 606–11.

Gray, Radford H. 1975. *Human Subjects in Medical Experimentation: A Sociological Study of the Conduct and Regulation of Research*. New York: John Wiley.

Guillemin, Jeanne H. and Lynda L. Holmstrom. 1986. *Mixed Blessings: Intensive Care for Newborns*. New York: Oxford University Press.

Halpern, Sydney. 2001. "Constructing Moral Boundaries: Public Discourse on Human Experimentation in Twentieth-Century America." Pp. 69–89 in B. Hoffmaster (ed.), *Bioethics in Social Context*. Philadelphia: Temple University Press.

Heimer, Carol A. and Lisa R. Staffen. 1998. *For the Sake of Children: The Social Organization of Responsibility in the Hospital and in the Home*. Chicago: University of Chicago Press.

Hedgecoe, Adam. 2004. "Critical Bioethics: Beyond the Social Science Critique of Applied Ethics." *Bioethics* 18: 120–43.

Hoffmaster, Barry (ed.). 2001. *Bioethics in Social Context*. Philadelphia: Temple University Press.

Hughes, E. C. 1958. *Men and Their Work*. Glencoe, IL: Free Press.

Illich, Ivan. 1971. *Deschooling Society*. London: Calder and Boyars.

Illich, Ivan. 1975. *Medical Nemesis*. London: Calder and Boyars.

In re Quinlan, 70 N.J. 10 (1976).

Jennings, Dana. 2008. "Person, Patient, Statistic." *New York Times*, December 16, Sciences Times, p. D1.

Jonas, Hans. 1966. *The Phenomenon of Life: Toward a Philosophical Biology*. New York: Harper and Row.

Jonsen, Albert R. 1998. *The Birth of Bioethics*. New York: Oxford University Press.

Katz, Jay. 1995. "The Consent Principle of the Nuremberg Code." Chapter 12 in Georges J. Annas and Michael A. Grodin (eds.), *The Nazi Doctors and the Nuremberg Code*. New York: Oxford University Press.

Kauffman, Sharon R. 1995. "Decision Making, Responsibility and Advocacy in Geriatric Medicine." *The Gerontologist* 35: 481–8.

Keith-Spiegel, Patricia and Gerald P. Koocher. 2005. "The IRB Paradox: Could the Protectors Also Encourage Deceit?" *Ethics and Behavior* 15: 339–49.

Marshall, Patricia. 2001. "A Contextual Approach to Clinical Ethics Consultation." Pp. 137–52 in B. Hoffmaster (ed.), *Bioethics in Social Context*. Philadelphia: Temple University Press.

Molewijk, Albert C., Anne Stiggelbout, W. Otten, H. Dupuis, and Job Kievit. 2003. "Implicit Normativity in Evidence-Based Medicine: A Plea for Integrated Empirical Ethics Research." *Health Care Analysis* 11: 69–92.

Morreim, E. Haavi. 2001. "From the Clinics to the Courts: The Role Evidence Should Play in Litigating Medical Care." *Journal of Health Politics, Policy and Law* 26: 409–28.

Muller, Jessica H. 1991. "Shades of Blue: The Negotiation of Limited Codes by Medical Residents." *Social Science and Medicine* 34: 885–98.

National Bioethics Advisory Council (NBAC). 2001. "Summary." In *Ethical and Policy Issues in Research Involving Human Participants*, August (www.ntis.gov).

National Commission for the Protection of Human Subjects of Biomedical and Behavioral Research. 1979. *The Belmont Report: Ethical Principles and Guidelines for the Protection of Human Subjects of Research* (ohsr.od.nih.gov/guidelines/belmont.html).

Nisbet, Robert. 1986. *The Making of Modern Society*. Brighton: Wheatsheaf.

Orfali, Kristina. 2004. "Parental Role and Medical Decision Making: Fact or Fiction? A Comparative Study of French and American Practices in Neonatal Intensive Care Units." *Social Science and Medicine* 58: 2009–22.

Pernick, Martin S. 1999. "Brain Death in a Cultural Context: The Reconstruction of Death 1967–1981." Pp. 3–33 in S. Youngner, R. Arnold, and R. Schapiro (eds.), *The Definition of Death: Contemporary Controversies*. Baltimore: Johns Hopkins University Press.

Pescosolido, Bernice A. and Carol A. Boyer. 2005. "The American Health Care Systems: Entering the Twenty-First Century with High Risk, Major Challenges and Great Opportunities." Pp. 180–98 in W. Cockerham (ed.), *The Blackwell Companion to Medical Sociology*. Oxford: Blackwell.

Quint, Jeanne C. 1972. "Institutionalized Practices of Information Control." Pp. 220–38 in E. Freidson, and J. Lorber (eds.), *Medical Men and Their Work*. San Francisco: Aldine.

Randall, Judith. 1983. "Are Ethics Committees Alive and Well?" *Hastings Center Report* 13(6): 10–12.

Rothman, David. 1991. *Strangers at the Bedside*. New York: Basic Books.

Rothman, David, Daniel Fox, and Stanley Reiser. 1974. "Three Views of the History of Bioethics." Birth of Bioethics Conference.

Schneider, Carl E. 1998. *The Practice of Autonomy: Patients, Doctors and Medical Decision*. New York: Oxford University Press.

Schneiderman, Lawrence J., Todd Gilmer, Holly D. Teetzel, Daniel O. Dugan, Jeffrey Blustein, Ronald Cranford, Kathleen B. Briggs, Glen I. Komatsu, Paula Goodman-Crews, Felicia Cohn, and Ernlé W. D. Young. 2003. "Effects of Ethics Consultations on Non-Beneficial Life-Sustaining Treatments in the Intensive Care Setting: A Randomized Controlled Trial." *Journal of the American Medical Association* 290: 1166–72.

Silverman, H., Sara C. Hull, and Jeremy Sugarman. 2001. "Variability Among Institutional Review Boards' Decisions within the Context of a Multi-Center Trial." *Critical Care Medicine* 29: 235–41.

Simmel, Georg. 1950. *The Sociology of Georg Simmel*, translated by K. Wolff. New York: Free Press.

Stevens, Tina M. L. 2000. *Bioethics in America: Origin and Cultural Politics*. Baltimore: Johns Hopkins University Press.

Stone, Deborah A. 1997. "The Doctor as Businessman: The Changing Politics of a Cultural Icon." *Journal of Health Politics and Law* 22: 533–56.

Strauss, Anselm and Barney G. Glaser. 1975. *Chronic Illness and the Quality of Life*. St. Louis, MO: Mosby.

Strong, Philip M. 1979. "Sociological Imperialism and the Profession of Medicine: A Critical Examination of the Thesis of Medical Imperialism." *Social Science and Medicine* 13A: 199–215.

SUPPORT Principal Investigators. 1995. "A Controlled Trial to Improve Care for Seriously Ill Hospitalized Patients: The Study to Understand Prognoses and Preferences for Outcomes and Risks of Treatments (SUPPORT)." *Journal of the American Medical Association* 274: 1591–8.

Toulmin, Stephen. 1982. "How Medicine Saved the Life of Ethics." *Perspectives in Biology and Medicine* 25: 736–50.

Touraine, Alain. 1995. *Critique of Modernity*. Oxford: Blackwell.

Van der Scheer, Lieke and Guy Widdershoven. 2004. "Integrated Empirical Ethics: Loss of Normativity?" *Medicine, Health Care and Philosophy* 7: 71–9.

Wainwright, Steven P., Clare Williams, Mike Michael, Bobbie Frasides, and Alen Cribb. 2007. "Ethical Boundary-Work in the Embryonic Stem Cell Laboratory." Pp. 67–82 in R. DeVries, L. Turner, K. Orfali, and C. Bosk (eds.), *The View from Here: Bioethics and the Social Sciences*. Oxford: Blackwell.

Wolf, Suzan M. 2004. "Law and Bioethics: From Values to Violence." *Journal of Law, Medicine and Ethics* 32: 293–306.

Wolpe, Paul R. 1998. "The Triumph of Autonomy in American Bioethics: A Sociological View." Pp. 38–59 in R. DeVries and J. Subedi (eds.), *Bioethics and Society: Constructing the Ethical Enterprise*. Upper Saddle River, NJ: Prentice-Hall.

Zussman, Robert. 1994. *Intensive Care*. Chicago: University of Chicago Press.

23

Medical Sociology and Genetics

Paul A. Martin and Robert Dingwall

Developments in genetics have attracted considerable interest from medical sociology over the last decade, partly because of the funding offered to examine the social implications of major scientific programs like the Human Genome Project (HGP). However, genetics also raises fundamental questions for medical sociology. Some are well established – the construction of disease, the experience of illness, and the nature of professional work – but others are new, concerning the nature of genetic knowledge, its implications for human identity, and the relationship between the biological and the social. In examining these, medical sociologists have taken up ideas from related fields, notably science and technology studies (STS). This has led to novel concepts, such as "geneticization," and new frameworks, as in the "dynamics of expectations."

This chapter offers an overview of medical sociology's work on genetics. It is organized into eight main sections, highlighting key research areas and major debates. The first two sections sketch the technical and historical background to genetic science and the legacy of eugenics. This leads into a consideration of genetics in the clinic, the genetic construction of disease, and the experience of living with our genotype, including a discussion of genetic discrimination and new genetic identities. The interface with STS is explored, in the area of expectations and the commodification of genetic knowledge, with a focus on important genetic technologies. Finally, the relationship between genetics and behavior is discussed before returning, in the conclusion, to consider the status of the geneticization thesis and the implications for medical sociology. Does genetics really have the potential to transform medicine, society, and identity? How have medical sociologists contributed to creating this expectation?

THE BASICS OF GENETIC SCIENCE

The rapid progress in genetic science has attracted considerable interest from medical sociologists (Conrad and Gabe 1999; Pilnick 2002a). Genetic science is founded on the observation that the biological constitution of all living things – plants, animals, fish, insects, bacteria, humans, and so on – is shaped by a chemical called DNA (deoxyribonucleic acid) found in the nuclear material of the cells from which they are all made. DNA is best thought of as an information-coding molecule that carries the instructions for the construction and operation of the living tissues that make up an organism. Genes are segments of DNA that carry a particular set of instructions to make molecules that can perform a specific task in relation to cell assembly or functioning. The totality of genes and related control sequences found in an organism is called its *genome*. The human genome is made up of about 25,000–30,000 genes, whose instructions combine to produce the varied bodies recognizable as members of our species, *Homo sapiens*.

An important early finding from classical genetics was that variations in an individual gene could lead directly to specific diseases. These, relatively uncommon, *monogenic* conditions, such as Huntington's disease, cystic fibrosis, and Duchenne muscular dystrophy, run in families where particular versions of single genes are passed from parent to child. Inheritance of a *dominant* gene from one parent, or a *recessive* gene from each parent, will almost invariably lead to the emergence of the disease. This "one gene = one disease" paradigm dominated genetic medicine until the 1980s. However, the development of recombinant DNA technology in the 1970s and 1980s created new possibilities for identifying genes and unraveling their role in common diseases. In the 1990s, the development of the new field of *genomics*, which catalogued the entire DNA sequence in humans and other species, allowed scientists and physicians to envisage a better understanding of the relationship between multiple genetic factors and disease pathology, a *polygenic* model.

Contemporary genetics sees genes as playing a determining role in many biological functions. Some scholars also claim that genes determine key aspects of human behavior and social life, such as reproductive choices, intellectual ability, sexuality, and aggression. Other scientists, both biological and social, stress the considerable element of indeterminacy in these processes.

The expression of genes is significantly influenced by both their physical and their social environments. These influences begin at the point of conception. During reproduction, a new combination of genes is assembled out of the set contributed by each parent, resulting in an organism that derives some features from each. The offspring is not identical to either parent and the novel combination may result in features that are not apparent in either parent. A first point of indeterminacy, then, is the combination of parents that actually occurs, which, in turn, reflects social and cultural opportunities to meet and reproduce. Sociologists have long established that our reproductive partners are most likely to be people like ourselves in terms of age, ethnicity, social status, and so on (Kalmijn 1994). Selection also has a cultural dimension, the ideals of "fitness" that we use to choose among potential partners. These ideals – body aesthetics, moral character, intellect, practical skills, and so on – reflect the thinking in a social group about what contributes to its members' adaptation to both the material and the cultural environments in which they live. If any of these have a genetic basis, reproductive selection will increase their prevalence within that group. Even if they do not have a genetic basis, though, their prevalence may still increase, if they are seen to be necessary for successful reproduction, by group members copying behaviors that seem to attract more, or more valuable, partners. This makes it extremely difficult to distinguish between biological and cultural forms of selection and undermines simple claims that many common social traits are under genetic control.

A second element of indeterminacy is the availability of nutrients and other chemicals *in utero*, affecting the resources on which gene products can operate. The famine experienced in the Netherlands during the winter of 1944–5, for example, when adult food intake fell to a quarter of recommended levels, had long-term intergenerational health consequences for babies born to women who experienced this shortage while they were pregnant (Academic Medical Centre 2008). A third is the interaction between genes, the way in which networks of genes constitute environments for each other that contribute to the development of a particular process or structure. A fourth is in the mutability of DNA itself, which can, rarely, lead to spontaneous and unpredictable changes (*mutations*), both at the cellular level and at the level of an organism's physical characteristics (its *phenotype*). Finally, there is the overall interaction between the combined expression of a genome and the social and physical environment within which an organism is located. For example, it is becoming increasingly clear that, in some animals, the expression of important genes that control the stress reaction is fundamentally influenced by the animal's infant environment (Francis et al. 1999).

The study of gene–environment interaction is rapidly becoming a major focus of investigation. This is an important shift away from the simple historic model that saw genes as major determinants of human development and behavior to one which sees the relationship between heredity and environment, nature and nurture, as complex, dynamic, and interactive. Nevertheless, contemporary genetics has been seen to have great potential as the basis of powerful new biotechnologies. Some commentators talk of a "biotechnology revolution" that could transform health care through the application of new diagnostics and therapies, including genetic testing, pharmacogenetics, gene therapy, and novel targeted therapeutics (Nightingale and Martin 2004).

GENETICS AND MEDICAL SOCIOLOGY

The development and implications of contemporary genetic science have become a major area of research and debate within medical sociology. A significant reason for this is the idea that many aspects of health and health care are becoming "geneticized." When genetic issues first took root in current popular and scientific discourse, they were associated with claims that they represented fundamental challenges to established institutions, practices, and professional interests. The term "geneticization" was coined, by analogy with medicalization, to describe the way in which health and disease were increasingly being understood by reference to genetic factors, with differences between humans being reduced to differences in their DNA (Lippman 1992). For example, rather than understanding the cause of common conditions, such as heart disease, in terms of structural inequalities, environmental hazards, and health-related behavior, it was argued that disparities simply reflected the distribution of gene variants within the population. The appropriate response would be clinical management based on biological science, rather than socioeconomic management, based on social science.

Closely related to geneticization is the notion of "genetic exceptionalism," the idea that genetic information is qualitatively different from other types of personal and health-related information because it can more accurately predict an individual's risk of getting ill. If this is so, then it could be socially problematic, raising issues for both individuals and institutions that may require new forms of governance to avoid unfair discrimination. In the case of rare monogenic conditions, such as cystic fibrosis, for example, genetic tests can identify individuals who will inevitably get this disease: genetic counseling has developed to help manage the delivery of this information. However, knowledge of the condition, with its consequent reduction in life expectancy and its costly implications for medical care, could lead to exclusion from access to long-term loans, such as mortgages, or health insurance programs.

Finally, one of the distinguishing features of genetics is its association with high expectations and social anxieties. It can be thought of as a *promissory field*, in which expectations, hopes, and fears about the future play a powerful role in shaping the present direction of science and technology, their clinical applications and social implications. Ideas from STS are increasingly being used by medical sociologists to analyze the role of expectations in the emergence of new technologies and clinical practices.

The development of genetic science has projected a transformation in medical practice, and in our understanding of health and illness. There are new opportunities for socioeconomic discrimination, new ideas about causes of human disease, the commodification of cells and tissues, new discourses concerning human identity and capabilities, such as intelligence and forms of social deviance, and new industries based on these new technologies. Many of these issues go beyond the traditional boundaries of medical sociology but may also raise questions about how those boundaries have been historically defined. Medical sociologists have, for example, been increasingly recruited to examine the governance issues that arise from the ethical, legal, and social implications (ELSI) of genetics. Government has been an important source of funding for research, but has also increasingly generated questions about the role and responsibility of social scientists and bioethicists who are being commissioned to supply legitimacy to a contested social field (Elliott 2002, 2004; Elliott and Lemmens 2005).

THE LEGACY OF EUGENICS

Two British scholars, Charles Darwin and Alfred Wallace, developed the basic ideas of evolution in the middle of the nineteenth century. Whereas previous scholars had thought that species were essentially fixed in their original form, the evolutionists showed that organisms were constantly subject to change through their interactions with their surrounding environment. The small variations that arose from sexual reproduction advantaged some members of the species and disadvantaged others. The advantaged members, the "fittest," would have more offspring and leave more descendants so that their characteristics were increasingly influential in defining the species. However, although the process could be demonstrated, the underlying mechanism was not known at the time. This only began to be recognized at the beginning of the twentieth century, when Dutch and German scientists appreciated the significance of the plant breeding studies carried out in the 1850s by a Czech monk, Gregor Mendel. The term "genetics" was introduced to describe the hereditary transmission of biological information by Patrick Bateson, a British academic, in 1905, and the concept of the gene was formalized by Wilhelm Johannsen, a Danish botanist, in 1909. The biological process involved was not fully established until the role of DNA was confirmed in the mid-1950s.

Although Darwin said little about the evolution of the human species, others were quick to take up the potential implications of his work in the form of *eugenics*, a social and intellectual movement based on the idea that humanity's development could be consciously controlled through direct intervention in human reproduction (Kevles 1995). Eugenicists believed that characteristics such as intellect or moral character were strongly determined by biology. They feared that social stability was threatened by the "degeneration" of race and nation caused by the excessive breeding of the genetically unfit – drunks, vagabonds, and delinquents, with little intelligence and low morals. This undermined the status and values of well-bred respectable people with secure lifestyles. The eugenics movement proposed to build a better society by encouraging the "best" humans to reproduce more (*positive eugenics*) and discouraging or preventing the "worst" from reproducing at all (*negative eugenics*). Planned Parenthood of America, for instance, was originally founded by Margaret Sanger with the aim of limiting reproduction among the lower classes by making contraception more readily available to them. Although eugenics was associated from the outset with social conservatism, it is important to recognize that early enthusiasts also included many people who would have described themselves as socialists or social democrats, like the British novelist H. G. Wells, or the Irish playwright George Bernard Shaw. Their ideals of progress were embodied in a vision of a planned society where individual breeding would also be regulated in the best interests of all. Aldous Huxley's 1932 novel, *Brave New World*, is often taken as an image of such a society, although Huxley's mechanism for producing different classes of human is chemical intervention in artificial wombs rather than selective breeding.

The limited success of voluntary measures to encourage those perceived to be genetically fit to have more children, and those seen as unfit to have fewer, led many eugenicists to advocate compulsion. Laws facilitating the sterilization of people who were considered to be physically, mentally, or morally unfit were passed in many Northern European countries, Canada, and 33 US states during the early twentieth century. The US Supreme Court upheld the constitutionality of compulsory sterilization in the case of *Buck v. Bell*, 274 U.S. 200 (1927). Carrie Buck was an 18-year-old woman who was said to have a mental age of 9 and was an inmate of the Virginia State Colony for Epileptics and Feebleminded, who had become pregnant in 1923. The Colony's medical superintendent applied to his Board for authority to use a new state law, passed in 1924, to carry out the procedure. The Board's approval was sustained through successive tiers of appeal. The Supreme Court's judgment was written by Oliver Wendell Holmes, who noted that Carrie's mother was said to be a prostitute with a mental age of 8 and declared: "Three generations of imbeciles is enough." Carrie's daughter was also sterilized as a child, although she seems to have performed well at school until her death at the age of 8. Later work has suggested that Carrie probably became pregnant as a result of rape by a member of her adoptive family (Lombardo 1985).

Holmes' judgment encouraged more enthusiastic use of sterilization laws until a later case, *Skinner v. Oklahoma*, 316 U.S. 535 (1942), introduced a degree of uncertainty about the legality of the practice, in an early judgment written by William O. Douglas, who was to become one of the longest-serving and most liberal Supreme Court Justices. Nevertheless, it is suggested that as many as one third of the 60,000 people estimated to have been involuntarily sterilized in the US between 1907 and 1963 experienced this procedure after the judgement in *Skinner* (Lombardo N.d.).

Eugenic ideas found their most powerful expression in the policies of Nazi Germany, which culminated in the Holocaust, although this had been preceded by the involuntary euthanasia of many people with learning disabilities or mental health problems from the late 1930s onwards. This experience discredited eugenics in the years following World War II, although sterilization laws and practices were only finally abandoned in Canada and some Scandinavian countries in the 1970s. The statute under which Carrie Buck had been sterilized, for example, was not repealed by Virginia until 1974 and Oregon had similar legislation as late as 1983.

The shadow of the Holocaust looms large in many contemporary discussions of genetics because of the renewed opportunities for intervention in the processes of human reproduction that have emerged from recent scientific developments. If, for example, examination of a human embryo's genome establishes the presence of Down's syndrome, is a woman's decision to terminate the pregnancy a eugenic one? Is there a real difference between a eugenic outcome determined by law and state policy and one determined by individual reproductive choice?

GENETICS IN THE CLINIC

Part of the answer to these questions may be found in the debates around *genetic counseling*. After World War II, geneticists continued to study the inheritance of rare monogenic conditions in affected families, as well as the impact of radiation damage and associated gene mutations, on the general population (Kevles 1995). Genetic health services were established around university research centers, offering diagnosis and counseling for affected families. By the 1980s, these local services had expanded in many countries into national networks of clinics employing specialists in genetics and testing for a wide range of monogenic conditions, and a smaller number of more common diseases, such as inherited forms of cancer. Population-based genetic screening programs were also introduced in some countries to help identify carriers of particular genetic defects such as the recessive genes for thalassemia in Cyprus or Tay-Sachs disease among Ashkenazi Jewish groups. Among the latter population, the tradition of arranged marriages offered opportunities to avoid reproduction between carriers of the gene, but the only interventions currently available for most other conditions are negative: the termination of a pregnancy or the non-implantation of an IVF embryo. Contemporary geneticists have tried to escape the stigma of the previous history of negative eugenics by emphasizing the role of individual choice, informed by non-directive genetic counseling, in acting on genetic information. Medical sociologists have questioned this in two ways.

Firstly, empirical studies of genetic counseling have shown that the interactional difficulties of giving sensitive and technical information in a neutral and non-directive fashion often result in what is effectively the manipulation of the recipients toward particular outcomes (Kolker and Burke 1998; Pilnick 2002b, 2004). These studies do not suggest that there is necessarily any malign intent, partly because the difficulties frequently arise from recipients looking for a direction in advice when the counselors are striving not to give one. Nevertheless, genetic counseling is frequently evaluated in terms of its success in reducing the number of births of babies with some genetic disability and it seems inherent in the enterprise that participants are encouraged toward individual outcomes that collectively add up to a policy of negative eugenics.

This has been the focus of the second current, which argues that "soft" eugenics is still eugenics (Shakespeare 1998). By permitting, and sometimes promoting, the termination of fetuses with genetic conditions, such as Down's syndrome, judgments are being made about the value of such human lives. Such judgments are insensitive to the rights of people with disabilities and the extent to which their difficulties are the result of disabling environments rather than essential properties of individuals. The consequence may be that disability is seen to be the result of flawed parental choices, for which the wider society bears no particular responsibility, rather than of the way that the society has chosen to organize itself, where those excluded by this decision may be able to make a claim for care and support in dealing with its impact on them.

THE GENETIC CONSTRUCTION OF DISEASE

The diagnosis of particular conditions has historically been the central task of clinical genetics, and the goal of most genetic testing. Many genetic disorders are hard to diagnose and require careful clinical examination of abnormal physical characteristics (Featherstone et al. 2005). However, as knowledge of the role of genetic factors in disease has grown, and a wider range of genetic testing has become available, new discourses have been constructed about the etiology of many diseases. Genes are being made central to accounts of the causation of common diseases, with the development of new taxonomies breaking up previously unitary disease entities, such as "cancer" or "cardiovascular disorder," into more specific subtypes, defined by a molecular pathology based on patterns of gene expression (Martin 1999). This promises to introduce more precise diagnostics and better disease management, and has opened up the idea of tailoring therapy to an individual's specific genotype – so called *personalized medicine*. In effect, the development of *pharmacogenetics*, the use of genetic testing to predict a person's response to a particular drug, is reverse engineering previously unitary disease concepts, such as asthma and heart disease, into genetically defined subtypes characterized by their different responses to therapy (Smart and Martin 2006).

Scholars at the interface between medical sociology and STS have examined the attempted geneticization of specific diseases. One example is work on the historical shifts in the understanding of cystic fibrosis, and the way it came to be seen as a genetic disease, with new forms of testing redrawing established definitions to include new symptoms (e.g., male infertility) (Hedgecoe 2003; Kerr 2005). This research emphasizes the complex relationship between new scientific knowledge and the development of both lay and clinical understandings of disease. Moreover, as innovation in genetic tests facilitates the identification of previously unknown, and unseen, forms of genetic disease, this can lead to an expansion of fetal screening and the range of findings seen as abnormal (Vailly 2008). The geneticization of common complex disorders has also been investigated. Hedgecoe's (2001) study of schizophrenia describes the subtle way in which scientists mobilize genetic ideas to create a cautious and responsible account of the place of genes in the etiology of the disease, a process he calls enlightened geneticization. Genes are reconstructed as individual risk factors, where the presence of a particular variation is seen as increasing the risk of developing a common disease: carriers do not necessarily develop the condition but have a greater chance of doing so (Prior 2001). One great hope of contemporary research is the identification of genetic risk factors associated with a wide range of diseases. The presence of BRCA1 or BRCA2 genes, for example, is now known to significantly increase the probability that a woman will develop breast cancer in early adult life.

This presents a range of social and ethical challenges: giving people information about their personal genetic status reveals information about the genotypes of their close kin, with whom they share many genes. How can patient confidentiality be sustained where those relatives may have chosen not to receive or share that information? This underlines the extent to which all medicine is ultimately family or community medicine rather than dealing with individuals outside their social and cultural environment. To the extent that risks can be managed, medical sociologists have examined the choices made, like decisions to undergo disfiguring surgery or to adopt long-term changes in diet or exercise regimes (Hallowell and Lawton 2002). Interactional studies have shown that many of the same problems emerge from these consultations as from those around reproductive decisions (Hallowell 1999). Women with a BRCA1 or 2 gene may be offered a theoretical choice about whether to undergo a prophylactic mastectomy, but find this hard to refuse. Knowledge of a person's genotype also raises possibilities of discrimination and social exclusion which we will look at later.

LIVING WITH OUR GENOTYPE

The experience of (genetic) illness: Risk and responsibility

A number of studies have examined the experience of living with the diagnosis of a genetic disease, including late onset disorders such as hereditary breast and ovarian cancer (Hallowell and Lawton 2002) and Huntington's disease (Cox and McKellin 1999; Novas and Rose 2000), as well as genetic diseases that manifest in childhood, such as cystic fibrosis (Lowton and Gabe 2003; Stockdale 1999) and sickle cell disease (Atkins, Ahmed, and Anionwu 1998). Other work has explored women's experience of prenatal diagnosis (Rapp 2000) and pre-implantation genetic diagnosis (Lavery et al. 2002). This body of research inves-tigates the meaning and experience of genetic disorders in the context of people's lives and explores issues of stigma and identity (Kerr 2004). It draws upon well-established ideas within medical sociology that conceptualize chronic illness as disrupting or reconstructing personal biographies (Williams 1984). In contrast to a dominant biomedical discourse that emphasizes the "fact" of disease, it appears that there is wide variation in how people choose to live their daily lives and negotiate risk in the face of an inherited condition. Being identified as having, or being at risk of getting, a genetic disease can only be fully understood in the context of family relationships and ideas about self-identity. For example, work on diagnostic testing of children with rare monogenic conditions suggests that parents, whilst accepting the existence of a syndrome, embrace uncertainty about how it might be expressed, the individuality of their child, and positive aspects of the situation to establish a complex meaning of how the diagnosis fits into their lives (Whitmarsh et al. 2007). In this respect, there are many continuities with, for example, Davis's (1963) discussion of uncertainty in the context of a diagnosis of poliomyelitis, which was a major childhood infection that sometimes led to severely disabling consequences. Nevertheless, the inherited nature of genetic disease does make for some distinctive features (Petersen 2006).

A major strand of research has centered on the idea of *genetic responsibility*, where an individual diagnosed as "at risk" acquires new responsibilities to both themselves and their kin. This work initially arose from studies of new reproductive technologies and the development of genetic testing services for rare monogenic conditions (Rapp 1998, 2000). There has been considerable concern about the implications of being tested for disorders that only become manifest later in life, like Huntington's disease, when there are no therapeutic options available (Hoff-mann and Wulfsberg 1995). These debates have recently extended to common complex disorders such as genetic predisposition to breast cancer, where the only intervention is prophylactic radical double mastectomy (Hallowell et al. 2003; Surbone 2001). Finkler, for example, has argued that the way in which women diagnosed with this condition are constructed as being at risk is renewing concerns about genetic determinism and leading to the medicalization of kinship (Finkler 2000; Finkler, Skrzynia, and Evans 2003). The experience of being diagnosed as "at genetic risk" can transform a healthy person into a "patient without symp-toms" and place increasing emphasis on the biological rather than social determi-nants of health and illness. This conclusion has been criticized for overstating the role of genetics, relative to social context, in shaping identity (Kerr 2004). However, other studies of this group of women have shown how their understandings about their responsibilities and their obligations to relatives shape their decisions about whether or not to manage this risk through a mastectomy (Hallowell 1999; Hal-lowell and Lawton 2002). Such choices must be located in the context of estab-lished, gendered, discourses about women's responsibilities as carers. Similarly, men who are carriers of the BRCA genes for increased risk of breast cancer are found to be involved in narrative reconstruction to manage feelings of guilt and blame and present themselves to their families as morally responsible (Hallowell et al. 2006).

Genetic discrimination

An important consequence of the predictive knowledge about an individual's risk of developing a monogenic genetic disorder, or being more vulnerable to a common disease, is its impact on access to personal insurance products – health insurance, disability insurance, or pensions (Ewald, McGleenan, and Wiesing 1999). The basis of insurance is that none of us know exactly when we are going to fall ill, become disabled, or die. People who stay fit or die young contribute to the costs of those who become ill or live longer. However, if we knew our fate in advance, low-risk people might not buy insurance and subsidize high-risk people. Conversely, high-risk people might cheat by buying more coverage than their current premium warrants. Predictive genetic knowledge reduces people's uncertainty about their fate and may make such behavior more likely. However, if purchasers are required to share their knowledge with insurers, high-risk people may find that coverage is unavailable or unaffordable. This is not a serious problem in many European countries, where personal insurance products are luxury goods and the whole population can be required to share risks through taxation or social insurance payments. However, it is a major issue for the US and other market-based systems of health care provision. The genetically disadvantaged may simply be excluded from personal insurance, and from linked financial products such as mortgages for house purchase.

Genetic discrimination may also occur in the field of employment. Those diagnosed as being at risk could encounter job discrimination, either to minimize employer-linked insurance costs or because their genotype affects their susceptibility to chemical or biological materials used in production processes. There are some examples where such discrimination has either taken place, or has at least been contemplated. Nevertheless, these are relatively rare, partly because many countries, including the US at both federal and state level, have introduced anti-discrimination statutes to ban such practices, although there is debate about the scope and effectiveness of these controls (Rothstein 2007).

New genetic identities

In contrast to the idea that genetic knowledge is dangerous and can threaten social identity or result in discrimination, some scholars have emphasized the way in which new genetic identities are being created that provide novel forms of (bio)sociality and citizenship (Rabinow 1996; Rose and Novas 2004). Much of this work comes from a neo-Foucauldian perspective. While genetics may place new responsibilities on people to look after their own health, if they are judged to be at risk, it may also grant them new rights to treatment and provide a basis for collective identity. Novas and Rose (2000), for example, argue that knowledge of genetic risk does not generate fatalism but creates new relations to oneself and one's future, with associated obligations and biological responsibilities. These new individual and collective identities may be embodied in and expressed through patient groups (e.g., for muscular dystrophy or Huntington's disease) and challenge stigma, social exclusion, and dominant biomedical discourses. Seen in this light, genetic knowledge can increase the potential for individuals to identify themselves in terms of innate biological characteristics and these may be used as the basis for association with people who have similar conditions. Other, non-medical, genetic technologies, such as the development of genetic ancestry testing, which claim to categorize people in terms of race and ethnicity, are also creating new forms of collective and individual identity (Nash 2004; Tutton 2004).

The emergence of new identities based on ideas of genetic susceptibility and risk, and discourses of rights and responsibilities that are being co-constructed through new screening and public health programs, may constitute a new form of biological or genetic citizenship (Rose and Novas 2004). For example, individuals may construct themselves as healthy and responsible citizens by fulfilling duties to know and manage their genetic risk in order to protect themselves and their families (Petersen 2002). Schaffer, Kuczynski, and Skinner (2008), for instance, show how mothers of children with genetic disorders have used Internet links to formulate their own, experiential, version of genetic citizenship. Others, however, have struck more skeptical notes. Taussig, Rapp, and Heath (2003) have explored a range of technological interventions (such as surgery or genetic testing) through research with the Little People of America, and noted that the rise of *flexible eugenics* may have both positive and negative implications for self-identity. Callon and Rabeharisoa (2004) also examined the ways in which people may resist the imposition of genomic identities and Vailly (2006) documents the potential for the political cooption of genetic citizenship in the service of governmentality.

While new genetic and genomic knowledge may be constituting distinct new forms of identity, subjectivity, and citizenship, it is unclear how far such transformations are actually occurring, outside very tightly defined niches (patient groups for rare genetic diseases), or represent a clear break with the past.

EXPECTATIONS AND THE COMMODIFICATION OF GENETIC KNOWLEDGE: THE BIOPHARMACEUTICAL AND GENOMICS INDUSTRY

A distinctive feature of contemporary genetics and genomics is the involvement of the private sector. This has been stimulated in large part by the high hopes that surround the potential of genetics to transform medicine, and the discovery and development of new diagnostics and therapeutics. These expectations have been shared by research scientists, clinicians, governments, industry, and venture capitalists, and have prompted billions of dollars of investment in both basic research and product development. At the heart of this project is a vision of a *molecular medicine* where knowledge of a person's genotype will allow physicians to increase the precision of their work. Such *personalization* will combine genetic, lifestyle, and medical information at an individual level to diagnose the risk of disease more accurately, to manage conditions more efficiently, and to target therapy more effectively. *Pharmacogenetics*, where genetic tests are used to predict an individual's response to specific medications, is one product of this vision (Martin et al. 2006). Medical sociology and the sociology of science and technology converge in a *sociology of expectations* that investigates the performative role played by such promises, visions, and hopes for the future in the mobilization of resources and enrollment of actors into present-day actions. Expectations are embedded and embodied in a wide range of biomedical institutions, practices, and artifacts, including the balance between science, commerce, and regulation in research and development, and the organization and ethics of trials (Brown 2003; Brown, Rappert, and Webster 2000; Hedgecoe and Martin 2003).

Particular visions for pharmacogenetics, for example, have played a key role in the design of clinical testing, regulatory regimes, and commercial strategies (Hedgecoe and Martin 2003). Expectations around the prospect of identifying genetic factors contributing to the causation of common conditions such as cancer, heart disease, Alzheimer's, and mental health disorders, including schizophrenia, have similarly mobilized heavy investment in the creation of biobanks and genetic association studies that attempt to correlate specific factors with particular disease symptoms. Researchers have examined the role of expectations in the construction of disease categories, the enrollment of public support and trust, and the governance of these big science projects (Petersen 2005).

At the same time, sociologists have been examining the extent to which the promise of such technologies is actually being translated into everyday clinical practice. There is a striking contrast, for example, between the expectations of the supporters of pharmacogenetics and the experiences and beliefs of professionals at the clinical "coal face" who have to put this technology into practice (Hedgecoe 2004). Clinicians are very knowledgeable about the specific drugs they use but remain doubtful and uncertain, and have important ethical reservations, about pharmacogenetics. Technologies portrayed as "revolutionary" in review articles that declare how they are "going to change the future of health care" look quite different as they become "ordinary" within a specific clinical context, where they must interact with current professional and organizational practice and with other technologies.

Molecular medicine has been slow to deliver on its promises for four main reasons. Firstly, the search for genetic factors involved in the etiology of common diseases and drug metabolism has proved much more difficult than initially imagined. Only a small number of identified genes are strongly correlated with common conditions. Secondly, the modern pharmaceutical industry exemplifies Fordism, with standardized products and huge economies of scale. In contrast, personalized medicine is predicated on niche markets and non-standard products. Large companies have consequently hesitated to invest in new technologies that threaten their dominant business model of creating blockbuster drugs for large undifferentiated markets. There are also important practical questions about how and where highly personalized therapies could be manufactured (Dingwall and Martin 2000; Martin et al. 2006). Thirdly, there have been major difficulties in getting the technologies to work in clinical settings. While gene therapy has been shown to cure serious inherited genetic diseases in principle, it has also been associated with very serious side effects. Only a handful of stem cell therapies have yet been introduced into the clinic, while very few genetic tests for common conditions, such as cancer, have reached the market and been widely adopted. A major reason for this lack of progress is the difficulty in establishing clinical utility. Within health economics, this is understood largely as cost effectiveness. However, the adoption of new technologies into routine medical work does not simply involve establishing an evidence base for safety and efficacy, but also requires the renegotiation of working practices, funding arrangements, complementary infrastructures, and patient concordance. Finally, a number of important social and ethical issues remain unresolved. Regulatory regimes for the control of personal genetic information are not yet fully trusted by those who fear genetic discrimination. Some promising areas, like cystic fibrosis, have seen considerable resistance from potential consumers, who have refused to participate in trials that may compromise their current health status for uncertain benefits, except to investigators who, they consider, are more interested in Nobel Prizes or corporate profit from selling new therapies back to them at high prices (Stockdale 1999). More generally, studies have shown that, while there is strong support for research involving human subjects and biological samples where there is a clear health benefit, the involvement of the private sector makes these projects more contentious (Haddow et al. 2007).

The introduction of new technology involves much more than the simple application of scientific knowledge implied in the phrase "from bench to bedside" commonly found in policy documents. Knowledge translation and technology adoption are complex processes involving the (re)alignment of actors and the (re)negotiation of organizational and institutional arrangements. The successful creation of new medical technologies also requires feedback from clinical knowledge into basic research (Martin, Brown, and Kraft 2008). This recasts the relationship between the laboratory and the clinic, and gives more respect to the tacit expertise embedded in medical practice.

Genetics and behavior

Early eugenicists were convinced that both intelligence and behavior were under strong genetic influences. Although this view was discredited by the early 1960s, it was never extinguished and has been revived alongside the other new developments in genetics. The publication of *The Bell Curve* in 1994, claiming a biological basis for the association between intelligence and social class in the US, provoked a wide international debate among social scientists (Duster 1995; Herrnstein and Murray 1994; Taylor 1995). The authors derived this claim indirectly, by seeking to eliminate other explanations, rather than by identifying specific genetic markers. However, others have claimed the discovery of particular genes for aggression, crime, and sexual orientation, leading to proposals for the pharmacological control of these behaviors. Medical sociologists have critically examined these claims. They have noted that the bioscientists' understanding of social action is often very crude: aggression may simply be assertiveness that offends bourgeois gentility; crime is not a universal but defined by the laws, rules, or other conventions established in a society; homosexuality is a very different phenomenon in environments where there is a free choice of sexual partners compared with those where there is not, like prisons. The complexity and plasticity of human social behavior make it implausible to suppose that there is a simple genetic foundation (Dingwall, Nerlich, and Hillyard 2003).

More recently studies have sought to move beyond simple genetic determinism by looking at the interaction between genetic and environmental factors in determining human behavior. However, much of this research is still predicated on a simple relationship, with genes still playing the key role, as in the emergence of "social neuroscience," which seeks to understand the genetic and biological basis of human sociality and social interaction (Cacioppo, Visser, and Pickett 2005; Frith and Wolpert 2004; Harmon-Jones and Winkielman 2007). This operates on a particular "theory of mind," the ability to empathize and "read" another person's mind, which is seen as the cognitive foundation of human social interaction. Where this breaks down, it may lead to important behavioral and health disorders, such as autism. As with behavioral genetics, there are fundamental problems with the idea of social neuroscience when seen from a sociological perspective. In particular, the idea that interaction is determined by the inner workings of the brain fails to address one of the central findings of sociology, namely, that interaction is socially embedded. The meaning of actions is not located in the brain of their author but in the responses of their recipients.

CONCLUSIONS: REFLECTIONS ON GENETICIZATION

This chapter started by describing why genetics has become a major area of study within medical sociology. Ideas like geneticization and genetic exceptionalism have been important elements in this work. However, it is worth reflecting on what the increasingly substantial literature on the production, use, and impact of new genetic knowledge has actually established. While the idea of geneticization still has considerable currency, it is now clear that the extent to which genetics can explain most aspects of human health and behavior has been overstated. Genes remain essential for the explanation of classical monogenic conditions. However, it is increasingly evident that their role in more common conditions is much more subtle and complex, depending on dynamic interactions with social and environmental factors. Work on a range of conditions, including familial hypercholesterolemia (Weiner and Martin 2008), heart disease (Hall 2005), schizophrenia (Hedgecoe 2001), and polycystic kidney disease (Cox and Starzomski 2003) is demonstrating the limits of genetics in accounting for etiology. Although geneticized models for common conditions may be emerging, these studies highlight problems with the utilization of genetic knowledge and technologies in routine clinical practice, and a lack of uptake of genetic ideas by doctors and patients.

Similarly, the extent to which genetic information is exceptional is very much dependent on how it is constructed and applied in particular clinical and social settings. Within clinical genetics, which deals largely with diseases caused by single gene defects, knowing an individual's genotype can be a very powerful predictor of future health status. However, in the context of more common conditions, where genetic factors are linked to increased risk of disease, such knowledge is significantly less valuable in prognosis. Genetic information may be little different from other medical information, such as the results of a blood pressure test.

An important question raised by the lack of progress concerns the role played by medical sociologists in the co-construction of expectations that genetics would transform medicine. Much early social science research in this area was quite uncritical about the claims made by genetic scientists and accepted common beliefs about the revolutionary power of this science. The result was a great emphasis on the potentially adverse consequences for individuals and society. By allowing themselves to be coopted, sociologists, particularly in the UK, gained access to considerable resources – in the US, funding went more into bioethics – to address these ethical and social issues and to supply legitimacy to this new social enterprise. However, they forgot to consider the basic reflexive questions that sociologists should always ask: What do these claims, and the credulity with which they are received, tell us about our society? Why is there a demand for knowledge of this kind? Whose interests are served by it? Instead of buying into the marketing effort for gene research, the challenge is to evaluate it.

The emerging reality looks much more mundane, with genetics being incrementally integrated into routine clinical practice in ways that, in most cases, make little difference to established procedures and institutions. It now seems unlikely that large numbers of people will either be discriminated against or assume new genetic identities based on their genotype. As further empirical work has been conducted, many of the supposedly unique features of genetic medicine have proved to be reincarnations of well-established topics within medical sociology like professional–patient communication, the nature of disease and its relation to other forms of deviance, the structuring of health services and the choice between public and private systems of funding, and so on. However, medical sociologists have also been reminded of the importance of the body as a material base for action or cultural interpretation, and of the need to acknowledge that it may be a real constraint on the possibilities for social construction.

None of this is to deny that genetics is likely to bring considerable health benefits in the longer term, but it is to suggest that the immediate challenge for medical sociologists is to avoid reinventing their own field just because others are reinventing theirs. It is not our role to be cheerleaders for the genetic revolution so much as to bring our own traditions of skeptical reflection to bear in a cool, critical, and reflexive assessment of the hype that others will supply in abundance.

References

Academic Medical Centre (AMC). 2008. "Dutch Famine Study." Retrieved February 22, 2009 (www.dutchfamine.nl).

Atkins, Karl, Waqar Ahmed, and Elizabeth Anionwu. 1998. "Screening and Counselling for Sickle Cell Disorders and Thalassaemia: The Experience of Parents and Health Professionals." *Social Science and Medicine* 47: 1639–51.

Brown, Nik. 2003. "Hope Against Hype: Accountability in Biopasts, Presents and Futures." *Science Studies* 16: 3–21.

Brown, Nik, Brian Rappert, and Andrew Webster (eds.). 2000. *Contested Futures: A Sociology of Prospective Techno-Science*. Aldershot: Ashgate.

Cacioppo, John T., Penny S. Visser, and Cynthia L. Pickett (eds.). 2005. *Social Neuroscience: People Thinking about Thinking People*. Cambridge, MA: MIT Press.

Callon, Michel and Vololona Rabeharisoa. 2004. "Gino's Lesson on Humanity: Genetics, Mutual Entanglements and the Sociologist's Role." *Economy and Society* 33: 1–27.

Conrad, Peter and Jonathan Gabe (eds.). 1999. *Sociological Perspectives on the New Genetics*. Oxford: Blackwell.

Cox, Susan M. and William McKellin. 1999. " 'There's This Thing In Our Family': Predictive Testing and the Construction of Risk for Huntington's Disease." Pp. 622–46 in P. Conrad and J. Gabe (eds.), *Sociological Perspectives on the New Genetics*. Oxford: Blackwell.

Cox, Susan M. and Rosalie C. Starzomski. 2003. "Genes and Geneticization? The Social Construction of Autosomal Dominant Polycystic Kidney Disease." *New Genetics and Society* 23: 137–66.

Davis, Fred. 1963. *Passage Through Crisis*. Indianapolis: Bobbs-Merrill.

Dingwall, Robert and Paul Martin. 2000. "Editorial: RCT – RIP? Or Can the Pharmaceutical Industry Survive the Genomic Revolution?" *Journal of Health Services Research and Policy* 5: 67–8.

Dingwall, Robert, Brigitte Nerlich, and Sam Hillyard. 2003. "Biological Determinism and Symbolic Interaction: Hereditary Streams and Cultural Roads." *Symbolic Interaction* 26: 631–44.

Duster, Troy. 1995. "Review of 'The Bell Curve'." *Contemporary Sociology* 24: 158–61.

Elliott, Carl. 2002. "Diary: The Ethics of Bioethics." *London Review of Books* 24(23): 36–7.

Elliott, Carl. 2004. "Six Problems With Pharma-Funded Bioethics." *Studies in History and Philosophy of Biological and Biomedical Sciences* 35: 125–9.

Elliott, Carl and Trudo Lemmens. 2005. "Ethics for Sale: For-Profit Ethical Review, Coming to a Clinical Trial Near You." *Slate*, December 13. Retrieved December 26, 2008 (www.slate.com/id/2132187/).

Ewald, François, Tony McGleenan, and Urban Wiesing (eds.). 1999. *Genetics and Insurance*. London: Garland Science.

Featherstone, Katie, Joanna Latimer, Paul Atkinson, Daniela T. Pilz, and Angus Clarke. 2005. "Dysmorphology and the Spectacle of the Clinic." *Sociology of Health and Illness* 27: 551–74.

Finkler, Kaja. 2000. *Experiencing the New Genetics: Family and Kinship on the Medical Frontier*. Philadelphia: University of Pennsylvania Press.

Finkler, Kaja, Cecile Skrzynia, and James P. Evans. 2003. "The New Genetics and its Consequences for Family, Kinship, Medicine and Medical Genetics." *Social Science and Medicine* 57: 403–12.

Francis, Darlene D., Josie Diorio, Dong Liu, and Michael J. Meaney. 1999. "Nongenomic Transmission Across Generations in Maternal Behavior and Stress Responses in the Rat." *Science* 286: 1155–8.

Frith, Christopher and Daniel M. Wolpert. 2004. *The Neuroscience of Social Interactions: Decoding, Imitating and Influencing the Actions of Others*. Oxford: Oxford University Press.

Haddow, Gill, Graeme Laurie, Sarah Cunningham-Burley, and Kathryn G. Hunter. 2007. "Tackling Community Concerns about Commercialisation and Genetic Research: A Modest Interdisciplinary Proposal." *Social Science and Medicine* 64: 272–82.

Hall, Edward. 2005. "The 'Geneticisation' of Heart Disease: A Network Analysis of the Production of New Genetic Knowledge." *Social Science and Medicine* 60: 2673–83.

Hallowell, Nina. 1999. "Advising on the Management of Genetic Risk: Offering Choice or Prescribing Action?" *Health, Risk and Society* 1: 267–80.

Hallowell, Nina, Audrey Arden-Jones, Ros Eeles, Claire Foster, Anneke Lucassen, Clare Moynihan, and Maggie Watson. 2006. "Guilt, Blame and Responsibility: Men's Understanding of their Role in the Transmission of BRCA1/2 Mutations within their Family." *Sociology of Health and Illness* 28: 969–88.

Hallowell, Nina, Claire Foster, Ros Eeles, Audrey Arden-Jones, Victoria Murday, and Maggie Watson. 2003. "Balancing Autonomy and Responsibility: The Ethics of Generating and Disclosing Genetic Information." *Journal of Medical Ethics* 29: 74–9.

Hallowell, Nina and Julia Lawton. 2002. "Negotiating Present and Future Selves: Managing the Risk of Hereditary Cancer by Prophylactic Surgery." *Health* 6: 423–44.

Harmon-Jones, Eddie and Piotr Winkielman. 2007. *Social Neuroscience: Integrating Biological and Psychological Explanations of Social Behavior*. New York: Guilford Press.

Hedgecoe, Adam. 2001. "Schizophrenia and the Narrative of Enlightened Geneticization." *Social Studies of Science* 31: 875–911.

Hedgecoe, Adam. 2003. "Expansion and Uncertainty: Cystic Fibrosis, Classification and Genetics." *Sociology of Health and Illness* 25: 50–70.

Hedgecoe, Adam. 2004. *The Politics of Personalised Medicine: Pharmacogenetics in the Clinic*. Cambridge: Cambridge University Press.

Hedgecoe, Adam and Paul A. Martin. 2003. "The Drugs Don't Work: Expectations and the Shaping of Pharmacogenetics." *Social Studies of Science* 33: 327–64.

Herrnstein, Richard J. and Charles Murray. 1994. *The Bell Curve: Intelligence and Class Structure in American Life*. New York: Free Press.

Hoffmann, Diane E. and Eric A. Wulfsberg. 1995. "Testing Children for Genetic Predispositions: Is it in Their Best Interest?" *Journal of Law, Medicine and Ethics* 23: 331–44.

Kalmijn, Matthijs. 1994. "Assortative Mating by Cultural and Economic Occupational Status." *American Journal of Sociology* 100: 422–52.

Kerr, Anne. 2004. *Genetics and Society: A Sociology of Disease*. London: Routledge.

Kerr, Anne. 2005. "Understanding Genetic Disease in a Socio-Historical Context: A Case Study of Cystic Fibrosis." *Sociology of Health and Illness* 27: 873–96.

Kevles, Daniel. 1995. *In the Name of Eugenics: Genetics and the Uses of Human Heredity*. Berkeley: University of California Press.

Kolker, Aliza and B. Meredith Burke. 1998. *Prenatal Testing: A Sociological Perspective*. Westport, CT: Bergin and Garvey.

Lavery, Stuart, R. Aurell, C. Turner, C. Castello, Anna Veiga, Pedro N. Barri, and Robert M. Winston. 2002. "Pre-Implantation Genetic Diagnosis: Patients' Experiences and Attitudes." *Human Reproduction* 17: 2464–7.

Lippman, Abby. 1992. "Led (Astray) by Genetic Maps: The Cartography of the Human Genome and Health Care." *Social Science and Medicine* 35: 1469–76.

Lombardo, Paul A. 1985. "Three Generations, No Imbeciles: New Light on *Buck v. Bell*." *New York University Law Review* 60: 50–62.

Lombardo, Paul A. N.d. *Eugenic Sterilization Laws*. Image Archive on the American Eugenics Movement. Cold Spring Harbor, NY: Dolan DNA Learning Center. Retrieved February 22, 2009 (www.eugenicsarchive.org/html/eugenics/essay8text.html).

Lowton, Karen and Jonathan Gabe. 2003. "Life on a Slippery Slope: Perceptions of Health in Adults with Cystic Fibrosis." *Sociology of Health and Illness* 25: 281–319.

Martin, Paul A. 1999. "Genes as Drugs: The Social Shaping of Gene Therapy and the Reconstruction of Genetic Disease." *Sociology of Health and Illness* 21: 517–38.

Martin, Paul A., Nik Brown, and Alison Kraft. 2008. "From Bedside to Bench? Communities of Promise, Translational Research and the Making of Blood Stem Cells." *Science as Culture* 17: 29–42.

Martin, Paul A., Graham Lewis, Andrew Smart, and Andrew Webster. 2006. *False Positive? Prospects for the Clinical and Commercial Development of Pharmacogenetics*. University of Nottingham/University of York.

McGee, Glenn. 2000. *The Perfect Baby: Parenthood in the New World of Cloning and Genetics*. Lanham, MD: Rowman and Littlefield.

Nash, Catherine. 2004. "Genetic Kinship." *Cultural Studies* 18: 1–33.

Nightingale, Paul and Paul A. Martin. 2004. "The Myth of the Biotech Revolution." *Trends in Biotechnology* 22: 564–9.

Novas, Carlos and Nikolas Rose. 2000. "Genetic Risk and the Birth of the Somatic Individual." *Economy and Society* 29: 445–69.

Nussbaum, Martha C. and Cass R. Sunstein (eds.). 1998. *Clones and Clones: Facts and Fantasies about Human Cloning*. New York: W. W. Norton.

Petersen, Alan. 2002. "The New Genetic Citizens." Pp. 180–207 in A. Petersen and R. Bunton (eds.), *The New Genetics and the Public's Health*. London: Routledge.

Petersen, Alan. 2005. "Securing our Genetic Health: Engendering Trust in UK Biobank." *Sociology of Health and Illness* 27: 271–92.

Petersen, Alan. 2006. "The Best Experts: The Narratives of Those Who Have a Genetic Condition." *Social Science and Medicine* 63: 32–42.

Pilnick, Alison. 2002a. *Genetics and Society: An Introduction*. Buckingham: Open University Press.

Pilnick, Alison. 2002b. " 'There Are No Rights and Wrongs in These Situations': Identifying Interactional Difficulties in Genetic Counselling." *Sociology of Health and Illness* 25: 66–88.

Pilnick, Alison. 2004. " 'It's Just One of the Best Tests That We've Got at the Moment': The Presentation of Screening For Fetal Abnormality in Pregnancy." *Discourse and Society* 15: 451–65.

Prior, Lindsay. 2001. "Rationing through Risk Assessment in Clinical Genetics: All Categories Have Wheels." *Sociology of Health and Illness* 23: 570–93.

Rabinow, Paul. 1996. "Artificiality and Enlightenment: From Sociobiology to Biosociality." Pp. 91–111 in P. Rabinow (ed.), *Essays on the Anthropology of Reason*. Princeton, NJ: Princeton University Press.

Rapp, Rayna. 1998. "Refusing Prenatal Diagnosis: The Multiple Meanings of Biotechnology in a Multicultural World." *Science, Technology and Human Values* 23: 45–70.

Rapp, Rayna. 2000. *Testing Women, Testing the Fetus: The Social Impact of Amniocentesis in America*. New York: Routledge.

Rose, Nikolas and Carlos Novas. 2004. "Biological Citizenship." Pp. 439–65 in A. Ong and S. Collier (eds.), *Global Assemblages: Technology, Politics, and Ethics as Anthropological Problems*. Malden, MA: Blackwell.

Rothstein, Mark A. 2007. "Genetic Exceptionalism and Legislative Pragmatism." *Journal of Law, Medicine and Ethics* 35: 59–65.

Schaffer, Rebecca, Kristine Kuczynski, and Debra Skinner. 2008. "A Place for Genetic Uncertainty: Parents Valuing an Unknown in the Meaning of Disease." *Sociology of Health and Illness* 30: 145–59.

Shakespeare, Tom. 1998. "Choices and Rights: Eugenics, Genetics and Disability Equality." *Disability and Society* 13: 655–81.

Smart, Andrew and Paul A. Martin. 2006. "The Promise of Pharmacogenetics: Assessing the Prospects for Disease and Patient Stratification." *Studies in the History and Philosophy of Biological and Biomedical Science.* 37: 583–601.

Stockdale, Alan. 1999. "Waiting for the Cure: Mapping the Social Relations of Human Gene Therapy Research." *Sociology of Health and Illness* 21: 579–96.

Surbone, Antonella. 2001. "Ethical Implications of Genetic Testing for Breast Cancer Susceptibility." *Critical Reviews in Oncology/Hematology* 40: 149–57.

Taussig, Karen-Sue, Rayna Rapp, and Deborah Heath. 2003. "Flexible Eugenics: Technologies of the Self in the Age of Genetics." Pp. 58–76 in A. H. Goodman, D. Heath, and M. S. Lindee (eds.), *Genetic Nature/Culture: Anthropology and Science Beyond the Two-Culture Divide*. Berkeley: University of California Press.

Taylor, Howard F. 1995. "Review of 'The Bell Curve'." *Contemporary Sociology* 24: 153–8.

Tutton, Richard. 2004. " 'They Want to Know Where They Came From': Population Genetics, Identity, and Family Genealogy." *New Genetics and Society* 23: 105–20.

Vailly, Joelle. 2006. "Genetic Screening as a Technique of Government: The Case of Neonatal Screening for Cystic Fibrosis in France." *Social Science and Medicine* 63: 3092–101.

Vailly, Joelle. 2008. "The Expansion of Abnormality and the Biomedical Norm: Neonatal Screening, Prenatal Diagnosis and Cystic Fibrosis in France." *Social Science and Medicine* 66: 2532–43.

Weiner, Kate and Paul A. Martin. 2008. "A Genetic Future for Coronary Heart Disease." *Sociology of Health and Illness* 30: 380–95.

Whitmarsh, Ian, Arlene M. Davis, Debra Skinner, and Donald B. Bailey. 2007. "A Place for Genetic Uncertainty: Parents Valuing an Unknown in the Meaning of Disease." *Social Science and Medicine* 65: 1082–93.

Williams, Gareth. 1984. "The Genesis of Chronic Illness: Narrative Reconstruction." *Sociology of Health and Illness* 6: 175–200.

24

New Developments in Neuroscience and Medical Sociology

Simon J. Williams

Developments in the brain or neurosciences pose a series of pertinent questions and challenges for sociology in general and medical sociology in particular. To the extent that the neurosciences provide or promise new understandings and explanations of human behavior, sociality, agency, affect, addiction, desire – and refashioned ideas about normality and abnormality, if not new forms of intervention or "control" – then they demand informed and robust sociological dialogue, discussion, and debate in medical sociology and beyond.

This chapter, therefore, maps these developments and potential "challenges" with particular reference to issues and agendas within medical sociology, both now and in the near future. On the one hand, as we shall see, these agendas feed into or build upon existing sociological concerns and long-standing preoccupations within medical sociology, this time albeit with a neuro-related focus. On the other hand, I will argue, developments in the neurosciences invite or encourage medical sociologists to move beyond these existing concerns and concepts, or at least to revise or rethink them, forging profitable new links to other areas of sociology, and to cognate areas such as science and technology studies (STS). All this, however, begs the obvious question: "What is neuroscience?" It is to this preliminary question, therefore, that we now turn as a backdrop to the sociological themes and issues that follow.

WHAT IS NEUROSCIENCE? CONTOURS, CHALLENGES, AND OPPORTUNITIES

The past two decades have witnessed important developments in the brain or neurosciences. The 1990s were declared the decade of the brain (courtesy of the White House), and a further series of hopes, fears, and aspirations were articulated concerning the brain and the neurosciences in the twenty-first century. These claims and concerns, to be sure, are themselves sociologically interesting in terms of the very construction or constitution of the field. What is equally clear is that neuroscience is a field which is best thought of in the *plural* rather than in the singular, given the diverse strands or branches of scientific inquiry that comprise it: areas of study which, all in their different ways, focus on the brain, its functions, and dysfunctions, but which do so "at many different levels and with many different paradigms, problematics and technologies" (Rose 2006: 3). This includes inputs and findings from molecular neuroscience, behavioral genetics, psychiatric genetics, neuroendocrinology, cognitive neuroscience, social neuroscience, brain imaging studies, psychopharmacology, the information sciences, and a host of other current or near future neurotechnologies.

Whilst these developments have already produced a wealth of data, facts, and experimental findings, at every level from the molecular or sub-molecular to the brain as a whole, they remain, as Steven Rose (2006: 5) wryly comments, "data-rich and theory-poor." The key problem, in other words, is how to *translate* this wealth of data into something like a coherent or comprehensive theory of the brain, let alone behavior. In part, as Rose himself recognizes, this stems from the paradoxes of the brain itself, which is simultaneously a "fixed structure" and a complex set of "dynamic processes" with functions that are both "localized" and "delocalized" (2006: 4). How all this, moreover, translates into consciousness (i.e., the so-called hard problem) remains, and will in all probability remain for the foreseeable future, a great mystery. On this big "C" question indeed, Rose boldly proclaims, neuroscientists (like himself) "don't have anything very much useful to say" and would as such, recalling Wittgenstein, "do better to keep silent" (2006: 4)! This, however, has not stopped the proliferation of neuro-spinoffs or hybrid (sub)disciplines such as neuroeconomics, neuromarketing, neuroaesthetics, neurotheology, neurodidactics, even neuropsychoanalysis, which all in their different ways seek to ally or align themselves with developments in the neurosciences.

What we have then, in effect, is a kind of neural map or network of the neurosciences and associated hybrids or spinoffs which in important respects mimics or models the complexities of the brain, with its neurons, axons, dendrites, synapses, and neurotransmitters communicating, configuring, and reconfiguring in various neurochemical ways, and with varying degrees of "long-term potentiation" and "neuroplasticity." It is equally clear nonetheless that neuroscience and neurotechnology are not only intimately bound up with one another, they are also deeply embedded in society: a fact which alerts us to the *social shaping* as well as the *social implications* of neuroscience and neurotechnology.

This in turn begs the related question of what role or roles sociologists in general and medical sociologists in particular might play in relation to these developments and debates regarding neuroscience and neurotechnology. To date, it seems, two main lines of research may be discerned here concerning the social aspects or dimension of neuroscience and neurotechnology, namely: (1) the *social neuroscience* (or *social cognitive neuroscience*) agenda, and (2) *the social studies of neuroscience* (or *neuroscience and society*) agenda.

Taking each of these in turn, the social neuroscience agenda is by far the most developed, albeit one with little sociological input or engagement to date. Social neuroscience, by definition, is an interdisciplinary field of inquiry – conducted mainly to date by experimental psychologists, cognitive psychologists, and neuropsychologists, but with newly emerging links to other branches of psychology and neuroscience, as well as economics, anthropology, and medical science. It aims to study the *neural correlates and substrates* of social cognition and social interaction. Harmon-Jones and Devine (2003: 590), for example, in their introduction to the special section of the *Journal of Personality and Social Psychology* on "Social Neuroscience," define it in broad terms as an:

> integrative field that examines how nervous, endocrine, and immune systems are involved in sociocultural processes. Being nondualist in its view of humans, it recognizes the importance of understanding the neural, hormonal, and immunological processes giving rise to and resulting from social psychological processes and behaviors. Social neuroscience also emphasizes the understanding of how the brain influences social processes as well as how social processes can influence the brain.

This includes research in areas such as face perception, emotion, the development of a theory of mind (which is said to enable us to empathize with the "minds" of others), and other basic social processes of categorizations, preference, prejudice and stereotyping, attention, language acquisition, memory, self-knowledge, imitation, and economic behavior as well as "disorders" such as autism and schizophrenia. An underlying premise is that we are intensely social beings with evolved neurophysiological mechanisms and systems to support and facilitate exchanges and interaction with others. As such, it is claimed, these systems and mechanisms warrant further study with potentially significant empirical if not therapeutic payoffs. This, moreover, involves the mobilization of diverse methodologies, including lesion methods, fMRI methods, hormonal methods, event-related brain potential methods, regional EEG methods, facial electromyographic methods, and cardiovascular methods (see Harmon-Jones and Winkielman 2007 for examples of all these methods).

Whilst sociological contributions to these social neuroscience agendas have been fairly limited to date, this is clearly an area ripe for sociological engagement, particularly concerning the role of social factors and social context in (neuro)biological processes – an issue we shall return to later in the course of this chapter in relation to inequalities in health research (cf. Marmot 2004; Wilkinson 1996, 2005). In this vein, one may also point to other recent calls for various kinds of "bridging work" between the neurosciences and social theory (Turner 2007), feminist work on the neurological body (Wilson 2004), attempts to forge or foster an explicit "neurosociology" of emotion (Franks and Smith 1999), and related work on the potential and pitfalls of "integrating" social science with neuroscience (Cromby 2007; Newton 2007).

The *social studies of neuroscience* or *neuroscience and society* agenda, in contrast, involves the mobilization of more critical, autonomous, independent sociological perspectives on the neurosciences and associated neurotechnologies. This includes critical analyses of new or novel configurations of knowledge, power, authority, and expertise associated with these developments, their role in changing conceptions of humanity, selfhood, citizenship, normality and abnormality, treatment and enhancement, the hopes and fears invested in neuroscience and the making of neuroscientific futures, and the broader social, cultural, political, and economic orders within which the neurosciences are embedded (Maasen and Sutter 2007; Rose 2007). A recent UK Economic and Social Research Council-funded seminar series, for example, entitled "Neuroscience, Identity, and Society" pursued precisely these sorts of issues. A new interdisciplinary Neuroscience and Society group has been established at the University of Warwick (Neuroscience and Society Group @ Warwick 2008), and a new interdisciplinary European Neuroscience and Society Network (ENSN) has also been established (ENSN 2009). In these and other ways, then, social studies of the neurosciences are beginning to emerge as a complementary if not critical field of inquiry. These developments, in part at least, rehearse familiar debates about the distinction between a sociology applied to or in the service of a particular problem, domain, or field of inquiry and a more autonomous sociological stance or perspective on these matters.

What we have, then, to summarize, are at least two main options for (medical) sociologists and other social scientists interested in neuroscience. In shorthand terms, they may profitably be referred to as "collaborative" (or integrative) and "critical" (or independent) agendas, options, or pathways. To this, moreover, drawing on the sociology of expectations (Brown and Michael 2003), we may add a related reflexive agenda that involves the reflexive commentary and analysis of sociologists themselves on their own role in the construction or co-construction of the hopes, fears, and futures associated with neuroscience and neurotechnologies.

This suggests that a number of options or possibilities are open to medical sociologists interested in these developments in the neurosciences and associated neurotechnologies. More specifically, in fleshing out these options and possibilities, it is possible to point to at least five key substantive areas and issues with which medical sociologists may profitably engage. These issues both consolidate and extend existing concerns and preoccupations within medical sociology, starting with the "challenge" of behavioral and psychiatric genetics.

BEHAVIORAL GENETICS/PSYCHIATRIC GENETICS: "NEUROGENETIC REDUCTIONISM" AND BEYOND

A considerable body of work now exists within medical sociology and cognate areas, on genetics and society (see, for example, Martin and Dingwall, Chapter 23 this volume). Profitable links or relays, in this respect, may be forged with recent developments in behavioral and psychiatric genetics (currently the largest branch of human behavioral genetics) on the role of genetic factors in the explanation of psychiatric and behavioral problems. Traditionally, behavioral geneticists have focused on the inheritance of certain behavioral traits – a tradition dating back to Francis Galton, Darwin's cousin and inventor of the term eugenics. Galton anticipated the field of modern behavioral genetics with his work on the inheritance of giftedness and talent and his studies of twins. Important developments, nonetheless, have taken place in this field since Galton's time, thereby serving to distance contemporary behavioral genetics from the shadow of its eugenic past. This, for example, in the era of molecular genetics includes work on the identification of so-called "susceptibility genes" associated with conditions such as schizophrenia and bipolar affective disorder, as well as attempts to find the genetic component of other human behavioral problems such as alcoholism, antisocial behavior, and eating disorders. Such work is part and parcel of the "rebiologization" of human behavior linked to a resurgence of interest in biological models in psychiatry (see, for example, Henderson 2008 for a recent study of the latter).

Despite important progress on these fronts, however, a key problem underpinning much of this work has been its poor predictive power in establishing or identifying reliable and robust associations or linkages between genes and behavior (i.e., the relationship between genotypes and phenotypes). A number of steps or strategies in this respect have been taken in order to address these problems, including the study of so-called endophenotypes (sub-categories of phenotypes) and other new approaches which recognize the complexity of these relationships and work with more sophisticated models, including the aforementioned notion of genetic susceptibility or risk and its interaction with social and environmental factors in triggering or causing behavioral problems of various kinds (i.e., gene–environment approaches) (e.g., Moffit, Avshalom, and Rutter 2005; Rutter 2007).

Expectations remain high in this respect, amongst behavioral geneticists at least, about the promise or potential of this research, not simply in terms of the explanation of human behavior and psychiatric disorders but in terms of the "translation" of this knowledge into clinical applications and new forms of therapeutic intervention – another alluring or tantalizing prospect which in large part has yet to materialize. In part these expectations themselves are fueled by appeals to the very notion of complexity. Complexity, in this respect, serves a dual purpose. On the one hand it provides a reassuring response to or rationale for the limited progress to date and a buffer against charges of "neurogenetic reductionism." On the other hand it provides the very impetus or spur for further research – a kind of rhetorical device and rallying call in effect (Featherstone 2008). What this does imply, nonetheless, is that the "one gene, one phenotype" – or the "one gene, one disorder" (OGOD) (Conrad 1999) – mantra or mentality has largely been abandoned in favor of a more "complex framework of interacting genetic, environmental, stochastic and emergent phenomena" (Frazzetto and Gross 2007: S4). It is equally clear, however, to date at least, that the ability to "catalogue genetic variations is rapidly outpacing our ability to link such changes with behavioural phenotypes" (Frazzetto and Gross 2007: S4).

These problems, prospects, and possibilities, and the claims with which they are associated, are well illustrated in a *Science and Society* special issue of *EMBO Reports* (published on behalf of the European Molecular Biology Organization) on "Genes, Brain/Mind and Behavior." Articles in this special issue include an introduction by Stefánsson (2007) on the scientific and ethical implications of the "biology of behavior"; Frazzetto and Gross's (2007) review of the complexity of relations between genotypes and phenotypes; and Roubertoux and Carlier's (2007) paper on the decline of gene–phenotype causality and the emergence of multifunctionality. (In this article, Roubertoux and Carlier [2007: S11] advocate that "no genes code for a behavioral trait," and that "at the very most, we can say that a gene is 'involved' in a behavioural trait, or that a phenotype has genetic correlates.")

There are also papers in this special issue by Singer (2007) on the brain as a complex non-linear system with emergent properties; Perreau-Lenz and colleagues (2007), who argue that a better understanding of "clock genes" can pave the way for new therapeutic approaches to drug addiction and depression; and Lesch (2007) on the role of the serotonin transporter in human social behavior. To this diverse ensemble we may add Canli's (2007: S31) bold claims that "the field of psychology is about to undergo another transformation that will affect all of its subfields, and that will push analyses further down to the level of the genome"; Kosfeld's (2007) paper on the neurobiology of trust based on the neurohormone oxytocin; Sandstrom's (2007) paper on a new so-called "chemical genomics" drug development strategy; and a variety of other papers on the social and ethical aspects of these and other developments in neuroscience, including claims that neuroscience can "help explain the mechanisms of normative judgement and how morality has evolved" (Evers 2007: S51).

In many ways, then, these developments in behavioral and psychiatric genetics echo and amplify, if not extend, ongoing debates in medical sociology and beyond concerning genetics and society in general, and medicalization and geneticization in particular (see, for example, Martin and Dingwall, Chapter 23 this volume). Medicalization and geneticization, of course, are far from synonymous. They cannot and should not, as such, be equated or conflated (see Shostak, Conrad, and Horwitz 2008 for a useful elaboration of these complex and multiple relations). Reciprocal or mutually reinforcing relations, nonetheless, may often occur. Frazzetto and Gross (2007: S5), for example, refer in this context to a "dynamic feedback loop" between behavioral genetics and medicalization, in which:

> Social contingencies and medicalization provide behavioural genetics with new objects for investigation, and, in turn, behavioural genetics contributes to the growing expansion of the medical realm. This intricate relationship artificially accentuates the view of psychiatric conditions as firm categories, and leads to an emphasis on genetic and neurochemical components rather than social factors.

Behavioral phenomena, as such, are abstracted from their social context and traits and phenotypes that are in "reality fluid and continuous concepts become reified in psychiatric categories" (Frazzetto and Gross 2007: S5; see also Press 2006 on these relations). Not only have the number of conditions regarded as mental illnesses mushroomed in recent years, so too have the numbers said to be suffering from them. Shyness, for example, as Frazzetto and Gross (2007) rightly note, is a prime case in point: a condition which has now been proposed as an endophenotype of anxiety disorders and for which several studies have found a significant genetic component. Shyness is now succumbing to processes of medicalization and pharmaceuticalization (Scott 2007).

These developments in turn link to new technologies which have grown out of behavioral genetics and the brain sciences, and which now provide powerful tools to help map or monitor the brain, if not influence or modify human behavior.

SCANNING THE BRAIN: VISUAL TRUTHS IN THE DIGITAL AGE

A rich and varied body of work already exists in medical sociology and cognate areas regarding both medical and health technologies in general (Brown and

Webster 2004; Nettleton 2004; Webster 2007; Williams 2003) and visual technologies in particular (Frank 1991; Waldby 2002). Profitable links again can be
made here with the development of powerful "new" visual or digital technologies
within the brain or neurosciences, technologies that enable us to visualize the
living brain or mind at work, as opposed to the examination of brain tissue,
scrutinized post-mortem under the (electron) microscope. This includes technologies such as computerized tomography (CT) in the 1960s, positron emission
tomography (PET) and magnetic resonance imaging (MRI) during the 1980s, and,
most recently of all, functional magnetic resonance imaging (fMRI). This latter
technology produces a map of the rate of oxygen use by different parts of the
brain. These technologies have generated not simply a proliferation of images of
the brain "at work," but an extraordinary range of claims and applications,
including attempts to map or "see" everything from clinical abnormalities and
drug responses to consumer choice, political preference, voting behavior, even
religious or spiritual experience, based on which part or parts of the brain "light"
up in response to these diverse stimuli.

These developments, in turn, rest on an assumption that in visualizing things
in this way, we are somehow providing "proof" of the biological existence of
the phenomenon under investigation in the brain. Perhaps more important than
this, as Dumit (2004) comments, they seem to have "persuasive power," particularly in popular culture, which far outstrips the actual data presented. These
digitalized brain images, in other words, are often depicted as "automatic, computed, and objective illustrations demonstrating insanity and incompetency"
(Dumit 2004: 15). Yet, as Dumit (2004: 15) rightly argues, this masks a far
deeper truth, namely, that each piece of experimental design, data generation,
and data analysis "necessarily builds in assumptions about human nature, about
how the brain works, and how person and brain are related." Behind the seeming
objective "reality" of brain scans, in other words, lies a complex chain of assumptions, tools, technologies, techniques, and data which somehow need to be assembled into meaningful data though a series of choices, including the very colors
used to depict any "differences" found.

Not only is neuroimaging indebted to assumptions about the localization or
modularization of brain functions, it also rests on a methodology which in the
service of these assumptions effectively eliminates overall brain activity in favor of
identifiable difference – i.e., a subtractive methodology based on the difference
between baseline measures of brain function and those associated with responses
to certain stimuli or the performance of certain tasks (see Crawford 2008, for
example, for a useful critique of this methodology). Assumptions in this respect, as
Dumit (2004) convincingly shows, are not simply designed into these scans, but
"read out" of them at every stage in the production, from selecting subjects and the
statistical techniques and mathematical models used to generate these "differences,"
to the decision over how to color them and which images to publish. Perhaps most
importantly of all, these technologies not only involve the visual generation or
depiction of graphically different brain-type images, they also become visual classifications or typologies that convey an impression of "natural kinds" of persons
– normal, healthy, anxious, obsessive, depressive, autistic, psychotic – which are
then taken as pictures of ourselves: pictures of personhood visibly and digitally

materialized in and through the brain (Dumit 2004). There are, however, other potent technologies on this neurofrontier with the power to transform us in more direct neurochemical ways.

THE PSYCHOPHARMACEUTICALIZATION OF EVERYDAY LIFE: FROM "THERAPY" TO "ENHANCEMENT"

We are, as already noted, in a new age or era of biological psychiatry in which previous psychological theories of mental illness or mental disorder, particularly the major psychoses, have been eclipsed, overshadowed, or overtaken by hypotheses, findings, and modes of explanation based on neurochemical foundations. This is a psychiatric landscape or terrain, as Rose (2007) comments, populated by diverse figures and entities such as: "brains" themselves; "brain chemicals" (e.g., adenosine, GABA, catecholamines, oxytocin, serotonin); "brain functions" (receptor sites, membrane potentials, ion channels, synaptic vesicles); "drugs" (tricyclic antidepressants, selective serotonin reuptake inhibitors or SSRIs); "experimental model systems" (human brains, cell cultures, animal models); "investigative techniques" (EEGs, PET scans, fMRIs); "diagnoses" (based on finer and finer classifications and distinctions through revised *DSMs*, such as biopolar affective disorder, schizophrenia, obsessive-compulsive disorder, attention deficit/hyperactivity disorder [ADHD], autistic spectrum disorder, social anxiety disorder [SAD], generalized anxiety disorder [GAD]); "human subjects" who participate in studies and clinical trials and undergo various forms of treatment; and finally, general "truth technologies" that "define and delimit how one can produce findings in psychiatry" (Rose 2007: 190–1; see also Henderson 2008 for a recent empirical study charting these biological transformations in psychiatry).

These developments have occurred in the context of a rapidly expanding market in psychopharmaceuticals over the past two decades, particularly in the advanced industrial societies of Europe and North America. We see this very clearly, for example, in the case of the new generation of selective serotonin reuptake inhibitors (SSRIs) for the treatment of depression. Prescriptions of antidepressants in both the United States and United Kingdom increased by around 200 percent over the decade from 1990 to 2000, with the SSRI family of drugs seeing a rise of over 1,300 percent in the United States (Rose 2006), resulting in a market estimated at around $10 billion. Translated into prescriptions for treatment of depression, in England alone this amounts to a rise from 1,884,571 NHS prescriptions in 1993 to 15,500,000 in 2002 (Department of Health 2003). The marketing of drugs such as Paxil for the anxiety market as well as the depression market, given the increasingly saturated depression market, has proved extremely successful, with US sales of approximately $2.1 billion and global sales of $2.7 billion in 2001 (Conrad 2007), although sales have been somewhat depressed since 2004 because of concerns over adverse effects and with the Food and Drug Administration (FDA) now issuing warning labels that these drugs may cause suicidal thoughts in children and adolescents. With some 19 million adult Americans suffering from clinical depression, and some 18 million prescription items dispensed for SSRIs in the UK in 2007 (DoH 2008), this remains nonetheless a significant and lucrative psychopharmaceutical market.

Considerable controversy has accompanied these psychopharmaceutical trends and transformations. In the case of ADHD, for example, concern has long been voiced about this diagnostic label as a way of medicalizing deviant behavior (Conrad 1976) given the remarkable growth in both the diagnosis of this condition and the prescription of drugs (Ritalin) to treat it. NHS prescriptions in England for Ritalin, for instance, grew from 3,500 to 161,800 between 1993 and 2002 (DoH 2003). Similarly, concerns have recently been expressed about the role of the pharmaceutical industry not simply in the manufacturing and marketing of drugs, but also in the manufacturing and marketing of disorders for these drugs to treat, a phenomenon that some critics have dubbed "disease mongering" (Moynihan, Health, and Henry 2002).

The aforementioned marketing of SSRIs for anxiety disorders such as social anxiety disorder and generalized anxiety disorder (SAD and GAD), for instance, seems to fit this pattern, particularly in countries such as the United States and New Zealand where direct-to-consumer advertising is permitted. This form of advertising invites individuals to question whether or not they would benefit from the advertised drug, or at the very least whether they fall into the advertised diagnostic category the drug promises to treat, and then go and talk to their doctor if they feel worried (Rose 2007). Yet concerns continue to be expressed about the efficacy and side effects of these drugs, including doubts (following reanalysis of trial data) as to the benefits of SSRIs in the treatment of mild to moderate depression and the risks of suicidal thoughts in children and adolescents taking these drugs.

A number of other key factors, however, complicate this picture still further. First, it is clear, in the case of drugs such as SSRIs at least, that they "do not so much seek to normalize deviant behaviour but to correct abnormalities, to adjust the individual and restore and maintain his or her capacity to enter the circuits of everyday life" (Rose 2007: 210). Second, taking these drugs, it is claimed, is not so much about masking the self or even creating or making a new self as a means of recovering, revealing, unlocking, or getting in touch with one's real, true, or authentic self: a viewpoint, it seems, which patients themselves often endorse. The effects of these drugs, moreover, are not limited to the mind or brain but radiate throughout the body as a whole (see, for example, Wilson 2006 on this point). As for these drugs themselves having something akin to personalities or person-like qualities, Martin (2007) shows that both patients and pharmaceutical marketers and advertisers, despite the "friendly" imagery of advertising, imbue or invest psychopharmaceuticals with deeply ambivalent meanings. Patients in this respect personify these drugs only weakly. Instead, she suggests, medications of these kinds are perhaps best viewed not simply in instrumental terms as "tools" or "precision instruments" but as "co-performers" or "teachers," enabling the person to experience new states and helping model new habits (Martin 2007: 171).

Third, and equally important, whilst the main drivers of these processes may well be the pharmaceutical industry, they nonetheless occur through complex, mobile, dynamic chains or networks of actors or agents, including drug companies, doctors, disease awareness campaigns, patient advocacy groups, media, regulators, policy makers, and so on. These networks involve alliances, allegiances, claims, controversies, hopes, fears about these disorders, and the drugs proposed or prescribed to treat them.

Another key area of controversy and concern pertains to so-called "cognitive enhancers." Here we encounter a further important set of developments in the neuro-field and beyond, namely, that we are not simply moving beyond the poles of health and illness. Rather, the boundaries between treatment or therapy and enhancement are themselves becoming increasingly blurred or unhelpful. Expressed most simply, enhancement technologies, including drugs, are technologies designed to improve us in some way beyond our current capacities or capabilities, to take us beyond therapy, to make us better than well if not better than "human" (Harris 2007; Kass 2002; Miller and Wilsdon 2006; Parens 1998). This includes attempts to boost our brainpower or enhance our cognition. But one may justifiably ask if this is a new story.

On the one hand, of course, it is part of a long, if not a "deep," history extending back into our evolutionary past, of attempts to supplement, extend, improve, or enhance human skills and capacities in one way or another, from tool use through schooling to the disciplines of the gym. On the other hand, what is perhaps new or novel here is that these enhancement technologies work in smarter, more direct ways to control or re-engineer vital biological processes themselves, opening up or altering their "normativity" in effect through the reconfiguration of "thresholds, norms, volatilities of affect, of cognition, of the will" (Rose 2007: 17). In doing so, moreover, as Rose (2007: 20) rightly notes, these technologies render us "all the more biological," thereby calling into question other more cyborgian readings or renditions of these matters (cf. Haraway 1991).

Caution is clearly needed here in relation to some of the claims being made about the advent and prospects of a new age or era of cognitive enhancement. Not only, for example, are there very few drugs of this kind on the market to date, but evidence of their efficacy or effectiveness is at best limited (based on relatively small effect sizes in trial data), and at worst equivocal – depending on which aspects of cognitive functioning are being measured and on initial baseline measures of cognitive functioning, with those with the poorest baseline measures showing most improvement. It is also debatable just how many healthy people would use (or are interested in using) any such drugs now or in the (near) future. There is partial or anecdotal evidence of use in certain specific situations (such as examinations), but, equally, other anecdotal or partial evidence suggests considerable resistance to chronic use amongst the general public.

Considerable concern nonetheless surrounds the promise or prospect of cognitive enhancement, with other drugs of this kind either currently in the pipeline or expected in the near future. Concern in this respect centers on the social, legal, and ethical aspects of these drugs, particularly the question of whether or not they should be regulated, and if so, to what degree (see, for example, Academy of Medical Sciences 2008; British Medical Association 2007; Department of Trade and Industry [DTI] 2005; Greely et al. 2008). The DTI (2005) drugs futures report, for example, claimed these drugs could be as "common as coffee" in the next decade or so. Similarly, the BMA (2007) report states this kind of drug use is likely to grow rapidly. Key questions posed here by the BMA include the following:

- How should society respond?
- Should individuals be free to make their own decisions about use, or are there good grounds to prevent them doing so?
- Should parents be free to choose cognitive enhancement agents (CEAs) for their children?
- Should the same principles apply to all CEAs?
- What, if any, regulation is needed?
- What role, if any, should doctors play in providing or monitoring CEAs?

A good example here is Modafinil, a drug that promotes wakefulness, manufactured by the Pennsylvania-based pharmaceutical company Cephalon under the brand name Provigil and its new-generation FDA-approved drug Nuvigil. Originally licensed to treat the sleep disorder narcolepsy, this is a drug which has already seen significant market expansion for the treatment of a range conditions, including FDA licensing for excessive sleepiness associated with obstructive sleep apnea (OSA) and so-called "shift work sleep disorder" (SWSD), and other "off-label" uses for the treatment of a range of other conditions in which sleepiness or fatigue are significant clinical features. The focus of concern, however, is centered less on these (expanding) clinical applications than on the broader lifestyle or recreational uses and abuses of Modafinil, including a reportedly growing market of uses in corporate culture, academe (late night students, jet-lagged academics), and amongst clubbers.

The rehearsal of these concerns, for example, is clearly evident in media coverage of this drug. Williams and colleagues (2008), for example, in a study of Modafinil in the British press, highlight the dual nature of this coverage. The clinical benefits of this drug in the treatment of conditions such as narcolepsy are extolled in a largely uncritical fashion, often accompanied by patient testimonies about the way in which the drug has helped transform their lives, lifting them from the fog of excessive sleepiness or reducing their daytime napping to manageable proportions. Yet, concerns are expressed about Modafinil as a drug that reflects and reinforces a 24/7 society and which threatens or promises to blur the boundaries still further between treatment and enhancement, including various military deployments or applications. The case has been made, however, that there may indeed be legitimate social circumstances, beyond any immediate clinical concern, when resort to such drugs may be beneficial. In safety-critical occupations, for example, the drugs might minimize sleepiness-related accidents or errors at work. Would you, for example, feel safer in the hands of a chemically enhanced physician or pilot, whose performance at the operating table or in the cockpit will not be affected by sleepiness? The first response, perhaps, may be that getting more sleep is the preferable non-pharmaceutical option, but demands and dictates of contemporary life and living, not least modern-day work cultures and around-the-clock schedules, do not always afford such luxuries even if they should.

These developments in turn resonate with Rose's (2007) contention that something significant or potentially significant is happening here, not simply in terms of new configurations of power/knowledge but in terms of new ways of understanding ourselves. To say we have become "neurochemical selves," he argues, is not to suggest the displacement or replacement of all other ways of thinking about ourselves. Rather, it is that a "neurochemical sense of ourselves is increasingly being layered onto other, older senses of the self, and invoked in particular settings and encounters with significant consequences" (Rose 2007: 222–3). This, to be sure, is a provocative suggestion that may well capture something important, if not vital, with regard to certain individuals, groups, or segments of the populace. To date, however, it remains a largely theoretical proposition, albeit a stimulating one, in need of further empirical investigation, refinement, or refutation, a point I shall return to in the conclusion to this chapter.

NEUROSCIENCE, (IN)EQUALITY, AND PUBLIC HEALTH

Whilst the foregoing themes and issues open up promising avenues of inquiry, in medical sociology and beyond, equally important sociological questions arise regarding neuroscience, (in)equality, and public health. What light, for example, can neuroscience shed on health inequalities and what role can or might it play in public health, both now and in the near future?

Answers to these questions will of course depend on the particular approach or stance taken. Returning to the more applied social neuroscience agenda, for example, it may be argued that a valuable contribution can be made here in relation to the so-called sociobiological translation: the translation, that is to say, of social and environmental factors into biological processes or pathologies. Wilkinson's (1996, 2000, 2005) work, for example, on unhealthy societies illustrates the power, promise, and potential of this synthesis or integration (see also Marmot 2004). In many respects, indeed, this approach to the corrosive effects of income inequalities, based on the primacy of psychosocial pathways, represents one of the most promising examples to date of integrative research on this neurosocial frontier in relation to public health.

The key contention for Wilkinson (1996, 2000, 2005), as many readers will no doubt recall, is that once countries pass a certain basic standard of living for the majority of the population and an "epidemiological transition" from acute to chronic conditions, then psychosocial factors (such as worry, stress, anxiety, invidious social comparisons) rather than material factors become the prime or most important determinants of health inequalities. It is not, moreover, as Wilkinson's comparative international data show, the wealthiest countries in the world that exhibit the best levels of population health, but those with the most equal or egalitarian income distributions. Britain and North America, in this respect, fare worse than countries such as Sweden or Japan when it comes to health inequalities. Wilkinson's work, in this respect, may be regarded as neo-Durkheimian given its emphasis on the corrosive effects of income inequalities for the social fabric. Societies with more equal income distributions are more socially cohesive, Wilkinson argues, which in turn explains not simply their better health records but also their lower crime rates, for certain types of crime at least such as violent or gun crime.

But what does this have to do with the brain? The answer is twofold. First, evolution of the human brain has ensured that we are intensely social beings, biologically primed or attuned, so to speak, to the significance of social bonds, social status, and social hierarchies (see Smail 2008, for example, for a fascinating deep history of the brain). Second, psychosocial factors are themselves mediated or translated through brain-based processes and mechanisms, including both direct neurohormonal or neurophysiological effects on the body and indirect effects through health-risking forms of behavior. Stressors of various sorts, such as status anxiety or lack of control in the workplace, may result in neurohormonal/neurophysiological arousal or perturbation of various kinds which, if prolonged or sustained, may have detrimental effects on health. Cortisol, for instance, a key stress hormone with a range of biological and physiological effects on the body, may have health-damaging consequences if levels remain raised over a significant period of time. Sustained stress may also damage the mechanisms by which insulin controls glucose levels in the blood and/or disrupt or compromise aspects of immune system functioning, thereby rendering individuals susceptible or prone to illness or disease (Marmot 2004; Wilkinson 1996, 2000, 2005). Alternatively, these psychosocial stressors may be expressed through health-damaging behaviors of various kinds such as excessive alcohol consumption, smoking, accident-prone behavior, self-destructive or self-abusing acts, violence, or aggressive behavior.

These issues, as I have argued elsewhere (Williams 1998, 2003), also provide some potentially promising connections to work in the sociology of emotions, including the role of positive emotions such as pride and negative emotions such as shame. Emotions, for example, may well be the catalyst to social transformation and change. They may also, however, help sustain or reproduce social structures and social hierarchies. Social conditions that create depression, as Freund (1990: 470) notes, may "construct an emotional mode of being in which the motivation to resist is blunted." As with the above examples, moreover, the neurohormonal or neurophysiological consequences of these emotional responses or modes of being may not be consciously known or experienced, despite their health-damaging effects (see Freund 1990, 1998 for an elaboration of these issues). Indeed, as neuroscientists such as LeDoux (1999) demonstrate, many processes and mechanisms in the emotional brain operate below the threshold of (self-)conscious awareness or attention, which in turn underpins the distinction writers such as Damasio (1994, 2003) and others draw between brain-based emotion and lived bodily feeling. Whether consciously experienced or not, it is nonetheless clear that both neuroscience and the sociology of emotion have much to contribute to our understanding of health inequalities, particularly the role of psychosocial pathways.

The public health remit or potential remit of neuroscience, however, extends to other important issues such as crime control and other security agendas. This includes current or future evidence regarding the (neuro)biological substrates or correlates of criminal behavior, particularly violent crime and antisocial behavior, gained through family histories, behavioral genetics, brain scans, and the like, and managed or treated through psychopharmaceuticals: the neurobiology of control, in effect. Biological factors, in this respect, take their place amongst a broader array or web of "predisposing factors," with "therapeutic interventions" couched in terms of the benefits for the individual and society alike (Rose 2007: 226).

Far from mitigating responsibility within the criminal justice system, however, these (neuro)biological explanations of conduct, Rose (2007: 226) stresses, have gone hand in hand with a renewed emphasis on the moral culpability of all offenders, irrespective of biological, psychological or social dispositions, and a move away from logics or reformation to those of social protection ... bound up with a new "public health" conception of crime control. This in turn requires the pre-emptive identification and management of "risky individuals" and risk-generating environments ... [which] ... seek to reduce the riskiness of individuals thought to be potential offenders where possible, and, where not, seek their indefinite containment in the name of public safety.

These developments in turn mesh with other military and security uses of neuroscience and neurotechnology in the twenty-first century. These issues, alas, are far beyond the scope of the present chapter to address in a sustained or meaningful fashion. Two important points nonetheless are worth stressing here on these latter two fronts. First, as with many other aspects of science, technology, and medicine, considerable funds are invested in the military applications of neuroscience and neurotechnology, from drugs to scanning technologies. The relays between medicalization and militarization, in this respect, are important sociological topics of investigation in relation to neuroscience/neurotechnology, as they are in all other areas of science and technology. Second, there are close if not symbiotic links here between these developments and their broader deployments in society at large in the name of public health, safety, and security. These deployments, without any hint of hyperbole, are likely to touch or affect us all in years to come, for better or worse. From here it is only a short step to questions of neuroethics, our last substantive theme in this chapter.

NEUROETHICS AND BEYOND

Many people are now familiar with the term bioethics, and its rapid professionalization and institutionalization (Fox 2002; Fox and Swazey 2008; see also Orfali and DeVries, Chapter 22 in this volume) – a new cadre of expertise, in effect, to advise on what is and is not acceptable in the new biological era from genetic therapy (somatic vs. germ line) to cloning (therapeutic vs. reproductive) and stem cell research. The developments discussed in the preceding sections of this chapter, however, have together promoted or resulted in the emergence of a new branch or subfield of bioethical inquiry – the birth or dawn, that is to say, of "neuroethics." A number of significant landmarks may be pointed to or discerned here in this respect, things commonly cited by commentators upon and proponents of neuroethics alike. These include consultation in Britain on the implications of behavioral genetics by the Nuffield Council on Bioethics (2002); a Wellcome-sponsored neuroethics summer school in 2005 (Martin and Ashcroft 2005); a recent major European technology assessment involving a European citizens jury on brain research (Citizen Participation in Science and Technology 2009); the President's Council on Bioethics "Meeting of Minds" (2005) and DANA foundation-sponsored discussions and events on neuroethics (see, for example, Marcus 2002).

As with any new area, attempts at definition and delineation may themselves be profitably viewed in part as constitutive of the field in question. The roots of neuroethics, moreover, are themselves multiple. Neuroethics relates to long-standing philosophical issues to do with will, intentionality, autonomy, agency, brain, mind, self, and society. The emergence of neuroethics can also be understood in the context of technological changes and transformations in the neuroscience field, the precedent of the ethical, legal, and social implications (ELSI) movement in genetics, and the challenges of reconciling or integrating findings from basic neuroscience research on neurons and neurotransmitters with "other more social neuroscience, and of communicating these advances to the wider scientific and public audience" (Martin and Ashcroft 2005: 3). Neuroethics, in this respect, as Martin and Ashcroft (2005: 3) rightly note, is best viewed as a "bundle of related strands" concerning:

- ethical and social issues regarding the conduct of research in neuroscience and biological psychiatry;
- the ethical and social implications of the transformed "models of man" or "humankind" arising from the neurosciences;
- the ethical and social aspects of the clinical and public treatment of psychiatric and neurological disorder;
- the impact of modern neuroscience for our understanding of the basis of morality and social behavior, including transformed notions of will, responsibility, culpability, and the psychological basis of moral knowledge.

Again, however, one needs to be mindful here of important continuities with the past as well as novel changes and developments in the present. Indeed, to repeat a point made earlier, one may be forgiven for questioning whether current developments in the neurosciences raise anything genuinely new in terms of moral or social issues or simply a reorganization of classical thinking on these matters, given that the relationship between brain, mind, and personality, if not personhood, has been a central topic of scientific, moral, and philosophical inquiry since at least the Renaissance (Martin and Ashcroft 2005). Even the so-called enhancement debate has a long historical pedigree behind it. We have always sought to improve or enhance our cognitive functioning from reading and schooling to eating the right foods and getting enough sleep. To the extent, however, that what we see developing before us are more direct neurochemical modes of intervention designed to manage, mend, modify, or manufacture brain states and associated thoughts, moods, emotions, and behaviors, then something new is possibly up for grabs or debate here.

Taking neuroethics as an object of sociological investigation, however, raises other critically important points and issues. Perhaps most contentiously, it can be argued that neuroethics thrives, if not depends, upon claims that developments and transformations in neuroscience and neurotechnology raise potentially profound ethical issues. These issues revolve around questions of autonomy, authenticity, free will, culpability, enhancement, and so forth which neuroethicists then seek to resolve or unravel, thereby fueling or feeding off the very problems in question in a largely self-fulfilling or self-sustaining fashion (De Vries 2007; Singh and Rose 2006). These issues, moreover, are frequently considered and discussed in an abstract fashion that decontextualizes and disembeds neuroscience and neurotechnology. Hence the focus on the social and ethical implications of neuroscience and neurotechnology and the neglect of questions regarding its social shaping and social embeddedness – what Corrigan (2003), in her critique of bioethical notions of informed consent, appositely terms "empty ethics" through this failure to contextualize and situate these issues in terms of ongoing power relations.

Two further directions of study are possible on this neuroethics front. One draws us further into the realms of neurosciences; the other involves an altogether different notion of ethics. Taking each of these in turn, attempts are now being made to identify the neural correlates or substrates of basic ethical decision-making, including the prospect of finding the brain correlates of (criminal) responsibility and the like (for a critique of the potential role of brain scans in relation to capital punishment, see Snead 2008; see also Morse 2004 on the implications, or lack of them, of neuroscientific evidence for existing legal concepts and principles). Again, we return here to some of the issues touched on in the previous section of this chapter regarding the role of neuroscience in new public health concepts of crime control.

Gazzaniga's (2005) book *The Ethical Brain*, for example, grapples or wrestles with some of these issues, including the implications of neuroscience for the law. In doing so, he flirts with the prospect or possibility of neuroscience providing us with a universally shared ethical culture or a universal ethics based on universal facts about neurological function from neuroscientific discoveries. With respect to notions of responsibility, however, Gazzaniga (2005: 90) wisely warns that "although brains are automatic, rule-governed, determined devices ... people are personally responsible agents, free to make their own decisions." "Responsibility," from this viewpoint, is a "social choice" and something we demand or attribute to our fellow citizens *qua* human beings, "the brain correlates of which neuroscience will chase in vain and has no real or realistic business searching for" (Gazzaniga 2005: 101).

The other stand of research, based on a critique of neuroethics, takes us in an altogether different biopolitical or neuropolitical direction. It draws our attention, as we have already seen, to the diverse and diffuse ways in which our "somatic, corporeal, neurochemical individuality now becomes a field of choice, prudence and responsibility" (Rose 2007: 40). This is an ethics, in other words, that is embodied in judgments, actions, choices, and decisions that individuals make regarding themselves and others in the context of their everyday lives and in their negotiations with biomedicine, bioscience, and biotechnology. It is an ethics, moreover, that is closely bound up with notions of biological citizenship, biological capital, and biovalue in the new bioeconomy of the neoliberal era (Rose 2007). As biopolitics, in short, "becomes entangled with bioeconomics, as biocapital becomes open to ethical evaluation, new spaces are emerging for the politics of life itself in the twenty-first century" (Rose 2007: 8).

CONCLUSIONS

What conclusions, then, can we draw from this necessarily selective tracing or mapping of the "neuro-" field in relation to medical sociology?

First and foremost, developments in neuroscience and neurotechnology raise a host of important issues for sociology in general and medical sociology in particular to engage with and address, whether through collaborative or integrative forms of inquiry or through more critical, reflexive sociological agendas.

A second closely related point follows, namely, that engagement with these issues and agendas regarding the social shaping and social implications of neuroscience both consolidates and extends existing work within medical sociology in profitable new ways. On the one hand, as we have seen, many of these issues and developments in neuroscience and neurotechnology may be approached through existing or familiar sociological frameworks such as medicalization debates and issues associated with pharmaceuticalization, geneticization, and the like. To the extent, however, that these very developments in neuroscience and neurotechnology are serving to blur or reconfigure if not move us beyond the poles of health and illness, normality and abnormality, therapy and enhancement, then they demand and necessitate new ways of thinking that potentially take us far beyond existing concerns within medical sociology to broader concepts and debates within sociology. Rose's (2007) work on biopolitics and neuropolitics, for example, as we have seen, is suggestive here. So too is other work within the sociology of expectations and cognate areas such as science and technology studies.

Clearly, however, we are at an early stage as far as sociological engagement with the neurosciences is concerned. A third conclusion, therefore, concerns the need for more theoretically informed empirical research – from a variety of different perspectives, positions, or viewpoints – on the neurosciences and associated neurotechnologies. This includes research on the social shaping as well as the social implications of neuroscience and neurotechnology; the expectations, hopes, and fears invested in neuroscience and neurotechnology and their role in the making or mobilization of various neurofutures; the meaning and use of neurotechnologies such as psychopharmaceuticals in everyday life; and the degree to which these developments in neuroscience/neurotechnology are in fact ushering in new neurochemical conceptions of selfhood, identity, and governance, as certain Foucauldian lines of inquiry suggest. Given the embryonic or promissory nature of many of these developments in neuroscience and neurotechnology to date, moreover, further detailed (ethnographic) work in localized settings, particularly on the challenges or problems of *translation* from the lab to clinic, the bench to the bedside, would be valuable.

Further sociological work too is needed on the implications of neuroscience for public health and the emergence of neuroethics as a distinct new branch of bioethics. And finally, in a more reflexive vein, sociologists themselves, returning to recent work within the sociology of expectations (Brown and Michael 2003), need to be aware of their own role within all this, not simply in terms of the co-construction of the very problems and issues under investigation, but also in the making or remaking of various technoscientific futures. This latter comment, to be sure, applies equally well to all forms of inquiry. It is particularly pertinent in the present case, however, given the considerable claims making that surrounds developments in neuroscience and neurotechnology as debates over so-called cognitive enhancement agents, for instance, clearly demonstrate.

Other promising avenues of future sociological research, not fully addressed in this chapter but pertinent nonetheless to medical sociology, include links to extant work on aging – from contributions to the social neuroscience of aging, touched on earlier, to other more full-blown critical sociological analyses of the "neurologization" of memory and the "Alzheimerization" of dementia – and work on the emergence of neuroculture as a point of articulation between popular discourses and practices and sciences of the brain. We know very little, for example, about the nature and status of neuroculture, its constituent elements or strands, its relations to other cultures such as genomic cultures, psy-cultures, cultures of aging, consumer culture, and neoliberal enterprise culture. To what extent, for example, is the brain becoming a "project," like other body projects in contemporary neuroculture? On the one hand, this question returns us to the (potential) uses and abuses of psycho-pharmaceuticals as so-called cognitive enhancers. On the other hand, it opens up a vast array of social and cultural practices with the brain in mind, so to speak – from brain-boosting books and computer games to the consumption of various nutraceuticals.

Herein, then, to conclude, lie the challenges and opportunities that current and near future developments in neuroscience and neurotechnology pose, not simply for current forms of inquiry in medical sociology and cognate areas, but for society at large. If the 1990s indeed were dubbed the decade of the brain, then the twenty-first century looks set to become, if not the century of the brain, then an era or age in which the neuro looms large in both scientific and popular culture. But, here again, we return to the (co-)construction of various neurofutures. A fitting note on which to end, perhaps, and a reflexive point to bear in mind concerning future sociological endeavors in the field, in medical sociology and beyond.

References

Academy of Medical Sciences (AMS). 2008. *Brain Science, Addictions and Drugs*. London: AMS.

British Medical Association (BMA). 2007. *Boosting Your Brain Power: Ethical Aspects of Cognitive Enhancements*. London: BMA.

Brown, Nik and Mike Michael. 2003. "A Sociology of Expectations: Retrospecting Prospects and Prospecting Retrospects." *Technology Assessment and Strategic Management*. 15(1): 3–18.

Brown, Nik and Andrew Webster. 2004. *New Medical Technologies and Society*. Cambridge: Polity Press.

Cacioppo, John and William Patrick. 2008. *Loneliness: Human Nature and the Need for Social Connection*. New York: W. W. Norton.

Canli, Turhan. 2007. "The Emergence of Genomic Psychology." *European Molecular Biology Organization Reports* 8 (Special Issue): S30–S34.

Citizen Participation in Science and Technology (CIPAST). 2009. *CIPAST Final Report and Recommendations*. Bonn: CIPAST. Retrieved February 14, 2009 (www.cipast.org).

Conrad, Peter. 1976. *Identifying Hyperactive Children: The Medicalization of Deviant Behavior*. Lexington, MA: D. C. Heath.

Conrad, Peter. 1999. "The Mirage of Genes." *Sociology of Health and Illness* 21: 228–41.

Conrad, Peter. 2007. *The Medicalization of Society*. Baltimore: Johns Hopkins University Press.

Corrigan, Oonagh. 2003. "Empty Ethics: The Problem of Informed Consent." *Sociology of Health and Illness* 25(7): 768–92.

Crawford, Michael R. 2008. "The Limits of Neuro-Talk." *The New Atlantis: A Journal of Technology and Society* (Winter): 65–78 (www.TheNewAlantis.com).

Cromby, John. 2007. "Integrating Social Science and Neuroscience: Potentials and Problems." *BioSocieties* 2: 149–69.

Damasio, Antonio. 1994. *Descartes' Error: Emotion, Reason and the Human Brain*. London: Picador.

Damasio, Antonio. 2003. *Looking for Spinoza: Joy, Sorrow and the Feeling Brain*. London: Vintage.

Department of Health (DoH). 2003. *Prescription Cost Analysis*. London: Government Statistical Service.

Department of Health (DoH). 2008. *Prescription Cost Analysis, England 2007*. London: Government Statistical Service.

Department of Trade and Industry (DTI: Office of Science and Technology). 2005. *Drugs Futures 2025*. London: DTI.

DeVries, Raymond. 2007. "Who Will Guard the Guardians of Neuroscience?" *European Molecular Biology Organization Reports* 8 (Special Issue): S65–S69.

Dumit, Joseph. 2004. *Picturing Personhood: Brain Scans and Biomedical Identity*. Princeton, NJ: Princeton University Press.

Eliot, Carl. 2003. *Better than Well: American Medicine Meets the American Dream*. New York: W. W. Norton.

European Neuroscience Society and Network (ENSN). 2009. *European Neuroscience Society and Network*. London: European Neuroscience Society and Network. Retrieved February 14, 2009 (www.neurosocieties.eu/).

Evers, Kathinka. 2007. "Towards a Philosophy of Neuroethics." *European Molecular Biology Organization Reports* 8 (Special Issue): S48–S51.

Featherstone, Katie. 2008. "*Genomics and Psychiatry: Neuroscience, Behavioural Genetics and Psychiatric Practice.*" Paper given as part of the Neuroscience and Medical Sociology Symposium at the British Sociological Association Medical Sociology Conference, University of Sussex, September.

Fox, Renée. 2002. "Medical Uncertainty Revisited." In Gillian Bendelow, Mick Carpenter, Caroline Vautier, and Simon J. Williams (eds.), *Gender, Health and Healing*. London: Routledge.

Fox, Renée and Judith P. Swazey. 2008. *Observing Bioethics*. New York and Oxford: Oxford University Press.

Frank, Arthur W. 1991. "Twin Nightmares of the Simulacrum: Jean Baudrillard and David Cronenberg." in William Stearns and William Chaloupka (eds.), *Jean Baudrillard: The Disappearance of Art and Politics*. London: Macmillan.

Franks, David D. and Thomas S. Smith (eds.). 1999. *Mind, Brain and Society: Toward a Neurosociology of Emotion*. Stamford, CT: JAI Press.

Frazzetto, Giovanni and Cornelius Gross. 2007. "Beyond Susceptibility." *European Molecular Biology Organization Reports* 8 (Special Issue): S3–S6.

Freund, Peter E. S. 1990. "The Expressive Body: A Common Ground for the Sociology of Emotions and the Sociology of Health and Illness." *Sociology of Health and Illness* 12(4): 452–77.

Freund, Peter E. S. 1998. "Social Performances and Their Discontents: Reflection on the Biosocial Psychology of Role Playing." Pp. 236–53 in Gillian A. Bendelow and Simon J. Williams (eds.), *Emotions in Social Life*. London: Routledge.

Gazzaniga, Michael. 2005. *The Ethical Brain*. London: Dana Press.

Greely, Henry, Barbara Sahakian, John Harris, Ronald C. Kessler, Michael Gazzaniga, Philip Campbell, and Martha J. Farah. 2008. "Towards Responsible Use of Cognitive-Enhancing Drugs by the Healthy." *Nature* 456 (December 10): 702–5.

Haraway, Donna. 1991. *Simians, Cyborgs and Women*. London: Free Association Press.

Harmon-Jones, Eddie and Patricia G. Devine. 2003. "Introduction to Special Section on Social Neuroscience: Promise and Caveats." *Journal of Personality and Social Psychology* 85(4): 589–93.

Harmon-Jones, Eddie and Piot Winkielman (eds.). 2007. *Social Neuroscience: Integrating Psychological Explanations of Social Behavior*. New York and London: Guilford Press.

Harris, John. 2007. *Enhancing Evolution: The Ethical Case for Making Better People*. Princeton, NJ: Princeton University Press.

Henderson, Julie. 2008. "Biological Psychiatry and Changing Ideas About 'Mental Health Prevention' in Australian Psychiatry: Risk and Individualism." *Health Sociology Review* 17(1): 4–17.

Kass, Leon. 2002. *Life, Liberty and the Defence of Dignity: The Challenge for Bioethics*. San Francisco: Encounter Books.

Kosfeld, Michael. 2007. "Trust in the Brain." *European Molecular Biology Organization Reports* 8 (Special Issue): S44–S47.

LeDoux, Joseph. 1999. *The Emotional Brain: The Mysterious Underpinnings of Emotional Life*. New York: Simon and Schuster.

Lesch, Klaus-Peter. 2007. "Linking Emotion to the Social Brain." *European Molecular Biology Organization Reports* 8 (Special Issue): S24–S29.

Maasen, Sabine and Barbara Sutter. 2007. *On Willing Selves: Neoliberal Politics and the Challenge of Neuroscience*. Basingstoke: Macmillan.

Marcus, Stephen J. (ed.). 2002. *Neuroethics: Mapping the Field*. New York: Dana Press.

Marmot, Michael. 2004. *The Status Syndrome: How Social Standing Affects Our Health and Longevity*. London: Bloomsbury.

Martin, Emily. 2007. *Bipolar*. Princeton, NJ: Princeton University Press.

Martin, Paul and Richard Ashcroft. 2005. "Neuroscience, Ethics and Society: A Review of the Field." Background paper prepared for the 2005 Wellcome Trust Summer School on "Neuroethics."

Miller, Paul and James Wilsdon (eds.). 2006. *Better Humans? The Politics of Human Enhancement and Life Extension*. London: Demos.

Moffit, Terry E., Caspi Avshalom, and Michael Rutter. 2005. "Strategy for Investigating Interactions Between Measured Genes and Measured Environments." *Archives of General Psychiatry* 62: 473–81.

Morse, Stephen J. 2004. "Neuroscience, Old Problems." Pp. 157–98 in Garland Brent (ed.), *Neuroscience and the Law: Brain, Mind and the Scales of Justice*. New York: Dana Press.

Moynihan, Ray, Iona Health, and David Henry. 2002. "Selling Sickness: The Pharmaceutical Industry and Disease Mongering." *British Medical Journal* 324: 886–91.

Nettleton, Sarah. 2004. "The Emergence of E-Scaped Medicine." *Sociology* 38(4): 661–80.

Neuroscience and Society Group @ Warwick 2008. "Neuroscience and Society Group @ Warwick." University of Warwick, Coventry, United Kingdom. Retrieved February 14, 2009 (www2.warwick.ac.uk/fac/soc/nsw).

Newton, Tim. 2007. *Nature and Sociology*. London: Routledge.

Nuffield Council on Bioethics. 2002. *Genetics and Human Behaviour: The Ethical Context*. London: Nuffield Council on Bioethics (www.nuffieldbioethics.org).

Parens, Erik (ed.). 1998. *Enhancing Human Traits: Ethical and Social Implications*. Washington, DC: Georgetown University Press.

Perreau-Lenz, Stéphanie, Tarek Zghoul, and Rainer Spanagel. 2007. "Clock Genes Running Amok." *European Molecular Biology Organization Reports* 8 (Special Issue): S20–S23.

President's Council on Bioethics. 2005. "*Meeting of the Minds*." Washington, DC: President's Council on Bioethics. Retrieved February 14, 2009 (bioethics/gov/topics_neuro_index.html).

Press, Nancy. 2006. "Social Construction and Medicalization: Behavioural Genetics in Context." Pp. 131–49 in Erik Parens, Audrey R. Chapman, and Nancy Press (eds.), *Wrestling with Behavioural Genetics: Science, Ethics and Public Conversation*. Baltimore: Johns Hopkins University Press.

Rose, Nikolas. 2007. *The Politics of Life Itself: Biomedicine, Power and Subjectivity in the Twenty-First Century*. Princeton, NJ: Princeton University Press.

Rose, Steven. 2006. *The 21st-Century Brain: Explaining, Mending and Manipulating the Mind*. London: Vintage.

Roubertoux, Pierre L. and Michèle Carlier. 2007. "From DNA to Mind." *European Molecular Biology Organization Reports* 8 (Special Issue): S7–S11.

Rutter, Michael. 2007. *Genes and Behaviour*. Oxford: Blackwell.

Sandstrom, Lars E. 2007. "Thinking Inside the Box." *European Molecular Biology Organization Reports* 8 (Special Issue): S40–S43.

Scott, Susie. 2007. *Shyness and Society: The Illusion of Competence*. Basingstoke: Macmillan.

Shostak, Sara, Peter Conrad, and Allan V. Horwitz. 2008. "Sequencing and its Consequences: Path Dependence and the Relationship Between Genetics and Medicalization." *American Journal of Sociology* 114 (Suppl.): S287–S316.

Singer, Wolf. 2007. "Understanding the Brain." *European Molecular Biology Organization Reports* 8 (Special Issue): S16–S19.

Singh, Ilina and Nikolas Rose. 2006. "Neuro-Forum: An Introduction." *BioSocieties* 1: 97–102.

Smail, D. L. 2008. *On Deep History and the Brain*. Berkeley: University of California Press.

Snead, O. Carter. 2008. "Neuroimaging and Capital Punishment." *The New Atlantis: A Journal of Technology and Society* (Winter): 35–63 (www.TheNewAtlantis.com).

Stefánsson, Halldór. 2007. "The Biology of Behaviour: Scientific and Ethical Implications." *European Molecular Biology Organization Reports* 8 (Special Issue): S1–S2.

Turner, Stephen. 2007. "Social Theory as Cognitive Neuroscience." *European Journal of Social Theory* 10(3): 357–73.

Waldby, Cathy. 2002. *The Visible Human Project*. London: Routledge.

Webster, Andrew. 2007. *Health Technology and Society: A Sociological Critique*. Basingstoke: Macmillan.

Wilkinson, Richard G. 1996. *Unhealthy Societies: The Afflictions of Inequality*. London: Routledge.

Wilkinson, Richard G. 2000. *Mind the Gap: Hierarchies, Health and Human Evolution*. London: Weidenfeld and Nicolson.

Wilkinson, Richard G. 2005. *The Impact of Inequality: How to Make Sick Societies Healthier*. London: Routledge.

Williams, Simon J. 1998. "Capitalising on Emotions? Rethinking the Inequalities Debate." *Sociology* 32(1): 121–39.

Williams, Simon J. 2003. *Medicine and the Body*. London: Sage.

Williams, Simon J., Clive Seale, Sharon Boden, Pam Lowe, and Deborah L. Steinberg. 2008. "Waking Up to Sleepiness: Modafinil, the Media and the Pharmaceuticalisation of Everday/Night Life." *Sociology of Health and Illness* 30(6): 839–55.

Wilson, Elizabeth A. 2004. *Psychosomatic: Feminism and the Neurological Body*. Durham, NC: Duke University Press.

Wilson, Elizabeth A. 2006. "The Work of Antidepressants." *BioSocieties* 1(1): 125–31.

Author Index

Subject Index